VISUAL RHETORIC IN A DIGITAL WORLD

A Critical Sourcebook

Carolyn Handa
Southern Illinois University
Edwardsville

BEDFORD / ST. MARTIN'S   Boston • New York

For Bedford / St. Martin's

Executive Editor: Leasa Burton
Executive Assistant: Brita Mess
Associate Editor, Publishing Services: Maria Teresa Burwell
Production Supervisor: Yexenia Markland
Project Management: DeMasi Design & Publishing Services
Text Design: Anna Palchik
Cover Design: Donna Dennison
Composition: Macmillan India Limited
Printing and Binding: Haddon Craftsmen, an RR Donnelley & Sons Company

President: Joan E. Feinberg
Editorial Director: Denise B. Wydra
Editor in Chief: Karen S. Henry
Director of Marketing: Karen Melton Soeltz
Director of Editing, Design, and Production: Marcia Cohen
Manager, Publishing Services: Emily Berleth

Library of Congress Control Number: 2003116942

Manufactured in the United States of America.

9 8 7
f e d

For information, write: Bedford / St. Martin's, 75 Arlington Street,
Boston, MA 02116 (617-399-4000)

ISBN-10: 0-312-40975-3
ISBN-13: 978-0-312-40975-3

ACKNOWLEDGMENTS
Acknowledgments and copyrights appear at the back of the book on pages 486–487,
which constitute an extension of the copyright page. It is a violation of the law to
reproduce these selections by any means whatsoever without the written permission
of the copyright holder.

ACKNOWLEDGMENTS

My heartfelt thanks go to Leasa Burton, my editor at Bedford/St. Martin's, for suggesting this project in February 2002, then bringing a poet's precision and careful eye to bear on this manuscript's numerous drafts and stages. Leasa always managed to find the right word, the right phrase. Would that I might always work with such a poetic editor. I wish to thank other members of the Bedford/St. Martin's family: Joan Feinberg, president, who encouraged this project from its inception; Nick Carbone and Paul Coleman for their friendship, support, and much appreciated senses of humor; Nelina Backman for important feedback, helpful suggestions, and engaging discussions; Brita Mess for invaluable editorial assistance; and finally, I thank production editors Emily Berleth and Linda DeMasi, who took such care coordinating this manuscript's production.

I am grateful to reviewers who commented on early stages of this project: Janice Walker, Cara Finnegan, Sibylle Gruber, Lester Faigley, and Jerry Blithefield. Christy Desmet, both a colleague and friend who understands, more than most, life's ups and downs, provided a detailed, insightful review.

Two teachers who influenced me above all others, Richard A. Lanham and Geoffrey Symcox, will find echoes of their scholarly ideals throughout this collection. My family brings me joy, fellowship, camaraderie, and the sense of belonging that comes only from close relatives. I am blessed with extraordinary siblings whose individual achievements inspire me daily. The memory of my father, George Handa, has been with me throughout the time I have worked on this project. My mother, Patricia Sakon Handa, has always been and continues to be an example of quiet strength and perseverance. I dedicate this book to "the girls," Alexa, Kira, Callie, Tegan, Lindsey, and Rori: in the spirit of Emily Dickinson, always "dwell in Possibility."

CONTENTS

INTRODUCTION

Placing the Visual in the Writing Classroom

To be deeply literate in the digital world means being skilled at deciphering complex images and sounds as well as the syntactical subtleties of words. Above all, it means being at home in a shifting mix of words, images and sounds (198, 200).

—RICHARD LANHAM, "DIGITAL LITERACY"

Not all that long ago our writing classrooms looked like any others in the university. They contained desks arranged in rows, a podium facing the class, and blackboards covering one or two walls. Technology may have existed only as an overhead projector displaying transparencies with additional class material. Occasionally, instructors would show films related to course topics. Some assignments might have asked students to analyze advertisements to study their rhetoric or to compare two products. Visuals were incidental props, tricks to spark students' interest in writing, more than viable communicative modes in themselves. Students wrote their compositions at home, typed them up, and then turned them in, using words and sentences — rather than images — to convey ideas.

Today, writing classrooms are more likely to be part of fully networked campuses with wired or wireless access to university servers and to the World Wide Web. Such easy access brings with it a flood of visual images, icons, streaming video, and various hybrid forms of images and text. Writing instructors are increasingly using classroom management programs and requiring students to maintain online portfolios. Students may work from CDs included as part of a textbook or from textbooks focusing completely on visuals and their importance in our lives. The landscape of composition — and the course itself — is beginning to *look* very different.

Even if writing classrooms are not wired, most of our students are: Many have home access to computers; the Internet; the World Wide Web; PDAs; cell phones with games and Web access; sophisticated word-processing packages; and software that allows them to draw, design, create movies, and edit or retouch photographs and videos. They can operate Photoshop and PageMaker; they can write in JavaScript and HTML. Our students' twenty-first-century lives are nothing if not visual.

For writing instructors raised on verbal texts, however, hybrid media, with their prominently featured visual components, can be an alien—and alienating—species, a source of much anxiety. Many of us who teach composition have been trained to read words closely, to explicate poems and longer texts, to consider the logic and linear organization of academic writing, to value the judgment of academic publishers and established print media, and to expect scholarly research to be contained within margins on linear pages. Some scholars may even be suspicious of work that incorporates images and sounds, which have traditionally been considered less authoritative than written text.

Composition as a discipline, however, has clearly begun to engage the visual more seriously as part of the pedagogy. In 2001, in the journal *Computers and Composition*, Sean Williams lamented, "How often, though, do we ask our composition students, particularly first-year students, to compose anything except verbal texts about whatever type of text they 'read'? This type of verbal bias disenfranchises students" (23). Only two years later, sessions on visual rhetoric and new media topics appear throughout the program for the Conference on College Composition and Communication, and a range of visual writing genres is increasingly assigned in composition courses across the country. Composition teachers are thinking about the visual, considering theories historicizing the separation of words and images, and understanding the place of classical rhetoric, design studies, and cultural studies in our pedagogy. However, there is still much work to be done.

The readings collected here are offered as a framework for thinking about the place of the visual in the composition course, especially in the context of the rhetorical tradition that undergirds the composition classroom's goals. Scholars such as Richard Lanham, Henrietta Nickels Shirk, Jay Bolter, and Susan Hilligoss have urged prophetically for years that we widen our understanding of the scope of rhetoric, that we include images in our study, along with words. First conceived of as a tool for orators, rhetoric developed into a tool for writers only after printed texts became the communicative medium of choice. Rhetoric's association with the written word is arbitrary, a by-product of print culture rather than the epistemological limits of rhetoric itself. We use rhetoric to help us think more clearly, write more elegantly, design more logically. Rhetoric works both to scaffold our ideas for clearer understanding and to structure our critical examinations of both visual and verbal objects. Rhetoric has always been important in the composition classroom, but we are only now beginning to understand how it might work as a device to help our students understand and create visually and verbally interwoven texts.

Visual rhetoric as an emerging field in composition owes much to the study of the visual in other disciplines. Articles collected in this volume originated in both books and journals from a wide variety of disciplines, not just composition studies. Their range suggests how broadly the study of the visual can extend, how broadly we can search in our own pursuit of the visual once we know where to look. They give us a starting place to begin listening to conversations ongoing in other disciplines about the visual. From fields as diverse as art history, design, philosophy, and graphic arts to ethnography, cultural studies, typography, and architecture, to name just a few, the authors' various disciplinary backgrounds show how important a multidisciplinary approach to our thinking is: The differing points of view about the visual, about rhetoric, about incorporating the visual in our teaching provide a rich foundation to begin building our own pedagogy of the visual.

Outside of our writing classrooms, students surround themselves with multimedia and cybertexts. At younger and younger ages, they become adept at playing entirely visual computer games and watch more television and movies than previous generations ever did. Tools like Adobe's Photoshop help them manipulate and edit images. When they construct their own highly sophisticated Web pages, they use Web browsers to create pages that almost always include visual elements. They may create their own visuals, even their own typography. For them, publishing Web pages without including images, graphics, movies, and creative typography is probably out of the question, not to mention unsophisticated. Our students, however, may be technologically sophisticated yet rhetorically illiterate.

Students who possess a high degree of technological skill may see the value in knowing how to create a document using the latest digital tool but not understand the importance of thinking carefully about rhetorical questions such as the appropriate audience, purpose, tone, and argument (Shauf). Here is where our experience as composition teachers becomes crucial. Preparing students to communicate in the digital world using a full range of rhetorical skills will enable them to analyze and critique both the technological tools and the multimodal texts produced with those tools. Visual rhetoric in the composition course then serves two ends: to help students better understand how images persuade on their own terms and in the context of multimodal texts, and to help students make more rhetorically informed decisions as they compose visual genres.

The readings collected here will hopefully serve to trigger necessary discussions about the impact of the visual and digital on the future of education. The very first piece, "Visualizing English," by Craig Stroupe, and the very last, "The Implications of Electronic Information for the Sociology of Knowledge," by Richard Lanham, come from scholars in English studies and work as framing devices for the entire volume. Stroupe looks back at the history of the discipline to identify curricular and cultural reasons for the tension between the visual and verbal that has marked English studies as a whole. By tracing this history, Stroupe argues that English studies can indeed be visualized—if only we keep open minds. Analyzing the codex book as the basic operating system for humanistic knowledge, Richard Lanham looks to the future. He asks us to discern ways that the sociology of knowledge will change once the codex book is replaced by the screen and pushes us to envision the ways in which educational institutions, curricula, and most humanistic enterprises will have to change.

Taking up this call to reimagine curricula in light of new media, Part One, "Toward a Pedagogy of the Visual," presents approaches to the visual ranging from the pedagogical to the epistemological, historical, technological, and typographical. Together they highlight the importance of the visual in our lives while underscoring the claim that the composition classroom is a proper place to study the visual because visual and verbal literacies have become increasingly interdependent. The readings will not resolve any major arguments about whether or not to bring visuals into our writing classes, but they will present positions worth thinking about. They also do not argue for a particular definition of a pedagogy of the visual. Instead they offer us places to start identifying what such a pedagogy would cover and how it would translate into actual classroom practice.

Part Two, "The Rhetoric of the Image," includes both time-honored and contemporary scholars whose range of theories about the visual helps us understand exactly how an image might work to convey specific information and even abstract concepts. From fields as diverse as semiology, science education, and comic book art, the readings in this section provide even stronger evidence for claims that the visual and verbal are increasingly interdependent. We begin to understand that the visual is every bit as valid a mode of communication as the verbal when we see how designers and illustrators can work with rhetorical concepts to picture ideas about science or drama or how the simple lines of comics can help an artist convey ideas to people, regardless of their different languages.

Part Three, "The Rhetoric of Design," presents theories from typographers, a new media designer, and rhetoricians who show us that rhetoric is a useful—and appropriate—critical tool for designers. Just as good writing involves more than putting words on a page, good design involves more than using words and pictures to convey information. Typography, punctuation, visual repetition, and apparently neutrally designed objects like e-mail all display a particular rhetorical position. These readings reinforce just how much there is to learn about rhetoric and the visual from other disciplines, such as graphic design, which shares the rhetorician's interest in how textual elements capture an audience's attention and convey a point of view.

Part Four, "Visual Rhetoric and Argument," examines how classical rhetoric might create a foundation for studying the visual. Readings from scholars in communications, forensics, philosophy, technical writing, and rhetoric address the problem of persuasion and argumentation through visuals, stress the importance of bringing a humanist's rhetorical perspective to electronic pedagogy, and show specific visual examples of rhetorical figures. Studying the visual in the context of the digital through a rhetorical lens means studying documents that are hybrids, not pure image. Besides considering whether visual arguments are theoretically and actually possible, the readings also give us a clearer idea of exactly what visually rendered rhetorical figures look like and how those visual portrayals work in documents.

Part Five, "Visual Rhetoric and Culture," shows culture's hold on the visual and rhetoric's power to illuminate that hold by helping us explicate historically and politically contingent points of view, revealing the anxieties these views produce, and showing how such anxieties can color what we see.

Many of these readings are rooted in "visual culture," a field that extends the work of cultural studies to analyze the social and political contexts of the visual. For example, in "The Wall, the Screen, and the Image: The Vietnam Veterans Memorial," Marita Sturken examines the social and political contexts that produced such negative reactions to a memorial that was designed to honor the men and women who lost their lives during the Vietnam War. Readings in this section not only illustrate the value for compositionists of visual literacy but also show how we can mistake the points of visual constructions if we cannot decipher their visual messages.

Composition Studies has a strong tradition of intellectual exploration in search of ways to understand our teaching and our students' learning. In 1984, Janice Lauer pointed out the willingness of early composition scholars to transcend theoretical boundaries and to explore multidisciplinary modes of inquiry:

> [One] shared trait of these early theorists [was] their willingness to take risks, to go beyond the boundaries of their traditional training into foreign domains in search of starting points, theoretical launching pads from which to begin investigating [questions about features of the discipline]. Some of this early work includes forays into classical rhetoric, transformational and tagmemic linguistics, semiotics, and speech act theory; into psychological studies of creativity, problem-solving, and cognitive development; into philosophical theories like those of Gadamer, Lonergan, Ricoeur, Habermas, Johnston, Perelman, Toulmin, Polyani, and Kuhn; and into such biological territory as hemisphericity. (21)

Lauer's words remind us that compositionists have traditionally widened their field of inquiry searching for ways to better understand how our students handle the writing process and the critical thinking necessary for good writing. Hopefully, the range of theories presented in this volume will provide helpful "launching pads," drawing on both rhetoric and an array of disciplines beyond composition's usual scope to inform our teaching and research practices.

REFERENCES

Lanham, Richard. "Digital Literacy." *Scientific American* 273:3 (September 1995): 198, 200.
Lauer, Janice. "Composition Studies: Dappled Discipline." *Rhetoric Review* 3:1 (September 1984): 21.
Shauf, Michelle S. "The Problem of Electronic Argument: A Humanist's Perspective." *Computers and Composition* 18:1 (2001): 33–37.
Williams, Sean. "Thinking out of the Pro-Verbal Box." *Computers and Composition* 18:1 (2001): 21–32.

PART ONE

Toward a Pedagogy of the Visual

Introduction to Part One

Before we, as composition instructors, can begin to construct a coherent pedagogy of the visual, we might ask ourselves what we need to understand about our discipline and what our assumptions about teaching are, exactly. Why do some writing curricula continue to focus only on words when today's documents are increasingly hybrids of words, images, and design? In what ways might we begin to address the visual on par with the verbal in our classrooms? The readings in this section offer a way to begin exploring these questions. Including a balance of theory, method, and praxis, they challenge us to look beyond the verbal, provide suggestions for classroom activities, situate the visual/verbal dichotomy historically, and finally even move beyond the immediate classroom to propose curricular changes that would conceive of rhetoric in an entirely different way.

Before drawing lines between those who would and wouldn't favor studying visuals in writing classes, we should keep in mind the reason why many instructors are not necessarily interested in teaching composition courses that take up visual genres: Because the first-year writing sequence is often the vehicle for conveying most universities' basic literacy requirements, writing instructors and program administrators often feel hard pressed to add yet another unit to an already crowded curriculum. The readings in this section support the claim not only that the visual is worth attending to in the composition course but also that finding space for the visual in the curriculum is possible without sacrificing the course goals of developing careful thinkers and thoughtful writers.

In "Visualizing English: Recognizing the Hybrid Literacy of Visual and Verbal Authorship on the Web," Craig Stroupe, who studies cultural and textual representations of writing and reading processes, asserts that English studies should reexamine its single-minded reliance on a predominately verbal rhetoric and literacy. Stroupe regards English studies, as "one of the more balkanized political interests on campus," marked by a "poetic-rhetoric divide." He traces the ideologic separation between types of verbal studies, then argues that the entire discipline of English studies must learn "from some of its more marginalized elements such as technical communication and cultural studies" to understand and then to set words and images in dialogic relation. Stroupe introduces critical ideas relevant to this collection. He enables us to recognize the distinctive literacies of both verbal and visual codes, the importance of cultural context in studying the visual, and the negative effect of the "poetic-rhetoric divide," an imagined border protecting the elaborated discourses of literary artistry and criticism from the more ordinary discourses of the workplace or popular culture.

While Stroupe suggests that we can set both words and images in a dialogic relationship, Gunther Kress stresses how different types of rhetorical functions are best carried out by different modes—verbal, visual, or aural—and that writing conveys certain types of acts more suitably than images, and vice versa. In "Multimodality, Multigenre, and Genre," Kress claims that we now face a range of epistemological choices when we create texts, choices that were unavailable to us just a few decades ago. Kress notes how, until recently, writing carried the main burden of communicating. Due to this burden, writing needed complex grammatical and syntactic structures to help convey complex messages. Kress speculates that today's multimodal communicative hybrids may allow simpler syntactic structures to evolve.

To illustrate his claims, Kress includes an accessible and memorable case study of the multimodal science reports of two English schoolgirls. One report consists of an abstract visual and a realistic text, while the other consists of a realistic diagram with an abstract report. Kress argues that the reports actually reflect different social relations between the teachers and the students who produced the texts. The level of abstraction in the hybrid visual and verbal texts reveals the extent to which the students report what they have been told exists or engage more deeply in the process of observing what is in front of them. Kress's findings suggest a new way of assessing students' critical thinking abilities by examining the relationship between the words and the images they create in multimodal texts.

The tension between words and images becomes evident when we look at how different historical eras contended with rhetorical and visual elements. In "Learning from the Past: Verbal and Visual Literacy in Early Modern Rhetoric and Writing Pedagogy," Catherine L. Hobbs addresses one of the crucial, ongoing dilemmas for many writing teachers today: whether paying attention to the visual and to a literacy combining images with words does not, in fact, undermine our objectives as teachers who, by virtue of being "writing" teachers, deal primarily with the written word. While not resolving the dilemma, Hobbs hopes that composition teachers today can take comfort in the fact that our dilemma is merely the latest transformation of an ancient conflict, an ongoing struggle since ancient times, persisting through the Middle Ages into modernity.

But even though this struggle between word and image has historical dimensions in Western culture, the balance, over the past three hundred years, has tipped squarely on the side of the word. According to J. L. Lemke, a professor of linguistics and education, what we have studied about literacy in the past has been too logocentric. Lemke would agree with Hobbs that we must study literacies of the past as well as literacy's past, but he would frame our vision by having us identify those cultural practices and ecosystems giving rise to certain material technologies that help people create meaning. The material technologies of pen and paper belonged to an ecosystem that included only a book and a reader, and possibly, as Lemke remarks, "eyeglasses." In a more sophisticated world, however, the material technologies of hardware and software form an ecosystem that also includes "new authoring skills and new interpretive skills." In "Metamedia Literacy: Transforming Meanings and Media," Lemke emphasizes the extent to which literacy depends upon material developments of the time. For instance, eons ago we relied on the technology of coloring pigments to trace images on walls; later, quills and inks constituted the extent of our material technology; today we use word processors loaded with capabilities for including images and sounds in our communications. Like many of the authors gathered in this collection, Lemke offers ways in which he feels we can improve learning today. In a critique of learning paradigms, Lemke moves from analyzing ways in which we can transform learning paradigms to explaining how transformed technologies can lead to what he calls "metamedia literacies," and then ultimately to a transformed humanity.

The final two readings in this section shift our focus from the more abstract philosophic and historic questions undergirding a visual pedagogy to a very specific view of how we might approach hybrid texts. Professor of technical communication Stephen Bernhardt in "Seeing the Text" helps us understand how both verbally informative and more visually informative texts are rhetorically constructed. By dissecting the ways in which these different types of texts establish rhetorical control, Bernhardt provides a concrete vocabulary for a pedagogy of the visual. Drawing from the work of John W. Cataldo, Bernhardt delineates four laws of a visual gestalt: equilibrium or *pragnanz*, good continuation or good figure, closure, and similarity. These laws offer ways of conceptualizing the visual equivalents of what have previously been considered verbal rhetorical constructs, devices such as transitional links, anaphoric place holders, coordination of smaller and larger blocks of information, topic sentences, and relations between generalizations and supporting information. Bernhardt feels that classroom practice must become much more familiar with and adept at understanding visual equivalents to verbal rhetorical cues. Classroom practices that do not, he states, will become increasingly irrelevant.

Charles Hill's "Reading the Visual in College Writing Classes" specifically addresses visual texts in the context of the first-year composition sequence. Hill, who teaches in several English studies disciplines, recommends bringing the visual into writing classes by asking students to analyze and experiment with typography and page layout. His overall argument echoes several of the other authors in this section, but he helps funnel the ideas to bear directly on composition pedagogy. Hill takes up the argument that visual texts have been neglected in our current educational system and that we are not training our students to be literate in a technological world containing more visual material than ever before. Hill argues that those of us who avoid the study of images in composition and rhetoric classes operate under several invalid assumptions: (1) that the visual and the verbal can be easily isolated from one another, (2) that visual images do not constitute meaningful texts despite the ubiquity and primacy of visual messages in our digital world, and (3) that images are just another way to convey information that can also be made clear through words. To ensure that verbal, visual, and oral literacies are attended to equally and not taught in isolation from one another, Hill extends John Trimbur's call to form multidepartmental writing programs and proposes that universities develop multidepartmental rhetoric programs.

A visual pedagogy for the digital world has yet to be thoroughly developed, but the time is especially right for us to do so. Pedagogies never emerge in a vacuum; they form as a result of particular historical contexts and particular historic and cultural tensions. We can, for example, trace the beginnings of basic writing pedagogy and feminist pedagogy to political events shaping the 1960s. At the beginning of the twenty-first century, technology has enabled the easy (re)production of images; all word-processing packages include the ability to import images or to draw on a file of clip art. Even if students are not themselves manipulating or using images, they should learn to contend with the visual in a sophisticated way because they are and will be constantly exposed to new media throughout their personal, academic, and professional lives.

1

Visualizing English: Recognizing the Hybrid Literacy of Visual and Verbal Authorship on the Web

CRAIG STROUPE

Early in his ground-breaking book, *Hypertext: The Convergence of Contemporary Critical Theory and Technology*, George Landow briefly notes — and, for his own purposes, dismisses — a distinction that may prove crucial to the future practice of English studies. Though he momentarily acknowledges the difference between the terms *hypertext* (a structure composed of blocks of text, or *lexias*, that are verbal) and *hypermedia* (which includes lexias with graphic and multimedia material as well), Landow concludes, "Since hypertext, which links a passage of verbal discourse to images, maps, diagrams, and sound as easily as to another verbal passage, expands the notion of text beyond the solely verbal, I do not distinguish between hypertext and hypermedia" (4). Landow's task of describing hypertext does not concern the internal workings of a Web page or single lexia (in which, he says, "conventional reading habits apply"), but rather the nonsequential functioning of a *network* of lexias, among which "new rules and new experience apply" — rules and experience that in 1992 demanded analysis and theorization (4).

Having seen this important critical work begun, however, those in English studies would benefit from revisiting the text/media dichotomy — particularly the dialogism between verbal and visual discourses on the single lexia. As more information is shared and cultural work performed via electronic environments — in June 1999, the size of the Web passed 300 million publicly accessible pages ("How Wide") — English studies will find its stock-in-trade of verbal rhetorics and literacies increasingly in competition and combination with extra-verbal codes and languages. Once a mere convenience in the print production or conventional verbal texts, for example, common word-processing applications such as Microsoft Word now allow users to insert digital images into documents, to create and display active Web links on the screen, to animate letters and words with such effects as twinkling

From *College English* 62:5 (May 2000): 607–632.

Christmas lights, and to save documents in HTML code for posting to Web servers rather than in formats for printing.

This encroachment of graphic, screen-based display—even into the word-, page-, and book-centered environment of word processing—presents English Studies with choices. The discipline needs to decide not only whether to embrace the teaching of visual and information design in addition to verbal production, which some of the more marginalized elements of English Studies have already done, but, more fundamentally, whether to confront its customary cultural attitudes toward visual discourses and their insinuation into verbal texts. W. J. T. Mitchell has characterized and critiqued these attitudes as combining an iconoclastic "contempt" for graphic images as uncritical "idolatry, fetishism, and iconophilia," a "fear" toward visual discourse as a "racial, social, and sexual other," and a tendency to see any genre that combines the two discourses, such as the theater, as a "battleground between the values associated with verbal and visual codes" (151, 157–58).

Such curricular and cultural tensions affect not only the future of the English Studies curriculum on campus, but the prospects of students who choose to identify and credential themselves as English majors. In an economy and culture increasingly mediated via Internet browsers, success in the "new work paradigm" described by Web-design expert David Siegel depends less upon the individual writer, or even collaborators, producing the well-wrought verbal text and more upon the coordination of a team whose members practice a variety of complementary technical, visual, verbal, and professional discourses. Among these, verbal literacy is not replaced or buried so much as layered *into* a more diverse amalgamation of literacies. In this new paradigm of communications work, writers become what Siegel terms "contentmasters," second-order editors, copywriters, and go-fers "in charge of rounding up the content and getting it ready to go on the site" (263). In contrast to Aristotle's *rhetor*, the verbal contentmaster is not necessarily the controller of the form and rhetoric of the site as a whole, but may work far down the chain of command, managing, in Siegel's words, "a particular set of assets on the site" (153). As has long been the case in television production and print advertising, Web-based communication makes verbal expertise only one among many forms of literacy and professional/rhetorical authority, any one of which may provide the primary vision for the production as a whole. A celebrated producer and critic of Web sites, Siegel himself comes from an undergraduate background in math with a master's degree in digital typography.

This article will describe a specific approach to reading, composing, and teaching the problematic combination of verbal and nonverbal features in texts conceived for or in electronic environments, a method by which English studies can address visual discourses while, most importantly, maintaining a critical consciousness of the distinctive literacies of both codes. I want to describe a disciplinary process I will call "visualizing English"—already underway in some English-department-based fields—which might allow English studies more generally to resist the critical and writerly impulse to subsume images under the dominant literacy of verbal culture (the use of graphics as supplemental "illustrations"). Conversely, visualizing English would also enable the discipline's teachers and scholars more seriously to critique the tendency in Web design, and popular media more generally, to handle verbal discourse as text-heavy gray chunks that must be made visually presentable (the use of words as iconographically dead weight, carried along on the energy of the images and design). The more hybrid approach of a visualized English would describe instead the potential for dialogically constitutive relations between words and images—in a larger sense, between the literacies of verbal and visual cultures—which can function as a singly intended, if double-voiced, rhetoric.

My point is that the practice and teaching of this hybrid literacy will require that those of us in English studies reexamine our customary distinctions and judgments about literacy in light of this historical challenge of the visual—not just in the extracurricular, top-down media of television and film, but in the more commonly accessible media of textual production and academic communication. The section that follows investigates these traditional assumptions as points of friction between verbal and visual discourses as they are taught in two instructional books. The remaining two sections, however, describe a number of *continuities* between visual digitality and the verbal literacy currently taught within the English Studies curricula of literary analysis, composition, or creative writing. These continuities, in other words, suggest that meeting the challenge of the visual need not become an occasion for English Studies further to divide and subdivide itself in another defensive effort to respond to social and historical needs by creating new, relevant, but "lite" Englishes on the margins in order to preserve a nostalgic fiction of pure English at the center. Instead, I will show how the challenge of the visual to the verbal can become an occasion to recognize the discipline's long-standing ideology of *elaborationism*, a set of cultural, pedagogical, and technical practices based on the idea that the formal composing or reading process can produce more critical forms of consciousness. As a fundamental assumption about the relation of language and thought, elaborationism represents a potential common thread that crosses not only the visual/verbal border, but also the boundaries that politically polarize and artificially stratify the discipline into curricular dichotomies of poetic and rhetoric, high and low, literature and composition.

To suggest that the loose confederation of scholarly and teaching interests called English studies should consciously visualize itself in these new terms is to argue that those at the discipline's prestigious center follow the lead of its more marginalized or controversial wings: technical communication, cultural studies, film, and popular culture. To pursue such a course would thus lead English to address its internal inequalities through this self-visualization and to recognize the mystified status of the privileged genres, discourses, and cultural narratives on which these inequalities rest. Historicizing these apparent eternal verities, however, also means exposing the political and pecuniary interests that underlie English studies' investment in and defense of verbal print culture and its customary dismissal of the popular, predominantly visual discourses of magazines and advertising as well as the more iconic media of movies, television, and the Internet.

The story of English studies' responses to computers is a case in point. Much of the early, negative reaction, which still persists among some in the discipline today, is based on the association of technology with the Cold War era's military-industrial buildup and the hawkish, conservative politics that supported it (Castells 5). The first wave of electronic theorists from English argued, as a necessary corrective to this stance, that the technologizing of writing would bear out English Studies' perennial relevance. In *The Electronic Word: Democracy, Technology and the Arts*, for instance, Richard Lanham declares that the anxieties of the Cold War viewpoint were unwarranted. Writing in approximately the same time period in which Landow's *Hypertext* appeared, Lanham argues that digital communication represents not the successor to the literacy traditionally taught by English (or at least rhetorical) Studies, but a vindication and salvation of it:

> To explain reading and writing on computers, we need to go back to the original Western thinking about reading and writing the rhetorical paideia that provided the backbone of Western education for 2,000 years. . . . Digital expression, in such a context, becomes not a revolutionary technology but a conservative one. It attempts to reclaim, and rethink, the basic Western wisdom about words. Its perils prove to be the great but familiar perils that have always lurked in the divided, unstable, protean Western self. (51)

Lanham deals specifically with the mingling of visual and verbal expression in his chapter "Digital Rhetoric and the Digital Arts." While he historicizes this hybridization by examining works of modernist and postmodernist art, Lanham never explicitly recognizes the potential for disciplinary and cultural challenge from outside this high-cultural world and its traditional hierarchies. "What happens when text moves from page to screen?" Lanham asks (31). With a glance back at "the history of illuminated manuscripts," Lanham illustrates the "struggle between icon and alphabet" with examples that reassure his largely academic audience of the centrality of their own cultural position, examining icono/typographical works by, among others, Filippo Tommaso Marinetti, Kenneth Burke, Roy Lichtenstein, and Christo Javacheff. Nowhere in the discussion does Lanham recognize the more egalitarian (and, for his audience, potentially threatening) sense of *iconic* defined not necessarily in terms of visual *forms*, but more generally as a code or style of expression characteristic of popular culture.[1] Constructed out of a vocabulary of socially agreed-upon symbols and roles—for example, celebrity images, mother figures, advertised visions of The Good Life—the iconic culture of display suggests that expressed meaning is immediate and denotative—cultural attitudes and assumptions that are very different from the iconoclastic, (post)modernist art works cited by Lanham. Indeed, works that emerge from the culture of elaborationism typically value complexity, irony, connotation, and deferred meanings, achieved through an awareness of the medium itself, whether visual or verbal. Lanham's examples thus suggest that the visualization of elaborated, verbal culture will happen via the high-culture world of the art gallery, overlooking the more genuine, popular visual rhetorics of television advertising, video-game animation, and Hollywood spectacle. In the next section, I will use specific examples to define terms in which these rhetorical and discursive challenges can be described and met.

POINTS OF FRICTION

As Cynthia and Richard Selfe have shown, the writing interfaces we sit down to every day are not "ideologically innocent or inert" utopias, but "complex political landscapes" (485, 481). Though the Selfes refer to electronic interfaces, the *metaphorical* interfaces constituted by composition theory and pedagogy also serve ideologically to structure the space between writer and writing project and to provide models of the writing process, its product, or its defining context. What, then, are the social consequences of composing through an interface that is visual and iconic in its focus, as opposed to one that is exclusively verbal in its procedures and results? What are the sources of dissonance when a writer brings both verbal and visual impulses to bear on a single page—whether in the case of Web authorship or the composition of any example of what W. J. T. Mitchell calls the "imagetext" (9)? What would be the tensions inherent within the hybrid products of a visualized English?

Almost any pairing of instructional interfaces could serve in the comparison that follows because we are concerned with what is happening on the level not so much of technique or even theory, but of cultural impulse: that of verbal development as opposed to visual display. These verbal and iconic approaches to composing are represented here by two popular books published twenty years apart. *Writing without Teachers* is one of the most influential pencil-and-paper composition texts of the 1970s and 1980s, in which Peter Elbow portrays the writing process as a passionately expressivist encounter between words and the self. On the other hand, Elizabeth Castro's *Netscape 3 for Macintosh* (a Visual Quickstart Guide) explains and aestheticizes features of Netscape's HTML Editor (later named the Composer) and analyzes how they constitute literacy on the more visually oriented Web. On first glance, this comparison would seem obviously loaded in favor of academic English studies: a rhetorical theorist versus a practical, how-to technical writer. The crucial distinction in the description that follows, however, does not oppose verbal depth with Web-site shallowness, but, more objectively, two cultural orientations—two historical modes of literacy as represented by "writing" manuals both intended for broad, popular audiences at their particular moments in history. Rather than viewing the comparison through the lens of academic culture, privileging Elbow's discourse as more advanced, evolved, or "later" than Castro's, despite their dates of publication, I will discuss each form of literacy in its own historical and cultural terms. To describe the essential points of friction between the layers of verbal and visual literacies in Web authorship, I will borrow a technique from Web authoring and "chunk" analyses of Elbow and Castro into four discrete categories: history, players, difficulty, and desires. These represent terms of potential rivalry between the verbal and iconic for discursive dominance on Web pages but also the possible unifying terms of a hybrid and dialogical sense of rhetoric that combines the visual and verbal in an "elaborated" discourse, a cultural and textual practice familiar to faculty and students who variously combine themselves under the rubric of "English."

1. History

Both Elbow and Castro agree with the Selfes that literacy is power, though their differences of medium and of historical context manifest themselves in a disagreement over how that power is to be seized and from whom. Elbow's preface begins, "Many people are now trying to become less helpless, both personally and politically: trying to claim more control over their own lives. One of the ways people most lack control over their own lives is through lacking control over words" (vii). Words in themselves are never any more or less powerful, of course. Elbow's prescription of verbal power as a cure for political helplessness, however, reflects particularly his historical moment of writing in February of 1973: the conviction of McCord and Liddy, on January 30, 1973, in the Watergate scandal that had made heroes of *Washington Post* journalists Bernstein and Woodward; the Vietnam Peace Agreement of January 22, 1973; the passage of the Equal Rights Amendment by twenty-two of the required thirty-eight states by the end of 1972. In journalism, diplomacy, and government, the written word seemed capable of defeating corruption, chaos, and inequality.

Though Castro's Netscape manual begins less loftily, she is no less historical in the sense she conveys of a moment of opportunity and change: "The beauty — and perils — of the World Wide Web is that everyone can publish their own information quickly and easily. As such, the Web is the fastest growing area in the computer world today. Each month thousands of new pages are added, by huge companies and private citizens alike" (ix). For Castro, the Web is not just "one of the ways" people contend for power and self-affirmation in a disempowering world; the Web *is* history, a rising tide that lifts "private citizens" and "huge companies" alike at a pace counted in months rather than years or generations. In both books, the notion of literacy is rhetorically presented not merely in terms of personal self-improvement, but as the ability and awareness to respond to a rare historical moment in which self-development and democratic social progress advance in step. Though Elbow and Castro present vastly different notions of good taste, writing competence, and discursive value, both claim the high ground of contemporary relevance and democratic progressivism.

2. Players

At the crux of these tensions between personal and social discourses stands the role of the "editor," a personification of the interface between writers and their social, rhetorical, and technological contexts. Elbow's now familiar innovation of freewriting separated the process of creation from the roles of editing and presenting:

> Editing, *in itself*, is not the problem. Editing is usually necessary if we want to end up with something satisfactory. The problem is that editing goes on *at the same time* as producing. The editor is, as it were, constantly looking over the shoulder of the producer and constantly fiddling with what he's doing while he's in the middle of trying to do it. No wonder the producer gets nervous, jumpy, inhibited, and finally can't be coherent. (5)

Elbow asserts the rights of authors' personal/productive sides against their complementary but puritanical public/editing sides, rhetorically authorizing his organic and domestic metaphors of true writing: growing and cooking.[2] "Growing" means "trying to help words grow" through a recursive and self-interrogational process (23). Drawn from the ideas of Ken Macrorie, "cooking" describes a process, more dialectical than growing, in which, says Elbow, "you have to let words talk to words" (26). This metaphor describes "the interaction of contrasting material" (49), which includes confrontations of contradictory metaphors, ideas, personal positions, cognitive perspectives, and genres as well as differences with real or potential readers (42–54). Cooking represents the essence of Elbow's system, whereby a potentially social sense of conflict and difference is textualized and internalized into the writer's private process of invention rather than dramatized by an encounter with an outside editor (that is, conventionalizing readers like the "teacher" of his book's title).

Netscape's Editor interface presents itself not in terms of Elbow's censorious "editor"/critic, but as a helpful and attractive array of editorial tool bars: buttons with icons of scissors, binoculars, links of chain, colorful checkerboards, and, most promising of all, a zigzagging blue lightning bolt shooting up from a piece of paper and labeled "Publish." In contrast to Elbow's metaphors of gradual and solitary verbal self-development, these inviting icons suggest that the business of "authoring" a Web page to be browsed is paradigmatically different from writing words on paper to be read. Because "everyone can publish" after the connectivity revolution, as the blue lightning bolt constantly reminds the writer, the Web page is less like public speaking — a commonplace metaphor for writing performance since Aristotle, which implies a one-speaker-at-a-time orderliness — and more like a shop window to the world, through which Web-page designers look outward to check the weather and which they stock and decorate to compete with all the other shops for attention from the street. On the Web, everyone "talks" at once, but this fact is not perceived as bedlam — as it would be in Elbow's metaphorically homey and intimate environment — because the Web's operational metaphors are spatial, iconic, and public, as implied in the preceding Main Street analogy. If Elbow's image for writing is slow home cooking, the Web's model is fast and convenient public takeout. In Castro's guide to this technological and iconographic retail landscape, the totality of Elbow's epic, personal, verbal struggle to gain control of life is relegated to one of the five steps listed under "Using paragraph styles": "1. Decide how you want to organize your information. Divide your page into sections, with descriptive headings. Apply the Heading styles to section heads" (183).

This is not to suggest, however, that the electronic, predominantly visual literacy imparted in Castro's manual does not raise significant issues of rhetoric, aesthetics, and ideology. Rather than Elbow's implied, dramatic struggle between the producer and editor in the writer's own mind, Castro's process of achieving personal power on the Web depends on learning to mediate among another cast of characters who lurk behind the scenes of Netscape's bright interface and whose relationships embroil the would-be Web-page designer in the Web's contentious combination of technology, human audience, and corporate capitalism. As Castro continually advises in *Netscape 3 for Macintosh*, "readers" on the Web receive the writer's text not just through a shared verbal language inscribed on a stable medium like paper, but through an intervening array of platforms, browsers, modems, invisible scripts, formatting languages, and corporate-specific extensions. Effects such as fonts, colors, tables, the wrapping of text around images, and images themselves may look fine on the writer's own browser but be invisible or incomprehensible to someone at the other end of this unpredictable chain of machines. Of all the effects possible on a Web page, the one least threatened by these vagaries is verbal text in paragraphs—what the Internet was originally designed to deliver and what the Editor's character-style box calls "normal." Web-literate and -illiterate authors can post sentences in paragraphs equally well. What distinguishes the truly powerful and effective Web author is the degree of control that he or she can have on the reader's experience of visual layout and graphic display as mediated through the intervening tangle of technologies.

3. Difficulty

Both Elbow and Castro define their different literacies according to the same standard—the degree of difficulty presented by a given effect in their respective writing environments. What is easy is never literate, whether it is prematurely submitting to one's own conventionalizing editor side or naively overloading a page with high-resolution graphics. Only those who resist the expedient and who master what is difficult will achieve personal empowerment. Since verbal production confronts the author with very different difficulties from Web designing, however, the two literacies in practice will constitute different tastes, values, and ideological standards.

As Richard Ohmann has shown, contemporary usage of the word *literacy* has its roots in the anxieties of nineteenth-century middle-class culture about the working classes, especially immigrants. As a social category, the notion of an exclusively "literate public" performed cultural work for diverse political persuasions: it was a means of exclusion by which cultural conservatives could distinguish themselves as fundamentally different from the "illiterate" masses, while liberals used it as a strategy of social containment whereby they could "help" the lower orders and thus exert paternalistic control over them (218–19). In Elbow's revolutionary struggle for personal empowerment, would-be writers must achieve literacy in writing by doing battle with their own self-repressive editorial impulses, especially early in the writing process, as well as by resisting an ideologically constituted aversion to verbal contradiction and self-argument:

> [E]ncourage conflicts or contradictions in your thinking. We are usually taught to avoid them; and we cooperate in this teaching because it is confusing or frustrating to hold two conflicting ideas at the same time. It feels like a dead end or a trap but really it is the most fruitful situation to be in. Unless you can get yourself into a contradiction, you may be stuck with no power to have any thoughts other than the ones you are already thinking. (50)

Echoing Keats's "negative capability," Elbow's metaphor of cooking—the creative "interaction of contrasting or conflicting materials" (49)—expresses a familiar narrative of development in elaborated, academic discourse: contradiction leads to more abstract, complex, and reflective thinking in which deferred meaning can be elaborated only through verbal connotations and ironies. In contrast, his elaborationist vision of "non-cooking" ("no power to have any thoughts other than the ones you are already thinking") describes an "iconic" writing process in which words serve as denotative pictures of pre-existing thought rather than "words talking to words" (26). In the unsuccessful, "non-cooking" version of the writing process, meaning is immediate, simple, and literal—and probably not very interesting unless "you already have brilliant fully-cooked material lying around in your head" (56).

In Castro's vision of a democratizing Internet, the illiterate Web page is not characterized by half-baked ideas and expression, but by a lack of friendliness and usability. Among Web sites dominated by "huge companies" and professional designers, the thoughtlessly constructed page reduces not only the author's effective connectivity, but cultural and economic competitiveness as well. Castro's manual devotes an entire page, set off visually with a gray background, to what she calls "The Page from Hell":

> The designer was so anxious to show you every image he's every [sic] created, that he placed them all on the same page. And no small images either—these are 24 bit color images. You're still on a 14.4 modem, but that's no excuse to make you wait this long to see the page. After a minute or two staring at the progress indicator at the bottom of the browser, you bag, and surf to a friendlier page. (195)

The defining difficulty lies in delivering this immediate, iconic content as attractively but quickly as possible with certain tricks that reconcile graphics with speed: for instance, the use of "a miniature version, or icon, of the image that links the user . . . to the full image" (195). Does the user need to see the full-sized image to understand the author's meaning? The *ethos* of Web literacy rejects such notions of intention and advocates relinquishing control of the presentation to the user — what Elbow's preface equates with control in life! For Castro, "information" needs merely to be chunked, organized, and made visually interesting. The illiterate "Page from Hell," on the other hand, represents an ill-advised HTML version of Elbow's verbal cooking: a dense, self-indulgent page produced in ignorance or defiance of technological (that is, editorial) standards.

4. Desires

Arguably, surfing and cooking exemplify diametrically opposed cultural desires. Peter Elbow's metaphor of cooking is decidedly homey and cozy. Like simmering chili in a pot, cooking is energy turned back on itself, under pressure, bringing about what he calls "the interaction of contrasting and conflicting material": "bubbling, percolating, fermenting, chemical interaction, atomic fission" (49, 48). The conflicting material may be found among different people, ideas, perspectives, metaphors, genres, or aspects of the same person (49–56), but everything is brought together under one lid to produce a verbal unity. Elbow's other metaphor of the writing process, growing, is dependent on cooking: "Cooking drives the engine that makes growing happen. It's because of cooking . . . that a writer can start out after supper seeing, feeling, and knowing one set of things and end up at midnight seeing, feeling, and knowing things he hadn't thought of before" (50). Elbow's example — down to his use of the old-fashioned *supper* rather than *dinner* — suggests that growing/cooking is a domestic and intimate site of literacy, a homey space for self-transformation, which eventual readers will discover only by reexperiencing the verbal process of cooking in their own easy chairs.

The defining desire on the Web, of course, is the restless user's thirst for constant novelty, variety, and potential surprise. Castro begins her early chapter "Surfing the Web,"

> This is what you've been waiting for: actually getting to surf the World Wide Web. Although *surf* seems like a strange way to describe your activities . . . in front of a computer . . . , it does capture the idea of jumping from one Web page to another, perhaps reading and exploring as you go along, perhaps just enjoying the spray of information. (21)

Surfing is part of a more general trope of travel by which flesh-and-blood users orient themselves in the virtual "environment." Landow's article "The Rhetoric of Hypermedia" likens the Web-site designer's task to that of an airport architect: "Drawing upon the analogy of travel, we can say that the first problem [of orienting readers of hypermedia] concerns *navigation* information necessary for making one's way through the materials. The second concerns *exit* or *departure* information and the third *arrival* or *entrance* information" (82).

The contrasting desires of the reflective culinary homebody and the footloose, stimulus-seeking globetrotter have profound textual implications. True to its elaborationist cultural roots, Elbow's chili is "well wrought." Every ingredient, every word, is equally dependent on the rest for its effect. In the electronic lexia, however, unlinked text can appear, to restless eyes, as merely a spatial matrix for the important linked words that allow readers to realize the full potential of hypertext and launch themselves to whatever other site that they have determined, for their own reasons, to be more relevant. Though barely large enough to read, a playful sample Web page in Castro's book suggests the rhetorical implications of linkable environments for Elbow's notion of good writing:

> My Home Page
>
> Is that an exciting title or what? Truly inspired. I should have some kind of personal statement here, but I'm totally stymied today for examples. I'll just blab on and on (that's not so unusual in a Web page) until the rest of the page is hidden, which is the point anyway, at least for this example. If you want to skip all this and get to <u>my favorite Web sites,</u> just go ahead. (209)

In this "uncooked" text, the colors and underlining visually distinguish the key words, making their iconic importance concrete, literal, immediate, and explicit. In this space between links, then, Castro's sample Web author is free to indulge in a breezy, self-conscious style that Elbow might excuse as freewriting, but that more conservative, verbal elaborationists would dismiss as illiterate chatter. The words themselves hardly make a greater claim for themselves: "If you want to skip all this and get to <u>my favorite Web sites,</u> just go ahead." Who am I, says the iconic style, to detain you here with a lot of mutually involved words?

A HYBRID LITERACY OF WORDS AND IMAGES

The historical mingling and dissonance of these histories, players, difficulties, and desires will define writing for generations to come. The evolutionary narrative from orality to written literacy to what Jean Baudrillard calls "digitality" suggests, perhaps, too linear a scheme to trace the broad history of human communication. Nonetheless, our own generation is involved in a paradigm shift as significant as the one Julian Jaynes has described as occurring in the second millennium BCE, when, he argues, the new technology of writing and other factors broke down the "bicameral mind," producing a modern sense of consciousness that we customarily assume to be inherently human and universal (208). And yet, even allowing for technology's accelerating pace of change, history suggests that the rhetorics of literacy and digitality will long be intertwined: "[E]ach medium arises by building recursively upon its predecessor," writes John McDaid, "taking the previous technology as 'content'" (209). More suggestively, as Gary Heba argues, new communication technologies appropriate not just the content of the older ones, but "the literacies required to read and interpret the earlier technologies in a process of 'repurposing' information, that is, using certain features of older communication technologies in the newer ones" (20).

This mingling and repurposing are evident historically in ways that orality has survived and insinuated itself into the conventions of writing and print culture during their emergence and dominance. Aristotle's rhetorical model of civic speech, for instance, has served as a means of conceptualizing and teaching written communication for two thousand years. For centuries after the invention of printing, the reading of the Bible or the recitation of poetry continued to be an oral practice in schools, in family parlors, and at social gatherings. Even Marcel Proust's densely verbal, high-literary performances have been visualized and understood by twentieth-century narratologist Gérard Genette in terms of speakers and speech (see Figure 1). These examples suggest that the new varieties of competence required by computer interfaces will not soon comprise pure digitality, but a hybrid of verbal and visual literacies, of textual integrity and hypertextual porousness. In the terms developed above, history suggests that Elbow's expressive, socially isolated ideals of growing and cooking will continue to function, in some form, within the highly interactive, fast-paced environment of iconic digitality. As Greg Ulmer observes, "People will not stop using print any more than they stopped talking when they became literate. But they will use it differently — will speak and write differently within the frame of electronics" (*Teletheory* 2). The challenge for the Web writer, then, is to understand the varieties of this hybridization of literacy and digitality and the possibilities they may offer for verbal authorship as well as iconic authoring.

In a visualized English Studies, writers are thus conscious of the need to resist the traditional impulse to isolate themselves in the cozy kitchen of verbal literacy and grow and cook in response to the public role the words must

FIGURE 1. From Gérard Genette's *Narrative Discourse Revisited*

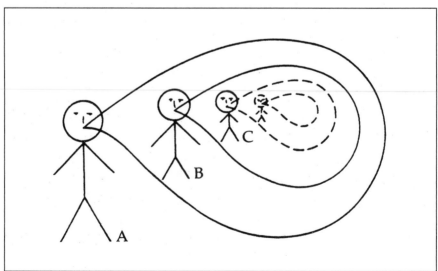

Trans. Jane E. Lewin. Ithaca: Cornell UP, 1988, 85.

play in the visual scheme of the page. Words don't simply talk to words, but to images, links, horizontal lines—to every feature of the iconographic page. While Web pages still partly replicate the left-to-right, top-to-bottom verbal literacy of the written page—just as postbellum American print culture repurposed oral narrative in the form of the regional dialect story—the most characteristic Web writing necessarily avoids the verbal purity and isolation that exemplifies *Writing without Teachers*. Such writing reconciles the struggle that Jay David Bolter describes as taking place between the values of nature and culture:

> The picture pretends to be a reflection of the visible world. . . . Therefore [Western artists assumed that] the space of the picture should reflect the space of nature. . . . In a verbal text, the space is wholly conventionalized, and learning to read means learning the conventions of the space. Pictorial space and textual space are therefore apparent opposites; one claims to reflect a world outside of it, the other is arbitrary and self-contained. (53)

In the synthesis, or at least orchestration, of these opposites into a hybrid composition, chunks of words that exemplify Elbow's ideal of verbal expressive literacy appear as distinct, internally organized structures within the matrix of non- and extra-verbal languages and codes, like crystals suspended in a liquid solution. Readers trained in the protocols of textual print culture want such words to talk to other words—to paraphrase Elbow—to combine into larger verbal structures, and to resist interruption by images, white space, hypertextual links, typographic effects, and multimedia. To such a reader and mode of reading, the chunking of sustained passages of words prevents elaboration and development as prose. Verbal structures in a hybrid environment like the Web appear to withhold themselves from the seeming discursive chaos and dissipation, to turn inward into what Bolter calls their own self-contained worlds, much as "poetic" discourse insulates itself from the "novelistic" play of languages in Mikhail Bakhtin's work:

> In poetic genres, artistic consciousness . . . fully realizes itself within its own language . . . sealing itself off from influence of extraliterary social dialects. Therefore such ideas as a special "poetic language," and "language of the gods," a "priestly language of poetry" and so forth could flourish [only] on poetic soil. (285, 287)

Even the "early" Peter Elbow of *Writing without Teachers* would undoubtedly object to this characterization as the very opposite of cooking's interaction of conflicting material. Conflicting words and images, he might argue, could be cooked together and grown just as readily as conflicting sets of words. What Bakhtin further offers a visualized English studies, however, is a theoretical vision of hybridization that goes beyond invention processes like growing and cooking, which metaphorically emphasize the text's and the writer's own internal development. That is, Bakhtin's "novelistic hybrid" refers simultaneously to the unifying, formal arrangement of languages *in* the novel as well as to profoundly social processes of cultural interaction operating around and through its creation—something at once inside and beyond the unitary, self-referential, self-determining world of words: "[T]he novelistic hybrid is an artistically organized system for bringing different languages in contact with one another, a system having as its goal the illumination of one language by means of another, the carving-out of a living image of another language" (361). Bakhtin's own choice of words is helpful in establishing the pedagogical and theoretical claims that a visualized English studies could make to hybrid composing environments such as those of electronic communication. By definition, Bakhtinian "novels" are characterized not by their purity, but by their dynamic, social hybridity. From this point of view, then, the mingling of verbal and visual elements so typical of Web authorship represents a potential realization of novelistic discourse rather than a necessary degradation of the literacy that the novel has come to signify. The mere juxtaposition of words and images, however, would not automatically result in the mutual "illumination" of languages or forms. Hybridity for Bakhtin must not simply be formal or generic, but ideological and historical. Words and images that come from the same "conception of the world" would constitute utterances in the same ideological language: "All words," writes Bakhtin (we might add "or images") "have the 'taste' of a profession, a genre, a tendency, a party, a particular work, a particular person, a generation, an age group, the day and hour. Each word [or image] tastes of the context and contexts in which it has lived its socially charged life; all words and forms are populated by intentions" (293). For Bakhtin, these intentions are the "force that stratifies and differentiates the common literary language, and not the linguistic markers . . . of generic languages, professional jargons and so forth—markers that are, so to speak, the sclerotic deposits of an intentional process" (292). Without an awareness of these intentions, "all we have left is the naked corpse of the word" or, we might suggest, of the word-image trope (292). Thus, wrapping text around an image in Netscape's Editor does not necessarily create novelistic hybridity in the Bakhtinian sense. It is not the mere juxtaposition of different genres, but the contact of underlying, contrasting intentions along the formal borders between words and images which produces the connotative, reflexive effects that we English-department elaborationists would generally value as "literary," "critical," or "complex." Ultimately, as I will show in the examples that follow, what distinguishes genuine "illumination" from mere "illustration" is a clash of living, social intentions rather than the formal arrangement of what Bakhtin calls those intentions' "sclerotic deposits"—whether they be verbal or visual.

The use of contrasting intentions and styles would seem to contradict the conventional wisdom, codified by George Landow in "The Rhetoric of Hypermedia," that words should provide faithful, navigational keys for hypertextual arrivals and departures. Do word-image hybrids currently on the Web manage to perform both functions: to conduct the user smoothly through the site as well as to illuminate mutually contrasting languages in a dialogical whole? Figure 2 shows a page from Landow's *Victorian Web*. At first glance, the presentation of verbal and visual texts seems entirely

FIGURE 2. George Landow's "Victorian Furniture Design"

Victorian Furniture Design

<u>George P. Landow,</u> **Professor of English and Art History, Brown University**

The VICTORIAN *Web*   literature, history, & culture in the age of Victoria

When many people think of the term Victorian, they envisage this kind of extremely ornate, even cluttered furniture proudly shown at the <u>1851 Crystal Palace exhibition</u>. During the decades of the twentieth century when the stripped-down, supposedly functional aesthetic of High Modernism ruled, most found it difficult to take seriously any Victorian furniture and design anything other than the proto-modern work inspired by <u>Ruskin</u> and <u>Morris</u>.

Look at the way the designers of this hideous furniture treat surface, overall design, and allusion and see how many similarities you can discern between this still unfashionable work and the writings of, say, <u>Carlyle</u>, <u>Dickens</u>, <u>Elizabeth</u> and <u>Robert Browning</u>, and <u>Trollope</u>. To begin with, what are the literary analogues of surface embellishment in this furniture?

Follow for more examples of <u>this kind of design</u> -- and the <u>reactions</u> against it.

The Victorian Web. <http://landow.stg.brown.edu/victorian/art/design/clutter1.html> (January 31, 1998).

monoglossic, without contrast or tension of any kind. The title, the image, and the text—even the thumbnail GIFs—converge on the notion of Victorianism. Landow's written prose makes this point explicit: "When many people think of the term Victorian, they envisage. . . . " Nothing here appears to disturb the user's preconceptions about Victorianism.

To be genuinely dialogical and "novelistic," Landow's words and images would need to illuminate one another mutually, rather than the image simply illustrating or illuminating the words. If the words talk to the images, do the images respond and resist? Certainly, Landow's prose is aggressive in referring to, framing, and containing the images of the chairs. The demonstrative pronouns *this* and the imperative voice ("Look at the way. . . ") represent verbal claims on the visual field of the images, Landow suggests an irony in the "ornate, even cluttered furniture" being "proudly shown at the 1851 Crystal Palace exhibition." He even terms "hideous" the designer's treatment of "surface, overall design, and allusion." Finally, Landow invites his reader to view the images as analogues of the literary styles of other written texts: that is, his words (questions) suggest new ways to produce words (analysis) about other words (the writings of Carlyle, etc.) via these visual texts. The images themselves do not and cannot respond. It is not because they are in themselves hideous or unworthy of pride, but because it is obvious in the context of Landow's page that the images are not *intended* to complicate or contradict the judgments of the written words. Long jaded to the sophisticated visual appeals of glossy magazine and television advertising, Landow's contemporary audience would recognize the "here's the chair" presentation of nineteenth-century advertising as pedestrian and deliberately quaint. Would the effect of Landow's prose be the same beside a photograph from a coffee-table book on Victorian furniture? Though historically and textually the images represent Victorian tastes, they are not intended here to "speak for" Victorian taste, in the way Bakhtin describes the "image of another's language and outlook on the world . . . [as] simultaneously represented and representing" in novelistic discourse (45). Instead, images and words function as part of the same, latter-twentieth-century academic discourse of Victorian studies.

Greg Ulmer's Web essay, "Metaphoric Rocks: A Psychogeography of Tourism and Monumentality," provides a suggestive example of a text that brings words and images into dialogical relation. In contrast to Landow's scholarly, word-dominated page, Ulmer's words and images are able to speak to one another because neither directly illustrates the other. The lack of an obvious, illustrative relation suggests the possibility, at least, of a mutually *illuminative* relation in the spirit of the dialogism that Bakhtin describes among languages in the novel. "Metaphoric Rocks" demonstrates how a genuinely dialogical verbal text can be integrated with a dialogical set of images — a principle of authorship with implications, I would argue, for both third-generation Web design and for a visualized English. In essence, rather than a page made monological by the dominance of either alphabetic or iconographic language, both verbal and visual elements are located within a dialogically animated field of contrasting (in this case, comically resonating) intentions. Conventional, formal word-image relations are disrupted by the unconventional, cultural play of voices and purposes.

The verbal text of Ulmer's essay is ostensibly addressed to the Florida Tourism Commission, on behalf of the "Florida Research Ensemble [or FRE] . . . a faculty group at the University of Florida that practices an experimental approach to arts and letters." Ulmer's narrator takes exception to the fact that the commission has paid $250,000 to the New York consulting firm Penn and Schoen to advise the state on its role in promoting tourism:

> If there is an agricultural problem the Institute for Food and Agricultural Sciences at the University of Florida is called on for advice. But when there is a cultural problem, why does no one ask the experts in culture at the University for advice? . . . This question is addressed as much to the professors as to the state agency, of course. . . . FRE is not "competing" with Penn and Schoen for the PR job; we offer a different expertise, which until now has not been applied to tourism except in the negative mode of critique.

From this not-unreasonable premise, Ulmer's modest proposal blossoms into an unlikely vision of a "Florida Rushmore" constructed in a sinkhole outside of Gainesville. Ulmer imagines a kind of underground, holographic drive-in movie theater where tourists take advantage of techniques of composite photography ("used by the FBI to update photographs of missing children, and by PEOPLE magazine to project the effect of age on celebrities") to construct mythic, national images out of the faces not of dead presidents, but of "figures with whom . . . [the tourists] identify—figures that represent their 'personalized' or internal Rushmores."

Ulmer's mingling of words and images is made possible by his very deliberate misunderstanding of the conventional, cultural distinctions between academic-critical and state-promotional discourses, which creates in "Metaphoric Rocks" a dialogical tension between these usually divergent languages and intentions. Despite the theoretical content of much of the essay's verbal text, the academic language never entirely subsumes or incorporates the public-relations discourse as it might in singly intended rhetoric. Nor does the essay obey the convention of the tall tale to give itself away. Under the businesslike heading "Project Pleasure-Dome," Ulmer describes the eighteenth-century travels of William Bartram through an area south of Gainesville now known as Payne's Prairie, "part," he hastens to add, "of the local formation in Alachua County that includes the Devil's Millhopper." Modulating then from the language of state historical promotion to that of literary scholarship—or, perhaps, parodies of these—Ulmer observes,

> It is said that Samuel Taylor Coleridge's reading of Bartram's *Travels* (one of the most popular books of its day) influenced the dream that led to the writing of the poem, "Kubla Kahn," about the place "Xanadu," in which "did Kubla Khan/A stately pleasure-dome decree: Where Alph, the sacred river, ran/Through caverns measureless to man/Down to a sunless sea/So twice five miles of fertile ground/with walls and towers were girdled round" (Coleridge).

Ulmer then associates Coleridge's Xanadu with Ted Nelson's model of an electronic, literary metatext, Project Xanadu—an early hypertextual experiment—which he in turn compares to the "network of underground rivers of Florida Karst," (*karst* being the soluble limestone topology of northern Florida which features caverns and sinkholes like the Devil's Millhopper, site of Ulmer's proposed "school of monumentality"). The languages of scholarly transhistorical synthesis and touristic promotion remain mutually opened and dialogical because it is never made explicit whether Ulmer's satire is aimed at the overreaching pedant or the overreaching salesman, or indeed if the proposal is satire at all.

What is most relevant about "Metaphoric Rocks," for the present purpose, is not the verbal text itself, of course, but its relation to the twenty-one visual graphics interspersed throughout. The capacity or trope of verbal-visual hybridity is made possible on the page by the very slipperiness of determining *which* of the verbal intentions the images might be illustrating. The verbal text here is, in Bakhtinian terms, highly double-voiced and stratified, and that internal dialogism among the words allows for a sense of independent play among the collective body of accompanying visual texts—all existing within what Bakhtin would call a disputed zone between languages/intentions in which the images, not just individually but in combination, objectify and "italicize" these dialogical tensions. These images, therefore, constitute an alternative, parallel text which doesn't simply follow the verbal text, but rises and falls independently on these same dialogical waves of discursive contention.

The first and second JPEG images, for example (see Figure 3), are obviously linked by their captions: the old and new Atlantis. They are connected spatially and intellectually by a paragraph in the essay arguing that "travel was an essential element of archaic theoria" and that the first tourists were, in fact, Greek philosophers and "theorists." At this point in the written text, scholarly language and intentions seem to dominate, methodically and univocally asserting the authority of modern theorists (that is, the academically affiliated Florida Research Ensemble's "New Consultancy") "to apply our knowledge to the design of an improved tourism." The image of "Plato's Plan of Atlantis" illustrates what the text defines as "Plato's effort to understand how to put into practice the principles of a just state outlined in the Republic." The legend of Atlantis, writes Ulmer, came to Plato from Solon, the first theorist/tourist, who had learned of the lost civilization on a visit to Egypt. In this sense, the image titled "Plato's Plan of Atlantis" is presented as illustratively as Landow's chairs: a map of the ideal state as well as a tourist's (or "Solonist's") souvenir.

The second image, "The New Atlantis," visually repeats the first image's symmetrical design, with right and left sides facing one another to create the effect of insularity and unity. Like the first image, it is both a map and a souvenir. What may first appear an artistic arrangement of different advertisements proves on closer examination to be a happy accident of the processes of mechanical reproduction and mass marketing: a tri-fold pamphlet advertising the Kennedy Space Center, spread out flat to show one complete side of the printed sheet. But does the suggested comparison work completely? Does the pamphlet also represent perhaps in its proclamation of "FREE ADMISSION AND PARKING!"—a visualization of the principles of a just society? The pairing and captioning of the images, as well as the academic argument of the verbal text, insist on this possibility. However, the "everyday," contextual distinction between the intentions of Platonic philosophy toward Atlantis in the *Timaeus* ("to understand . . . the just state") and the intentions of the promotional ad ("Florida's Best Visitor Value . . .") exemplify and "italicize" strains among these differing languages which the verbal argument at this point would suppress.

"Ulmer's "Metaphoric Rocks," then, represents a larger, dynamic structure in which both the verbal text *and* the string of images are dialogical. The role played by the images, however, is not simply illustrative because the zigzagging lines of dialogical development—the explicit shifts and juxtapositions between these languages/intentions in verbal and visual terms—are roughly parallel but not precisely synchronous. At just the point when the

FIGURE 3. Plato's Plan of Atlantis and the New "Atlantis"

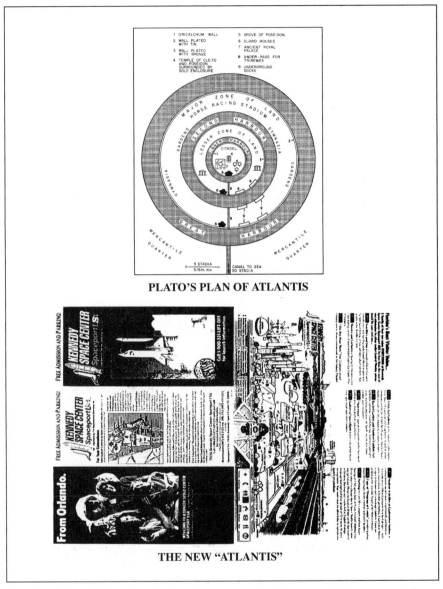

PLATO'S PLAN OF ATLANTIS

THE NEW "ATLANTIS"

From Greg Ulmer's "Metaphoric Rocks: A Psychogeography of Tourism and Monumentality."
Rewired. *<http://www.clas.ufl.edu/clas/departments/rewired/ulmer.html> (February 1, 1998).*
Plato's plan of Atlantis reprinted from The End of Atlantis *(1969) by J. V. Luce by permission of*
the publisher (London: Thames and Hudson Ltd.).

verbal essay deploys its most monoglossic, academic language (and the loftiest and most sustained appeal to Classical learning), the images "spoil things" by presenting a jarring, playful contrast of the intellectual/philosophical and touristic/commercial. This is the very same contrast, however, that the verbal text makes manifest elsewhere: in the New Consultancy's feigned begrudging of the state's $250,000 payment to Penn and Schoen or in the deliberate absurdity of its proposing a "Tourist Hall of Fame commemorating tourist sacrifices to chance" in a state now internationally famous for out-of-state visitors' falling prey to random highway shootings and public robberies. In essence, the visuals zig where the verbal text zags.

This analysis of Ulmer's "Metaphoric Rocks" demonstrates the elaborationist possibilities of visual-verbal hybridity — dialogical capabilities that desktop publishing programs, Web-page authoring tools, and even word-processing applications make increasingly available and inviting to nonprofessional composers. Whether users become critically aware of these implications and possibilities, however, depends upon the availability of a theoretical language and a critical tradition for describing these effects and a pedagogical apparatus for teaching them. Such effects are not the inevitable result of mingling words and images, but the product of a degree of consciousness in reading and composing — an expressed purpose in many an English Studies course syllabus. Consider for example a sentence from earlier in this article:

> . . . [O]ur own generation is involved in a paradigm shift as significant as the one Julian Jaynes has described as occurring in the second millennium BCE, when, he argues, the new technology of writing and other factors broke down the "bicameral mind," producing a modern sense of consciousness that we customarily assume to be inherently human and universal.

What kind of image might be set beside these words not simply to illustrate them, but to invoke the spirit of mutually illuminating dialogue? One of the products of the breakdown of the bicameral mind, according to Jaynes, was the emergence of virtually all of the current world's major religions within a relatively brief span of time. On first consideration, then, a conventional religious symbol — perhaps Jesus on the cross — might seem visually to invite the reader to consider the cultural and historical implications produced by the rise of writing as a culturally dominant discourse.

Such a visual reference, however, would illuminate only the paradigm shift described by Jaynes, the invoked historical authority, and would ignore more dialogical instabilities suggested in the apparent slippage (at least for some of us) between "modern . . . consciousness" and the assumption of its essential universality. An image used dialogically would not passively illustrate the passage's unquestioned opposition of ancient and modern cultures, but speak to and elaborate the verbal text's perhaps accidental insinuation of doubt ("that we customarily assume") about modernity's claims of universal relevance. If we pair the passage with the Aubrey Beardsley illustration in Figure 4, for instance, modernity is both illustrated and questioned. Though the *Yellow Book* cover specifies London of the 1890s, the graphic's primary elements — the bookshop window, the fashionable shopper, the street lamp — all evoke an urban individual in a cosmopolitan cityscape, a mode of life and consciousness which is not only modernist in the early-twentieth-century

FIGURE 4. Aubrey Beardsley, Prospectus Design for the *Yellow Book*

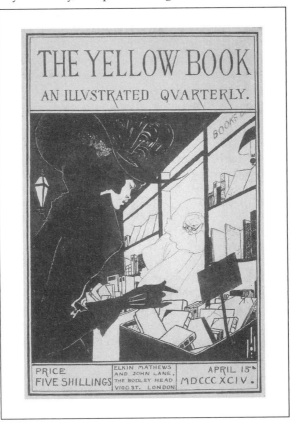

Victoria & Albert Museum, London. Art Resource, NY.

sense, but characteristic of an older historical phase of modernity. The solitary browser in the city suggests an individual who presumably is not bound by local provincialism (the circulating library or the traditional domestic bookshelf), but who is free to choose among alternatives in this open marketplace of ideas and tastes.

In contradiction, however, to the norms of nineteenth-century representation, which would have invited readers to infer that any woman alone at night in the street was a prostitute, Beardsley's browser is obviously a well-to-do woman. The image itself suggests a conflict between the post-Renaissance sense of modernity — personified by the caricatured capitalist proprietor/Pierrot blocking the doorway — and the consciously iconoclastic, *fin de siècle* modernism represented by the emancipated woman customer. Indeed, Beardsley's rendering makes the attitude of the woman toward the books she finds there ambiguous (her fingers are both extended toward and withheld back from the bin), as is the gaze (forbidding? anxious? surprised?) of the Pierrot figure toward the woman and his stock (Fletcher 97–98). Both figures, as well as the city environment they share, are products of the modern, individualist culture of the written word which Jaynes describes emerging from the breakdown of the bicameral mind, but the image contradicts and complicates the assumption—which the verbal passage barely questions—that the resulting modernity is unitary and universal.

Thus, the seams and margins between visual and verbal elements can become contact zones between the roles of digital editor and literate writer in which the hybrid composition practices can be pursued. In Bakhtin's words,

> the intention of the author, refracted as it passes through these planes, does not wholly give itself up to any of them. It is as if the author has no language of his own, but does possess his own style, his own organic and unitary law governing the way he plays with languages and the way his own real semantic and expressive intentions are refracted through them. (311)

To theorize how authorship can be expressed in these gaps, Bakhtin's implied metaphor of the prism could be extended to another optical phenomenon: pinhole projection. As the tiny spaces between the leaves of a tree cast hundreds of crescent-shaped dapples on the ground during a solar eclipse, the gaps between words and images can project the shape of the author's intentions, which may not be directly expressed in either the verbal or visual process/text alone. As we have seen in the case of Landow's "Victorian Furniture Design," not all combinations of visual editing and verbal writing express these dialogical tensions or gaps and thus these suggestive projections. The suitably illustrative nature of Landow's images, vis-à-vis the verbal commentary, makes this page monoglossic and authoritative, despite the hypertext user's democratic power to click elsewhere at will. In a hybrid, dialogical composition, however, the appropriateness of the author's choice and placement of the visual text is not obviously clear, creating a suggestive difficulty, an insinuating gap that raises questions not only about the graphic or the verbal text itself, but about the rhetorical, cultural, and historical intentions that bring them together.

REPURPOSING ELABORATIONISM

Early in this essay, I introduced the contrast of Peter Elbow's *Writing without Teachers* and Elizabeth Castro's *Netscape 3 for Macintosh* by claiming that the literacy exemplified by Elbow's ideal of verbal ability would not be privileged over that of Castro's model of electronic, visual competence. Indeed, with the subsequent contrast of Landow's and Ulmer's texts, I have attempted to demonstrate one way that "depth" or "cooking" is not exclusive to traditional elaborationists' versions of writing. I have tried to suggest how the practical skills and hybrid medium described in Castro's book can also produce texts that embody the complex, ironic, and connotative effects valued by the dominant, "modernist" tradition of English studies.

With the examples of Castro and Ulmer, I have shown how, in these electronic or hybrid contexts, modernist practice does not simply disappear into postmodern fragments, but is repurposed beyond literary, high-cultural, or even "literate" practice. In this repurposed form, this connotative, self-reflexive discourse assumes a life beyond the historically specific or genre-bound rubrics of "modernism" or "literature" or even "A+ student writing," which necessitates a more general term such as "elaborationist." When we acknowledge that elaborationism is expressed outside its traditionally recognized forms and media, we discover continuities between traditionally defined English studies and certain possibilities in the hybrid practices of popular and Web cultures.

All that is well enough. However, what is more challenging to English Studies—admittedly one of the more balkanized political interests on campus—are the continuities that a term such as "elaborationism" reveals between persistent curricular and theoretical differences within the discipline between poetic and rhetorical discourses, which James Berlin has located as the crux of the English profession's ongoing crisis of identity (xi). Indeed, it is the mystification of this sense of poetic or "critical" elaborationism—versus a presumed rhetorical instrumentalism—that has traditionally served as a means to separate the sheep and goats in English studies, a bifurcation that Berlin characterizes as the "governing scheme" of the profession founded on "the division between sacred and profane texts, the division between the priestly class and the menial class, the placing of beauty and truth against the utilitarian and commonplace" (85). In essence, this poetic-rhetoric divide marks a protective border imagined between ordinary discourses of the workplace or popular culture and an ideal of elaborated discourse as a special province of literary artistry or critical literacy—an ideal attainable only by those practicing certain higher formal genres in select cultural situations or perhaps by the occasional auteur.

While "Metaphoric Rocks" is written from within this protective circle of academic English, it also reflects an effort, expressed in entirely serious terms or not, to reach beyond its confines to a wider relevance. Working parallel to these cultural politics, Ulmer's visual/verbal technique not only exemplifies the hybrid possibilities of electronic composition, but demonstrates a synthesis of poetic and rhetoric, the aesthetic and practical, which cuts across the lines of the English curriculum's traditional "governing scheme." As commentators from Raymond Williams to Manuel Castells have argued, technological innovations such as the Internet have not functioned simply as determinates of global change, but as occasions for "local" cultures to reproduce and reinvent themselves—or not—in postindustrial terms. Consider, for instance, the very different social and cultural results seen in the development of network television in Britain in contrast to the United States (Williams 120–21), or the divergent effects produced by the integration of globalizing technologies into the culture of 1960s Japan in contrast to their irrelevance to the centralized, "statist" culture of the former Soviet Union (Castells 11–13). In light of this latter example especially, it seems crucial that the "local" culture of English studies, first, look beyond its internal dissensions and begin to recognize its own peculiar literacies and logics in the hybrid practices of everyday, nonprofessional composers, even if we can no longer strictly call them "writers." Doing so requires that the discipline also recognize elaborationism not as a special, higher, historically more advanced literacy—available only through a rejection of the visual, electronic, or popular—but as one among other literate possibilities in a wider, emergent networked culture. By visualizing its mostly verbal practices, English studies could both recognize its continuities with these extra-verbal cultures and, looking inward, really see the priestly and profane words that divide us.

NOTES

1. My association of the term *iconic* with popular, situational discourses draws, most obviously, on Basil Bernstein's now controversial distinction between "elaborated and restricted" language codes, since applied by Patricia Bizzell in her critique of academic culture's customary responses to the problems of basic writers. Though largely discounted today, Bernstein's distinction is extremely useful in differentiating "elaborated" discourse from verbal discourse generally; for instance, a novel may present an iconographic narrative that does not necessarily invoke the connotative, self-reflexive effects of verbal language. Thus, not all verbal discourse is elaborated, which also implies that not all elaborated discourse needs to be verbal. I too resist, however, the drift of Bernstein's theory, despite his best efforts to the contrary, which appears to perpetuate the very social-class assumptions that he was attempting to describe and expose. The problem with both Bernstein's and Bizzell's assumptions lies in placing iconic discourse in an historical position *prior*, and thus inferior, to a verbal or "elaborated" discourse, in assumed narratives of individual and cultural development. In *Literacy Into Cultural Studies*, Anthony Easthope contrasts iconic representation of imperialism in *Tarzan of the Apes* with a more critical, "elaborated" one from Conrad's *Heart of Darkness* and questions academe's customary privileging of the latter discourse. In essence, Easthope attempts to reverse the time line by placing elaborationist (or what he terms "modernist") discourse in a narrative position prior to postmodern iconic practice, a historical process that he explicitly connects with his own experiences on university campuses in the 1960s and 1970s. In the years since Easthope's book, the Web and its visual discourse have become integrated into academic life to a degree that this privileging of elaborated discourse as a "later" and thus more advanced stage of cultural development is more obviously open to question.

2. Peter Elbow's notion of a teacherless writing class does recognize social aspects of writing in *Writing without Teachers*. However, chapters 4 and 5, which deal with this social process, follow those defined as "the process of writing" itself: chapter 1, "Freewriting Exercises"; chapter 2, "The Process of Writing—Growing"; and chapter 3, "The Process of Writing—Cooking."

WORKS CITED

Bakhtin, Mikhail. *The Dialogic Imagination*. Trans. Caryl Emerson and Michael Holquist. Austin: U of Texas P, 1981.

Baudrillard, Jean. *Simulations*. New York: Semiotext(e), 1983.

Berlin, James A. *Rhetorics, Poetics, and Cultures: Refiguring College English Studies*. Urbana: NCTE, 1996.

Bernstein, Basil. *Class Codes and Control*. Vol. 1. London: Routledge, 1973.

Bizzell, Patricia. "College Composition: Initiation into the Academic Discourse Community." *Curriculum Inquiry* 12.2 (1982): 191–207.

Bolter, Jay David. *Writing Space: The Computer, Hypertext, and the History of Writing*. Hillsdale, NJ: Lawrence Erlbaum, 1991.

Castells, Manuel. *The Rise of the Network Society*. Malden, MA: Blackwell, 1996. Vol. 1 of *The Information Age: Economy, Society and Culture*. 3 vols.

Castro, Elizabeth. *Netscape 3 for Macintosh*. Visual Quickstart Guide. Berkeley: Peachpit Press, 1996.

Easthope, Anthony. *Literary Into Cultural Studies*. London: Routlege, 1991.

Elbow, Peter. *Writing without Teachers*. London: Oxford UP, 1973.

Fletcher, Ian. *Aubrey Beardsley*. Boston: Twayne, 1987.

Genette, Gérard. *Narrative Discourse Revisited*. Trans. Jane E. Lewin. Ithaca: Cornell UP, 1988.

Heba, Gary. "HyperRhetoric: Multimedia, Literacy, and the Future of Composition." *Computers and Composition* 14 (1997): 19–44.

"How Wide Is the Web? *CyberAtlas*. 23 September 1999 <http://cyberatlas.internet.com/big_picture/ demographics/article/0,1323,5931_199701,00.html>.

Jaynes, Julian. *The Origin of Consciousness in the Breakdown of the Bicameral Mind*. Boston: Houghton Mifflin, 1976.

Landow, George P. *Hypertext: The Convergence of Contemporary Critical Theory and Technology*. Baltimore: Johns Hopkins UP, 1992.

———. "The Rhetoric of Hypermedia: Some Rules for Authors." *Hypermedia and Literary Studies*. Ed. Paul Delany and George P. Landow. Cambridge, MA: MIT P, 1991. 81–103.

———. "Victorian Furniture Design." *The Victorian Web*. 31 January 1998 <http:// landow.stg.brown.edu/victorian/art/design/clutter1.html>.

Lanham, Richard. *The Electronic Word: Democracy, Technology and the Arts*. Chicago: U Chicago P, 1995.

McDaid, John. "Toward an Ecology of Hypermedia." *Evolving Perspectives on Computers and Composition Studies: Questions for the 1990s*. Ed. Gail E. Hawisher and Cynthia Selfe. Urbana, IL: NCTE and *Computers and Composition*, 1991. 203–23.

Mitchell, W. J. T. *Iconology: Image, Text, Ideology*. Chicago: U Chicago P, 1986.

Ohmann, Richard. *Politics of Letters*. Middletown, CT: Wesleyan UP, 1987.

Selfe, Cynthia, and Richard Selfe. "The Politics of the Interface: Power and Its Exercise in Electronic Contact Zones." *College Composition and Communication* 45.4 (1994): 481–504.

Siegel, David. *Secretes of Successful Web Sites Project Management on the World Wide Web*. Indianapolis: Hayden Books, 1997.

Ulmer, Greg. "Metaphoric Rocks: A Psychogeography of Tourism and Monumentality." *Rewired*. 1 February 1998 <http://www.clas.ufl.edu/Clas/departments/rewired/ulmer.html>.

———. *Teletheory: Grammatology in the Age of Video*. New York: Routledge, 1989.

Williams, Raymond. *The Politics of Modernism: Against the New Conformists*. Ed. Tony Pinkney. London: Verso, 1989.

2

Multimodality, Multimedia, and Genre

GUNTHER KRESS

A MULTIMODAL VIEW OF GENRE

So far I have treated the category of *genre* more or less as though it were obviously and naturally realized in language, either in speech or in writing. Much of the work done over the last twenty or thirty years assumes that genres are linguistic phenomena. Yes, film, or video and television, have been described by using this category, and of course they consist of much more than "just" language. And literary texts have been described in genre-terms for a very long time. But in the broad area of literacy the work that underpins the interest in genre treats it as a purely linguistic phenomenon. This needs to be expanded a bit by saying that the assumption that genre is a linguistic category does not really surface into explicitness: it is simply there. Yet as so many of the text-objects in the contemporary world—as my example of the small card in the previous chapter—make use of modes other than speech or writing, or make use of many modes at the same time, the question must arise of whether "genre" is a category that applies to texts or textlike objects realized in other modes, in image, gesture, 3D representations, or in relation to multi-modally constituted texts. Is genre a linguistic category first and foremost, or most plausibly? Or is it a category that applies to all forms of representation and communication?

The problem which arises is that the theoretical categories developed to understand and describe genre are linguistic categories, developed by linguistics for linguistically realized objects. The question then is whether categories that are specific to the modes of speech or writing, to texts which are (predominantly) linguistic, can be apt, appropriate, or useful for describing texts which are realized in other modes. Does it matter if we use linguistic categories to describe visual or three-dimensional texts? Can that which is realized in language—that is, the kinds of meaning that I discussed in relation to

From *Literacy in the New Media Age* by Gunther Kress. London: Routledge, 2003. 106–121.

written genres—be realized in other modes, in image, for instance, or in combinations of image and writing? Can the meanings of negation, overt and covert, that I discussed be realized other than in speech or writing? Or, to turn it the other way around, are there social meanings which can be realized in the mode of image but not in the mode of speech or of writing? We can make the question quite specific and ask, how do images represent social relations and social interactions?

The materiality of the different modes—sound for speech, light for image, body for dance—means that not everything can be realized in every mode with equal facility, and that we cannot transport mode-specific theories from one mode to another without producing severe distortions. This is somewhat difficult to express clearly, because I want to say that meanings, in the broad sense, can be realized in any mode, but that when they are, they are realized in mode-specific articulations. This means that we need to attend to that which is mode-specific and to that which is not. Our past understanding of meaning has not raised that question, and therefore our attention does not go in that direction. Rather we have been told that that which is meant is realized, and that that which is realized is that which has been meant. Instead we need to understand that meaning is articulated in this way in a specific mode, and in this other way in another mode. From here we have questions which go on the one hand in the direction of "meaning," loosely speaking, and on the other hand in the direction of theory. From the point of view of meaning the question is, what is the meaning to be realized? From the point of view of theory one question is, what are the affordances of different modes, and how do different modes therefore realize meanings of a certain kind? The other is about genre as a category: is it a mode-specific category or not?

The question about the social meaning is readily answered: it is not possible to imagine communication which does not encompass the meanings realized in genre. That is, no message or text is conceivable which does not respond to such social facts. Hence all representation and communication must be generically shaped; it must carry these social meanings. "Meaning" is inevitably and necessarily realized differently in different modes. And so the question here is, what is our sense of the social givens realized in genre, and how will they appear in this modal articulation? Does the category of genre remain important, useful, necessary; does it become more or less important in the era of multimodal communication? The answer is that the category of genre is essential in all attempts to understand text, whatever its modal constitution. The point is to develop a theory and terms adequate to that.

The question is, what is it that we want to mean, and what modes and genres are best for realizing that meaning? That leads us to the social givens which we want to realize in a genre, and a question more like, what social, representational and communicative function do genres have? I will return to this throughout this discussion, but here I wish to make this concrete by looking at two texts.

The texts are entirely usual. They come from a science classroom in a secondary school in inner-city London. The children in this class are in year eight which means that they are twelve to thirteen years of age. The series of lessons in which the texts were produced had as its topic "plant cells." Four children — all girls — had worked together in a group around a microscope, first preparing a slide with a piece of the epidermis of an onion, then looking at this slide through a microscope, and afterwards carrying out the task, given by the teacher, of "doing a report." Each had to "record" the experiment: to draw what they had seen through the microscope and to write what they had done in conducting the experiment. The teacher had given them just two specific instructions: "put your writing at the top of the page" (the teacher was anxious that the drawing should not take up too much of the space, so as to leave enough room for writing), and "use only your lead pencil — do not use colored pencils in your drawings" (to distinguish "scientificness" — black-and-white drawing — from "artisticness" — using color pens — or from "everyday realism"). Here I will look at two of the four texts produced. I am particularly interested in the meanings of formal aspects — the genre — of the texts.

The first example (Figure 1) has the drawing at the top of the page (as did another one of the four), and the written part of the text at the bottom. Image and writing are clearly separated on the page; each has its own, slightly differing, heading. The written text is in the generic form of a "recount." That is, it is a temporally ordered or sequenced presentation of events reported in sentences. The image part of the text has the form of a line-drawing; it is not clear that there is a suitable generic label available to name it.

Here I will first say something briefly about the written part of the text as a "recount," then I will attempt to uncover the generic form of the visual part, and then speculate on the generic form of the text as a whole. My intention is to answer the question, "Is the category 'genre' useful in a multimodal text and, if so, how is it useful?"

As I have mentioned, I treat genre as that category which realizes the social relations of the participants involved in the text as interaction. The social relations which are realized in the recount are of three types: first, those of the relations of the actors, objects and events which are *reported in* the recount; second, those of the relations between the participants in the act of communication, which are *implied by* the recount. The third type concerns the social world that is *represented in* the recount. The question here is, how is (the institution of) science represented or constructed as a social activity? Here we are in large part in the realm of the discursive organization of the activity, in the sense of Foucault's use of "discourse."

The relations "in" the recount are of actors acting in events with and on objects, either singly (I collected all the equipment) or jointly (we then sorted the microscope out). This is recounted "realistically," that is, it is presented as being a recount of the actual, significant events, in the temporal sequence in which they happened, with a clear enough implication that no other (significant) events occurred. The recount is "complete"; there is closure: it is a completed, finished, rounded-off textual entity. The recount, as genre, makes an implicit claim about the relation of the events or practices recounted to other practices in the world, and of the relation of the domain of the practices

FIGURE 1. Student Drawing of a Plant Cell 1: "Like a Brick Wall"

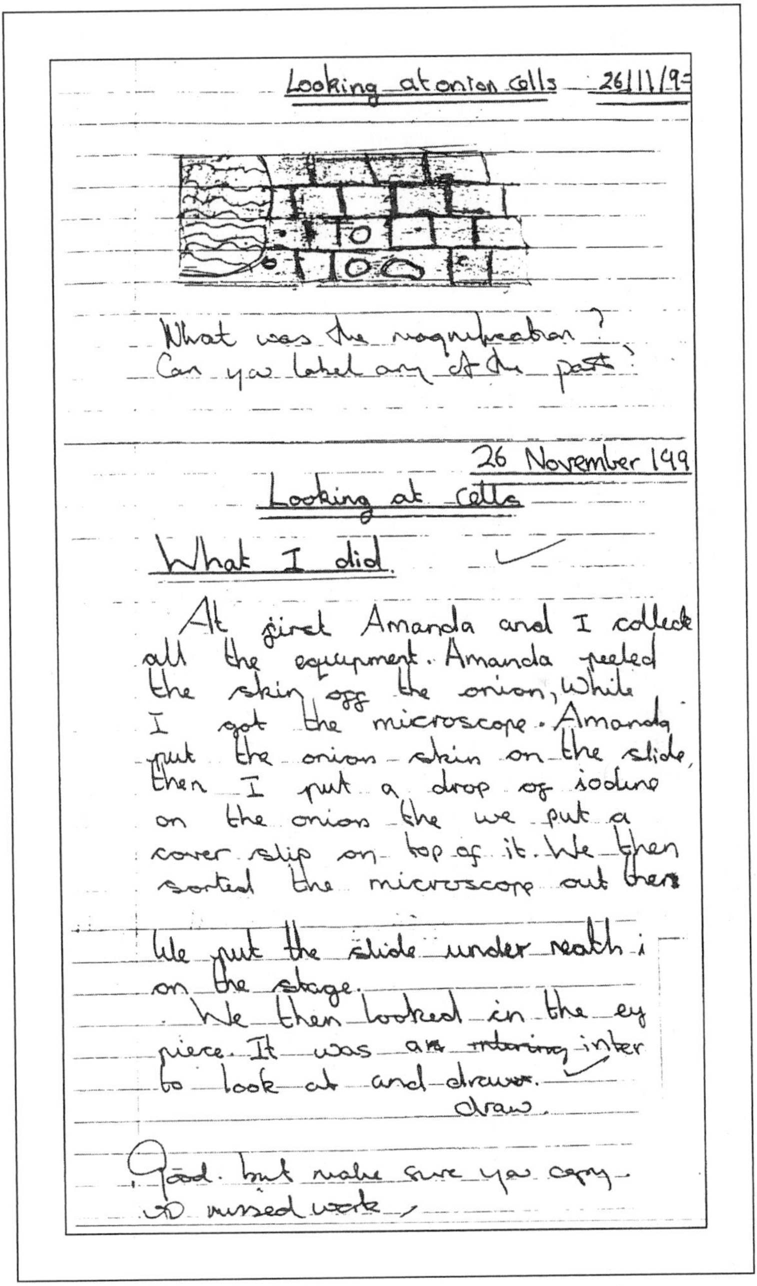
Looking at onion cells 26/11/9-

What was the magnification?
Can you label any of the parts?

26 November 199
Looking at cells
What I did

At first Amanda and I collect
all the equipment. Amanda peeled
the skin off the onion, While
I got the microscope. Amanda
put the onion skin on the slide,
then I put a drop of iodine
on the onion the we put a
cover slip on top of it. We then
sorted the microscope out then

We put the slide under neath i
on the stage.
We then looked in the ey
piece. It was an ~~intering~~ inter
to look at and drawer.
draw.

Good. but make sure you copy
up missed work.

to other domains. It is the claim of realism, in the everyday world. It makes the claims, implicitly: "this is, simply, how it was; these were the main participants, the main events and they occurred in this order." It claims, specifically, that "practices in the science classroom are practices in the everyday world." (A narrative, by contrast, makes a different claim: "that is how I have (re)constructed the world for you," and "practices in the everyday world may be different to the way they are narrated here."

The social roles and relations established and implied by the *genre of recount as message* (that is, genre oriented towards communication) are, if *I* am presenting the recount, those of "recounter" — I am someone who knows that which is being recounted — and "recountee" — you are someone whom I regard as wishing to have the events recounted to you. If I am receiving the recount, the roles are those of myself being someone who is interested in having these events recounted to me, in being the "recountee," and accepting you as the "recounter." The recount presents a world of action/event, temporally ordered and complete.

In asking about the generic form of the drawing, we bump up against a problem: there are no genre-terms for describing what this drawing is or does, either in terms of the presentation of material — the content — or of its representation of the social relations between the "participants" in the production and reproduction of the text, the participants in the communicational event. What are these relations, as they are realized in the drawing, as they appear here? (To some extent what appears here will become clearer by comparison with the next example.) In answering this I will make use of the same types of relation as I used just above. First, what is shown "in" the drawing (analogous to what is shown "in" the recount) and by the drawing as a whole? The drawing shows a rectangular block with clearly distinct elements within it. The block is strongly framed along the top and the bottom, but is "open" at each end, suggesting that it is "a part of," "an extract from," "a fragment of" a larger entity. This suggests that while the drawing is not textually complete, it is conceptually complete: any other part of the larger entity of which this is a fragment will also be like this fragment. The elements themselves are drawn as being broadly uniform in shape and size. One of the handouts used in the lead-up lessons had suggested to the students that they would see something resembling "bricks in a brick-wall," and quite clearly that metaphor has guided this student's "seeing." On the left-most edge there is a large "irregularity" — the circular shape — and there are small bubble-like elements within the bricks.

This is a structure of relatively uniform elements in regular arrangement: the blocks are arranged in even layers, arranged regularly. While the recount presents a world of *happenings*, of *actions* or *events*, what is displayed here is a world of *entities as they are*: static, stable, regular elements in regular arrangement. While the world of the recount is complete in that *it represents all there is to recount*, the world of this display is complete in that *it represents all there is to know* — to show more would be to show more of the same, and while the world of the recount is set in time and *is* completed — it has happened — the world of this display is out of time — it just is — and it is complete in *being*.

The relation between the participants in the act of communication is an "objective" one. The viewer is presented with this text-element "front on." It is objectively there, with maximal "involvement" of the viewer, that is, the viewer is positioned as confronting this image straight on, at eye-level. The positioning is neither to the side — which would indicate lesser involvement, nor is the viewer below or above the element shown, something that would indicate difference in power. The entity is presented to the viewer in a maximally neutral manner: it is simply "there," *objectively*. Instead of the relations of "recounter" and "recountee" of that which is "recounted," we have the relation of "displayer" and "viewer" of that which is "displayed."

At this stage we would need to look back at the written recount and attempt an assessment of kinds of involvement there. We can, however, make comments on the third level, the relation between the world of practices represented here and that of the everyday world. The mode of drawing is not a realist one: it is generalized away from everyday realism, both through the means of using the soft black pencil on the white page (rather than the use of color, as in one of the other pieces of work) and the abstracting, diagrammatic form of representation. The former tells us that certain aspects of the everyday world, such as the color of the viewed entity, are not relevant here, and similarly with other aspects, such as the actual, "real" boundaries of the object. These all provide pointers to the kind of social world into which we are invited. "Diagram" is closer to serving as a genre-label, in that it suggests both a particular social purpose, and social relations, of those who use the diagram and those who make it. "Diagram" also suggests a particular coding-orientation: not the realism of the everyday world, but the realism of the scientific-technological world.

MEANINGS OF GENRES IN MULTIMODAL TEXTS

So what is the genre of this text overall? And what consequences does all this have not just for a view of writing, but for the actual uses of writing, and for likely changes to the uses, forms, and values of the technology of writing?

To answer the first question, we can say that there is a clear difference between the "naturalism" (within the realism of everyday life) of the written genre of recount, and the abstraction (within the world of scientific theorizing) of the visual genre of diagram-drawing. The first positions me as someone who hears an account of a completed, ordered sequence of events, recounted as though they form part of my everyday life. That sense is reinforced by the syntax of the writing, which is close to the clausal structures of everyday speech, as is its use of words — "we then *sorted* the microscope *out*" from a quite casual register. Doing science, in this account, is like doing cooking, or doing the dishes. The second form, the visual, positions me as someone who is given a view of a fragment of an entity, but understands that the fragment "stands for" the structure of the whole entity, in a form which is not part of the everyday world. I am positioned in a different domain, out of time, in a world of regularity produced by the theory that I am applying.

The task of the science curriculum is, still, to induct young people into the practices that constitute "doing science." That practice is presented in two distinct ways here: "doing science" in the recount presents me with a world of ordered actions or events which are like actions or events in the everyday world. "Doing science" in the drawing/diagram is presented as being about

another world, not one of actions and events, but of states of affairs with reg-
ularities, abstracted away from the everyday world. If this multimodal text-
entity "has" a genre, then it is a mixed genre, in which differently organized
worlds appear differently: one a world of actions where the actors are like you
and me, the other a world without actors, a world of things as they are. If one
is the world of the everyday, then the other is the world of theory, abstraction.
One draws me in by suggesting that I am like the actors in a world that is
familiar to me. The other positions me as a neutral observer of an objectively
present world, but an observer with a special status and a special lens.

This is the meaning of this genre; these are the social relations and the
social roles of the participants projected by the combined genre. Of course, this
is a genre produced by a non-expert. The fact that she mixes the social relations of the world of the everyday with the social relations of the world of scientific work may be an effect of the teaching that she has had, or it may be her
response to what she has taken from that teaching. She is able to form her own
generic response, to see science her way and to represent it her way: actions
which are like those of the everyday, in relation to a world which is differently constituted. The genre overall seems to position her somewhere between
the everyday and the special world of technical/theoretical endeavor.

Mixed genres are commonplace, though the kind of disjunction presented here would appear as a severe problem if both texts were written texts, or
if this was the text of an expert. Because the two generic positions are realized
in different modes, the disjunction is not readily apparent, or does not become
a problem; it does not appear as a contradiction. In fact it may well be a very
good representation of the social relations as they exist in the science teaching
that she is experiencing. Is it a problem that we do not have labels for these
"mixes," or indeed do not have labels for many kinds of generic organization?
This is not, I think, the main issue at all; if we find that we need labels, we will
make them up. What is important is to recognize that texts realize, among
other things, the kinds of social relation pointed to here.

In this text too we see design at work. This young woman has made a
number of design decisions in a multimodal representation: a decision about
layout, in where to place which element; a decision about generic (epistemological) form—everyday or scientific—for each of the two elements; a decision about which mode to use for the realization of each of the distinct
positions; and no doubt others.

As far as labels for the mixes are concerned, my analysis of the next example (Figure 2) will show that this may be even less of a useful aim.

Several differences are immediately apparent. The "diagram" (with the
teacher's written comment, "Diagram needs to be much larger") is below the
written text, as the teacher had asked. There is a division between the written
part and the visual; they are separated by a heading—"What We Saw." But
the image partly protrudes into its heading, and the heading is very tightly
linked to the written text, insisting, as it were, on a connectedness, even a
unity, of writing and image. Where in the first example they had been clearly
separate, here there is a real move physically to integrate them.

FIGURE 2. Student Drawing of a Plant Cell 2: The Lens of the Microscope

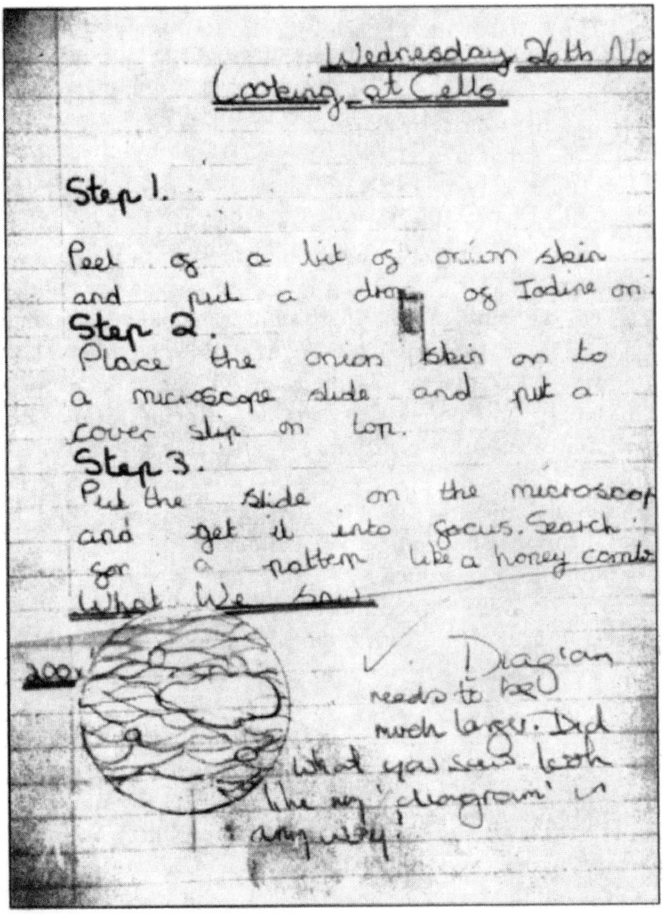

The genre of the written text is that of *procedure*: a sequence of distinct (in this case numbered) steps which, when followed, will lead to the achievement of the intended aim. The social relations expressed "in" the procedure differ from those in the recount. The recount told what happened, and the assumption was that there might be those who would wish to reproduce those actions. Here there are those with the power or authority to order actions to be taken, and those who carry out the actions. This is very different to the recount. It is no longer the friendly telling of what happened so that you might do the same; this is being told what to do. The claim made implicitly in the procedure is one of relations of power, actions, and intended outcomes. This is not a realist genre in the manner of the recount; it is not a report of real events or actions of actual people, of events which have happened. It is a set of commands (in the syntactic form of imperatives) for actions that are to happen.

As in the first example, the written text-part is generically complete. Its relation to the world of the everyday is different; it is not the world of everyday happenings. This is a world in which power exists, and those with power can insist on actions being taken in a specific way and in a certain sequence. These are social relations of a very different kind. In the recount we could be sure that all the *significant* events were there, even though there might also be others. For instance, in the recount we are told that "it was interesting to look at and draw." In the procedure we have only those potential actions (as commands) which are essential to the carrying out of a task which already exists as a prestructured schema.

In terms of communicational roles, there is a big difference: the text overall is a set of instructions, and the individual segments are commands to carry out the instructions as they are indicated. Consequently, the roles here are of a different kind: to act in a world in accord with the commands of some other with power, with clear procedures and in accordance with those procedures. The reader is not in the world of their everyday life. My role is to carry out commands issued by some (institutional) authority.

That also describes the relation between the world of this written text and the everyday world: they are different. In this world I have less power than others. The manner in which I am drawn into the text is by command, by means of power, and not as before, by the pleasure or interest of the recount. The world projected here is the world of precise procedures which those who are a part of this world must follow. It is not the everyday world of these students: There is no (implicit) claim here that the world of scientific practices is like the world of their everyday practices.

The drawing differs from that in the first example. One clue is provided in the instructions: "Search for pattern like a honeycomb." In his talk the teacher had provided the metaphor, among others, of the honeycomb: "it might look like a honeycomb." In the case of both texts, a metaphor provided in language—in writing in the one instance—"what you will see will be like bricks in a brick wall"—and in talk in the other—has been transducted by the pupils into visual form. Let me follow the steps that I took in analyzing both the written and the visual elements of the first example. The drawing shows a strongly delineated circle, with elements of different kinds contained in the circle. What is represented "in" the image, and what is represented by the image overall, as a whole? Like her fellow students, this young woman saw air-bubbles, larger and smaller ones. However, the cell-entities which she saw are far less regular in shape, and their arrangement is not in any way as orderly as in the "brick wall" example. Regularity of the elements or of their arrangements is not a feature of this image. The drawing differs from that in the first example in that what it shows is complete: here we have the whole world that is to be represented. The implication is that this is what she actually saw through the microscope: everything that was there to see is there, as she saw it. It is textually as well as representationally complete.

In the drawing in the first example scientificness lay in abstraction away from that which appeared in view in the microscope, abstraction in the direction of theory and generalization. There was no representation of the lens of the microscope, and in fact no real pretense that the drawing represented what the "eye" had seen. That drawing represented what the "eye of theory" had seen. Here, by contrast, scientificness lies in the precision of representing that which is there in view, that which the human eye can see. In the first example truth is the truth of abstraction, the truth of theory; here truth is the truth of actuality, of that which is there, the truth of the empirically real world. We are shown not only what she saw, but the means by which she saw what she saw, hence we see the eyepiece through which the young woman looked — we see everything that she saw. For her, being scientific resides in the accuracy of observation and representation.

The relation of the written text and the image is inverted in relation to that in the first example. There the written text was broadly realistic and the visual broadly non-realistic, theoretical. Here the written text is not an account of events as they happened, but of a schema as it exists in the world of science, which might lead to a set of actions in that world. The visual part, by contrast, is realistic. The two aspects of the text jointly seem to suggest that the meaning of "scientificness" here might be that the world of science is ordered by schemata for action which organize and underlie action, and that the essential task of science is to achieve an accurate account of the empirically real, aided by these schemata of actions.

If we contrast the two examples, they are nearly an inversion of each other: in the first, the written part of the text is realist; in the second it is schematic/theoretical; in the first text, the visual part is theoretical/abstract, while in the second it is empirical/realist. Scientificness is carried in distinctively different ways in the two cases. Underlying this is the action and the process of design of an overall message-entity.

What is the role of writing in these multimodal ensembles? Even though the written parts of the two ensembles are *generically* different from each other, they do share a significantly common feature: both are focused on action and event, even if differently so; both of the visual elements by contrast are focused on "what is," the visual display of the world that is in focus. Each of the two texts overall is incomplete without both written and visual parts; each mode, writing and image, does distinctly different and specific things. The specificity is the same at one level: the affordance of the logic of time governs writing, and the affordance of the logic of space governs the image. Within that, there is the possibility of generic variation. And the generic variation of the ensembles, in each case, produces an overall difference of a significant kind.

GENRE AS DESIGN: TEXT AND THE NEW MEDIA

As I suggested, the two texts that I have discussed here . . . are examples of *ensembles of modes*, brought together to realize particular meanings. The fact that the two school-texts are made by unpracticed designers is in one way an advantage in that it shows how an untutored maker of such ensembles uses the affordances of the modes for their ends. The purpose of the science curriculum is, in one important way, to induct young people into the idea of scientificness. Here we see the response of two students to this demand, expressed through what we can see as design decisions in the realization of that meaning. They are faced with the question of "what is it to act or be scientific?" and each gives a distinct answer, which is expressed through choice of modes, and choice of genres, more than through what aspects of curriculum content to represent. Both students understand the affordances of writing—best of all it does the job of representing action and event—though of course the teacher's demands and previously encountered models will have given them resources in that respect. The teacher's inexplicit or "open" framing of the task leaves much of the design decision to the students: how to interpret the relatively open request "write what you did" in generically specific terms, and to do the same for the request "draw what you saw."

The first of the two examples shows a decision to go for realism in the written genre: to be truthful to science means that I am expected to report things as they were; I have to stay true to the empirically real. But this student also realized that science is about constructing general accounts of what this aspect of the world is (like), and she does that in her drawing: the truth of this world lies in this abstraction, which generalizes away from the messiness of the empirical and to a general truth. The truth of actions is reached via the mode of writing, and the truth of how the world looks is reached via the mode of image.

For the second student there is a similar question, though she answers it differently: the truth of science lies in the generality of the procedures, in the generality of the practices, which must be the same each time they are performed and not open to the chance of contingent event. This truth is reached via the mode of writing. The truth of what the world is like is reached via the mode of image and the precise recording of what there actually is in that world, without concession to anything but strict observation.

These are epistemological decisions, but they are realized through design decisions focused on the use of modes and the truth they harbor, the use of genres and the truths that they contain. On the face of it, these decisions have nothing to do with the existence of the new information and communication media. In reality they absolutely do: the manner in which these young people encounter school science owes much to the revolution in representation which has already in their world altered the status, the function, the uses, and the forms of writing. The "books" which they use are transformed already by the joint effects of the emergence into central representational use of the mode of image, and the effect on the page of the organizations of the screens of the new media. The fact that there is now a design decision to be made, and that decisions about genre are now relatively open, is both a direct effect of the new media via their effect on the look of the page, and also an indirect effect of the new media in that teachers as much as designers of textbooks know that the young are attuned to a differently configured communicational world.

In that new communicational world there are now choices about how what is to be represented should be represented: in what mode, in what genre, in what ensembles of modes and genres, and on what occasions. These were not decisions open to students (or teachers or textbook-makers) some twenty years earlier. Of course, with all this go questions not only of the potentials of the resources, but also of the new possibilities of arrangements, the new grammars of multimodal texts. These new grammars, barely coming into conventionality at the moment, and certainly very little understood, have effects in two ways at least. On the one hand they order the arrangements of the elements in the ensembles; on the other hand they design the functions that the different elements are to have in the ensembles. These are the kinds of decision that I pointed to: writing used for the representation of event structures, and image used for the representations of displays of aspects of the world. This is what I call the "functional specialization" of the modes, and that in turn has the profoundest effects on the inner organization and development of the modes.

Where before, up until twenty or thirty years ago, writing carried all the communicational load of a message, and needed to have grammatical and syntactic structures that were equal to the complexities of that which had to be represented in that single mode, now there is a specialization which allows each of the modes to carry that part of the message for which it is best equipped. This brings with it the possibilities of great simplification of syntax for writing, for instance. It leads to some new questions, such as I have mentioned: What are the elements which come together in the multimodal ensembles? In the two text examples discussed above, there are image blocks and writing blocks, and it is these which form the first level of conjunction. At the first level of reading we note that the text is composed of "blocks," and at that level it is not immediately relevant what modal realization these elements have, whether they are image or writing. They are treated as elements of the same order. This is a bit like the analysis of a sentence where we might want to know what the main verb is, what its subject noun might be, and what complements—if any—there are. Reading at the next level down would then focus on the internal elements of these higher-level elements.

If we take Figure 3 . . . as an example, it is clear that there are three elements or blocks at the first level. These are predominantly visual, but the point is that in our first engagement with and analysis of ("scanning" might be another useful term) the page we note the three blocks. We then note that each image has accompanying it a written bolded label. So at the next level down our analysis reveals that each block consists of two elements, in a particular relation. That relation is in part defined in mode terms—large image, relatively small label—and in part by proximity—the label is at a certain distance from the image, indicating that it "goes with" the image. At the third level down, the analysis reveals lower-level elements both in the visual mode and in writing, and here too the relation is that of labelling. Because the relationship is not so obvious—the elements are smaller, and the "goes with" relation could be misinterpreted—it is indicated by a connecting line.

FIGURE 3. The Eye: Biology in the Secondary School

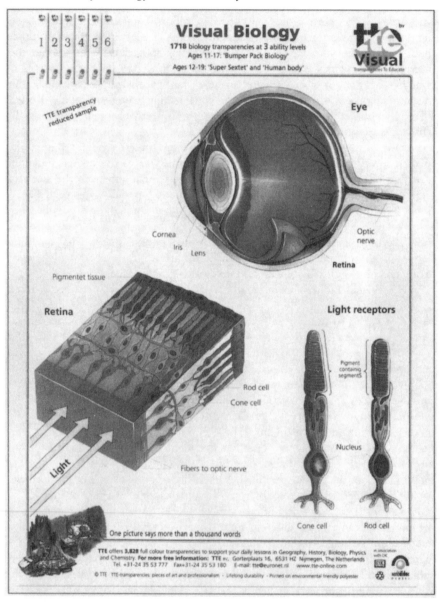

It is clear that here the question of genre no longer rests with the written mode. If we wish to understand the social relations realized in this text, we need to look predominantly at the visual mode. The verbal mode supplies text elements, namely "labels," and labels do of course also have generic effect — they supply the information of "name," and supplying information is to take and assign a specific social role. In the original, the images are in heavily saturated color, deep reds, purples, yellows, some green — all close to the primary part of the color spectrum. We are not in the same domain as the black-and-white drawing of the students, nor in that of the student who used color pencils. Nor are we in the coding orientation of the circuit diagrams in Chapter 9.* This is the world of excitement, entertainment, pleasure, the world of consumer culture, and science has become a part of that. That is perhaps the first thing to note about this page/screen. We are shown the retina from the side, signalling lower involvement with what we are looking at than in either the onion-cell drawings, which were front-on, or the circuits, which also were. We are looking down on the square which is a hypothetical slice out of the retina. *Standing apart* (signalling low involvement) and *looking down on* (signalling greater power of the viewer) bring highly affective subjective elements into the social relation. These objects or entities do not demand our attention by the front-on objective demand — of the circuit diagram or of the onion-cell drawing. We, the viewers, are in control here, it is our will and our pleasure which dictates what we do. The distance at which these entities are presented is at mid-range: a distance which can signal some engagement, but not too close.

Generically this image suggests a social relation like that of the report; this is what there is; this is all there is; I have shown you all. However, the image, through its spatial affordances, can bring aspects of social relations into the text which might be problematic in a written genre in school science. For instance, there is a clear appeal to the viewer in the angles I mentioned, in the social domain signalled by the hyper-realist representation, including the intense saturation of the colors, and by the dynamism indicated by the angle of the retina segment. It is a "display," but for a viewer with power — the power of the consumer in the market society.

GENRE LABELS

These examples raise again something of a recurring problem: what do we call "mixed genres"? There is in any case the problem that there are very few commonly used labels for genres; only really prominent ones have well-understood names — whether literary (the novel) or non-literary (the interview) or texts of popular culture (romance, film noir). That problem is somewhat compounded by the differences in theoretical practice — where genre can be used as the naming of the text as a whole or, as in my approach here, as the naming of an aspect of text. One of the solutions that has been adopted at times is that of inventing subcategories. So we have "interview" but also then "job-interview," "media-interview," "radio-interview," and so on. In these three cases qualifying adjective names quite different things, a very good reason for avoiding this strategy. But even if we kept the categories steady, using one category, say "what medium?" (radio, TV,

---

* This chapter number refers to the original volume from which this chapter is reprinted.

newspaper, and so on), we would end up proliferating types, and end up with an unprincipled list.

My preferred solution is to accept, to begin with, that *mixing* is normal, in whatever domain, and at whatever level. In writing we can have clauses functioning as subjects of a sentence, taking a quasi-noun role. We can have single words or two-word structures functioning as complete message units, taking a quasi-sentence role, and indeed functioning as complete texts — as in "No" or "No Smoking." Mixed genres exist in written text, though they have been somewhat of a theoretical embarrassment. Mixed genres exist in multimodal, or mono-modal, non-verbal texts. The question is, what do we call generically mixed texts in writing? We have no problem accepting generically hugely mixed texts such as the novel as a genre. No one disputes that "novel" is a genre label. Or is it perhaps a matter of the intensity and the degree of mixing? If all genres are mixed genres — as I suggested earlier — what is a "genre," a pure genre; how and where would it occur; and how would we recognize it?

In my approach, where genre does not name the text, but an aspect of the text's organization (though I am happy to name the whole text after its dominant generic features — as in "interview"), there is no problem in saying that a text can be and in many cases will be genetically mixed. If we see this as a matter "levels" then there is no problem at all: we have genres and generic fragments embedded in, forming a part of, the text overall. The real issue in any case is not really to have labels, though they can be useful devices, and it is clear that bad labels can be importantly misleading. The science teacher's use of the label "diagram" might be one case in point. But the real issue is to understand the generic nature of the text — what meanings does the text realize, what social meanings are at issue?

GENRE AND EDUCATIONAL STRATEGIES

The profound cultural diversity of all contemporary "Western" post-industrial societies, as much as the new demands for education for participation in a fully globalized economy, has specific educational consequences. It means that an "outcomes-based curriculum" or, to use a better formulation, a curriculum which focuses on skills, disposition, essential processes, and understanding of resources for representing and communicating, may be what all of "us" in the anglophone and ever more globalizing world will need to consider urgently. This will be a curriculum which focuses above all on "dispositions," a return to quite traditional notions of education — not training — on something akin to the German notion of *Bildung*, but refocused clearly on the real features of the new globalizing world and its demands. I am not here thinking of the facile and deeply mistaken ideas around skills-training, but focusing rather on giving students a full awareness of what might be possible, beyond both the suggestions of current politics and the seductions of the market-led consumption. Such an education would provide them with the means both for setting their goals and for achieving them in the contexts of their lives. This is the ability for which I use the term "design." Much more goes with that change in curriculum from either content as stable knowledge or content as the training for skills, to dispositions to "design."

A new theory of text is essential to meet the demands of culturally plural societies in a globalizing world. In my *Writing the Future: English and the Making of a Culture of Innovation* (1995) I suggested that the school-subject English needed an encompassing theory of text, in which the texts of high culture could be brought into productive conjunction with the banal texts of the everyday. If the literary texts which have been seen as "the best" are to have real effects on all texts, they cannot be treated as separate. I suggested three categories of text, within the one theory: the aesthetically valued text — the texts treated by any one cultural group as the texts which embodied for them what they saw as best; the culturally salient text — texts which were significant for a society for any number of reasons, but which might not meet the criteria of aesthetic value; and the mundane text — texts of the everyday, entirely banal texts . . . are significant because they constitute, reproduce, and remake the "everyday." All these will have to be dealt with within one theory of text, within one culture, across cultures in one society, and across historical periods. But what is quite clear is that even the production of the banal text . . . requires much more than competent knowledge. That text is based, however imperfectly, on the understandings of design: an understanding of what the social and cultural environment is into which my text is to fit, the purposes it is to achieve, the resources of all kinds that I have to implement and realize my design, and the awareness of the characteristics of the sites of appearance of that text.

That educational environment will deal with banal texts, culturally salient texts (from all the cultures represented in one society), and aesthetically valued texts, in all modes and in all kinds of modal combination. Translations, transformations, and transductions will be entirely normal, and made more so by the affordances of the new information and communication technologies which make modal transformation and transduction, as well as the co-appearance of modes, entirely normal.

Theories of meaning will have to be rethought and remade. There is a reality to genre, but the conceptions from former social arrangements with their (relative) stabilities have left us with both the wrong theory and the wrong vocabulary. The wrong theory led us to believe that stability of language or of text-form (as indeed of other social phenomena) is a feature of texts, when it had always been — as it appears now — a feature of these phenomena in a particular historical period, when relative social stability had obtained. So, for instance, to speak of "generic mixes" is really to conceive of genre in the older fashion — of stable genres which can be and are mixed. A newer way of thinking may be that within a general awareness of the range of genres, of their shapes and their contexts, speakers and writers newly make the generic forms out of available resources. This is a much more "generative" notion of genre: not one where you learn the shapes of existing kinds of text alone, in order to replicate them, but where you learn the generative rules of the constitution of generic form within the power structures of a society. And you learn what the shapes of these texts are, coming out of those social conditions. That will permit (and account for) constant change, and makes the actions of the producer of the genre innovative and transformative. It encourages and normalizes "design" of text in response to the perceived needs of the maker of the text in a given environment. In such a theory all acts of representation are innovative, and creativity is the normal process of representation for all.

There will need to be a new evaluation and description of the resources for representation and communication, the means for making texts, which are available and in use in a particular society. For in a plural society the generic forms of all cultural groups will need to be brought into the market of communication.

Literacy and communication curricula rethought in this fashion offer an education in which creativity in different domains and at different levels of representation is well understood, in which both creativity and difference are seen as normal and as productive. The young who experienced that kind of curriculum might feel at ease in a world of incessant change. A social theory of genre is one essential element in bringing about that shift.

3

Learning from the Past: Verbal and Visual Literacy in Early Modern Rhetoric and Writing Pedagogy

CATHERINE L. HOBBS

The history of culture is in part the story of a protracted struggle for dominance between pictorial and linguistic signs, each claiming for itself certain proprietary rights on a "nature" to which only it has access. . . . Among the most interesting and complex versions of this struggle is what might be called the relationship of subversion, in which language or imagery looks into its own heart and finds lurking there its opposite number.

–MITCHELL (1986, p. 43)

Print-imprinted intellectuals, including professors, must relearn the world of the graphic, a word which derives from the Greek graphe and refers both to the written and the pictorial. The humanities/posthumanities/literacies must relinquish semiconscious resistance to pictorial communication and its technologies.

–WELCH (1999, p. 208)

Writing teachers today are living through a revolution in literacy brought about by the capability of computers to combine blocks of text—or verbal *lexias*—with graphic images, sounds, video, and other multimedia (see Landow, 1992, on *lexias*). We are forced—at times by our failures—to grapple with the potential relationships between the ubiquitous and chaotic new visual and the comfortingly familiar, more linear verbal. Awash in both good and bad examples—on the Web, but also on TV and, lest we forget, still in traditional print—we are discovering that it is no longer enough to fragment our concepts of literacy, bracket off our traditional blocks of text, and just stick to what we know. To condone and contribute to visual illiteracy contradicts our purpose of teaching effective and ethical written communication. Yet as we often tell ourselves, we are still trying to figure out how to teach just our traditional, single piece of the puzzle—nothing to sneeze at in its full complexity.

This chapter starts from the premise that our project of rethinking literacy in light of new technological capabilities might be done more easily with

From *Language and Image in the Reading-Writing Classroom*. Ed. Kristie Fleckenstein, Linda T. Calendrillo and Demetrice A. Worley. Mahwah, NJ: Lawrence Erlbaum, 2002. 27–44.

some historical context. This is because the translation of visual images into verbal text—and vice versa—has always been a part of writing and speaking instruction. Furthermore, as Mitchell (1986) noted in the epigraph, there have always been conflicts between the two media, as well as subversion of the one by the other. Why does the verbal find the visual lurking and vice versa? Perhaps this is because of the long history of translation of one into the other and the presumed convertibility of one to the other. Yet as with two circles overlapping, not quite congruent, there is, nonetheless, a *wild zone* each has to itself that has nothing to do with the other.

What interests me in this cultural history is how shifts in this long conflict/subversion affect writing instruction. For example, breakthroughs in the science of optics and vision occurred in the same time frame as interest in the image and imagination intensified in language pedagogy. This was before and during the seventeenth and eighteenth centuries, just as modernity coalesced and the Scientific Revolution occurred. Ideas developed at that time provided some of the historical foundation for our twentieth-century values, beliefs, and practices in writing instruction. This chapter attempts to show that language arts teachers have always incorporated visual theory of one kind or another in their teaching. Yet verbal-visual relationships keep transforming as technologies change and our understanding of vision grows (see Faigley, 1999, for more on these changes). In the next section, I show that rhetorical arts always incorporated practice in translation from the visual to the verbal. Then, I present some significant developments in optics and vision science, followed by a discussion of how rhetoricians and writers responded to these developments in their pedagogical values and practices.

VISUALS IN ANCIENT ARTS

The Greeks systematized the art of rhetoric or public persuasive speaking over the same long historical period as the alphabet and writing developed (eighth century B.C.E. for the alphabet). Genres developed linked with the sites of the speaking—the public forum, the courts, the legislatures—and by Plato and Aristotle's days (at least by 450 B.C.E.), schools were in operation to teach boys (almost always boys) first grammar and literary studies beginning to involve instruction in writing (see Welch, 1990). Boys worked on language arts until they reached the pinnacle of learning—rhetoric, or the public, persuasive oration. From the beginning, vision and description were important to persuasion and were overtly taught, as is made clear in the term from the art of style, *ecphrasis*—delineation, or description used in teaching. There had always been descriptions in Homer and the poets, and later in the early Sophists and pre-Socratics, who attempted to use language to put a magical spell on listeners to transport them and used vivid descriptions in the process.

Aristotle said little about description in the *Rhetoric*, although his emphasis on metaphor and visualization linked to poetics and description. The more poetic Plato, who banned poets from his *Republic*, placed a great deal of emphasis on light, vision, and knowledge, first in the realm beyond the sensory and in this world. His banning of the poets from the *Republic* gives us a glimpse of how powerful the poets were in Greek society. Indeed, in Greek society, poetry vied with rhetoric for pride of place in education, with rhetoric and prose composition building on and growing out of earlier studies of Homer and the poets led by the *grammatikos* or grammar instructor. Greek writers whose texts reveal the teaching of description include Theon, Hermogenes, Aphthonius, and Libanius, who discussed "bringing before the eyes what is to be shown" in a clear and vivid manner or, in the generic term, *enargia* (Lanham, 1991, pp. 64–65).

In his encyclopedic rendering of Roman education, based on the Greeks they emulated, Quintilian mentioned student writing of descriptions only to try to diminish the activity, which must have grown to elaborate proportions. By this time, the teaching of writing and rhetoric had become completely intertwined. In Roman education, the first century before Christ saw a shift to a systematic rhetorical program of (like the Greeks) male education. Quintilian, a master teacher, published the most extensive description of this system in 95 C.E. (see Kennedy, 1980).

Quintilian, who summarized the Greek and Roman arts of rhetoric, believed emotional appeals to be perhaps the most powerful arguments to sway an audience. Visualization is the key to the most powerful means of arousing emotion. "A powerful effect may be created if to the actual facts of the [legal] case we add a plausible picture of what occurred, such as will make our audience feel as if they were actual eyewitnesses to the scene," he explained (1921, p. 117).

Tracing the experience back to the Greeks, he discussed daydreamlike visions, hallucinations, in which absent experiences are revived in the imagination, a phenomenon common to all. He cited Cicero on the use of this as a rhetorical art. This involves not only a translation from visual scenes to verbal, but also a transformation to visual body language as the orator becomes actor moving the audience with physical depictions of the emotion his words attempt to arouse:

> [For,] if we wish to give our words the appearance of sincerity, we must assimilate ourselves to the emotions of those who are genuinely so affected, and our eloquence must spring from the same feeling that we desire to produce in the mind of the judge. Will he grieve who can find no trace of grief in the words with which I seek to move him to grief? Will he be angry, if the orator who seeks to kindle his anger shows no sign of labouring under the motion which he demands from his audience? Will he shed tears if the pleader's eyes are dry? It is utterly impossible. (Quintilian, 1921, p. 433)

The words are never separate from the performance of them in the rhetorical arts. Quintilian (1921) believed this power of vivid imagination is natural and can be cultivated, although some are more sensitive and can produce emotion to great persuasive effect. The method is "not so much to narrate as to exhibit the actual scene, while our emotions will be no less actively stirred than if we were present at the actual occurrence" (pp. 436–437). We must cultivate this power of daydreaming and also identify ourselves with those for whom we are pleading, to "for a brief space feel their suffering as though it were our own, while our words must be such as we should use if we stood in their shoes" (p. 437). Quintilian advised that a student declaiming in school "be moved by his theme, and should imagine it to be true" when "impersonating an orphan, a shipwrecked man, or one in grave peril. What profit is there in assuming such a role unless we also assume the emotions which it involves?" (p. 439).

In addition to the words and images, Greco-Roman judicial cases (as do ours today — remember O.J.'s glove?) made heavy use of actual visual pre-sentations — the showing of a scar, a wound, a bloody weapon, or a toga. The audience's senses were all called on in this oratorical culture, rather than being fragmented and addressed in a single focus, the pictorial eye for seeing art, the ear for hearing music, the eye and intellect for reading, the nose for food and perfume.

Although the parts of Quintilian's educational system were Greek, the systematization was Roman. Roman education also emphasized a set of grad-ed composition exercises called the *progymnasmata*, not treated in detail by Quintilian. These exercises, which began with the retelling of fables (such as Aesop's) and other tales, worked up to declamation of fictitious speeches (see Friend, 1999).

An advanced exercise was description as a self-contained unit that could be dropped into place in a discourse (*ecphrasis*). Quintilian (1921) discussed this in Book VIII as *enargeia* or vivid illustration. Of course, during this time of systematization, Roman education became based on translation and transliteration. These exercises in particular depended on translation of the Greek poets and writers and subsequent paraphrase or other transformation of those texts by students. For example, students would read a fable, for instance, as in Theon, "the fable of the dog and his reflection," and, as histo-rian of Roman education Bonner (1977) explained, would subsequently para-phrase it or transform it in other ways:

> [C]arrying a piece of meat, the dog was walking beside a river, when he thought he saw another dog beside him, also carrying a piece of meat; the temptation was too great, and in attempting to acquire two pieces of meat, he lost what he had, or in Theon's version, was drowned. Here was an opportunity to describe the placid stream, the brightness of a sunny day, and the clarity of reflection in the water. All this encouraged the young to use their imaginations and at the same time developed their powers of expression. (p. 155)

Bonner also told us that poetry and history provided a broader scope for description than rhetoric, especially in the declamations in which descriptions became a stock theme. These later influenced the taste for what Horace called *purple patches* and were linked with transformations of Virgil and Ovid.

MEDIEVAL AND RENAISSANCE IMAGES

In his book on literature in the Latin Middle Ages, Curtius (1973) told how *ecphrasis*, popular in late antiquity under the Roman empire, became important in medieval times. The genre of rhetoric called *epideictic* — ceremonial speeches of praise and blame — became more important than deliberative, legislative rhetoric under tyrannical Roman emperors who were often praised. Thus, the Latin curriculum abounded in elaborate delineation of people, places, monuments and buildings, as well as sculpture and painting. From this great archive of descriptions, French writers later developed the romance, whose interest in nature and its creations created a cliché based on word-picture translation: "Nature created a beautiful being as a picture" (Curtius, 1973, pp. 181–182). Descriptions of beautiful men and women in courtly poetry were turned out in accordance with *recipes*, as Curtius wrote.

Landscape description was always important, but became especially so after Virgil had transformed Greek poetry in his Arcadian eclogues. The emphasis on pastoral landscape grew out of the epideictic praise of landscape and the rhetorical topics of *place* and *time*. For example, this pastoral description of Arcadia is filled with description of pleasurable topography (*topoi*) such as springs, hills, and animals:

> Springs bubble out, brook joined with brook runs streaming,
> Already gorge and slope and mead are green.
> Where the plain heaves into a hundred hillocks,
> The woolly sheep in scattered flocks are seen.
>
> Beyond, with step as careful as 's certain,
> The horn-browed herds toward the cliffside graze;
> There could they shelter every one, for there
> The stone is hollowed in a hundred caves.
>
> There Plan protects, there vivifying nymphs
> Dwell in the dripping, green-clad crevices —
> And there aspire to higher airs forever
> The intertangled ranks of branchy trees. (Curtius, 1973, p. 188)

Yet landscape descriptions in genres such as the medieval epic linked with pastoral poetry were soon challenged by the courtly romance, which appears in about 1150. Atmospheric scenery — in particular, the wild forest of chivalric romance — called forth new efforts in the classical *topos* of "situation" or "description of a place" (Curtius, 1973).

Notions of image and place were central in another medieval art drawn from rhetoric — the art of memory. Yates (1966) first elaborated on this art, pointing out that ancient memory systems were based on the principle that memory could be strengthened by linking it to the emotions through striking images. Architectural "places" in particular became imaginary sites for storing images to remind one of facts or, harder yet, the words of a poem or speech. This is the source of our locution, "in the first place."

This art of memory, first described in the pedagogical text *Ad Herennium* (long mistakenly attributed to Cicero), was a standard part of ancient rhetoric. The Sophists may have invented memory arts, and these were easily linked to the occult because they could produce such amazing feats of memory. Plato objected to artificial memory arts, but based his philosophy on vision and memory — knowledge became a remembering of archetypal forms visually glimpsed in the realm before birth and innately present in human minds. Overall, in the medieval period, memory arts from classical texts were progressively complicated and made into elaborate puzzles or games. These elaborate, visually based memory arts in the Renaissance became linked with Platonism; for example, Camillo's Memory Theatre tried to organize memory according to universal archetypes of reality, not trivial memory of speeches and facts. This helped incorporate classical arts of memory into the Hermetic-Cabalist tradition (see Calendrillo, 1995–1996).

In the Renaissance, memory arts became marginalized as they linked with occult thought, although they still had a place in pedagogy. The images produced by the memory systems were more likely to be expressed in print in illustrated emblem books. Here one can see images from classical fables and myths as well as spiritual or pedagogical reminders. The familiar assignment to tell a story from a picture is one that links us closely to writing teachers from the earliest times. More often, however, the process was reversed — illustrations and actual images (e.g., in emblem books) — were fashioned from oral and textual descriptions. For example, an early textbook on the liberal arts, the third- to fourth-century allegory of *The Marriage of Philology and Mercury* by Capella, spawned many popular emblems (see Moseley, 1989). In the book, seven elaborately described bridesmaids give summaries of their liberal arts to the guests at the wedding. This book also spurred early scientific illustration, such as drawings of the textually described motion of Venus and Mercury centered on the sun — a motion Copernicus cited 1,100 years later to support his own system.

Emblem books were used for entertainment, education, spiritual instruction, and memory aids. Words and pictures worked together as equals in many of these books, although they center on the elaborate narrative-bearing emblems. Many editions of Ripa's *Iconologia* (1611/1976) appeared or were imitated on the Continent or in Britain in the sixteenth and seventeenth centuries. Ripa included the goddess Eloquence, helmeted and in armor, holding thunderbolts in her right hand and a book in her left. A word picture follows — an explanation that the end of eloquence is persuasion and that her arts, youth, and beauty contribute to that end.

Bacon's (1970) texts are a significant site on which to examine the various threads of imagery from memory arts to textual imagery because they come together to reveal a fault line — a point of slippage in how images and texts were transforming. Bacon, who knew and used arts of memory well, wanted to reform the art so it would better function for investigation or for ordering and classifying knowledge. Subverting the distinction and calling images *emblems*, he fully accepted the principle that images were more memorable than words:

> Emblems bring down intellectual to sensible things; for what is sensible always strikes the memory stronger, and sooner impresses itself than the intellectual . . . And therefore it is easier to retain the image of a sportsman hunting the hare, of an apothecary ranging his boxes, an orator making a speech, a boy repeating verses, or a player acting his part, than

the corresponding notions of invention, disposition, elocution, memory, action. (cited in Yates, 1966, p. 371)

Bacon (1970) also relied on a system of faculties for the mind, originally from Plato's division of the mind and body into the reason (head), the passions (heart), and the appetites (liver). Bacon's faculties include: (a) understanding and reason; (b) the will, appetite, and affection; and (c) the imagination, which gets messages from the sense and reason and shuttles them as a messenger among faculties. Because of his emphasis on sense imagery and the central role of the imagination, his definition and goals for rhetoric shift; Rhetoric's end becomes to "fill the imagination with observations and images, to second reason, and not to oppress it" (Book IV, p. 456). Rhetoric for Bacon is visually insinuative; thus, he wrote of "coloring" an argument, piling together illustrations and observations that support a chosen aspect of the subject under consideration (Book VII, p. 77). His definition of *rhetoric* sets up a cognitive chain depending on imagery: "Rhetoric is subservient to the imagination as Logic is to the understanding; and the Duty and Office of Rhetoric, if it be deeply looked into, is no other than to apply and recommend the dictates of reason to imagination in order to excite the appetite and will" (Book IV, p. 455).

I focus on this shift because it is so key to the seventeenth and eighteenth centuries and their theories of rhetoric. The faculty of imagination, intertwined with memory, becomes central to the very definition of rhetoric, which carries with it a cognitive model. It forms the background of discoveries in vision and optics and is linked with the notion that we gain knowledge through observation. This centrality of vision and imagination is breathed in with the very air that formed the period its shapers called The Enlightenment.

Yet these themes of vision and imagination were transformations of the Renaissance preoccupation with emblems and pictorial representations. Vico (1668–1744) was on the cusp of the Enlightenment, but drew his intellectual energy from his forebears in the Renaissance. He named Bacon as one of his four major influences. Platonic in his orientation to vision and knowledge, Vico (1744/1984) believed that divine knowledge was like a sculpture, whereas human knowledge was flat like a picture. He traced the development of human culture from the image and imagination to rationality and the philosophical concept. A key turning point in his history — perhaps the beginning of a decline — is when the pictorial emblem failed to communicate to the culture as a whole and needed a written motto of explanation. Language originated with visuals — real things used as signs or visual gestures — a frog to signal place in the earth, a mouse to mean fertility, a sword to threaten violence. The very motive of language began when the beasts in the field after the flood heard a crash of thunder and *looked up* at what they took to be the thundering belly of Jove. Language, institutions such as religion and law, and society began with that act of fear and wonder involving vision (but also sound). Thus, language was metaphoric, imagistic, and poetic from its inception. Myths and fables with their magnificent images and figures were nothing more or less than true history.

Language for Vico traversed three stages — that of the gods, that of heroes, and finally that of men before decaying into barbarism, which returned humans to the age of gods. The languages of the first two stages were imaginative and full of symbolic imagery. In the age of heroes, thought was based on the imaginative universal (e.g., Ulysses, a figure who stood for a concept) (Verene, 1981). Each nation had its Ulysses, its heroic founder figure. The heroic age was the age of visuals, blazonry, crests, shields, images, rebus figures, and human symbols, such as Homer, a metaphor for collective poetry rather than a unique human being. With this elevation of symbolic language came the reverence for acute and witty sayings, language that could strike quickly and emulate the all-at-onceness of an instantaneous picture — what Vico (1996) called *sublime rhetoric* in his rhetoric manuals. That trend grew from the Renaissance into the eloquent salon language of the French Enlightenment and the wit and erudition of the English coffeehouses of the eighteenth century.

OCULARISM IN THE ENLIGHTENMENT

Vico sent an early version of his masterwork *New Science* based on his historical cultural cycle to Isaac Newton, but it is not known whether Newton ever received the book (see Dobbs & Jacob, 1995). Newton (1643–1727) is the figure most people think of when they think of the Enlightenment and the beginnings of modern science, as well as the modern study of color and light. As Pope (1954) wrote in an epitaph intended for Newton:

Nature and Nature's Laws lay hid in Night,
God said, "*Let Newton be!*" and All was Light. (p. 317)

In 1666, when Newton started thinking about color and light, theories from Descartes described light as a pressure on the eyeball of the ether that filled the universe. Newton rejected this, working with a notion of light as a particle, thus having velocity. Hooke's *Micrographia* (1665), which was a collection of illustrations made under the microscope, at that time discussed color as pulses of light. Newton used a prism to determine that white light was a mixture of various colors that were refracted in different angles. This was not published until 1704, but was wildly popular. Later, the Italian professor, Bassi, who in the mid-eighteenth century was the first woman to be offered an official university teaching position in Europe, taught the *Opticks* at Bologna (Dobbs & Jacob, 1995). Light became a key concept across fields; for example, architects tried to open up buildings to reveal the light of Newton's *Opticks*. Investigations into light and vision of all sorts multiplied in the Enlightenment period.

That "construction is the essence of vision" has long been known, Hoffman (1998) argued. The notion first appeared in Ptolemy in the second century A.D., who wrote an *Optics*. Aristotle, Euclid, and Ptolemy all wrote on light and vision. The Islamic scholar Alhazen (Ibn al-Haytham, ca. 965–ca. 1040) wrote on the constructed nature of vision in his seven-volume *Optics*. His work, which refuted weaker Greek theories and synthesized stronger ones, was translated into Latin in the late twelfth and early thirteenth centuries and became influential in vision theory (see Lindberg, 1992). Others mastered both the Greek and Islamic vision theory. The inferences from vision seemed so instantaneous that Malebranche (1638–1715) believed that God produces them (Hoffman, 1998). Molyneux (d. 1698) published the first English text on optics, *Dioptrika Nova*, and asked the famous question Locke repeated in his *Essay*: How would a man born blind see if he were suddenly given his sight? Would he recognize on sight the shapes he had heretofore felt? Many speculated on the answer, but Cheselden (1688–1752), the famous physician who cared for Newton in his last illness, published a famous case that began to answer the question. Having performed cataract surgery on a young man born blind, he discovered that the man had to learn to interpret what he saw at first only as colored patches. Berkeley (1685–1753) wrote about the ambiguity of vision and the need for interpretation. As the Cheselden case confirmed, he predicted that one born blind could not recognize shapes. The French encyclopedists led the Continental interest in vision, especially Locke's admirer Condillac and the better known Diderot, who wrote controversial treatises on the blind and deaf that also argued that we actively construct what we see.

How does seeing work? Early thinkers based their new theories of vision on what they already knew—aesthetic theories of the imagination and natural philosophies like those of Epicurus. In 1604, Johannes Kepler had a theory of the retinal image that used the analogy of a camera—but the Kodak was as then unknown. However, philosophers played with the new pinpoint camera, like the ones we played with as children, which projected an image upside down. This was an exciting development, and they explained it by referring to the mind's eye and the imagination. The camera obscura image was found in Locke's *Essay* (1699–1705) as an explanation of how the mind took in images. The Greek atomists had a long-standing explanation that became deeply intertwined with rhetoric and the teaching of writing.

Kroll's (1991) history of language revisited the seventeenth century with its return to classical notions of the Epicureans and their visual theories of the image. During the Scientific Revolution, there was a "neo-Epicurean revival" centering on Lucretius' (1946) *De Rerum Natura (On the Nature of Things)*. This amazing classical poem, which dramatically and abruptly ended in midstream just as the author visually described the sweep of the plague through Athens, was a staple of the educational canon and had particularly captured the imagination of Renaissance readers. Written in the first century before Christ, it is a verse explication for the Roman world of the Greek system of philosophy. It was popular in the early modern period despite its antireligious outlook based on a rationalist Epicurean theory of nature, optics, and vision.

Later blended with faculty psychology as in Bacon's rhetoric, Epicurean theory suggested that using language to present images to the intellect through the imagination (*phantasia*) is the way to arouse the passions and motivate the will. This is based on the theory of optics in the philosophy of Epicurus, as interpreted through Lucretius' poem: The atomic and dynamic constitution of bodies causes them continually to throw off microscopically thin representations of themselves (*eidola*), which almost instantaneously strike the eye or another sense organ, producing a presentation (*phantasia*). The mind can then take hold of the image by an act (*epibole*). Thus, the entire basis of Epicurus' mental economy presumes the mediating function of the *phantasia* as well as an active construction (Kroll, 1991).

Although the images that we see are true in that they exist, they are not presumed to match the actual nature of things. In the Lucretian version of Epicurean philosophy, mental images are in cognition the equivalent of the atom or minima in physics. They result from the things of the world's continual throwing off of images that strike our minds whether we are asleep or awake. This was called the *intromission theory*, in opposition to Plato's notion that the eyes shoot out rays to see—called the *extromission theory*. The intromission theory came to dominate in early modern science.

Epicureans believed that, in fact, the mind cannot think without images or ideas (significantly, the Greek word for "to see"). Images, the atoms of thought, were combined to make thoughts the way notes make up music or the alphabet makes up language. Lucretius' analogy between atoms and letters of the alphabet found its way into nearly every major consideration of natural science at the turn of the seventeenth century, found in Bacon and Boyle and extended to rhetorical topics in Vico's use of topics in scientific inquiries. This image is a familiar one in Gassendi, an atomist whose language theory is Epicurean. For Gassendi, words are *ostensive* (Kroll, 1991), analogically pointing to things. Utterances partake of symbolic action, pointing to the cognitive image. Locke's language theory, in touch with Boyle, resonates with the spirit if not the letter of Epicurean thought, as he was steeped in French thought, especially Gassendi. In Locke's *Essay*, the notion of "idea" is central, which fed into the growing interest in the faculty of imagination. Locke's popular abbreviated logic and his educational advice for the son of a friend helped put these ideas into the mainstream of pedagogy.

In part, a return to Augustine (Kroll, 1991) was at the heart of this new emphasis on imagination, converging with notions of the Epicurean image. According to an Augustinian Biblical view, humans once were spiritual creatures, but since the Fall, they must live a predominantly physical existence. The imagination, the faculty of storing and reviving images, was often thought of as the intermediary between humans' physical and spiritual natures, between the senses and pure thought. It was, significantly, the faculty of representation. The centrality of the imagination as intermediary was held by many throughout the century, and it became key to rhetorical persuasion. It also became central to the rhetorical description, which is of so much value in the modern novel. As such, description became a key pedagogical tool in early modern writing instruction, which more and more exemplified French belles lettres rather than the classical rhetorical canon.

DESCRIPTION IN MODERNITY

During the eighteenth century, when it became clear that print and writing and associated book literacy were spreading, teachers worked to understand

and teach how to translate visual scenes and images into text. One such teacher was a self-proclaimed follower of Locke, the French philosopher Condillac (1714–1799). His work influenced the Scottish Enlightenment rhetoricians, especially Smith, Blair, and Campbell. For many years, Condillac was tutor to the young Prince of Parma and associate of the French encyclopedist Diderot and Rousseau. In his pedagogy, Condillac liked to place his pupil before a window with shutters that were opened to give a brief view of the landscape. As Aarsleff (1982) summarized:

> In remembering and talking about this landscape, the young man was forced to analyze the instantaneous unitary tableau into elements he recalled as single units — trees, shrubbery, bushes, fences, groves, and the like. He was forced to think sequentially because discourse is linear. (p. 30)

Condillac explained the differences between the visual and verbal in this way: The visual world is holistic and is seen instantaneously as a picture. Verbal language is linear, occurring sequentially in units over time. Language decomposes holistic reality, allowing writers to convey what is really seen out there in the world into the mind, where we can once again recompose it to represent the holistic world. It also analyzes that reality by breaking it into bits. For Condillac and others in French belles lettres, the most expressive text is one that tries to re-create this all at onceness — this powerful tableau effect of prelinguistic, visual thought. This is because it hearkens back to the original language of gesture, a bodily visual art that was the first human communication. Gesture and body language were the first systems of human communication and analyzed or broke apart the holistic idea. Language, both gestural and verbal, was formed on the basis of analogy to earlier signs in a process of translation. Thus, the keys to the later process of translation from visual imagery to written text were memory and imagination, closely linked. They allowed the language user to recall and visualize past sights and experiences and link them to signs. This theory presumes a split between analytical and expressive language — a split that helps enact a separation of scientific from poetic text in the future. Like Vico's theories, the earliest language was more expressively poetic and imagistic, whereas language became more analytical, abstract, and philosophical over time.

Later in the eighteenth century, about the time of the American Declaration of Independence, French theory hybridized with earlier British thought in Scotland to produce what was called *new rhetoric* of the Scottish Enlightenment. Key figures are the economist Smith, Blair (the first professor of English), Lord Kames, and Campbell (see Miller, 1997). The Baconian shift to make imagery and imagination central was apparent in the work of all these figures. To illustrate, we can examine Campbell's discussion of the ends of rhetoric as "to enlighten the understanding, to please the imagination, to move the passions, or to influence the will" (Golden & Corbett, 1968, p. 145). This was a classification system, but also an ascending progression: The intellect feeds the "fancy" or imagination, the fancy transforms and presents materials to affect the passions, then the passions spur the will to act (p. 146).

Thereby, the imagination becomes the hinge, catalyst, or fulcrum for persuasion. For Campbell, the imagination is linked to painting:

> The imagination is addressed by exhibiting to it a lively and beautiful representation of a suitable object. As in this exhibition, the task of the oratory, in some sort, be said, like that of the painter, to consist in imitation, the merit of the work results entirely from these two sources; dignity, as well in the subject or thing imitated, as in the manner of imitation; and resemblance, in the portrait or performance. (p. 146)

Campbell linked the most perfect discourse to the sublime — "those great and noble images, which, when in suitable colouring presented to the mind, do, as it were, distend the imagination with some vast conception, and quite ravish the soul" (pp. 146–147).

Rhetoricians concerned with style and those building their rhetorics around models of texts also turned to the late Greek rhetorician pseudo-Longinus, whose *On the Sublime* was translated into French by Boileau-Despreaux in the seventeenth century. These stylistic rhetorics also formed the backbone of the Continental belles lettres movement transformed by Scots such as Campbell over the century (see Howell's [1971] classifications).

The interest in vision and imagination formed the heart of the Enlightenment belles lettres movement, with its paradigm shift in language arts pedagogy to an aesthetics of taste (see Miller, 1997). This ultimately spread from France to Britain and, from both those countries, quite naturally to the United States. Belles lettres included written forms such as history, essays, and poetry, but also such visual arts as architecture and landscape gardening. The goal *sublime rhetoric* (Vico's term) was often not to persuade as much as to transport an audience, and word painting of nature was a key method used. As a result, in British and American composition, textual description became an even more important mode, especially descriptions of landscapes. These were inevitably tied to moral values and were a continuation of the kind of oratory practiced at public ceremonials from classical times, epideictic rhetoric.

The development of the novel in the eighteenth century made use of these traditions of landscape description, as we can see in Austen's descriptions in *Pride and Prejudice* (1993) and again in *Emma* (2000). In the first book, when Elizabeth visits Darcy's Pemberley, Austen sets the reflective mode appropriate not only for landscape, but for consideration of values: "They gradually ascended for half a mile, and then found themselves at the top of a considerable eminence, where the wood ceased, and the eye was instantly caught by Pemberley House, situated on the opposite side of a valley into which the road with such abruptness wound" (p. 156). The passage not only reveals the imbrication of landscape design with its contrived views and picturesque writing, but also provides a tone that suits Elizabeth's full state of mind on entering the estate of the man whose hand she had rejected. Descriptions of Pemberley's buildings and grounds not only create a reflective tone, but also help support the ideals of reason, solidity, unity, and permanence of the structure: "It was a large, handsome, stone building, standing well on rising ground, and backed by a ridge of high woody hills; and in front, a stream of some natural importance was swelled into greater, but without any artificial appearance (p. 156).

After describing Donwell Abbey and environs in a similar style in *Emma*, Austen revealed Emma's feelings on looking down on Abbey-Mill Farm, "with meadows in front, and the river making a close and handsome curve around it" (p. 236), all suffused with patriotic values and sentiments: "It was a sweet view—sweet to the eye and the mind. English verdure, English culture, English comfort, seen under a sun bright, without being Oppressive" (p. 236). The three-part (tricolon) structure harmoniously and reasonably emphasized the values Austen wanted to forward.

Although my analysis stops with the long eighteenth century in Great Britain, Clark and Halloran (1993) wrote about how such picturesque discourse in nineteenth-century American writing was a transformation of classical epideictic discourse, carrying the values of Romanticism and also its class hierarchy. In landscape description, harmonious composition makes the writing seem like a painting or actual landscape, but the language also increases adherence to certain values, Halloran explained, similar to what we see in the Austen passages. Such descriptive writing abounds in Emerson, Thoreau, Whittier, Longfellow, and J. Fenimore Cooper, helping form a sense of American identity. An overflow of "mass produced prints and boilerplate prose" poured over the nation as a result of this movement, and books such as *Picturesque America* (1874) combining engravings and essays became popular (Clark & Halloran, 1993, p. 245).

One significant element not examined in this chapter is the effect of technological advances on rendering visual images on writing. Yet it is clear that the invention of mechanical print—the book—and improvements such as the high-speed press in the nineteenth century all shaped the uses of graphics and affected how students were taught to write or interact with pictures in print. Although there were perhaps fewer pictures and graphic elements when they were more difficult and expensive to print, pictures, engravings, and even simple line drawings have always been cherished by readers to relieve the difficulty of reading.

Written language was always a chief way of translating the visual world. Yet in the eighteenth century, more and more literature in the vernacular was produced, and education began to shift to the vernacular. Translation as a central educational activity began a slow decline. That century saw the first literary criticism of literature in English and the appointment of the first professor of English literature in Scotland. In another shift involving the Scientific Revolution, some saw written language as a representation of the world rather than a translation into a different system of signs or a transformation of symbols serving as an interface to a mysterious reality. Thus, they feared metaphor and other rhetorical devices as distortions of the objective representation of a visual reality. They insisted on "clear and distinct" prose that would carry the writer's vision of reality into the reader's mental structure. This notion of prose as clear as a window that would allow a primarily visual reality to be seen became a dominant strand of writing instruction. It led to pedagogies encouraging good observational skills and clarity in style and structure. The scientific urge also led to the movement to classify and describe types of writing as if writing were a form of natural history.

This urge to taxonomize led to the pedagogy based on the "Four Horsemen," widely deplored when I was in graduate school, but tenaciously hanging on since. That form-based pedagogy evolved to present students with writing centered not on aims, but on genres or forms of exposition, argument, narrative, and, most important for this analysis, description. This pedagogy has been traced to figures like the nineteenth-century Scottish Bain's response to both the discourse of scientific classification, clarity, and belles lettres. The hybridizing of the old belles lettres theories with the newer scientific models produced the first modern rhetorics. Those first Scottish rhetorics were also part of the transformation that led to modern English literary studies (see Miller, 1997, for this history in detail).

How to understand and teach language and literature in an age of technical transformation that renews the age-old interest in the image is a significant issue that connects us to these rhetorical predecessors. We might also wonder how transformations currently taking place will change the current English studies model. We may not know how, but we can surmise that English studies in the new century will offer a very different product from traditional twentieth-century print pedagogy (see Stroupe, 2000). The more we learn about both those elements, the more prepared we will be to teach our students how to make better meaning and communicate in the new era. The tension between graphic elements and text may not go away, but it can be a more creative and *interinanimating* tension if we know how to translate between modes (Richards, p. 47). We can do no better than emulate the Renaissance's da Vinci, who saw so much and wrote so well he could carelessly confuse the one with the other in his prolific notebooks during the Renaissance of learning. We might cajole our students as he prompted himself:

> Write [he reminded himself, for to him writing and drawing are all one], write the tongue of the woodpecker and the jaw of the crocodile. Write the flight of the fourth kind of chewing butterflies, and of the flying ants, and the three chief positions of the wings of birds in descent. . . . Write of the regions of the air and the formation of clouds, and the cause of snow and hail, and of the new shapes that show forms in the air, and of the trees in cold countries with the new shape of the leaves. . . . Write whether the percussion made by water upon its object is equal in power to the whole mass of water supposed suspended in the air or no. (cited in de Santillana, 1956, pp. 67–70)

Such sublime vision as Leonardo's presents us with the gift of a moment in which scientific terminology and poetry are one and neither word nor image is valued as more sacred. If they once were divorced by print culture, the remarriage of word and image performed by digital technology signals the rebirth of literacy in the twenty-first century, a hybrid literacy in which we all may hope to share more of the potential of Leonardo.

REFERENCES

Aarsleff, H. (1982). *From Locke to Saussure: Essays on the study of language and intellectual history*. Minneapolis: University of Minnesota Press.

Austen, J. (1993). *Pride and prejudice* (D. Gray, Ed.). New York: Norton.

Austen, J. (2000). *Emma* (S. M. Parrish, Ed.). New York: Norton.

Bacon, F. (1970). *The philosophical works of Francis Bacon* (Reprinted from J. Spedding, R. L. Ellis, & J. M. Robertson, Eds.). Freeport, NY: Books for Libraries.

Bonner, S. F. (1977). *Education in ancient Rome: From the elder Cato to the younger Pliny*. Berkeley: University of California Press.

Calendrillo, L. (1995–1996). Mental imagery, psychology, and rhetoric: An examination of recurring problems. *JAEPL: The Journal of the Assembly for Expanded Perspectives on Learning*, 3, 74–79.

Clark, G., & Halloran, S. M. (1993). *Oratorical culture in nineteenth-century America: Transformations in the theory and practice of rhetoric*. Carbondale: Southern Illinois University Press.

Curtius, E. R. (1973). *European literature and the Latin middle ages* (W. R. Trask, Trans.) Princeton, NJ: Princeton/Bollingen Books.

de Santillana, G. (1956). *The age of adventure: The Renaissance philosophers*. New York: Mentor Books.

Dobbs, B. J. T., & Jacob, M. C. (1995). *Newton and the culture of Newtonianism*. Atlantic Highlands, NJ: Humanities Press.

Faigley, L. (1999). Material literacy and visual design. In J. Selzer & S. Crowley (Eds.), *Rhetorical bodies* (pp. 171–201). Madison: University of Wisconsin Press.

Friend, C. (1999). Pirates, seducers, wronged heirs, poison cups, cruel husbands, and other calamities: The Roman school declamations and critical pedagogy. *Rhetoric Review*, 17, 300–319.

Golden, J. L., & Corbett, E. P. J. (1968). *The rhetoric of Blair, Campbell, and Whately*. New York: Holt.

Hoffman, D. D. (1998). *Visual intelligence: How we create what we see*. New York: Norton.

Hooke, R. *Micrographia, or Some physiological descriptions of minute bodies made by magnifying glasses with observations and inquiries thereupon*. London: Printed for James Allestry, 1665.

Howell, W. S. (1971). *Eighteenth-century British logic and rhetoric*. Princeton, NJ: Princeton University Press.

Kennedy, G. A. (1980). *Classical rhetoric and its Christian and secular tradition from ancient to modern times*. Chapel Hill: University of North Carolina Press.

Kroll, R. W. (1991). *The material word: Literate culture in the Restoration and early eighteenth century*. Baltimore: Johns Hopkins University Press.

Landow, G. (1992). *Hypertext: The convergence of contemporary, critical theory and teachnology*. Baltimore: Johns Hopkins University Press.

Lanham, R. A. (1991). *A handlist of rhetorical terms* (2nd ed.). Berkeley: University of California Press.

Lindberg, D. C. (1992). *The beginnings of Western science: The European scientific tradition in philosophical, religious, and institutional context, 600 B.C. to A.D. 1450*. Chicago: University of Chicago Press.

Lucretius. (1946). *On the nature of things* (C. E. Bennett, Trans.). Roslyn, NY: Walter J. Black.

Miller, T. P. (1997). *The formation of college English: Rhetoric and belles lettres in the British cultural provinces*. Pittsburgh, PA: University of Pittsburgh Press.

Mitchell, W. J. T. (1986). *Iconology: Image, text, ideology*. Chicago: University of Chicago Press.

Mitchell, W. J. T. (1994). *Picture theory: Essays on verbal and visual representation*. Chicago: University of Chicago Press.

Moseley, C. (1989). *A century of emblems: An introductory anthology*. Hants, England: Scolar Press.

Pope, A. (1954). *The Twickenham edition of the poems of Alexander Pope* (N. Ault, completed by J. Batt, Eds.). London: Methuen.

Quintilian. (1921). *The institutio oratoria of Quintilian II* (H. E. Butler, Trans.). Cambridge, MA: Harvard University Press.

Richards, I. A. (1936). *The philosophy of rhetoric*. New York: Oxford University Press.

Ripa, C. (1976). *Iconologia*. New York: Garland. (Original work published 1611)

Stroupe, C. (2000). Visualizing English: Recognizing the hybrid literacy of visual and verbal authorship on the Web. *College English*, 62, 607–632.

Verene, D. P. (1981). *Vico's science of imagination*. Ithaca: Cornell.

Verene, D. P. (1991). *The new art of autobiography: An essay on the* Life of Giambattista Vico. Written by Himself. Oxford: Clarendon.

Vico, G. (1984). *The new science of Giambattista Vico* (T. G. Bergin & M. H. Fisch, Trans., abridged from 3rd ed.). Ithaca, NY: Cornell University Press. (Original work published 1744)

Vico, G. (1996). *The art of rhetoric (Institutiones Oratoriae, 1711-1741)* (G. A. Pinton & A. W. Shippee, Trans. & Eds.). Amsterdam: Rodopi.

Welch, K. E. (1990). Writing instruction in ancient Athens after 450 B.C. In J.J. Murphy (Ed.), *A short history of writing instruction: From ancient Greece to twentieth-century America* (pp. 1–18). Davis, CA: Hermagoras.

Welch, K. E. (1999). *Electric rhetoric: Classical rhetoric, oralism, and a new literacy.* Cambridge, MA: MIT Press.

Yates, F. (1966). *The art of memory.* Chicago: University of Chicago Press.

4

Metamedia Literacy: Transforming Meanings and Media

J. L. LEMKE

Literacies are legion. Each one consists of a set of interdependent social practices that link people, media objects, and strategies for meaning making (Gee, 1990; Lemke, 1989b). Each is an integral part of a culture and its subcultures. Each plays a role in maintaining and transforming a society because literacies provide essential links between meanings and doings. Literacies are themselves technologies, and they give us the keys to using broader technologies. They also provide a key link between self and society: the means through which we act on, participate in, and become shaped by larger "ecosocial" systems and networks (see examples in the following and in Lemke, 1993a, 1995c). Literacies are transformed in the dynamics of these larger self-organizing systems, and we—our own human perceptions, identities, and possibilities—are transformed along with them.

That, at least, is the Big Picture as I would sketch it today. Let me try to fill in a few of the details that are particularly relevant to our concerns here. The notion of literacy as such seems to me to be too broad to be useful. I do not think we can define it more precisely than as a set of cultural competences for making socially recognizable meanings by the use of particular material technologies. Such a definition hardly distinguishes literacy from competence at cooking or choosing your wardrobe, except for the particular semiotic resources used to make meaning (language vs. the cuisine or fashion system) and the particular material artifacts that mediate this process (vocal sounds or written signs vs. foods or clothes). There was a time perhaps when we could believe that making meaning with language was somehow fundamentally different, or could be treated in isolation from making meaning with visual resources or patterns of bodily action and social interaction. But today our technologies are moving us from the age of writing to an age of multimedia authoring in which voice-annotated documents and images, and written text

From *Handbook of Literacy and Technology: Transformations in a Post-Typographic World.* Ed. David Reinking, Michael C. McKenna, Linda D. Labbo, and Ronald D. Kieffer. Mahwah, NJ: Lawrence Erlbaum Associates, 1998. 283–301.

itself, are now merely components of larger meaning objects. The meanings of words and images, read or heard, seen static or changing, are different because of the contexts in which they appear—contexts that consist significantly of the other media components. Meanings in multimedia are not fixed and additive (the word meaning plus the picture meaning), but multiplicative (word meaning modified by image context, image meaning modified by textual context), making a whole far greater than the simple sum of its parts (see Lemke, 1994b, 1997a). Moreover all literacy is multimedia literacy: You can never make meaning with language alone; there must always be a visual or vocal realization of linguistic signs that also carries nonlinguistic meaning (e.g., tone of voice or style of orthography). Signs must have some material reality in order to function as signs, but every material form potentially carries meanings according to more than one code. All semiotics is multimedia semiotics, and all literacy is multimedia literacy.

The European cultural tradition, among others, has long recognized and made use of these multimedia principles even in ordinary printed texts (cf. Alpers, 1983; Bellone, 1980; Eisenstein, 1979; Olson, 1994). whether in manuscript illustration or the use of diagrams in technical writing. But there has been a certain modern logocentrism (Derrida, 1976) that has identified language alone as a reliable medium for logical thought, and written language as the primary medium of, first, authoritative knowledge, and lately of all higher cognitive capacities (see Olson, 1994, for a reprise of these arguments and Lemke, 1995b, for a critique).

If we are required to specify exactly which semiotic resources and which material technologies define a particular literacy, then we have as many literacies as there are multimedia genres (cf. Gee, 1990). These can perhaps be further subdivided (and so the number of functional literacies further multiplied) by considering whether competence with both the technologies of production and the technologies of use are to be included. When writing required pen and paper or typewriter, and reading required only the book (and maybe your eyeglasses) these distinctions were simple to maintain. But today whether you wish to read hypertext or write it, you still need much the same hardware and software technologies, and you need both new authoring skills and new interpretive skills to use them.

Finally, in the spirit of Latour's (1987, 1993) work on actor networks in the study of technologies in society, we need to count other people as part of the technological ecology of literacy practices. (Latour constructed social networks from both the human and the nonhuman actors, such as technical artifacts in a social ecology of cultural practices.) The network of interactions that renders a text or multimedia object meaningful is not limited to those between the author or user and the object, but must also include those with teachers, peers, and communities of people who embody the practices that make a particular sign combination meaningful. Isolated from all social interaction, humans do not learn to talk or write. However appealing the ideology of individualism may make the stereotype of the lone writer or reader, the fact that texts and signs are socially meaningful is what gives them their usefulness and makes them possible. What looks like the same text or multi-media genre on paper or on screen is not functionally the same, follows different meaning conventions, and requires different skills for its successful use, when it functions in different social networks for different purposes, as part of different human activities. A literacy is always a literacy in some genre, and it must be defined with respect to the sign systems deployed, the material technologies involved, and the social contexts of production, circulation, and use of the particular genre. We can be literate in the genre of the scientific research report or the genre of the business presentation; in each case the specific literate skills and the relevant communicative communities are very different.

In the study of written language literacy, there is still considerable debate about how important it is that the material signs of writing are relatively more permanent or more evanescent, how they are organized in space and time, and what counts as writing (Mathematics? Braille? Videotapes of American Sign Language?). Some of these questions remain of interest for particular genres and technologies, but few of them have yet been reconceptualized in the context of the new multimedia technologies (see Harris, 1995, and Lemke, 1997b).

We also need to reconceptualize the relations between literacies and the societies in which they operate, and the role of people in these larger processes (e.g., Lemke, 1995b; Olson, 1994). We need to improve our older ways of talking about these phenomena. It is no longer sufficient to imagine that societies are made up of isolated human individuals, tentatively linked by voluntary social contacts, with individual and autonomous minds somehow dissociated from the material world. We cannot get by anymore thinking that there is just one thing called literacy or that it is simply what individual minds do when confronted with symbols one at a time.

Every time we make meaning by reading a text or interpreting a graph or picture we do so by connecting the symbols at hand to other texts and other images read, heard, seen, or imagined on other occasions (the principle of general *intertextuality*; cf. Lemke, 1985, 1992, 1995a). Which connections we make (what kind and to which other texts and images) is partly individual, but also characteristic of our society and our place in it: our age, gender, economic class, affiliation groups, family traditions, cultures, and subcultures.

Literacies are always social: We learn them by participating in social relationships; their conventional forms evolved historically in particular societies; the meanings we make with them always tie us back into the fabric of meanings made by others.

Literacies are legion. Each different register, genre, or discourse formation (Bazerman, 1988, 1994; Foucault, 1969; Gee, 1990; Halliday, 1977, 1978; Lemke, 1995c; Martin, 1992) is the product of some particular subcommunity going about its special business. Being a native speaker, knowing the grammar, and checking the dictionary are not enough to understand the texts of these specialized communities as their members understand them, unless we also know their contexts of use. Broadcast accounts of cricket test matches are mostly incomprehensible to me even with a rudimentary knowledge of terms and rules and an hour or two watching, even when watching a match as I hear the commentary. I am not sufficiently a member of this community, do not have enough experience, have not heard enough commentaries, seen enough matches, or understood the strategies of the game and the culture of this community. It is no different if you pick up a research article on quantum cosmology or biotechnology development, or a technical report on needed equipment repairs in an electrical generating station, or a Japanese *manga* comic book. It does not matter if the medium is voice or video, diagram or text. What matters is knowing how to make meaning like the natives do.

Literacies cannot be understood as passive receptivities. Making sense with a printed text is a complex and active process of meaning making not so different from writing the original of that text (say by editing and modifying a previous draft, or cobbling together from sets of notes a final coherent text). Both reading and writing are meaning-making processes of the same kind. They are in no sense inverse to one another (Harris, 1995; Lemke, 1989b). All that is different are the situational affordances. The other human or inanimate players we interact with to make our meanings — be they writing partners or marks scratched on paper.

It has been a long time since the technologies of literacy were as simple as pen, ink, and paper; and in the era of print, as before, literacy has rarely meant verbal text alone. Many of the genres of literacy, from the popular magazine article to the scientific research report, combine visual images and printed text in ways that make cross-reference between them essential to understanding them as their regular readers and writers do. No technology is an island. Every literate meaning-making practice is interdependent with skills from keyboarding to page turning, typesetting to bookbinding, and copyediting to marketing and distribution (in the case of print technologies). As our technologies become more complex they find themselves situated in larger and longer networks of other technologies and other cultural practices (Latour, 1993).

Publishing yourself on the World Wide Web may cut out many of the old print middlemen, human and machine, but in addition to simple writing and typing skills, you need to be able to operate the software and hardware to get your work formatted properly in HTML (hypertext markup language), loaded on a server, and connected to the Internet. Someone has to write and update those programs; design, manufacture, sell, and deliver the hardware; configure it; maintain the network; develop the protocols; and offer technical assistance and service. As a universal information processor, the same computer can serve many of these purposes, which makes the process look simpler; but what people have to know to use the computer, and to design and maintain this whole system of practices, becomes far greater, both materially and semiotically. Some people somewhere have to manipulate more different kinds of matter in more different ways. We have to know how to do more different sorts of things (collectively and individually).

Literacies cannot be adequately analyzed just as what individuals do. We must understand them as part of the larger systems of practices that hold a society together, that make it a unit of dynamic self-organization far larger than the individual. In fact, if we think the word *society* means only people, then we need another term, one that, like *ecosystem* includes the total environment; machines, buildings, cables, satellites, bedrock, sewers, farms, insect life, bacteria, and everything with which we are interdependent in order to be the complex community that we are. We could not be the community we are unless we did the things we do, and most of what we do depends not just on the physical and biological properties of all these system partners, but on what they mean to us.

Dynamically, the total system we are talking about, the one within which we need to analyze changes in literacies and technologies, is not of course a system of things at all. It has to be a system of interdependent processes in which these things participate, and which link them, and us, together into a system. Biological and geological processes, human activities, and social practices—are regarded as one system of interdependent goings on: an "ecosocial" system (Lemke, 1993a, 1995c). Within this system we have to follow out the links and networks of interdependence: which practices where and when are interdependent with which other practices elsewhere and elsewhen. Critical among these processes, insofar as human action matters to the dynamics of the system, are the meaning-making practices by which we humans interpret, evaluate, plan, and cooperate, including our many literacy practices. (The boundary between literacy practices as such and meaning making, or semiotic signifying practices in general is a fuzzy one. Core literacy practices are usually distinguished by code, language, and by medium, spatial, visible, and durable. (For efforts to deal with the limitations of such definitions, see Harris, 1995; Lemke, 1997b.)

We no longer have to separate our material technologies so radically as we once did from our cognitive strategies. People with bodies participate in activities and practices, such as jointly authoring a multimedia Web document, in which we and our appliances are partners in action; in which who we are and how we act is as much a function of what is at hand as of what is in head. This is the powerful new viewpoint on human activity and society that many disciplines today are converging toward, whether they speak of actor networks (Latour, 1987; Lynch & Woolgar, 1990), situated or social cognition (Hutchins, 1995; Lave, 1988; Rogoff, 1990), ecosocial semiotics (Lemke, 1993a, 1995c), mediated activity (Engestrom, 1990; Wertsch, 1991), or cyborg transgressions (Bryson & deCastell, 1996; Haraway, 1991; Sofia, 1995). Instead of theorizing causal relations from one autonomous domain to another (technologies to literacies, literacies to minds, minds to societies), if we unite all these domains as participants in the myriad subnetworks of an ecosocial system, we can give detailed accounts of their interdependencies and the self-organizing dynamics of this complex system. We need to break down the artificial boundaries we have tried to create between the mental and the material, the individual and the social aspects of people and things interacting physically and semiotically with other people and things.

Today new information technologies are mediating the transformation of our meaning-making communities. We can communicate more often and more intimately with more geographically and culturally diverse communities than ever before. Online conferences and listserv groups, the denizens of chat rooms, and the pioneers of MUDs and MOOs (Day, Crump, & Rickly, 1996; Harrison & Stephen, 1996; Unsworth, 1996) are extending old communities and creating new ones (Rheingold, 1993). People who corresponded a few times a year and met once or twice at conferences can now be in regular contact by e-mail, by inexpensive (we hope) voice Internet, and perhaps soon, bandwidth, and the regulators willing, by videoconferencing. You can have a more significant dialogue with someone in Australia than with someone across the hall, and sustain it just as easily. You can don a new gender or identity, in masquerade or for exploration of possible selves (Day et al., 1996; Stone, 1991). You can experience new kinds of relationships to people and be treated differently by them. You can lurk and listen in communities you might someday want to join. You can have a first taste without risk or commitment, and you will hear viewpoints expressed that you might not otherwise have come into contact with, or might have discounted prematurely out of prejudice if you identified their source in other ways than what cyberspace makes possible.

Every new community, every transformed community, potentially represents a new literacy. Every new system of conventional practices for meaningful communication already is a new literacy embedded in new technologies. All participation in new communities, in new social practices, potentially makes available to us new identities as individuals and new forms of humanity as members of communities. Insofar as education is initiation into communities, and especially into their generic and specialized literacy practices, new information technologies, new communication practices, and new social networks make possible new paradigms for education and learning, and call into question the assumptions on which the older paradigms rest.

Old practices migrate en masse to new or transformed ecosocial systems: We re-create much that is already familiar. Our Web documents initially look like print documents. Our online communities initially grow out of familiar institutional groupings. But our new online homes come equipped with new appliances, our old practices take on new meanings in these new settings, new opportunities will get taken up, and new serendipities become likely. Change and transformation are at work.

TRANSFORMING LITERACIES

What are the new literacies that new information technologies are making both necessary and possible? The generic literacies of the Information Age will certainly include multimedia authoring skills, multimedia critical analysis, cyberspace exploration strategies, and cyberspace navigation skills (Lemke, 1996b).

But there is also an even more important question to consider. How can we understand what they demand of us, and how can adopting and adapting them transform social relationships and social structures? I discuss in the following some larger themes that go beyond specific literacy skills and that I believe will define the most radical transformations in literacy and literacy education that the new technologies may bring.

Multimedia Literacies

Multimedia authoring skills and multimedia critical analysis correspond closely to traditional skills of text writing and critical reading, but we need to understand how narrowly restrictive our literacy education traditions have been in the past in order to see how much more students will need in the future than we are now giving them. We do not teach students how to integrate even drawings and diagrams into their writing, much less archival photo images, video clips, sound effects, voice audio, music, animation, or more specialized representations (mathematical formulas, graphs, and tables, etc.). For such multimedia productions it does not even really make sense any more, if it ever did, to speak of integrating these other media into writing. Text may or may not form the organizing spine of a multimedia work. What we really need to teach, and to understand before we can teach it, is how various literacies and various cultural traditions combine these different semiotic modalities to make meanings that are more than the sum of what each could mean separately. I have called this multiplying meaning (Lemke, 1994b, 1997a) because the options for meanings from each medium cross-multiply in a combinatorial explosion; in multimedia meaning possibilities are not merely additive.

At least this is so in principle. In practice, every multimedia genre and every multimedia literacy tradition restricts the enormous set of possibilities to only some allowed or favored combinations, but there are still always more than what one would get just by adding those of each medium separately. No text exactly duplicates what a picture means to us: Text and picture together are not two ways of saying the same thing; the text means more when juxtaposed with the picture, and so does the picture when set beside the text.

We need also to realize that these multimedia skills are not advanced skills that should only follow learning the separate media literacies. Young children's early modes of communication integrate vocal articulations with large-motor gestures; they only gradually learn to differentiate gestures from drawing, and drawing from writing, as independent systems for making meaning. They are perfectly ready to learn integrated multimedia literacies from the start, and of course they do: They learn to read picture books while talking with adults and playing with toys that resemble images in the books. They begin to write and draw while telling stories and leaving traces of their gestures on paper, walls, and refrigerator doors (cf. Dyson, 1991;

Hicks & Kanevsky, 1992; Lemke, 1994b). However, our theories and teaching of literacy have long been too logocentric. Whereas children are learning to distinguish different semiotic resources (e.g., drawing from writing), thus opening up larger combinatorial spaces for using them in coordinated ways, we are only teaching them to use one: written language. When we do teach other modes, such as singing, drawing, or mime, we still do not teach students about the traditions and possibilities for combining these with writing and with each other. That needs to change, very quickly and very thoroughly, if we are to help students develop sophisticated multimedia literacies. Their new authoring skills will hopefully enable students to create multimedia portfolios that will help teachers remove the logocentric bias from our evaluations of their understanding and competence, as well as enable them to produce the kinds of meanings they really want to mean.

Likewise, critical interpretive skills must be extended from the analysis of print texts to video and film, to news photos and advertising images, to statistical charts and tables, and mathematical graphs. We must help students understand exactly how to read the text differently and interpret the image differently because of the presence of the other. We even need to understand how it is that we know which text is relevant to the interpretation of which image, and vice versa. All of this requires, at least for teachers and media specialists, a useful understanding of multimedia semiotics.

I am currently trying to develop such a general theory of multimedia based on seeing how three universal semiotic functions — presentation (creating or describing a world), orientation (taking a stance toward the presentation and its audiences), and organization (linking parts into wholes) — draw on the resources of each available semiotic modality (language, typography, images, music, etc.) to produce a meaning effect (Lemke, 1989a, 1995c, 1997a), For instance representational imagery in painting presents the world, but figure perspective orients the view to it, and the composition of masses and vectors of edges and lines organize its parts into a coherent whole. In text, we present with propositional content, orient with mood (command vs. question) and modality (*may* vs. *must*), and organize with genre structure (introduction, body, conclusion) and cohesion (*John* . . . becomes . . . *he* . . .).

Other related work in social semiotics is also contributing to this understanding (e.g., Kress & van Leeuwen, 1996; O'Toole, 1990, 1994). With such a functionally motivated framework for describing what is possible in multimedia, it should be possible not only to analyze particular multimedia works, but to compare different approaches and traditions in terms of which possibilities they make use of and which they do not. We may even be able to identify new combinations worth trying out.

Both authoring skills and critical interpretive skills for multimedia potentially transform not just the ways students and teachers communicate information and ideas, but also the ways in which we learn and teach. Kinzer and Risko report on ways in which prospective teachers can learn by producing multimedia analyses of their initial teaching experiences. Goldman-Segall (1992) and Tierney and Damarin provide analogous case studies of students learning through multimedia production. In both cases, the integration of video and pictorial realism, providing context and complexity, with textual analysis, providing focus and conceptualization, help define and transform viewpoints on our own and others' experiences.

Informatic Literacies

The literacies of the Information Age are not just about making and using multimedia. They also include *informatic literacies*: the skills of the library user as well as those of the text user. These are skills for categorizing and locating information and multimedia objects and presentations. Cyberspace will be many things: the world's ultimate shopping mall, humanity's most enticing playground, the university of universities, and, especially from a literacy point of view, the library of all libraries. Search and retrieval strategies will be subsumed in the arts of exploration and navigation; we will replace a metaphor in which texts come to us (e.g., downloading them from a remote server) with one in which we go to them (navigating though virtual 3-D worlds that represent servers and their contents). What strategies are useful for finding out what kinds of knowledge exist in the world? How do you browse the library of cyberspace? Once you pick an area of interest, how do you systematically explore it? Once you decide where you want to go, what do you have to know to get there? Librarians spend years learning how information is classified and sorted according to the conventions of a hundred disciplines and interest areas. What do they know that we all need to know? How can we represent the topography of information in ways that will make it easier for all of us to navigate around in it?

Without all these skills, future citizens will be as disempowered as those who today cannot write, read, or use a library. These are the necessary skills of our future literacies, those we will all need. However, new information technologies also open up possibilities for extending our literacies in other ways, and many of us will choose to develop additional kinds of literacies that perhaps not everyone will need, but that will confer great benefits on those who acquire them. I discuss in the following two potentially important categories of such value-added literacies: quantitative-mathematical literacy and cross-cultural literacy.

Typological and Topological Meaning.   Analyzing multimedia semiotics has led me to ask some old questions in new ways and to begin to see the history of writing, drawing, calculating, and displaying images visually in a different light (Lemke, 1994b, 1997a). I am coming to believe that we make meaning in two fundamentally complementary ways: (a) by classifying things into mutually exclusive categories, and (b) by distinguishing variations of degree (rather than kind) along various continua of difference. Language operates mainly in the first way, which I call *typological*. Visual perception and spatial gesturing (drawing, dancing) operate more in the second, *topological* way. As I have already argued, real meaning making generally involves combinations of different semiotic modalities, and so also combinations of these two rather general modes. The semantics of words in language is mainly categorical or typological in its principles, but the significant visual distinctions in handwriting (e.g., writing more boldly or in slightly larger letters) or calligraphy, or the acoustic effects of speaking a bit more loudly or forcefully, make sense along a continuous spectrum of possibilities, topologically. (In mathematics, topology studies matters of relative nearness, connectedness, continuity, etc.). Even in specialized subject areas like science, mathematics, art, or music, the educational curriculum has followed the logocentric tradition in emphasizing conceptual categories and semantic distinctions and has neglected to educate students about topological principles of making meaning by creating and interpreting differences of degree as well as differences of kind. I believe that the new multimedia technologies will make the salience and importance of topological kinds of meaning far greater, and that an emphasis on these two complementary modes of meaning making may help students grasp kinds of meanings (e.g., those based in quantitative and mathematical reasoning) that have tended to elude many of us in the past.

What is it that pictures, drawings, diagrams, graphs, tables, and equations do for us that verbal text alone cannot? What can we do far better still with combinations of texts and these other media? What is it exactly about a picture that even a thousand words cannot say as well? Or about a diagram and its caption that tell us far more than a drawing or a text alone could do? Why has natural science chosen to speak so often in the language of mathematics? And is mathematics really a language? Should mathematical and quantitative literacies be considered integral parts of a multimedia literacy for today and tomorrow?

To answer these questions it helps to distinguish these two rather different kinds of meaning, or strategies for making meaning, that all human cultures seem to have evolved. We make meaning by contrasting types or categories of things, events, people, and signs. For instance, we distinguish right from left, up from down, male from female, fruit from vegetable, motion from rest, red from blue, x from y, ahh from ohh, buying from selling, live from dead, and writing from drawing. This is the basis of the semantics of natural language, and of the analogous representations of identifiable types, kinds, categories, qualities, and so on, in other media. Most are based on a logic of either–or. Within a category we can often distinguish and contrast many different subcategories, and so on to great delicacy of typological categorization and description. Our verbal sentences construct a small number of semantic relations among categorical processes, participants, and circumstances (cf. Halliday, 1985; Martin, 1992), and from this comes our conceptual reasoning. However, this is not the whole story of human meaning.

Some of these categorical distinctions also allow differences by degree, so that there is now a possibility of intermediate cases that are in some measurable or quantitative sense in between others: higher and lower, nearer and further, faster and slower, or more reddish orange. However, there is nothing that is in between motion and rest, or living and dead, and no mix of the letters x and y. Language does recognize difference by degree, but has very few and quite limited resources for describing such differences. Other forms of meaningful human action, however, are wonderful at indicating shades of intermediate degree: the rise of an eyebrow, the tension in a voice, the breadth of a gesture, the depth of a bow. Space and time, movement, position, and pacing define for us the possibility of meanings that are more topological, matters of degree, of almost-the-same, and just-a-bit-more-or-less, of what is *like* because it is near to or almost equal to, rather than *like* because it does or does not possess certain criterial properties for membership in a category, for being of some type. Typological and topological meaning are complementary in many fundamental ways.

Because language is so heavily biased toward the construction of typologically grounded meanings, it requires complementary partners that are better at constructing topological meaning, especially when what we are trying to make sense about is a phenomenon that changes in important ways by degree. You cannot readily describe in words the shape of a draped bolt of fabric, but you can gesture that shape and you can draw it (if you have learned the necessary skills). If the shape represents data on the pressure at different places inside a nuclear reactor system, it is not good enough to say the pressure is increasing very quickly near the containment dome: You want to measure the rate of increase and extrapolate it graphically or algebraically.

Many cultural phenomena seem to be strictly typological, but topological or quantitative analysis can undermine this illusion (e.g., biology finds no quantitative basis for racial categories). Other phenomena (like the phonemes of our native language) we learn to perceive typologically, even though a topological or quantitative analysis may be hard pressed to see how (e.g., the acoustic spectra of language sounds on an oscilloscope screen do not neatly fit phoneme categories, so you cannot "see" where particular letters or even whole syllables begin or end—and sometimes cannot see them at all). Many natural phenomena, however, yield rather directly to analysis by degree, in space, in time, in movement or change, in mass, in temperature, and in all the other quantitative variables that science has found so useful.

Our concepts tend to depend on the typological semantics of language or other media of representation, but our experience in the world as material bodies in space and time interacting with an environment shows us the importance of topological meaning as well. It is no accident that the most systematic extension of natural language into topological domains of meaning, known to us as mathematics, has arisen historically as a kind of bridge between conceptual language and quantitative measurement and description. Or that mathematics has been built from both sides: from language through arithmetic to algebra and functions, and from continuous variation in the environment to visual depiction to geometric diagrams and Cartesian graphs. The modern unification of algebra and geometry is only one chapter in the long history of the semiotic integration of typological and topological meaning.

Many people experience great difficulty with quantitative and mathematical reasoning, beginning from just those points where, historically, mathematics went beyond what natural language could comfortably deal with, inventing notions like complex ratios and fractions, partially compensating operations and reciprocal inverses, continuously varying functions and equations with multiple factors and operations. Natural language has no problem with integers, with simple fractions or ratios, and with addition and subtraction. It can just barely get around multiplication, and begins to give up with division. Many mathematical concepts that are confusing or resist easy explanation and learning in natural language alone become far clearer with visual representations and manipulatives combined *with* natural language. It is not a matter of substituting one for the other, but of combining them together: conceptual typological reasoning and quantitative topological accounting.

Not every aspect of human cultural life yet requires sophisticated quantitative and mathematical reasoning. It is not yet part of the literacy skills of most nontechnical genres. For many purposes the combination of visual-image representations, including abstract ones like graphs and tables, and verbal ones is sufficient. However, I suspect that extending multimedia literacy to include mathematical representations could become much easier with new information technologies. Expanded use of and familiarity with visual representations will make it easier for students to deal with quantitative relations expressed also in more formal mathematical terms (numerical or algebraic). If the time comes when a new generation's multimedia literacy is as much at home with quantitative reasoning and representation as with depiction and verbal text, then ideological oversimplifications based purely on category names, like White versus Black, straight versus gay, or masculine versus feminine will be vulnerable to quantitative deconstruction for far more people than the few technical specialists who understand these arguments today. The cultures, attitudes, and characteristics of real people have never fit the pigeonhole categories of our typologies and stereotypes. Too many real people have claims, to some degree and in some ways, to fit both sides of these dichotomies, to be members of many categories whose names and definitions make them seem mutually exclusive. Our lived realities cannot be faithfully represented in purely typological ways; too many people have no voice where there are no other ways to make sense. The topological potential of multimedia literacy can help give voice, dignity, and power to real hybrid people. It can undermine an ideological system that limits personal identities to a few available and approved social pigeonholes and let us see and show one another the much larger multidimensional universe of real human possibilities.

Global Cultural Literacies.   Information exchange, academic and business collaboration, and even entertainment and shopping, are very soon going to be much more global and cross-cultural than ever before in human history. The dominance of cyberspace by the European American cultural tribes will inevitably be short-lived. Asian societies have the technology and the confidence in their cultural traditions to ensure that global exchange will not take place entirely on our terms, as it has for the past couple of centuries. We may not welcome the loss of our economic hegemony and our impossibly exaggerated standard of living relative to the rest of the world's population, but we should certainly welcome new ways of making meaning. English may or may not survive as the lingua franca of the Internet (a lot depends on whether machine translation ever becomes effective, fast, and cheap), and although it would not hurt Americans particularly to learn a non-Indo-European language with a nonalphabetic script, what seems most likely is that non-European traditions of visual design and aesthetics (e.g., Asian-European hybrids in multimedia) will become extremely important to the evolving genres of cyberspace. In time other cultural traditions will join the mix in substantial ways as well, as African-European cultural hybrids already have in music and visual arts styles.

Increasingly, members of our online communities are going to come from non-European-American cultural backgrounds. We are going to have to learn to communicate effectively with them, and to learn effectively from them. Our economic success, our intellectual opportunities, and perhaps the long-term cause of world peace and harmony depend on our success in this. Because we have been on top for so long, it will be harder for many upper-middle-class Americans and Europeans to learn how to listen across cultural differences. Most of the rest of the world has long since had to learn how to listen to us.

As we face the many tasks of communication and design, of combining and integrating text with graphic images both abstract and iconic, not to mention animations, videos, sound, and so forth, we will want to consider all the resources, all the traditions, and all the possibilities in the human repertoire. We will need to do this as the next phase of world cultural evolution speeds up. We will be moving beyond the era of national and ethnic cultures to an era of diverse cultural hybrids, each with a global community of members and aficionados. The new world cultural order will be no less diverse and complex than our present one, but its basis will extend beyond geography and family heritage to encompass shared interests and participation in activity-centered communities.

The global human heritage provides more than just geocultural diversity as a resource for new ways of making meaning: It also provides the historical diversity within each of our cultural traditions. Visual and textual forms and the conventions for combining them have passed through many interesting historical turns, some of them largely lost to present-day awareness. The study of the history of semiotic media is likely to become an increasingly important part of scholarship, and a richer resource in the curriculum. In my own work I have been greatly impressed by what can be learned from the rich resource of a comprehensive, global history of mathematical notations (Cajori, 1928), or from the growing literature on the history of visual representations in many fields (e.g., Alpers, 1983; Bellone, 1980; Eisenstein, 1979; Skelton, 1958; Tufte, 1983, 1990; see also Olson, 1994). Vast as this underappreciated literature is, there is more still on the representational conventions of non-Western cultures, Both Western and non-Western media history are likely, in my opinion, to richly reward study, appreciation, and appropriation for the purposes of constructing and teaching our future multimedia literacies. These then are the key directions for transformation of our contemporary literacies as we enter the Information Age: We certainly need generalized multimedia and informatic literacy skills now, and we will probably also need more quantitative topological and more global historical literacies for the near future.

TRANSFORMING LEARNING PARADIGMS

With so much to be learned, we need to give some thought to how new information technologies may transform our institutional habits of teaching and learning. There are two paradigms of learning and education contending in our society today, and the new technologies will, I believe, shift the balance between them significantly (Lemke, 1994a).

The *curricular learning paradigm* dominates institutions such as schools and universities. The curricular paradigm assumes that someone else will decide what you need to know and will arrange for you to learn it all in a fixed order and on a fixed schedule. It is the educational paradigm of industrial capitalism and factory-based mass production. It developed simultaneously with them, and in close philosophical agreement; it feeds into their wider networks of employment and careers, and resembles them in its authoritarianism, top-down planning, rigidity, economies of scale, and general unsuitability to the new information-based fast capitalist world (discussed later). It is widely refused and resisted by students, and its end results provide little more of demonstrated usefulness in the nonacademic world than a few text literacies and certification as a member of the middle class.

The *interactive learning paradigm* dominates such institutions as libraries and research centers. It assumes that people determine what they need to know based on their participation in activities in which such needs arise, and in consultation with knowledgeable specialists; that they learn in the order that suits them, at a comfortable pace, and just in time to make use of what they learn. This is the learning paradigm of the people who created the Internet and cyberspace. It is the paradigm of access to information, rather than imposition of learning. It is the paradigm of how people with power and resources choose to learn. Its end results are generally satisfying to the learner, and usually useful for business or scholarship. It is perhaps also the paradigm of *fast capitalism* (Gee, 1996; Lemke, 1996a), in which economies based on the production and circulation of information favor rapidly changing work groups of flexible individuals engaged in projects that produce "just-in-time" results for niche-market customers. It may tend to produce less common learning among the members of a society and favor specialization over liberal arts education.

These two educational paradigms are in fundamental conflict, and many disappointments that schools are not more eager to adopt computer-mediated information technologies may perhaps be laid at the door of this largely unrecognized conflict (Hodas, 1994).

The curricular paradigm is failing disastrously in the United States today. Anyone who has spent time in urban schools, even the better ones, can tell you that things are even worse than standardized tests and statistics indicate. Most students really do not see the usefulness of most of what they are being expected to learn. Many know they are unprepared for what they are scheduled to learn this year. The nation is trying to develop a national curriculum at a time when only the most rudimentary elements of school-based learning (say up to Grade eight) are demonstrably of value to most citizens when they leave school. Beyond that, whatever some will use, others will not need at all. We are trying to impose uniform learning at a time when there has never been more radical inequality of every kind among students of a given age. Fortunately, the institutional arrangements for schooling in the United States are so decentralized that a national curriculum in practice (as opposed to agreements in principle) seems unlikely ever to actually happen. I believe that the effort to create a uniform content-centered national curriculum may in fact seriously hamper our transition to more effective and appropriate educational models for the globally competitive future.

What seems to be generally agreed among educators and many citizens and prospective employers is that we want people, of whatever age, who can guide their own learning and who know enough to know how to learn more, including where and to whom they should turn for useful advice and relevant information. We want people who know things that they want to know, and people who know things that are useful in human enterprises outside schools. We want people who are at least a little critical and skeptical about information and points of view, and have some idea how to judge their reliability. Beyond this, however, there is no general social consensus about the content of education beyond what could be learned in the first eight or nine years of schooling, and there is no basis in empirical research for deciding what every citizen would actually find it useful to know after leaving school. My personal view is that if such research were done it would not find much of anything universally necessary beyond what could be taught in those basic years. It is perhaps time that we put behind us the U.S. preoccupation with nation building and common culture. We are indissolubly tied together by our interactions with and interdependencies on one another, and it really does not matter, except for ideological purposes, how much alike we are or are taught to pretend we are.

Every effort to construct a common curriculum is an effort by some people to impose their values on others who probably do not agree. Only demonstrated necessity or substantial usefulness to most people can morally justify curricular uniformity, especially in the context of a coercive educational system (i.e., one in which participation is not voluntary and resistance is punished by sanctions that go beyond the inevitable consequences of our own actions). It is particularly morally questionable that curricular education is imposed on the weakest members of our society: those who are forbidden many of the political and legal rights of all other citizens, solely because of their age. Fully empowered adults would not tolerate the faults of many of our schools: their authoritarianism, their educational incompetence, their inadequate resources, and their physical conditions. The very young may have little choice about their helplessness; they cannot yet operate the machinery of our complex society at even the most basic levels. We cannot empower them. But from an age somewhere between ten and thirteen years old, depending on the individual (and governed at least a little by the extent of opportunities afforded), we know that increasing numbers of younger citizens can exercise adult rights and want to, but are not permitted to, and are prevented from doing so by law and by force. It is arguable that the curricular paradigm survives in our schools mainly because of, and perhaps in part in the service of, the political domination of citizens in their second decade by older and more powerful adults.

New information technologies will make it possible for students to learn what they want, when they want, and how they want, without schools. Not all students will have equal or even immediate access to these technologies, but those who do will surely see the possibilities. Curricular education will not be able to compete for sheer educational effectiveness or economic efficiency with the learning services that will become available online and in portable media for interactive education. The interactive paradigm need not be one of isolated learning, or even of exclusively computer-mediated learning. Social interaction among peers and between learners and mentors and other experts will take place online, one on one and in groups of various sizes, Some of this interaction will be live in real time, and some will be asynchronous, as with listservs and newsgroups. Face-to-face groups will still play an important role, as will direct interaction with teachers. However, the proportions of time spent in each of these learning modes will change radically, and the diversity of approaches to learning will increase.

What will necessarily be radically different, however, is the single issue of control. In the interactive paradigm, students will pursue topics, interests, problems, and agendas of their own and of the groups they participate in. They will encounter the fundamental categories, concepts, and principles of all the basic disciplines, whatever trails they blaze through the forests of knowledge, precisely to the extent that these notions really are fundamental and widely applicable and therefore necessarily to be found wherever we travel. But they will all fashion for themselves essentially different educations, with only that degree of commonality that arises from interaction with others and from the common usefulness of common notions.

The interactive learning paradigm, once its information technology infrastructure is in place, will also very likely be a lot cheaper than the present schools and curricula arrangements. We will not need a separate material infrastructure for education nearly to the extent that we do today; education will be one function of a multipurpose technology. We will not need to buy all the working time of so many teachers, but only to compensate sufficiently the people who make themselves available to students online, and the few specialists who will staff more specialized learning facilities. Those who produce great interactive learning environments will be well paid by the marketplace. A great deal of productive labor potential now tied up in chalking-and-talking curricula to captive classroom audiences will be liberated to enrich the general information economy.

What will the new information technologies be that can best support an interactive learning paradigm and make use of those multimedia and informatic literacies that will genuinely be needed by everyone?

TRANSFORMING TECHNOLOGIES: TOWARD METAMEDIA LITERACIES

The first generation of interactive learning technologies has mostly been, not unexpectedly, simply a transposition of the textbook model of education to a new display medium. Trees may be grateful, but little about the nature of learning changes, perhaps only the increased motivation for some students generated by novelty. But as soon as online text becomes digital (as opposed to bitmapped images of the page), it is easily searched, and if it can be searched, it can be indexed and cross-referenced. Now the text is also simultaneously a database, and hypertext is born (Bolter, 1991; Landow, 1992; Nelson, 1974). If we can use a word or phrase in the text as an index entry to find other occurrences, and also add cross-references to other specific items in the same text, why not then make links to other texts? In the simplest cases, hypertexts offer us only one link per item, but there is no inherent limitation of this kind in the concept or the technology. If we can jump from one text to another, and to multiple landing points from each jumping-off point, we will need some navigational assistance in order to backtrack and to get a sense of the text space we are mapping out and traversing. Because the topography of these links is nonlinear, a two- or three-dimensional image or map is a useful navigational tool. It can be established by an author and later customized or reconstructed by each reader.

Now learning changes. Instead of being the prisoners of textbook authors and their priorities, scope, and sequence, we are free agents who can find more about a topic they skimped on, or find alternative interpretations they did not mention (or agree with, or even consider moral or scientific). We can shift the topic to match our judgments of relevance to our own interests and agendas, and we can return to a standard, textbooklike development later. We can learn as if we had access to all these texts, and as if we had an expert who could point out to us most of the relevant cross-references among them. We now have to learn to exercise more complex forms of judgment and we get a lot of practice doing so.

The next generation of interactive learning environments adds visual images and then sound and video and animation, all of which became practical when speed and storage capacity can accommodate these information-dense topological forms of meaning. From the typological point of view, text has very low redundancy, it does not code in much more than is needed to make the key distinctions between one word and another, but visual images typically contain all sorts of typologically irrelevant information—which is for that very reason potentially critical to their topological meaning capacity. (Compression strategies need to be careful not to be overly biased toward preserving typological meaning at the expense of potentially valuable topological meaning. If you reduce the number of bytes allotted to Aunt Hilda's voice message as much as you could for her e-mail message, you could probably still make out the words, but it would not sound like Aunt Hilda anymore.) These more topological media cannot be indexed and cross-referenced for their internal content (what the picture shows, say) but must be treated as whole objects. Even so, as objects they can become nodes for hyperlinks, and so hypermedia is born (see Bolter, 1998; Landow & Delany, 1991). The importance of the corresponding multimedia literacies has already been discussed, but it is worth noting that it is not only using hypermedia, but authoring them that the new technologies make easier. Today anyone can edit audio and video at home, produce good-quality animations, shape three-dimensional objects and environments, combine them with text and still images, add music and voice, and produce works far beyond what any publisher or movie studio could have done until a few years ago.

The key to interactive learning paradigms, however, is neither hyperlinks nor multimedia, but interactivity itself. Interactive media present themselves differently to different users depending on the user's own actions. This can be as simple as seeing one image rather than another after clicking on a link, but it becomes educationally useful to the extent that the result of the interactions accumulates intelligently, so that the whole history of my interaction with a program influences what it shows me when I click on that link. This is the basic principle of *intelligent tutoring systems* (ITS; see Wenger, 1987), a parallel development to educational hypermedia, but still mainly within the curricular paradigm. An ITS program constructs a model of the user over time and customizes its responses to lead the user optimally to a fixed learning goal. Each different user potentially follows a different pathway, but all end up in the same place.

What would we get if we combined the dynamic user-customization of an ITS with the learning paradigm of exploring and navigating interactive hypermedia? The purpose of a user model then would not be to create a path to a fixed goal; goals would be emergent for the user as a result of interacting with the media. The user model would catalog where we had been, our learning styles and preferences, our prior background in different subjects, and could offer us a filtered set of choices for each next jump or link that would optimize their potential value for us. The program could be set to offer narrow or wider ranges of choices, index the options by various criteria useful to us in making the ultimate choice ourselves, and include a certain percentage of serendipitous surprises. Like a human tutor, the program would get to know us, and in effect make suggestions to help us make the most of our time in cyberspace. It could tailor the text and images it generated to our needs (cf. Hovy, 1987). It would also need to be able to reconfigure information from one medium to another, to the extent that this is possible, varying the relative emphasis of text, voice, still images, videos, animations, and degrees of abstraction, either by selection from available items, or by conversion from one to another. This would, accordingly, be in fact a *metamedia* system.

With such a technology we could be free to learn in the language and dialect of our choice, with the visual-aesthetic styles of our choice, and the mix of media we learn from best. Just as various document definition languages (such as SGML, HTML, and VRML; Hockey, 1996) allow different browsers to customize how they present the same text and image files, one can imagine our metamedia system's source files to contain data in abstract representations that could be variously displayed as text, chart or table, graph, diagram, visual image, video, and so on (cf. Arens, Hovy, & Vossers, 1992) according to user preference and ITS tutor recommendation.

Original source media are thus going to be relinked and their displays transformed endlessly by different individual and group users who are sharing files. Systems will need to keep track of user annotations and overlays (backing up earlier versions), user-added links, user transformations of medium, user-defined sequencings, and so on so that any original source file or complete metamedia work will exist in many customized versions, each with a traceable history. Some of these versions will conceivably become more popular with new users than the originals, and some may come to be recognized as classics, even as all of them get endlessly modified. Various user communities will determine what constitutes value-added in this process, and what is transient or idiosyncratic. Intelligent metamedia tutoring systems will, of course, have to be able to sort through the many available versions as they seek optimization for their user. Users will inevitably gain some sophistication in this process as well, as they provide the tutor with explicit instructions and responses to queries, as well as statistical patterns of past and continuing choices, to which the tutoring program will be sensitive.

TRANSFORMING HUMANITY

The ultimate display medium is reality itself: what we see and hear, touch and feel; what we manipulate and control; where we feel ourselves to be present and living. Our bodies are integral parts of larger ecosocial systems: We live in those systems materially as sensory signals and motor feedback, heat exchanges and nutrient and waste flows link us into them; and we live in them semiotically as we make culturally and personally meaningful sense of our participation. Reading a text, our verbal and visual imaginations can begin to conjure a second world of meanings in addition to the usual realistic ones. Watching a film on a large screen, the divergence between sense data and fictional illusion diminishes; we can experience terror or a sensation of falling while watching a fabric screen and sitting in a fixed chair. It is possible to intercept many of the signals by which our bodies locate themselves in space, time, and reality and replace them by other signals. To do this we have to monitor our actions and efferent motor signals as well as supply new inputs, because our bodies create reality out of the relation between outgoing efferent and incoming afferent nerve impulses. A fast enough computer can simulate reality well enough to fool a large part of our body's evolved links with its environment. We can create virtual realities, and we can feel as if we are living in them. We can create a sense of full presence (cf. Benedikt, 1991; Rheingold, 1991).

Within a virtual reality (VR) environment, all other media can be presented and coordinated. What VR technologies add is greater interactivity: We can make more things happen in VR worlds, and that is partly why we feel that they are more real. However, they do not have to happen according to the laws of normal physics, or the constraints of our normal ecological environment, provided the timing of action and reaction is precise enough to make them seem equally real. In principle in VR we can learn by doing, without consuming proportional material resources as we would in the normal world, without the attendant risks to life and limb, or the consequences to our life-sustaining ecosystem. And we can do what is simply not normally possible: We can change reality by acts of will or small motor commands, we can be the sorcerers of our dreams and our nightmares.

We can also learn to be a different sort of human being (Lemke, 1993b). We can walk, not through a simulated Martian valley, but by telepresence and a robot sensor system, on the actual surface of Mars. We can sound with whales and soar with eagles. We can observe the earth from space in real time, and zoom in to any place that is visible and monitored. We can observe on our normal human time scale the changes in a rainforest over decades as seen from space. We can burrow with insects. We can grasp biological molecules and do chemistry by hand as the molecules react according to their quantum laws. We can expand the scale of direct human experience in space and time to the limits of our technology. And we can do all these things as children.

What kinds of humanity are possible for us if we can learn in these ways and have these experiences from our childhood? What are the possibilities, and what are the dangers?

The literacies of VR converge with, and indeed go beyond, the literacies and wisdoms of human life itself. What is a literacy when the distinction between reading and living itself is nominal? When a reality becomes our multimedia text, enhanced by the sorcery of hyperlinks that can carry us not just from page to page or text to text, but from place to place, from time to time, and from the cosmological scale to a world of quarks? Is this a dream or a nightmare?

Yes, we could become lost in this cyberspace, not for want of navigational aids, but because we may prefer the worlds of our own imaginations to those within which we evolved. Literacy confers both power and vulnerability: the power to add a second meaning world to the one our bodies are enmeshed in, but also the vulnerability of mistaking the former for the latter. The power comes when we add one to the other; the danger if we substitute VR for ecological reality. The semiotic capacity of human beings makes us infinitely adaptable in terms of the meanings we attach to our experience, but not all of those possible adaptations will allow our species to survive. In the lifetimes of students now in our schools, these issues will have to be faced. Will the literacies we teach today help them choose wisely?

No one can predict the transformations of twenty-first-century society during the information technology revolution. We certainly cannot afford to continue teaching our students only the literacies of the mid-twentieth century, or even to simply lay before them the most advanced and diverse literacies of today. We must help this next generation learn to use these literacies wisely, and hope they will succeed better than we have.

REFERENCES

Alpers, S. (1983). *The art of describing*. Chicago: University of Chicago Press.
Arens, Y., Hovy, E., & Vossers, M. (1992). On the knowledge underlying multimedia presentations. In M. Maybury (Ed.), *Intelligent multimedia interfaces* (pp. 280–306). Stanford, CA: AAAI Press.
Bazerman, C. (1988). *Shaping written knowledge*. Madison: University of Wisconsin Press.
Bazerman, C. (1994). Systems of genres and the enactment of social intentions. In A. Freedman & P. Medway (Eds.), *Rethinking genre* (pp. 79–101). London: Falmer.
Bellone, E. (1980). *A world on paper: Studies on the second scientific revolution*. Cambridge, MA: MIT Press.
Benedikt, M. (1991). *Cyberspace: First steps*. Cambridge, MA: MIT Press.
Bolter, J. D. (1991). *Writing space*. Hillsdale. NJ: Lawrence Erlbaum Associates.
Bolter, J. D. (1998). Hypertext and the question of visual literacy. In D. Reinking, M. C. Mckenna, L. D. Labbo, and R. D. Kieffer (Eds.), *Handbook of literacy and technology: Transformations in a post-typographic world* (pp. 3–13). Manwah, NJ: Lawrence Erlbaum Associates.
Bryson, M., & de Castell, S. (1996). Learning to make a difference: Gender, new technologies and in/equity. *Mind, Culture, and Activity, 3*(2), 119–135.
Cajori, F. (1928). *A history of mathematical notations*. Chicago: Open Court.
Day, M., Crump, E., & Rickly, R. (1996). Creating a virtual academic community. In T. M. Harrison & T. D. Stephen (Eds.), *Computer networking and scholarship in the 21st-century university* (pp. 291–314). Albany: State University of New York Press.
Derrida, J. (1976). *Of grammatology*. Baltimore: Johns Hopkins University Press.
Dyson, A. H. (1991). Toward a reconceptualization of written language development. *Linguistics and Education, 3*, 139–162.
Eisenstein, E. (1979). *The printing press as an agent of change*. Cambridge, UK: Cambridge University Press.
Engestrom, Y. (1990). *Learning, working, and imagining*. Helsinki: Orienta-Konsultit.
Foucault, M. (1969). *The archeology of knowledge*. New York: Random House.
Gee, J. P. (1990). *Social linguistics and literacies*. London: Falmer.
Gee, J. P. (1996). On mobots and classrooms. *Organization, 3*(3). 385–407.
Goldman-Segall, R. (1992). Collaborative virtual communities. In E. Barrett (Ed.), *Sociomedia: Multimedia, hypermedia, and the social construction of knowledge* (pp. 257–296). Cambridge, MA: MIT Press.
Halliday, M. A. K. (1977). Text as semantic choice in social contexts. In T. A. van Dijk & J. Petöfi (Eds.), *Grammars and descriptions* (pp. 176–225). Berlin: de Gruyter.
Halliday, M. A. K. (1978). *Language as social semiotic*. London: Edward Arnold.
Halliday, M. A. K. (1985). *An introduction to functional grammar*. London: Edward Arnold.
Haraway, D. (1991). *Simians, cyborgs, and women*. New York: Routledge.
Harris, R. (1995). *Signs of writing*. London: Routledge.
Harrison, T. M., & Stephen, T. D. (1996). Computer networking, communication, and scholarship. In T. M. Harrison & T. D. Stephen (Eds.), *Computer networking and scholarship in the 21st century university* (pp. 3–38). Albany: State University of New York Press.
Hicks, D., & Kanevsky, R. (1992). Ninja Turtles and other superheroes: A case study of one literacy learner. *Linguistics and Education, 4*, 59–106.
Hockey, S. (1996). Computer networking and textual sources in the humanities. In T. M. Harrison & T. D. Stephen (Eds.), *Computer networking and scholarship in the 21st century university* (pp. 83–94). Albany: State University of New York Press.

Hodas, S. (1994). Technology refusal and the organizational culture of schools. In *Cyberspace super-highways: Access, ethics, and control: Proceedings of the Fourth Conference on Computers, Freedom, and Privacy* (pp. 54–75). Chicago: John Marshall Law School.

Hovy, E. H. (1987). Generating natural language under pragmatic constraints. *Journal of Pragmatics, 11*(6), 689–719.

Hutchins, E. (1995). *Cognition in the wild.* Cambridge, MA: MIT Press.

Kinzer, C. K., & Risko, V. J. (1998). Multimedia and enhanced learning: Transforming preservice education. In D. Reinking, M. C. McKenna, L. D. Labbo, & R. D. Keiffer, (Eds.) *Handbook of literacy and technology: Transformations in a post-typographic world* (pp. 185–202). Mahwah, NJ: Lawrence Erlbaum Associates.

Kress, G., & van Leeuwen, T. (1996). *Reading images: The grammar of visual design.* London: Routledge.

Landow, G. P. (1992). *Hypertext: The convergence of contemporary literary theory and technology.* Baltimore: Johns Hopkins University Press.

Landow, G. P., & Delany, P. (Eds.). (1991). *Hypermedia and literary studies.* Cambridge, MA: MIT Press.

Latour, B. (1987). *Science in action.* Cambridge. MA: Harvard University Press.

Latour, B. (1993). *We have never been modern.* Cambridge, MA: Harvard University Press.

Lave, J. (1988). *Cognition in practice.* Cambridge, UK: Cambridge University Press.

Lemke, J. L. (1985). Ideology, intertextuality, and the notion of register. In J.D. Benson & W. S. Greaves (Eds.), *Systemic perspectives on discourse* (pp. 275–294). Norwood, NJ: Ablex.

Lemke, J. L. (1989a). Semantics and social values. *WORD, 40*(1–2), 37–50.

Lemke, J. L. (1989b). Social semiotics: A new model for literacy education. In D. Bloome (Ed.), *Classrooms and literacy* (pp. 289–309). Norwood, NJ: Ablex.

Lemke, J. L. (1992). Intertextuality and educational research. *Linguistics and Education, 4*(3–4), 257–268.

Lemke, J. L. (1993a). Discourse, dynamics, and social change. *Cultural Dynamics, 6*(1), 243–275.

Lemke, J. L. (1993b). Education, cyberspace, and change. Information Technology and Education Electronic Salon, Deakin University, Australia. (ERIC Document Reproduction Service, No. ED 356 767)

Lemke, J. L. (1994a). The coming paradigm wars in education: Curriculum vs. information access. In *Cyberspace superhighways: Access, ethics, and control: Proceedings of the Fourth Conference on Computers, Freedom, and Privacy* (pp. 76–85). Chicago: John Marshall Law School.

Lemke, J. L. (1994b). *Multiplying meaning: Literacy in a multimedia world* [Paper presented at the National Reading Conference, Charleston SC]. (ERIC Document Reproduction Service No. ED 365 940)

Lemke, J. L. (1995a). Intertextuality and text semantics. In M. Gregory & P. Fries (Eds.), *Discourse in society: Functional perspectives* (pp. 85–114). Norwood, NJ: Ablex.

Lemke, J. L. (1995b). Literacy, culture, and history: Review of *The World on Paper*. *Communication Review, 1*(2), 241–259.

Lemke, J. L. (1995c). *Textual politics: Discourse and social dynamics.* London: Taylor & Francis.

Lemke, J. L. (1996a). Emptying the center. *Organization, 3*(3), 411–418.

Lemke, J. L. (1996b). Hypermedia and higher education. In T. M. Harrison & T. D. Stephen (Eds.), *Computer networking and scholarship in the 21st century university* (pp. 215–232). Albany: State University of New York Press.

Lemke, J. L. (1997a). Multiplying meaning: Visual and verbal semiotics in scientific text. In J. R. Martin & R. Veel (Eds.), *Reading science* (pp. 87–113). London: Routledge.

Lemke, J. L. (1997b). Review of: *Roy Harris, Signs of writing. Functions of Language, 4*(1), 125–129.

Lynch, M., & Woolgar, S. (Eds.), (1990). *Representation in scientific practice.* Cambridge, MA: MIT Press.

Martin, J. R. (1992). *English text.* Philadelphia: John Benjamins.

Nelson, T. H. (1974). *Dream machines/Computer Lib.* Chicago: Nelson/Hugo's Book Service.

Olson, D. R. (1994). *The world on paper.* Cambridge. UK: Cambridge University Press.

O'Toole, M. (1990). A systemic-functional semiotics of art. *Semiotica, 82,* 185–209.

O'Toole, M. (1994). *The language of displayed art.* London: Leicester University Press.

Rheingold, H. (1991). *Virtual reality.* New York: Simon & Schuster.

Rheingold, H. (1993). *The virtual community: Homesteading on the electronic frontier.* Reading, MA: Addison-Wesley.

Rogoff, B. (1990). *Apprenticeship in thinking.* New York: Oxford University Press.

Skelton. R. A. (1958). *Explorers' maps: Chapters in the cartographic record of geographical discovery,* London: Routledge & Kegan Paul.

Sofia, Z. (1995). Of spanners and cyborgs. In B. Caine & R. Pringle (Eds.), *Transitions: New Australian feminisms* (pp. 147–163). New York: St. Martin's.

Stone, A. R. (1991). Will the real body please stand up: Boundary stories about virtual cultures. In M. Benedikt (Ed.), *Cyberspace: First steps* (pp. 81–118). Cambridge, MA: MIT Press.

Tierney, R., & Damarin S. (1998). *Technology as enfranchisement and cultural development: Crisscrossing symbol systems, paradigm shifts, and social-cultural considerations.* In D. Reinking, M. C. McKenna, L. D. Labbo, and R. D. Kieffer, (Eds.). *Handbook of literacy and technology: Transformations in a post-typographic world* (pp. 253–268). Mahwah, NJ: Lawrence Erlbaum Associates.

Tufte, E. R. (1983). *The visual display of quantitative information.* Cheshire, CT: Graphics Press.

Tufte, E. R. (1990). *Envisioning information.* Cheshire, CT: Graphics Press.

Unsworth, J. (1996). Living inside the operating system: Community in virtual reality. In T. M. Harrison & T. D. Stephen (Eds.), *Computer networking and scholarship in the 21st century university* (pp. 137–150). Albany: State University of New York Press.

Wenger, E. (1987). *Artificial intelligence and tutoring systems.* Los Altos, CA: Morgan Kaufmann.

Wertsch, J. (1991). *Voices of the mind.* Cambridge, MA: Harvard University Press.

5 Seeing the Text

STEPHEN A. BERNHARDT

The physical fact of the text, with its spatial appearance on the page, requires visual apprehension: a text can be seen, must be seen, in a process which is essentially different from the perception of speech. The written mode necessitates the arrangement of script or typeface, a process which gives visual cues to the verbal organization of the text. We might think of texts arranged along a continuum, from texts at one end which convey relatively little information visually, to texts at the opposite end which reveal substantial information through such visible cues as white space, illustrations, variation in typeface, and use of nonalphabetic symbols, such as numbers, asterisks, and punctuation. In terms of this continuum, an essay would fall well toward the non-visually informative end. Certainly, paragraph indentation, margins, capitalization, and sentence punctuation provide some information to the reader, but such information is extremely limited, with most of the cues as to organization and logical relations buried within the text. At the other extreme of the continuum would be texts which display their structure, providing the reader/viewer with a schematic representation of the divisions and hierarchies which organize the text.

If we were to encourage students to experiment with visible features of written texts, we would increase their ability to understand and use hierarchical and classificatory arrangements. Because of the opportunities it offers for visual inspection, writing heightens awareness of categories and divisions, changing the ways people conceive classificatory relations. Goody has suggested that the earliest uses of writing in a society — making lists, keeping accounts, recording events — sharpen awareness of categories and classes through the very fact of placing items physically on a page where they can be inspected and arranged. The graphic quality of writing, in contrast to the flow of speech, underscores the discontinuity, the boundaries, and the order which is possible in visual organization.[1] Ong derives similar conclusions concerning the introduction of typography, suggesting that printing "gave urgency to

From *College Composition and Communication* 37:1 (Feb. 1986): 66–78.

the very metaphor that ideas were items which could be 'spread,'" in two senses: the printing press spread books throughout the culture, but also opened new possibilities for spreading type on the page, possibilities which were not open to scribes.[2] Writing, especially when visually informative, encourages the writer to be exact about grouping related ideas, delineating beginnings and endings, and using cues to signal to the reader a graphic representation of cognitive organization. By studying and writing texts which display their structures through white space, graphic patterning, enumerative sequences, and so on, student writers can gain a heightened sense of categories, divisions, and orderly progression.[3]

Though classroom teaching often assumes essay organization as the norm, outside the classroom visually informative prose is pervasive, and not just in scientific or technical fields. As a starting point, we might consider the ubiquitous, insistent presence of advertising, with its continual striving for attractive and convincing visual/verbal stategies. The graphic arts generally attend to the intersection of print and graphic media.[4] Texts designed for public audiences typically adopt visually informative strategies. Thousands of informational pamphlets, brochures, and forms flow from government agencies, special interest groups, businesses, and community groups, attempting to gather information, to sell ideas, to explain programs, to describe rights and responsibilities to an affected public, or to seek support for one program or any another.

Legal writing also displays a "tendency to make more and more use of layout and other graphetic and graphological devices as a means of revealing structure, content, and logical progression."[5] Business writing exhibits similar visual patterning in everything from formal reports, to procedures, to correspondence, to memos—all make liberal use of conventional partitioning, white space, headings, schematics, lists, and other visible cues. The same can be claimed for writing in scientific and technical fields, much of which follows familiar formats with text layout determined by conventional practices.

At all levels of structure, texts which are highly informative visually share features not characteristic of texts which do not exploit the graphic potential of written language. We can assume that visually informative texts achieve rhetorical organization, just as do texts which are relatively noninformative visually. Both types must provide direction to the reader as to how the text is to be read: what transaction is intended, what the major divisions are, what is considered important, and what relations exist amongst the various subpoints. But the manner in which visually informative texts achieve rhetorical control differs in important ways from that in the non-visually informative text, at all levels of organization: in the whole discourse, in the paragraph, and in the sentence.

In a non-visually informative expository text, rhetorical control is typically exercised through the familiar strategies of essay composition. Introduction/body/conclusion partitioning is frequently in evidence, with each section performing predictable functions. Topics are introduced and broken down in the initial section; the sequence for the following paragraphs is anticipated by statements that preview the full text or announce a plan of organization. Paragraph-to-paragraph movement is often facilitated by transitional links to show logical connection. From time to time, readers are reminded of their place in the progression of the text, reminded anaphorically of what has come before and prepared cataphorically for what is to follow. Topic or core sentences enter into coordinate relations with other topic or core sentences in other paragraphs, and into relations of generalization and support with sentences within the paragraph. Sentence to sentence relations are controlled semantically through cohesive ties: one must actually read what is written to get any sense of how one point is related to the next. The net effect, or at least that which is intended, is one of smooth progression from beginning to end, a careful leading of the reader through the text to the final acceptance of and satisfaction with the conclusion. Linear progression characterizes both the execution and the intended-reader's approach to the text.

In sentences, the non-visually informative text evidences a consistency of structure. The vast majority of sentences are major syntactic forms as opposed to minor; they exhibit typical patterns of subject/verb/object, cast in a preponderance of declarative mood constructions. Minor forms or use of fragments is generally rare, as are uses of interrogative or imperative mood. The typical classroom essay is composed of sentences which resemble each other in their full, declarative structures, arranged in paragraphs with low visual identity (except for boundaries, signalled by indentation). The essay appears on the page as essentially unbroken, undifferentiated print, an effect which is heightened by printing processes which justify margins and further homogenize the texture of the page.

Admittedly, this characterization of expository text is based on one sort of writing, that enshrined in the handbooks of our trade. But this characterization does seem sufficiently influential within our discipline to be considered the norm, the product we encourage in our practice within the "current-traditional paradigm."[6] The control of rhetorical relations is strictly internal to the text, integrated within the paragraph and sentence structures. And the closer our models come to literary norms, to the norms of the polite, personal, anthologized essay typical of the Eastern literary "establishment," the greater are the demands on the student to produce essays which are subtle in their organizational schemes, leading rather than showing and telling, with no authorial recourse to meta-discoursal commentary on the structure or logic of the exposition.

To gain a sense of just how divergent these rhetorical values are from those evidenced in other, more visually informative prose patterns, it is necessary to look at and think about the achievement of rhetorical control in a visible text. The sample text reproduced below as Figure 1, a fact sheet on wetlands, is part of a larger project, *The Great Lakes Notebook*, undertaken by the Great Lakes Basin Commission.[7] *The Great Lakes Notebook* was conceived and composed by Sandra Gregerman, information officer for the Commission and a graduate of the University of Michigan's School of Natural Resources Master's degree program in Environmental Communications. Those in the

FIGURE 1. Reduced Photocopy of Wetlands Fact Sheet from *The Great Lakes Notebook*

Wetlands

Every year in the Great Lakes region an estimated 20,000 acres of valuable wetlands are filled, drained, or developed for residential, commercial and other uses. No one is certain how many acres of wetlands remain in the Great Lakes region, because the last complete national inventory was done in 1955, but losses have been significant. The most common types of wetlands found in the Great Lakes are coastal wetlands, marshes, wet meadows, shrub and wooded swamps, ponds, and bogs - all remnants of the shallow lakes left by the glaciers. These areas are wet all or part of the year.

Wetlands are valuable to the Great Lakes because they provide many free and natural environmental services. These services range from helping preserve water quality in the lakes to shoreline protection to providing a habitat for valuable wildlife such as waterfowl, fur bearing animals, and spawning fish - all important to the regional economy.

But despite their potential value, incremental losses of wetlands continue. Why? One reason is that the public has historically been ignorant about the value of wetlands, seeing them as useless property - swamps filled with mosquitoes. Secondly, many wetlands are found along the coastline of the Great Lakes or in the region's rich agricultural areas. Therefore, they are economically desirable land for development and agriculture. Thirdly, few studies exist which quantify the economic and environmental value of wetlands. And lastly, there is no comprehensive and coordinated state or federal policy for the management of wetlands.

The importance of wetlands to the Great Lakes

Free and natural water treatment	Wetlands purify surface and groundwater by filtering and absorbing sediments, nutrients, and chemicals from runoff.
Flood control	Wetlands can absorb and hold large quantities of water from flooding rivers and streams, effectively regulating extreme water levels which often occur in the Great Lakes.
Shoreline erosion prevention	The thickly rooted aquatic vegetation in wetlands can buffer the shore against waves in sheltered lakes and bays.
Tourist and recreation areas	Wetlands are rich natural areas which are good for birdwatching, fishing, and hunting.
Produce food crops	Wetlands are excellent growing and gathering areas for wild rice, cranberries, and blueberries.
Produce wildlife	Wetlands provide a habitat for waterfowl, fish, like northern pike, large-mouthed bass, and muskies, and other wildlife such as valuable fur bearing muskrats, racoons, and minks.
Replenish groundwater supplies	Wetlands act like natural reservoirs trapping rain and melting snow which later flows into underground water systems.

environmental sciences know that to be successful they must communicate with diverse audiences, and this text attempts to increase public awareness of the importance of wetlands protection in the Great Lakes area. The importance of this sheet was heightened by the fact that at the time of its release,

FIGURE 1. (continued)

How can wetlands be protected?

- By legislation which prevents the drainage, filling, or development of wetland areas without state review and permit.

- By state or federal acquisition of private wetlands in order to protect important wetlands.

- By tax reductions and other incentives to private owners to protect and preserve their wetlands.

- By identification of wetlands which have special environmental importance.

- By educating people about the many values of wetlands.

Status of Federal Wetlands Protection

There are no comprehensive federal laws to protect wetlands, however limited protection is found under: 1) section 404 of the Clean Water Act which requires permits to dredge and fill in wetlands and prohibits construction of wastewater treatment plants in wetlands; 2) the National Flood Insurance Program which limits development in wetlands near floodplains; 3) the U.S. Fish and Wildlife Coordination Act which requires consultation on all water projects to protect rare habitats; and 4) Executive Order 11990 of May 1977 which instructs federal agencies to implement programs to protect wetlands.

Great Lakes Region — status of wetlands protection

ILLINOIS: Few wetlands in Great Lakes portion of state. Limited protection through floodplain management and dredging legislation.

INDIANA: One third of the state's wetlands are in the Great Lakes basin. Limited wetlands protection under the state's Natural Scenic and Recreational Rivers Act and Nature Preserve Program.

MICHIGAN: One half of all Great Lakes wetlands are in Michigan. The wetlands Protection Act enacted in 1979 regulates the filling, dredging, development or drainage of wetlands primarily 5 acres or more and smaller significant wetlands.

MINNESOTA: The state owns or controls many of the state's numerous and important wetlands. The Public Waters Act and several other acts indirectly protect many wetland areas.

NEW YORK: Has one of the most comprehensive state wetlands protection laws, the Freshwater Wetlands Act of 1975. The act protects wetlands larger than 12.4 acres and those with special significance.

OHIO: One-half of the state's wetlands are in the Great Lakes basin. The Nature Preserve Program which acquires land for endangered species habitat and the Critical Areas Program are used to protect wetlands.

PENNSYLVANIA: Special wetlands area along Lake Erie. Floodplain management legislation and the state's administrative code which allows state acquisition of valuable wetlands afford protection.

WISCONSIN: The state has many wetland areas in the basin. The Shoreland Zoning Act limits development in shoreland wetlands, and the Floodplain Management Act and other legislation offer protection of other wetlands.

ONTARIO: Two thirds of the province's wetlands are located in the Great Lakes basin. These are protected under the provincial Beach Protection Act which requires permits for, and review of, any work in wetlands.

Prepared by the Great Lakes Basin Commission, Box 999, Ann Arbor, MI 48106   1/81.

conservation groups and interested legislators in Michigan were working to pass a wetlands protection act. The primary audiences for the text were legislators, educators and their students, and the general public. Gregerman's purpose was larger than public relations: she hoped to convey important, substantial information in an intelligent manner in order to influence the ecological administration of the region.

These multiple considerations of audience and purpose functionally constrain the text, influencing its shape and structure. The intention was to produce a document which would satisfy a number of functional considerations of cost and distribution, while being attractive enough to draw reader attention and substantial enough to encourage the reader to keep the sheet, compile it with others in the series, and use it. Especially in legislative and bureaucratic spheres, where the flow of print information is heavy, documents compete for attention, and to be effective readers must be drawn into the text.[8] The wetlands fact sheet insured attention through the use of high quantity, heavy-weight paper and crisp, well-defined print, qualities chosen to encourage the reader to notice and keep the sheet. Though each sheet of the Notebook was a different color (the wetlands sheet a light brown), all attained a high visual identity through headings across the top and sides and identifying symbols in the upper right hand corners.[9] The sheets were distributed one at a time in an effort to shorten initial production time and to allow for subsequent revisions, so it was important that they be recognized as part of a series. Their compilation was encouraged by the use of punched paper, and headings spaced vertically along the right margin increased the identity of the sheets and usefully served as a thumb index once the sheets were compiled.

Also important in the design of the fact sheet was the distribution of printed information on the page. To attend to the layout of the text requires considering the text as a visual gestalt, focusing attention on the total visual impact of the text on a prospective reader. Cataldo suggests that the principles codified by experiments in perception can be usefully applied to the visual/verbal design of graphic texts.[10] Perhaps the most relevant law is that of equilibrium, or *pragnanz*, which suggests that items in a visual field strive for balance or equilibrium with other items in the field. The wetlands text works well, in part, because the distribution of print on the first page achieves equilibrium simultaneously along several axes: horizontally, vertically, and diagonally. A horizontal axis balances the material above and below the widely spaced heading: *The importance of wetlands to the Great Lakes.* A vertical axis divides the lower half of the page, balancing the widely spaced headings along the left side against the explanatory material on the right. Finally, diagonal axes work toward symmetry; the lined margins on the top and right balance each other, the continuous text in the upper-left balances the shorter, detached statements on the lower right, and the logo in the upper-right balances the spaced headings of the lower-left.

A second law of gestalt, that of *good continuation*, or good figure, suggests that visual perception works to pull figures out of the background, to give them definition against the undistinguished field in which they are located. In the sample text on wetlands, good continuation is achieved through the clear black print on a light-brown background, through the headings, and through the groupings of related information which are set off by blank space. The typeface variation further reinforces the high definition of figure against ground. With a poorly reproduced text with low contrast of figure to ground, the reader has to strain to make out the text, in the process invoking a third law of gestalt, that of *closure*. When good continuation or good figure is not provided by the visual stimulus, the perceiver has a tendency to fill in the missing gaps, to provide the missing definition, as evidenced by the ability of readers to process even highly degraded copy, in which much of the information provided by the shape of letters is missing. In the sample text reproduced here, the quality of the printing and the arrangement of type on the page make for good figure and the reader need not strive for closure.

The law of good continuation or good figure also underlies the effect of emphasis in a visible text. Figures which are more strongly defined against their field will tend to appear more important than other figures which share the same ground. On the first page, an emphasis on wetland values is achieved by isolating the list under a major heading in the middle of the page and then calling attention visually to the list of functions and values with bold-faced headings along the left margin. The emphasis on this section may be further increased by its location in the lower-left area of the visual field, an area which, it has been suggested, is favored by visual stress.[11]

A fourth law of gestalt, the law of *similarity*, suggests that units which resemble each other in shape, size, color, or direction will be seen together as a homogenous grouping. The groupings of the wetlands sheet are highly distinct, reinforced by spacing between sections and headings in various type sizes which clearly delineate boundaries, allowing the text to display its structure. Good use of the law of similarity, as obvious a principle as it may seem, is an accomplishment, not a given, as has been amply demonstrated by Anderson's discussion of the visual organization of written texts.[12] Anderson shows how texts which fail to convey to the reader the intended groupings of information under the law of similarity can be profitably rewritten.

The sample text on wetlands makes good use of "visual syntax," to use Dondis' phrase, in the creation of a harmonious, balanced, attractive text which conveys information to the reader about textual organization through visible means. The visual impact of the front side is certainly greater than which of the reverse, but that is as it should be, for if the reader is sufficiently engaged with the text to flip the sheet over and look at the reverse, then the visual appeal has already proven effective.

Through these laws of gestalt, visual features take over the load of structuring and organizing the reader's processing, thus reducing the role of those semantic features which organize a form like the essay. Instead of a smooth, progressive realization of the text through initial previewing and a chain of logic which ties each paragraph or section to the preceding or following one, the visible text relies on localization, on a heightening of the boundaries, edges, and divisions of the text. In an integrated, non-visually informative text, the desideratum is a seamless text. In the visible text, the goal is to call the reader's attention visually to semantically grouped information, focusing the reader's attention on discrete sections. Fowler captures the distinction well in his contrast between progressive and localized text structures:

> A text is progressive if its structure leads the reader onwards, projects him forward from one segment of text to a succeeding one. Textual surface structure may be said to be localizing when it operates to hold up the reader's attention at a specific place in the total syntagm.[13]

Each section of the wetlands text is its own locale; it has its own function, which is likely to differ from previous and subsequent sections. Instead of a cumulative movement, the text has a localized focus in each section, with separateness rather than integration characterizing the text both semantically and visually.

In the sample text on wetlands, each section is self-contained and available to the reader without reference to other sections. Unconstrained by linear presentation, the reader can move about, settle on certain sections, read some sections lightly, some intently, some not at all, and still have a good idea of what the text is about. The legal audience, for example, may be less interested in or already familiar with the values of wetlands, but very interested in existing state and federal legislation. Students in a biology class may be highly motivated to look at the information on the first page, but uninterested in that on the second. The localization of the text makes possible the selective use of the text by varied audiences for varied purposes.

With a visible text, it may not be fruitful to talk about paragraphs in terms of topic sentences and support, or opening and closing sentences, or sentences of transition. In fact, it may not be useful to speak of paragraphs at all, but of sections or chunks. In the visible text, the headings take over the task of generalizing or identifying the topic. Levels of subordination are indicated by variation in typeface, type size, or placement of headings, rather than through subordinators or cohesive ties which indicate semantically dependent relations. For example, the initial section, written in integrated paragraphs, makes heavy use of deictics (*the, these*), pronominals (*their, they*), conjuncts (*but, one, secondly, thirdly, therefore, and lastly*), and ellipsis (*Why?, One reason is . . .*), to link each sentence to the next through some expressed logical relation or through the carrying over of the topic. But in sections two, three, and five, with the exception of lexical ties, there are no cohesive ties indicating logical relations, nor any transitional ties between sections. With subordinate relations indicated visually, the contents of each section tend to be a series or list of coordinate points, each item having equal status.

The move toward serial, coordinate development of sections exerts a shaping influence over the syntax of the listed items. Parallel grammatical structures tend to predominate, as in the second section of the wetlands text, wherein each statement of the values or functions of wetlands, with one exception, begins with the word *wetlands*, which serves simultaneously as the topic for the following comment, the subject of the sentence, and the agent of the actions or qualities described. The visual isolation of the information interrupts the flow of discourse, exerting a localizing effect which is reflected in parallel syntax. The sentence beginning *The thickly rooted aquatic vegetation* calls attention to itself because it does not fit the abstract context, that is, a visible parallel list. A better fit would be provided by beginning the sentence like the others, with initial phrasing such as *Wetlands buffer*, with *vegetation* planted within an instrumental clause later in the sentence. Traditional advice to vary sentence structure or sentence openings to avoid boring the reader or to keep sentences from sounding choppy would be misdirected here, where structural isomorphism must be maintained.

In addition to heightening the demands for parallel form, localization tends to reduce syntax from full sentences to phrases. In the third section of sample text, for instance, the question *How can wetlands be protected?* is followed by a list of prepositional phrases beginning with *by*, each of which answers the question. Each carries over elliptical information from the lead question, which would take the form "*Wetlands can be protected . . .*" were it written out in full form. In this instance, the individual items do not complete a syntactic structure begun in a lead sentence, even though the items are punctuated like sentences. The fourth section of the text offers a contrast, in that the syntax of a single sentence is carried over from item to item in the list, resulting in one long sentence which is at once a single sentence and a list of sentences. It is worth noting that no term for this sort of construction exists, to my knowledge, in the lexicon of composition, rhetoric, or linguistics, and yet the pattern is extremely widespread in writing from many fields. Such *expanded sentences* require careful control, demanding a series of elements which are syntactically parallel, each completing a sentence by adding a phrase which complements the initiating phrase.

The sentences of the final section of the sample text evidence still another kind of syntactic patterning. This section demonstrates an easy movement from full sentences to fragments in an unpredictable sequence. The effect is a casual tone, almost as though we were reading someone's notes rather than a finished written product.

The wetlands fact sheet thus offers quite a contrast to texts composed within traditional essay format, employing as it does a variety of strategies on both large (full text and sectioning) and small (sentence and section development) scales. It avoids linear, progressive organization, allowing a reader to break in at any point in the text with full comprehension. It combines graphic techniques of layout and typeface variation with verbal passages which achieve cohesion in a variety of ways through integrated paragraphs, expanded sentences, isolated sentences, and organized fragments of various sorts. The text reflects decisions by the author to adopt a variety of strategies in response to varying ideational content and in the interest of assembling the information attractively for various audiences. Any of the sections might have been written in integrated paragraphs, but the choices made capitalize on the visual potential of written language.

Table 1 summarizes those features which distinguish visually informative from non-visually informative texts. Not all features will necessarily be present in any given text, but texts at one end of the continuum or the other are likely to share some combination of these features.

There are no hard-and-fast rules for designing effective visually informative texts, though empirical research has begun to offer some tentative findings. For example, in studies at the Document Design Center, complicated FCC regulations were rewritten and simplified through a visually informative format of questions and answers. The new rules enabled readers to find information more quickly and more accurately.[14] Not all research findings are so clear, however. A report by Frase and Schwartz made a strong claim which bears directly on visual design:

> Our results show that lines may be short or they may be long, a page may have neat margins or ragged margins. No matter. What is critical is whether the lines represent meaningful groups of information. It is this matching of visual design to the constraints of cognitive processing that makes for efficiency.[15]

The conclusion seems logical and is not qualified by the authors. And yet an attempt to replicate the study under similar conditions did not find significant gains in comprehension which could be attributed to visual, semantically-based groupings.[16] Great difficulties beset the researcher who attempts to demonstrate changed reader behavior as a function of text design, since texts which fall toward the visually informative end of the continuum encourage selective reading and extracting of information. The design strategies make the texts accessible at various depths to suit the purposes of various readers. This aspect of interaction between text and reader is difficult to evaluate or build into experimental design.[17]

Instead of attempting to base teaching practice on scant and tentative results, we may find it more expedient to view the rhetoric of visual design as an evolving art. As is true of other arts, more profit can be gained in the early stages of research from looking at what practitioners do than from attempting to induce and measure changes in experimental variables. If teachers would begin to look at naturally occurring discourse forms which have evolved outside the classroom, they would begin to develop a descriptive base for visual design. A preoccupation with conventional essay format allows little attention to visual features. Instead of helping students learn to analyze a situation and determine an appropriate form, given a certain audience and purpose, many writing assignments merely exercise the same sort of writing week after week, introducing only topical variation. Texts with visually organized, localized development, and features such as headings, expanded sentences, meaningful white space, or question-and-answer strategies are typically neglected.

Classroom practice which ignores the increasingly visual, localized qualities of information exchange can only become increasingly irrelevant. Influenced especially by the growth of electronic media, strategies of

TABLE 1. Visual Organization of Written Texts

Visually Informative		Non-visually Informative
	Rhetorical Control	
varied surface offers aesthetic possibilities; can attract or repel reader through the shape of the text; laws of equilibrium, good continuation, good figure, closure, similarity.	Visual Gestalt	homogenous surface offers little possibility of conveying information; dense, indistinguished block of print; every text presents the same face; formidable appearance assumes willing reader.
localized: each section is its own locale with its own pattern of development; arrests reader's attention.	Development	progressive: each section leads smoothly to the next; projects reader forward through discourse-level previewing and backwards through reviewing.
iconic: spacing, headings reveal explicit, highly visible divisions; reader can jump around, process the text in a non-linear fashion, access information easily, read selectively.	Partitioning	integrated: indentations give some indication of boundaries, but sections frequently contain several paragraphs and sometimes divisions occur within paragraphs; reader must read or scan linearly to find divisions.
emphasis controlled by visual stress of layout, type size, spacing, headings.	Emphasis	emphasis controlled semantically through intensifiers, conjunctive ties; some emphasis achieved by placement of information in initial or final slots in sentences and paragraphs.
subordinate relations signaled through type size, headings, indenting.	Subordinate Relations	controlled semantically within linear sequence of paragraphs and sentences.
signalled through listing structures, expanded sentences, parallel structures, enumerated or iconically signalled by spacing, bullets, or other graphic devices.	Coordinate Relations	controlled semantically through juxtaposition, parallel structures, and cohesive ties, especially additive ties.
linkage controlled visually; little or no use of semantic ties between sentences and sections; reliance on enumerative sequences or topicalization of a series.	Linking/ Transitional/ Intersentential Relations	liberal use of cohesive ties, especially conjunctives and deictics; frequent interparagraph ties or transitional phrases.
variety in mood and syntactic patterning; much use of Q/A sequences, imperatives; fragments and minor forms; phrases used in isolation.	Sentence Patterns	complete sentences with little variation in mood; sentences typically declarative with full syntax.

rhetorical organization will move increasingly toward visual patterns presented on screens and interpreted through visual as well as verbal syntax. Written texts will gain flexibility in organization through branching and recursion, characteristics more closely associated with speech than writing. Further use of isolated, localized passages also seems likely, with information called up in short snatches in interactional patterns, rather than in extended, rhetorically integrated, progressive texts.

By studying actual texts as they function in particular contexts, we can gain an improved understanding of what constitute appropriate, effective strategies of rhetorical organization. At the same time, we can learn from such studies how successful texts are composed and what part schools can play in encouraging students to become able, creative composers.

NOTES

1. Jack Goody, *The Domestication of the Savage Mind* (Cambridge, England: Cambridge University Press, 1977), p. 81.

2. Walter J. Ong, S. J., *Rhetoric, Romance, and Technology* (Ithaca: Cornell University Press, 1971), p. 167.

3. See Anne Ruggles Gere, "A Cultural Perspective on Talking and Writing," in *Exploring Speaking-Writing Relationships: Connections and Contrasts*, ed. Barry M. Kroll and Roberta J. Vann (Urbana, IL: National Council of Teachers of English, 1981), pp. 111–123.

4. See especially John W. Cataldo, *Graphic Design and Visual Communication* (Scranton: International Textbook Company, 1966); Arthur T. Turnbull and Russell N. Baird, *The Graphics of Communication* (New York: Holt, Rinehart & Winston, 1975).

5. David Crystal and Derek Davy, *Investigating English Style* (Bloomington: Indiana University Press, 1969), p. 198. See also David Mellinkoff, *The Language of the Law* (Boston: Little, Brown and Company, 1963).

6. Richard Young, "Paradigms and Problems: Needed Research in Rhetorical Invention," in *Research on Composing: Points of Departure*, ed. Charles R. Cooper and Lee Odell (Urbana, IL: National Council of Teachers of English, 1978), pp. 29–47.

7. A commission which has, unfortunately, but like so many other environmental advocacy groups, been eliminated by Federal budget cuts.

8. Roland Harweg draws a nice distinction between texts which must seek out an audience vs. those which have an assured audience, outlining characteristic ways of beginning for each: "Beginning a Text," in *Discourse Processes*, 3 (October–December, 1980), 313–326.

9. It is unfortunate that the attractive qualities of the sheet cannot be appreciated in the reduced, black-and-white version printed here. Standard print journalism, with its homogenization of the text's surface and reduction of the physicality of the text, levels qualities active in more graphic media. For examples of how print journalism can extend the possibilities of the printed page, see any issue of *Visible Language: The Research Journal Concerned with All That Is Involved in Our Being Literate*.

10. Cataldo, Chapters 2, 3, 4, and 5.

11. Donis Dondis, *A Primer of Visual Literacy* (Cambridge: MIT Press, 1973), pp. 28–29.

12. Paul V. Anderson, "Organizing Is Not Enough," in *Courses, Components, and Exercises in Technical Communication* (Urbana, IL: National Council of Teachers of English, 1981), pp. 163–184.

13. Roger Fowler, "Cohesive, Progressive, and Localizing Aspects of Text Structure," in *Grammars and Descriptions*, ed. Teun A. Van Dijk and János Petöfi (Berlin: de Gruyter, 1977), pp. 64–84.

14. Reported by Robin Battison and Joanne Landesman in "The Cost Effectiveness of Designing Simpler Documents," *Simply Stated*, 16 (April 1981), pp. 1, 3.

15. L. T. Frase and B. J. Schwartz, "Typographical Cues that Facilitate Comprehension," *Journal of Educational Psychology*, 71 (April 1979), p. 205.

16. James Hartley, "Spatial Cues in Text," *Visible Language*, 14 (1980), 62–79.

17. Experimental studies on text design are reported in P. A. Kolers, M. E. Wrolstad, and H. Bouman, ed., *Processing of Visible Language*, 1, 2 (New York: Plenum, 1979, 1980); D. Wright

reviews the research and concludes "there is no ubiquitously good way of presenting technical information" in "Presenting Technical Information: A Survey of Research Findings," *Instructional Science*, 6 (April, 1977), 93–134. For an overview of writings on visual literacy, see Dennis W. Pett, "Visual Literacy," in *Classroom Relevant Research in the Language Arts*, ed. Harold G. Shane and James Walden (Washington, DC: Association for Curriculum Development, 1978), pp. 8–17.

6

Reading the Visual in College Writing Classes

CHARLES A. HILL

For about a decade now, scholars have been declaring that the age of printed text is all but over. Jay Bolter claims that we are now in "the late age of print" (2) and in 1994, Sven Birkerts estimated that printed books would be dominant for about another fifty years (121), to be replaced almost entirely with online hypermedia forms of communication. But regardless of whether one agrees with these and other obituaries of the print medium, it would be difficult to deny the importance of electronic and other visual media in today's society. The students now entering our classrooms have grown up with one hundred channels of television, and the World Wide Web is no longer a novelty, but part of their social, academic, and working lives. If we include nonelectronic sources of visual communication such as billboards, print advertisements, and the ubiquitous packaging that has taken such an important place in our consumer culture, then we have to conclude that most of the information that our students are exposed to is in a visual form.

There is little doubt that the increasing ubiquity of visual and aural forms of communication is one of the reasons that so many students arrive at the university with apparently little experience with the written word. However, while our students might engage relatively rarely with print text, we should not therefore conclude that their lives are devoid of information or of expression. Quite the opposite is true. Our students may have been exposed to more "texts" than any other generation in history, and many of these texts are dense with cultural information. One might argue that most of these texts are designed primarily to entertain or to sell something rather than to offer information or increase one's understanding of complex issues; nevertheless, our students are exposed to a broad range of information daily. So far, our educational system has failed to take seriously and to adequately respond to the fact that so much of this information is in visual form. As Barbara Stafford notes,

From *Intertexts: Reading Pedagogy in College Writing Classrooms*. Ed. Marguerite Helmers. Mahwah, NJ: Lawrence Erlbaum Associates, 2003. 123–150.

"In most American university curricula, graphicacy remains subordinate to literacy" (5).

THE NEGLECT OF THE VISUAL

One might assume—or at least hope—that a major goal of the educational system is to help students develop the abilities necessary to comprehend, interpret, and critically respond to the textual forms that they will encounter as members of the culture. Since so many of the texts that our students encounter are visual ones, and since visual literacy is becoming increasingly important for everyday social functioning and even for success in the workplace (Kress and van Leeuwen 2–3), it would seem obvious that our educational institutions should be spending at least as much time and energy on developing students' visual literacies as these institutions spend on developing students' textual literacy. However, both in the classroom and in literacy research, the amount of time and effort devoted to developing students' abilities to comprehend, analyze, and critique visual messages is relatively miniscule.

As a result, Americans tend to act as passive consumers rather than as critics or analysts of visual messages. While we are all being increasingly exposed to highly manipulated images meant to influence our beliefs, opinions, and behaviors, very few of us are adequately prepared to analyze and critique these images in order to make informed decisions about them. In fact, many people seem unaware of the rhetorical power of images and of their mediated nature. The adage "seeing is believing" is often applied, not just to natural objects that are being directly perceived, but often to visual representations of objects, people, and events, as well. Photographs and video, in particular, are typically treated as "direct copies of reality" rather than as representations designed to influence viewers in particular ways (Messaris, vi).

The field of rhetoric in general, and the subfield of composition in particular, have largely ignored visual types of expression, especially in the classroom. This is true for many reasons, largely historical. It could be argued that visual forms of rhetorical expression have not become predominant until recently, and that the methodological and theoretical work necessary for the analysis of visual rhetoric is in the process of catching up to its increasing presence and importance. But this argument cannot fully explain the scholarly neglect of visual information. From the iconography of the medieval church to the propaganda posters of the two world wars, it cannot be denied that visual forms of rhetoric have always existed and have always served important functions in society (Purves). Why, then, has visual rhetoric been so neglected, especially as its power and influence have grown steadily over the last century?

Perhaps this neglect can be largely attributed to a widespread and traditional dislike and disparagement of mass culture, and from our fears that visual and other modes of communication will overtake, replace, or diminish the importance of the print medium (Stafford; Stroupe; Welch). When most people think of visual media, they think of the "vast wasteland" of television (including the much-derided music video), comic books, picture books (produced for young children who have not yet "progressed" to purely verbal texts), "coffee table books" (usually considered more decorative than informative or scholarly), and Hollywood cinema (though, of these genres, film is generally assumed to have more promise as a "serious" medium). Despite our supposed postmodern rejections of canonical hierarchies that would place literary and scholarly texts above such commercially produced and widely disseminated "texts," we still tend to favor words over images, and we worry defensively that our students are spending too much time watching television and surfing the Web, and not enough time reading books. Stafford describes the present situation in the scholarly community eloquently: "The passionate visualist, roaming the labyrinth of the postdisciplinary age, is haunted by the paradoxical ubiquity and degradation of images: everywhere transmitted, universally viewed, but as a category generally despised" (11).

When educators discuss among themselves the role of visual forms of communication (especially the culturally dominant, mass-produced forms), it is usually to express and reinforce the worry that students are already too reliant on the visual, in many cases almost to the exclusion of written forms, and that educators should be trying to arrest that trend in their classrooms, not reinforce it. Dealing with visual texts in university classrooms might seem like surrendering to the inevitable "dumbing down" of our society's discourse or pandering to our students' lazy tendencies (Stafford 3). However, the avoidance of taking images seriously in general education, and especially in writing classrooms, is based on some assumptions that may not be valid.

The most basic, and perhaps the most misguided, of these assumptions is that we could ever draw a distinct line between the visual and the verbal, or that concentrating on one can or should require ignoring the other. As W. J. T. Mitchell argues, "recent developments in art history, film theory, and what is loosely called 'cultural studies' make the notion of a purely verbal literacy increasingly problematic" (6). Communication has always been a hybrid blending of visual, written, and aural forms, and the new electronic technologies are making this melding of media easier and more common, requiring readers and writers to have a richer understanding of how words and images work together to produce meaning (Stroupe 618; Welch 131, 157). James Elkins argues that "mixed images" (incorporating some combination of pictures, words, and/or notations) are the norm rather than the exception (91). He goes on to argue that, while it may be useful to make a conceptual distinction between a "pure" image (requiring no verbal interpretation) and a "pure" text (with no meaningful visual element), we should recognize that this purity does not exist in the real world, and pedagogical efforts should be aimed toward helping students deal with combinations of picture, word, and symbol. Perhaps Mitchell makes the case most adamantly: "all media are mixed media, and all representations are heterogeneous; there are no 'purely' visual or verbal arts" (5).

Even if we could make a clear-cut and reasonable distinction between purely verbal texts and purely visual ones, it would still be a mistake to concentrate our teaching efforts on reading and writing to the exclusion of other modes of communication and to neglect visual forms. Most students enter the university unable to articulate any principles about how visual messages work and without any of the skills or habits necessary to critically analyze such messages. In fact, largely because they have adopted the prejudices and fears of their educators and of the larger culture, many university students need to be convinced that visual images constitute meaningful texts at all in the sense that people are used to thinking about written texts. The very dominance and ubiquity of visual messages suggest that our students should develop at least a basic understanding of how they work. Students also need to develop both the ability and the inclination to examine their own reactions to such messages, if they are to have any real independence and effectiveness as social agents.

Finally, images should be studied and understood because of the unique epistemic power they possess. As Stafford argues, images are not "just more efficient conveyors of extant verbal information"; rather, they are "indispensable in discovering that which could not otherwise be known" (40). In other words, images are not just another method for expressing propositions that could otherwise be expressed in verbal form. Rather, they are essential for expressing, and therefore for knowing things that cannot be expressed in any other form. To ignore images is to ignore all of the knowledge that they can help us develop, knowledge that cannot be logically deduced or proven; they "help us to organize and make sense of that floating world, that milieu, stretching considerably below certitude and somewhat above ignorance" (Stafford 39).

The public's general inability to interpret and analyze visual images has not gone entirely unnoticed. At its November 1996 meeting, the National Council of Teachers of English passed a resolution to "support professional development and promote public awareness of the role that viewing and visually representing our world have as forms of literacy" ("NCTE Passes Visual Literacy Resolution"). And educators are developing curricular units and materials on nearly every educational level to help students interpret and accurately respond to visual messages. Still, these initiatives are often treated as add-on units, subordinated to the larger goal of developing students' reading and writing abilities. For a variety of reasons, educators in general, and perhaps those of us in the humanities above all, continue to neglect visual sources of communication in favor of verbal texts.

If literacy development were a zero-sum game, in which our time and energies must necessarily be spent on *either* written *or* visual literacies, then this neglect would be understandable, perhaps even defensible. However, ignoring the visual aspects of rhetoric, even the visual aspects of written texts, hinders our efforts to help students develop an accurate understanding of the nature of rhetorical practice, including an adequate understanding of the potential, as well as the limitations, of written discourse.

TOWARD A PEDAGOGY OF VISUAL RHETORIC

It is one thing to argue that university students should be exposed to more explicit instruction about the uses of visual communication, and it is quite another to develop a workable pedagogy for dealing with visual rhetoric. Such a pedagogy has not yet been developed, partly because no one recognizable discipline has staked a claim around the immense and vaguely defined area that is variously referred to as "visual communication," "visual rhetoric," or "visual literacy." Research and scholarship in the production, comprehension, interpretation, and analysis of visuals continually takes place in fields as diverse as art history, anthropology, education, semiotics, film studies, political science, psychology, and cultural studies, but none of these disciplines can claim the study of visual communication as its own, and there is little coordination among the various fields that study it. Roy Fox proposes an interdisciplinary endeavor that would be called "Image Studies," and that would draw from the sciences, social sciences, humanities, and arts. But until such a formalized collaboration exists, we have nowhere to look for a highly developed pedagogy of visual rhetoric.

In fact, because visual communication does not yet have a formalized disciplinary framework, we do not even have generally accepted definitions and parameters within which to work. For example, what sorts of visual input should be included in a pedagogy of "visual communication"? Or, working from the process of elimination, what sorts of visual input are we willing to say are *not* communicative? Humans process visual input continuously, and much of this input is consciously interpreted as carrying meaning or implying something beyond the specific empirical data being observed. For example, a viewer who sees a tree bending in a sudden wind may interpret the image to mean that a storm is approaching. Similarly, a viewer may see a person in ragged clothing pushing a shopping cart through a downtown area, and interpret these signs as indicating that the person is homeless (Worth and Gross). However, while these kinds of visual images are interpreted as carrying meaning beyond the visual data they provide, they would not generally be considered instances of visual *communication* because they are not images created by an agent for the purpose of communicating some particular information or ideas to others. Worth and Gross call these kinds of events "natural signs"—imagistic events that the viewer might consciously interpret, but without making any assumption that an agent is creating or distributing these images in order to communicate an idea.

On the other hand, a *painting* of a tree bending in the wind would be interpreted, not as a natural event, but as a conscious representation of such an event. The viewer interprets such images with the assumption that a deliberate intent to communicate is driving the production and distribution of the image. Worth and Gross call such image-events "symbolic signs." So, for example, if we are watching a documentary, and we see in the documentary a shot of a person in ragged clothing pushing a shopping cart through a downtown area, we assume that the producer of the documentary has consciously chosen to include that image in the film in order to influence the viewer's reactions. It is this intent (or, more precisely, the viewer's assumption that this intent exists) that makes this shot in the documentary a *symbolic* sign.

These classifications are not objective ones. What distinguishes a natural sign from a symbolic sign is the viewer's interpretation of the image event. For example, if two people see a homeless person walking down the street, the first viewer may determine that the homeless person is merely going about his or her business, unmindful of how the image he or she is projecting may be interpreted by others, while the second viewer may decide that the person being viewed is deliberately "playing up" the image of homelessness in order to affect the reactions of passersby. (A viewer could also suspect that the "homeless" person is a performance artist, a sociological researcher, or an undercover police officer, deliberately creating an image of homelessness in order to produce a specific reaction in passersby.) In this case, the first viewer would see the ragged clothing and the shopping cart as elements of a natural sign, while the second viewer would see the same elements as constituting a symbolic sign (a deliberate attempt to project an image of homelessness).

It is relatively easy to exclude naturally occurring events, those that are not produced or influenced by humans, from the category of symbolic signs (unless one posits some nonhuman entity deliberately attempting to communicate with us through these events). But it seems impossible to say of almost any human action that it is not in any way influenced by a communicative intention. Almost any human action (even sitting still or some other form of nonaction) could be interpreted as resulting from a communicative intent. However, if our aim is to develop a workable pedagogy of visual rhetoric, we will have to draw the boundaries around our subject matter a little more tightly.

Walker and Chaplin follow many theorists in distinguishing between mediated and unmediated vision (23). When we look at a cow standing in a field, we are directly perceiving the cow, unmediated by any outside filter. But when we see a painting or a drawing or a photograph of a cow, or see it in a film, then we are seeing, not the cow itself, but a representation of it. The representation works by instantiating our memories of cows we have seen firsthand, along with any of our feelings or attitudes about cows that the producer of the image would like to instantiate. Even if the viewer has never seen a real, unmediated cow, the viewer understands that such creatures exist, and that they have particular traits and associations that the creator of the image would like to bring to the forefront of the viewer's consciousness.

From a purely theoretical perspective, of course, it is highly problematic to speak of concrete objects as being unmediated images. Too many people make the mistake of insisting on a rigid binary distinction between mediated and "real" objects, in essence positing two separate worlds—the "real" world, which we can walk through or drive through, looking at cows and barns and trees—and the world of created images, consisting of paintings or photographs or drawings of these objects, as well as movies and television shows that include images of them.

In almost every instance in which the physical, "real" world and the world of representations are compared, the physical world is assumed to be the preferable, superior, the more "authentic" of the two, and therefore more epistemologically trustworthy. The assumption behind this hierarchy of values is that, while images are a representation of someone else's perception of an event, and therefore tainted by that person's biases and imperfections, the physical world provides the opportunity for pure, untainted perception. This assumption, though, cannot begin to stand up to the considerable challenges that face it. First, a vast amount of scientific research on the subject of perception makes clear that we perceive events around us very imperfectly and incompletely. Because we cannot possibly process all of the visual information that bombards us on a continual basis, we actively filter and prioritize the visual information we are exposed to, and this filtering and prioritizing process is driven by our own preconceptions, desires, biases, and value judgments.

The second challenge to the assumption of the purity of direct perception consists of a simple recognition that all of our perceptions are influenced by cultural values and assumptions. One of the most succinct and persuasive accounts of this recognition is given in a work of fiction: Don DeLillo's *White Noise*. In DeLillo's novel, Murray Siskind, a professor of popular culture studies, accompanies the novel's narrator to "a tourist attraction known as the most photographed barn in America" (12). The narrator and Murray watch as crowds of tourists take pictures of the barn.

> Murray maintained a prolonged silence, occasionally scrawling some notes in a little book.
>
> "No one sees the barn," he said finally. "Once you've seen the signs about the barn, it becomes impossible to see the barn." [. . .]
>
> "Being here is a kind of spiritual surrender. We see only what the others see. The thousands who were here in the past, those who will come in the future. We've agreed to be part of a collective perception. This literally colors our vision." [. . .]
>
> "What was the barn like before it was photographed?" he said. "What did it look like, how was it different from other barns, how was it similar to other barns? We can't answer these questions because we've read the signs, seen the people snapping the pictures. We can't get outside the aura. We're part of the aura. We're here, we're now."
>
> He seemed immensely pleased by this. (12–13)

What the fictional Murray Siskind understands is that no visual perception is a pure apprehension of objective reality. Comprehending and interpreting any image, whether it is a barn seen through a car window or a painting of a barn, requires an active mental process that is driven by personal and cultural values and assumptions. When we look at an object, no matter how mundane, our perception of the object is filtered through, and transformed by, our assumptions about it and attitudes toward it, assumptions and attitudes that may be highly idiosyncratic or widely shared within the culture. Seeing a rusted car on blocks in someone's front yard may signal any range of assumptions about the owner, whether the car is seen in a photograph or painting, or whether one is seeing the actual car. To use a quite different example, it is impossible for members of our culture to view a sunset without it bringing to mind a range of associations from literary and other cultural sources. As Murray Siskind would say, we're part of the aura, and we can't escape it.

Having said all of this, though, I think it is valid and useful to make a distinction between looking at an object and looking at a representation of an object. Though both may be activities involving mediating influences, there *is* a difference between the act of seeing an object "first-hand" and seeing a visual representation of it. In the first case, the mediation results from the individual's past experiences with similar objects, experiences that are largely culturally shared but sometimes idiosyncratic. In the second case, there is an added layer of mediation—the conscious and sometimes unconscious choices that the producer of the image has made in order to further his or her own goals as a communicator. These choices can only influence—not determine—the viewer's interpretation of and emotional responses to the object. But these choices *can* determine what the viewer actually sees, and this mundane fact should not be overlooked.

At some point in their careers, students should come to understand something about visual semiotics in a broad and inclusive sense, one that includes consideration of the ways in which even direct apprehension of concrete objects is influenced by cultural values and personal experiences. However, in order to deal with more immediate concerns—or at least ones

that teachers of rhetoric and communication are more prepared to deal with — it might make sense to restrict our efforts, at least initially, to visual representations — objects meant to "stand in for" or to create in the viewer's mind a representation of something else, whether that something else be a concrete object or an abstract idea. Visual objects that could be studied as representations include paintings, sculptures, murals, photographs, drawings, videos and films, logos, icons, symbols, and multimedia art.

It is necessary, before moving on, to make one more point about the category of visual objects we are dealing with. I have been discussing the difference between concrete objects and visual representations of those objects, but rhetorical images do not necessarily have to portray an object, or even a class of objects, that exists or ever did exist. A picture of a unicorn can carry meaning because the viewer has been exposed to other representations of unicorns, both visual and verbal, and can associate the new representation with memories of those encountered previously. And, like words, visual representations can stand in for abstract ideas. Many symbols (e.g., a swastika or a peace sign) are designed primarily to represent an idea or an institution or an ideology without attempting to look like any concrete object. But just like representations of concrete objects, these abstract symbols depend on the viewer's ability and willingness to attach some particular meaning to them, and they will likely be treated as "symbolic signs" — that is, the viewer will likely assume that the producer of the visual symbol is attempting to instantiate within the viewer some shared cultural meanings that are commonly attached to the symbol (Worth and Gross). (The various controversies over the display of the confederate flag in some southern states powerfully demonstrate the symbolic nature of some abstract icons, and demonstrate also that the meanings of these symbols are not fixed.)

Even after narrowing the range of visual objects to deliberate representations, we are still left with the most basic pedagogical question — what, exactly, do students need to know about representational images? In other words, what exactly should we be doing with visual representations in our writing and rhetoric classes?

Of course, many instructors already deal with visuals in writing classrooms, and textbook publishers are beginning to take visual information more seriously as a rhetorical mode. In fact, a recent first-year composition textbook deals almost entirely with visual communication (*Seeing & Writing*, by Donald and Christine McQuade, published by Bedford/St. Martin's). But there is nothing even approaching a consensus about what types of visuals should be used in writing classrooms or exactly what students should be doing with them. Perhaps, given the nature of the discipline, no such consensus will ever emerge. Nevertheless, as a point of discussion, I offer here some thoughts about how visuals can be profitably used in a writing and rhetoric curriculum. I consider these ideas to be an early step in the development of a coherent undergraduate pedagogy of rhetoric, a pedagogy that combines the visual and the verbal without subordinating either mode of rhetoric to the other.

THE PLACE OF VISUAL INFORMATION IN AMERICAN CULTURE

First, students can and should be taught about the cultural work of images in our society. Many of our most powerful and influential cultural concepts are encoded within what Richard Weaver called "God words" (e.g., "freedom," "motherhood," and "justice"). But we are a largely visual society, and many of these powerful cultural concepts are encoded within easily recognizable images (e.g., representations of George Washington, the Statue of Liberty, the Madonna and child, and the American flag). And besides these common images, advertisers and others continually create new images designed to exploit many of our society's predominantly held values and assumptions. Visuals are also used both to take advantage of and to reinforce roles and stereotypes defined by gender, race, and socioeconomic status.

Students need to learn to appreciate the power of images for defining and for reinforcing our cultural values and to understand the ways in which images help us define our individual roles within society. Students also need some understanding of the many ways in which the producers of images take advantage of these cultural values and use them for their own persuasive purposes.

The advertisement in Figure 1 is an example of an image that takes advantage of common cultural values for persuasive purposes. The advertisement constitutes an appeal to readers to purchase and maintain an amount of life insurance that is adequate to cover their family members' needs. In the narrative at the bottom of the ad, we are told that, while "life suddenly changed for Mark when his father died," his father's foresight in purchasing adequate life insurance allowed his mother to pay the mortgage so Mark "can remain with his friends in the community where he grew up." The picture at the top of the ad (processed in a blue-gray duotone, to give the scene an old-fashioned, slightly dreamy quality) shows two boys (one of whom is presumably Mark, but we don't know which one) laughing as if sharing a joke. The point, presumably, is to demonstrate the claim that Mark is relatively happy, given the unfortunate circumstances of his father's death. (Clearly, the advertisement is not trying to claim that Mark is unaffected by his father's death—just that having adequate life insurance did not make matters even worse than they had to be.)

Seen as a piece of evidence (albeit a fictional one, given that the picture is obviously posed), the image can be treated rather straightforwardly as evidence to support the author's claims. However, as with any picture, the producers of the image had many decisions to make, and their decisions reflect some of the values and assumptions of the current American culture.

One of these values is racial integration and harmony. The picture portrays a European-American boy and an African-American boy playing and laughing together. (Their stance indicates that they are having a conversation.) While I hope and believe that interracial friendships among children are relatively common, it is almost certainly more common to see close friendships among children of the same race. But the creators of the advertisement are not interested in showing the world as it most typically is, but in creating

FIGURE 1. Insurance Company

a scene that will appeal to its target audiences—parents, and most specifically, fathers. Portraying children of two races playing together as friends helps fathers of both of those races identify with the children in the picture, and it also makes the scene more positive (if slightly idealized) by evoking one of the more positive values in American culture—a desire for racial harmony.

Given the target audience, it is also no surprise that the creators of the advertisement chose to pose one of the boys with a baseball glove (held up to his chin, in order to situate it prominently in the middle of the frame) and the other one with a baseball bat over his shoulder. When it comes to fathers interacting with their sons, perhaps no activity is more iconic in American culture than baseball. From Hollywood movies like *Field of Dreams* and *City Slickers*, to Ken Burns's PBS miniseries, to the countless novels and nonfiction books extolling its virtues and celebrating its Americanness, the message is clear—if you're a father and you want your son to think back on your time together with fond remembrance, take him to a baseball game.

It is easy for an analysis like this to begin to sound cynical, painting the use of cultural values as a manipulative process. But it's important to point out, especially to students who may be exposed to such an analysis for the first time, that this need not be the case. It may be true that the picture in this advertisement is deliberately designed to portray an idealized version of American boyhood; the point is to present boyhood as a parent *would like it to be* for his or her son. In order to accomplish this, the advertisers must necessarily play to their audience's ambitions, dreams, and values. But this is true for any type of persuasive appeal; visual rhetoric is not unique in this regard.

Certainly, professional persuaders should be criticized when they appeal to some of the more negative aspects of American culture, including our fears and prejudices. And we can certainly find things to critique about the advertisement in Figure 1 if we are so inclined, such as the traditional gender roles that it represents. But we can just as certainly analyze the persuasive strategies being used and point out the use of common cultural values without the analysis turning into a condemnation of the agents behind it, and it is possible to find some instances of this strategy to be relatively benign. (And would we really prefer that the advertisers use surly, tough-looking teenagers, playing violent video games and smoking cigarettes, in a more "honest" attempt to stir fathers' emotions?) An analysis of a persuasive appeal need not always become a criticism of its source, and an analysis of visual messages in which cultural values are reflected and reinforced need not, in every case, become a criticism of those values. These points are especially important to keep in mind when dealing with young university students, who may grow suspicious or weary of rhetorical analysis if they see it as inevitably leading to a criticism of the values they have been raised to accept.

Of course, this does not mean that a critique of widely cherished American values has no place in the classroom. And there are other types of ethical questions in respect to visual rhetoric that we should prompt students to explore. In the case of Figure 1, even if the ultimate goal of the ad is to increase the revenues of insurance companies, convincing parents to carry an adequate amount of life insurance seems largely unobjectionable. But we might feel differently if the picture were being used in an advertisement for cigarettes, or for a political campaign in which we thought that the candidate's policy goals were actually harmful to American children. Such ethical questions are not trivial, and preparing students to deal with such questions should be a central goal of rhetorical education. But my point is that an instructor faced with a classroom of students who have never been asked even to think of images as rhetorical appeals, let alone to analyze the rhetorical strategies being used in them, does not necessarily have to cover all of this ground in one leap. The first step, the one that must be taken before such ethical and moral questions can be fruitfully addressed, is to get students to understand and accept that, more often than not, images used in persuasive messages both reflect and reinforce common cultural assumptions, biases, and values, and that examining these images reflectively can tell us a lot about our own culture that we might not otherwise notice.

Of all the ways in which images could be used in writing classes, writing instructors as a group are probably most comfortable with examining the ways in which images reflect and help shape current cultural assumptions. Many first-year composition readers contain articles in which cultural critics attempt to do this. Still, despite some individual success stories, getting students to analyze images for cultural assumptions can be extremely difficult. In a sense, we're asking students to step outside of themselves and to see these familiar images as strange and exotic objects. Unfortunately, the more familiar the image, the more difficult it is for students to examine it reflectively. (I've shown the image in Figure 1 to several groups of students and asked them what American values and icons were being used in it, and not one has mentioned the reference to baseball.)

One method for overcoming this difficulty is to ask students to look first at images from cultures that are foreign to them, before asking them to examine more familiar images as cultural markers. The assumption behind this method is that, once students have gained some practice looking at images from foreign cultures, experiencing those images as outsiders of the culture, it may be easier for them to then take an outsider's relatively disinterested stance when examining visuals from their own culture. However, the tendency to see a familiar image or cultural concept as transparent is a powerful one, and there is no significant amount of evidence that methods such as these can overcome the difficulty students have in analyzing images that they would normally take for granted. More effort needs to be applied to the development and assessment of methodologies that will help students make this kind of conceptual leap.

IMAGES AS RHETORICAL CONSTRUCTS

In addition to understanding the importance of images as cultural artifacts, students need to understand the psychological processes by which images persuade. Any advertiser, attorney, or political advisor—in short, anyone who engages in rhetorical practice for a living—knows that images can be extremely powerful persuasive devices. In terms used by Chaim Perelman and Lucie Olbrechts-Tyteca, including an image of an object in a persuasive appeal can enhance the "presence" of the object being represented, thereby enhancing its value or importance in the viewer's mind (117–120). Objects or ideas that are merely discussed, especially in abstract terms, have a low level of psychological presence, whereas objects or ideas that are pictured or represented in concrete, visual terms are given added presence, thereby becoming more real to the reader/viewer. "As far as possible," say Perelman and Olbrechts-Tyteca, "such an effort is directed to filling the whole field of consciousness with this presence" (118). In other words, when particular objects are given enough presence, they can crowd out other considerations from the viewer's mind, regardless of the logical force or relevance of those other considerations.

Perelman and Olbrechts-Tyteca's notion of presence is similar to what has been labeled by psychologists as the concept of *vividness*. In psychological studies, vivid information is identified as information that is emotionally interesting and concrete (Nisbett and Ross). Vivid information, which may take the form of imagistic language, personal narrative, or a representational picture, has been shown in experiments to be more persuasive than nonvivid information (Block and Keller; Smith and Shaffer; Wilson, Northcraft, and Neale). Vivid information tends to overwhelm information presented in abstract or technical language and to be given more weight than a coldly rational analysis would justify: Thus, a picture of a single starving child might move masses to action, while an abstract technical argument about crop yields and nutritional requirements might fail to instigate any action at all.

Kenneth Burke points out another way in which images can be rhetorically powerful. He claims that an evocative image is often associated in each individual's mind with "many kindred principles or ideas" and that, when referring to the image, the rhetor implicitly brings all of these ideas to bear without having to explicitly argue for their relevance (87). (Burke is discussing the use of verbal imagery, as in poetry, but his observations are undoubtedly even more true when applied to the use of actual representational images.) For example, the famous picture of U.S. Marines raising the American flag on the Pacific island of Iwo Jima (Figure 2) may instantiate in an American viewer feelings of patriotism, pride, or even nostalgia. If an institution such as a bank or insurance company includes this picture in its promotional literature, the hope is that the image and the values that it evokes in the viewer (e.g., patriotism, valor, courage, sacrifice) will become associated with the institution itself. No explicit ethical arguments need be made for why the institution might deserve to be associated with such an event and, since the relationship between the institution and the attitudes and feelings associated with the image is not explicitly stated, it is not likely to be questioned or challenged.[1]

This process of building associations between an image and a specified product, institution, political candidate, or ideological concept may be the most common way that images are used persuasively. Whether the image represents a scene from a well-known battle, a sexy model, a cuddly puppy, a beautiful sunset, or a farmer standing in his field, the objective is to prompt the viewer to associate the values and emotions that he or she feels toward the object represented in the image with the product being sold. Unfortunately, we do not yet have a well-developed pedagogy for helping students analyze and evaluate such associative arguments.

Over the past century, we have developed a variety of tools for analyzing and evaluating verbal arguments. We can take such arguments apart piece by piece and show where the flaws are. Recently, several argumentation scholars have argued that at least some persuasive images can be analyzed using the conceptual tools that have been developed to analyze verbal arguments, but J. Anthony Blair and David Fleming offer convincing refutations of that position.

FIGURE 2. U.S. Marines of the 28th Regiment of the Fifth Division Raise the American Flag atop Mt. Suribachi, Iwo Jima, on February 23, 1945

AP/Wide World Photos.

Because persuasive images are most often used, not to support arguments with logic and evidence, but to prompt viewers to develop new associations, the logical apparatus that has been developed to analyze and evaluate verbal arguments does not seem to apply to visual forms of persuasion.

The analysis of visual rhetoric does not yet have a detailed vocabulary and methodology on the scale of the ones that have been developed for the analysis and critique of persuasive verbal texts. There is, as yet, not an established and widely disseminated pedagogy for discussing persuasive images with students. But a substantial amount of theoretical work is being undertaken in a variety of fields to try to fill this gap (Walker and Chaplin 1–3), and while that work is ongoing, we can help students understand, at least in broad outline, the psychological processes that are brought to bear while interpreting and reacting to persuasive images, if only to try to build students' awareness of some basic truths about the nature of such images as rhetorical constructs (e.g., that they work through prompting the viewer to develop associations rather than through building linear, rational arguments). Concentrating on such an endeavor can provide several important benefits. First, it can help students understand that images are not just ornamental supplements to written texts, but complex texts in their own right, often relying on powerful and subtle psychological processes in order to be comprehended and to be rhetorically effective. Second, even with the relatively limited analytical tools that we have for working with images, providing students with such tools can go far toward empowering them to analyze persuasive images and to reflect on their own responses to such images — not just in the classroom, but in their daily lives as consumers, political agents, and social beings.

THE VISUAL ASPECTS OF WRITTEN TEXT

When students are faced with the task of interpreting and analyzing images in the classroom, they may resist. At the least, they will face some uncomfortable dissonance, perhaps confusion, when asked to treat images as another kind of "text." This is true for several reasons, all of which have been discussed above. First, students are simply not used to working with images in this way; both in secondary and in postsecondary education, the curriculum in the United States concentrates almost solely on written or oral modes of communication, so the act of dealing with visuals as informational and persuasive texts will be unfamiliar to most students. Second, images have been given a degraded status in our culture. Students may see a move to introduce visuals into the classroom as a "dumbing down" of the content, or they may not understand that the instructor expects serious work and sustained analysis to be applied to these types of texts. Finally, students may feel lost or inadequate when they realize that the familiar methods of analyzing verbal text cannot be applied to images.

One strategy for avoiding such obstacles and initial difficulties is to introduce visual analysis into the writing class by first demonstrating how writing itself is partly a visual medium. Too many people, including many writing instructors, think of the visual elements of written texts as mere ornamentation, or perhaps as aids to comprehension. What many people fail to understand is that visual elements are powerful and essential features of almost any written text. Even when all of the propositional content is expressed in verbal form, the design of the page or the screen on which the text resides, the relative location and proximity of textual elements, and even the font used can not only enhance readability, but be part of the message that is conveyed. Overall, the visual aspects of writing can have as much to do with the effectiveness of one's message as choosing an appropriate tone or sentence structure.

Yet general-education writing courses pay almost no attention to issues of page design. By specifying a particular format and font (almost always the default Times New Roman) in their assignments, instructors control issues of page design, and therefore pretend that these issues don't matter. But by making design elements a nonissue in our courses, we leave students unprepared to analyze visual elements as readers and to use them effectively as writers, and we implicitly send the erroneous message that these visual elements are unimportant. Now that digital technologies have given all writers the ability to easily manipulate design elements in their texts, it is past time for teachers of writing to begin to pay serious attention to the communicative and rhetorical aspects of page and screen design.

One obstacle to the teaching of text design in writing classrooms is that many writing instructors themselves have little or no background in text or page design. Changes need to be made in the education of high school teachers and university writing instructors to remedy this lack of knowledge. However, in the meantime, any writing instructor can learn enough to introduce some basic design concepts to students, if only to trigger in them an awareness that text design issues are not insignificant aspects of the rhetorical process.

There are several good introductory texts that any writing instructor could use to introduce students to text design issues, Kostelnick's and Robert's *Designing Visual Language* being a notable example. Almost any good technical writing or business writing textbook will also contain some information about design, and even first-year composition rhetorics and writing handbooks are beginning to include some information about page design (though their treatment of the subject sometimes makes an interest in design seem like an afterthought). For a basic introduction to some broad design concepts, an interested instructor could begin with Robin Williams's *The Non-Designer's Design Book*. In that book, Williams explains four basic elements of text design: proximity (manipulating and varying the amount of space between and around various text elements), contrast (using design features to indicate a hierarchy of importance among text elements), alignment (varying the alignment of text elements with different rhetorical functions), and repetition (consistently applying the same design features to text elements with similar rhetorical functions). Every general-education writing course could easily incorporate some instruction and practice in basic design elements such as these.

A simple example of how the first two of these elements can be introduced is demonstrated in Figures 3 to 6, which are variations of a title slide that I have used when giving presentations on the subject of this chapter.

FIGURE 3.

Reading the Visual in College Writing Classes
Charles Hill
Department of English
UW Oshkosh

In Figure 3, the text elements are placed together and are all in the same font and style, with no variation in proximity and no use of contrast.

FIGURE 4.

Reading the Visual in College Writing Classes

Charles Hill

Department of English
UW Oshkosh

In Figure 4, students can easily see that implementing the principle of proximity (placing elements close together or farther apart to indicate their relationships to each other) can greatly improve readability even of a very simple page and, Figure 5 demonstrates that varying the color, size, and text style of the different textual elements (thereby enhancing contrast) can increase readability even more.

FIGURE 5.

Reading the Visual in College Writing Classes

Charles Hill

Department of English
UW Oshkosh

But comparing Figures 5 and 6 demonstrates that using such format features not only increases readability, but can affect the meaning and rhetorical effectiveness of the verbal text. As my name increases in relation to the type size of the title, my sense of self-worth appears to increase, as well. I overwhelm the subject of the essay.

There may be situations in which emphasizing the speaker's name in such a fashion would be appropriate (e.g., if the speaker is a "star," likely to attract listeners by his or her very identity), but it is clear (and students can easily understand) that it would not be appropriate in many situations, and a speaker or writer who uses format elements inappropriately could elicit highly negative reactions from listeners or readers.

FIGURE 6.

Reading the Visual in College Writing Classes

Charles Hill

Department of English
UW Oshkosh

Instruction in text design need not be technical and dry—quite the opposite. In fact, I've found that even discussions about typefaces can be lively, and students enjoy the "eureka" moments that occur when they realize how much meaning is often carried by this most mundane textual element. Working from materials (advertisements, flyers, instruction manuals, labels, etc.) that they collect and bring to class, students begin by discussing the "tone" of different typefaces that they have found, until they come to some agreements about particular examples. (This usually results in vague assertions that a particular typeface seems more "playful" or "serious" or "modern" than others.)

Once students find some examples that they agree on, I have them try to determine why the writer/designer decided to use a typeface with those qualities—which necessarily involves a discussion of the writer/designer's rhetorical goals and assumptions about his or her audience. Only after this discussion do we try to determine the specific concrete elements in the typeface that might be influencing the students' judgments. In this final discussion, we touch on many concepts that experienced typeface designers would find familiar, though we might not use their technical terms.

Given the current state of word-processing programs, students can also easily practice manipulating the design elements in their own texts and instructors can use these features for a variety of creative purposes such as allowing students to experiment with typefaces, color, and design in their written work in order to express their reactions to particular texts. For instance, students who have read Mary Shelley's novel *Frankenstein* are often inspired to represent their interpretation of the novel visually through typeface choice. The first example uses a Gothic style font, illustrating the student's sense that the novel is a dark tale of dungeons and death:

FIGURE 7.

𝔉𝔯𝔞𝔫𝔨𝔢𝔫𝔰𝔱𝔢𝔦𝔫

The second typestyle choice, however, seems to indicate a more favorable view of the text as a "classic" work of literature:

FIGURE 8.

Frankenstein

Dealing with elements such as typography and page layout may be one way to begin to break down the overly rigid distinction between verbal and visual communication that characterizes both scholarly thought and commonly held assumptions in our society. Another way is to recognize and discuss the many ways in which images and text work together in contemporary communication. Examples to analyze can be found everywhere and could include business correspondence, scientific research reports, cartoons, newspaper articles, and all types of advertisements. (Figure 1 is an example in which neither the picture nor the verbal text, if offered alone, would be rhetorically effective.) Kathleen Welch argues that new electronic technologies are making the hybrid text, in which words and images work together, the dominant mode of discourse in our society (131), and Mitchell argues that nearly all texts have both a verbal and a visual element (5). A brief, random perusal of commercially published texts should be enough to convince students of the truth of these statements.

FIRST-YEAR COMPOSITION AND THE VISUAL

Welch argues convincingly that every university student should be taught to interpret, analyze, and produce texts that incorporate visual elements, and I have taken up that argument here. Welch goes on to argue that the composition classroom is the appropriate place to accomplish this, since it is the primary site "for teaching articulation and power" (134). In a more practical vein, it could be argued that, for many of our students, the general-education writing course is the only real exposure to rhetorical theory and principles that they will have. Arguably, the primary purpose of a rhetorical education is to teach students to respond to the messages that they will likely encounter in their lives as part of this culture. Given this objective, and given that so many of the communicative expressions that our students encounter are and will continue to be visual in nature, it no longer seems viable for the instructors of our students' only rhetoric course to ignore issues of visual literacy and visual rhetoric in their classes.

Another reason for placing discussions of visual communication into the writing class is that the boundary separating text from images has always been little more than a convenient fiction, and as new computer technologies become more sophisticated and more dominant, this fiction is becoming quite inconvenient. For a long time, embedding any kind of visual into one's writing was possible only for professional writers, it often involved the work of several people with distinct sets of skills, and it was a complex and expensive process. Today, anyone who uses a standard word processor can manipulate text faces, styles, sizes, and colors and easily embed graphs, drawings, photographs, and even video clips. And the World Wide Web, which is quickly becoming the standard mode of transmission for many types of texts, relies largely on visual elements for its impact and its attraction. It is true that the typical university writing assignment in many disciplines still requires no design elements beyond discrete paragraphs and a centered title. However, with the increasing availability of digital imaging technology, this situation is changing, and it will continue to change. And outside of the academy, such non-visual texts are relatively and increasingly rare. Ignoring graphics and visual design elements in writing classes, even in first-year composition, is quickly becoming anachronistic.

Still, even given all these arguments, one could reasonably ask if university writing instructors can realistically take on the task of teaching students to interpret, analyze, and produce visual texts. General-education writing courses are already typically overburdened with goals and objectives, and such courses tend to suffer from "mission creep," taking on more and more responsibilities as notions of critical literacy and empowerment continue to broaden. The goals statement for the first-year writing program at my university includes eight objectives, including the following:

- Teaching students to use new writing technologies.
- Encouraging students to interact reflectively with their peers.
- Developing students' critical reading skills.
- Teaching the conventions of academic discourse.
- Teaching students to evaluate sources of information.

And the goals statement doesn't even discuss issues that nearly everyone in the university assumes will be covered in first-year composition, including research strategies, proper citation and documentation, and grammatical and mechanical correctness. Other composition courses across the country take on tasks such as teaching students to analyze literature, raising students' critical consciousness, and teaching them to argue soundly and logically. Clearly, the expectations placed on the first-year writing course are already too great, partly as a result of our own ambitions as instructors and program coordinators, and partly because of the unrealistic expectations of others in the university community. Why, then, should instructors of such courses accept the additional task of helping students learn to interpret and analyze visual images? More important, can they do so effectively, without resulting in an incoherent and watered-down curriculum, miles wide but an inch deep? Given what writing instructors are already faced with, how can we hope to accomplish the additional tasks of helping students learn to interpret and analyze images, create their own rhetorical images, and manage the visual elements of their written texts?

A UTOPIAN PROPOSAL: THE RHETORICAL CURRICULUM

In a recent essay in the journal *Writing Program Administration*, John Trimbur addresses the problem of overburdened general-education writing courses and proposes that such courses be replaced with multidepartmental, multicourse writing *programs*. Each program would look different and involve a different set of academic departments, depending on the needs and inherent strengths present on each campus. Trimbur's proposal is a response to what many in the discipline already perceive as a set of expectations that no one university course could hope to meet.

I would go one step further, and say that we should have multidepartmental *rhetoric* programs — programs built on the recognition that writing, visual literacy, and oral communication are all essential skills, but that, in the real world, they work together in complex ways, not in isolation. Scholarship and research related to visual communication is already being accomplished on most American campuses, in departments such as art, journalism, communication, political science, and anthropology, and we can probably find colleagues in history and even literature professors in English who use visuals extensively in their classes. However, on most campuses, the only required general-education courses in rhetorical analysis or practice are in written composition and speech. Though a considerable amount of expertise exists in various areas of visual analysis and critique, students are exposed to this expertise only if they elect to take certain majors that prepare them for professional work in a related area. In other words, the only students who get exposed to principles of visual rhetoric are those who decide that their careers will largely involve the production of some form of visual communication. This leaves the rest of the students, the ones who will presumably make up the audience for these professional communicators, helpless to analyze or critique their messages. The university system is doing a good job of training a select group of students to produce persuasive visual messages. But shouldn't we be at least as concerned with helping the rest of our students respond to these messages in an informed and critical way? If we can tap into the experience, expertise, and interest in visual communication that exists across campus, then we can build a new paradigm, one that takes rhetorical education seriously and that recognizes it for the multidisciplinary endeavor that it is.

Though it may seem like a drastic step, what is needed is a bottom-up reconfiguration of the notion of rhetorical education. As with Trimbur's proposed writing program, what this reconfiguration will look like in curricular terms will vary from one campus to the next. On some campuses, it might involve sharing resources among departments such as journalism, art, and communication. On others, it might involve the creation of a new, stand-alone administrative unit. On still others, it might be accomplished solely within an existing department. What is important is that the interested people within the university work together to decide what their goals are for their students, identify the available resources on campus for achieving those goals, identify the unique set of institutional constraints that must be negotiated on their campus, and figure out the best way, given these resources and constraints, for addressing the issue of developing students' critical and rhetorical literacy in a multimedia world.

No doubt many of us with a vested interest in the general education composition program as it now stands will feel threatened by such a proposal. However, for those of us who see composition as a course in rhetoric, I think implementing such a proposal would represent a new opportunity—an opportunity to have, perhaps for the first time, a campuswide discussion about what rhetoric is, what it means to make students rhetorically aware and rhetorically proficient, and what students need to know about rhetorical theory and practice in order to thrive as citizens in the information age. Following through on this proposal would be risky because it would force us to confront the myths about first-year composition that we have profited from (such as the myth that first-year composition will "clean up" students' grammar). For perhaps the first time, we would have to lay all of our cards on the table. We should be worried only if we are not sure of our hand.

NOTE

1. A potential problem with such persuasive strategies is that the image being used may not be as familiar to a broad audience as one might expect. For instance, Messaris reports that only fourteen students in a class of twenty-nine undergraduates could name "even an approximate place and time (e.g., World War II battle) for Joe Rosenthal's original photograph of the flag-raising," one of the most famous American photographs of the twentieth century. Messaris reports similar recognition rates among U.S.-born graduate students (*Visual Persuasion* 94).

WORKS CITED

Birkerts, Sven. *The Gutenberg Elegies: The Fate of Reading in an Electronic Age*. Boston: Faber, 1994.

Blair, J. Anthony. "The Possibility and Actuality of Visual Arguments," *Argumentation and Advocacy* 33 (1996): 23–39.

Block, Lauren G., and Punam Anand Keller. "Effects of Self-Efficacy and Vividness on the Persuasiveness of Health Communications." *Journal of Consumer Psychology* 6 (1997): 31–54.

Bolter, Jay David. *Writing Space: The Computer, Hypertext, and the History of Writing*. Hillsdale, NJ: Erlbaum, 1991.

Burke, Kenneth. *A Rhetoric of Motives*. 1950. Berkeley: U of California P, 1969.

DeLillo, Don. *White Noise*. New York: Penguin, 1991.

Elkins, James. *The Domain of Images*. Ithaca: Cornell UP, 1999.

Fleming, David. "Can Pictures Be Arguments?" *Argumentation and Advocacy* 33 (1996): 11–22.

Fox, Roy F. "Image Studies: An Interdisciplinary View." *Images in Language, Media, and Mind*. Ed. Roy F. Fox. Urbana: NCTE 1994. 3–20.

Kostelnick, Charles, and David D. Roberts. *Designing Visual Language: Strategies for Professional Communicators*. Boston: Allyn, 1997.

Kress, Gunther, and Theo van Leeuwen. *Reading Images: The Grammar of Visual Design*. London: Routledge, 1996.

McQuade, Donald, and Christine McQuade. *Seeing & Writing*. Boston: Bedford/St. Martin's, 2000.

Messaris, Paul. *Visual Persuasion: The Role of Images in Advertising*. Thousand Oaks, CA: Sage, 1997.

Mitchell, W. J. T. *Picture Theory: Essays on Verbal and Visual Representation*. Chicago: U of Chicago P, 1994.

"NCTE Passes Visual Literacy Resolution." *Kairos* 2.1 (1997). 31 August 2000 <http://english.ttu.edu/kairos/2.1/news/briefs/nctevis.html>.

Nisbett, Richard E., and Lee Ross. *Human Inference: Strategies and Shortcomings of Social Judgment.* Englewood Cliffs, NJ: Prentice-Hall, 1980.

Perelman, Chaim, and L. Olbrechts-Tyteca. *The New Rhetoric: A Treatise on Argumentation.* Trans. John Wilkinson and Purcell Weaver. Notre Dame, IN: U of Notre Dame P, 1971.

Purves, Alan C. *The Web of Text and the Web of God.* New York: Guilford, 1998.

Smith, Stephen M., and David R. Shaffer. "Vividness Can Undermine or Enhance Message Processing: The Moderating Role of Vividness Congruency." *Personality and Social Psychology Bulletin* 26 (2000): 769–79.

Stafford, Barbara Maria, *Good Looking: Essays on the Virtue of Images.* Cambridge: MIT P, 1997.

Stroupe, Craig. "Visualizing English: Recognizing the Hybrid Literacy of Visual and Verbal Authorship on the Web." *College English* 62 (2000): 607–32.

Trimbur, John. "The Problem of Freshman English (Only): Toward Programs of Study in Writing." *Writing Program Administration* 22.3 (1999): 9–30.

Walker, John A., and Sarah Chaplin. *Visual Culture: An Introduction.* Manchester: Manchester UP, 1997.

Weaver, Richard M. *The Ethics of Rhetoric.* 1953. Davis, CA: Hermagoras, 1985.

Welch, Kathleen E. *Electric Rhetoric: Classical Rhetoric, Oralism, and a New Literacy.* Cambridge: MIT P, 1999.

Williams, Robin. *The Non-Designer's Design Book.* Berkeley, CA: Peachpit, 1994.

Wilson, Marie G., Gregory B. Northcraft, and Margaret A. Neale. "Information Competition and Vividness Effects in On-Line Judgments." *Organizational Behavior and Human Decision Processes* 44 (1989): 132–39.

Worth, Sol, and Larry Gross. "Symbolic Strategies." *Studying Visual Communication.* Ed. Larry Gross. Philadelphia: U of Pennsylvania P, 1981. 134–47.

PART TWO

The Rhetoric of the Image

Introduction to Part Two

The essays in this section focus on the visual at its most basic level, the picture, as a way to clarify visual theory and visual rhetoric in practice. Images communicate powerfully whether they function on their own, in relation to words, or in multimediated forms combining images, words, and sounds. But what is the source of this power? Working from various disciplinary perspectives and analytic angles, including the psychology of art, semiotics, graphic design, science, cartoon illustration, and art history, the readings here can help us answer this question by exploring the ways in which images communicate, both similarly to and differently from, words. They also help us to think about how images communicate in combination with words and to identify a possible grammar and rhetoric belonging specifically to images. Finally, the essays push us to consider whether different types of images or images presented in different media, such as painting, illustration, photography, scientific diagrams, advertisements, films, and cartoons, function in distinguishable but predictable ways.

Understanding exactly how images function rhetorically and the specific visual "grammars" they use to operate will allow us to develop a composition pedagogy that empowers students to become more sophisticated viewers and producers of the kinds of hybrid texts emerging in the digital age. A visual rhetoric could help our students understand asyndetic (or associative) forms of argument where otherwise "missing" conjunctions could be supplied iconically by images or graphic elements. In other words, visual elements could serve as transitional links between concepts or ideas. They could also compare ideas or show parallel, hierarchical, subordinate, or coordinate relationships — all structural manifestations of critical thinking skills that form the basis of rhetoric. For example, graphic elements and images used throughout Web texts to inform readers may work metaphorically or metonymically.

Writing in 1969, professor of Psychology of Art, Rudolph Arnheim provides a classic and helpful introduction to the rhetoric of the image in "Pictures, Symbols, and Signs." Devising a scheme for each of these three types of images, Arnheim discusses a wide sampling of image types from seventeenth-century Dutch landscape paintings to figure drawings in novels, scientific drawings, surrealist paintings, street signs, and more. For the author, a predictable relation exists between the level of visual complexity or abstraction of the image itself and the complexity or abstraction of the concept represented by that image. Arnheim contends that images, far from serving as mere illustrations for complex ideas stated in words, can convey these difficult, even abstract ideas on their own. He also invites us to think in rhetorical terms about the effect of images that "depict" versus those that "symbolize."

Arnheim's piece raises questions about the levels on which the images in our multimediated texts operate today. Do our hybrid texts incorporate images that do little justice to the complexity of their verbal elements? By analyzing images in the ways Arnheim outlines and gauging their rhetorical impact, can we construct more intellectual or visually intelligent hybrid texts than those we are accustomed to creating? Do we think about the degree of abstraction existing in or needed for images included in hybrid texts? According to Arnheim, finally, the nature of a given culture's images have serious implications. To him, a society that privileges one kind of image making over another (for instance, abstraction over realism, or vice versa) likely suffers from an unhealthy imbalance of thought in relation to feeling. Understanding the visual, then, is critical as a way to discern and insure a culture's psychological well-being.

"Rhetoric of the Image," published in 1977 by the noted semiotician Roland Barthes, lays a foundation for any critical work examining images in their cultural contexts. He begins by asking the question: "How does meaning get into the image?" He notes how a visual image's precise meaning can be difficult to guarantee in the absence of a verbal "anchor" and then distinguishes carefully between types of visuals and the messages they communicate: A pure image presented on its own is essentially denotative, an image presented in conjunction with words offers a linguistic message that is both denotative and connotative, and semiotic signifiers are connotative and heavily cultural. One of Barthes' fundamental points is that in the vast majority of cases, cultures work hard to assure that images do not simply connote, but are clearly anchored, "denoted" either by verbal text or cultural context, so that their connotative powers do not exert unpredictable effects on their audiences. For Barthes, the classic instance of the "denoted image" is the magazine photo advertisement designed to maximize simultaneous connotative visual (ideological) and denotative verbal power.

Hanno Ehses's "Representing Macbeth: A Case Study in Visual Rhetoric" moves us through theory into practice. The author, a professor of design, considers rhetoric surprisingly adaptable to design curricula and worth considering in regard to images. Visual rhetoric for Ehses is thus not just an intellectual possibility but a professional necessity: Designers need to study rhetoric and its figures as intellectual tools that can help create graphic structures built on higher levels of thought, persuasion, and eloquence. Ehses' selection includes charts of phrases and figures from classical rhetoric and thought-provoking visual portrayals of rhetorical figures as they appear in different theater posters constructed by design students to illustrate

Shakespeare's play *Macbeth*. The visual portrayals of ten figures are divided into four classes: contrast (or antithesis and irony); resemblance (or metaphor and personification); contiguity (or metonymy, synechdoche, periphrasis, and puns); and gradation (or amplification and hyperbole). Ehses demonstrates that the exercise of asking students to think through the abstract categories of classical rhetoric and the concrete visualizations of graphic design proved a source of great creativity rather than a stifling, artificial assignment. Developing an expertise in rhetorical figures increased the students' awareness of the number of creative options available to them.

Students working in the scientific disciplines need to appreciate the rhetoric of images just as much as those in the arts and humanities. In "The Role of Abstraction in Scientific Illustration," Punyashloke Mishra approaches the study of images as a science educator. Mishra analyzes the pedagogical function of scientific illustrations to show that these images, as representations of particular concepts, carry histories as well as particular cultural and ideological biases. Mishra surveys the landscape of work from the psychology of art (including that of Rudolph Arnheim) to the sociology of scientific knowledge and then reminds us that we need to account for individual differences in perception when we consider how images function pedagogically in scientific contexts. Novices and experts "see" differently when examining or drawing scientific diagrams.

While focusing on scientific images, Mishra introduces concepts that are crucial for studying the rhetoric of the image. In order to understand how images speak to us and why we may or may not grasp the ideas they are attempting to portray, we must acknowledge three important concepts. (1) Illustrations follow and depend on conventions so that we can understand them. (2) Illustrations fall within disciplinary matrices encapsulating particular biases and building on assumptions commonly held at particular historic times. (3) Illustrations are "handed down"; that is, later generations reproduce an earlier generation's illustrations and, in the reproduction, "recopy" the images but insert changes that bring the image closer to prevalent social ideals. Mishra offers one particularly interesting example from an article by Stephen Jay Gould comparing dinosaur iconology of the Victorian age to dinosaur iconology today. The Victorian illustrations represented predatory scenes of lumbering animals while today's images show herding scenes and scenes of familial cooperation and caring by sleek and elegant creatures. The preferences of an age infuse images; in other words, images are ideological. The rhetoric of the image needs to delineate ways to account for such ideology when we teach our students to analyze images.

Comic books, with their interplay of icons, symbols, typography, space, and caricature, offer yet another way to understand the rhetoric of images. The excerpt from "The Vocabulary of Comics" by cartoonist Scott McCloud shows how cartoons, by simplifying an image, can amplify ideas in ways that realistic pictures cannot. McCloud not only helps us to understand how images impart ideas but also offers brief examples of cartoon styles that have arisen in different countries and analyzes their particular effects. McCloud's insistence that cartoons are not simply frivolous forms of drawings intended for children echoes the call by other readings in this chapter to take images seriously as a form of communication. He suggests that in a visual and "increasingly symbol-oriented" world, comics and iconography could approach a universal language. In fact, it is the very simplicity of comics that may make them an ideal medium through which to introduce composition students to the logic of hybrid rhetorical forms and to impress on them the considerable rhetorical power of abstraction.

Art historian Barbara Stafford labels "Visual Pragmatism for a Virtual World," her introductory chapter to the volume *Good Looking*, a manifesto. Stafford's arguments provide a fitting end to this section examining the image and its rhetoric: Stafford urges humanities scholars still unwilling to regard the visual as anything but ancillary and superficial to think differently about images or become academically anachronistic. In the wake of the visual blitz effected by technology's ubiquity, her appeal rings even more insistently. Stafford's strong language challenges students and teachers of both the visual and the verbal to abandon concepts that only work to impede our ability to function intelligently in this visual world. Stafford, most importantly, challenges teachers to reconceptualize education, to remake our curricula. Her stance toward the visual in our culture is thus, above all, a practical one because she faces the implications of visual technology's explosion head on. Stafford argues for more interdisciplinary or multidisciplinary study, as does the cumulative argument weaving through the other articles collected here. "I believe," she says, "we must finally renounce the institutionalized notion that only the 'pure' study of anything, including images . . . is admirable." The question remaining is whether or not the practitioners of these inherited proclivities and disciplines are prepared to face such a new reality.

7 Pictures, Symbols, and Signs

RUDOLPH ARNHEIM

Simple line drawings can give visible shape to patterns of forces or other structural qualities. The drawings in the preceding chapter* described the nature of a good or bad marriage or of democracy or of youth as conceived by the person who drew them. Highly abstract social or psychological configurations appeared in visible shape. However, images can also depict the things of our environment themselves, for example, a husband and a wife or a town meeting in a democracy. They commonly do so in a style that is more abstract than the way these persons, objects, or happenings would register on a photographic plate. Images, then, regard the world in two opposite directions. They hover somewhere above the realm of "practical" things and below the disembodied forces animating these things. They can be said to mediate between the two.

THREE FUNCTIONS OF IMAGES

In order to clarify and compare various relations of images to their referents I shall distinguish between three functions performed by images. Images can serve as pictures or as symbols; they can also be used as mere signs. This sort of distinction has been made by many writers on the subject. Some have used the same terms or similar ones, but the meanings they have given them overlap complexly with the distinctions I need for our purpose. Instead of analyzing these similarities and differences, I shall try to define the three terms so tangibly that the reader will know what I mean by them.

The three terms—picture, symbol, sign—do not stand for kinds of images. They rather describe three functions fulfilled by images. A particular image may be used for each of these functions and will often serve more than one at the same time. As a rule, the image itself does not tell which function

From *Visual Thinking*. Berkeley: U of California P, 1969. 135–144.
*The drawings and chapter mentioned in this selection can be found in the original volume from which this chapter is reprinted.

is intended. A triangle may be a sign of danger or a picture of a mountain or a symbol of hierarchy. We need to know how well or badly various kinds of images fulfill these functions.

An image serves merely as a *sign* to the extent to which it stands for a particular content without reflecting its characteristics visually. In the strictest sense it is perhaps impossible for a visual thing to be nothing but a sign. Portrayal tends to slip in. The letters of the alphabet used in algebra come close to being pure signs. But even they stand for discrete entities by *being* discrete entities: a and b portray twoness. Otherwise, however, they do not resemble the things they represent in any way, because further specification would distract from the generality of the proposition. On the other hand, signs possess visual characteristics derived from requirements other than those of portrayal, that is to say, they appear as they do for good reasons. The 1926 international convention on road signs decided that all traffic signs warning of danger should be given a triangular shape. Perhaps the sharpness of a triangle makes it look a bit more like danger than would, say, a circle, but its shape was chosen mainly because it is easily identified in itself and distinguished from other signs. In written language, the variety of letter groups used to designate words serves similar purposes of identification and distinction, and therefore letters and words are, to this extent, signs. Many words fail to fulfill their function well because languages are not created rationally but grow informally and produce accidental, arbitrary, adulterated shapes. Words can be ambiguous; for example, *pupil* refers to schoolchildren and to holes in the eyes, since the original connotation of smallness has been split up into different meanings. Apart from such imperfections, however, the characteristics of signs tend to be selected in such a way as to serve their function. In this sense, they are not arbitrary. The previously mentioned "innate releasing mechanisms" in biology are signs. Konrad Lorenz says of these visual releasers that their simplicity of shape and color makes them distinct in appearance and "improbable" in occurrence, that is, unlikely to be confused with other things visible in the environment.

To the extent to which images are signs they can serve only as indirect media, for they operate as mere references to the things for which they stand. They are not analogues, and therefore they cannot be used as media for thought in their own right. This will become evident in the discussion of numerals and verbal languages, which are the sign media *par excellence*.

Images are *pictures* to the extent to which they portray things located at a lower level of abstractness than they are themselves. They do their work by grasping and rendering some relevant qualities—shape, color, movement—of the objects or activities they depict. Pictures are not mere replicas, by which I mean faithful copies that differ from the model only by random imperfections.

A picture can dwell at the most varied levels of abstractness. A photograph or a Dutch landscape of the seventeenth century may be quite lifelike and yet select, arrange, and almost unnoticeably stylize its subject in such a way that it focuses on some of the subject's essence. On the other hand, a totally non-mimetic geometrical pattern by Mondrian may be intended as a picture of the turmoil of New York's Broadway. A child may capture the character of a human figure or a tree by a few highly abstract circles, ovals, or straight lines.

Abstractness is a means by which the picture interprets what it portrays. This precious accomplishment is ignored if one pretends that an abbreviated representation invites the beholder to fill in the missing realistic detail. If this were true, a simply drawn cartoon or caricature would produce a particularly active response of this kind. The assertion is based on no evidence; it is simply inferred from the traditional notion that perception consists in a complete recording of the visual field and that therefore a percept of "incomplete" material will be completed by the mind from the stores of past experience. If this were so, all pictures would be transformed subjectively by the beholder into mechanically faithful replicas. The "incompleteness" would be remedied. But abstractness is not incompleteness. A picture is a statement about visual qualities, and such a statement can be complete at any level of abstractness. To be sure, when the picture is incomplete, imprecise, or ambiguous with regard to these abstract qualities, the observer is called upon to make his own decisions about what he sees. (This is true, for instance, for the inkblots of the Rorschach Test or the pictures of the Thematic Apperception Test, used by psychologists to induce subjective interpretations.)

Fortunately, "completion" by "imagination" is all but impossible and the desire to attempt it quite rare. A cartoon is seen at exactly the level at which it is drawn. Its forceful liveliness does not derive from supplements contributed by the observer but is made possible, on the contrary, by the intense visual dynamics of simplified line and color. It is true that the abstract style of such pictures removes their subject matter from physical reality. Human traits and impulses appear, unencumbered by physical matter and free from the tyranny of gravitation and bodily frailty. A blow on the head is an abstract assault responded to by an equally abstract expression of distress. In other words, the pictorial interpretation emphasizes the generic qualities with which all thinking is concerned — a kind of unreality quite different from that of miraculous, superhuman tales, which are generally represented with realistic faithfulness. The latter endow nonexistent forces with material bodies whereas the former extract constituent forces from physical substance.

An image acts as a *symbol* to the extent to which it portrays things which are at a higher level of abstractness than is the symbol itself. A symbol gives particular shape to types of things or constellations of forces. Any image is, of course, a particular thing, and by standing for a kind of thing it serves as a symbol, e.g., if it presents a dog in order to show what the concept *dog* is. In principle, any specimen or replica of a specimen can serve as a symbol, if somebody chooses to use it that way. But in such cases, the image leaves the effort of abstracting entirely to the user. It does not help him by focusing on relevant features. Works of art do better. For example, Ambrogio Lorenzetti's murals in the town hall of Siena symbolize the ideas of good and bad government by showing scenes of struggle and of prosperous harmony; and being works of art, they do so by inventing, selecting and shaping these scenes in ways that display the relevant qualities more purely than random views of town and country life would. Or, to use another example, Holbein's portrait of Henry VIII is a picture of the king, but it also serves as a symbol of kingship and of qualities such as brutality, strength, exuberance, which are located at a higher level of abstraction than is the painting. The painting, in turn, is more abstract than the visual appearance of the king in flesh and blood because it sharpens the formal features of shape and color which are analogues of the symbolized qualities.

Symbolic functions can also be fulfilled by highly abstract images. The amateur drawings I discussed in the preceding chapter gave visible geometrical shape to the dynamic patterns characterizing ideas or institutions. The arrows by which physicists depict vectors show relevant qualities of forces, namely, their strength, direction, sense, and point of application. Musical notation operates partly by means of symbols; that is, it represents the pitch level of sounds by the structurally analogous location of the notes on the staff. In a similar way, drawings can symbolize a state of mind by translating some of its dynamic properties into visible patterns. Figure 1 shows a page from Sterne's *Tristram Shandy*, depicting the hero's straightforward intention modulated by a more or less erratic spirit.

FIGURE 1.

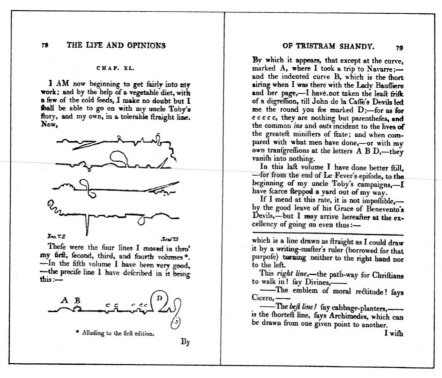

IMAGES TO SUIT THEIR FUNCTIONS

Since images can be made at any level of abstraction, it is worth asking how well different degrees of abstractness suit the three functions here under discussion. I will limit myself to a few examples taken from the two extremities of the scale of abstraction. How about highly realistic images? As mentioned before, mere replicas may be useful as raw material for cognition but are produced by cognitive acts of the lowest order and do not, by themselves, guide understanding. Paradoxically, they may even make identification difficult, because to identify an object means to recognize some of its salient structural features. A mechanically produced replica may hide or distort these features. One of the reasons why persons brought up in cultures that are unacquainted with photography have trouble with our snapshots is that the realistic and accidental detail and partial shapelessness of such images do not help perception. It is a problem we shall meet again when we look at the so-called visual aids in education. Faithfulness and realism are terms to be used with caution because a bona fide likeness may fail to present the beholder with the essential features of the objects represented.

The human mind can be forced to produce replicas of things, but it is not naturally geared to it. Since perception is concerned with the grasping of significant form, the mind finds it hard to produce images devoid of that formal virtue. In fact, it is by the structural properties of lines and colors that even some "material" desires are best satisfied. For example, the mechanical faithfulness of artless color photography or painting is not the surest way of arousing sexual stimulation through the sense of sight. Sensuous pleasure is aroused more effectively by the smoothness of swelling curves, the tension animating the shapes of breasts and thighs. Without the dominance of these expressive forces the picture is reduced to the presentation of pure matter. To offer matter devoid of form, which is the perceptual carrier of meaning, is pornography in the only valid sense of the word, namely, a breach of man's duty to perceive the world intelligently. A harlot (Greek, *porné*) is a person who offers body without spirit.

As symbols, fairly realistic images have the advantage of giving flesh and blood to the structural skeletons of ideas. They convey a sense of lifelike presence, which is often desirable. But they may be inefficient otherwise because the objects they represent are, after all, only part-time symbols. A newspaper reported that one day, some time ago, the Reverend January of the Zion Hill Baptist Church in Detroit took his four-year-old son, Stanley, to view a large mural, which had just been painted in the auditorium of a local school. "I see a train," said Stanley. "That track," said the Reverend January, "is the future coming toward us. The train is this country's unity, far off but bearing down on us." "No," said Stanley, "it's a train."

This disagreement between father and son arose because a train is not a full-time symbol. It is a piece of railway equipment, first of all, and acts as a symbol only by moonlighting—as an avocation, not advertised and therefore not necessarily recognized by the four-year-olds of our time nor by quite a few of their elders. The more lifelike a piece of sculpture or painting, the more difficult may the artist find it to make his point symbolically. Courbet's painting, *L'Atélier*, of 1855, presented groups of realistically painted persons surrounding the artist himself at work in his studio. The painting was subtitled *une allégorie réelle* and intended to show on one side the people of the practical life and on the other those concerned with feeling and thought, both equally arrested in a state of dreamlike suspension, while the painter alone, vigorously at work on a canvas, held the center as the only person actively dealing with reality. Werner Hofmann, in an extensive analysis of this painting, mentions that "the realists felt the allegorical implications to be superfluous, the symbolists thought them out of keeping with the very robustness of the style." Only by a careful and unprejudiced examination of the whole painting will the viewer come to realize that, for example, the nude woman watching the artist at work in his studio is not only his model, at the realistic level of the representation, but also the muse, the traditional allegory of truth, the fullness of life, all at the same time.

The dilemma becomes particularly poignant when an artist aspires to fantasy and deeper meaning but lacks the pictorial imagination to make such qualities visible. Examples can be found among the more pedestrian Surrealists. There is a painting by René Magritte showing a tediously painted tobacco pipe on empty ground and the inscription: *Ceci n'est pas une pipe.* Unfortunately a pipe is all it is. A similar problem arises from the unskillful use of *objets trouvés* in collages or sculpture. The beholder is confronted with the untransfigured presence of refuse. What he sees may inspire him to think, but the thought is not in the work. Yet, Picasso can evoke the very nature of a bull's head by simply combining the handlebar and the saddle of an old bicycle.

The more particular a concept, the greater the competition among its traits for the attention of the user. This becomes evident when traffic signs, posters, and similar pictorial indicators try to symbolize a limited point by means of a complex image. Martin Krampen has pointed to the example of a snail used in an older pictographic traffic sign to call for a reduction of speed. The fairly lifelike picture of the snail may indeed engage the driver's mind more vividly than the message "Reduce Speed," but Krampen notes that a snail is not only slow but also slimy, easily frightened, etc. Of course, the highway setting helps in picking out the relevant aspect, but the image itself offers no guidance for the selection.

The specificity of an image also calls for correspondingly specific knowledge in the person who is to understand it. Rudolf Modley notes that a traffic sign showing a pedestrian in Western clothing may be puzzling or unwelcome to drivers in a non-Western country and that the picture of an old-fashioned locomotive may let a driver of the young generation expect a museum of historical railroad engines rather than a crossing. Specific characterization can make it easier to identify the particular kind of thing if it is known to the observer but harder to draw forth a more abstract meaning.

At the other extremity of the scale of abstraction are highly stylized, often purely geometrical shapes. They have the advantage of singling out particular properties with precision. A simple arrow concentrates more efficiently on pointing than does a realistically drawn Victorian hand with fingernails, sleeve, cuff, and buttons. The arrow is also more nearly a full-time symbol and therefore invites the beholder to treat it as a statement rather than a piece of the practical world. However, highly abstract concepts, although narrow in intention, are broad in extension, that is, they can refer to many things. A drawing of two overlapping circles may be a picture of some physical object such as a new type of pretzel or eyeglasses. It may be the ground-plan for a two-ring circus. It may also be a symbol of a good marriage or the brotherhood of nations. Still more generically, it may be meant to show the logical relation of any two overlapping concepts. Which of these meanings is aimed at, only the context can reveal.

This creates a problem in a civilization which constantly throws things together that do not belong together or puts them in places contradictory to their function. All the mobility, transportation, transmission, and communication in our century removes things from their natural location and thereby interferes with their identification and efficiency. An apple makes its point more easily when seen in an orchard or fruit store. Placed in the company of hundreds of other household items, or advertised in the midst of heterogeneous matter, or talked about in places that have no relevance to fruit, the apple must make a much greater effort to be recognized and responded to. A palace or church crowning a hilltop town or introduced by an imposing vista, a triumphal arch placed at the crossing of a star of avenues are defined and helped by their location; whereas a traditional church building buried among New York skyscrapers not only receives no help but is refuted and derided by its setting. We pay for lack of redundancy in the environment by spending a greater effort on identifying the particular item or on making it identifiable.

A highly abstract design that bears little or no obvious resemblance to its referent must be restricted to a unique application or rely heavily on explanatory context. It is the context that will decide whether a cross is to be read as a religious or an arithmetical sign or symbol or whether no semantic function at all is intended, as in the crossbars of a window. It may take a powerful and prolonged effort to endow a simple design with a particular meaning, and even the most determined indoctrination may not exclude unwelcome associations. I remember that when Hitler visited Mussolini's Rome and the whole city was suddenly covered with Nazi flags an Italian girl exclaimed in horror: "Rome is crawling with black spiders."

The simple design of the swastika was sufficiently free of other associations to make it acceptable as a carrier of a new meaning. The imposition was so effective that in time the emblem came visually to contain and exude a highly emotional connotation it did not possess before. To be sure, the design was extremely well chosen. It met the ethological requirements of distinctness and striking simplicity. It conveyed the dynamics of the "Movement" by its tilted orientation in space. The black figure in a white and red setting helped revive the colors of the German Empire and thereby appealed to nationalism. In the Nazi flag, red became the color of revolution, and the black was frightening like the storm-troopers' shirts. The swastika had the straight-edged angularity of Prussian efficiency, and its clean geometry was, ironical-ly, in keeping with the modern taste for functional design. For the educated, there was also the reference to the Aryan race evoked by the symbol from India. The pressures of the social context did the rest. No wonder a recent writer, Jay Doblin, has credited Hitler, "the frustrated artist," with having become "the trademark designer of the century."

WHAT TRADEMARKS CAN TELL

Commercial trademark designers cannot rely on the powerful social forces that were at Hitler's command. What makes their task all the more difficult is that in most cases they cannot make their designs self-explanatory. The taste and style of our time associates successful business with clean-cut, starkly reduced shape, and the disorder and rapidity of modern living calls for stim-uli of split-second efficiency. The problem is that a pattern of high abstract-ness fails to specify its referent, whereas the identification of a particular company, brand, institution, idea, is the purpose of advertising. Doblin cites experiments to show that the "logotype," that is, the verbal name or slogan presented in commercial design, is identified by consumers more readily than the brandmark. In fact, the presence of the brandmark may decrease the num-ber of correct responses to the logotype. Doblin concludes that "from a com-munications viewpoint a brandmark, for most companies, is not only a waste of time but can actually become a detriment." Whatever the validity of this argument, it illustrates the peculiar character of highly abstract patterns.

The inability of such patterns to specify a particular application brings to mind similar findings in experiments on the meaning of music. For example, in order to determine whether the "intentions of composers" can be gathered from their works, Melvin G. Rigg played a number of recordings, taken most-ly from classical opera, and asked listeners to match them with descriptions listed on a questionnaire as to their generic mood (sorrowful, joyful), their overall subject category (death, religion, love, etc.), and their specific program (farewell, prayer, Good Friday music, spinning song, moonlight, etc.). The lis-teners did well at the highest level of abstraction but poorly at the lowest. To conclude from that, as Rigg did, "that the intentions of composers usually do not 'get over' in any specific way to the cultural strata of our population" is to misinterpret the nature of music and its relation to specific program content. The cognitive virtue of music derives precisely from the high level of abstract-ness at which it depicts patterns of forces. These patterns in themselves do not point to any particular "application" but can be made to interpret such instances. Program music, the portrayal of narrative subject matter by sounds, has never been more than an awkward curiosity, exactly because it attempts to depict a particular content through a generic medium. Inversely, in an opera or as accompaniment to a theater play or film, music serves to give shape to the generic inherent in the particular. In the words of Schopenhauer, "music demonstrates here its power and higher aptitude by offering the deepest, ultimate, and most secret revelations about the feelings expressed in the words or the action which the opera represents, and discloses their proper and true essence. Music acquaints us with the intimate soul of the happenings and events of which the stage gives us no more than the husk and body."

Visual images have similar virtues and weaknesses. Just as Saint-Saëns' music cannot hope to identify *Omphale's Spinning Wheel*, trademarks and other such emblems cannot identify a particular product or producer. Identification can only be obtained by what the men in the trade call "strong penetration," that is, insistent re-inforcement of the association of signifier and referent, as exemplified by religious emblems (Cross, Star of David), flag designs (Canada's maple leaf, Japan's rising sun), or the Red Cross. Therefore, to test the value of trademarks independently of the context that ties them to their owners is like evaluating a diagram on the classroom blackboard without reference to the professor's explanatory speech.

The color blue a lady is wearing may be experienced by an observer as an essential feature of her personality; but that color by itself may in no way invoke the image of the lady. Thus, a good trademark can strengthen the individual character of its wearer by a striking sensory supplement without evoking that reference by itself. When I meet the trademark designed by Francesco Saroglia for the International Wool Secretariat (Figure 2) I may not identify it, because its supple, flexible, smooth shapes portray a very generic quality. It has an elegance deliberately chosen to counteract the connotation of stodgy tweeds, but it is not specific to wool. In the proper context, the simple design focuses on these essential and desirable properties in a tangible, concentrated fashion, helpful to the intended message.

A good modern trademark interprets the character of its wearer by associating it with sharply defined patterns of visual forces. The well-known emblem of the Chase Manhattan Bank designed by Chermayeff and Geismar may serve as an example (Figure 3). The inner square and the outer octagon produce a centrically symmetrical figure, conveying the sense of repose, compactness, solidity. Closed like a fortress against interference and untouched by the changes and vicissitudes of time, the little monument is built of sturdy

FIGURE 2.   FIGURE 3.

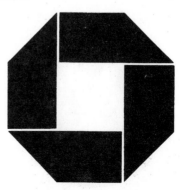

blocks defined by parallel straight edges and simple angles. At the same time, it has the necessary vitality and goal-directedness. The pointed units contribute dynamic forces which, however, do not displace the figure as a whole but are confined within the stable, directionless framework. The antagonistic movements compensate each other to an overall enlivened stillness or add up to the steady, contained rotation of a motor. Furthermore, the four components are tightly fitted into the whole but at the same time preserve an integrity of their own, thus showing multiplicity of initiative, executed by elements, whose individuality is limited, however, to a difference of position in the whole. In addition, the figure is usefully ambiguous in the connection of the four elements. Seen as right-angular blocks with a corner clipped off, the four fit each other like bricks in a wall. Seen as four symmetrical prisms they overlap each other and thereby interlock. The delicate balance between adjoining each other and interacting with each other by cooperative clasp further illustrates the nature of the internal organization.

To some extent, so highly abstract an image will always have the chill of remoteness. It cannot give the sensuous fluffiness of wool conveyed by a good color photograph or realistic painting. It cannot show the bustle of the bank, its people, its splendid halls. On the other hand, it need not limit itself to the mere identification of relevant structural properties. Any design has dynamic qualities, which contribute to characterizing the object. Simple shapes can evoke the expressive qualities of suppleness or vitality or harmony. This sort of evocation is indispensable in art. The emblems here discussed dwell curiously between art and the cognitive functions of mere identification and distinction. An emblem may be a perfectly acceptable analogue of the referent for which it stands, and yet it may not intend to evoke its dynamic impact or not succeed in doing it.

This is particularly evident when the referent has strong emotional connotations. Figures 4 and 5 give two examples, the one Ernst Roch's proposal of an emblem for the Canadian World's Fair of 1967, the other designed by Saul Bass for the Committee for a Sane Nuclear Policy. Both are most distinctive and display attractive intelligence in reducing the objects they depict to simply defined visual patterns. Roch's design, in which Leonardo's famous

FIGURE 4.   FIGURE 5.

drawing of the Vitruvian man reverberates, was intended to illustrate the theme of the exhibition: Man and His World. Bass shows protective hands trying to contain an atomic explosion. While both designs focus on essential elements of their subject matter with great precision, Roch's terrestrial globe does not attempt to convey a sense of vastness, and there is no real reaching, embracing, or upholding in the arms, no power in the straddled legs. Similarly in the Bass emblem, the exploding fragments have little destructive power, and the hands may not look actively protective to some observers.

This reduction of expressive dynamics to a mere hint may be exactly appropriate. The principal function of an emblem is not that of a work of art. A painting or piece of sculpture is intended to evoke the impact of a configuration of forces, and the references to the subject matter of a work are only a means to that end. Inversely a design, meant to serve identification and distinction, uses dynamic expression mainly for this principal purpose; just as the three strokes of the Chinese character for "mountain" hint not only at peaks but also at their rising and thereby make the reference a bit more lively. Of course, even the most sober and neutral design can unleash violent passion through the meaning associated with it. But the dynamics inherent in a visual object—in a Baroque painting, for instance—is one thing; the emotions released by it—such as by hammer and sickle—are quite another.

EXPERIENCE INTERACTING WITH IDEAS

Pictorial analogues, I said earlier, fulfill a mediating position between the world of sensory experience and the disembodied forces underlying the objects and events of that experience. A portrait by Rembrandt is a picture, interpreting a particular inhabitant of Amsterdam as a kind of person, characterized by a particular pattern of physical and psychical forces—a man, let us say, battered but upright, vigilant but thoughtful. At the same time, the unknown man from a past century is of lasting interest as a symbol because his image gives animated appearance to those more abstract qualities of oppression and resistance, outward-directedness and inner containment. The same is true for a good "abstract," i.e., non-mimetic work of art. Since it does not portray the external shape of physical objects, it is closer to the pure forces it presents symbolically; but it portrays at the same time the inherent nature of the things and events of the world and thereby maintains its relevance to human life on earth. In sum, every pictorial analogue performs the task of reasoning by fusing sensory appearance and generic concepts into one unified cognitive statement.

How essential it is that these two aspects of the image should complement each other constantly, not only in the arts but everywhere in human thinking, has been pointed out by Goethe in an eloquent passage of his *Theory of Color:*

> With regard to figurative speech and indirect expression, poetry has great advantage over all the other ways of language. It can use any image, any relation to suit its own character and convenience. It compares the spiritual with the physical and vice versa: thought with

lightning, lightning with thought, whereby the interdependence of the matters of our world [das Wechselleben der Weltgegenstände] is expressed in the best way. Philosophy, too, in its climactic moments, needs indirect expressions and figurative speech, as witnessed by its use of symbolism, which we have often mentioned, both censuring and defending it. Unfortunately, history tells us that the philosophical schools, depending on the manner and approach of their founders and principal teachers, suffer from employing one-sided symbols in order to express and master the whole. In particular, some of them insist on describing the physical by spiritual symbols while others want physical symbols for the spiritual. In this fashion, subjects are never worked through; instead, a disjunction comes about in what is to be represented and defined and therefore also a discrepancy among those concerned with it. In consequence, ill will is created on both sides and a partisan spirit establishes itself.

There are paintings and sculptures that portray figures, objects, actions in a more or less realistic style, but indicate that they are not to be taken at their face value. They make no sense as reports on what goes on in life on earth, but are intended primarily as symbolic vehicles of ideas. The beholder is overcome by the uncanny feeling of which Hegel speaks with regard to the symbolism of ancient oriental art: "Wir fühlen, dass wir unter Aufgaben wandeln" (We have the sensation of wandering among tasks.) Since the picture does not simply interpret life, the beholder faces the task of telling what it symbolizes. Picasso's early painting *La Vie* is called by Wilhelm Boeck a tribute to the secularized philosophical symbolism of art around the turn of the century. Boeck describes this representation of "Life" as follows:

A barefoot woman is standing at the right, her serious face in profile, with a sleeping infant in the folds of her draped garment. At the left stands the graceful nude of a young couple, seeking each other's protection as though suddenly frightened; the man is larger, with the high forehead of an intellectual, the tender woman is all devotion. They face the mother but their glance is turned inward; engrossed in their own destiny, they do not see her, although the index finger of the man's sensitive left hand points emphatically to the child. Behind the foreground figures we see two painted studies: the lower one shows a squatting nude lost in a reverie; the upper one, a seated couple whose attitude echoes that of the couple standing in the foreground.

Clearly, the painter has undertaken to represent an idea of the kind directly expressed as a theoretical schema, for example, in Keats' sonnet *The Human Seasons* or in the riddle of the Sphinx ("What creature goes on four feet in the morning, on two at noonday, on three in the evening?") Clearly also, the painter treads on dangerous ground. Explicitly symbolical representations are common in all cultures. But since they take their principal cue from an idea, the style of the presentation must warn the beholder that he is not in the realm of earthly happenings. On the other hand, in this twilight area between diagram and art, there is always the risk of ideas coercing the life of the image.

The so-called allegory travesties the task of the symbol by illustrating ideas through standardized clichés. Conceptual norm becomes poverty of imagination. Hence the chilling effect of overly cerebral novels, in which unconsummated theorems are draped over the characters as though they were the dummies of a dressmaker. Hence also the ludicrousness of schematic symbolism in some amateur art, cheap oratory, or dreams. Roger Fry has poked fun at the poor artistic quality of the dreams cited by the psychoanalyst Oskar Pfister, who wished to show that poetic inspiration derives from the same source as do dreams. Here is an example:

> A youth is about to leap away from a female corpse onto a bridge lost in a sea of fog, in the midst of which Death is standing. Behind him the sun rises in bloodred splendor. On the right margin two pairs of hands are trying to recall or hold back the hurrying youth.

I suspect that the repulsiveness of amateur fantasy, which Freud noted in reactions to daydreams and cheap fiction, is aroused not so much because desires and fears are revealed in their nakedness, but because preconceived ideas and hackneyed imagery are permitted to interfere with the truthfulness of the statement. These products of the mind are cognitively unclean.

Two Scales of Abstraction

What I have tried to say about the functions of pictorial analogues is summed up in Figure 6. Pictures and symbols depict experience by means of images in two complementary ways. In a picture, the abstraction level of the image is higher than that of the experience it represents; in a symbol the opposite is the case.

Figure 6.

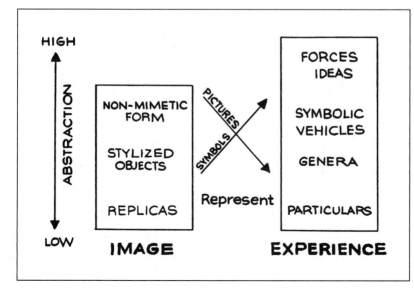

While every image connects two specific levels of the two scales, it is most desirable for the particular purposes of art that the whole range of both scales reverberate in each instance of pictorial representation. This means for the Image Scale that although a painting may be entirely "abstract" (non-mimetic), it needs to reflect some of the complexity of form by which realistic works depict the wealth of human experience. Inversely, a realistic portrayal, in order to be readable, generic, and expressive, must fit its presentation of objects to the pure forms, more directly embodied in non-mimetic art.

For the Experience Scale this condition demands that while focusing upon the ultimate forces inherent in existence, the mind view them as creating the richness of empirical manifestation; and vice versa, the teeming multiplicity of particular phenomena must be seen as organized by underlying general principles.

This doctrinaire demand will appear justified if one thinks of what happens when the two scales are not fully extended or not fully permeable. Under such pathological conditions, a scale is trimmed or cut through at some level, leaving the mind with a restricted range. Restriction to the bottom of the image scale may lead to the thoughtless imitation of natural objects. At the top end, isolation makes for a rigid geometry, orderly enough, but too impoverished to occupy the human brain, the most differentiated creation of nature. On the side of experience, limitation to the bottom of the scale makes for a materialistic, utilitarian outlook, unrelieved by guiding ideas. At the top we get anaemic speculation, the purely formal handling of theoretical propositions or norms.

Any such restriction of thought and expression weakens the validity of artistic statements. In an ideal civilization, no object is perceived and no action performed without an open-ended vista of analogues, which point to the most abstract guiding principles; and, inversely, when pure, generic shapes are handled, there reverberates in human reasoning the experience of particular existence, which gives substance to thought.

REFERENCES

Boeck, Wilhelm, and Jaime Sabartés. *Picasso*. New York: Abrams, 1955.
Doblin, Jay. *Trademark Design. Dot Zero #2*. New York: Finch, Pruyn and Co., 1966.
Freud, Sigmund. "Der Dichter und das Phantasieren." *Gesammelte Werke*, vol. 7. London: Imago, 1940. (Creative writers and day-dreaming. Standard ed. of the complete psychol. works of Sigmund Freud, vol. 9. London: Hogarth Press, 1959.)
Fry, Roger. *The Artist and Psychoanalysis*. London: Hogarth Press, 1924.
Goethe, Johann Wolfgang von. *Naturwissenschaftliche Schriften*, vol. 2. Leipzig: Insel Verlag, n. d. (Goethe's theory of colors. London: Murray, 1840.)
Hofmann, Werner. *The Earthly Paradise*. New York: Braziller, 1961.
Kamekura, Yusaku. *Trademarks and Symbols of the World*. New York: Reinhold, 1965.
Kepes, Gyorgy (ed.). Vision and value series: 1. Education of vision; 2. Structure in art and in science; 3. The nature and art of motion; 4. Module, proportion, symmetry, rhythm; 5. The man-made object; 6. Sign, image, symbol. New York: Braziller, 1965/66.
Kramer, Edith. The problem of quality in art, II: stereotypes. *Bul. of Art Therapy*, July 1967, vol. 6, pp. 151–171.
Krampen, Martin. Signs and symbols in graphic communication. *Design Quarterly* 1965, no. 62.
Langer, Susanne K. *Philosophy in a New Key*. Cambridge: Harvard Univ. Press, 1960.
Lorenz, Konrad Z. The Role of Gestalt Perception in Animal and Human Behavior. In *Whyte* (303) pp. 157–178.

Modley, Rudolf. "Graphic Symbols for World-Wide Communication." In *Kepes* (143) vol. 6, pp. 108–125.

Mondrian, Piet. *Plastic Art and Pure Plastic Art.* New York: Wittenborn, 1945.

Pfister, Oskar. *Expressionism in Art.* New York: Dutton, 1923.

Pratt, Carroll C. *Music as the Language of Emotion.* Washington, D.C.: Library of Congress, 1952.

Rigg, Melvin Gillison. "The expression of meanings and emotions in music." *Philos. Essays in Honor of Edgar Arthur Singer, Jr.* Philadelphia: Univ. of Pennsylvania Press, 1942.

Schopenhauer, Arthur. "Die Welt als Wille und Vorstellung." *Sämtliche Werke*, vol. 1. Leipzig: Insel, n.d. (The World as Will and Representation. New York: Dover, 1966.)

8   *Rhetoric of the Image*

ROLAND BARTHES

According to an ancient etymology, the word *image* should be linked to the root *imitari*. Thus we find ourselves immediately at the heart of the most important problem facing the semiology of images: can analogical representation (the "copy") produce true systems of signs and not merely simple agglutinations of symbols? Is it possible to conceive of an analogical "code"(as opposed to a digital one)? We know that linguists refuse the status of language to all communication" by analogy—from the "language" of bees to the "language" of gesture—the moment such communications are not doubly articulated, are not founded on a combinatory system of digital units as phonemes are. Nor are linguists the only ones to be suspicious as to the linguistic nature of the image; general opinion too has a vague conception of the image as an area of resistance to meaning—this in the name of a certain mythical idea of Life: the image is re-presentation, which is to say ultimately resurrection, and, as we know, the intelligible is reputed antipathetic to lived experience. Thus from both sides the image is felt to be weak in respect of meaning: there are those who think that the image is an extremely rudimentary system in comparison with language and those who think that signification cannot exhaust the image's ineffable richness. Now even—and above all if—the image is in a certain manner the *limit* of meaning, it permits the consideration of a veritable ontology of the process of signification. How does meaning get into the image? Where does it end? And if it ends, what is there *beyond*? Such are the questions that I wish to raise by submitting the image to a spectral analysis of the messages it may contain. We will start by making it considerably easier for ourselves: we will only study the advertising image. Why? Because in advertising the signification of the image is undoubtedly intentional; the signifieds of the advertising message are formed *a priori* by certain attributes of the product and these signifieds have to be transmitted as clearly as possible. If the image contains signs, we can be sure that in

From *Image – Music – Text*. Sel. and Trans. Stephen Heath. New York: Hill and Wang, 1977. 32–51.

advertising these signs are full, formed with a view to the optimum reading: the advertising image is *frank*, or at least emphatic.

THE THREE MESSAGES

Here we have a Panzani advertisement: some packets of pasta, a tin, a sachet, some tomatoes, onions, peppers, a mushroom, all emerging from a half-open string bag, in yellows and greens on a red background.[1] Let us try to "skim off" the different messages it contains.

The image immediately yields a first message whose substance is linguistic; its supports are the caption, which is marginal, and the labels, these being inserted into the natural disposition of the scene, "*en abyme*." The code from which this message has been taken is none other than that of the French language; the only knowledge required to decipher it is a knowledge of writing and French. In fact, this message can itself be further broken down, for the sign *Panzani* gives not simply the name of the firm but also, by its assonance, an additional signified, that of "Italianicity." The linguistic message is thus twofold (at least in this particular image): denotational and connotational. Since, however, we have here only a single typical sign,[2] namely that of articulated (written) language, it will be counted as one message.

Putting aside the linguistic message, we are left with the pure image (even if the labels are part of it, anecdotally). This image straightaway provides a series of discontinuous signs. First (the order is unimportant as these signs are not linear), the idea that what we have in the scene represented is a return from the market. A signified which itself implies two euphoric values: that of the freshness of the products and that of the essentially domestic preparation for which they are destined. Its signifier is the half-open bag which lets the provisions spill out over the table, "unpacked." To read this first sign requires only a knowledge which is in some sort implanted as part of the habits of a very widespread culture where "shopping around for oneself" is opposed to the hasty stocking up (preserves, refrigerators) of a more "mechanical" civilization. A second sign is more or less equally evident; its signifier is the bringing together of the tomato, the pepper, and the tricolored hues (yellow, green, red) of the poster; its signified is Italy or rather *Italianicity*. This sign stands in a relation of redundancy with the connoted sign of the linguistic message (the Italian assonance of the name *Panzani*) and the knowledge it draws upon is already more particular; it is a specifically "French" knowledge (an Italian would barely perceive the connotation of the name, no more probably than he would the Italianicity of tomato and pepper), based on a familiarity with certain tourist stereotypes. Continuing to explore the image (which is not to say that it is not entirely clear at the first glance), there is no difficulty in discovering at least two other signs: in the first, the serried collection of different objects transmits the idea of a total culinary service, on the one hand as though Panzani furnished everything necessary for a carefully balanced dish and on the other as though the concentrate in the tin were equivalent to the natural produce surrounding it; in the other sign, the composition of the image, evoking the memory of innumerable alimentary paintings, sends us to an aesthetic signified: the *"nature morte"* or, as it is better expressed in other languages, the "still life"[3]; the knowledge on which this sign depends is heavily cultural. It might be suggested that, in addition to these four signs, there is a further information pointer, that which tells us that this is an advertisement and which arises both from the place of the image in the magazine and from the emphasis of the labels (not to mention the caption). This last information, however, is co-extensive with the scene; it eludes signification insofar as the advertising nature of the image is essentially functional: to utter something is not necessarily to declare *I am speaking*, except in a deliberately reflexive system such as literature.

Thus there are four signs for this image and we will assume that they form a coherent whole (for they are all discontinuous), require a generally cultural knowledge, and refer back to signifieds each of which is global (for example, *Italianicity*), imbued with euphoric values. After the linguistic message, then, we can see a second, iconic message. Is that the end? If all these signs are removed from the image, we are still left with a certain informational matter; deprived of all knowledge, I continue to "read" the image, to "understand" that it assembles in a common space a number of identifiable (nameable) objects, not merely shapes and colors. The signifieds of this third message are constituted by the real objects in the scene, the signifiers by these same objects photographed, for, given that the relation between thing signified and image signifying in analogical representation is not "arbitrary" (as it is in language), it is no longer necessary to dose the relay with a third term in the guise of the psychic image of the object. What defines the third message is precisely that the relation between signified and signifier is quasi-tautological; no doubt the photograph involves a certain arrangement of the scene (framing, reduction, flattening) but this transition is not a *transformation* (in the way a coding can be); we have here a loss of the equivalence characteristic of true sign systems and a statement of quasi-identity. In other words, the sign of this message is not drawn from an institutional stock, is not coded, and we are brought up against the paradox (to which we will return) of a *message without a code*.[4] This peculiarity can be seen again at the level of the knowledge invested in the reading of the message; in order to "read" this last (or first) level of the image, all that is needed is the knowledge bound up with our perception. That knowledge is not nil, for we need to know what an image is (children only learn this at about the age of four) and what a tomato, a string-bag, a packet of pasta are, but it is a matter of an almost anthropological knowledge. This message corresponds, as it were, to the letter of the image and we can agree to call it the literal message, as opposed to the previous symbolic 'message.

If our reading is satisfactory, the photograph analyzed offers us three messages: a linguistic message, a coded iconic message, and a non-coded iconic message. The linguistic message can be readily separated from the other two, but since the latter share the same (iconic) substance, to what extent have we the right to separate them? It is certain that the distinction between the two iconic messages is not made spontaneously in ordinary reading: the viewer of the image receives *at one and the same time* the perceptual message and the cultural message, and it will be seen later that this confusion in reading corresponds to the function of the mass image (our concern here). The distinction, however, has an operational validity, analogous to that which allows the distinction in the linguistic sign of a signifier and a signified (even though in reality no one is able to separate the "word" from its meaning except by recourse to the metalanguage of a definition). If the distinction permits us to describe the structure of the image in a simple and coherent fashion and if this description paves the way for an explanation of the role of the image in society, we will take it to be justified. The task now is thus to reconsider each type of message so as to explore it in its generality, without losing sight of our aim of understanding the overall structure of the image, the final inter-relationship of the three messages. Given that what is in question is not a "naive" analysis but a structural description,[5] the order of the messages will be modified a little by the inversion of the cultural message and the literal message; of the two iconic messages, the first is in some sort imprinted on the second: the literal message appears as the *support* of the "symbolic" message. Hence, knowing that a system which takes over the signs of another system in order to make them its signifiers is a system of connotation,[6] we may say immediately that the literal image is *denoted* and the symbolic image *connoted*. Successively, then, we shall look at the linguistic message, the denoted image, and the connoted image.

THE LINGUISTIC MESSAGE

Is the linguistic message constant? Is there always textual matter in, under, or around the image? In order to find images given without words, it is doubtless necessary to go back to partially illiterate societies, to a sort of pictographic state of the image. From the moment of the appearance of the book, the linking of text and image is frequent, though it seems to have been little studied from a structural point of view. What is the signifying structure of "illustration"? Does the image duplicate certain of the informations given in the text by a phenomenon of redundancy or does the text add a fresh information to the image? The problem could be posed historically as regards the classical period with its passion for books with pictures (it was inconceivable in the eighteenth century that editions of La Fontaine's *Fables* should not be illustrated) and its authors such as Menestrier who concerned themselves with the relations between figure and discourse.[7] Today, at the level of mass communications, it appears that the linguistic message is indeed present in every image: as title, caption, accompanying press article, film dialogue, comic strip balloon. Which shows that it is not very accurate to talk of a civilization of the image — we are still, and more than ever, a civilization of writing,[8] writing and speech continuing to be the full terms of the informational structure. In fact, it is simply the presence of the linguistic message that counts, for neither its position nor its length seem to be pertinent (a long text may only comprise a single global signified, thanks to connotation, and it is this signified which is put in relation with the image). What are the functions of the linguistic message with regard to the (twofold) iconic message? There appear to be two: *anchorage* and *relay*.

As will be seen more clearly in a moment, all images are polysemous; they imply, underlying their signifiers, a "floating chain" of signifieds, the reader able to choose some and ignore others. Polysemy poses a question of meaning and this question always comes through as a dysfunction, even if this dysfunction is recuperated by society as a tragic (silent, God provides no possibility of choosing between signs) or a poetic (the panic "shudder of meaning" of the Ancient Greeks) game; in the cinema itself, traumatic images are bound up with an uncertainty (an anxiety) concerning the meaning of objects or attitudes. Hence in every society various techniques are developed intended to *fix* the floating chain of signifieds in such a way as to counter the terror of uncertain signs; the linguistic message is one of these techniques. At the level of the literal message, the text replies — in a more or less direct, more or less partial manner — to the question: *what is it?* The text helps to identify purely and simply the elements of the scene and the scene itself; it is a matter of a denoted description of the image (a description which is often incomplete) or, in Hjelmslev's terminology, of an *operation* (as opposed to connotation).[9] The denominative function corresponds exactly to an *anchorage* of all the possible (denoted) meanings of the object by recourse to a nomenclature. Shown a plateful of something (in an *Amieux* advertisement), I may hesitate in identifying the forms and masses; the caption ("*rice and tuna fish with mushrooms*") helps me to choose *the correct level of perception*, permits me to focus not simply my gaze but also my understanding. When it comes to the "symbolic message," the linguistic message no longer guides identification but interpretation, constituting a kind of vise which holds the connoted meanings from proliferating, whether towards excessively individual regions (it limits, that is to say, the projective power of the image) or towards dysphoric values. An advertisement (for *d'Arcy* preserves) shows a few fruits scattered around a ladder; the caption ("*as if from your own garden*") banishes one possible signified (parsimony, the paucity of the harvest) because of its unpleasantness and orientates the reading towards a more flattering signified (the natural and personal character of fruit from a private garden); it acts here as a counter-taboo, combatting the disagreeable myth of the artificial usually associated with preserves. Of course, elsewhere than in advertising, the anchorage may be ideological and indeed this is its principal function; the text *directs* the reader through the signifieds of the image, causing him to avoid some and receive others; by means of an often subtle *dispatching*, it remote-controls him towards a meaning chosen in advance. In all these cases of anchorage, language clearly has a function of elucidation, but this elucidation is selective, a metalanguage applied not to the totality of the iconic message but only to certain of its signs. The text is indeed the creator's (and hence society's) right of inspection over the image; anchorage is a control, bearing a responsibility — in the face of the projective power of pictures — for the use of the message. With respect to the liberty of the signifieds of the image, the text has thus a *repressive* value[10] and we can see that it is at this level that the morality and ideology of a society are above all invested.

Anchorage is the most frequent function of the linguistic message and is commonly found in press photographs and advertisements. The function of relay is less common (at least as far as the fixed image is concerned); it can be seen particularly in cartoons and comic strips. Here text (most often a snatch of dialogue) and image stand in a complementary relationship; the words, in the same way as the images, are fragments of a more general syntagm and the unity of the message is realized at a higher level, that of the story, the anecdote, the diegesis (which is ample confirmation that the diegesis must be treated as an autonomous system[11]). While rare in the fixed image, this relay-text becomes very important in film, where dialogue functions not simply as elucidation but really does advance the action by setting out, in the sequence of messages, meanings that are not to be found in the image itself. Obviously, the two functions of the linguistic message can co-exist in the one iconic whole, but the dominance of the one or the other is of consequence for the general economy of a work. When the text has the diegetic value of relay, the information is more costly, requiring as it does the learning of a digital code (the system of language); when it has a substitute value (anchorage, control), it is the image which detains the informational charge and, the image being analogical, the information is then "lazier": in certain comic strips intended for "quick" reading the diegesis is confined above all to the text, the image gathering the attributive informations of a paradigmatic order (the stereotyped status of the characters); the costly message and the discursive message are made to coincide so that the hurried reader may be spared the boredom of verbal "descriptions" which are entrusted to the image, that is to say to a less "laborious" system.

THE DENOTED IMAGE

We have seen that in the image properly speaking, the distinction between the literal message and the symbolic message is operational; we never encounter (at least in advertising) a literal image in a pure state. Even if a totally "naive" image were to be achieved, it would immediately join the sign of naivety and be completed by a third — symbolic — message. Thus the characteristics of the literal message cannot be substantial but only relational. It is first of all, so to speak, a message by eviction, constituted by what is left in the image when the signs of connotation are mentally deleted (it would not be possible actually to remove them for they can impregnate the whole of the image, as in the case of the "still life composition"). This evictive state naturally corresponds to a plenitude of virtualities: it is an absence of meaning full of all the meanings. Then again (and there is no contradiction with what has just been said), it is a sufficient message, since it has at least one meaning at the level of the identification of the scene represented; the letter of the image corresponds in short to the first degree of intelligibility (below which the reader would perceive only lines, forms, and colors), but this intelligibility remains virtual by reason of its very poverty, for everyone from a real society always disposes of a knowledge superior to the merely anthropological and perceives more than just the letter. Since it is both evictive and sufficient, it will be understood that from an aesthetic point of view the denoted image can appear as a kind of Edenic state of the image; cleared utopianically of its connotations, the image would become radically objective, or, in the last analysis, innocent.

This utopian character of denotation is considerably reinforced by the paradox already mentioned, that the photograph (in its literal state), by virtue of its absolutely analogical nature, seems to constitute a message without a code. Here, however, structural analysis must differentiate, for of all the kinds of image only the photograph is able to transmit the (literal) information without forming it by means of discontinuous signs and rules of transformation. The photograph, message without a code, must thus be opposed to the drawing which, even when denoted, is a coded message. The coded nature of the drawing can be seen at three levels. Firstly, to reproduce an object or a scene in a drawing requires a set of *rule-governed* transpositions; there is no essential nature of the pictorial copy and the codes of transposition are historical (notably those concerning perspective). Secondly, the operation of the drawing (the coding) immediately necessitates a certain division between the significant and the insignificant: the drawing does not reproduce *everything* (often it reproduces very little), without its ceasing, however, to be a strong message; whereas the photograph, although it can choose its subject, its point of view and its angle, cannot intervene *within* the object (except by trick effects). In other words, the denotation of the drawing is less pure than that of the photograph, for there is no drawing without style. Finally, like all codes, the drawing demands an apprenticeship (Saussure attributed a great importance to this semiological fact). Does the coding of the denoted message have consequences for the connoted message? It is certain that the coding of the literal prepares and facilitates connotation since it at once establishes a certain discontinuity in the image: the "execution" of a drawing itself constitutes a connotation. But at the same time, insofar as the drawing displays its coding, the relationship between the two messages is profoundly modified: it is no longer the relationship between a nature and a culture (as with the photograph) but that between two cultures; the "ethic" of the drawing is not the same as that of the photograph.

In the photograph — at least at the level of the literal message — the relationship of signifieds to signifiers is not one of "transformation" but of "recording," and the absence of a code clearly reinforces the myth of photographic "naturalness": the scene *is there*, captured mechanically, not humanly (the mechanical is here a guarantee of objectivity). Man's interventions in the photograph (framing, distance, lighting, focus, speed) all effectively belong to the plane of connotation; it is as though in the beginning (even if utopian) there were a brute photograph (frontal and clear) on which man would then lay out, with the aid of various techniques, the signs drawn from a cultural code. Only the opposition of the cultural code and the natural non-code can, it seems, account for the specific character of the photograph and allow the assessment of the anthropological revolution it represents in man's history. The type of consciousness the photograph involves is indeed truly unprecedented, since it establishes not a consciousness of the *being-there* of the thing (which any copy could provoke) but an awareness of its *having-been-there*. What we have is a new space-time category: spatial immediacy and temporal anteriority, the photograph being an illogical conjunction between the *here-now* and the *there-then*. It is thus at the level of this denoted message or message without code that the *real unreality* of the photograph can be fully understood: its unreality is that of the *here-now*, for the photograph is never experienced as illusion, is in no way a *presence* (claims as to the magical character of the photographic image must be deflated); its reality that of the *having-been-there*, for in every photograph there is the always stupefying evidence of *this is how it was*, giving us, by a precious miracle, a reality from which we are sheltered. This kind of temporal equilibrium (*having-been-there*) probably diminishes the projective power of the image (very few psychological tests resort to photographs while many use drawings): the *this was so* easily defeats the *it's me*. If these remarks are at all correct, the photograph must be related to a pure spectatorial, consciousness and not to the more projective, more "magical" fictional consciousness on which film by and large depends. This would lend authority to the view that the distinction between film and photograph is not a simple difference of degree but a radical opposition. Film can no longer be seen as animated photographs: the *having-been-there* gives way before a *being-there* of the thing; which omission would explain how there can be a history of the cinema, without any real break with the previous arts of fiction, whereas the photograph can in some sense elude history (despite the evolution of the techniques and ambitions of the photographic art) and represent a "flat" anthropological fact, at once absolutely new and definitively unsurpassable, humanity encountering for the first time in its history *messages without a code*. Hence the photograph is not the last (improved) term of the great family of images; it corresponds to a decisive mutation of informational economies.

At all events, the denoted image, to the extent to which it does not imply any code (the case with the advertising photograph), plays a special role in the general structure of the iconic message which we can begin to define (returning to this question after discussion of the third message): the denoted image naturalizes the symbolic message, it innocents the semantic artifice of connotation, which is extremely dense, especially in advertising. Although the *Panzani* poster is full of "symbols," there nonetheless remains in the photograph, insofar as the literal message is sufficient, a kind of natural *being-there* of objects: nature seems spontaneously to produce the scene represented. A pseudo-truth is surreptitiously substituted for the simple validity of openly semantic systems; the absence of code disintellectualizes the message because it seems to found in nature the signs of culture. This is without doubt an important historical paradox: the more technology develops the diffusion of information (and notably of images), the more it provides the means of masking the constructed meaning under the appearance of the given meaning.

RHETORIC OF THE IMAGE

It was seen that the signs of the third message (the "symbolic" message, cultural or connoted) were discontinuous. Even when the signifier seems to extend over the whole image, it is nonetheless a sign separated from the others: the "composition" carries an aesthetic signified, in much the same way as intonation although suprasegmental is a separate signifier in language. Thus we are here dealing with a normal system whose signs are drawn from a cultural code (even if the linking together of the elements of the sign appears more or less analogical). What gives this system its originality is that the number of readings of the same lexical unit or *lexia* (of the same image) varies according to individuals. In the *Panzani* advertisement analyzed, four connotative signs have been identified; probably there are others (the net bag, for example, can signify the miraculous draught of fishes, plenty, etc.). The variation in readings is not, however, anarchic; it depends on the different kinds of knowledge — practical, national, cultural, aesthetic — invested in the image and these can be classified, brought into a typology. It is as though the image presented itself to the reading of several different people who can perfectly well co-exist in a single individual: *the one lexia mobilizes different lexicons*. What is a lexicon? A portion of the symbolic plane (of language) which corresponds to a body of practices and techniques.[12] This is the case for the different readings of the image: each sign corresponds to a body of "attitudes" — tourism, housekeeping, knowledge of art — certainty of which may obviously be lacking in this or that individual. There is a plurality and a co-existence of lexicons in one and the same person, the number and identity of these lexicons forming in some sort a person's *idiolect*.[13] The image, in its connotation, is thus constituted by an architecture of signs drawn from a variable depth of lexicons (of idiolects); each lexicon, no matter how "deep," still being coded, if, as is thought today, the *psyche* itself is articulated like a language; indeed, the further one "descends" into the psychic depths of an individual, the more rarified and the more classifiable the signs become — what could be more systematic than the readings of Rorschach tests? The variability of readings, therefore, is no threat to the "language" of the image if it be admitted that that language is composed of idiolects, lexicons and sub-codes. The image is penetrated through and through by the system of meaning, in exactly the same way as man is articulated to the very depths of his being in distinct languages. The language of the image is not merely the totality of utterances emitted (for example at the level of the combiner of the signs or creator of the message), it is also the totality of utterances received:[14] the language must include the "surprises" of meaning.

Another difficulty in analyzing connotation is that there is no particular analytical language corresponding to the particularity of its signifieds — how are the signifieds of connotation to be named? For one of them we ventured the term *Italianicity*, but the others can only be designated by words from ordinary language (*culinary preparation, still life, plenty*); the metalanguage which has to take charge of them at the moment of the analysis is not specialized. This is a difficulty, for these signifieds have a particular semantic nature: as a seme of connotation, "plenty" does not exactly cover "plenty" in the denoted sense; the signifier of connotation (here the profusion and the condensation of the produce) is like the essential cipher of all possible plenties, of the purest idea of plenty. The denoted word never refers to an essence for it is always caught up in a contingent utterance, a continuous syntagm (that of verbal discourse), oriented towards a certain practical transitivity of language; the seme "plenty," on the contrary, is a concept in a pure state, cut off from any syntagm, deprived of any context and corresponding to a sort of theatrical state of meaning, or, better (since it is a question of a sign without a syntagm), to an *exposed* meaning. To express these semes of connotation would therefore require a special metalanguage and we are left with barbarisms of the *Italianicity* kind as best being able to account for the signifieds of connotation, the suffix *-icity* deriving an abstract noun from the adjective: *Italianicity* is not Italy, it is the condensed essence of everything that could be Italian, from spaghetti to painting. By accepting to regulate artificially — and if needs be barbarously — the naming of the semes of connotation, the analysis of their form will be rendered easier.[15] These semes are organized in associative fields, in paradigmatic articulations, even perhaps in oppositions, according to certain defined paths or, as A. J. Greimas puts it, according to certain semic axes:[16] *Italianicity* belongs to a certain axis of nationalities, alongside Frenchicity, Germanicity or Spanishicity. The reconstitution of such axes — which may eventually be in opposition to one another — will clearly only be possible once a massive inventory of the systems of connotation has been carried out, an inventory not merely of the connotative system of the image but also of those of other substances, for if connotation has typical signifiers dependent on the different substances utilized (image, language, objects, modes of behaviour) it holds all its signifieds in common: the same signifieds are to be found in the written press, the image or the actor's gestures (which is why semiology can only be conceived in a so to speak total framework). This common domain of the signifieds of connotation is that of *ideology*, which cannot but be single for a given society and history, no matter what signifiers of connotation it may use.

To the general ideology, that is, correspond signifiers of connotation which are specified according to the chosen substance. These signifiers will be called *connotators* and the set of connotators a *rhetoric*, rhetoric thus appearing as the signifying aspect of ideology. Rhetorics inevitably vary by their substance (here articulated sound, there image, gesture, or whatever) but not necessarily by their form; it is even probable that there exists a single rhetorical *form*, common for instance to dream, literature, and image.[17] Thus the rhetoric of the image (that is to say, the classification of its connotators) is specific to the extent that it is subject to the physical constraints of vision (different, for example, from phonatory constraints) but general to the extent that the "figures" are never more than formal relations of elements. This rhetoric could only be established on the basis of a quite considerable inventory, but it is possible now to foresee that one will find in it some of the figures formerly identified by the Ancients and the Classics:[18] the tomato, for example, signifies *Italianicity* by metonymy and in another advertisement the sequence of three scenes (coffee in beans, coffee in powder, coffee sipped in the cup) releases a certain logical relationship in the same way as an asyndeton. It is probable indeed that among the metabolas (or figures of the substitution of one signifier for another[19]), it is metonymy which furnishes the image with the greatest number of its connotators, and that among the parataxes (or syntagmatic figures), it is asyndeton which predominates.

The most important thing, however, at least for the moment, is not to inventorize the connotators but to understand that in the total image they constitute *discontinuous* or better still *scattered traits*. The connotators do not fill the whole of the lexia, reading them does not exhaust it. In other words (and this would be a valid proposition for semiology in general), not all the elements of the lexia can be transformed into connotators; there always remaining in the discourse a certain denotation without which, precisely, the discourse would not be possible. Which brings us back to the second message or denoted image. In the *Panzani* advertisement, the Mediterranean vegetables, the color, the composition, the very profusion rise up as so many scattered blocks, at once isolated and mounted in a general scene which has its own space and, as was seen, its "meaning": they are "set" in a syntagm *which is not theirs and which is that of the denotation*. This last proposition is important for it permits us to found (retroactively) the structural distinction between the second or literal message and the third or symbolic message and to give a more exact description of the naturalizing function of the denotation with respect to the connotation. We can now understand that *it is precisely the syntagm of the denoted message which "naturalizes" the system of the connoted message*. Or again: connotation is only system, can only be defined in paradigmatic terms; iconic denotation is only syntagm, associates elements without any system: the discontinuous connotators are connected, actualized, "spoken" through the syntagm of the denotation, the discontinuous world of symbols plunges into the story of the denoted scene as though into a lustral bath of innocence.

It can thus be seen that in the total system of the image the structural functions are polarized: on the one hand there is a sort of paradigmatic condensation at the level of the connotators (that is, broadly speaking, of the symbols), which are strong signs, scattered, "reified"; on the other a syntagmatic 'flow' at the level of the denotation—it will not be forgotten that the syntagm is always very close to speech, and it is indeed the iconic "discourse" which naturalizes its symbols. Without wishing to infer too quickly from the image to semiology in general, one can nevertheless venture that the world of total meaning is torn internally (structurally) between the system as culture and the syntagm as nature: the works of mass communications all combine, through diverse and diversely successful dialectics, the fascination of a nature, that of story, diegesis, syntagm, and the intelligibility of a culture, withdrawn into a few discontinuous symbols which men "decline" in the shelter of their living speech.

NOTES

1. The *description* of the photograph is given here with prudence, for it already constitutes a metalanguage. The reader is asked to refer to the reproduction (XVII).

2. By *typical sign* is meant the sign of a system insofar as it is adequately defined by its substance: the verbal sign, the iconic sign, the gestural sign are so many typical signs.

3. In French, the expression *nature morte* refers to the original presence of funereal objects, such as a skull, in certain pictures.

4. Cf. "The photographic message," above pp. 15–31, R. Barthes, *Images – Music – Text*. Sel. and Trans. Stephen Heath. New York: Hill and Wang. 1977.

5. "Naive" analysis is an enumeration of elements, structural description aims to grasp the relation of these elements by virtue of the principle of the solidarity holding between the terms of a structure: if one term changes, so also do the others.

6. Cf. R. Barthes, *Eléments de sémiologie, Communications* 4, 1964, p. 130 [trans. *Elements of Semiology*, London 1967 & New York 1968, pp. 89–92].

7. Menestrier, *L'Art des emblèmes*, 1684.

8. Images without words can certainly be found in certain cartoons, but by way of a paradox; the absence of words always covers an enigmatic intention.

9. *Eléments de sémiologie*, pp. 131–2 [trans. pp. 90–4].

10. This can be seen clearly in the paradoxical case where the image is constructed according to the text and where, consequently, the control would seem to be needless. An advertisement which wants to communicate that in such and such a coffee the aroma is "locked in" the product in powder form and that it will thus be wholly there when the coffee is used depicts, above this proposition, a tin of coffee with a chain and padlock round it. Here, the linguistic metaphor ("locked in") is taken literally (a well-known poetic device); in fact, however, it is the image which is read first and the text from which the image is constructed becomes in the end the simple choice of one signified among others. The repression is present again in the circular movement as a banalization of the message.

11. Cf. Claude Bremond, "Le message narratif," *Communications* 4, 1964.

12. Cf. A. J. Greimas, "Les problèmes de la description mécanographique," *Cahiers de Lexicologie*, 1, 1959, p. 63.

13. Cf. *Eléments de sémiologie*, p. 96 [trans, pp. 21–2].

14. In the Saussurian perspective, speech (utterances) is above all that which is emitted, drawn from the language-system (and constituting it in return). It is necessary today to enlarge the notion of language [*langue*], especially from the semantic point of view: language is the "totalizing abstraction" of the messages emitted *and received*.

15. *Form* in the precise sense given it by Hjelmslev (cf. *Eléments de sémiologie*, p. 105 [trans, pp. 39–41]), as the functional organization of the signifieds among themselves.

16. A. J. Greimas, *Cours de Sémantique*, 1964 (notes roneotyped by the Ecole Normale Supérieure de Saint-Cloud).

17. Cf. Emile Benveniste, 'Remarques sur la fonction du langage dans la découverte freudienne', *La Psychanalyse* 1, 1956, pp. 3–16 [reprinted in E. Benveniste, *Problèmes de linguistique générale*, Paris 1966, Chapter 7; translated as *Problems of General Linguistics*, Coral Gables, Florida 1971].

18. Classical rhetoric needs to be rethought in structural terms (this is the object of a work in progress); it will then perhaps be possible to establish a general rhetoric or linguistics of the signifiers of connotation, valid for articulated sound, image, gesture, etc. See 'L'ancienne Rhétorique (Aide-mémoire)', *Communications* 16, 1970.

19. We prefer here to evade Jakobson's opposition between metaphor and metonymy for if metonymy by its origin is a figure of contiguity, it nevertheless functions finally as a substitute of the signifier, that is as a metaphor.

Representing Macbeth: A Case Study in Visual Rhetoric

HANNO H. J. EHSES

INTRODUCTION

The creative process of finding appropriate design solutions to visual problems would become more accessible and more probable, and could be enriched if designers were more conscious of the underlying system of concept formation. Instead, they seem to use it intuitively. In adapting contemporary semiotic and rhetoric theory, the following study of Macbeth posters endeavors to present an operational model of concept formation that is often identified with the creative process. Semiotics, the doctrine of signs, explains the principles that underlie the structure of signs and their utilization within messages, and rhetoric, the art of persuasion, suggests ways to construct appropriate messages.

Speaking out on concept formation and the problems involved in designing a poster for a theater play, J. Shadbolt, the designer, remarked: "The psychological problem was what slowed down the process. I would read the actual play, consider carefully its overall impact, and then try to convey with the totality of my design something of that precise import. It's easy to make an elegant decoration, but quite another thing to evoke exact implication."[1]

Shadbolt's remark addresses some fundamental problems in the design activity, and directs special attention to the following questions: How is meaning created visually in design? What is the routing that leads from the text of a play (or any other statement) to a concept and its visualization in a poster (or a book cover or trademark)? What is the nature of the relationship between the figurative image and the text? These questions are all related to the process of signification, that is, the coding dimension that precedes all message transfer and communicative interaction.

To find answers to these questions and to illuminate the process of arriving at a design solution, this article will examine the relevance of rhetoric to

From *Design Discourse: History/Theory/Criticism*. Ed. Victor Margolin. Chicago: U of Chicago P, 1989. 187–197.

design and explore some of its basic principles. The semiotic structure of coding and the rhetorical characteristic that governs the visual appearance of a poster will also be discussed. In addition, the operational potential of rhetorical procedure for design in conjunction with the outcome of a recent case study is demonstrated.

DESIGN AND RHETORICAL PRINCIPLES

Rhetoric, generally speaking, is concerned with the functional organization of verbal discourse or messages. It operates on the basis of logical and esthetic modes to affect interaction in both a rational and emotional way. According to Aristotle, rhetoric is concerned with "discovering all the available means of persuasion in any given situation" either to instruct an audience (rational appeal), to please an audience and win it over (ethical appeal), or to move it (emotional appeal). The object of rhetoric is eloquence, which is defined as effective speech that makes it possible to determine the attitude of people in order to influence their actions. The possibility of influencing and being influenced presupposes the possibility of choice. Choice is a key term in rhetoric as well as design, as both pertain to making appropriate selections of means to achieve a desired end. Design, as a communication-oriented discipline, is governed by and must pay attention to pragmatic motivations and functional considerations. Inasmuch as the spirit of rhetoric is also pragmatic, this situation gives design a rhetorical dimension.

Despite all the negative connotations, persuasion is not necessarily an underhanded device, but rather a socially acceptable form of reasoning. During the past few decades, I. A. Richards and C. Perelman in particular have been influential in freeing rhetoric from articulated prejudices.[2]

At present, the exponents of the "new rhetoric" contend that even the simplest utterances are pragmatic, that is, functionally determined and, therefore, persuasive. According to this school of thought, "Almost all human reasoning about facts, decisions, opinions, beliefs, and values is no longer considered to be based on the authority of Absolute Reason but instead intertwined with emotional elements, historical evaluations, and pragmatic motivations. In this sense, the new rhetoric considers the persuasive discourse not as a subtle fraudulent procedure but a technique of "reasonable human interaction controlled by doubt and explicitly subject to many extralogical conditions."[3]

Because all human communication is, in one way or another, infiltrated rhetorically, design for visual or verbal communication cannot be exempt from that fact.

Although rhetoric has developed as a method that deals fundamentally with speaking and writing, rhetorical principles have been transferred into various other media, as well. This has been indicated by E. R. Curtius[4] and R. Lee,[5] both of whom refer to rhetoric and its relationship to painting, architecture, and music. The potential value of the rhetorical system within a semiotic framework was also realized by G. Bonsiepe, who published the article "Visual/Verbal Rhetoric" in 1965.[6] Essentially concerned with analyzing advertisements, Bonsiepe demonstrated that visual rhetoric is possible on the basis of verbal rhetoric. In 1968, M. Krampen remarked that "a careful study of classical rhetoric could lead to a catalog of rhetorical devices that are capable of visual duplication."[7] In light of these suggestions, ten figures of speech were selected for this case study. The ten that were chosen suggest an obvious potential for visual duplication. What precisely constitutes such a rhetorical figure, and what is its position within the rhetorical system?

The system of classical rhetoric formulates precepts for the production of a message and traditionally is divided into five phases (see Figure 1).

FIGURE 1.

I   **Inventio: Discovery of ideas/arguments**
Concerned with finding and selecting material in support of the subject matter and relevant to the situation.

II   **Dispositio: Arrangement of ideas/arguments**
Concerned with organizing the selected material into an effective whole (statement of intent).

III   **Elocutio: Form of expressing ideas/arguments**
Stylistic treatment or detailed shaping of the organized material in consideration of the following criteria:
- Aptum: appropriateness with reference to subject matter and context
- Puritas: correctness of expression
- Perspicuitas: comprehensibility of expression
- Ornatus: deliberate adornment of expression

IV   **Memoria: Memorization of speech**

V   **Pronunciatio: Delivery of speech**
Concerned with voice and gestures, but also with appropriate setting.

The third phase is of particular interest, as it covers the stylistic features that have already been referred to as figures of speech. According to Quintilian, rhetorical figures generate rules that can be looked upon as means of "lending credibility to our arguments" and "exciting the emotions." He also considered the use of these figures as "the art of saying something in a new form" to give a message greater vitality and impact. The essence of a rhetorical figure is an artful departure from the ordinary and simple method of speaking. It should be added that these figures do not refer to ready-made expressions; rather, they should be viewed as abstract operational terms that can be filled out.

The notion that stylistic devices are simply the "dress of thought" needs to be erased. According to E. Corbett, "Style does provide a vehicle for thought, and style can be ornamental; but style is something more than that. It is another of the available means of persuasion, another of the means of arousing the appropriate emotional response in the audience, and another of the means of establishing the proper ethical image. If the student adopts this functional notion of style . . . he will begin to regard style in the way Stendhal conceived of it: 'Style is this: to add to a given thought all the circumstances fitted to produce the whole effect that the thought is intended to produce.'"[8]

Rhetorical figures are usually divided into two groups, schemes and tropes. Whereas the former are defined as departures from the ordinary positioning of words in a sentence ("Uncomplicated are young people, sometimes," as opposed to "Young people are sometimes uncomplicated"), the latter are defined as departures from the ordinary signification of words or idioms ("The ground thirsts for rain," as opposed to "The ground is very dry and needs rain").

To delineate building blocks of concept formation, this article must concentrate on the tropes. The nature of the trope can be explained by the following example. In "He was a lion in battle," the term lion is the departed substitute referring to the substituted expression "undaunted unconquerable fighter." The person is not a lion in actuality, but only in some transferred sense. Although the substitute word appears only rarely or occasionally, the substituted words represent the ordinary or habitual mode of expression. The occasional departure involves a change in meaning because it results in effects that are different from the ordinary mode of expression.

Different classifications of figures of speech have been adopted by various writers in the past. In adopting a classification for this study, DeMille's *Elements of Rhetoric*[9] and Corbett's *Classical Rhetoric for the Modern Student* served as guides. The classification is as follows:

Figures of contrast
- *Antithesis:* the juxtaposition of contrasting ideas, for example, "By the time the wallet is *empty*, life will be *full*."
- *Irony:* an expression that conveys a meaning opposite to its literal meaning, for example, "Robbing a widow of her life savings was certainly a *noble act*."

Figures of resemblance
- *Metaphor:* an implied comparison between two things of unlike nature, for example, "The colorful display was a *magnet* for anybody in the room."
- *Personification:* a comparison whereby human qualities are assigned to inanimate objects, for example, "The thatch-roofed cottages in the valley *seemed to be asleep*."

Figures of contiguity
- *Metonymy:* the substitution of terms suggesting an actual relationship that can be of causal, spatial, or chronological nature (cause instead of effect, instrument for agent, author for work, container for contained, and produce for producer), for example, "*The White House* (President of the United States) reduced her troops in Europe," or "He had always been a great lover of *gold* (money)."
- *Synecdoche:* the substitution of a more inclusive term for one that is less inclusive or vice versa, the nature of which is quantitative, for example, "*Canada* (Canadian team) won the competition" or "He lived for a week *under my roof* (house)."
- *Periphrasis:* circumlocution, the indirect reference by means of well-known attributes or characteristics, for example, "*to go to a better world*" instead of "to die."

- *Puns:* a play on words, using words that sound alike but have different meanings, for example, "Check in here for the *rest* of your life (Wandlyn Motel)."

Figures of graduation

- *Amplification:* the expansion of a topic through the assemblage of relevant particulars, for example, "He used all the means at his disposal: *radio, TV, brochures, posters, advertisements, and so forth.*"
- *Hyperbole:* the exaggeration of an object beyond its natural and proper dimensions, for example, "Jan's friends tracked a *ton of mud* through the hallway."

Any departure from the ordinary way of expression endows the expression with a strong dynamic tension directed either toward the ordinary (making the hallway terribly dirty) or away from it (tracked a ton of mud through the hallway). The less known the trope, the longer the tension span.

It is a necessary condition for all figures of speech that they presuppose a basic understanding of grammatical forms and lexical content from which departure is possible. Figurative variations cannot ignore the grammar of the language inasmuch as any change for a greater effect must respect grammatical possibilities. Because the basic understanding is determined by the grammar and rhetoric is built upon its fundamentals, rhetorical procedure is also referred to as constituting a secondary grammar.

Furthermore, both grammars participate in successive generations of order. However, in using the aforementioned rhetorical figures, a lower literal order is transformed into a higher rhetorical order, giving the expression more vitality. The difference is characterized by the word *money* depicting an image of coins and bills (literal order) as opposed to *money* being illustrated metonomically by the trademarks of several major Canadian banks (rhetorical order). Thus, the effectiveness of a rhetorical figure always depends on the audience's ability to perceive the difference between the substitute and the substituted way of expression.

Whether the literal or rhetorical order is used depends on the number of structured relationships that have materialized, which also implies reference to pre-existing cultural knowledge that predates a design. The connection between both orders is one of balancing two oppositional forces, the obvious and the new. Whereas the obvious tends toward satisfying expectations by responding to existing standards, the new moves toward upsetting those standards by way of a novel and atypical approach with lesser relation to existing expectations. This situation may be described as a state of mutual equilibrium between both preservative and changeable forces. In responding to existing expectations and supplying something unexpected at the same time, a design produces a challenge (a pleasant or unpleasant surprise) in addition to a renewed and extended perspective.

From Concept Formation to Visual Form

Visual communication takes place on the basis of more or less conventionalized signs belonging to many kinds of codes of disparate languages. A theater poster is seen as a message representing a complex of signs built on the basis of codes, conveying certain meanings that are interpretable on the basis of either those same codes or different ones. Concept formation coincides with the process of coding insofar as the designer assumes and activates codes by correlating selected graphic devices with selected culturally sanctioned meanings, thus binding something present with something absent. The process of coupling these two opposed units is called *signification*, an act whose product is a sign. A sign according to C. S. Peirce is "something that stands to somebody for something [else] in some respect or capacity."[10] Thus, the possession of codes allows readers to draw relationships, for example, between a poster titled "Macbeth" and an actual play by Shakespeare. Codes can stimulate a variety of interpretations by allowing the designer to draw relationships between the play *Macbeth* itself and concepts such as "crowned beast," "sinister king," "curse of evil actions," "scene from an actual theatre production," and many more.

Signification operates on the basis of denotative as well as connotative codes, both of which draw upon different experiences. Anything derived from the visual perception of a literal reading of a theater poster is denotative, while anything derived from additional experiences and associations or symbolic readings is connotative. Whereas denotation is referential and direct and tends toward monofunctionality (a theater poster as a vehicle whose sole function is to announce the play), connotation is suggestive and indirect and tends toward polyfunctionality (a theater poster suggests a whole host of shared assumptions and possible functions).

Thus, while the posters shown at the end of this article refer to the play *Macbeth* and are denotatively interchangeable in announcing the play, they are connotatively quite different. It follows, then, that any act of signification—in addition to conventionalized denotations—must consciously take into account the breadth and complexity of connotations.

An inquiry into concept formation and rhetorical coding must proceed backward from the result toward a hypothetical model that explains the process. To this end, a theater poster is the result of the interplay of two sign systems—title of play and graphic image—that elucidate and complement each other. This is possible in theater posters because the signification of the image is assumed to be intentional; the signifieds of the message correspond to certain attributes or associations of the play that are graphically transmitted in the clearest way. Therefore, the graphic image is seen as a series of signs replacing a statement about the play or about a specific theatrical interpretation of the play. It represents a concept analogous to a written précis.

Having a more focused object of study, the next step involves outlining the elementary conditions of graphic signification, which also includes a wider application than that of the design of theater posters. A visual system such as that of theater posters is the result of two coordinated sets: the set of possible graphic forms and the set of plays to be announced (see Figure 2). According to a scheme proposed by L. Hjelmslev,[11] all graphic forms correspond to level of expression; all plays to level of content. On both levels, a

FIGURE 2.

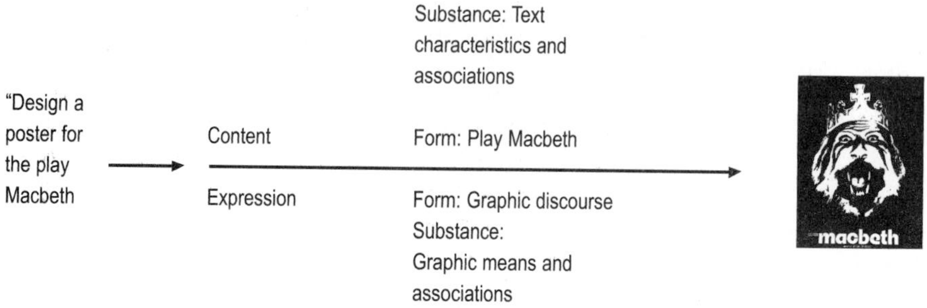

		Substance: Text characteristics and associations
"Design a poster for the play Macbeth	Content	Form: Play Macbeth
	Expression	Form: Graphic discourse Substance: Graphic means and associations

form (play/graphic representation or discourse) is distinguished from a substance (text characteristics/graphic means). The coupling of the two oppositionally structured sets of forms determines the semiotic structure of the visual system. The structure itself becomes semiotic, since each of the two forms involved contains information over and above that pertaining to its own set. The additional charge of information is obtained through the correlation of the signified play and signifying graphic image, thus determining the deliberately fixed signification of a poster.

The next step of analysis must be to identify the plot or chosen visual concept that is equivalent to the meaning nucleus of a given graphic image. In decoding the meaning of the Macbeth poster in terms of ideas conveyed or suggested feelings expressed and connoted, a summarizing statement could read "King Macbeth, a human beast" (see Figure 3). This graphically encoded statement should be seen as the designer's chosen visual concept that was skillfully and clearly encoded. It should be pointed out that the identified visual concept is not only the result of a literal reading of the perceptible units (crown, face, fangs), but also the result of denotative and connotative reading which, in turn, is influenced by a familiarity with this particular play and by a certain visual literacy.

The remaining question concerns the designer's method of arriving at such a concept. The text of the play itself contains a large stock of suitable material for conceptualization, such as references to certain locations and events, key objects and scenes, main characters, cause-effect relations, and so forth. However, in the text of the play, there is no direct reference to King Macbeth as a human beast. But there are enough indications to constitute an image of Macbeth as a despot. In the example, the designer went one step further in reaching a solution that clearly mirrors the dialectic of comprehensibility and attractiveness to stimulate interest and to represent a high degree of information, the full extent of which can only be discerned by the attentive reader. Referring back to the process that led to the concept, the initial interpretation of Macbeth as a despot has been replaced and dramatized by a visual concept that displays King Macbeth as a human beast.

FIGURE 3.

The relation of the form of expression to the form of content is regulated by specific figures of speech. To reveal the rhetorical figure that governs the concept formation, it is necessary to look at the relationship "title of play = Macbeth" and the concept "King Macbeth, a human beast." In this particular poster, the relation follows a metaphorical structure. A metaphor is defined as an implied comparison between two things of unlike nature, which in this case is Macbeth being implicitly compared to a beast.

Figure 4 indicates that the signification process in visual design involves two major operations: formation of the visual concept, as well as its graphic encoding. Although in the former, the central problem of design involves finding an idea that expresses the play in some respect or capacity, the concern of the latter is in the visual translation of this concept. Both operations are equally important.

Although graphic encoding is beyond this study, it is likewise governed by rhetorical figures. This point can be illustrated by looking at the visual treatment of the poster previously discussed. To express the concept of the human beast graphically, the designer omitted certain features of a human face and replaced them with features of a particular predatory animal. This graphic manipulation, the departure from a common face—human or animal—adds considerably to the graphic interpretation of beastness. The underlying rhetorical figure at work here is called oxymoron, defined as the yoking of two terms that are ordinarily contradictory. Transferred to this example, it is the yoking

FIGURE 4.

Graphic encoding

| | King Macbeth | |
Content	as human beast	
= result of	———————————————————	= result of
Expression? (graphic image)		

Concept formation

Content	Play Macbeth	Rhetorical
----------	---------------------	pattern:
Expression?	(King Macbeth as	Metaphor
	human beast)	

of the facial features of a human being with those of an animal. By combining contradictory elements, the designer produced a startling effect, especially as the figure is used in such an obviously fresh and apt way. Finally, in addition to a clear expression of the concept, the designer's command of different media and techniques of visual treatment also allows for modification of the degree of human beastness, which is similar to the use of adjectives to modify nouns or adverbs to modify verbs in a sentence.

VISUAL DUPLICATION OF RHETORICAL FIGURES

From a design viewpoint, rhetoric has classified numerous patterns of signification. However, rhetoric does not say metonymy exists when a king is represented by a crown. Instead, it formulates a kind of equation by saying that metonymy is a substitution for one another of terms suggesting an actual relationship that can be of causal, spatial, or chronological nature.

A common criticism that arises when dealing with rhetorical figures is that discourse manifests itself as concrete, particular, and individual, whereas these terms are abstract, general, and universal. How then can they be useful for the study of design? Their usefulness, according to K. Burke, resides in the fact that they can be re-individuated into different subject matter, that is, a particular figure can be filled out with a completely different subject. As Burke explains it: "A *metaphor* is a concept, an abstraction, but a specific metaphor, exemplified by specific images, is an *individuation*. Its appeal as form resides in the fact that its particular subject matter enables the mind to follow a metaphor-process."[12]

Thus, from a pragmatic viewpoint, rhetorical figures manifest themselves in vividly concrete ways, for example, Macbeth as a human beast. From a logical viewpoint, however, they represent only different abstract terms, for example, a metaphor that can be revitalized in numerous ways. Rhetorical figures should be viewed as construction principles that can assist designers in their search for visual concepts.

To conduct the case study, second-year graphic design students at the Nova Scotia College of Art and Design were introduced to rhetorical methodology. They were encouraged to adopt and test rhetorical figures in conjunction with the designing of a Macbeth poster for the local theater company. It was anticipated that this approach would help to shed more light on the process of concept formation, sparking a greater diversity of interpretations, and, therefore, a greater range of original poster designs. They read the play, viewed the movie *Macbeth* directed by Roman Polanski, and formed study groups around ten listed rhetorical figures. With the construction principle of a specific rhetorical figure as a guideline, each group looked for potential themes that fit the term and had visual potential. Finally, a theme was selected and visually executed; the results then were compared. The feedback from the students was enthusiastic; several mentioned that, for the first time, they felt as if they had produced something that deserved to be labeled "creative." The posters show the visual duplication of one specific rhetorical figure together with the concept statement (see Figures 5–14).

Rhetorical figures do not by any means represent specific recipes. They are exploration tools that can spur lateral thinking, giving designers the awareness of possibilities to make the best choice. However, the creative

FIGURE 5. Antithesis

FIGURE 6. Irony

Juxtaposition of Macbeth, the loyal general, with Macbeth, the visciously evil king (Joseph McDonald).

The amiable couple, Her Highness Lady Macbeth and His Highness King Macbeth (Marilyn Dyke).

FIGURE 7. Metaphor

Comparison between events in the play Macbeth and contemporary events of a similar nature portrayed as we would learn of them today, for example, in a newspaper (Nat Connacher).

FIGURE 8. Personification

Human qualities are assigned to animate and inanimate objects bearing historical significance, bleeding armor (Ian Mason).

FIGURE 9. Metonymy

The crown and the blood suggest an actual relationship with the tragic theme of the play (Julien LeBlanc).

FIGURE 10. Synecdoche

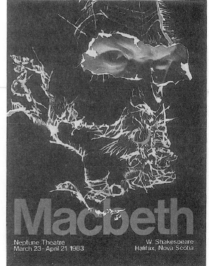

Substitution of a part for the whole, a portrayal of Macbeth's sinister character through concentration on the eyes (Cynthia Henry).

FIGURE 11. Periphrases

Macbeth's fatal strategy to attain power and crown is indirectly referred to by a "baited trap" (Siuw Ying Soo).

FIGURE 12. Pun

A play on the three witches, who spur Macbeth's ambition to attain the crown, and the crown itself (Steve Durning).

FIGURE 13. Amplification

Selection of key elements of the play to enhance its nature (Dave Roe).

FIGURE 14. Hyperbole

Exaggeration of the crown, which turns out to be an unbearable burden for Macbeth (John Murphy).

process will not become mechanized, because each concrete task requires a different solution. The real problem continues to be that of bringing together the abstract construction principles with original ideas within the confines of a specific task. Concerning design curricula, it would be worthwhile to consider consciously once again the surprising adaptability of rhetoric, especially in light of the new rhetoric movement and in the context of contemporary society, for this society is informed by visual discourse through a wide variety of media to a degree incomparable with any other time.

NOTES

1. Quoted in R. Stacey, *The Canadian Poster Book* (Toronto: Methuen, 1979), 58.

2. Edward P. J. Corbett, *Classical Rhetoric for the Modern Student*, 2nd ed. (New York: Oxford University Press, 1971), 625–30.

3. Umberto Eco, *A Theory of Semiotics* (Bloomington: Indiana University Press, 1976), 277–78.

4. E. R. Curtius, *European Literature and the Latin Middle Ages* (Princeton: Princeton UP, 1953), 77–78.

5. Renssalaer Wright Lee, *Ut Pictura Poesis: The Humanistic Theory of Painting* (New York: W. W. Norton, 1967).

6. G. Bonsiepe, "Visual/Verbal, Rhetoric," *Ulm* 14/15/16 (1965).

7. Martin Krampen "Signs and Symbols in Graphic Communication." *Design Quarterly* 62 (1968): 18.

8. Corbett, *Classical Rhetoric*, 415.

9. J. DeMille, *The Elements of Rhetoric* (New York: Harper and Brothers, 1878).

10. Quoted in Eco, *Theory of Semiotics*, 15.

11. See Eco, *Theory of Semiotics*, 51–57.

12. Kenneth Burke, *Counter-Statement* (Los Altos, CA: Hermes Publications, 1953), 143.

10   *The Role of Abstraction in Scientific Illustration: Implications for Pedagogy*

PUNYASHLOKE MISHRA

> In examining visual messages, as in examining other forms of messages, it is necessary to take into account the hidden assumptions which are inevitably adopted both by their producers and their users.
>
> – MOORHOUSE (1974)

> It is important to clarify the potentialities of the image in communication, to ask what it can do and what it cannot do. . . In comparison with the importance of the question, the amount of attention devoted to it is disappointingly small.
>
> – GOMBRICH (1960)

> There is more to seeing than meets the eye.
>
> – GREGORY (1970)

INTRODUCTION

Illustrations are often seen as a very significant part of educational materials. From the earliest stages of elementary school to the advanced college level, illustrations are used profusely and in many cases may be the most striking feature that distinguishes one set of learning materials from another. In fact, the perceived effectiveness of the illustrations clearly plays an important role in the marketing of many educational materials.

Diagrams, accompanied by text, have been a common means of recording and conveying scientific and technical information since the fifteenth century. While the use of illustrations in more secular texts actually goes back much further in time (Ford, 1992; Robin, 1992), the invention of the printing press in the fifteenth century made these illustrated books available to a large audience. Their availability may have been a major cause of the large

From *Journal of Visual Literacy* 19:2 (Autumn 1999): 139–158.

technological advances between the sixteenth and eighteenth centuries. As McLuhan, the late guru of media theory, said:

> The art of making pictorial statements in a precise and repeatable form is one that has long been taken for granted in the West. But it is usually forgotten that without prints and blueprints, without maps and geometry, the world of modern science and technology would hardly exist (1964, p. 145).

In recent years there has been an analogous advance in the capabilities of graphic technologies, as well as their availability. Technologies, such as animation software, computer-aided drawing, and plotting programs have made the techniques of graphic communication available to an ever growing community of users. Scientific visualization has become an important tool for scientists in all disciplines.

However, given the importance of visual displays in science, there has been little research into this area. There has been research on the use of imagery and mental models in scientific thinking (Brown, 1991), as well as some interesting debate on whether human thinking is visual or propositional in nature. But apart from supporting our notion that imagery plays an important role in scientific thinking and creativity, much of this work is quite peripheral to the issue of how scientific illustrations are used and understood. Verbal propositions, arguments, references, analogies, metaphors, and "ideas" have received much greater attention as constituents of scientific reasoning and rhetoric. This imbalance may be due to the fact that methods for analyzing verbal materials are more developed than those for analyzing pictures. Lynch argues that, the fact that writing is the dominant medium of academic discourse is not incidental:

> While pictorial subject matter is alien to written discourse, and requires a reduction to make it amenable to analysis, written subject matter can be iterated without any "gap" within the textual surface that analyzes it. Nevertheless, visual displays are distinctly involved in scientific communication and in the very "construction" of scientific facts (1991a, p. 207).

Gould argues that this neglect can have serious consequences:

> Iconography comes upon us like a thief in the night—powerful and remarkably efficacious, yet often so silent that we do not detect the influence. Pictorial imagery catches us unawares because, as intellectuals, we are trained to analyze text and to treat drawings or photographs as trifling adjuncts. Thus, while we may pore over our words and examine them closely for biases and hidden meanings, we often view our pictures as frills and afterthoughts, simple illustrations of a natural reality or crutches for those who need a visual guide. We are most revealed in what we do not scrutinize (1993, p. 108).

This lack of scrutiny can cause problems at multiple levels—from the design of incorrect visuals to the causing (or the strengthening or existing) misconceptions in the minds of students.

MISCONCEPTIONS OR ALTERNATIVE CONCEPTIONS

Current research in science education has generated a growing body of evidence showing that students come to science classes with theories about how the natural world works. These theories are generally less coherent, less precise, and less extensive than accepted scientific theories and often hinder students' learning.

These cognitive structures that students have prior to instruction have been variously called misconceptions, alternative frameworks, alternative conceptions, or naive theories (Hewson & Hewson, 1984). A great deal of research has documented alternative conceptions of topics as varied as motion, friction, gravity, heat and temperature, electricity, light, evolution, heredity, etc. A good review of such research is given by Driver, Guesne, and Tiberghien (1985). Research in cognitive science and the history and philosophy of science has produced a general consensus on the nature of science learning that can help in understanding why alternative conceptions occur. As Hewson and Hewson (1984) state:

> The emerging picture is of a learner who actively constructs his or her own meaning by looking for regularity and order in the events of the world. On the one hand, learning can happen only by relating the unknown to what is already known, and thus all learning depends on the prior knowledge of the learner . . . On the other hand, learning involves the active generation of new links between new information and the existing knowledge by the learner . . . each learner generates links between new and old for him or herself, it is not surprising to find that different learners construct alternative conceptions of the same phenomena (p. 12).

Most of the misconception research has focused on textual materials. There is little research on how scientific images can hinder or enhance the development of such misconceptions. This paper offers a framework for further research into this area.

MISCONCEPTIONS AND SCIENTIFIC ILLUSTRATIONS

The scope and applicability of previous educational research into illustrations is limited primarily due to the narrow band of ideas that were considered amenable to scientific questioning. There are two good reviews of research into scientific illustration, a 1979 paper by Fleming and a 1984 book by Goldsmith. In reviewing the work of the previous twenty years Fleming notes that though research has improved, because it has become more analytical and advances in psychology have contributed to our understanding of these issues, much of the work seems to have only limited relevance to answering any questions about the value of illustrations in assisting science learning.

Goldsmith's book (1984), *Research into Illustration: An Approach and a Review*, is a comprehensive review of the research on the understanding of factors affecting the comprehensibility of illustration. It is interesting, though somewhat depressing, to note the absolute lack of any research into how read-ers may comprehend (or miscomprehend) illustrations. Most of the research focuses on the formal aspects of illustrations, such as the perception of color, shapes, faces etc. Rarely are illustrations seen within the larger context of ful-filling some specific educational purpose. For example, among the more than 650 books and papers referenced in this book, just one paper mentions some specific subject area (biology). However, a closer perusal reveals that the paper is concerned more with the effect of color on children's pictorial com-prehension than with biology. The illustrations used could very easily have been from any other discipline within science.

The Goldsmith book does, however, set forth in great detail all the research on picture perception conducted up to 1984. Though the author admits that the findings of the research are conflicting, there are some inter-esting conclusions about the perception of images in general that are of inter-est. The research on children's perceptions is quite exhaustive and can be quite useful to textbook designers and illustrators.

Representations of statistical data, and the misconceptions that it can lead to, have been studied in depth in Tufte's (1983) classic work, *The Visual Display of Quantitative Information*. Tufte points out misconceptions that can arise due to the manner in which data are displayed. Such errors may be deliberate in that the designer or statistician willfully presents the data in a manner meant to mislead the reader, or they may be unplanned.

Some of the more interesting work in this area has been done by psy-chologists of art. Critics such as Ernst Gombrich and Rudolf Arnheim have combined a deep understanding of art and illustration with the psychology of perception to develop theories of how people see and understand art, carica-ture, and illustrations. Their work is of great relevance to the scientific illus-trator and educator. Unfortunately, their work has been largely ignored by educational researchers, and that is a sad commentary on the exclusive nature of intellectual boundaries.

Another approach that has gained prestige and following in recent years is that practiced by the people studying the "sociology of scientific knowl-edge" (SSK) (Ashmore, 1989). They see illustrations as just one of the many forms of scientific representation and study it within a large societal and dis-course matrix. The distinction between what the psychologists of art and the sociologists of science can tell us is an interesting one. The psychologists focus on the more formal and perceptual elements of visuals, while sociolo-gists stress the process of science and knowledge formation, and how that process affects visual representation. Knowledge of both the elements and process is essential if we are to understand how people "read" illustrations.

Following this rather extended introduction, the rest of the paper is devoted to developing a broad framework for studying the manner in which images are used in communicating science. I begin first by looking at the psy-chology of art and perception. This is followed by sketching out what the soci-ology of science approach has to say about how scientific representation functions within scientific discourse. Finally, I focus on seeing how these two very different perspectives can help us understand scientific illustration specifically within an educational context.

PSYCHOLOGY OF ART AND PERCEPTION

There are two different approaches to how pictures are interpreted. According to the standard view, a picture is defined in structural terms as, "any two-dimensional artifact that attempts a veridical representation of an object or the relationships between objects" (Reid, 1990). Theorists in this camp see picture interpretation skills in terms of the development of more general cognitive, linguistic, and psycho-motor skills. Pictorial representation depends upon visual correspondence or "likeness" with the object depicted.

Usually pictures are supposed to represent reality — directly. The word "horse" is an arbitrary sequence of phonemes. Any other sequence of phonemes would have done as well. However with respect to images, it is felt, that there is no such randomness. An image is iconic, i.e. there is a one to one mapping between the object with its image.

The other camp (Gombrich, 1960, 1982; Arnheim, 1969, 1974; Gregory, 1970, 1973), however, postulate abilities more specific to the process of "picture interpretation" and attribute the advancement of picture "reading" skills to the learning of pictorial conventions. One can trace the roots of this contentiousness to disagreements about the nature of pictures themselves. While the former position sees development in picture interpretation skills as the increasing ability to make intelligent judgments about pictures which have "imperfect fidelity" with the object depicted, the latter explains progress by postulating a growing vocabulary of pictorial symbols and conventions (see Figure 1). Implications of the second view are that some pictorial conventions need more learning than others and some illustrations pose difficulties because they make greater use of conventions than others. The second view has become increasingly popular especially due to studies into the history of art and the psychology of perception (Gombrich. 1960; Gregory, 1970).

FIGURE 1. Perception as Hypothesis Testing: A Perceived Object Is a Hypothesis, Suggested and Tested by Sensory Data. A Single Line Can Serve Many Purposes.

Illustration by author, based on work by Saul Steinberg.

According to this perspective, seeing is not tacking different interpretations to one and the same precept. The experienced physician, mechanic, or physiologist looking at a wound, an engine, or a microscopic preparation "sees" things the novice does not see. If both experts and laymen were asked to make exact copies of what they see, their drawings would be quite different. Perception involves "going beyond the immediately given evidence of the senses": this evidence is assessed on many grounds and generally we make the best bet, and see things more or less correctly. But the senses do not give us a picture of the world directly; rather they provide evidence for checking hypotheses about what lies before us. Indeed we may say that "a perceived object is a hypothesis, suggested and tested by sensory data" (Gregory, 1970).

There is a great commonalty between the views espoused by the psychologists of art and some contemporary post-positivist philosophers of science. Prominent among them is Russell Hanson (1965) with his emphasis of the idea that all observation is theory laden. According to him, there are indefinitely many ways in which a constellation of lines, shapes, patches, may be seen. Why a visual pattern is seen differently is a question for psychology, but that it may be seen differently is important in any examination of the concepts of seeing and observation. As Gregory (1970) puts it, "Perceiving and thinking are not independent: 'I see what you mean' is not a puerile pun, but indicates a connection which is very real." Similarly interpreting illustrations is also a creative task. Illustrations also have pasts and futures; they change and influence each other, and have hidden aspects which emerge under different conditions.

However, perceiving illustrations is, in a very fundamental way, different from perceiving the world around us. Pictures are not natural. Gregory contends that no eyes before man's were confronted by pictures. Previously, all objects in themselves were important or could be safely ignored. But pictures, though trivial in themselves, mere patterns of marks, are important in showing absent things. Biologically this is most odd since for millions of years animals had been able to respond only to present situations and the immediate future. Pictures, and other symbols, allow responses to be directed to situations quite different from the present; and may give perceptions perhaps not even possible for the world of objects. This is their strength, yet it may be where they can go wrong as well. Gregory states:

> Pictures have a double reality. Drawings, paintings, and photographs are objects in their own right, patterns on a flat sheet, and at the same time entirely different objects to the eye. We see both a pattern of marks on paper, with shading, brush strokes or photographic "grain", and at the same time we see that these compose a face, a house or a ship on a stormy sea. Pictures are unique among objects; for they are seen both as themselves and as some other thing, entirely different from the paper or canvas of the picture. Pictures are paradoxes (Gregory, 1970. p. 128).

The paradoxical nature of pictures is that they must convey information about a three-dimensional world through marks on a two-dimensional surface. There are various ways of doing this, as a survey of world art will show, and almost no two ways are alike. For a long time art historians felt that geometrical perspective was the right way of representing the world. However, geometrical perspective was unknown until the Renaissance. In the highly developed world of the ancient Egyptians, heads and feet are shown in profile, never foreshortened by perspective, which offers a certain resemblance to children's art. Chinese drawing and painting curiously goes against the formal rules of perspective in that lines actually diverge with increasing distance. As Gombrich (1960) says, "It is an extraordinary fact that simple geometrical perspective took so long to develop—far longer than the wheel or fire—and yet in a sense it has always been present for the seeing" (p. 143). But he asks, "Is perspective present in nature? Is perspective a discovery, or an invention of the Renaissance artists?" The answer he suggests is that perspective is an invention, an invention whose implicit conventions we now take for granted. He argues that all art and representation depends on a series of conventions and to place one over the other may be wrong. Geometric perspective may be appropriate for the way the image of the world is formed on the retina, but it need not be the way we actually perceive. "When an artist employs geometrical perspective he does not draw what he sees, he represents his retinal image." Representational realism is not a static phenomenon. Artistic realism includes an abundance of painterly techniques and stylistic conventions which do not simply fall in line along a continuum from "nonrealistic" to "completely realistic" (Gombrich, 1960, p. 144). Scientific realism is no different, and scientists use artistic conventions and techniques for documenting observations and illustrating texts.

This notion of abstraction and the creation of symbol systems (visual conventions) is of crucial importance in the argument that Arnheim and Gombrich are making. Winn argues that diagrams use "notational" symbol systems. Winn says that "in notational symbol systems an unambiguous relationship exists between each symbol in the diagram and the object to which it refers. Some diagrams contain hierarchies of symbols and symbol groups that illustrate domains of reference at varying levels of complexity" (1993, p. 163).

The symbols used for electronics since the beginning of this century parallel the development of the pictograms of ancient languages. At first the symbols were realistic drawings of the components. Within a few years, the electronic "pictograms" became simpler: the emphasis was placed on the functionally important features of the components, while the outward shapes were lost. The symbols pictured their functional significance. Each symbol is a kind of abstract cartoon. An early (1884) drawing of a Wheatstone bridge circuit shows that the components are drawn as they appear, without emphasis on their functional characteristics. A later (1890) drawing of the same circuit is somewhat more stylized, with emphasis on the functional features of the components. A still later (1898) drawing shows that by this time the components are not drawn as they appear: they are drawn with conventionalized symbols. But such symbols are meaningless to those with no understanding of, in this case, electrical theory (see Figure 2). Symbols only have meaning for those who share perceptual hypotheses, or abstract theories.

Another example, this time from biology — human anatomy to be specific — is given in Miller (1978). Anatomical textbooks give the misleading impression that everything in the chest is immediately distinguishable. In the illustrations, the heart is artificially distinguished from its vessels by a bold graphic outline and sometimes a special color. The aorta is printed in scarlet, the great veins in sky-blue, the nerves are usually represented in green and yellow (see Figure 3). Miller says:

> The unsuspecting student plunges into the laboratory carcass expecting to find these neat arrangements repeated in nature, and the blurred confusion which he actually meets often produces a sense of despair. The heart is not so clearly distinguished from its vessels as the textbook implies, and at first sight the vessels are practically indistinguishable from one another. A practiced eye can readily recognize the gristly pallor of an artery as opposed to the purple flabbiness of a vein, but what

FIGURE 2. Abstract Symbol Systems: Symbols Only Have Meaning for Those Who Share Perceptual Hypotheses, or Abstract Theories.

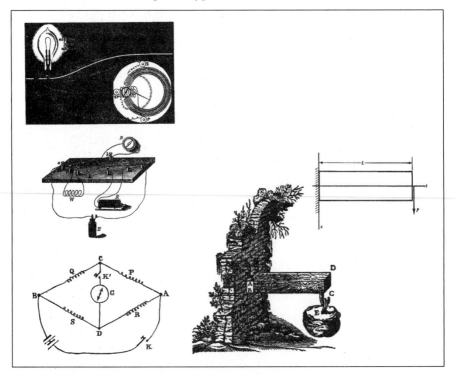

Wheat-stone bridge diagram as represented in 1888, 1890, and 1898 and Cantilever beam as shown by Galileo and as depicted in today's textbooks.

FIGURE 3. Abstraction and Reality: Anatomical Textbooks Give the Misleading Impression that Everything in the Chest Is Immediately Distinguishable. Diagram of a Human Heart Along with Actual Photograph

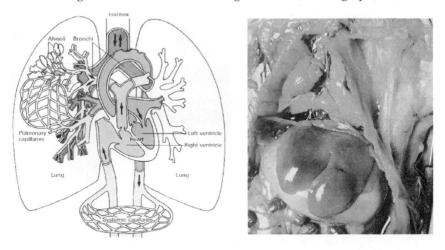

makes the eye practiced are the theories or presuppositions which direct its gaze — and one of the leading theories of anyone now looking into the chest is one which says that arteries are different because the blood flows through them in different directions. The color-codes which illustrate students' textbooks are not simply vivid illustrations of what there is to be seen, but graphic conventions which illustrate theories about the functions of what there is to be seen (p. 177).

The psychology of art approach tells us that there are artistic conventions that have to be learnt in order to understand pictures. These conventions are not "natural" but rather are creations of time and culture. However, scientific illustration is more than art. The term scientific graphics is the marriage of two very different notions, science and art, often felt to be antithetical to each other. Arnheim (1969) sees artistic activity as a form of reasoning, in which perceiving and thinking are indivisibly intertwined. Noting similarities between art and science, he feels that both are "bent on the understanding of the forces that shape existence, and both call for an unselfish dedication to what is. Neither of them can tolerate capricious subjectivity because both are subject to their criteria of truth. Both require precision, order, and discipline because no comprehensible statement can be made without these." However, there are significant differences especially in the criteria of exactness as applied to both disciplines. In a scientific demonstration, the particular appearance of what is shown matters only to the extent to which it is symptomatic of the facts.

The shape of the containers, the size of the dials, the precise color of a substance may be irrelevant, Similarly, the particular proportions, angles, colors of a diagram may not matter. This is because in science the appearance of things are mere indicators, pointing beyond themselves to hidden constellations of forces. The laboratory demonstration and the diagram in the textbook are not scientific statements but only illustrations of such statements. In the arts the image is the statement . . . The arts tell the student about the significance of direct experience and of his own response. In this sense, they are complimentary to the message of science, where direct experience must be transcended and the individual outlook of each observer counts only to the extent to which it contributes to shaping the conception of the phenomenon under investigation (Arnheim, 1969, p. 132).

All scientific illustration has to chart this line between the Scylla of scientific abstraction and the Charybdis of visual specificity of illustrations. This is one level at which misconceptions can occur in scientific illustrations. Students may see a visual in specific terms, as referring to something unique when the concept being dealt with is a more general one. As Lynch (1991b) says:

Even when a picture obviously resembles an object, just how it does so can be far from obvious when the picture is viewed in isolation. For instance, a picture of a seagull inflight can variously be used to illustrate the aerodynamics of flight, to display the characteristic field marks of a particular species or age-class or gull, to exemplify the basic anatomical features of birds, to demonstrate techniques of nature photography, or to give a pictorial inventory of typical constituents of a shoreline habitat. An appreciation of the picture's conceptual and documentary functions can be gained only when one places it within a cross-referential network. This network includes various other textual features—captions, headings, narratives, and other tables, graphs, photographs and pictures—as well as the practices within which these textual features have a role. The polysemous properties of pictures are readily grasped when one flips through an illustrated text and examines the pictures while covering-up the captions (p. 204).

This is similar to what Gould (1993, p. 211) says while describing the problems with biological illustrations. One of the problems, he feels, is the fact that by intending to "capture the entire time period" illustrators are forced to wedge in as many animals and ecosystems within a single picture as they possibly can. This leads to a false view of prehistoric life, showing it to be more active and crowded than it really was. This is a misconception, since "at most natural moments at most places nothing much is happening."

THE SOCIOLOGY OF SCIENTIFIC KNOWLEDGE

In contrast to the psychologists of art, the sociologists of science reject (at least temporarily) the idea of representation from an individualistic cognitive foundation, and attempt to "replace a preoccupation with images on the retina . . . with a focus on the 'externalized retina.' . . . [Pictures are used] as evidence of methodic practices, accomplished by researchers working together in groups, which transform previously hidden phenomena into visual displays for consensual 'seeing' and 'knowing'" (Lynch, 1991a, p. 206).

A similarity of viewpoint can be seen in recent developments in "distributed cognition." (Salomon, 1993). This view reexamines the traditional view that sees cognition as existing solely "inside" a person's head and attempts to consider social, physical, and artifactual surroundings in which cognition takes place. The claim is that a "clearer understanding of human cognition would be achieved if studies were based on the concept that cognition is distributed among individuals, that knowledge is socially constructed through collaborative efforts to achieve shared objectives in cultural surroundings, and that information is processed between individuals and the tools and artifacts provided by culture" (Salomon, 1993, p. 14). According to this framework, illustrations, diagrams, and other visual displays must be considered as carrying information within a context contingent on the history and social practices of the domain under consideration. A newcomer into the field may not "see" the same thing since a sharing of concepts has not taken place. Thus it is the business of the educator and the illustrator, to take care of the preconceptions of the students.

Lynch (1991a, p. 217) argues that there is more to the "transformational process" in the creation of diagrams than mere simplification and abstraction (as argued by the psychologists of art). This process synthesizes form as well. Most importantly, it strives to identify in the particular specimen under study "universal" properties which "solidify" the object in reference to the current state of the discipline. In comparing photographs to diagrams of the same object, he argues that while a photograph is "unique, situationally specific, perspectival, and instantaneous" a diagram is "essential, synthetic, constant and veridical." It could be said (quite counter-intuitively) that, within the context of a given scientific discourse, a photograph is an imperfect representation of an actual object, while a diagram represents it more faithfully (see Figure 4). Thus the conventions of representation are more than artistic devices, they take their authority from previous experience and the state of

FIGURE 4. Abstraction Defines Reality: Within the Context of a Given Scientific Discourse, a Photograph Is an Imperfect Representation, While a Diagram Represents It More Faithfully. Photograph and Diagram of a Mitochondrion.

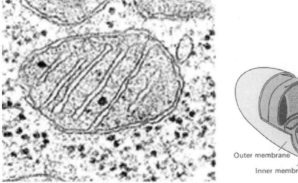
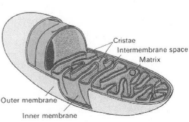

the scientific field to competently build on a body of assumptions about the represented structures.

The variety of illustration styles used in scientific communication (such as diagrams, photographs, sketches, tables, graphs, instrumental displays, animations, simulations, and so on) are not isolated representations, but they all work within a framework of verbal and written discourse. Although many sketches and pictures can easily be seen to resemble a familiar object of interest (a cell organelle, animal, or plant, of a particular species etc.) what a picture "is doing in a textual representation is not disclosed by naming what it resembles" (Lynch, 1991a, p. 217). Many diagrams take the form of "conceptual models" of, for instance, a flow of ions across a membrane, a cycle of biochemical transformations, or a molecular sequence. At times such images include symbolic, iconic, and even fantastic features; for example, vectors, cartoon figures, chemical formulas, and labels. Such hybrid combinations of "schematic, pictorial and verbal constituents" make up what Gilbert and Mulkay call "working conceptual hallucinations." (see Figure 5)

A historical approach to graphic conventions in science can reveal which conventions change and which persist, and whether the meaning of persistent conventions remains constant. Many graphic conventions have survived centuries of change in both scientific practice and technology of pictorial reproduction. Some of "these conventions have so much and such enduring power that they can be deployed to effect, and can also pass unremarked" (Gould, 1993, p. 109). O'Hara's (1991) investigation into some of these "invisible" conventions in nineteenth century biological illustration shows a strong emphasis on the geometric ideal of order portrayed through symmetry and numerical regularity. Maienschein (1991) reports similar findings in his work on illustration style in E. B. Wilson's work on cytology *The Cell*. He traces an increased abstraction in Wilson's use of diagrams from the first publication in 1896 to the last publication in 1925. Moreover, he also notices "an enduring premium on symmetry." These conventions are "hardly neutral" and embed within them certain ideas and notions that may not even be apparent to scientists and designers themselves. Hanson (1958) said that one cannot remove the context (speaking of the context in very general terms) from the image: "The context is part of the illustration itself. Such a context, however, need not be set out explicitly, Often it is 'built into' thinking, imagining and picturing. We are set to appreciate the visual aspect of things in certain ways" (Hanson, 1958, p. 15).

Illustrations have a history. Often they are copied and passed on without thought. Illustrations once created develop a life of their own and are repeated indiscriminately in spite of changes in scientific theories. Ford (1992) documents how illustrations have changed over time, sometimes due to improvements in technology, sometimes due to plagiarism.

> The thousand words that a picture is supposed to tell are a small part of the tale. There are hidden influences and cultural pressures underlying what people choose to illustrate, and fashionable constraints on how they make their representation. . . . Plagiarism has been rife in science since the discipline emerged. . . . Each generation of copying takes one

FIGURE 5. Conceptual Hallucinations: Hybrid Combinations of Schematic, Pictorial, and Verbal Elements Make Working Conceptual Hallucinations. The Process of Protein Synthesis.

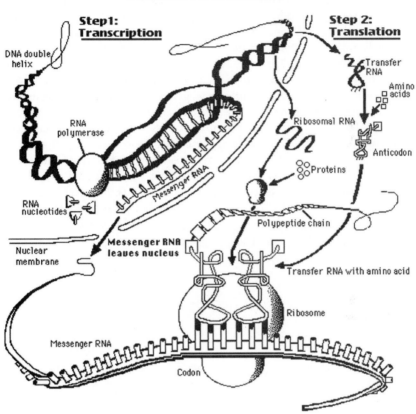

PROTEIN SYNTHESIS

further from reality. A living specimen, well portrayed, becomes wooden and stiff as it is copied and re-copied. Scientific realities mutate: six-pointed snowflakes become eight-pointed, [something that just does not exist in nature] just as carefully delineated bacteria transpose themselves into species that seem to exist only in textbooks . . . there are "icons" that stand out in scientific literature: illustrations to attract respect for learning, but which cannot be intended to represent reality. Scientific illustration may be scientific in nature, but it may be far from scientific in application. (p. 164)

There may be a feeling that such plagiarism and hidden influences may have existed in earlier more imperfect times, but do not take place today. However, these factors are so deeply ingrained that it may be impossible to even feel their presence except in hindsight. Gould in his chapter on dinosaur iconography shows the changes that have been taking place in pictorial representation of dinosaurs over the last few centuries. Scenes of predation, the staple of Victorian iconography are replaced by scenes of herding and caring. Dinosaurs are no longer slow lumbering giants but rather are sleek, fast, efficient animals. Commenting on these changes Gould says, "I am intrigued to note how closely the trends in prehistoric iconography match the winds of change labeled 'postmodernism' in so many other fields from literature to architecture—so we are once again taking part in a general social movement, not merely following the local norms of science by responding to improvements in factual knowledge." (Gould 1993, p. 109)

Another example of scientific illustrations copied indiscriminately and thus restricting other interpretations is given in a Mazurs (1974) book in which he documents some 450 different ways the periodic table has been portrayed in the past 100 years, all of them "correct" yet different from each other (see Figure 6). Most people however, know just one version of the periodic table, the Mendeleev version. These multiple representations of the periodic system have been used as a basis for developing a multi-media hypertext for teaching complex concepts in chemistry (Mishra & Nguyen-Jahiel, 1997;

FIGURE 6. Missing Representations: Some Alternative Representations of the Periodic System Not Usually Seen in Textbooks. From Left: Treptow's Atomic Table; Janet's Spiral and Pyramid Table.

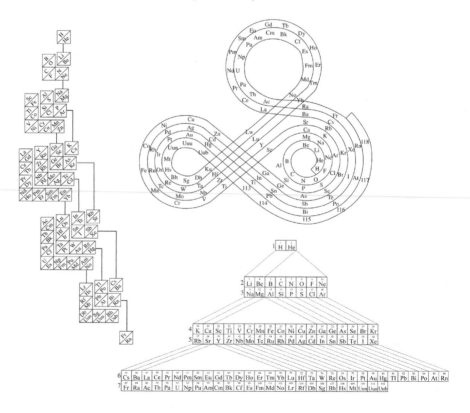

Mishra, 1998). As Root-Bernstein (1989) says in his book on scientific discovery and creativity:

> Pictures, tables, graphs can be dangerous things. Revealing one point, they hide assumptions, eliminate possibilities, prevent comparisons — silently, unobviously. Thus, a pattern makes sense of data but also limits what sense it can make (p. 142).

The reasons for this conservatism on the part of artists and scientists are many — ranging from lack of knowledge about other interpretations to political, social, and personal factors that abhor change. The conservative nature of the publishing industry (with economic pressures to stick to the acceptable and proven) are also issues to consider.

MISCONCEPTIONS AND SCIENTIFIC ILLUSTRATIONS: REVISITED

It must be obvious that despite apparent differences there are certain fundamental similarities between what psychologists of art and the sociologists of science have to say about the use and perception of images. However, we must remember that science is a very broad term and is used to describe a large variety of practices and products. The word "products" is used in a very general way as the specific result of scientific activity. It may be a theory, a host of data, a new piece of technology, and so on. It does not necessarily mean some specific material object. Different subdisciplines in science need different strategies and "ways of doing." If we are to understand how illustrations can lead to misconceptions it is important to focus on individual topics in science. It is important for us to ground our theoretical work in the actual educational situation. Misconceptions in science do not happen independent of the content of what is to be taught and learned. Each situation will be unique in the way in which it affects students and their prior beliefs.

One of the first references to these issues of misunderstanding illustrations is given by Arnheim (1969). He shows a figure that was used by Piaget to test the comprehension of children (see Figure 7). Do they understand how a tap works? When the handle is turned horizontally, the canal is open and lets the water run through; otherwise it is closed. The child's performance will largely depend on whether the drawing is recognizable as a tap. The pipe, flat rather than cylindrical, hangs in space. It does not continue on top, nor does it receive water from anywhere. The hatching does not indicate liquid filling a hollow and shows little relation to the dark stripe, meant to be the canal. The canal is in front of the handle rather than behind it, and the handle is not in front of the pipe. Does *b* show a vertical handle outside a pipe or rather a kind of bob, swallowed by a rectangle or possibly a tube? As Arnheim (1974) says, "But surely, if a child passes the test he does so in spite of the drawing, not with the help of it; and if he fails, he has not shown that he does not understand the working of a tap. He may simply be unable to extricate himself from a visual pitfall" (p. 120).

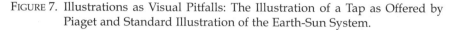

FIGURE 7. Illustrations as Visual Pitfalls: The Illustration of a Tap as Offered by Piaget and Standard Illustration of the Earth-Sun System.

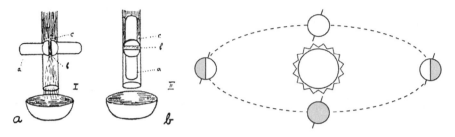

Deficient pictures of this kind can be found at any level of abstractness. The drawings could be much more realistic and still be unsuited to present the relevant features of the physical situation. They fail not because they are not lifelike or devoid of detail but because they are ambiguous and misleading.

The next example is based on Gould's (1993) analysis of fossil iconography. He feels that the artistic conventions used in these paintings/illustrations create an enormous departure between scenes as sketched and any conceivable counterpart in nature. He sees a fundamental difference between artistic genres in general and the nature of fossil iconography in specific. All artistic genres follow social conventions, but few also "grapple with the assumption that finished products represent a natural reality" (p. 108). Gould identifies a series of conventions (all of which can be defended) that "distinguish painted fossil scenes from inferred actualities." He argues that certain fundamental misconceptions that many people have about evolution can be traced to these conventions.

Another example is related to astronomy. Most people seem to have consistent misconceptions about how the seasons are caused. The standard belief is that seasons are caused by the elliptical nature of earth's orbit around the sun. The further the earth is from the sun the colder it gets and vice versa. It is summer when the earth is closest to the sun and winter when it is furthest away. However, this theory does not explain why the southern hemisphere switches seasons with the northern hemisphere nor does it explain why we do not have two winters and two summers every year. It is provocative to think of this misconception as being caused by the standard illustration seen in textbooks and science writings. The orbit of the earth is described as being "shaped like a stretched out circle" (quoted in Michaels & Bruce, 1989). However, they ignore the fact that the ratio between the major and the minor axis of the ellipse that is the earth's orbit is so close to unity that no diagram (at least one that fits in a regular textbook) can show its elliptical nature. This is compounded by the way in which these illustrations are usually drawn — from a viewpoint above and at an angle over the plane within which the planets lie. This point of view exaggerates the elliptical nature even more. Michaels and Bruce enumerate a few more "problems":

The distorted scale in the figure presents the sun as smaller than the earth (when in fact the sun has 100 times the diameter of the earth). It shows the earth/sun distance as less than one earth diameter, when in fact it should be 100 times the diameter of the sun. These representations may contribute to the misconception that variations in energy received between the poles and the equator are due to differences in distance to the sun (p. 7).

CONCLUSION

To conclude, visual representations are powerful tools to communicate ideas. However, in spite of their effectiveness and importance very little research has been focused on how they work in an educational situation. This paper identifies three areas that are possible "danger areas" for students. The first is that all forms of illustration depend on artistic conventions — conventions that are not "natural" and have to be learnt. Students unaware of these conventions can easily misunderstand illustrations and other visual representations. Second, apart from artistic conventions, scientific illustrations function within the matrix of science, with its hidden assumptions and biases. Quite often these biases are invisible to us at this moment in time and thus are quite insidious in their effect. Illustrations in a given domain are very dependent on the theory they are based on. This is not a one way street — a theory helps us "see" certain facts and then illustrate them; and these illustrations, in turn, support the theory. And third, illustrations have a contingent, zig-zag history and their copying and recopying leads them to evolve far from what they began with — any diagram of amoeba or a paramecium in school-textbooks can show this "evolution." (See Ford, 1993, for some excellent examples.) Apart from the above factors, we must also consider the fact that illustrations are treated (created/read) differently by different domains or subdisciplines within science. Biological illustrations have a very different look and feel from tracks of subatomic particles or from geological maps. Even within biology, genetics requires a different kind of visual skills than paleontology. Thus, understanding how illustrations work in science cannot be done in a generalized manner, it must be grounded in the dynamics of a specific discipline.

REFERENCES

Arnheim, R. (1969). *Visual thinking*. Los Angeles: University of California Press.

Arnheim, R. (1974). Introduction: Lemonade and the perceiving mind. In Moorhouse, C. E. (Ed.) *Visual education*. Carlton, Vic.: Pitman Australia.

Ashmore, M. (1989). *The reflexive thesis: Wrighting sociology of scientific knowledge*. Chicago: University of Chicago Press.

Brown, J. R. (1991). *The laboratory of the mind: Thought experiments in the natural sciences*. London: Routledge.

Driver, R., Guesne, E. & Tiberghien, A. (1985). *Children's ideas in science*. Philadelphia: Open University Press.

Fleming, M. L. (1979). On pictures in educational research. *Instructional Science, 8*, 235–251.

Ford, B. J. (1992). *Images of science: A history of scientific illustration*. London: The British Library.

Goldsmith, E. (1984). *Research into illustration: An approach and a review*. Cambridge: Cambridge University Press.

Gombrich, E. H. (1960). *Art and illusion: A study in the psychology of pictorial representation.* New York: Pantheon Books.

Gombrich, E. H. (1982). *The image and the eye: Further studies in the psychology of pictorial representation.* Ithaca, NY: Cornell University Press.

Gould, S. J. (1993). Dinosaur deconstruction. *Discover, 14* (10), 108–113.

Gregory, R. L. (1970). *The intelligent eye.* New York: McGraw-Hill.

Gregory, R. L. (1973). *Eye and brain: The psychology of seeing.* New York: McGraw-Hill.

Hanson, R, N. (1958). *Patterns of discovery.* Cambridge: Cambridge University Press.

Hewson, P. W. & Hewson, M. G. A. (1984). The role of conceptual conflict in conceptual change and the design of science instruction. *Instructional Science, 13,* 1–13.

Lynch, M. (1991a). Science in the age of mechanical reproduction: Moral and epistemic relations between diagrams and photographs. *Biology and Philosophy, 6,* 205–226.

Lynch, M. (1991b). The externalized retina: Selection and mathematization in the visual documentation of objects in the life sciences. *Human Studies, 11,* 201–254.

Maienschein, J. (1991). From presentation to representation in E. B. Wilson's *The Cell. Biology and Philosophy, 6,* 227–254.

Mazurs, E. G. (1974). *Graphic representations of the periodic system during one hundred years.* Tuscaloosa: University of Alabama Press.

McLuhan, M. (1964). *Understanding media: The extensions of man.* New York: McGraw-Hill.

Michaels, S. & Bruce, B. (1989). Discourses on the seasons. Paper presented at the *Annual Meeting of the American Educational Research Association,* San Francisco, CA.

Miller, J. (1978). *The body in question.* New York: Random House.

Mishra, P. & Nguyen-Jahiel, K. (1997). Multiple visual representations of the Periodic System of elements: Epistemological and pedagogic implications. *Proceedings of the 1997 IVLA Conference,* State College, PA.

Mishra, P. (1998). Flexible learning in the Periodic System with multiple representations: The design of a hypertext for learning complex concepts in chemistry. *Unpublished doctoral dissertation.* University of Illinois at Urbana-Champaign.

Moorhouse, C. E. (1974). *Visual education.* Carlton, Vic.: Pitman Australia.

O'Hara, R. J. (1991). Representations of the Natural System in the nineteenth century. *Biology and Philosophy, 6,* 255–274.

Reid, D. (1990). The role of pictures in learning biology: Part 1. Perception and observation. *Journal of Biological Education, 24* (3), 161–172.

Reid, D. J. & Miller, G. J. A. (1980). Pupil's perception of biological pictures and its implications for the readability studies of biology textbooks. *Journal of Biological Education. 14* (1), 59–69.

Robin, H. (1992). *The scientific image: from cave to computer.* New York: Harry N. Abrams.

Root-Bernstein, R. S. (1989). *Discovering: Inventing and solving problems at the frontiers of scientific knowledge.* Cambridge, MA: Harvard University Press.

Salomon, G. (1993). (Ed.) *Distributed cognitions; Psychological and educational considerations.* Cambridge, Cambridge University Press.

Tufte, E. R. (1983). *The visual display of quantitative information.* Cheshire, CT: Graphic Press.

Winn, W. (1993). An account of how readers search for information in diagrams. *Contemporary Educational Psychology, 18,* 162–185.

11 From *The Vocabulary of Comics*

SCOTT MCCLOUD

From *Understanding Comics: The Invisible Art*. New York: HarperCollins, 1994. 24–37.

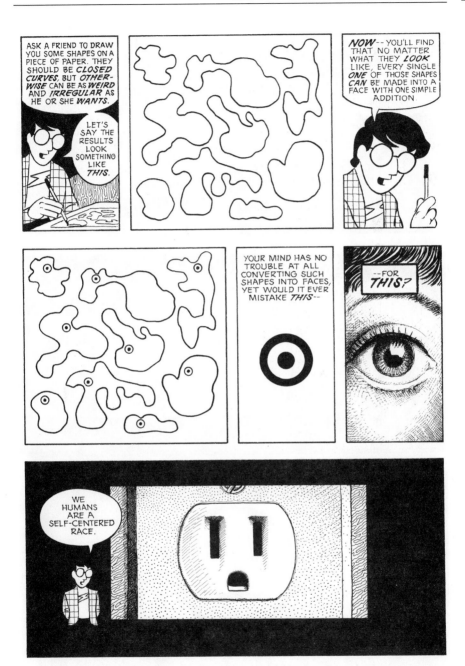

12   *Visual Pragmatism for a Virtual World*

BARBARA STAFFORD

A Constructivist Manifesto

Recent academic rhetoric is saturated with terms of rejection, revision, revolution; but manifestos, even of renunciation, remain in short supply. Writing about what is wrong in old optical formats and new imaging technologies is relatively easy. Harder is proposing mind-opening analogies between historical displays of visual intelligence and computer-age information viewed through the eyes. Being digital requires designing a post-Gutenbergian *constructive* model of education through vision. But I am not convinced, with Nicholas Negroponte, that a hypermedia future entails obliterating the past.[1] The crux of the matter, I think, seems more Darwinian than cataclysmic. Today's instructional landscape must inevitably evolve or die, like biological species, since its environment is being radically altered by volatile visualization technologies. This ongoing displacement of fixed, monochromatic type by interactive, multidimensional graphics is a tumultuous process. In the realm of the artificial, as in nature, extinction occurs when there is no accommodation. Imaginative adaptation to the information superhighway, even the survival of reflective communication, means casting off vestigial biases automatically coupling printed words to introspective depth and pictures to dumbing down.[2]

The bound book has led a charmed existence since typesetting was invented in mid-fifteenth-century Mainz. This longevity, no doubt partially owing to a Darwinian flexibility, makes me optimistic about its mutated persistence. Become more virtual informational space than stable artifact, the traditional volume can find another life as an interconnective environment. Lines of copy interface with users very differently when presented in hybrid Web pages, and acquire unsettling mobility when reformatted, amended, and emended electronically. The digital imaging revolution is crucially

---

From *Good Looking: Essays on the Virtues of Images.* Cambridge, MA: MIT Press, 1996. 3–15.

reconfiguring how we explore and comprehend ideas from urban planning to photograph.[3] Yet in spite of the arrival of what I have termed the "age of computerism"[4] — rapidly replacing modernism and even postmodernism — a distorted hierarchy ranking the importance of reading above that of seeing remains anachronistically in place. All the while, computers are forcing the recognition that texts are not "higher," durable monuments to civilization compared to "lower," fleeting images. These marvelous machines may eventually rid us of the uninformed assumption that sensory messages are incompatible with reflection.

I have serious trouble with the deprecating rhetoric that stakes out bookish literacy as a moral high ground from which to denounce a tainted "society of spectacle." Contemporary iconoclasm, like early modern versions, rests on the puritanical myth of an authentic or innocent epistemological origin. Clinging to the Rousseauean fantasy of a supposedly blotless, and largely imageless, print ecology ignores not only contrary evidence from the past but the real virtues of colorful, heterogeneous, and mutable icons, whether on or off screen.

These essays, then, are unfashionably positive and frankly polemical. Their perspective is simultaneously pragmatic and theoretical. As practical acts of affirmation, they challenge an implacable system of negative dialectics arcing from the moral denunciations of Plato to the coercive aesthetics of Adorno to the war metaphors of Foucault.[5] In short, they offer case studies, stretching from the lens to the computer era, presenting an alternative view of the pleasures, beauties, consolations, and, above all, *intelligence* of sight. They argue that imaging, ranging from high art to popular illusions, remains the richest, most fascinating modality for configuring and conveying ideas. More broadly, they prismatically interconnect seers and seeing within a sensory web productive of cultural signification.

Yet it is not enough to show the intellectual, spiritual, and physical demands of making, observing, and exhibiting spatialized media, whether pre- or postmodern. I want to combat the sophism that images do only destructive work within our institutions. By engaging the epistemological uncertainties and educational upheavals of an electronic future, I seek to demonstrate their capacity for good interventions. Further, I ask how the practice of image study can regain pertinency at a moment when the traditional visual disciplines, like all the rest, are coming unmoored from their original purposes. From this dual perception of revolutionary opportunity and impending Armageddon, the following essays call on established and aspiring imagists across disciplinary boundaries to confront the fundamental task of remaking the image of images. Freeing graphic expression from an unnuanced dominant discourse of consumerism, corruption, deception, and ethical failure is a challenge that cuts across the arts, humanities, and sciences.

As manifestos on the knowingness of visual communication, from scientific illustration to on-line interactivity, these studies have another immediate context. They specifically counter the hierarchical "linguistic turn" in contemporary thought. The totemization of language as a godlike agency in western culture has guaranteed the identification of writing with intellectual potency. Ferdinand de Saussure, the early twentieth-century founder of structuralism, strengthened the biblical coupling of meaning with naming by formulating the opposition of signifier/signified.[6] These verbalizing binaries turned noumenal and phenomenal experience into the product of language. Not only temporal but spatial effects supposedly obeyed an invisible system, the controlling structure of an inborn ruling *écriture*.

Forcing human cognition to become synonymous both with computational codes or abstruse texts and with the ability to decipher them resulted in downgrading sensory awareness to superficial stimuli and false perceptions. Most damagingly, Saussure's schema emptied the mind of its body, obliterating the interdependence of physiological functions and thinking. It is not surprising that, up to now, an educational economy materially based on language has either marginalized the study of images, reduced it to a subaltern position, or appropriated it through colonization.[7] In most American university curricula, graphicacy remains subordinate to literacy. Even so-called interdisciplinary "visual culture" programs are governed by the ruling metaphor of reading. Consequently, iconicity is treated as an inferior part of a more general semantics.

Establishing a universal linguistic unconscious was central to Noam Chomsky's much publicized debates in the mid-1950s with B. F. Skinner.[8] The often-maligned father of behaviorism had tried to erase consciousness from psychology's subject matter. Skinner spent most of his beleaguered career measuring how rats pressed down levers and pigeons pecked at disks, seeking in these reinforced operations the explanation for why organisms do what they do.[9] Chomsky, on the contrary, tied mental concepts to innate "computationalist" discourse in which an automaton neurology manufactured strings of prepositional symbols. The equally controversial linguist's theory inspired the invidious comparison of algorithms used to write computer programs with human conceptualization.[10] What was left out of this, and the subsequent rationalist cognitive science quest for a parsing grammar of the mind, was the developmental link between perception and thought. This vital omission, now being rectified in the metaphor and mental imagery research of Lakoff and Johnson among others,[11] contributed significantly, I believe, to poststructuralism's "linguistic turn" and its splintering strategies of differentiation. While the intellectual work of criticism assumed the status of a superior generative language, its base physical object was fragmented into a multiplicity of scattered and uprooted propositions.[12]

Modeling comprehension as a kind of ascetic, even anaesthetic, information processing allowed influential academic areas such as semiotic and deconstructive literary theory or interpretive anthropology to reconceive the material subjects of their inquiry as decorporealized signs and encrypted messages requiring decipherment. So Clifford Geertz's narrational view of ethnography as "thick description" — influential on new historicist tendencies in recent scholarship — treated artifacts, behavior, and culture as if they were layered pages in a book demanding sustained decoding.[13] Although himself a persistent critic of the single-minded quantifying pretensions of the social sciences, Geertz paradoxically reduced communication to inscription. Not unlike Chomsky, his cultural textology assumed that language provided the most basic grid for getting at the meaning of what, after all, were intricately patterned ceremonies, rituals, and gestures.

While the problem of consciousness has returned to cognitive science after its Skinnerian banishment,[14] the conjunction of *psyche* with *logos* — especially in artificial intelligence systems — has not helped the status of images. An unfortunate consequence of the metaphor that treats brain function as modular, but ruled by a common syntax, is the intellectual imperialism of collapsing diverse phenomenological performances, whether drawings, gestures, sounds, or scents, into interpretable texts without sensory diversity. Cartesian reductive tendencies, intensified by advances in high-tech instrumentation, have leaked out of robotics into the humanities. The example of cybernetic disembodiment lurks behind unbiological abstractions such as "spectacle," "spectatorship," "gaze." Derived from observational apparatus, these static concepts ignore the variability of optical sensations in different times, places, and individual beholders.

I am arguing that we need to disestablish the view of cognition as dominantly and aggressively linguistic. It is narcissistic tribal compulsion to overemphasize the agency of *logos* and annihilate rival imaginaries. Martha Nussbaum's subtle remark about dogmatic Stoicism's guarding itself against the lure of poetry applies to the obsession with language in contemporary methodologies.[15] Semiotic, poststructuralist, and deconstructivist translations of the pictorial can be equally self-protective and unidirectional. Typically, these interpretive systems do not allow the "reader" of the depiction to be changed or gain insight through an avenue of expression different from the literariness of the criticism. Derrida's perverse praise of blindness provides a case in point. Claiming that drawing is inadequate to render the "sufferings of sight," he extols the superiority of writing "without seeing."[16]

Culture studies are no less problematic when they disseminate a bifurcated and essentializing world picture of observed annexed subjects and narrating free agents. Thus, in a reprise of Derrida, one hears that the invisible depths of postcolonial identity emerge only through discourse since the true self eludes surveillance. Homi Bhabha, echoing Frantz Fanon, reduces visuality to an evil, doubling colonial eye that either strips the individual of her proper representation or negatively mirrors the alien appearance projected by an oppressor.[17] In the face of such sweeping schematizations, knowledgeable artists and art, architectural, or design historians should ask what ever happened to the notion of *complex* imagery and revealing portraits. The facile complaint that images are merely and always trumping reproductions drowns any memory of their originality and plenitude. Since when does working with surfaces qualify as shallowness? It's a bizarre logic, indeed, that tautologically identifies mimesis with copying whatever sits on a plane (as if that were a simple process!), and, from this restricted definition of resemblance, leaps to conclude the inherent superficiality of imitation.

Anne Hollander's intuition that western fashion offers a visual escape from the trap of unquestioning custom suggests a compelling optical counterpoint to the inscription of racial or ethnic stereotypes.[18] A world rather than a national literature, according to Goethe, had the obligation to make available works from different times, places, cultures.[19] But this desirable effort of translation is not the sole, or even the most effective, means for facilitating exchange. I consider an unforeseen benefit of media "disembedding"[20] to be precisely the global traffic in fugitive visions. Large populations, from both "traditional" and "modern" societies, are being exposed and educated to the hybrid ways in which people everywhere wish to, and do in fact, look. Recognizing alternative styles of being and manifold appearances undermines false assumptions about constant meanings and inherited roles. As a confessed enthusiast for images, then, I deplore the one-sided estimation of language that has installed it as the paradigm for depth, seriousness, thought, even our very identity.

It is not hard to see that the multifaceted campaign to establish the primacy and innateness of our linguistic faculty is challenged by the materialist approach to the mind. Intense debates over Darwin's theory that organisms were born of blind chance and evolved according to the quirks of matter have refocused attention on the origin and configuration of all species. Both adaptationist and ultra-Darwinian investigations into human and animal reasoning[21] open up the question of the sensorium's role. The philosopher Daniel Dennett is a spokesman for the latter camp, stating that to have evolved a capacity for awareness, living creatures must have a sophisticated, unified informational organization endowing them with cognitive capabilities. Empirical processes like learning, in this account, are a tool by which natural selection has created complex biological systems. This new turn in the study of consciousness proposes that life is more than selfish genes by bringing the formative powers of perception into productive engagement with a no longer discrete and hierarchical organ of thought. Urging humanity to "grow up," he comments that Darwin's great legacy consists in his distribution of design throughout nature.[22] The lesson in this for imagists is that, if there is no hope of discovering an absolute trace or essential mark in life's processes that counts more than the rest, then, similarly, we must select, conserve, invent, and compose our artificial environment so that it becomes humane for all.

Yet, in spite of his Darwinian conviction about the importance of design, Dennett remains strangely language-centered. For him, the unfolding stream of human consciousness occurs in a massively parallel-processing brain, a virtual James Joycean linguistic machine. Only now, with the integrative neuroscientific philosophy of Paul and Patricia Churchland, "the body-minded brain" of Antonio Damasio, or Owen Flanagan's insistence on "the missing shade that is you," is the iron grip of a univocal language-like prototype for cognitive activity starting to erode.[23] Understanding, imagined as a combinatorial and synthetic physical function, has the potential for taking into account a broad range of multisensory endeavors. This suggests that truly enlarging the horizon of the emergent sciences of the mind (cognitive science, neurobiology, linguistics, AI, philosophy) should entail learning from the transactional visual arts about the experiential structures of thought. Ironically, the aesthetic, historical, and humanistic dimensions of perception remain virtually absent from the new interdisciplinary matrix in which cognitive being is about to become embedded.[24]

The controversy over who or what is designing nature, then, has been at the heart not only of genetic and reproductive research but of neurobiology. The much-publicized "decade of the brain," bridging the 1980s and 1990s, spectacularly opened a window onto the living mind. Multidimensional medical imaging (CT, PET, MRI) transparently displayed both the permanent neural anatomy and the acrobatics of evanescent emotion. Seeing neurons firing and witnessing localized functions in simultaneous performance suggest that it is more accurate to speak, not of separate art, artists, or art historians, but of interconnective images, imaging, imagists. Bennett Reimer's insistence that the application of arts education must be extended by showing its pertinency to every symbol sphere is even more true in light of this lately revealed cross-cortical power.[25] An array of devices, discoveries, and practices, then, are encouraging us to relocate narrowly categorized "art objects" elsewhere, into what I have termed "imaging." In this borderless community without physical territory, spatialized phenomena belong to larger constellations of events. Creating a map of ongoing debates, organized around central issues or substantial questions arising from this evolving geography, will be a major task confronting the new imagist. Such a "hypermediated" person will have become a reality when we are hard-pressed to say what his or her discipline is.

Optical technology itself is spurring an integrative revolution. Yet it is staggering how loath we visualists have been to transform ourselves. Where are our blueprints, blue-sky or realistic, for guiding media convergence on screen?[26] The conservatism of the supposedly new and old art history, its secondhand reliance on "discourse," on recirculating other fields' methodologies, tropes, rhetoric, has meant the loss of any intellectual and moral leadership that we might have exerted. If we have nothing particular to contribute to formerly linguistic fields and professions now undergoing radical *visual* metamorphosis, we confirm our irrelevance both within institutions of higher learning and in a decentralized electronic society.

These essay-manifestos, then, are constructivist in another sense as well. They call for some real risk-taking. It is one thing to embrace the agendas, definitions, and theories provided by other disciplines—themselves, ironically, in the throes of blurring or dissolving—and quite another to reconceptualize visuality historically, and in the light of that past lens culture to devise crosscutting projects for the emergent cyberspace era. We no longer face the nagging question of whether and how we might establish boundaries for art history, as Victor Margolin remarks about design studies.[27] Rather, we confront mutable fragmenting and coalescing forms of humanistic, scientific, and technological knowledge that temporarily converge because of imaging—an activity itself constantly changing. It seems infeasible, either intellectually or financially, to sustain multiple, linear specializations in art, craft, graphic, industrial, film, video, or media production and their separate histories. Instead, we need to forge an imaging field focused on transdisciplinary *problems* to which we bring a distinctive, irreducible, and highly visible expertise.

If Gianni Vattimo is correct that the effect of networked mass media is a "weakening" of immutable or Heideggerian Being,[28] then giving shape to metamorphic Becoming is the challenge. Suddenly, possibilities for configuring a shifting artificial environment open up. Bodynet, part of the innovative Things that Think project of the MIT Media Lab, implicitly challenges Baudrillard's claim that the simulacrum killed reality.[29] In an uncanny permutation of the premodern notion that there is no inanimate matter, explored in my *Voyage into Substance*,[30] this research center envisages designing intelligence into everyday products. A new sensing, networking, and automating technology is to vivify "dead" objects, making them responsive to human needs or emotions. Doorknobs, chairs, toasters, even jewelry will contain implanted silicon chips to perform smart operations by perceiving the desires of their owners. Clothing could recover a patient's vital signs and transmit them to a doctor's database, or adjust to the thermal conditions of different climates, obviating the need for a large wardrobe.[31]

All told, when freed from nihilism and liberated from asymmetrical relationships, material artifacts and graphic presentations can regain their rightful cognitive share. In the magical era of ubiquitous computing, art history's mission to retell the story of conventional media without a consideration of their future is over. Even its disciplinary name sounds archaic. But the efficacy of appearances — whether old or new — and the imaginative possibilities of thinking in, through, and with them is not anachronistic. Imaging may even begin to formulate its own questions and confidently say something about its own ends. It might think about itself instead of just being thought about by others. In spite of incessant talk concerning interdisciplinarity, something is wildly out of kilter when, at the end of the twentieth century, no alternative metaphor of intelligence counters the nineteenth-century standard of the printed book.

THE THROWAWAY MEDIUM

The passionate visualist, roaming the labyrinth of the postdisciplinary age, is haunted by the paradoxical ubiquity and degradation of images: everywhere transmitted, universally viewed, but as a category generally despised. Spectatorship itself has become synonymous with empty gaping, not thought-provoking attention. Some might object to this inclusiveness, replying that disdain is reserved for machine-generated simulations, or that most people value medical scans, or that, surely, canonical works of art in museums are exempt. Yet none of these caveats gets at the heart of a deeper problem. We have lost faith in the creation of good images; we have no confidence that good looking can be agreed upon or fostered. Already in *Body Criticism* and *Artful Science*, I uncovered an entrenched antivisualism pervading western neoplatonizing discourse from the Enlightenment forward.[32] Will enthusiasm for etherealized environments, data glasses or gloves, and Internet epiphanies automatically change the reflex that associates graphics with illiteracy, delusion, shape-shifting, and coloring emotion? I fear not.

This Orwellian disenchantment with the iconic affects not only a broad spectrum of the educated public but, more disturbingly, those of us in colleges or universities professing to know something about how imagery functions. No matter where one looks, a balanced, let alone a constructive, demonstration of the power of sophisticated images to communicate something other than misinformation, violence, pornography, and callous consumerism to tuned-in viewers is absent. Their visionary role in speculating about the conduct of life is obliterated by a relentless discourse of voyeurism and trickery. John Dewey's perceptive remark, in *Experience and Nature*, that the fine arts as well as industrial technologies are affairs of practice molders forgotten.[33]

But why should it concern those of us working in the visual arts, film, video, computers, and design, or anyone else for that matter, that spatializing media are declared to be *intrinsically* prone to ethical violations? Even as the din grows louder over plagiarism, misappropriation of written evidence, incomplete research, and errors of fact, images are perceived as more treacherous, requiring greater control, tougher proscriptions, than verbal modes. Why, in short, is the view of optically presented material as more corruptible and less mindful than typeset texts the most intractable bias? Equally the most ancient and the most modern of discriminations, aniconicity is also the most fundamental, underlying harassments against women, people of color, other races, different classes. The unfair assessment of representations as always unfair is itself the first bias for many. Consciously or unconsciously grounded in a faulty sight, this initial misperception is reified into an absolute judgment about the taintedness of the instrument and not the fallibility of the errant perceiver.

Beyond exposing the dubious assumption that pictures, their creators, and their beholders *essentially* lack integrity, or basically are not as cognizant as language purveyors,[34] there are other pressing reasons for making public the affirmative actions of images throughout time and across civilizations. The exhilaration of living in the on-line era is dampened for me by the worry that manipulable graphics will again, and more resolutely than ever, be identified with the unethical modifications possible in *any* replicating medium. Will we ever dig ourselves out of Plato's irrational shadow realm? Escaping from the cave involves, not outlawing the ghosts, but recognizing that such infringements are as old and as new as human nature.

The venerable plight of appearances turned me into an essayist. Their dissolution in the all-purpose solvent of wired fraud changed me into a public advocate. In the age of the throwaway image, when digital "banks" stockpile, license, and sell volatile conglomerated media to customers through CD-ROM catalogs, or subscribers download, use, and reuse hybrid graphics through the agency of commercial servers, it becomes impossible to divorce thinking about past illusion-producing art from contemporary imaging modalities. Digital plagiarism and the illegal redistribution of printed works, pictures, and photographs evoke historical problems concerning the ownership, transmission, and display of material objects. To date, the legal discussion over who owns the rights to immaterial cyberproperty transferred over the national information infrastructure ignores this potentially illuminating avenue of inquiry.[35]

But how to wed the study of the early modern period with reflections on the science-fictionalized realm of distance learning, telecomputing, animation, video, home shopping, and court TV? Why not abandon the chronological enterprise entirely and embrace the here and now? Ultimately, I was reluctant to forsake a stretch of time that had inspired and sustained my work over the last twenty years. Without its anchoring example, the electronic web of America OnLine, Prodigy, and CompuServe fragmented into instantaneous Post-It notes and intangible connections. So I just made the long eighteenth century longer.

Reckoning with shattered categories and crumbling institutions suggests an even greater reason for integrating historical knowledge with current events. As graduate education everywhere grows imperiled and traditional employment opportunities dwindle for highly trained and focused students, what kinds of embodied knowledge will survive the corporate tendency to convert individual aptitudes into remote expert systems? On one hand, we are faced with the specter of narrow "consultants" (without permanent jobs), and, on the other, with "generalists" (a euphemism for people with minimal skills). Donna Haraway's myth of a new species, a synthetic blend of human and machine, does not exhaust the implications of such pay-for-use utilitarianism.[36]

The trend toward automation has moved from the factory into the office, blueing the white collar. In a deregulated society, citizens find themselves as deregulated as industries. Jobs are being taken away not just from auto assembly line laborers but from the service and management force, from secretaries, sales personnel, telephone operators, bank tellers, lawyers, journalists, publishers, editors. Can professors and their students lag far behind? Mind you, the work all these people perform has not disappeared. On the contrary, it is being done directly between customers and robotic systems. In light of increasing layoffs across all sectors and the steady squeezing of survivors to produce even more, home shopping aptly epitomizes the destabilizing directness accompanying the spread of the Net. Such computerized immediacy will certainly cause other types of employment — from stockbrokering to in-class instruction — to vanish if it is not thoroughly reconceptualized and the value of *mediated* encounters stressed.

Add to this ubiquitous telemarketing impulse the threat of abolishing the NEA and the NEH, or even the proposal that the NSF be privatized, and we have the permanence of impermanence reified. The vulnerability of higher education, where even college degrees offer no guarantee of entry to secure jobs, further underscores a general sense of the decrepitude of the humanities and the sciences, their perceived lack of compelling aim or clear intellectual purpose within an ironically named "information society." I do not see that we are preparing our students for the reality that the Information Superhighway is a brand-new toll road and not the same old freeway.

Startlingly, the emergence and convergence of media is simultaneously a wholly ancient and an utterly modern phenomenon. As a deliberate shock tactic, then, these essays brusquely juxtapose distant periods and earlier types of graphic communication with those of the present. I do this believing the eighteenth century uncannily recuperates what we have repressed about our own times. Hal Foster's nuanced analysis of the Surrealist fascination for the outmoded[37] pertains to my invocation of the Enlightenment. The auratic-explosive eruption of an old-fashioned epoch into the contemporary scene disrupts both a Luddite nostalgia for the pretechnological era and the empty ecstasy of netsurfing. Like André Breton's melancholic flea markets or Walter Benjamin's ruined arcades, obsolete optical apparatus and discarded mechanisms are the ghostly remains of lost practices we need to redeem. Relics from an artisanal age haunt current ephemera. To spark a connection between the supplanted and the alien, I have mounted remote scenes in a futuristic frame and edged our virtual world with forgotten representational strategies.

The "In-Viewness of Ends"

But even this transdisciplinary and transtemporal initiative does not go far enough. I believe we must finally renounce the institutionalized notion that only the "pure" study of anything, including images (whether defined as formal, theoretical, critical, historical, cultural, neurological, psychological, biographical, museological), is admirable. If not for its intellectual merits alone, then because of the recent spate of books damning the beleaguered university,[38] serious consideration should be given to the proposition that a great part of our most meaningful inquiry goes on precisely because it gives thought to practical ends. The Princeton sociologist Donald Stokes convincingly argues for developing a national agenda of understanding-driven and use-inspired science.[39] His central thesis urges joining "pure" inquiry to applied ends following a nonlinear model of research.

Independently, but likemindedly, I have resisted oppositional dualisms. The more we can demonstrate real functions for images, and the greater the comprehension they foster across disparate dimensions—running the gamut from virtual museums, to hypothetical surgery, to a revolutionary visual model of the law[40]—the more integral they, and we, will become to our digital age. The longing for renewal and reinvention, shimmering in every corner of the academy, stems partially from the sense of living at a precarious juncture where supplanting people, businesses, and traditional skills has become the norm. Engaging new equipment at the design and content level means we will less likely be split across irreconcilable generational divides or be outpaced by an inhuman nanosecond immediacy.

Dewey's evocative phrase, "the in-viewness of ends," captures this projection in real time of the possible consequences of any mental or physical operation.[41] At present, an arbitrary theory, offered as a candidate for aesthetic contemplation in competition with its own subject matter,[42] and an avant-garde opticality, conceived as self-enclosed visual plenitude,[43] have played themselves out. Pursuing these romantic roads terminated in frustration at the limits stopping freewheeling subjectivity. But they also led to a boundless cynicism condemning all forms of persuasion as specious and manipulative.[44] Pulled both by the ideological power struggles accompanying the disintegration of the "canonical" disciplines and by dangerous administrative drives to tailor the curriculum solely to the marketplace, teachers need to demonstrate more effectively how images contribute to the informed conduct of life.

Neither an unimaginative utilitarianism nor a constricting instrumentalism, classical American pragmatism struggled to overcome the unproductive conflict between ideas and experience. Peirce, James, Royce, and Dewey insisted that human endeavors were not diminished when steered by a purpose. In differing ways, their philosophies exemplified transactional process and Emersonian presence.[45] By overturning the wholesale skepticism of the British empiricists, Dewey, in particular, developed a more generous, juster apprehension of sensory phenomena beyond aesthetic trumpery. His educational philosophy stands in stark contrast to a neo-Kantian, postwar model of art history that removed the discipline from democratic social goals and the amelioration of existing circumstances.[46] Following his lead, I suggest that images should be freed from the idealist identification with *trompe l'oeil*, the contemptuous judgment that they always pretend to fool the viewer into thinking that unreal things are real. Such a nonabstract, anti-Platonic stance would have as its touchstone the cumulative somatic and spiritual experiences felt by interconnected organisms coexisting in a material world. Developing an integrated, nonpolarized view of the varieties of visual experience means that the good, bad, and mixed properties of imaging would never be a foregone conclusion. As is true for any other human production, decisions about value would depend upon individual and community use during the course of a lifetime.

NOTES

1. Although Nicholas Negroponte, in *Being Digital* (New York: Alfred A. Knopf, 1995), is enthusiastic about the digital age, he, as well as other more critical writers on the future of information technology such as Jeremy Rifkin and Clifford Stoll, make no attempt to link our high-tech reality with historical examples of visuality from which we might usefully learn.

2. Doomsayers for the book include Neil Postman, *Technopoly: The Surrender of Culture to Technology* (New York: Knopf, 1992); and Sven Birkerts, *The Gutenberg Elegies: The Fate of Reading in the Electronic Age* (Winchester, Mass.: Faber & Faber, 1994).

3. See William J. Mitchell, *The Reconfigured Eye: Visual Truth in the Post-Photographic Era* (Cambridge, Mass., and London: MIT Press, 1994); and his *City of Bits: Space, Place, and the Infobahn* (Cambridge, Mass., and London: MIT Press, 1995).

4. See my *Artful Science: Enlightenment Entertainment and the Eclipse of Visual Education* (Cambridge, Mass., and London: MIT Press, 1994), xxiv.

5. For its modern instantiation see, especially, Adorno. Rolf Wiggershaus, *The Frankfurt School: Its History, Theories and Political Significance* (Cambridge: Polity Press, 1994), 597–608.

6. Murray Krieger, *Theory of Criticism: A Tradition and Its System* (Baltimore and London: Johns Hopkins University Press, 1976), 220.

7. Linda Brodkey, "The Value of Theory in the Academic Marketplace: The Reception of *Structuralist Poetics*," in *Rhetoric in the Human Sciences*, ed. Herbert W. Simons (London, Newbury Park, and New Delhi: Sage Publications, 1989), 168.

8. Noam Chomsky, *Syntactic Structures* (Cambridge, Mass.: MIT Press, 1957).

9. Dean Keith Simonton, *Greatness: Who Makes History and Why* (New York and London: The Guilford Press, 1994), 55–56.

10. Marcel Danesi, *Giambattista Vico and the Cognitive Science Enterprise* (New York: Peter Lang, 1994), 36, 46–49.

11. See, especially, Mark Johnson, *The Body in the Mind: The Bodily Basis of Meaning, Imagination, and Reason* (Chicago and London: University of Chicago Press, 1987), xxxvi–xxxviii; and George Lakoff, *Women, Fire, and Dangerous Things: What Categories Reveal about the Mind* (Chicago and London: University of Chicago Press, 1987), 8.

12. Interestingly, philosophers are now lamenting this same fragmenting process that accompanied the death of the Cartesian foundational subject. See Michel Meyer, *Of Problematology: Philosophy, Science, and Language*, trans. David Jamison with Alan Hart (Chicago and London: University of Chicago Press, 1995), 8.

13. For the importance of Geertz's conception of culture as "an historically transmitted pattern of meanings embodied in symbols," see Robert Darnton, *The Kiss of Lamourette: Reflections in Cultural History* (New York and London: W. W. Norton, 1990), 336.

14. See, for example, Paul M. Churchland, *The Engine of Reason, the Seat of the Soul: A Philosophical Journey into the Brain* (Cambridge, Mass., and London: MIT Press, 1995), 264–170; and William G. Lycan, *Consciousness* (Cambridge, Mass., and London; MIT Press, 1995), 1–8.

15. Martha C. Nussbaum, "Poetry and the Passions: Two Stoic Views," in *Passions and Perceptions: Studies in Hellenistic Philosophy of Mind*, Proceedings of the Fifth Symposium Hellenisticum, ed. Jacques Brunschwig and Martha C. Nussbaum (Cambridge: Cambridge University Press, 1993), 148–149.

16. Jacques Derrida, *Memoirs of the Blind: The Self-Portrait and Other Ruins*, trans. Pascale-Anne Brault and Michael Naas (Chicago and London: University of Chicago Press, 1993), 4.

17. Homi Bhabha, *The Location of Culture* (New York and London: Routledge, 1994), 48–51.

18. Anne Hollander, *Suits and Sex* (New York: Alfred A. Knopf, 1995), 19.

19. Cited by Alain Finkielkraut, *The Defeat of the Mind*, trans. Judith Friedlander (New York: Columbia University Press, 1995), 35.

20. The term is from Anthony Giddens, *The Consequences of Modernity* (Stanford: Stanford University Press, 1990), 21.

21. Liz McMillen, "The Meaning of Animals," *Chronicle of Higher Education* (April 21, 1995), A12.

22. Daniel C. Dennett, *Darwin's Dangerous Idea: Evolution and the Meaning of Life* (New York: Simon & Schuster, 1995), 512–513.

23. Churchland, *Engine of Reason*, 11–19, 298. For the importance of the emotions and feelings in neural representations, see Antonio R. Damasio, *Descartes' Error: Emotion, Reason, and the Human Brain* (New York: G. P. Putnam's Sons, 1994), 223–244; and Owen Flanagan, *Consciousness Reconsidered* (Cambridge, Mass., and London: MIT Press, 1992), 102.

24. See, for example, Francisco J. Varela, Evan Thompson, and Eleanor Rosch, *The Embodied Mind: Cognitive Science and Human Experience* (Cambridge, Mass., and London: MIT Press, 1993), xvi–xvii.

25. Bennett Reimer, "What Knowledge Is of Most Worth in the Arts?" in *The Arts, Education, and Aesthetic Knowing: Ninety-First Yearbook of the National Society for the Study of Education*, ed. Bennett Reimer and Ralph A. Smith (Chicago and London: University of Chicago Press, 1992), 20–50.

26. One such blueprint is Robert N. Beck, *Center for Imaging Science: A Plan for the Future* (Chicago: University of Chicago, 1995).

27. Victor Margolin, "Design History or Design Studies: Subject Matter and Methods," *Design Issues*, 11 (Spring 1995), 9–11.

28. Gianni Vattimo, *The End of Modernity: Nihilism and Hermeneutics in Post-Modern Culture*, trans. Jon R. Snyder (Cambridge: Polity Press, 1988), 47.

29. Jean Baudrillard, *Simulacra and Simulation*, trans. Sheila Faria Glaser (Ann Arbor: University of Michigan Press, 1994), 55–56.

30. See my *Voyage into Substance: Art, Science, Nature, and the Illustrated Travel Account, 1760–1840* (Cambridge, Mass., and London: MIT Press, 1984), chapter 2: "The Natural Masterpiece."

31. John Markoff, "And Now Computerized Sensibility," *New York Times* (May 15, 1995), C4. For the eclipse of keyboard-centric views of word processors by that of computers as small, smart objects or even spaces you enter, see David Weinberger "In Your Interface," *Wired* (September 1995), pp. 134–135.

32. My last two books analyzed in different ways the durability with which vision is coupled with negative metaphors. This *préhistoire* is given inadequate and short shrift in Martin Jay's *Downcast Eyes: The Denigration of Vision in Twentieth-Century French Thought* (Berkeley, Los Angeles, and London: University of California Press, 1993); see especially chapter 2, "Dialectic of Enlightenment," 85ff., which is cursory and derivative in its assessment.

33. John Dewey, *Experience and Nature*, 2d ed. (La Salle, Ill.: Open Court, 1961), 288.

34. See, for example, Neil Postman, *Conscientious Objections: Stirring Up Trouble about Language, Technology, and Education* (New York: Alfred A. Knopf, 1988), xiv.

35. Barbara Hoffman, "Digital Technology, Cyberspace, and the Arts," *CAA News* (May/June 1995), 6–7.

36. Donna Haraway, "A Manifesto for Cyborgs: Science, Technology and Socialist Feminism in the 1980's," *Socialist Review* 15 (March–April 1985), 65–107.

37. Hal Foster, *Compulsive Beauty* (Cambridge, Mass., and London: MIT Press, 1993), 158–159, 163–164.

38. See, for example, George H. Birch, *Education without Impact: How Our Universities Fail the Young* (New York: Lane Press, 1994); Robert and Jan Solomon, *Up the University: Recreating Higher Education in America* (New York: Wesley Publishing Company, 1994); and Eli M. Noam, "Electronics and the Dim Future of the University," *Science*, 270 (October 13, 1995), 247–249.

39. Donald E. Stokes, "The Impaired Dialog between Science and Government and What Might Be Done about It," paper delivered at the Nineteenth Annual AAAS Colloquium on Science and Technology Policy (Washington, D.C., April 7, 1994). Also see his forthcoming *Pasteur's Quadrant: Basic Science and Technological Innovation* (Washington, D.C.: The Brookings Institution, 1996).

40. Ethan M. Katsch, *Law in a Digital World* (New York and Oxford: Oxford University Press, 1995), has suggested that law must join other disciplines in entering a graphic world opened up by the computer. See pp. 152–153.

41. Dewey, *Experience and Nature*, 86.

42. Elizabeth W. Bruss, *Beautiful Theories: The Spectacle of Discourse in Contemporary Criticism* (Baltimore and London: Johns Hopkins University Press, 1982), 79. Also see Daniel Herwitz, *Making Theory/Constructing Art: On the Authority of the Avant-Garde* (Chicago and London: University of Chicago Press, 1993), 195, for Arthur Danto's pervasive notion that theory is the defining ingredient of art. Peter Brooks, "Aesthetics and Ideology: What Happened to Poetics?" *Critical Inquiry*, 20 (Spring 1994), 515, asserts that ideological criticism has degenerated into self-importance and posturing.

43. Rosalind E. Krauss, *The Optical Unconscious* (Cambridge, Mass., and London: MIT Press, 1993), 2.

44. For the confusion of power with persuasion in the new sophistic propounded by Stanley Fish, see Martha C. Nussbaum, *Love's Knowledge: Essays on Philosophy and Literature* (New York and Oxford: Oxford University Press, 1990), 222.

45. For the distinctions between the old pragmatism and the "new pragmatism" of Richard Rorty, with its emphasis on script, vocabulary, and constructed narration, see the excellent discussion by John E. Smith, *America's Philosophical Vision* (Chicago and London: University of Chicago Press, 1992); and John Pattrick Diggins, *The Promise of Pragmatism: Modernism and the Crisis of Knowledge and Authority* (Chicago and London: University of Chicago Press, 1994), 492. For the Emersonian connection, see Cornel West, *The American Evasion of Philosophy: A Genealogy of Pragmatism* (Madison: University of Wisconsin Press, 1989), 73–74.

46. Thomas F. Reese contrasts the more hierarchical pedagogical models of German emigrés, such as Panofsky, with Dewey's call for a study that integrates art into our lives. See his "Mapping Interdisciplinarity," *Art Bulletin* (forthcoming).

47. See, for example, John La Puma & David Shiedermayer, *Ethics Consultation: A Practical Guide* (Boston: Jones & Bartlett Publishers, 1994).

PART THREE

The Rhetoric of Design

Introduction to Part Three

Once we begin analyzing the arrangement of individual elements on a page — not only words and images but also graphic elements such as layout and typography — we enter the realm of design. In the digital world where text so often combines words and images, where word-processing packages contain varieties of fonts, where drawings, table applications, and page elements are easily available, where anyone can add clip art or digital photos to a document, design choices are becoming an integral part of the writing process. "Writing" is even beginning to be reconceived as a process of "composing," returning to the roots of the term "composition" in order to acknowledge that writing involves more than text. Just as we teach students to consider rhetoric in writing, we need also to teach them to consider the rhetoric of design choices.

Words, clauses, or sentences are not the only elements that can be yoked in a faulty way; so can images and visual elements. Colors, fonts, line thickness — all can connote feelings and attitudes. Mere punctuation marks can make statements. Typeface sets a tone. Visual elements on a page can be designed to function metaphorically, to use repetition for emphasis, or to provide transitions. Designed elements can be coordinated with or subordinated to each other. For example, elements in a list can suggest that the parts of the list are equal or that those on the top are more important than those on the bottom.

The readings in this section suggest new ways of thinking and talking about design choices with our students and provide a foundation for understanding the ways in which design might also function rhetorically. Because the design field is no longer the restricted purview of graphic artists, writers of all kinds — journalists and Web developers alike — are required to think about design as part of the process of writing. This section covers a variety of topics connected to design, from general design theory to the materiality of writing to typography, as well as the rhetorical effectiveness of both punctuation and a figure such as repetition.

In "Rhetoric, Humanism, and Design," Richard Buchanan, who teaches the history and philosophy of rhetoric, catalogs various approaches to design and argues that scholars need to consider design as an enterprise that is essentially humanistic and analytically grounded in rhetoric. Buchanan arrived at his theory because he asked a simple question: whether the many products and fields requiring design expertise, from graphic communications to crafted objects, shared a discipline of design. If we reconceive of design as a "humanistic enterprise," as Buchanan asks us to, then we can recognize "the inherently rhetorical dimension of all design thinking." Design's rhetoric becomes especially relevant for us in composition studies, then, as new media present us with more and more hybrid texts.

Rhetorician John Trimbur analyzes typography to foreground the materiality and, by extension, the visuality of writing. In "Delivering the Message: Typography and the Materiality of Writing," Trimbur asserts that "typography has been ghettoized in technical communication" so that its concerns, "document design, page layout, fonts, infographics, and reading paths," are dismissed by compositionists as vocational and commercial. Trimbur traces notions of texts and scopophobia, fear of the visual, from the "great Alphabetic Literacy Narrative" and its concept of the transparent text through the process movement in composition pedagogy. These concepts of writing neglect to study writing's materiality and the technologies writers use during the actual labor of writing. Trimbur argues that notions of literacy have focused on elevating the alphabet as a writing system, meanwhile relegating pictographs and visual images to the level of illiteracy and considering such visual attempts to communicate as "immature, ephemeral, and manipulative." Digital technologies, however, are pressuring and dismantling previous divisions of labor between author, designer, and printer. Trimbur argues that we cannot continue to maintain such distinctions if we are to encourage true literacy. By establishing that "typography links writing to delivery—the fifth canon of rhetoric," Trimbur aims to make space for typography in the composition curriculum.

We can see the divisions between author, designer, and printer eroding in the field of typography. Printers and typographers no longer have a lock on typeface. Anyone today can design any kind of typeface. For a few traditional typographers, this design freedom is an aggravating if not a threatening affront to a highly developed, studied taste and style. In "The Rules of Typography According to ~~Crackpots~~ Experts," type designer Jeffery Keedy sets the study and design of type into cultural and historical contexts. In a postmodern age, he feels, typography connoisseurs will need to give way to the so-called "postmodernist hacks" who are infusing typography with a long-missing energy and creativity. Our digital era uses technology that has thus democratized information and type design. Like other theorists in this section, Keedy stresses that type design today must reflect context and culture, thereby adding to "cultural diversity and empowering other voices," rather than retrenching and designing only according to preferences held over from past ages.

Looking more closely at literacy issues, new media designer Jessica Helfand examines the shift from "the printed word as the emissary of spoken communication" to digitization's effect on typography in "Electronic Typography: The New Visual Language." Computerized typography adds previously unconsidered dimensions to writing while lessening the impact of traditional type conventions such as capitalization and font. If we can, for example, make type move, give it a sound, or frame it with background music when it appears onscreen, the power of the traditional capital letter seems nearly insignificant in comparison. Ultimately, Helfand challenges typographers to reexamine their own understanding of what it means to be literate in a digital environment. She uses the "drive-thru design" of e-mail to show how designers risk becoming irrelevant when they are not engaged in developing new digital forms of communication. Helfand's concerns lead her to wonder, finally, about visual thinking that springs from a method of communication like sign language. What researchers can tell us about such an established nonlinear language may help typographers—and multimedia designers—better understand thinking based on multiple points of view.

Focusing on print media, Martin Solomon, a graphic designer and typographer, examines the rhetorical effect of punctuation marks in "The Power of Punctuation." These marks are often overlooked as insignificant elements in the context of the composing process. Classifying punctuation as *mechanics* may even reinforce the idea that the small marks deserve little thought. Solomon shows that punctuation directs the pacing or tempo—the "voice"—of typography, and, even more, that it can make statements in itself—for example, as an enlarged period at the end of a sentence or after a single word would do. In digital environments, designing and shaping punctuation have become ridiculously easy. But greater ease requires greater rhetorical care. Students need to be able to recognize the rhetorical potential of these smallest of marks.

If students can recognize the rhetorical possibilities of punctuation, they may be able to recognize the rhetorical power of a figure such as repetition. Designers often use repetition to establish transitions in their work; the rhetorical form "anaphora" can work both as an organizational device and as a way to emphasize a repeated word or phrase. In a longitudinal study, rhetoricians James Porter and Patricia Sullivan observed a graduate of their technical writing program as he created a tutorial for Aldus PageMaker and then tested the document with five users. Porter and Sullivan's "Repetition and the Rhetoric of Visual Design" shows us how using visual repetition without careful rhetorical consideration of the ways it will direct a reader visually and whether or not the repetition best serves the design's rhetorical intent almost always leads to disastrous design consequences for any document.

Whether or not college writing classes are taught in computer classrooms, students own or have access to computers outside of school, enabling them to design any written text in ways we may or may not require for class. Many of our students have already designed their own Web pages, may have created class Web pages, and may even be required to compile a Web-based portfolio as part of a course or job application. For our students' sake, we need to understand the degree to which the rhetorical principles we teach them to use when developing written text also apply to the visual and digital texts they compose.

13 *Rhetoric, Humanism, and Design*

RICHARD BUCHANAN

INTRODUCTION

Confronted with the vast array of products in the contemporary world, an observer is justified in wondering whether there really is a discipline of design shared by all of those who conceive and plan such things as graphic communications, the physical objects produced by craft and machine, structured services and activities, and the integrated systems which range in scale from computers and other forms of technology to urban and humanly managed natural environments. The scope of design appears to be so great, and the range of styles and other qualities of individual products within even one category so diverse, that the prospects for identifying a common discipline seem dim. To compound the problem, histories and theories of design are also exceptionally diverse, representing a wide range of beliefs about what design is, how it should be practiced, and for what purpose. For example, design histories typically identify their subject matter as the history of objects, or the careers of individual designers who have influenced society, or the development of the technical means and processes of a specialized branch of design practice such as graphic design, industrial design, or engineering, or the influence of broad cultural ideas on the practice of all of the fine and useful arts. Similarly, designers and design theorists present a seemingly endless array of special procedures and maxims required for what they believe to be effective designing. And, finally, design critics, as well as historians, designers, and theorists, offer a great variety of incompatible, if not contradictory, principles and slogans to explain what designers should and should not seek to accomplish through their work.

What is needed to reduce the welter of products, methods, and purposes of design to an intelligible pattern is a new conception of the discipline as a humanistic enterprise, recognizing the inherently rhetorical dimension of all

From *Discovering Design: Explorations in Design Studies*. Ed., Richard Buchanan and Victor Margolin. Chicago: U of Chicago P, 1995. 23–66.

design thinking. The key to such a conception lies in the subject matter of design. There is a tendency among theorists to reduce design to a form of science, as if there is a fundamental predictive quality in designing that has eluded practicing designers. The assumption is that design has a fixed or determinate subject matter that is given to the designer in the same way that the subject matter of nature is given to the scientist. However, the subject matter of design is not given. It is created through the activities of invention and planning, or through whatever other methodology or procedures a designer finds helpful in characterizing his or her work. Of course, one may argue that the subject matter of the sciences is not entirely given; it must be discovered in the activities of scientific inquiry. But discovery and invention are essentially different. Discovery implies that there is something constantly available, waiting passively to be uncovered, and that the discovery will yield only one result, which may be confirmed by other experimental techniques for questioning nature. In other words, there is a determinacy in natural science, and the goal of inquiry is knowledge of properties and predictability of processes.

There is no similar determinacy in the activity of designing. The subject matter of design is radically indeterminate, open to alternative resolutions *even with the same methodology.*[1] One may speak of "discovering design" because one is concerned with determining what design and the products of design are, or have been, in the twentieth century. The issue is a question of fact, and observations may be verified if someone else examines the evidence from the perspective of the claim. But of the designer, one speaks most often of creation and invention, and only casually or mistakenly of discovery. The scientist *discovers* a natural process or a natural law, but the engineer or designer *invents* a possible application or a new use suited to a particular product. There are many determinate constraints on the work of the designer, but the consideration of constraints is only a background for the invention or conception of a new product.

Why is the indeterminacy of subject matter in design significant? There are several reasons. First, it immediately serves to distinguish design from all of the natural and social sciences, which are directed toward the understanding of determinate subject matters. (With this in mind, appeals to science among design theorists must be viewed with caution, because the appeal may be only a rhetorical tactic that conceals a personal preference or interest that has nothing to do with the necessities of science.) Second, it directs attention to the exceptional diversity of the products created by designers and to the continual change going on among those products. The subject matter of design is not fixed; it is constantly undergoing exploration. Individual designers extend their vision to new areas of application or focus on one area of application and refine a vision. In general, design is continually evolving, and the range of products or areas where design thinking may be applied continues to expand. Third, indeterminacy of subject matter serves to characterize design as a discipline fundamentally concerned with matters that admit of alternative resolutions. Designers deal with matters of choice, with things that may be other than they are. The implications of this are immense, because it reveals the domain of design to be not accidentally but essentially contested. The essential nature of design calls for both the process and the results of designing to be open to debate and disagreement. Designers deal with possible worlds and with opinions about what the parts and the whole of the human environment should be. Any authority of the designer comes from recognized experience and practical wisdom in dealing with such matters, but the designer's judgment and the results of his or her decisions are open to questioning by the general public, as are all matters of public policy and personal action, where things may be other than they are.

What is the consequence for the discipline of design of the indeterminacy of its subject matter? Does it mean that there can be no discipline or art of design thinking, as the diversity of descriptions of design seems to suggest? Quite the opposite. There can be a discipline of design, but it must be different in kind from disciplines which possess determinate subject matters. Design is a discipline where the conception of subject matter, method, and purpose is an integral part of the activity and of the results.

On the level of professional practice, the discipline of design must incorporate competing interests and values, alternative ideas, and different bodies of knowledge. This is nothing new to designers, who have understood that they must be persuasive in dealing with others and find concrete techniques for assessing the many perspectives from which products are viewed by clients, manufacturers, business and other technical experts, and potential users. What is new is the possibility of systematizing the discipline of design to explain how designers invent and develop the arguments contained in their products and how designers may present their ideas persuasively to clients and other members of product development teams. However, the elements of a new discipline of design do not have to be created entirely anew. Nearly a century of exploration and reflection have provided the materials for a synthesis which is, arguably, underway today in contemporary design thinking.

If the subject matter of design is indeterminate—potentially universal in scope, because design may be applied to new and changing situations, limited only by the inventiveness of the designer—then the subject matter of design studies is not products, as such, but the art of conceiving and planning products. In other words, the *poetics* of products—the study of products as they are—is different from the *rhetoric* of products—the study of how products come to be as vehicles of argument and persuasion about the desirable qualities of private and public life. The interplay between the rhetoric and poetics of products is a significant issue in design studies, but the orientation in logical sequence is from rhetoric to poetics. Recognition of this is important because designers, and those who study design, often confuse the qualities of existing products with the problems of designing new products. There is a tendency to see determinacy in existing products and project that determinacy back into the activity and discipline of designing. This is what Kenneth Burke means when he discusses "prediction after the fact" in literary studies. Prediction after the fact is what designers and design theorists do when they conclude that design is a determinate activity—an activity of discovery—rather than an activity of invention concerned with the indeter-minate. A designer's beliefs are sometimes elevated to the status of determi-nate principles governing all of design, rather than personal visions infused into a rhetorical art of communication and persuasion. From this perspective, design history, theory, and criticism should balance any discussion of prod-ucts with discussion of the particular conception of design that stands behind the product in its historical context. Indeed, different conceptions of design also carry with them different conceptions of history, further complicating the task of design studies. For this reason, one way to investigate the different forms of the discipline of design in the twentieth century is to consider different accounts of the origins of design.

THE ORIGINS OF DESIGN

Serious discussions of design seldom omit some reference to the origins of the discipline. Such passages are perhaps regarded by the casual reader as cere-monial rather than substantive, but the treatment of this commonplace reveals a great deal about a writer's perspective on the nature of design and the significance of contemporary practice. There is a surprising pattern in accounts of the origins of design, revealing the systematic pluralism of the discipline in the twentieth century.

The origins of design are usually traced to one of only four beginnings. Some argue that design began in the twentieth century with the formation of new disciplines of design thinking. Others argue that design began in the early days of the Industrial Revolution with the transformation of the instru-ments of production and the social conditions of work. Still others argue that design began in the prehistoric period with the creation of images and objects by primitive human beings. And, finally, some argue that design began with the creation of the universe, the first act of God, who represents the ideal model of a creator which all human designers, knowingly or unknowingly, strive to imitate. The alternative origins may be represented in a schematism which suggests interesting relations and potential oppositions (Figure 1).

Such wide disparity in a matter which on first consideration seems to admit only a single answer suggests, at once, that the issue at stake cannot be resolved by a simple appeal to facts or historical data. What is at stake is not

FIGURE 1. Schematism of the Origins of Design

Creation of the Universe

Industrial Revolution ——— **ORIGINS OF DESIGN** ——— *Early Twentieth Century*

Prehistoric Images & Objects

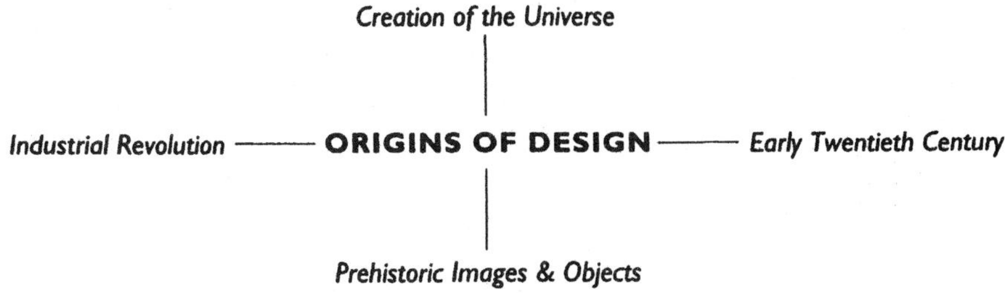

fact, as such, but the principle which gives meaning to data and allows the assertion of factual claims: the principle by which facts are established and made pertinent to the practice, study, and experience of design. This is confirmed to the degree that whatever principle is selected by a writer, the data which are primary in other accounts of the origins of design are not excluded or ignored but merely given lower priority and different meaning; the data of alternative accounts do not bear directly on the question of the origins of design but on other factors related to human nature, social conditions, cultural myths, and so forth. In short, the way a writer identifies the origins of design indicates a broad rhetorical perspective on the nature of design. Such perspectives are perhaps endless in their subtle differences, but they may be grouped into four kinds, each indicating a *rhetorical commonplace* which may be made fundamental in the practice and study of design. These commonplaces are represented in the schematism of Figure 2.

The history, current practice, and theory of design are presented differently from each perspective, accounting for the pluralism of conflicting approaches to design that are evident in the contemporary period. However, this pluralism does not undermine the possibility of understanding the common discipline of design shared by all designers. The scope and nature of design in the contemporary world are determined by two considerations: the pluralism of principles which have guided designers in exploring the human-made world, and the pluralism of conceptions of the discipline which have provided new instrumentalities for such explorations. The principles of design are grounded in spiritual and cultural ideals, or in material conditions, or in the power of individuals to control nature and influence social life, or in the qualities of moral and intellectual character which stand behind the integrative discipline of design thinking and the productive arts. Such principles are presupposed and pre-existent in the concerns of each designer. They are expressed as *theses, maxims, or slogans* to guide practice, and their elaboration and adaptation to new circumstances is a process of discovery.

However, the discipline of design is in a process of formation in a way that principles are not. The discipline is being invented through the

FIGURE 2. Schematism of the Commonplaces of Design Practice and Theory

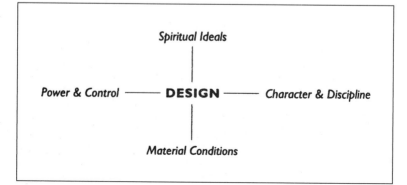

exploration of instrumentalities, technologies, and specific methods which are suited to the changing circumstances of contemporary culture. The discipline of design, in all its forms, empowers individuals to explore the diverse qualities of personal experience and to shape the common qualities of community experience. This makes design an essential element in a new philosophy of culture, replacing the old metaphysics of fixed essences and natures which Dewey critiqued throughout a lifetime of work directed toward the experimental nature of inquiry after the philosophic and cultural revolution at the beginning of the twentieth century.[2]

To investigate the various forms of the discipline of design in the twentieth century, we may take as our beginning point the perspective which specifically focuses on design as a discipline. Later, we may consider how the other perspectives on design have also contributed to the standing of design as a liberal art of technological culture.

CHARACTER AND THE FORMATION OF THE DISCIPLINE OF DESIGN

When the origins of design are traced to the first decades of the twentieth century, the principle lies in human character. Design rests on the ability of human beings to reason and act with prudence in solving problems that are obstacles to the functioning, development, and well-being of individuals and society. Furthermore, design is inquiry and experimentation in the activity of making, since making is the way that human beings provide for themselves what nature provides only by accident. There is a deep reflexive relation between human character and the character of the human-made: character influences the formation of products and products influence the formation of character in individuals, institutions, and society.

Integrative Arts in the Ancient World

Although design emerged as a distinct discipline only in the twentieth century, its precursors may be traced from the ancient world through the disciplines of art and changing attitudes toward production and making. In the ancient world, Aristotle discovered a science of production directed toward an understanding of the differences among all of the arts and their products due to the specific *materials, techniques of production, forms*, and *purposes* that are relevant to each kind of making.[3] He called this "poetic science," or poetics, derived from the Greek word for making. The only remaining example of this science, as it was explored by Aristotle, is the *Poetics*, a treatise on the literary arts and, specifically, the art of tragedy. (Reportedly, there was a parallel treatise on the art of comedy, but it is lost.) There are many references to mechanical objects, domestic implements, and other products of the useful arts throughout Aristotle's other treatises. These references and brief analyses provide tantalizing hints about how he would have investigated design, but there is no evidence that he ever wrote a treatise specifically devoted to a poetic analysis of what we, in the modern world, would regard as the result of design. Nonetheless, Aristotle's method of studying the artificial—even limited to the literary arts, as the most important examples are—exerted a strong influence on all subsequent discussions of making in Western culture. If not his specific philosophy, then the terms and distinctions of his analysis directly or indirectly provide the basis for how we discuss design in the contemporary world.

For Aristotle, the differences among the various literary and constructive arts depend on a fundamental understanding of the human capacity to make, considered to be independent from the specialization of a particular art. All making is an integrative, synthetic activity. It is what he describes as an intellectual virtue: a reasoned state of the capacity to make, different from, but closely related to, the intellectual virtue that stands behind the theoretical sciences and the moral virtues that stand behind action.[4] However, Aristotle also found it important to distinguish the element of *forethought* from the specific considerations and activities that are relevant to each kind of making.[5] Forethought in making is a kind of universal art, in the sense that it is independent of any particular art of making and, therefore, able to range over all potential considerations and subjects that may enter into the making of this or that kind of product. Forethought is an "architectonic" or "master" art, concerned with *discovery* and *invention*, *argument* and *planning*, and the purposes or ends that guide the activities of the subordinate arts and crafts.

The element of forethought in making is what subsequently came to be known as design, although no distinct discipline of design emerged in the ancient world, perhaps because forethought and making were most often combined in the same person, the master builder or craftsman. However, one exception was in the diverse arts of language and literature. A core art of rhetoric provided the basis for systematic forethought in all of the distinct forms of making in words: history, drama, poetry, political and legal speeches, prayers, and religious sermons.[6] Rhetoric served as the design art of literature; it provided the organization of thought in narrative and argument as well as the composition and arrangement of words in style. Yet rhetoric was not conceived by Aristotle as an art of words. It was an art of thought and argument whose product found *embodiment* in words as a vehicle of presentation.

However, since words refer to things, and the use of words has consequences for action and understanding, even the literary form of rhetoric has often provided a way of connecting ethics, politics, and the theoretical sciences with the activities of making. Indeed, the themes of rhetorical thinking have exerted a powerful influence on those arts of making which employ materials other than words. For example, rhetoric and the intellectual virtues associated with rhetoric—the humanism established by Cicero in the Roman republic—stand behind Vitruvius's account of architecture.[7] His portrait of the architect parallels Cicero's portrait of the well-educated rhetorician, except with regard to the type of product that follows from the art. The architect is an individual trained in the liberal arts and sciences of his day, prepared to practice the integrative liberal art of architecture for the fabrication of buildings, instruments for measuring time, and the devices of war.

Integrative Arts in the Renaissance

The relation between rhetoric and the arts of making, whether in words or things, is one of the most complex themes in Western culture. However, the development of this theme in the Renaissance has special significance for the subsequent understanding of design in the twentieth century. In the Renaissance, the fine arts were distinguished from the practical arts in a fashion more complete — or, at any rate, with greater cultural impact — than at any time in the past.[8] The reason for this was an unusual confluence of Platonic and Aristotelian ideas, along with a rebirth of rhetoric through the direct or mediated influence of Cicero, Horace, Quintilian, and Longinus.[9] New readings of Plato supported an intense interest in the imitation of ideal models. In conjunction with the rebirth of rhetoric as a cultural art, this led in turn to the imitation of ideal literary models. Finally, the translation of Aristotle's *Poetics* into a variety of languages in the sixteenth century "provided a technical vocabulary, a statement of problems, and an array of literary data" that was adjusted to the rhetorical tradition of poetry, stemming from Horace and Longinus.[10] The result was the rhetorical humanism of the Renaissance, directed toward the creation of the new liberal art of belles lettres as the highest achievement of culture. This was conceived as a return to the ancient union of the arts of making in words and things. However, it was, in fact, a departure from classical and modern ideas that decisively reoriented culture toward the literary arts.

It is no contradiction that some Renaissance artists explored the practical arts of *architectura* and *grafice* (including the art of *pittura*) at the same time that they explored new literary arts, because the practical arts were conceived as an extension of poetic vision. The highest forms of making remained rhetoric and poetry, since these arts were regarded as closest to the spirit of the ideal. Nor is it a contradiction that the creation of the liberal art of beaux arts soon followed the creation of belles lettres: the beautiful arts, similarly based on rhetoric, provided a new way for exploring the delightful and noble, thereby extending the subject matter and concepts of beautiful letters.[11] Thus, the first academies of art were created in the sixteenth century, "based originally on the assumption that the visual arts may be analyzed intellectually, and criticized and improved according to laws not different from those governing literature codified by Aristotle and other authors of the ancient world."[12]

The great achievement of the Renaissance was the creation of belles lettres and beaux arts, along with a rebirth of rhetorical thought. This influenced all areas of culture and all arts of making, yielding a secularized humanism which influenced the sciences, as well. Yet this achievement, particularly as carried forward in the seventeenth and eighteenth centuries, ultimately eroded the intellectual foundations of rhetoric and the practical arts of making, with nearly disastrous consequences for the conception and practice of design. Although the Renaissance artist distinguished the rational arts of rhetoric and poetry from the practical or useful arts, he also understood and appreciated their relation, and frequently cultivated the practical arts of making in innovative ways. Leonardo da Vinci's speculations on mechanical devices were simply another expression of his poetic and visual imagination. But the successors of the Renaissance artist, inheriting a reified distinction between the fine and practical arts, progressively lost understanding of, and interest in, the fertile connective link.[13]

Renaissance inventions were based on an architectonic art of rhetoric. However, what was invented by means of rhetoric — the new subject matters of culture, identified as literature, history, the fine arts, science, and philosophy — gradually attracted more interest and attention than the integrative art from which they emerged.[14] For example, Galileo was inspired by the design arts practiced in the great arsenal of Venice, but he directed his work not toward the nature of design but toward the creation of the two new sciences of mechanics. The result is easy to see: the arts of making were progressively distinguished, specialized, and fragmented into many forms; the practical arts were developed without sound intellectual foundations which could be integrated into a humanistic conception of making; and the theoretical sciences underwent explosive growth, often relying on the industrial, mechanical, and practical arts for inspiration and devices of investigation, but without a framework for relating theoretical knowledge to its practical impact on the development of human character and society. As for rhetoric, it became one more technical, specialized branch of the literary arts, ultimately dissociated by Descartes, Newton, and others from philosophy, practical reasoning, and the new sciences.[15]

It is true that in the period from the Renaissance to the early days of the Industrial Revolution the invention of techniques for mass production in support of the practical arts allowed — and required — a separation of designing from making. However, design was also separated from the intellectual and fine arts, leaving it without an intellectual foundation of its own. Therefore, instead of becoming a unifying discipline directed toward the new productive capabilities and scientific understanding of the modern world, design was diminished in importance and fragmented into the specializations of different types of production, leaving its connection with other human enterprises and bodies of knowledge vague and uncertain. Design was rescued periodically by exceptional individuals with natural talent who could provide examples of successful design thinking, based on an intuitive grasp of broader considerations. But these individuals could not provide a systematic discipline with principles and methods appropriate to the tasks of design.

Following the Renaissance, the consequence of separating the theoretical from the practical, the ideal from the real, and the cognitive from the noncognitive was a loss of the essentially humanistic dimension of production. The forms of making which had the widest impact on the daily life of society — engineering and the other practical arts — were guided merely by a narrow profit motive or by military necessity,[16] rather than a deeper consideration of the interplay between human character and products.[17] Design was practiced by chance and intuition as a trade activity or military occupation, rather than in its full potential as an architectonic master art that guides all of the diverse forms of making which are central to human culture. In short, design became a servile activity rather than a liberal art. It was not conceived as an art which could promote the freedom of men and women in the circumstances of the newly emerging technological culture.

Integrative Arts in the Twentieth Century

Efforts to reunite design with the arts of making began in the nineteenth century, when Ruskin, Morris, and others attempted to elevate the status of craft production as an alternative to mass production by machines. However, the most significant efforts to rejoin design and making came with the cultural and philosophic revolution at the beginning of the twentieth century. The origins of design are reasonably traced to the early decades of the twentieth century because it was in this period that individuals began to formulate new disciplines of design thinking that would combine theoretical knowledge with practical action for new productive purposes.[18]

Walter Gropius was among the first to recognize in design a new liberal art of technological culture. In the wake of the First World War, he realized that he had a responsibility to train a new generation of architects who could help to overcome the disastrous gulf which had emerged between idealism and reality. The basis of that training would be a "modern architectonic art" of design.

> Thus the Bauhaus was inaugurated in 1919 with the specific object of realizing a modern architectonic art, which like human nature was meant to be all-embracing in its scope. It deliberately concentrated primarily on what has now become a work of imperative urgency — averting mankind's enslavement by the machine by saving the mass-product and the home from mechanical anarchy and by restoring them to purpose, sense and life. This means evolving goods and buildings specifically designed for industrial production. Our object was to eliminate the drawbacks of the machine without sacrificing any one of its real advantages. We aimed at realizing standards of excellence, not creating transient novelties. Experiment once more became the center of architecture, and that demands a broad, coordinating mind, not the narrow specialist.[19]

The ground of the new art of design was not to be found in the principles of idealism, materialism, or "art for art's sake."[20] It was to be found in human character and in the essential unity of all forms of making in the circumstances of a new cultural environment strongly influenced by engineering, technology, and commerce.[21]

> What the Bauhaus preached in practice was the common citizenship of all forms of creative work, and their logical interdependence on one another in the modern world. Our guiding principle was that design is neither an intellectual nor a material affair, but simply an integral part of the stuff of life, necessary for everyone in a civilized society. Our ambition was to rouse the creative artist from his other-worldliness and to reintegrate him into the workaday world of realities and, at the same

time, to broaden and humanize the rigid, almost exclusively material mind of the businessman. Our conception of the basic unity of all design in relation to life was in diametric opposition to that of "art for art's sake" and the much more dangerous philosophy it sprang from, business as an end in itself.[22]

However, the significance of the new architectonic art of design lay precisely in encouraging the cultivation of alternative and often conflicting principles as hypotheses for making. Gropius did not claim that the new art of design provided an ultimate solution to the problems of industrialized society. What he claimed was that it revitalized design thinking by initiating a new path of experimentation and pluralistic exploration grounded in art and human character. Aside from the broad principle that an architectonic art of design connected the arts, the path or discipline presented by Gropius did not presuppose or require any particular principles of art. Rather, it was a way to explore a variety of principles in order to discover their potential consequences for making and practical life: "Modern painting, breaking through old conventions, has released countless suggestions which are still waiting to be used by the practical world. But when, in the future, artists who sense new creative values have had practical training in the industrial world, they will themselves possess the means for realizing those values immediately. They will compel industry to serve their idea and industry will seek out and utilize their comprehensive training."[23]

It is easy to confuse the idea of design that gave purpose to the Bauhaus with the separate directions in which it was developed by the faculty in the short period of the school's institutional existence. Gropius, Moholy-Nagy, Klee, Kandinsky, and others developed individual visions that favored one or another principle of making. But to substitute particular visions and consequent results for the concept of a new discipline of design thinking misses the point of the liberal art that Gropius sought to establish. The goal was to provide a concrete connection between artistic exploration and practical action, where artists could learn how their conceptions of art might be carried forward as experiments in shaping the broad domain of the artificial in human experience, extending beyond traditional forms of artistic expression into making in all phases of life, supported by new technologies and advances in science.

Interpreted in its weakest form, this is "aesthetic" exploration in the reductive sense of the term, leading toward decoration and styling that appeals only to the senses.[24] However, interpreted in the strongest sense, it is "artistic" exploration in the sense that Dewey speaks of art, as the quality of unity and satisfaction belonging to any experience, whether the experience is primarily intellectual, practical, or aesthetic. Art should not be something outside of experience or segregated to a small area of experience. It *is* experience in its most vital and essential form.[25] Mechanization has tended to diminish the human qualities developed in all phases of life, but the new art of design sought by the Bauhaus offered a way to discover and express human qualities and values, to make them an integral part of the human-made environment.

The most important practical criticisms of the Bauhaus do not concern its effort to establish a new architectonic art of design thinking. Rather, they concern what the nature of that art should be. Evidence for this is that subsequent discussion turned toward the proper methodology of design. Unfortunately, "methodology" was interpreted in its narrow form as *specialized techniques or methods* rather than in its architectonic form as *systematic disciplines of integrative thinking,* within which diverse techniques and methods are given direction and purpose.[26] The proper question should have been, what is *forethought* in the new circumstances of twentieth-century culture? The leaders of the Bauhaus expressed a new attitude toward making that was consistent with the cultural and philosophic revolution that began in the early days of the twentieth century. Indeed, the Bauhaus was part of that revolution precisely because of its effort to establish a new architectonic art of design grounded in character and making. However, the Bauhaus did not fully develop the new disciplines of design thinking. It left the architectonic art of design with open-ended possibilities that required further concrete development in order to be effective. It is no surprise, therefore, that the issue for debate in evaluating the contribution of the Bauhaus soon became whether it succeeded in providing the necessary intellectual tools for integrating the arts of making with knowledge gained from the natural and social sciences, and whether it succeeded in integrating design thinking with industry and the world of practical action.

The Bauhaus opened paths in these directions, but it lacked instrumentalities of forethought essential for further exploration and development—instrumentalities that were required to complete the revolution in attitude and direction of thinking that it helped to initiate. Forethought at the Bauhaus derived its strength from the creative imagination of artists. And, despite debunking by critics, the leaders of the Bauhaus went to a correct source, because all making is, in essence, an artistic, not merely an aesthetic, activity.[27] But the *thought* that must stand behind *making* in the new circumstances that have emerged in the twentieth century was only partly grasped in the vision and preparation of artists that existed at the Bauhaus. When Gropius spoke of the "comprehensive training" of the new artist, it was more an expression of optimism about future possibilities than accurate reporting about the reality of the Bauhaus program.

Considering the relation between rhetoric and making, which has been an ongoing source of innovation in Western culture, it is reasonable to suggest that what the Bauhaus lacked was a revolutionary vision of rhetoric to match its revolutionary vision of making. This would be rhetoric as a broad intellectual discipline, expanded from an art productive of words and verbal arguments to an art of conceiving and planning all of the types of products that human beings are capable of making. Without such a discipline for integrating design and making with science and practical action, the accomplishments of the Bauhaus were necessarily limited. Thus, design may have had its origin at the beginning of the twentieth century, but it required further development appropriate to the new circumstances of culture.

Moholy-Nagy took an important step in this direction when he established the New Bauhaus in Chicago in 1937. As part of the new program, he invited a philosopher from the University of Chicago, Charles W. Morris, to design a component of the curriculum suited to prepare students with a broader understanding of the relations among art, science, and technology that the school was attempting to explore in practice.[28] Morris accepted the challenge with enthusiasm and promptly recruited distinguished colleagues from the university to assist. The resulting curriculum followed the pattern of general education at the University of Chicago, with courses in the subject matter and methods of the physical and biological sciences, the social sciences, and the humanities, as well as two interdisciplinary courses: "intellectual and cultural history," and "intellectual integration."[29]

Morris taught the course in intellectual integration, using the uncorrected galley proof of his *Foundations of the Theory of Signs* as a background reading. His goal was to use "the theory of signs and the results of the unity of science movement to obtain a philosophical perspective on human activity," and thereby broaden the understanding of design students who were active in the workshops and studios of the school.[30] Unfortunately, this experiment was cut short because of financial difficulties, which forced the school to close for a short period. When it reopened, Morris and his colleagues continued to teach for a short time without compensation, but there is little documentation to suggest that the venture in intellectual integration reached its potential. Nonetheless, Moholy-Nagy viewed such explorations as an essential part of the new liberal art of design that he sought to develop and that he described in detail in *Vision in Motion*.[31] Relying on the contingent of professors from the University of Chicago to teach subject matters and methods of intellectual integration, he viewed the overall program of the New Bauhaus as a further integration in the activity of making. This was a concrete development of the original Bauhaus idea, although the significance of the innovation has passed largely unnoticed because it lasted only a short time and few results were immediately evident.

Without a Bauhäusler at once sensitive to the connection between design and making *and* prepared to explore new disciplines of forethought, further development of the Bauhaus idea was difficult, if not impossible. This is illustrated in the fate of the Hochschule für Gestaltung (HfG) Ulm, widely regarded as the most important and influential school of design since World War II. Founded in 1953 by Max Bill and others to promote the principles of the Bauhaus, HfG Ulm was soon racked by irreconcilable differences between Bill and those among the staff who wanted to pursue new methods suited to the needs of industry. Bill, an alumnus of the Bauhaus, resigned after a short time, succeeded by his deputy, Tomás Maldonado, who encouraged the development of scientific planning more deeply informed with mathematics and analytical techniques.

The differences between Bill and his colleagues are usually described as methodological, but they were far more. The combined influence of the Frankfurt School and the Vienna Circle on Maldonado and his colleagues helps to explain the unusual and, at times, explosive contradictions that formed the atmosphere at HfG Ulm, representing a shift away from the principles of an integrative discipline of design sought by Bill and the leaders of the Bauhaus. The contrast of principles is evident in the confidence displayed by Maldonado that HfG Ulm could tell the world what forms should and should not be created to serve social goals. "The HfG we are building in Ulm intends to redefine the terms of the new culture. Unlike Moholy-Nagy in Chicago, it does not merely want to form men who would be able to create and express themselves. The school at Ulm . . . wants to indicate what the social goal of this creativity should be; in other words, which forms deserve to be created and which do not."[32] While the Bauhaus based its work on a belief in the essential freedom of individual human character in a society and culture influenced by industrialization, Maldonado viewed industry itself as the central agency shaping culture. Indeed, for Maldonado industry was culture.

> Ulm was based on one basic idea, which we all shared in spite of disagreeing on absolutely everything else: the idea that industry is culture, and that there exists the possibility (and also the necessity) of an industrial culture. . . . At that time I was particularly receptive to some of the thinking of the Frankfurt School. Although my own cultural orientation was strongly marked at that time by Neopositivism (I was eagerly reading Carnap, Neurath, Schlick, Morris, Wittgenstein, Reichenback, etc.), the presence of Adorno in Frankfurt represented for me, as it were, a contradictory intellectual stimulation.[33]

Focus on methodology was a way of introducing a collection of scientific methods and techniques into design. It promoted the idea of a new science of design, grounded in neopositivist and empiricist philosophy, which some in the theoretical wing of HfG Ulm perhaps naively believed could be harnessed to serve a particular social, political, and intellectual agenda.

> What must be remembered is not only the limitless curiosity that we had in those years about anything that was — or seemed — new. That was a feverish, insatiable curiosity directed above all at the new disciplines that were then coming up: cybernetics, information theory, systems theory, semiotics, ergonomics. But our curiosity went further than this: it also extended, in no small measure, to established disciplines such as the philosophy of science and mathematical logic.
>   The mainspring of all our curiosity, or reading, and our theoretical work was our determination to find a solid methodological basis for the work of design.
>   This was a highly ambitious undertaking, admittedly: we were seeking to force through, in the field of design, a transformation equivalent to the process by which chemistry emerged from alchemy.[34]

However, the result of the work at HfG Ulm was not a new integrative science of design, but a further exploration of the relation between design and the natural and behavioral sciences begun at the Bauhaus and continued at the New Bauhaus.[35] Furthermore, without the humanistic orientation of the

Bauhaus, the tendency at HfG Ulm was toward specialization, somewhat along the lines developed by Hannes Meyer in the closing days of the Bauhaus,[36] involving a belief in the ability of experts to engineer socially acceptable results through industry.[37] HfG Ulm should not be credited with initiating the "design methods movement" or the effort to find a neopositivist science of design thinking. It was a meeting ground for individuals from around the world who held such interests. It was a place where design educators could experiment with potentially useful techniques generally invented elsewhere.

However, neopositivism and empiricism are not inherently opposed to the concept of an integrative liberal art of design. This is evident in one of the most important works of design theory in the twentieth century, Herbert Simon's *The Sciences of the Artificial*. The problem addressed by Simon is the relation between the *necessary* in natural phenomena and the *contingent* features of the human-made: "The contingency of artificial phenomena has always created doubts as to whether they fall properly within the compass of science. Sometimes these doubts are directed at the teleological character of artificial systems and the consequent difficulty of disentangling prescription from description. This seems to me not to be the real difficulty. The genuine problem is to show how empirical propositions can be made at all about systems that, given different circumstances, might be quite other than they are."[38] His insight was not the reduction of design to any one of the established theoretical sciences—as appears to have been the goal at HfG Ulm. Rather, it was a recognition of the theoretical substance of design *distinct* from the substance of its supporting sciences. The result was the discovery of a new kind of science, radically distinct from the sciences of nature.

> Finally, I thought I began to see in the problem of artificiality an explanation of the difficulty that has been experienced in filling engineering and other professions with empirical and theoretical substance distinct from the substance of their supporting sciences. Engineering, medicine, business, architecture, and painting are concerned not with the necessary but with the contingent—not with how things are but with how they might be—in short, with design. The possibility of creating a science or sciences of design is exactly as great as the possibility of creating any science of the artificial. The two possibilities stand or fall together.[39]

The problem identified by Simon is surprisingly similar to the problems discussed by Aristotle in the first chapter of the *Rhetoric* and in the first chapter of the *Poetics:* how human beings reason and reach decisions about matters which may be other than they are, and how the artificial or human-made is different from, but related to, the natural.[40] Simon's proposed solution is a science of design, with features that are both *rhetorical*—an emphasis on deliberation and decision making—and *poetic*, in the sense that all products made by human beings are subject to analysis and understanding based on the nature of the activity of making.[41] Like the leaders of the Bauhaus, Simon is not concerned with a trenchant Renaissance distinction between the fine and practical arts. He is interested in the elements of forethought operating behind all arts of making.

> The real subjects of the new intellectual free trade among the many cultures are our own thought processes, our processes of *judging, deciding, choosing*, and *creating*. We are importing and exporting from one intellectual discipline to another ideas about how a serially organized information-processing system like a human being — or a computer, or a complex of men and women and computers in organized cooperation — solves problems and achieves goals in outer environments of great complexity.
>
> The proper study of mankind has been said to be man. But I have argued that man — at least the intellective component of man — may be relatively simple, that most of the complexity of his behavior may be drawn from man's environment, from man's search for good designs. If I have made my case, then we can conclude that, in large part, the proper study of mankind is the science of design, not only as a professional component of a technical education but as a core discipline for every liberally educated person.[42]

The basis for the integration that Simon seeks for design is the new discipline of decision making, and he explores this discipline in the context of neopositivist and empiricist philosophy. However, the particular philosophic orientation of Simon's approach should not distract from appreciation of the broader direction of design thinking toward which he points. Simon is investigating the themes and arts of rhetoric in their relation to new arts of making.

Rhetoric and the New Technologies of Design Thinking

The effort to establish a new liberal art of design at the Bauhaus has given way to a search for a plurality of design arts which can provide suitable instrumentalities of forethought for a discipline which increasingly requires the incorporation of diverse kinds of knowledge. Since the search is still underway and no conventions of terminology, description, or formulation have emerged with clarity, the precise nature of these arts remains uncertain and open to debate. Yet, central themes are evident throughout contemporary explorations of design and reflections on design practice, and the roots of those themes in rhetoric and poetics is an indication of the shape that the new integrative disciplines of design thinking may eventually take.

When Herbert Simon refers to the thought processes of creating, judging, deciding, and choosing as the real subjects of the new intellectual free trade among cultures and disciplines, he is giving new voice to the traditional arts and themes of rhetoric. However, the foundation of these processes of forethought in the disciplines of rhetoric is not yet widely recognized or understood. Rhetoric is still perceived by many people in its Renaissance orientation toward poetry, belles lettres, and beaux arts, rather than in its twentieth-century orientation toward technology as the new science of art, where theory is integrated with practice for productive purposes and where art is no longer confined to an exclusive domain of fine art but extends to all forms of making. Nonetheless, the themes of rhetoric have emerged in twentieth-century design precisely because they provide the integrative connections that are needed in an age of technology.

The pattern of rhetoric in twentieth-century design builds on distinctions which were established early in the formation of rhetorical theory and developed to meet changing circumstances. In earlier periods of Western culture, when rhetoric was oriented toward words and verbal arguments, the traditional divisions of rhetoric were *invention, judgment, disposition* (planning the sequence of argument), *delivery* (choosing the appropriate vehicle for presenting arguments to different audiences), and *expression* (choosing the appropriate stylistic embodiment of arguments). In the expanded rhetoric of Francis Bacon, who sought to overcome the separation between words and things in order to explore science and technology, the traditional divisions of rhetoric survived in the groundplan for the advancement of learning and in the four intellectual arts needed to carry out that advancement: the arts of *invention, judgment, custody*, and *tradition*. Significantly, the fifth division of rhetoric, expression, did not disappear. It was distributed by Bacon among the four intellectual arts, integrated into the larger task of intellectual exploration in each area.

In the new rhetoric of twentieth-century design and technology, where the effort is also to overcome the separation between words and things, the traditional divisions of rhetoric have emerged once again to give coherence to inquiry. The investigation of design in theory and practice centers around four themes, which may be stated briefly and ambiguously as *invention and communication, judgment and construction, decision making and strategic planning,* and *evaluation and systemic integration*. These themes may be represented in the form of a matrix in order to suggest issues and problems that stand behind the shifting debate about design in the past seventy years (Figure 3).

In this framework, the fifth division of rhetoric, *expression and styling,* emerges as a persistent issue in each of the disciplines. Few designers are content to describe their work as mere styling. Yet, most recognize that the appearance and expressive quality of products is critically important not only in marketing but in the substantive contribution of design to daily living. The problem is how to accommodate sensitivity to expression with the intellectual and analytical issues belonging to communication, construction, strategic planning, and systemic integration. The neopositivist approach is to distinguish sharply between emotion and cognition, leaving expression as something emotive, irrational, intuitive, and noncognitive. However, in the context of a rhetorical approach, the expressive appearance or styling of a product carries a deeper argument about the nature of the product and its role in practical action and social life. Expression does not clothe design thinking; it *is* design thinking in its most immediate manifestation, providing the integrative aesthetic experience which incorporates the array of technical decisions contained in any product.

The disciplines or arts of design have their counterparts in the intellectual virtues of designers. Designers should be (1) curious and inventive beyond

FIGURE 3. Matrix of Abilities and Disciplines in Design

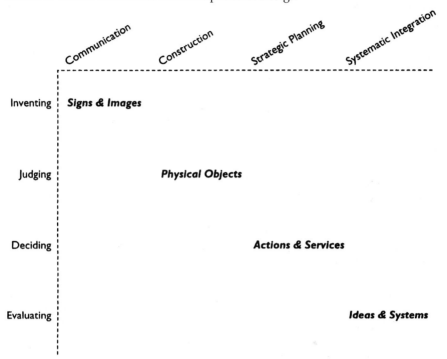

the bounds of specialization in addressing design problems; (2) able to judge which of their inventions are and which are not viable constructs in particular circumstances and under given conditions; (3) able to participate with others, including technical specialists from many fields, in decision-making processes which develop products from conception to production, distribution, disposal, and recycling; (4) able to evaluate the objective worth of products in terms of the needs of manufacturers, individual users, and society at large; and (5) able to embody ideas in appropriately expressive forms throughout the process of conception and planning. The disciplines of design are *enabled* by the rhetorical abilities of designers.

Design has become an art of deliberation essential for making in all phases of human activity. It applies to the making of theories which attempt to explain the natural operations of the world. It applies to making policies and institutions which may guide practical action, as in a constitution for a newly emerging state or in political, social, and economic institutions relevant to new circumstances. And, it applies to making all of the objects in the domain of production that the Renaissance arbitrarily divided into belles lettres, beaux arts, and the practical arts. Deliberation in design yields arguments: the plans, proposals, sketches, models, and prototypes which are presented by designers as the basis for understanding, practical action, or production.

Design is the art of shaping arguments about the artificial or human-made world, arguments which may be carried forward in the concrete activities of production in each of these areas, with objective results ultimately judged by individuals, groups, and society.

EXPANDING THE DISCIPLINE OF DESIGN

Three other perspectives have also exerted strong influence on the formation of design thinking in the twentieth century. However, they have shifted attention away from the discipline of design, toward different types of philosophic or cultural content. This has sometimes led to new characterizations of the method of designing that are more closely aligned with politics, science, or dialectic. Nonetheless, the discipline has expanded quite easily to accommodate such interests, demonstrating the potential of design to adapt to different rhetorical purposes and objectives.

Power to Control Nature and Influence Social Life

When the origins of design are traced to the Industrial Revolution, the principle lies in the power of individuals to control their surroundings, satisfy needs and desires, and influence social life through mechanization and technology. For example, John Heskett begins his history of industrial design with a description of the quantitative and qualitative change that has taken place in the last two hundred years.

> In the last two centuries, human power to control and shape the surroundings we inhabit has been continuously augmented, to the extent that it has become a truism to speak of a man-made world. The instrument of this transformation has been mechanized industry, and from its workshops and factories a swelling flood of artefacts and mechanisms has poured out to satisfy the needs and desires of an ever-greater proportion of the world's population. The change has not only been quantitative, but has also radically altered the qualitative nature of the life we live, or aspire to live.[43]

For writers such as Heskett, the origins of design are best traced to the Industrial Revolution, because it was during this period that the power to invent and shape useful products was distinguished from the laborious physical activities of making them. Prior to this period, design was closely associated with craft methods of production, and the crafts, in their most refined forms, were instruments to satisfy the desire of princes and kings for luxury. With the advent of new techniques for mass production, design became an instrument of merchant princes in a new world of technological capabilities, economic competition, political and social ideas, and masses of consumers from all social classes. Design and designers came into existence within the competitive organization of production, distribution, and consumption.

From this perspective, design is an instrument of power.[44] It is the art of inventing and shaping two-, three-, and four-dimensional forms that are intended to satisfy needs, wants, and desires, thereby effecting changes in the attitudes, beliefs, and actions of others. Of course, after two hundred years of development, design is no longer the exclusive instrument of merchant princes. Yet, it is still significantly dependent on the interests of businesses and corporations, making products that are competitive in the global marketplace. The competitive environment of business provides the framework for understanding the diverse roles of professional designers today. Some work within corporate structures; some work outside, in design consultancies; and some work alone, with even greater independence, serving their own interests, working with only marginal concern for the interests of corporations, content with personal satisfaction in small-scale work or quietly seeking to bypass corporate intermediaries in order to serve the long-term interests of the general public.[45] Indeed, one aspect of the qualitative change in culture that has followed the Industrial Revolution is the widening range of individuals who may exercise the power of design.

From the perspective of design as power, a variety of traditional themes in design history and theory take on special significance. In *Objects of Desire*, Adrian Forty emphasizes the role of design in society. He argues that excessive concentration on design as an art of making things beautiful has severed design from its function in making profit and in transmitting ideas. In effect, it "has obscured the fact that design came into being at a particular stage in the history of capitalism and played a vital part in the creation of industrial wealth. Limiting it to a purely artistic activity has made it seem trivial and relegated it to the status of a mere cultural appendix."[46] For Forty, design is indeed concerned with the look of things, but the look of things is more than a matter of pure, idealized beauty: "Those who complain about the effects of television, journalism, advertising and fiction on our minds remain oblivious to the similar influence of design. Far from being a neutral, inoffensive artistic activity, design, by its very nature, has more enduring effects than the ephemeral products of the media because it can cast ideas about who we are and how we should behave into permanent and tangible form."[47] Forty argues that design is the preparation of instructions for the production of manufactured goods. However, these instructions include more than information about formal shapes. They inevitably include an expression of ideas or myths about the world in which we live. "Every product, to be successful, must incorporate the ideas that will make it marketable, and the particular task of design is to bring about the conjunction between such ideas and the available means of production. The result of this process is that manufactured goods embody innumerable myths about the world which in time come to seem as real as the products in which they are embedded."[48]

Throughout his work, Forty seeks to establish a better understanding of the balance that exists among various influences on the design process. On the one hand, he warns against excessive emphasis on the creative power of the individual professional designer, observing that the entrepreneur's final selection among alternative design proposals is just as important a design decision as any decision made by the formally designated designer.[49] On the other hand, he warns against excessive emphasis on "extremely general dominating ideas" at the social or cultural level. This is a clear criticism of dialecticians who attempt to trace the significance of design to broad cultural ideas grounded in the spirit of the time, without adequate recognition of the diversity of specific ideas held by designers and entrepreneurs or of the variety of desires operating among individuals and groups within society at any moment in history.[50] Design is part of a social process in which there are professional designers and many others who are not formally described as designers but who make design decisions — whether in the process of product development, manufacturing, or distribution and consumption.

Material Conditions and Aesthetic Appeal

When the origins of design are traced to the creation of images and objects by primitive human beings, the principle lies in the material conditions of life. The origins of design in prehistory will never be fully understood because the surviving evidence is fragmentary. Nonetheless, based on images and objects which have survived, the broad outlines of an account are possible, throwing light on the problems of design in the twentieth century. The earliest examples of design are tools, images drawn on cave walls, and ornamental objects with images drawn on bone or other materials. These objects reveal rudimentary technical skills in shaping materials into useful forms and, at the same time, an added psychological factor: aesthetic delight in the sensuousness of materials, patterns, and forms. The development of design throughout prehistory and recorded history is an elaboration of the technical and aesthetic considerations which have contributed to a satisfying physical and emotional life for mankind.[51]

Characteristic of this approach, human life is seen as progressively complicated by a hierarchy of needs, ascending from the physical and biological, to the emotional and psychological, to the spiritual — the most refined of the emotional needs of the human animal.[52] Design is the natural ability of human beings to shape and use materials to satisfy all of these needs.[53] However, design is partly rational and cognitive, and partly irrational, emotive, intuitive, and noncognitive. It is rational to the extent that there is conscious understanding of the laws of nature; it is irrational to the extent that the sciences have not yet succeeded in revealing the laws of complex phenomena. Indeed, there is reason to believe that design will always retain an irrational or intuitive component, because there are properties of materials and forms that possess aesthetic and spiritual appeal for which no scientific explanation seems possible. However, this is not a confirmation of the existence of a transcendental realm, since the spiritual is regarded by the materialist merely as a complex emotional state of mind.

There are three basic elements that contribute to the development of design in the contemporary world. The first element is the technique or technology of craft production, supported by a gradual accumulation of scientific understanding of the underlying principles of nature that guide construction.[54] This has led to the technology of machines, mass production, and computers. Indeed, engineering, with its reliance on natural science and mathematics, is the basic form of design for the materialist.[55] The second element is our understanding of the psychological, social, and cultural needs that condition the use of products.[56] (Practical mechanics and engineering may provide the fundamental example of design, but industrial designers are quick to argue that they have special expertise in addressing the behavioral considerations that are associated with products.) The third element is awareness of the aesthetic appeal of forms. This sometimes leads to proposals for a "science of art" which grows out of perceptual psychology and other branches of social science.[57]

The treatment of aesthetics from this perspective may be illustrated by Herbert Read, whose book *Art and Industry* was a standard text in many design schools in the United States and Britain and served as an exceptionally influential introductory work on design for general readers.[58] Although Read is associated with the Bauhaus movement, and was a friend and strong supporter of Moholy-Nagy, his book represents a different philosophic orientation that deserves careful consideration.[59] Relying on similar themes and many of the same commonplaces of design history as told by Moholy-Nagy, he tells a subtly different story about the history of design and introduces a different thread into the history of the Bauhaus and into design thinking in the twentieth century.[60]

For Read, the problem of design in the twentieth century is precisely the consequence of developments that have followed in the linear progression of history through advances in the technology of production and efforts to add aesthetic value to products.

> For more than a hundred years an attempt has been made to impose on the products of machinery aesthetic values which are not only irrelevant, but generally costly and harmful to efficiency. Those aesthetic values were associated with the previously prevailing handicraft methods of production, but they were not essential even to these. Actually they were the superficial styles and mannerisms of the Renaissance tradition of ornament. Nevertheless, the products of machinery were at first judged by the standards of this tradition, and though there have been attempts, notably the one led by Ruskin and Morris, to return to the more fundamental aspects of handicraft—that is to say, to the forms underlying ornament—yet the problem in its essentials remains unresolved. For the real problem is not to adapt machine production to the aesthetic standards of handicraft, but to think out new aesthetic standards for new methods of production.[61]

The method proposed by Read to address this problem indicates a sharp reversal of the dialectician's concern for spirit and culture. Instead of seeking an explanation for design in the unifying ideas of a particular cultural epoch, he seeks to strip away cultural irrelevancies and reduce design to its essential elements in art and industrial production.

> [W]hat is required as a preliminary to any practical solution of the division existing between art and industry is a clear understanding, not only

of the processes of modern production, but also of the nature of art. Not until we have reduced the work of art to its essentials, stripped it of all the irrelevancies imposed on it by a particular culture or civilization, can we see any solution of the problem. The first step, therefore, is to define art; the second is to estimate the capacity of the machine to produce works of art.[62]

This involves a twofold use of reasoning that leads to a "science of art" that is coordinate with the natural sciences: first, a decomposition to fundamental parts, elements, or essentials; second, a subsequent construction of understanding by the progressive addition of the complicating factors that eventually yield an approximation of the complexity that is possible in design.

> The work of art is shown to be essentially formal; it is the shaping of material into forms which have a sensuous or intellectual appeal to the average human being. To define the nature and operation of this appeal is not an easy task, but it must be faced by anyone who wishes to see a permanent solution of the problem that concerns us.
>
> The problem, that is to say, is in the first place a logical or dialectical one. It is the definition of the normal or universal elements in art.
>
> It is then complicated by the purposes which the objects we are shaping have to serve. That is to say, we are concerned, not with the works of art whose only purpose is to please the senses or intellect, but with works of art which must in addition perform a utilitarian function.[63]

The result is recognition of a type of art which is abstract or non-figurative, with "no concern beyond making objects whose plastic form appeals to the aesthetic sensibility." Furthermore, the nature of this appeal may be either rational or intuitional—the former obeying rules of symmetry and proportion, the latter appealing to "some obscurer unconscious faculty."[64] "We must recognize the abstract nature of the essential element in art, and as a consequence, we must recognize that design is a function of the abstract artist. The abstract artist (who may often be identical with the engineer or the technician) must be given a place in all industries in which he is not already established, and his decisions on all questions of design must be final."[65] Designers construct objects to satisfy fundamental human needs that are susceptible to some level of scientific or engineering analysis.[66] However, the constructions are inevitably complicated by arbitrary factors of taste and preference which the designer is often able to address only by emotional sensitivity and intuitive understanding. Design is based on science, but it extends its reach in addressing emotional needs through aesthetics.

Spiritual Life: Hellenism and Hebraism in Design

There is a persistent thread of spirituality in twentieth-century art and design which has never found an adequately articulate voice in modern design theory. This is disappointing, because the widespread discontent with the fruits of science, technology, and business cannot be easily dismissed. Judged by the ideals of Western and Eastern cultures, the obsessive materialism, injustice, warfare, environmental degradation, and inhumanity of the past century of progress is a cruel denial of something fundamental in the human spirit, a betrayal of reason and conscience, of right thinking and right acting. Ironically, the two great theories of design in Western culture — one embedded in Hellenism, the other in Hebraicism — have exerted little explicit influence on the development of design thinking in the period when design is most widely practiced and discussed as a cultural art.[67] Yet, traces of these theories emerge occasionally as a reminder of a resource that remains available to illuminate the work of those designers who are not content with pragmatic design and insist that design has a more important role to play in promoting human well-being.

Distinguished designer George Nelson argues that the design process is integrated in the principle of appropriateness, and he grounds this principle in the model provided by God and natural order.

> Going through the entire design process, which includes the important collaborations all the way down the line, with materials people, engineers, technicians in specialized areas, and marketing people, the steady movement is in the direction of a solution that is ultimately seen, not as beautiful, but as *appropriate*. The creation of beauty cannot be the aim; beauty is one of the aspects of appropriateness, and it still lies pretty much in the eye of the beholder, which makes it a by-product rather than a goal.
>
>   There is very powerful support for this view in nature, which is always the best model to be followed, for God, so to speak, is still the best designer. People who work with natural organisms at any scale, such as biologists, are invariably the expression of some function or other. . . . Everything in organic nature functions in relation to survival needs; we find these things beautiful, because as creatures of nature we are programmed to respond to evidence of appropriateness as an expression of beauty. For mathematicians, and for scientists generally, words like "elegant," "appropriate," and "beautiful" are synonymous.[68]

The spiritual feature of Nelson's work is sometimes neglected by design critics and historians who interpret "function" in a narrow, mechanistic way, rather than as a connection between human beings, products, and the broader system of nature and the universe. The principle of appropriateness, regarded as a spiritual quality, serves to explain some features of Nelson's writings which otherwise appear paradoxical. For example, he offers harsh criticism of excessively narrow concepts of "functional" design; so-called "good" design, as judged by aesthetic standards such as those once promoted by Edgar Kaufmann, Jr. at the Museum of Modern Art; the pretensions of design for design's sake; and the equally pretentious idea of the designer as creator and purveyor of social meanings. Yet, he argues for a vision of design as communication and of the designer as artist. The only explanation is that he regards the designer as an artist in the Platonic sense, an enlightened practitioner seeking unity and harmony among the disparate elements of every product. Indeed, he argues that products which internally achieve harmony and balance serve the ethical life of human beings, who are actively seeking their own place in a unity of social experience and nature — precisely at a time when culture appears to be disintegrating.[69]

The elements of Hellenism and Hebraicism which are balanced in Nelson's work — a concern for right thinking and for right acting, consciousness and conscience — are echoed whenever the origins of design are traced to the creation of the universe. The principle lies in spiritual life and the natural order. Unfortunately, scholars have exercised little ingenuity in exploring the rich, complex theory of design provided by Plato in the *Timaeus* and the *Republic*, or in rethinking the Christian tradition represented, for example, by St. Augustine.[70] Until this material is rediscovered, the spiritual discontent with design and technology will remain inchoate. We will speak of an environmental crisis, when we mean a spiritual crisis in the relation of human beings to natural order. We will be charmed by some products and infuriated by others, while remaining oblivious to their spiritual meaning. We will be mystified by the absence of an adequate cultural critique in design theory which is based on more than materialist economics and the conflict of social classes. Finally, we will be puzzled by the failure of systems theory to reach beyond its materialist origins and explore unifying cultural ideas and values as the core of all systems.

CONCLUSION

The four perspectives identified in this essay are based on rhetorical commonplaces in the study and practice of design. Each commonplace orients our ideas about design in a different direction, opening up a broad avenue for exploration and integration. The purpose in identifying these perspectives is to gain a more adequate representation of the pluralism of twentieth-century design thinking. The diversity of design in the contemporary world is less bewildering than it appears to the casual observer. Products embody the intentions and purposes of their makers, and there is an intelligible pattern in the ongoing development and application of design. The essential humanism of design lies in the fact that human beings determine what the subject matter, processes, and purposes of design shall be. These are not determined by nature, but by our decisions.

In the contemporary world, design is the domain of vividly competing ideas about what it means to be human. However, the exploration of design does not break our connection with the past. The central themes and commonplaces of design — power and control, materialism and pleasure, spirituality, and character — reveal deep continuities with ancient philosophic traditions. Indeed, the pluralism of design in the twentieth century is inteligible because it rests on a pluralism of philosophic assumptions which are familiar. The exploration of design is therefore, a contribution to the philosophy of culture in our time.

NOTES

1. Richard Buchanan, "Wicked Problems in Design Thinking," *Design Issues*, 8, no. 2 (Spring 1992): 5–21.

2. John Dewey, "By Nature and by Art," *Philosophy of Education* (*Problems of Men*) (1946; rpt. Totowa, NJ: Littlefield, Adams, 1958), pp. 286–300.

3. Philosopher Richard McKeon provides a useful interpretation of Aristotle's position on the arts. "The productive sciences are differentiated according to their products, and there are no sharply defined lines imposed by nature to separate the arts or to differentiate the kinds of artificial things. The Greeks did not differentiate the fine arts from the mechanical in the fashion that has been customary since the Renaissance, and they have therefore been criticized by humanists for confusing arts and trades, thereby degrading the artist, and by pragmatists for separating science from art, thereby reducing operations and mechanical contrivances to a servile level. The arts as conceived by Aristotle include not only such arts as painting, music, and poetry, but medicine, architecture, cobbling, and rhetoric. Since the arts imitate nature, they may be differentiated by consideration of the object, means, and manner of their imitation, and therefore, although he has no words for fine arts, Aristotle is able, in the opening chapter of the *Poetics*, to assemble the arts which we call fine by isolating their means of imitation and to differentiate tragedy from the other arts. Aristotle did, however, have a word by which to differentiate the liberal arts from the mechanical, and he sought their differentiation in the educative influence of the arts in the formation of men for freedom." Richard McKeon, ed., *Introduction to Aristotle* (New York: Modern Library, 1947), pp. xxiii–xxiv.

4. Aristotle, *Nicomachean Ethics*, 4.4.1140a1–23. Also, *Metaphysics*, 1.1.980a20–982a1.

5. Aristotle, *Poetics*, 1450b5–12. For a discussion of this issue, see Richard McKeon, "The Uses of Rhetoric in a Technological Age: Architectonic Productive Arts," in *Rhetoric: Essays in Invention and Discovery*, ed. Mark Backman (Woodbridge, CT: Ox Bow Press, 1987), p. 4. The balanced relation between rhetoric and poetics in Aristotle's philosophy gave way in the work of his successors to an emphasis on rhetoric and a rhetoricized poetics. This led to a reading of the *Poetics* as a body of rules or laws of making to guide the literary artist, rather than a scientific analysis of made things, as Aristotle intended. Such an approach, evident in Horace and Longinus, has dominated Western literary theory in many periods, including the Renaissance.

6. Aristotle defined rhetoric as the faculty of finding the available means of persuasion with regard to any subject about which we deliberate. Along with its counterpart, dialectic, rhetoric supplied the arguments and thought which could be used by the artist to shape a particular form. Aristotle, *Rhetoric*, 1.2.

7. Vitruvius, *The Ten Books on Architecture*, trans. Morris Hicky Morgan (New York: Dover, 1960), 1.1.

8. For an extensive discussion of the classification of poetry among the sciences in the Renaissance, with useful observations on the practical arts, see Bernard Weinberg, *A History of Literary Criticism in the Italian Renaissance* (Chicago: University of Chicago Press, 1961), 1.1–37.

9. For a discussion of these three traditions in the context of the arts, see Weinberg, *A History of Literary Criticism*, 2.797–813. For a broader discussion of these traditions and representative texts by Petrarca, Valla, Ficino, et al., see Ernst Cassirer, Paul Oscar Kristeller, and John Herman Randal, Jr., eds., *The Renaissance Philosophy of Man* (Chicago: University of Chicago Press, 1948).

10. Richard McKeon, "Imitation and Poetry," in *Thought, Action, and Passion* (Chicago: University of Chicago Press, 1954), p. 175. Includes a useful discussion of the Platonic, Aristotelean, and rhetorical traditions in the Renaissance.

11. See Leon Battista Alberti, *On Painting*, trans. John R. Spencer (New Haven: Yale University Press, 1966). Also, John White, *The Birth and Rebirth of Pictorial Space* (Cambridge: Harvard University Press, 1987), pp. 121, 126. White discusses the invention of "artificial perspective" in the Renaissance and observes the emerging tendency to connect painting with mathematics, science, and theory: "It is in Alberti's *Della Pittura*, which he wrote in 1435, that a theory of perspective first attains formal being outside the individual work of art. Theoretical discussion replaces practical demonstration. The way is open, in art also, for that separation of theory and practice; that particular kind of self-consciousness which, in the wider view, showed itself most significantly in the growing realization of the historical remoteness of antiquity, and which underlies modern scientific achievement." White also notes the effort to elevate painting to the status of the liberal arts. "The innate pictorial qualities of artificial perspective were not the only sources of its popularity and prestige. Already in the *Della Pittura*, it is used as a lever with which to ease the humble craft of painting into the lordly circle of the liberal arts. With this ascent the formerly humble, but now scientific, painter was to move into the sphere of princely patrons and attendant men of letters." The transposition of themes from mathematics (Euclidean geometry) into painting should be

compared with Galileo's use of mathematics to treat the new science of mechanics. Compare also the use of mathematics in the disciplines of design in the twentieth century.

12. Joshua C. Taylor, ed., *Nineteenth Century Theories of Art* (Berkeley: University of California Press, 1987), p. 11.

13. The increasing separation of art academies from the practical arts is well illustrated in the founding of the Royal Academy in London in 1768. Joshua Reynolds epitomizes the extent of the division. "An institution like this has often been recommended upon considerations merely mercantile; but an Academy, founded upon such principles, can never effect even its own narrow purposes. If it has an origin no higher, no taste can ever be formed in manufactures; but if the higher Arts of Design flourish, these inferior ends will be answered of course." Also, "The rank and value of every art is in proportion to the mental labor employed in it, or the mental pleasure produced by it. As this principle is observed or neglected, our profession becomes either a liberal art, or a mechanical trade. In the hands of one man it makes the highest pretensions, as it is addressed to the noblest faculties: in those of another it is reduced to a mere matter of ornament; and the painter has but the humble province of furnishing our apartments with elegance." Sir Joshua Reynolds, *Discourses on Art* (New York: Collier Books, 1966), pp. 19, 55.

14. The central themes of rhetoric provided the ground plan and intellectual disciplines for Francis Bacon's *The Advancement of Learning* and *The New Organon*. The goal was "the invention not of arguments but of arts; not of things in accordance with principles, but of principles themselves; not of probable reasons, but of designations and directions of works," with the effect not of overcoming an opponent in verbal argument, but "to command nature in action." What Bacon called the "operative part of the liberal arts," the mechanical arts and the crafts which have not yet grown into arts properly so called, provided experimental data for the investigation of the principles of nature. Francis Bacon, *The New Organon* (New York: Bobbs-Merrill, 1960), pp. 19, 25. For a discussion of rhetoric in Bacon, see R. S. Crane, "Shifting Definitions and Evaluations of the Humanities from the Renaissance to the Present," in *The Idea of the Humanities and Other Essays Critical and Historical* (Chicago: University of Chicago Press, 1967), 1.64–65. Also, John C. Briggs, *Francis Bacon and the Rhetoric of Nature* (Cambridge: Harvard University Press, 1989). For an important account of changes in the liberal arts from the Renaissance to the twentieth century, see Richard McKeon, "The Transformation of the Liberal Arts in the Renaissance," *Developments in the Early Renaissance*, ed. Bernard S. Levy (Albany: State University of New York Press, 1972), pp. 158–223.

15. For a discussion of the decline of rhetoric as an intellectual art and its rebirth in the twentieth century, see Chaim Perelman, "The New Rhetoric: A Theory of Practical Reasoning," in *The New Rhetoric and the Humanities* (Dordrecht, Holland: D. Reidel, 1979), pp. 1–42.

16. This is illustrated in the development of the engineering profession in the French and British traditions after the Renaissance. The military provided the primary base of employment for engineers in Europe. The *Corps du génie* was created in the French army in 1676. The need for suitable deployment of troops also led to the creation by the French government of the *Corps des ponts et chaussées* in 1716. For a brief but useful discussion of the rise of engineering as a profession after the Renaissance, see Terry S. Reynolds, "The Engineer in Nineteenth-Century America"; and John B. Rae, "Engineers Are People," in *The Engineer in America: A Historical Anthology from Technology and Culture*, ed. Terry S. Reynolds (Chicago: University of Chicago Press, 1991). Also, Bertrand Gille, *Engineers of the Renaissance* (Cambridge: Harvard University Press, 1966). For another useful discussion of the discipline of engineering, see Carl Mitcham, "Engineering as (Productive) Activity: Philosophical Remarks," in *Critical Perspectives on Non-Academic Science and Engineering*, ed. Paul T. Durbin (Bethlehem, PA: Lehigh University Press, 1990).

17. In the twentieth century, the narrow interpretation of the principle of "profit first" in Western culture has been attacked from within and without. Criticisms of "profit first" voiced at the Bauhaus were easily dismissed as socialist ideology, but the movement of "quality first" has gained force in the business community in recent decades, suggesting that profit and quality are not opposites. For an account of the "quality control" movement that explains some of the connections between Western and Asian thinking, see Kaoru Ishikawa, *What Is Total Quality Control: The Japanese Way* (Englewood Cliffs, NJ: Prentice-Hall, 1985), p. 74. Marketing expert Philip Kotler provides a suggestive analysis of the growing perception of the relation between business practices and human character. Philip Kotler, "Humanistic Marketing: Beyond the Marketing Concept," in *Philosophical and Radical Thought in Marketing*, ed. A. Fuat Firat, N. Dholakia, and R. P. Bagozzi (Lexington, MA: D. C. Heath, 1987), pp. 271–88.

18. For a discussion of this revolution and its influence on the emergence of new disciplines of design, see R. Buchanan, "Wicked Problems in Design Thinking." The rise of design in the twentieth century could be regarded as a completion of the Baconian project to command nature in action, after a three-century detour into the theoretic sciences to discover the principles of natural

processes. For a discussion of the relations among art, science, and technology at the beginning of the twentieth century, see John Dewey, "By Nature and by Art."

19. Walter Gropius, "My Conception of the Bauhaus Idea," *Scope of Total Architecture* (New York: Collier Books, 1962), pp. 19–20.

20. For Aristotle, art for art's sake would be unintelligible and dangerous. It would be a vice, representing excessive preoccupation with one or another pleasure without the balance of moral and intellectual virtues found in well-formed character. Art is not an end in itself but serves human beings as a means for supplying what nature provides only by chance. In the variety of its forms, art is directed toward the range of functions which the human being must perform in order to sustain life and further the well-being of the individual and community in a complex environment. There is a sense in which art possesses autonomy and integrity as an expression of the soul of the artist and the object of imitation, but "art for art's sake" is the formula of power without responsibility. It is the basis of sophistry.

21. Criticism of the Bauhaus has become quite fashionable in recent decades. However, the criticism comes from individuals who hold precisely the principles rejected in Bauhaus writings. The most paradoxical criticism comes from idealists: some complain about an overemphasis on art (beauty detached from rational function), while others complain about an overemphasis on the practical arts (to the detriment of the spiritual aspect of fine art). In contrast, materialists criticize the Bauhaus for naively seeking to advance utopian idealism while neglecting scientific "realism" and true functionalism. Finally, individuals who believe that design should be judged by its power to influence social life criticize the Bauhaus for a failure to influence the practices of industry to a sufficient degree. Judged by principles that it did not hold, it hardly comes as a surprise that the Bauhaus fails to measure up to the wishes of its critics. The controversy surrounding the Bauhaus suggests that Gropius and his colleagues did, indeed, seek to establish a different principle for design, resisting the reduction of design to idealism, materialism, or the sophistic power represented by "art for art's sake" and its more dangerous expression, "business for business's sake."

22. Gropius, *Scope of Total Architecture*, p. 20.

23. Walter Gropius, "The Theory and Organization of the Bauhaus," *Bauhaus: 1919–1928*, ed. Herbert Bayer, Walter Gropius, and Ise Gropius (New York: Museum of Modern Art, 1938), p. 29.

24. "An esthetic conception, so to speak, has fatally displaced a creative conception of art. Creative art and history of art should no longer be confused. 'Creating new order' is the artist's task; that of the historian, to rediscover and explain orders in the past. Both are equally indispensible, but they have entirely different aims." Walter Gropius, "Blueprint of an Architect's Education," *Scope of Total Architecture*, pp. 47–48.

25. Dewey recognized the importance of those experiences that are predominantly aesthetic, but he argued that such experiences should not prevent one from recognizing the aesthetic quality of predominantly intellectual or practical experiences. John Dewey, *Art at Experience* (New York: Capricorn, 1958), pp. 38–39, 55, et passim.

26. Christopher Alexander is often regarded as a leader of the "design methods movement" of the 1960s. However, he rejected the idea in 1971, rebuking those who read his important book only for its contribution to methodology. Noting the tendency of readers to miss his central idea, he writes:

> "But I feel it is important to say it also here, to make you alive to it before you read the book, since so many readers have focused on the *method which leads to* the creation of the diagrams, not on the *diagrams themselves*, and have even made a cult of following this method. Indeed, since the book was published, a whole academic field has grown up around the idea of 'design methods'—and I have been hailed as one of the leading exponents of these so-called design methods. I am very sorry that this has happened, and want to state, publicly, that I reject the whole idea of design methods as a subject of study, since I think it is absurd to separate the study of designing from the practice of design. . . . No one will become a better designer by blindly following this method, or indeed by following any method blindly. On the other hand, if you try to understand the idea that you can create abstract patterns by studying the implications of limited systems of forces, and can create new forms by free combinations of these patterns—and realize that this will work if the patterns which you define deal with systems of forces whose internal interaction is very dense, and whose interaction with the other forces in the world is very weak—then, in the process of trying to create such diagrams or patterns for yourself, you will reach the central idea which this book is all about."

Christopher Alexander, *Notes on the Synthesis of Form* (Cambridge, MA: Harvard University Press, 1971). It is the central idea of this book that elevates Alexander's approach from methodology toward a form of architectonic integrative discipline.

27. A frequent observation about the Bauhaus and the New Bauhaus is that their graduates tended to become artists rather than designers and that both institutions found their primary influence in the reform of education for artists rather than in concrete programs for the education of designers. How is one to evaluate this? On the one hand, the observation tends to confirm the suggestion that the Bauhaus discovered an architectonic art of *making* rather than an architectonic art of *design thinking*. On the other hand, is it without ultimate influence on design that the Bauhaus and the New Bauhaus served as institutions of basic research in the arts of making?

28. For a brief discussion of this event, see Alain Findeli, "Design Education and Industry: The Laborious Beginnings of the Institute of Design in Chicago," *Journal of Design History* 4, no. 2 (1991): 97–113.

29. Present and Former Members of the Faculty, *The Idea and Practice of General Education: An Account of the College of the University of Chicago* (Chicago: University of Chicago Press, 1950).

30. Charles W. Morris, Proposed Course Descriptions, 1937, University of Illinois at Chicago, Special Collection. (Typewritten.) See a selection by Charles Morris, "The Contribution of Science to the Designer's Task" from the prospectus of the New Bauhaus. Reprinted in Hans M. Wingler, *The Bauhaus: Weiman Dessau, Berlin, Chicago* (Cambridge, MA: MIT Press, 1969), p. 195. Moholy-Nagy relied on Morris and his colleagues to provide substantive content and connections between design and the arts and sciences, but he did not share the neopositivist philosophy of Morris and Rudolph Carnap. Moholy-Nagy's views were much closer to the pragmatic philosophy of John Dewey. However, Morris, Moholy-Nagy, and Dewey were able to cooperate in supporting the New Bauhaus because of a shared vision of the contribution that broader artistic education could bring to twentieth-century society and culture. See Wingler, *The Bauhaus*, pp. 195–99.

31. L. Moholy-Nagy, *Vision in Motion* (Chicago: Paul Theobald, 1947). Although usually ignored by scholars trained in the remnants of the Renaissance liberal arts of belles lettres and beaux arts, this book is an important contribution to the development of the liberal arts in the twentieth century. Moholy-Nagy remarks that the conventional form of contemporary liberal education has tended to separate words from things, with the result that students are too often trained in verbalisms and lack experience and understanding of the things to which words refer. "'Liberal' education, which is considered a positive step to counteract a one-sided vocationalism, is at present not much different from it. Vocational education provides external skills while liberal education furnishes the skill in verbalization, both usually a mechanical accumulation." Moholy-Nagy, *Vision in Motion*, p. 21.

32. Quoted in Kenneth Frampton, "Apropos Ulm: Curriculum and Critical Theory," *Oppositions*, May 1974: 35.

33. Tomás Maldonado, "Looking Back at Ulm," *Ulm Design: The Morality of Objects*, ed. Herbert Lindinger (Cambridge, MA: MIT Press, 1990), p. 223.

34. Ibid., p. 222.

35. "Our efforts were, as we now know, historically premature. The bits of methodological knowledge that we were trying to absorb were too 'hand-crafted'; and our instrumentation was virtually nonexistent. We did not have what we have today: the personal computer. We also lacked a full understanding of the notion of 'limited rationality,' which Herbert Simon was just beginning to develop. And so we remained prisoners of the theoretical generalities of a form of 'problem solving' that was nothing more than a Cartesian 'discourse upon method.' But in the midst of our limitless faith in method—and we were already dimly aware that it might have a negative aspect in 'methodolatry'—there lay some powerful intuitions that the evolution of information technology, especially since 1963, has to a large extent confirmed." Ibid. Regarding the Bauhaus and science, see Walter Gropius, "Is There a Science of Design," *Scope of Total Architecture*, pp. 30–40.

36. Some of the interests at HfG Ulm appear to have been foreshadowed in the reductive approach of Hannes Meyer, director of the Bauhaus in its final period. "All things on this earth are a product of the formula: (function times economy) . . . building is a biological process. Building is not an aesthetic process . . . architecture which produces effects introduced by the artist has no right to exist. Architecture which 'continues a tradition' is historicist . . . the new house is . . . a product of industry as much as such is the work of specialists: economists, statisticians, hygienicists, climatologists, experts in . . . norms, heating techniques . . . the architect? He was an artist and is becoming a specialist in organization . . . building is only organization." Hannes Meyer, quoted in Frank Whitford, *Bauhaus* (London: Thames and Hudson, 1984), p. 180. Meyer's approach is obviously the antithesis of that taken by Gropius and the other leaders of the Bauhaus, most of whom left before or shortly after Meyer's appointment as director.

37. This appears to come close to a form of the technocracy movement of the 1930s. For a brief discussion of this movement in the context of the history of technology, see Alan I. Marcus and Howard P. Segal, *Technology in America: A Brief History* (New York: Harcourt Brace Jovanovich, 1989), pp. 263–64. This book also provides a useful account of the development of systems thinking in the nineteenth and twentieth centuries.

38. Herbert Simon, *The Sciences of the Artificial* (1969; rpt. Cambridge, MA: MIT Press, 1981), pp. x–xi. Simon studied with philosopher Rudolph Carnap at the University of Chicago. He also taught economics in Chicago in the 1940s to architecture students of a former Bauhäusler, Mies van der Rohe.

39. Simon, *The Sciences of the Artificial*, p. xi.

40. Some of the rhetorical features of Simon's approach are discussed in a critical manner in Carolyn R. Miller, "The Rhetoric of Decision Science, or Herbert A. Simon Says," in *The Rhetorical Turn: Invention and Persuasion in the Conduct of Inquiry*, ed. Herbert W. Simon (Chicago: University of Chicago Press, 1990), pp. 162–84.

41. Traces of Aristotle's four causes are discernable in the four indicia employed by Simon to distinguish the artificial from the natural and set the boundaries for the sciences of the artificial. Simon, *The Sciences of the Artificial*, p. 8.

42. Ibid., p. 159. (Emphasis mine.)

43. John Heskett, *Industrial Design* (New York: Oxford University Press, 1980), p. 7.

44. The ancient precursor of this perspective lies in the philosophy of the Greek sophists, who present an approach to rhetoric that is strikingly different from the Platonic or Aristotelean. In Plato's *Protagoras*, the sophist presents an elegant myth of the origin and distribution of powers among human beings. These powers are held in the form of arts and technologies. Some individuals possess the techniques for creating images and objects for survival and pleasure, while others possess the political art of words, suitable for creating societies and civilization. In a later period, Machiavelli presents a vivid account of the power of princes to design their city-states through words and actions. A contemporary example of this perspective illustrates the turn from words to things: "Engineering schools continued to train generation after generation of possibly the most powerful agents of change that our planet has ever produced." George Bugiarello and Dean B. Doner, eds., *The History and Philosophy of Technology* '(Urbana: University of Illinois Press, 1979), p. vii. The concept of engineering as power echoes the sophistic account of technology by Protagoras.

45. For a useful survey of views on the place of design within corporate structures, see Mark Oakley, ed., *Design Management: A Handbook of Issues and Methods* (Oxford: Basil Blackwell, 1990). For a discussion of design and the design process in the context of corporate operations and values, see John Heskett, "Product Integrity," *Design Processes Newsletter* 4 (1991). For a view of design as power outside the corporate domain, see Victor Papanek, *Design for the Real World: Human Ecology and Social Change* (New York: Pantheon, 1972).

46. Adrian Forty, *Objects of Desire: Design and Society from Wedgwood to IBM* (New York: Pantheon, 1986), p. 6.

47. Ibid.

48. Ibid., p. 9. Forty suggests an affinity between his approach and structuralism, but he notes the mechanical quality that often accompanies structuralist analysis. In personal conversation, he recently acknowledged that his approach perhaps shares more with rhetorical analysis than structuralism.

49. Ibid., p. 241. "It is the entrepreneur not the designer who decides which design most satisfactorily embodies the ideas necessary to the product's success, and which best fits the material conditions of production."

50. Ibid., p. 240. This is an appropriate criticism of Siegfried Giedion, who proposes a dialectical study in anonymous cultural history. "Anonymous history is directly connected with the general, guiding ideas of an epoch. But at the same time it must be traced back to the particulars from which it arises. Anonymous history is many sided, and its different departments flow into one another. Only with difficulty can they be separated. The ideal in anonymous history would be to show simultaneously the various facets as they exist side by side, together with the process of their interpenetration." This is an excellent statement of a dialectician's approach, but from Forty's perspective it fails to capture the give-and-take of individual points of view in social life, constituting a debate that advances competing ideas and myths. Siegfried Giedion, *Mechanization Takes Command: A Contribution to Anonymous History* (1948; rpt. New York: W. W. Norton, 1969), p. 4.

51. Herbert Read's account of the origin and development of ornamentation parallels his account of the origins of design and clearly points toward the materialist perspective. Psychological necessity combines with the technology of construction, complicated by the further factor of utilitarian purpose.

Whatever physiological and psychological necessities may exist for ornament, its actual origin and development can be explained in simple materialist terms. It is true that
for the sake of simplicity we have to neglect certain anomalous types of ornament
belonging to the earliest phase of human civilization—the paleolithic period. To this
period belong a few objects mostly of bone, and for the most part apparently objects of
personal adornment, which bear incised lines, chevrons, and curves, for which no obvious explanation exists. A utilitarian explanation seems out of the question, and the suggestion that they are primitive tallies for counting does not carry much conviction;
some of the forms of decoration are too complicated for such a purpose. Historically,
therefore, one must begin with a psychological explanation. But when we pass to a later
stage in pre-history, to the neolithic age, the evidence is much more plentiful and much
less equivocal. We are able to conclude without any doubt, that whatever the purpose
and appeal of the ornament, its forms arose in, and were determined by, the material
and the process of manufacture. We may still assume a previous psychological necessity; but the fulfillment of this necessity was inevitable. It was inherent in the material or
in the constructive form assumed by the material.

Herbert Read, *Art and Industry: The Principles of Industrial Design* (1934; rpt. London: Faber
and Faber, 1947), pp. 165–67.

52. In this sequence of primary, secondary, and tertiary needs, the latter grow out of the psychological but are sometimes described as spiritual. The materialist account of spiritual needs is
easily recognized. These needs vary greatly from period to period and from place to place among
human societies. They are sometimes manifested as superstitions, sometimes as religions, and
sometimes in the most refined forms of art and poetry. But these needs are fundamentally psychological. On the one hand, they represent the desire to express pure, universal feelings and values that are independent of practical purpose. On the other hand, they represent the desire to
excite unalloyed emotional response within ourselves and within others.

53. The ancient precursors of this perspective were the Epicureans and atomists, who equate
art with pleasure.

54. In the *Principia*, Newton describes the rise of universal mechanics out of practical mechanics. The latter is based on manual arts, the former on mathematics. H. S. Thayer, ed., *Newton's
Philosophy of Nature: Selections from His Writings* (New York: Hafner, 1953), pp. 9–11. Compare this
account with Galileo's account of the rise of mechanics. He describes a visit to the great arsenal of
Venice, where the constant activity of artisans and architects, intent on making weapons of war,
"suggests to the studious mind a large field for investigation, especially that part of the work
which involves mechanics." Galileo Galilei, *Dialogues Concerning Two New Sciences* (New York:
Dover, 1954), p. 1.

55. For an introductory discussion of design as engineering, see M. J. French, *Invention and
Evolution: Design in Nature and Engineering* (Cambridge: Cambridge University Press, 1988). For a
practical discussion of engineering design, see Gorden L. Glegg, *The Selection of Design*
(Cambridge: Cambridge University Press, 1972). Also, Harry Petroski, *To Engineer Is Human: The
Role of Failure in Successful Design* (New York: St. Martin's Press, 1985), and Harry Petroski, *The
Evolution of Useful Things* (New York: Knopf, 1993).

56. Examples include Donald Norman, *The Psychology of Everyday Things* (New York: Basic
Books, 1988); and Edward T. Hall, *The Hidden Dimension* (Garden City, NY: Doubleday, 1969). The
latter is not explicitly about design, but it has influenced design thinking in a variety of ways.

57. The effort to explain art and design by a reductive approach that links art with aesthetics
and psychology is well represented in the twentieth century. It involves themes such as pleasure,
exercise of the senses, recognition of pattern and form, and the "hushed reverberations" of associ-
ated meanings. In addition to Herbert Read, see George Santayana, *The Sense of Beauty: Being the
Outline of Aesthetic Theory* (New York: Dover, 1955); and "The Rationality of Industrial Art," in *The
Life of Reason: Or, The Phases of Human Progress* (New York: Charles Scribner's Sons, 1953); Rudolph
Arnheim, *Art and Visual Perception: A Psychology of the Creative Eye* (Berkeley: University of
California Press, 1974); and E. H. Gombrich, *The Sense of Order: A Study in the Psychology of
Decorative Art* (Ithaca, NY: Cornell University Press, 1979).

58. Read's book was employed, for example, by Alexander Kostellow at Brooklyn's Pratt
Institute and served as a text for students at Chicago's Institute of Design in the early years, during the influence of Moholy-Nagy.

59. Read's philosophic position should be compared with that of David Hume, represented
in works such as "Of the Standard of Taste," "Of Refinement in the Arts," and "Of the Rise and
Progress of the Arts and Sciences," in *Of the Standard of Taste and Other Essays*, ed. John W. Lenz
(New York: Bobbs-Merrill, 1965). While he could never be regarded as a neopositivist, Read's

emphasis on a science of art, which is allied with various natural sciences in solving the problems of industrial production, appears to support the Unity of Science movement, guided by Rudolph Carnap, Charles Morris, and others.

60. See Herbert Read, "A Great Teacher," in *Moholy-Nagy: An Anthology*, ed. Richard Kostelanetz (New York: Praeger, 1970), pp. 203–6. This excellent review of Moholy-Nagy's *Vision in Motion* represents a subtle reinterpretation of Moholy-Nagy's ideas in terms of Read's own philosophy.

61. Read, *Art and Industry*, p. 9.

62. Ibid.

63. Ibid., p. 10.

64. Ibid., p. 51.

65. Ibid., p. 55.

66. For a discussion of aesthetics and ergonomics (sometimes referred to as "human engineering"), see Niels Diffrient, "Design and Technology," in *Design since 1945*, ed. Kathryn B. Hiesinger (Philadelphia: Philadelphia Museum of Art, 1983), pp. 12–16.

67. For a discussion of the two traditions of spirituality in Western culture, see Matthew Arnold, "Culture and Anarchy," in *Poetry and Criticism of Matthew Arnold*, ed. A. Dwight Culler (Boston: Houghton Mifflin, 1961), pp. 407–75. The chapter "Hellenism and Hebraism" is particularly useful in distinguishing the spiritual relation between thinking and doing.

68. George Nelson, "The Design Process," in *Design since 1945*, p. 10.

69. George Nelson, "The Enlargement of Vision," *Problems of Design* (New York: Whitney, 1957), p. 59.

70. The Hellenistic perspective on design, products, and the spiritual life is best represented by Plato in the *Timaeus* and the *Republic* (11.369c ff.). The *Timaeus* is an account of the creation of the world and of all things within the world. The *Republic* is an account of the origin and development of the city, with extensive discussions of the nature of products and the role of products in human life. The Hebraic perspective on design, products, and spirituality is illustrated in an exquisite passage by St. Augustine, *On Christian Doctrine* (New York: Bobbs-Merrill, 1958), pp. 9–10. One of the best examples of the Hebraic tradition in nineteenth- and twentieth-century design is Shaker furniture.

14   *Delivering the Message: Typography and the Materiality of Writing*

JOHN TRIMBUR

In recent years, those of us involved in the study and teaching of writing have been trying to adjust to life after the process movement. To be sure, the slogan "process not product" long ago lost any critical edge it might have possessed in the 1970s, and the once enabling notion that composing is the critical object of inquiry now seems, in Karl Marx's words, a "one-sided" view of the production of writing. One can no longer read, for example, Janet Emig's or Donald Graves's pioneer composing research without reading into it representations of their research subjects as gendered and racialized subjects of class society. And yet, the moment writing theorists are starting to call "post-process" must be seen not just as a repudiation of the process movement but also as an attempt to read into composition precisely the material conditions of the composer and the material pressures and limits of the composing process. As Robert J. Connors once remarked, the reason we feel we're living in a post-process era is that process has been so fully assimilated, so exhaustively read into and written over that we forget about the traces it has left in our theories and practices.

The dominant representations of writing typically offered by the process movement—voice, cognition, conversation—despite the crucial differences among them, all picture writing as an invisible process, an auditory or mental event that takes place at the point of composing, where meanings get made. In my contribution to this volume, I want to reread these dematerialized representations of writing in terms of the materiality of literacy, from the perspective that writing is a visible language produced and circulated in material forms. To put it another way, I want to suggest that the process movement's emphasis on the composer as the maker of meaning (whether that figure entails self-expression, mental activity, or participation in communal discourses) has obscured the composer's work in producing the resources

From *Rhetoric and Composition as Intellectual Work*. Ed. Gary A. Olson. Carbondale: Southern Illinois University Press, 2002. 188–202.

of representation in order to signify at all, to make the special signs we call writing.

THE MATERIALITY OF WRITING

The line of thinking I propose holds that the figure of the composer we inherit from the process movement can still provide a generative topos in writing studies. The task, however, requires a thoroughgoing reconceptualization of the writer at work—one that locates the composer in the labor process, in relation to the available means of production. In certain respects, of course, such a project has already begun. No doubt the leading impetus to materialize literacy comes from the emergence of digital communication. Marshall McLuhan says that we can see human-made environments only once they have changed, and this is very much the case, I think, regarding the current shift from print to digital literacy. These changes in the technology of writing allow us to compare, say, mechanical means of production such as the typewriter or the Linotype machine and hot type of the late nineteenth-century print shop to the cool cybersurface and digital signals of the computer screen and digital signals. As Christina Haas points out, it is no longer quite so easy to treat the technologies of writing as transparent, to efface the material tools and embodied practices involved in the production of writing.

One of the main obstacles to *seeing* the materiality of writing has been the essayist tradition and its notion of a transparent text. (It is no accident that the process movement's favored genre has always been the essay, be it literary, journalistic, or academic.) I argued a few years ago that essayist literacy—from the scientific prose of the Royal Society to the essay of the coffeehouse and salon—emerged in the early modern period as a rhetoric of deproduction: a programmatic effort to reduce the figurative character of writing, minimize the need for interpretation, and thereby make the text more transparent ("Essayist"). What I was not aware of at the time, however, is how essayist literacy's compulsion to eliminate metaphor is linked to Old Testament warnings about graven images and to a Protestant desire to purge writing of all traces of visuality, a desire to replace, as Lester Faigley puts it, the "'mindless' auditory, visual, and olfactory credulity of Catholicism with the power of reason expressed in print" (174–75).

In Faigley's view, the notion of transparent text results from a great Alphabetic Literacy Narrative that runs through the work of Harold Innis, Jack Goody, Eric Havelock, and Walter Ong. This grand narrative identifies "'true' literacy" with the "abstract representation of sounds—a presupposition that subordinates syllabic and logographic writing systems and banishes pictographs and images to the status of illiteracy" (174). As the graphic design theorists J. Abbott Miller and Ellen Lupton say, "Westerners revere the alphabet as the most rational and transparent of all writing systems, the clearest of vessels for containing the words of speech" (21). By this account of literacy, the suppression of visuality in the alphabet's abstract coding system provides the groundwork for normative representations of both cultural and individual development as matters of overcoming a dependence on the visual that is taken to be immature, ephemeral, and manipulative. Accordingly, it should be no surprise that David Olson would want to make the essay into the culmination of alphabetic literacy precisely because it appears to transcend the visuality of writing by organizing the speech-sound abstractions of the alphabet into highly integrated grammatical and logical structures, forming self-sufficient, autonomous texts capable of speaking for themselves. The texts of essayist literacy, by Olson's account, appear to transmit meanings transparently, without reference to their mode and medium of production.

The fatal weakness of the Alphabetic Literacy Narrative and its commitment to textual transparency, however, is its scopophobia and how its fear of the visual causes it to align writing with speech. In this sense, the irony of the grand narrative is that it suppresses the full upshot of its own discovery — namely, that writing amounts to be less a recording of speech than a visual coding system that communicates by employing a range of nonphonetic elements such as spacing, punctuation, frames, and borders, not to mention the eccentricities in codes, such as in written English where different words can have the same sound (its/it's, meet/meat) and silent letters seem to defy phonetic strategies of pronunciation (might, paradigm). Haunted by suspicions of the visual (and hence of the visibility of writing), at just the moment when it elevates alphabetic literacy to a preeminent position in Western cultural history, the Alphabetic Literacy Narrative comes unglued, reminded by the very visuality of the alphabet, as Miller and Lupton say, that writing can only be a "faulty reflection of speech, an artificial by-product of the otherwise natural workings of the mind" (24).

Now, you don't have to be much of a Derridean (I'm certainly not) to recognize a metaphysics of presence at work in such disappointment with writing, the overwhelming sense that what promised to be the vehicle for rational discourse is, in the end, a treacherous medium that continually betrays its own ostensible transparency by thickening into metaphor and material form. My view, perhaps uncharacteristically, is to follow Derrida out of the morass created by the Alphabetic Literacy Narrative and to picture writing not as a derivative of speech at all but instead as a typographical and rhetorical system of sign making. After all, as the turn-of-the-century Austrian architect and graphic designer Adolf Loos put it so concisely, "One cannot *speak* a capital letter" (qtd. in Helfand 50).

For post-process theorizing to rematerialize writing, we need to recast the figure of the composer and its essayist legacy — to see writers not just as makers of meaning but as makers of the means of producing meaning out of the available resources of representation. To understand more fully the work of the composer in the labor process of writing, we must see, as Gunther Kress has argued, that individuals do not simply *acquire* literacy but actually *build* for themselves the tools to produce writing. As Kress shows in *Before Writing*, the multimodal activity of young children working with images, shapes, letterforms, the directionality of writing, the page, and an emergent understanding of genre amounts to an active incorporation of sign-making tools into their practices of signification. By the same token, instead of thinking of writers as "users" who confront computers as machines that they must learn to operate in order to write, we might think in terms of how individuals, through the labor process of writing, appropriate the means of digital literacy, in highly variable ways, into their own repertoire of sign-making tools. In either case, by locating the composer in a labor process that includes assembling the means of making meaning, we can begin to see, as Kress suggests, how writing transforms the signifying resources at hand by consuming them in the act of production and, in turn, how the material practice of writing transforms the composer's subjectivity and the world in which newly made signs appear.

TYPOGRAPHY AND WRITING STUDIES

The line of thinking I want to advance starts with the recognition that the major images of writing from the process era (voice, cognition, conversation) neglect the materiality and visuality of writing. The next step is to devise a more adequate account. My claim is that studying and teaching typography as the culturally salient means of producing writing can help locate composers in the labor process and thereby contribute to the larger post-process work of rematerializing literacy. Typography, of course, has been a longtime topic in the writing curriculum. The problem is that, by and large, typography has been ghettoized in technical communication, where many compositionists think of it as a vocational skill. The concerns of typography — such as document design, page layout, fonts, infographics, and reading paths — are associated with at best commercial art and career training and at worst complicity with corporate culture. To put it bluntly, typography, for all practical purposes, has been assigned in the writing curriculum to the marketplace, at a far remove from the belletristic, critical, and academic work of the essay so cherished by the process movement.

There are good reasons to reconsider this marginalization and to bring typography into the mainstream of writing studies. For one thing, typography — quite literally "writing with type" — can help rematerialize literacy by calling attention to the visual design of writing, be it handwritten, print, or electronic. Typography enables us to *see* writing in material terms as letterforms, printed pages, posters, computer screens. It helps to name the available tools of representation that composers draw on to make their own means of production. For another, typography links writing to delivery — the fifth canon of rhetoric. Like typography, delivery has been neglected by the process movement, isolated from invention, arrangement, style, and memory, and, when mentioned at all, reduced to such afterthoughts as neat handwriting and manuscript preparation. From a typographical perspective, however, the visual design of writing figures prominently as the material form in which the message is delivered. That is, typography offers a way to think of writing not just in terms of the moment of composing but also in terms of its circulation, as messages take on cultural value and worldly force, moving through the Marxian dialectic of production, distribution, exchange, and consumption.[1] From the mass circulation of periodicals to the way junior high school girls write and fold the notes they pass in class (see Finders), the visual design of writing enters consequentially into the activity of composition.

Modern typography is associated with the rise of mass communication, consumer culture, and the society of the spectacle, with roots in both the popular culture of the metropolis and the agitations of the high modernist vanguard in art and politics. Typographical theory and practice developed largely within graphic design movements, from the art nouveau lithographs of Toulouse-Lautrec and Jules Cheret, William Morris, and the Viennese Secession at the turn of the previous century to the avant-garde of Futurism, Dada, and Soviet Constructivism, Jan Tschichold "new typography," Bauhaus, and the federal WPA posters of the 1920s and 1930s to the postwar ascendancy of Swiss Modern and its current postmodern challengers. Though now collected and displayed in art museums (see Friedman; Rothschild, Lupton, and Goldstein; and Lupton for catalogues of major exhibits), typographical work has typically occurred outside the art world, in the realm of commerce and politics—or, in some instances, such as with Futurism and Dada, as an anti-art.

Only recently has there been an organized academic investigation of graphic design theory and history. During the 1980s, the professional journals *Print* and *AIGA Journal of Graphic Design* started to feature historical and critical articles. *Visible Language*, founded in 1967 as the quarterly *Journal of Typographical Research*, and journals started in the 1980s such as *Design Issues* and *Journal of Design History* have worked to make typography and graphic design, along with other types of design, into respectable objects of scholarly inquiry. Victor Margolin gives a sense of design history from 1977 to 1987 in an important review essay ("A Decade"). Two textbooks, Philip Meggs's *A History of Graphic Design* and Richard Hollis's *Graphic Design: A Concise History*, and Robin Kinross's *Modern Typography: An Essay in Critical History*, give overviews of graphic design movements and theories, and the three volumes of *Looking Closer* (edited by Michael Bierut et al.) collect both contemporary critical perspectives in the first two volumes and classic statements in the third. Book-length studies, such as Victor Margolin's *The Struggle for Utopia* (a study of the Soviet constructivists El Lissitzky and Alexander Rodchenko, as well as the associated figure Laslo Moholy-Nagi) and Johanna Drucker's *The Visible Word: Experimental Typography and Modern Art, 1909-1923*, have started to appear, providing both critical accounts and an alternative to the expensive, coffee-table productions that contain extensive illustrations but little analysis—publications that have tended to dominate publishing on typography and graphic design.

I offer this quick bibliographical tour as an outsider to the field of graphic design and with considerable misgivings. What I hope to suggest is the intellectual ferment that is currently taking place around what we might call in its most general sense "design studies." There are two points to be made. The first is that graphic designers and typographers have started to interrogate design theory and history in ways that are potentially of great interest to those of us who work in writing. I will look at a few of the specific questions they raise in the final section of this chapter. The second point is more general, for it has to do with the relevance of the very notion of "design" to writing theorists.[2] Design studies and design history are relatively new interdisciplinary fields that take not only typography and graphic design as their objects of inquiry but more broadly "the conception and planning of all the products made by human beings" (Buchanan and Margolin x). In other words, "design" has to do with the work of architects, urban planners, engineers, computer scientists, psychologists, sociologists, anthropologists, marketing and manufacturing experts, as well as industrial and graphic designers and communication specialists (see, for example, Buchanan and Margolin; and Margolin, *Design*). The various efforts to identify a discipline of design that can organize such a range of activities into intelligible patterns go far beyond the scope of this paper. For our purposes, what is worth noting is the persistent quest in modern design theory for "the essential unity of all forms of making in the circumstances of a new cultural environment strongly influenced by engineering, technology, and commerce" (Buchanan 36).

Importantly this search for what Richard Buchanan calls a "new architechtonic art of design" emerges in the modern era not so much out of the profit motive of the market as from a utopian vision of the designer's relationship to mass production, on the one hand, and to the fine arts, on the other. As Walter Gropius says of the Bauhaus:

> Our guiding principle was that design is neither an intellectual nor a material affair, but simply an integral part of the stuff of life, necessary for everyone in a civilized society. Our ambition was to arouse the creative artist from his other-worldliness and to reintegrate him into the workaday world of realities and, at the same time, to broaden and humanize the rigid, almost exclusively material mind of the businessman. Our conception of the basic unity of all design in relation to life was in diametric opposition to that of "art for art's sake" and the much more dangerous philosophy it sprang from, business as an end in itself. (20)

Gropius's desire to "humanize" the business classes may sound naïve, particularly after so much of modernist design has been assimilated by advertising, mass media, the "corporate identity" programs of the postwar period, and the current "branding" campaigns of global capital. Nonetheless, like the aspirations of Morris, Lissitzky, and others to design for social ends, the Bauhaus's utopian goal of dismantling the boundaries between fine and applied art and of designing for social usefulness and the enrichment of everyday life still retains its critical edge.[3]

The desire to design for life has particular relevance to the study and teaching of writing. Not only does it emphasize the rhetoricity of design as deliberation and argument about the possible worlds we might construct, it also calls attention to genres of writing that have traditionally fallen outside the mainstream of writing instruction. As Walter Benjamin says:

> Significant literary work can only come into being in a strict alternation between action and writing; it must nurture the inconspicuous forms

> that better fit its influence in active communities than does the preten-
> tious, universal gesture of the book—in leaflets, brochures, articles, and
> posters. Only this prompt language shows itself actively equal to the
> moment. (qtd. in Kinross xv)

If we substitute here the "universal gesture" of *the essay* for that of *the book*, we can read Benjamin's remarks as a pertinent critique of contemporary writing instruction (and the residual hold of its essayist legacy). Benjamin's notion of "prompt language" amounts to the design of messages for mass circulation, timely responses to the twists and turns of class struggle "actively equal to the moment." Long considered ephemeral and beneath notice by writing teach-ers, Benjamin's "inconspicuous forms" break with the "universal gesture" of the essay to deliver messages in the history of the contemporary. And in this light, typography and the visual design of writing can no longer be margin-alized in the writing curriculum as afterthoughts or preprofessional training; they appear instead as essential elements in an emergent civic rhetoric. If any-thing, the call to write for the social good found in public and community service writing can help to materialize Benjamin's figure of the author-as-producer as a post-process representation to replace the process movement's composer as the essayist maker of meaning.

TYPOGRAPHY IN THEORY AND PRACTICE

Three issues in typographical theory and practice seem to me to be of partic-ular interest to writing studies: the narrativity of letterforms, the page as a unit of discourse, and the division of labor that produces written text. The comments that follow are meant to be suggestive rather than programmatic, to indicate some of the paths typography opens to further investigation in our own intellectual work.

THE NARRATIVITY OF LETTERFORMS

The history of letterforms is a complex one involving changing philosophies, technologies, and social uses of writing. In Gutenburg's fifteenth-century print shop, handmade letterforms imitated the calligraphy of the older scrib-al tradition. During the Renaissance, humanist designers departed from the naturalistic pen strokes of handwriting to fix the ideal proportions of the alphabet by using the tools of geometry; and in 1693, Louis XIV commis-sioned a study of the Roman alphabet that imposed a rational grid on letter-forms, resulting in the *romain du roi* that was meant to embody the authority of scientific method and bureaucratic power. Hopes for such an absolutist, idealized system of letterforms, however, disappeared within a century. According to Lupton and Miller, the Enlightenment typographers Giambattista Bodoni and Françoise Ambroise Didot broke the "ancestral bond between contemporary typefaces and a divine classical past" by reducing the alphabet to "a system of oppositions—thick and thin, vertical and horizontal, serif and stem," in effect paving the way to an understanding of letterforms "as a set of elements open to infinite manipulation" (55). From the nineteenth-century proliferation of display type to modernist experimentalism and now the vast repertoire of computer fonts (including inexact and degraded forms and bi-fontal crossbreedings), the alphabet has changed, as Miller and Lupton point out, from a "pedigreed line of fixed, self-contained symbols" to a "flexible system of difference." The emphasis in typography has shifted "from the individual letter to the overall series of characters," exchanging the "fixed identity of the letter for the relational system of the font" (23).

What this shift enables us to see is the figurative, narrative character of letterforms. We might read, for example, Josef Alber's 1925 stencil typeface, Herbert Bayer's 1925 "universal," and Tschichold's "new typography" not simply as failed modernist master codes to produce a rational font out of standardized, interchangeable parts but also as expressions of technological and humanistic optimism about to be shattered by the atavistic nationalism of black letter type under Hitler's Third Reich. By the same token, we can find the story in the use of vernacular forms by current typographical designers such as Jeffrey Keedy, whose 1990 Manuscript "combines an anti-heroic amalgam of Modernist geometry and grade-school penmanship" to recall the "naïve yet normative scenario of learning to write" — an exercise that results "not only from external technologies but from the disciplinary socialization of the individual" (Lupton and Miller 24).[4] And finally, to bring things closer to home, we can read the manuscript conventions of the student essay as the story of the transparent text, where the neatness and clarity of standardized type on the printed page seek to efface the visuality of writing and bring the teacher-reader in direct and unmediated touch with the student's mind.

The Page as a Unit of Discourse

The standard units of discourse in writing instruction are the word, sentence, paragraph, and essay; and there is a sad — though now largely repudiated — history of arranging them as a developmental sequence. In the essayist tradition, the page itself is of little account, for as readers we are supposedly not looking at the visual design of writing but following the writer's thoughts. Typography, on the other hand, calls attention to how the look of the page communicates meaning by treating text as a visual element that can be combined with images and other nonverbal forms to produce a unit of discourse. Early printed books, for example, often sought to emulate the multimodal capacities of illuminated manuscripts by using borders, rules, columns, marginalia, textual inserts, and woodblock illustrations to design the page. Typography in the modern period has, in many respects, been eager to recover the visuality of the page from the monotony of standardized letterforms and dense monochromatic blocks of text by incorporating onto the printed page the available means of visual communication, from the engravings in such nineteenth-century periodicals as *Frank Leslie's*

Illustrated Newspaper and *Harpers Weekly* to the mid-twentieth-century photo essays in *Life* and the computer infographics of *USA Today*. In addition, poets such as Stephane Mallarme, Guillaume Apollinaire, and Filippo Marinetti sought to free the word and the poetic line from the conventional horizontal and vertical structures of the printed page by mixing size, weight, and style of type and pasting letters and words in visual patterns to create nonlinear compositions. More recently, Dan Friedman's now famous design exercise, drawing on the mundane text of a weather report, raised questions about the emphasis on clarity, orderliness, and simplicity in the modernist use of the grid, rules, and information bands as the basis of page design to explore how "legibility (a quality of efficient, clear, and simple reading) is often in conflict with readability (a quality which promotes interest, pleasure, and challenge in reading)" ("Introductory" 139). And, with the advent of computers, designers such as Rudy VanderLans at *Emigre* magazine, April Greiman, and Katherine McCoy at Cranbrook Academy of Art have made use of the new digital technologies to give the page a formerly unimagined depth, layering and overlapping images and text in deep perspective in ways that confound the traditional opposition between seeing and reading and that call on reader/viewers to participate in making sense of the page.

The complicated relationship between reading and seeing text and image raises interesting questions for writing studies about how we might think about the page as a unit of discourse—about how, say, the juxtaposition of articles, photographs, and advertisements on a newspaper or magazine page creates larger messages than any single item can convey (see Kress, "Text," for an analysis of how the articles on a single newspaper page articulate complex and contradictory representations of poverty); about how "hyperactive" pages encourage browsing rather than reading (see Giovannini's warnings about the "capitulation of text to layout" [204]); and about how individuals find their own reading paths to negotiate the page. Finally, we might ask what is at stake in writing instruction by the common practice of taking articles and essays off the printed page on which they appear (along with other articles, images, and advertising) and reproducing them in handouts or anthologies.

Division of Labor

Typography was traditionally a craft, an artisan's labor that belongs to the print shop. In the early modern period, printing was often thought of as "black magic," and its secrets were guarded by guilds of craftsmen who passed their hermetic arts from master to apprentice. As printing spread, however, "a new occupational culture associated with the printing trades" began to appear, in which the print shop provided "a new setting for intellectual activity," and the master printer became a "hybrid figure"—by turns entrepreneur, lexicographer, editor, cultural impresario, sponsor of scientific research, and political activist—who "presided over the rise of a lay intelligentsia" (Eisenstein 24, 25). If printers like Benjamin Franklin played a central role in the scientific and democratic revolutions of the modern era, in the twentieth century, typography settled into the division of labor under corporate capital, becoming a career path for graphic artists in design studios, publishing, the media, advertising, and academia—another profession with its associations and publications.

I recount this brief historical overview to sketch a typical (if oversimplified) pattern of specialization in professional life and to suggest ways in which such specialization is now under pressure. With the rise of desktop publishing, the division of labor is beginning to flatten, and the distinctions between author, designer, and printer are starting to collapse. For example, the design, composition, production, and distribution of a memo or report may well be the continuous activity in virtual space of a single figure at a connected computer terminal. In the contemporary workplace, this is what new-age management gurus call "multitasking," where digital literacy overcomes the divisions of labor in the era of mechanical reproduction, eliminating secretarial pools and mimeograph machines and transforming managers into information designers.

But the pressure on specialization can do more than serve the ends of corporate restructuring. Benjamin's essay "The Author as Producer" anticipates the progressive possibilities inherent in a collapsing division of labor:

> What we require of the photographer is the ability to give his picture the caption that wrenches it from modish commerce and gives it revolutionary useful value. But we shall make this demand most emphatically when we—the writers—take up photography. Here, too, therefore, technical progress is for the author as producer of the foundation of political progress. (230)

Writing in 1934, Benjamin must have had in mind the work of revolutionary artists such as John Heartfield, whose photomontages used the airbrush, captions, and cut-and-paste techniques to turn the apparent transparency of the photograph into revolutionary messages ("prompt language") in the struggle against fascism (see Pachnicke and Honnef). At the same time, Benjamin raises questions for us today about how, with the rise of digital typography and online communication, we might imagine new possibilities for designers and authors to become producers, to take over the available tools of representation in order to transform the distribution and use of messages. Given the recent eruption of interest in visual culture within composition, Benjamin offers a way to think about how the study and teaching of writing might take up the visual (and the visibility of writing) as more than just new texts and topics for theorists and students to write about in interpretive and critical essays—though I certainly endorse the value of such work.[5] What remains to be seen, in theory and practice, is how typography—the productive art of writing with type—can be "actively equal to the moment."

NOTES

1. For an extended argument on the importance of circulation to the study and teaching of writing, see Trimbur, "Composition."

2. The notion of "design" is already seeping into writing studies, as a possible replacement for "composing." See Kaufer and Butler; Petraglia; and Cope and Kalantzis. The view of "design" in this essay is aligned in important respects with the latter volume, but I think, at this point, it is important to keep the idea of "design" an open one—to see where it might lead us.

3. In this regard, see the three *Looking Closer* volumes (Bierut et al.) for the ongoing discussion of the social responsibilities of graphic designers. Also see Daniel Friedman, *Radical*, for an heroic attempt to join design and everyday life (as well as negotiate the demands of modernism and postmodernism on the contemporary designer), and *Adbusters* magazine and Web site <www.adbusters.org>.

4. In this narrative vein, typographer Jonathan Barnbrook has designed a Nixon typeface "to tell lies" and Prozac to "simplify meanings."

5. *Reading Images: The Grammar of Visual Design* (Kress and van Leeuwen) provides, in my view, the preeminently useful social semiotic analysis of the "look of the page," but I can't resist pointing out the irony that it "explains" visual structures in terms of Hallydean linguistic ones.

WORKS CITED

Benjamin, Walter. "The Author as Producer." 1934. *Reflections: Essays, Aphorism, Autobiographical Writings.* Ed. Peter Demetz. New York: Schocken, 1978. 220–38.

Bierut, Michael, William Drenttel, Steven Heller, and D. K. Holland, eds. *Looking Closer: Critical Writings on Graphic Design.* Vols. 1–2. New York: Allworth, 1994, 1997.

Bierut, Michael, Jessica Helfand, Steven Heller, and Rich Poynor, eds. *Looking Closer: Classic Writings on Graphic Design.* Vol. 3. New York: Allworth, 1999.

Buchanan, Richard. "Rhetoric, Humanism, and Design." *Discovering Design: Explorations in Design Studies.* Ed. Richard Buchanan and Victor Margolin. Chicago: U of Chicago P, 1995. 23–66.

Buchanan, Richard, and Victor Margolin. Introduction. *Discovering Design: Explorations in Design Studies.* Ed. Richard Buchanan and Victor Margolin. Chicago: U of Chicago P, 1995. ix–xxvi.

Cope, Bill, and Mary Kalantzis, eds. *Multiliteracies: Literacy Learning and the Design of Social Futures.* London: Routledge, 2000.

Drucker, Johanna. *The Visible Word: Experimental Typography and Modern Art, 1909–1923.* Chicago: U of Chicago P, 1994.

Eisenstein, Elizabeth. "On the Printing Press as an Agent of Change." *Literacy, Language, and Learning: The Nature and Consequences of Reading and Writing.* Ed. David R. Olson, Nancy Torrance, and Angela Hildyard. Cambridge: Cambridge UP, 1985. 19–33.

Faigley, Lester. "Material Literacy and Visual Design." *Rhetorical Bodies.* Ed. Jack Selzer and Sharon Crowley. Madison: U of Wisconsin P, 1999. 171–201.

Finders, Margaret. *Just Girls: Hidden Literacies and Life in Junior High.* New York: Teachers College P, 1997.

Friedman, Daniel. "Introductory Education in Typography." *Visible Language* 7.2 (1973): 129–44.

———. *Radical Modernism.* New Haven: Yale UP, 1997.

Friedman, Mildred, ed. *Graphic Design in America: A Visual Language History.* Minneapolis: Walker Art Center, 1989.

Giovannini, Joseph. "A Zero Degree of Graphics." *Graphic Design in America: A Visual Language History.* Ed. Mildred Friedman. Minneapolis: Walker Art Center, 1989. 200–13.

Goody, Jack, and Ian P. Watt. "The Consequences of Literacy." *Comparative Studies in Society and History* 5 (1963): 304–45.

Gropius, Walter. "My Conception of the Bauhaus Idea." *Scope of Total Architecture.* Ed. Walter Gropius. New York: Colliers, 1962. 6–19.

Haas, Christina. *Writing Technology: Studies on the Materiality of Literacy.* Mahwah, NJ: Erlbaum, 1996.

Havelock, Eric. *The Literate Revolution in Greece and Its Cultural Consequences.* Princeton: Princeton UP, 1982.

Helfand, Jessica. "Electronic Typography: The New Visual Language." Bierut et al., vol. 2, 49–51.

Hollis, Richard. *Graphic Design: A Concise History.* London: Thames and Hudson, 1994.

Innis, Harold A. *The Bias of Communication.* Toronto: U of Toronto P, 1951.

Kaufer, David S., and Brian S. Butler. *Rhetoric and the Arts of Design.* Mahwah, NJ: Erlbaum, 1996.

Kinross, Robin. Introduction. *The New Typography: A Handbook for Modern Designers*. Jan Tschichold. Trans. Ruari McLean. Berkeley: U of California P, 1998. xv–xliv.

———. *Modern Typography: An Essay in Critical History*. London: Hyphen, 1992.

Kress, Gunther R. *Before Writing: Rethinking the Paths to Literacy*. London: Routledge, 1997.

———. "Text and Grammar as Explanation." *Text, Discourse, and Context: Representations of Poverty in Britain*. Ed. Ulrike H. Meinhof and Kay Richardson. London: Longman, 1994. 24–46.

Kress, Gunther R., and Theo van Leeuwen. *Reading Images: The Grammar of Visual Design*. New York: Routledge, 1996.

Lupton, Ellen. *Mixing Messages: Graphic Design in Contemporary Culture*. New York: Princeton Architectural P, 1996.

Lupton, Ellen, and J. Abbott Miller. "Laws of the Letter." *Design Writing Research: Writing on Graphic Design*. Ed. Ellen Lupton and J. Abbott Miller. London: Phaidon, 1996. 53–61.

Margolin, Victor. "A Decade of Design History in the United States, 1977–88." *Journal of Design History* 1.1 (1988): 51–72.

———, ed. *Design Discourse: History, Theory, Criticism*. Chicago: U of Chicago P, 1989.

———. *The Struggle for Utopia: Rodchenko, Lissitzky, Moholy-Nagy, 1917–1946*. Chicago: U of Chicago P, 1997.

Meggs, Philip B. *A History of Graphic Design*. 3rd ed. New York: Wiley, 1998.

Miller, J. Abbott, and Ellen Lupton. "A Natural History of Typography." Bierut et al., vol. 1, 19–25.

Olson, David R, "From Utterance to Text: The Bias of Language in Speaking and Writing." *Harvard Educational Review* 47 (1977): 257–81.

Ong, Walter J. *Orality and Literacy: The Technologizing of the Word*. New York: Methuen, 1982.

Pachnicke, Peter, and Klaus Honnef, eds. *John Heartfield*. New York: Abrams, 1992.

Petraglia, Joseph. *Reality by Design: The Rhetoric and Technology of Authenticity*. Mahwah, NJ: Erlbaum, 1998.

Rothschild, Deborah, Ellen Lupton, and Darra Goldstein. *Graphic Design in the Mechanical Age: Selections from the Merrill C. Berman Collection*. New Haven: Yale UP, 1998.

Trimbur, John. "Composition and the Circulation of Writing." *College Composition and Communication*" 52 (2000): 188–219.

———. "Essayist Literacy and the Rhetoric of Deproduction." *Rhetoric Review* 9 (1990): 72–86.

15   *The Rules of Typography According to ~~Crackpots~~ Experts*

JEFFERY KEEDY

The first thing one learns about typography and type design is that there are many rules and maxims. The second is that these rules are made to be broken. And the third is that "breaking the rules" has always been just another one of the rules. Although rules are meant to be broken, scrupulously followed, misunderstood, reassessed, retrofitted, and subverted, the best rule of thumb is that rules should never be ignored. The typefaces discussed in this article are recent examples of rule-breaking/making in progress. I have taken some old rules to task and added some new ones of my own that I hope will be considered critically.

> Imagine that you have before you a flagon of wine. You may choose your own favorite vintage for this imaginary demonstration, so that it be a deep shimmering crimson in colour. You have two goblets before you. One is of solid gold, wrought in the most exquisite patterns. The other is of crystal-clear glass, thin as a bubble, and as transparent. Pour and drink; and according to your choice of goblet, I shall know whether or not you are a connoisseur of wine. For if you have no feelings about wine one way or the other, you will want the sensation of drinking the stuff out of a vessel that may have cost thousands of pounds; but if you are a member of that vanishing tribe, the amateurs of fine vintages, you will choose the crystal, because everything about it is calculated to reveal rather than to hide the beautiful thing which it was meant to contain. . . . Now the man who first chose glass instead of clay or metal to hold his wine was a "modernist" in the sense in which I am going to use the term. That is, the first thing he asked of this particular object was not "How should it look?" but "What must it do?" and to that extent all good typography is modernist.

> Beatrice Warde, from an address to the British Typographers' Guild at the St. Bride Institute, London, 1932. Published in *Monotype Recorder*, Vol. 44, No. 1 (Autumn 1970).

From *Looking Closer 2: Critical Writings on Graphic Design*. Ed. Michael Bierut, William Drentell, Steven Heller, and D. K. Holland. New York: Allworth Press, 1997. 49–52. Originally published in *Eye* No. 11, November 1993.

Beatrice Warde's address is favored by members of a vanishing tribe—typography connoisseurs who "reveal" beautiful things to the rest of us (modernists). Such connoisseurs are opposed to typographic sensationalists who have no feelings about the material they contain with their extravagance (postmodernist hacks). In short, the typographers with "taste" must rise above the crass fashion-mongers of the day. Connoisseurship will always have its place in a capitalist, class-conscious society and there is nothing like modernism for the creation of high and low consumer markets. The modernist typophile-connoisseur should rejoice in the typefaces shown here because they reaffirm his or her status as being above fleeting concerns. After all, if there was no innovation to evolve through refinement to tradition, then where would the connoisseur be?

Beatrice Warde did not imagine her crystal goblet would contain Pepsi-Cola, but some vessel has to do it. Of course, she was talking in terms of ideals, but what is the ideal typeface to say: "Uh-Huh, Uh-Huh, You got the right one baby"? There is no reason why all typefaces should be designed to last forever, and in any case, how would we know if they did?

The art of lettering has all but disappeared today, surviving at best through sign painters and logotype specialists. Lettering is being incorporated into type design and the distinction between the two is no longer clear. Today, special or custom letterforms designed in earlier times by a letterer are developed into whole typefaces. Calligraphy will also be added to the mix as more calligraphic tools are incorporated into type-design software. Marshall McLuhan said that all new technologies incorporate the previous ones, and this certainly seems to be the case with type. The technological integration of calligraphy, lettering, and type has expanded the conceptual and aesthetic possibilities of letterforms.

The rigid categories applied to type design in the past do not make much sense in the digital era. Previous distinctions such as serif and sans serif are challenged by the new "semi serif" and "pseudo serif." The designation of type as text or display is also too simplistic. Whereas type used to exist only in books (text faces) or occasionally on a building or sign (display), today's typographer is most frequently working with in-between amounts of type—more than a word or two but much less than one hundred pages. The categories of text and display should not be taken too literally in a multimedia and interactive environment where type is also read on television, computers, clothing, even tattoos.

> Good taste and perfect typography are suprapersonal. Today, good taste is often erroneously rejected as old-fashioned because the ordinary man, seeking approval of his so-called personality, prefers to follow the dictates of his own peculiar style rather than submit to any objective criterion of taste.
>
> Jan Tschichold, 1948, published in *Ausgewählte Aufsatze über Fragen der Gestalt des Buches und der Typographie* (1975).

"Criteria of taste" are anything but objective. Theories of typography are mostly a matter of proclaiming one's own "tastes" as universal truths. The typographic tradition is one of constant change due to technological, functional, and cultural advancement (I use the word "advancement" as I am unfashionably optimistic about the future).

In typographic circles it is common to refer to traditional values as though they were permanently fixed and definitely not open to interpretation. This is the source of the misguided fear of new developments in type design. The fear is that new technology, with its democratization of design, is the beginning of the end of traditional typographic standards. In fact, just the opposite is true, for though typographic standards are being challenged by more designers and applications than ever before, this challenge can only reaffirm what works and modify what is outdated.

The desktop computer and related software have empowered designers and nonspecialists to design and use their own typefaces. And with more type designers and consumers, there will obviously be more amateurish and ill-conceived letterforms. But there will also be an abundance of new ideas that will add to the richness of the tradition. Too much has been made of the proliferation of "bad" typefaces, as if a few poorly drawn letterforms could bring Western civilization to its knees. Major creative breakthroughs often come from outside a discipline, because the "experts" all approach the discipline with a similar obedient point of view. The most important contribution of computer technology, like the printing press before it, lies in its democratization of information. This is why the digital era will be the most innovative in the history of type design.

The more uninteresting the letter, the more useful it is to the typographer.

Piet Zwart, *A History of Lettering, Creative Experiment and Letter Identity* (1986).

Back in Piet Zwart's day most typographers relied on "fancy type" to be expressive. I don't think Zwart was *against* expression in type design as much as he was *for* expression (an architectonic one) in composition. Zwart's statement epitomizes the typographic fundamentalists' credo. The irony is that the essentially radical and liberal manifestos of the early modernists are with us today as fundamentally conservative dogma.

I suspect that what is most appealing about this rhetoric is the way the typographer's ego supersedes that of the type designer. By using uninteresting "neutral" typefaces (created by anonymous or dead designers), typographers are assured that they alone will be credited for their creations. I have often heard designers say they would never use so-and-so's typefaces because that would make their work look like so-and-so's, though they are apparently unafraid of looking like Eric Gill or Giambattista Bodoni. Wolfgang Weingart told me after a lecture at CalArts in which he included my typeface Keedy Sans as an example of "what we do not do at Basel" that he likes the typeface, but believes it should be used only by me. Missing from this statement is an explanation of how Weingart can use a typeface such as Akzidenz Grotesk so innovatively and expertly.

New typefaces designed by living designers should not be perceived as incompatible with the typographer's ego. Rudy VanderLans's use of Keedy Sans for *Emigre* and B.W. Honeycutt's use of Hard Times and Skelter in *Details* magazine are better treatments of my typefaces than I could conceive. Much of the pleasure in designing a typeface is seeing what people do with it. If you are lucky, the uses of your typeface will transcend your expectations; if you are not so fortunate, your type will sink into oblivion. Typefaces have a life of their own and only time will determine their fate.

> In the new computer age, the proliferation of typefaces and type manipulations represents a new level of visual pollution threatening our culture. Out of thousands of typefaces, all we need are a few basic ones, and trash the rest.
>
> > Massimo Vignelli, from a poster announcing the exhibition "The Masters Series: Massimo Vignelli," (February/March 1991).

In an age of hundreds of television channels, thousands of magazines, books, and newspapers, and inconceivable amounts of information via telecommunications, could just a few basic typefaces keep the information net moving? Given the value placed on expressing one's individual point of view, there would have to be only a handful of people on the planet for this to work.

Everything should be permitted, as long as context is rigorously and critically scrutinized. Diversity and excellence are not mutually exclusive; if everything is allowed it does not necessarily follow that everything is of equal value. Variety is much more than just the "spice of life." At a time when cultural diversity and empowering other voices are critical issues in society, the last thing designers should be doing is retrenching into a mythical canon of "good taste."

> There is no such thing as a bad typeface . . . just bad typography.
>
> > Jeffery Keedy

Typographers are always quick to criticize, but it is rare to hear them admit that it is a typeface that makes their typography look good. Good typographers can make good use of almost anything. The typeface is a point of departure, not a destination. In using new typefaces the essential ingredient is imagination, because unlike with old faces, the possibilities have not been exhausted.

Typographers need to lighten up, to recognize that change is good (and inevitable), to jump into the multicultural, poststructural, postmodern, electronic flow. Rejection or ignorance of the rich and varied history and traditions of typography are inexcusable; however, adherence to traditional concepts without regard to contemporary context is intellectually lazy and a threat to typography today.

You cannot do new typography with old typefaces. This statement riles typographers, probably because they equate "new" with "good," which I do not. My statement is simply a statement of fact, not a value judgement. The recent proliferation of new typefaces should have anyone interested in advancing the tradition of typography in a state of ecstasy. It is always possible to do *good* typography with old typefaces. But why are so many typographers insistent on trying to do the impossible — *new* typography with old faces?

Inherent in the new typefaces are possibilities for the (imaginative) typographer that were unavailable ten years ago. So besides merely titillating typophiles with fresh new faces, it is my intention to encourage typographers and type designers to look optimistically forward. You may find some of the typefaces formally and functionally repugnant, but you must admit that type design is becoming very interesting again.

16   *Electronic Typography: The New Visual Language*

JESSICA HELFAND

In 1968, Mattel introduced Talking Barbie. I like to think of this as my first computer. I remember saving up my allowance for what seemed an eternity to buy one. To make her talk, you pulled a little string; upon its release, slave-to-fashion Barbie would utter delightful little conversational quips like "I think mini-skirts are smashing" and "Let's have a costume party." If you held the string back slightly as she was talking, her voice would drop a few octaves, transforming her from a chirpy soprano into a slurpy baritone. What came out then sounded a lot more like "Let's have a *cocktail* party."

I loved that part.

What I loved was playing director—casting her in a new role, assigning her a new (albeit ludicrous) personality. What I loved was controlling the tone of her voice, altering the rhythm of her words, modulating her oh-so-minimal (and moronic) vocabulary. What I loved was the power to shape her *language*—something I would later investigate typographically, as I struggled to understand the role of the printed word as an emissary of spoken communication.

Twenty-five years later, my Mac sounds a lot like my Barbie did then— the same monotone, genderless, robotic drawl. But here in the digital age, the relationship between design and sound—and in particular, between the spoken word and the written word—goes far beyond pulling a string. And don't be fooled by voice recognition software: The truth is that the computer's internal sound capabilities enable us to design *with* sound, not in imitation of it. Like it or not, the changes brought about by recent advances in technology (and here I am referring to multimedia) indicate the need for designers to broaden their understanding of what it is to work effectively with typography. It is no longer enough to design for readability, to "suggest" a sentiment

From *Looking Closer 2*. Eds. Michael Bierut, William Drenttel, Steven Heller, and D.K. Holland. New York: All Worth Press, 1997. 49–52. Originally published in *Print*, May/ June 1994.

or reinforce a concept through the selection of a particular font. Today, we can make type *talk*: in any language, at any volume, with musical underscoring or sci-fi sound effects. We can sequence and dissolve, pan and tilt, fade to black, and spec type in Sensurround. As we "set" type, we encounter a decision-making process unprecedented in two-dimensional design. Unlike the kinetic experience of turning a printed page to sequence information, time becomes a powerful and persuasive design element. Today, we can visualize concepts in four action-packed, digital dimensions.

Multimedia has introduced a new visual language, one which is no longer bound to traditional definitions of word and image and form and place. Typography, in an environment that offers such diverse riches, must redefine its goals, its purpose, its very identity. It must reinvent itself. And soon.

Visual language, or the interpretation of spoken words through typographic expression, has long been a source of inspiration to designers, artists, and writers. Examples abound, from concrete poetry in the twenties to "happenings" in the sixties, and in graphic design, dating as far back as the incunabula. Visual wordplay proliferates, in this century in particular, from F. T. Marinetti's *Parole in Liberià*, to George Maciunas's Fluxus installations, to the latest MTA posters adorning the New York subway walls. Kurt Schwitters, Guillaume Apollinaire, Piet Zwart, Robert Brownjohn—the list is long, the examples inexhaustible. For designers, there has always been an overwhelming interest in formalism, in analyzing the role of type as medium (structure), message (syntax), and muse (sensibility). Throughout, there has been an attempt to reconcile the relationship between words both spoken and seen—a source of exhilaration to some and ennui to others. Lamenting the expressive limitations of the Western alphabet, Adolf Loos explained it simply: "One cannot *speak* a capital letter." Denouncing its structural failings, Stanley Morison was equally at odds with a tradition that designated hierarchies, in the form of upper- and lower-case letterforms. Preferring to shape language as he deemed appropriate, Morison referred to CAPS as "a necessary evil."

Academic debate over the relationship between language and form has enjoyed renewed popularity in recent years, as designers borrowed from linguistic models in an attempt to codify and clarify their own typographic explorations. Deconstruction's design devotees eagerly appropriated its terminology and theory, hoping to introduce a new vocabulary for design: it was the vocabulary of signifiers and signifieds, of Jacques Derrida and Ferdinand de Saussure, of Michel Foucault and Umberto Eco.

As a comprehensive model for evaluating typographic expression, deconstruction proved both heady and limited. Today, as advances in technology introduce greater and more complex creative challenges, it is simply arcane. We need to look at screen-based typography as a *new language*—with its own grammar, its own syntax, its own rules. What we need are new models, better models, models that go beyond language or typography, per se—models that reinforce rather than restrict our understanding of what it is to design electronic media. "What we need," says design and new-media consultant Wendy Richmond, "are extreme and unusual metaphors."

Learning a new language is one thing; fluency, quite another. We've come to equate fluency with literacy — another outdated model for evaluation. "Literacy should not mean the ability to decode strings of alphabetic letters," says Seymour Papert, director of the Epistemology and Learning Group at MIT's Media Lab, who refers to such a definition as "letteracy." And language, even to linguists, proves creatively limiting as a paradigm. "New media promise the opportunity to offer a smoother transition to what really deserves to be called literacy," says Papert. Typography, as the physical embodiment of such thinking, has quite a way to go.

The will to decipher the formal properties of language, a topic of great consequence for communication designers in general, has its philosophical antecedents in ancient Greece. "Spoken words," wrote Aristotle in *Logic*, "are the symbols of mental experience. Written words are the symbols of spoken words." Today, centuries later, the equation has added a new link: what happens when written words can speak? when they can move? when they can be imbued with sound and tone and nuance and decibel and harmony and voice? As designers probing the creative parameters of this new technology, our goal may be less to *digitize* than to *dramatize*. Indeed, there is a theatrical component that I am convinced is essential to this new thinking. Of what value are bold and italics when words can dance across the screen, dissolve, or disappear altogether?

In this dynamic landscape, our static definitions of typography appear increasingly imperiled. Will the beauty of traditional letterforms be compromised by the evils of this new technology? Will punctuation be stripped of its functional contributions, or ligatures of their aesthetic ones? Will type really matter?

Of course it will.

In the meantime, however, typography's early appearance on the digital frontier doesn't speak too well for design. Take e-mail for example. Gone are the days of good handwriting, of the Palmer Method and the penmanship primer. In its place, electronic mail — which, despite its futuristic tone, has paradoxically revived the Victorian art of letter writing. Sending electronic mail is easy and quick. For those of us who spend a good deal of our professional lives on the telephone, e-mail offers a welcome respite from talking (though it bears a closer stylistic resemblance to conversational speech than to written language). However, for those of us with even the most modest design sense, e-mail eliminates the *distinctiveness* that typography has traditionally brought to our written communiqués. Though its supporters endorse the democratic nature of such homogeneity, the truth is, it's boring. In the land of e-mail, we all "sound" alike: everyone speaks in Monaco.

Oddly, it is laden with contradictions: ubiquitous in form yet highly diverse in content, at once ephemeral and archival, transmitted in real time yet physically intangible. E-mail is a kind of aesthetic flatland, informationally dense and visually unimaginative. Here, hierarchies are preordained and non-negotiable: passwords, menus, commands, help. Networks like America OnLine require that we title our mail, a leftover model from the days of interoffice correspondence, which makes even the most casual letter sound like a corporate memo. As a result, electronic missives all have headlines: titling our letters makes us better editors, not better designers. As a fitting metaphor for the distilled quality of things digital, the focus in e-mail is on the abridged, the acronym, the quick read. E-mail is functionally serviceable and visually forgettable, not unlike fast food. It's drive-thru design: get in, get out, move on.

And it's everywhere. Here is the biggest contribution to communication technology to come out of the last decade, a global network linking an estimated 50 million people worldwide, and designers—communication designers, no less—are *nowhere in sight*.

Typography, in this environment, desperately needs direction. Where do we start? Comparisons with printed matter inevitably fail, since words in the digital domain are processed with a speed unprecedented in the world of paper. Here, they are incorporated into databases or interactive programs, where they are transmitted and accessed in random, nonhierarchical sequences. "Hypertext," or the ability to program text with interactivity (meaning that a word, when clicked upon or pointed to, will actually do something), takes it all a step further: by introducing alternate paths, information lacks the closure of the traditional printed narrative. "Hypertextual story space is now multidimensional," explains novelist Robert Coover in a recent issue of *Artforum*, "and theoretically infinite."

If graphic design can be largely characterized by its attention to understanding the hierarchy of information (and using type in accordance with such understanding), then how are we to determine its use in a nonlinear context such as this? On a purely visual level, we are limited by what the pixel will render: the screen matrix simulates curves with surprising sophistication, but hairlines and idiosyncratic serifs will, to the typophile, inevitably appear compromised. On a more objective level, type in this context is both silent and static, and must compete with sound and motion—not an easy task, even in the best of circumstances. (Conversely, in the era of the TV remote, where the user can mute at will, the visual impact of written typography is not to be discounted.)

To analyze better the role(s) of electronic typography, we might begin by looking outside—not to remote classifications imported from linguistic textbooks, or even to traditional design theories conveniently repackaged—but to our own innate intelligence, our own distinctive powers of creative thought. To cultivate and develop adequately this new typography (because if we don't, no one else will), we might do well to rethink language altogether, to consider new and alternative perspectives. "If language is indeed the limit of our world," writes literary critic William Gass in *Habitations of the Word*, "then we must find another, larger, stronger, more inventive language which will burst those limits."

In his book *Seeing Voices*, author and neurologist Oliver Sacks reflects on sign language and looks at the cognitive understanding of spatial grammar in a language that exists without sound. He cites the example of a deaf child learning to sign and describes in detail the remarkable quality of her visual awareness and descriptive, spatial capabilities. "By the age of four, indeed, Charlotte had advanced so far into visual thinking and language that she was able to provide new ways of thinking—revelations—to her parents." As a consequence of learning sign language as adults, this child's parents not only learned a new language, but also discovered new ways of thinking as well—*visual thinking*. Imagine the potential for multimedia if designers were to approach electronic typography with this kind of ingenuity and openmindedness.

William Stokoe, a Chaucer scholar who taught Shakespeare at Gallaudet College in the 1950s, summarized it this way: "In a signed language, narrative is no longer linear and prosaic. Instead, the essence of sign language is to cut from a normal view to a close-up to a distant shot to a close-up again, and so on, even including flashback and fastforward scenes, exactly as a movie editor works." Here, perhaps, is another model for visual thinking: a new way of shaping meaning based on multiple points of view, which sees language as part of a more comprehensive communication platform—time-sensitive, interactive, and highly visual. Much like multimedia.

Addendum: In gathering research for this article, I posted a query on Applelink's typography board. I received the following response:

> As a type designer, I am sort of surprised to find myself NOT VERY CONCERNED with how type is used in the fluid context of multimedia. In a way, type is as flexible as photography or illustration in a mm context . . . i.e., it's a whole new ballgame for everyone.

Though my link-pal claimed not to be concerned, he did take the time to respond. And as I read his reply, I realized how important it will be for all of us to be concerned: not merely to translate the printed word to the screen, but to transcend it.

Then I found myself wondering: what would Stanley Morison have thought of all those CAPS?

17 *The Power of Punctuation*

MARTIN SOLOMON

Punctuation (pŭngk'chōō-ā shən) *n.* The use of standard marks and signs in writing and printing to separate works into sentences, clauses, and phrases in order to clarify meaning.

The American Heritage Dictionary

One of the first rules of grammar we learn is the proper use of punctuation marks. Their application abides by traditional standards, indicated in the style guides that dictate punctuation usage in formal texts. In general writing, however, most of us use punctuation in a more flexible manner. We omit, substitute, improvise, and alter many of the given rules. Application is determined by both tradition and the writer's personal style. Because of this casual treatment, punctuation is often taken for granted.

Most punctuation marks are composed to be seen but not heard. These subtle, often understated, devices are quite important, however, for they are the meter that determines the measure within the silent voice of typography (Figure 1). Punctuation directs tempo, pitch, volume, and the separation of words. Periods signify full stops. Commas slow the reader down. Question marks change pitch. Quotation marks indicate references.

Symbols in music perform comparable functions (Figure 2). During the performance of a piece of music, each conductor interprets the intensities and durations of these notations according to his or her own style. Similarly, designers can improvise upon the standards of punctuation.

Punctuation marks have tonal value just as letter forms do; they also have mass and energy, which may vary according to their structure. The various marks can be classified as major ? ! [], intermediate : ; " " () /, and minor - ' * in correspondence with their mass. Full-bodied punctuation marks, such as question marks and exclamation points, contain the definite characteristics of their type style. Intermediate and minor punctuation marks, although in keeping with their type style, correspond more closely with the typeface weight.

From *The Idea of Design: A Design Issues Reader* Ed. Victor Margolin and Richard Buchanan. Cambridge, MA: MIT Press, 1995. 113–117.

FIGURE 1.

,	COMMA
;	SEMICOLON
:	COLON
.	PERIOD
—	DASH OR EM DASH
-	DASH OR EN DASH
~	SWING DASH
-	HYPHEN
?	QUESTION MARK
¿ ?	QUESTION MARKS, SPANISH
!	EXCLAMATION POINT
¡ !	EXCLAMATION POINTS, SPANISH
'	APOSTROPHE
( )	PARENTHESIS
[ ]	BRACKETS
< >	BRACKET ANGLE
{ }	BRACES
" "	QUOTATION MARKS
` '	DOUBLE & SINGLE
...	ELLIPSIS

FIGURE 2.

pp	(pianissimo) — very soft
p	(piano) — soft
mp	(mezzopiano) — sort of soft
mf	(mezzoforte) — sort of loud
f	(forte) — loud
ff	(fortissimo) — very loud

FIGURE 3.

Punctuation marks vary widely from one type style to the next. A period, for example, is round in Futura, square in Helvetica, diamond shaped in Goudy, and oval in Ultra Bodoni (Figure 3).

Designers need not be confined to using only the punctuation included in a type font. They can utilize punctuation from other fonts or Pi sorts. However, they must consider compatibility between type and punctuation (Figure 4).

With punctuation marks designers can create illustrations without pictures. A single line of copy set in a light typeface contrasted with a bold, larger period creates a more dramatic stop than a period of conventional size and weight. Exaggerated quotation marks flanking a message offer another example of illustrative punctuation. The contrast in size and weight indicates to the reader, primarily through design rather than grammatical intent, that an important message is being presented (Figure 5 and 6).

FIGURE 4. Cover Design by Martin Solomon

FIGURE 5. From a Poster Designed by Martin Solomon

Asterisks function as visual movers, telling the reader to go to another location for a reference or definition (Figure 7). When this direction is coupled with the energies within the asterisk's geometric design, a bold or enlarged asterisk becomes a strong statement. The area surrounding exaggerated punctuation marks should be supportive of the size and weight of these images. Exaggerated punctuation should not be used with all messages. The indiscriminate display of punctuation for the sake of design turns these marks into

FIGURE 6.

> **❝**The player must know how to relieve
> the soft with the loud and
> how to apply each of these in its
> proper place, for following the familiar
> expression in painting, is called light and shade**❞**
> *Leopold Mozart*

FIGURE 7. Poster Designed by Martin Solomon

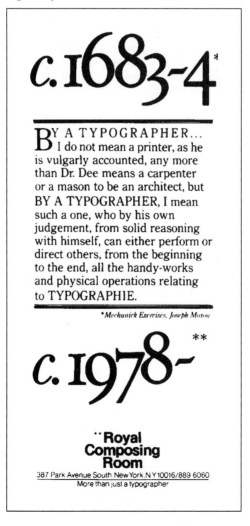

devices unrelated to concept; punctuation used out of context can diminish the effect of a message (Figure 8).

A greater or more interesting arrangement within any typographical composition can be created through the positioning of punctuation. An example is the abbreviation of the word *number*. By aligning the lower case *o* with the top of the capital *N* and inserting a small horizontal dash or rule beneath it, letters and punctuation work in concert to form a design unit: Nº. Although rules and underscores are not punctuation, they can be used to support or intensify characters or words. A period can replace the dash or rule, Nº. This simple usage of supporting punctuation creates a personality that can be more effective in endorsing a theme than the commonly used No. configuration (Figure 9).

FIGURE 8. Advertisements Designed by Martin Solomon

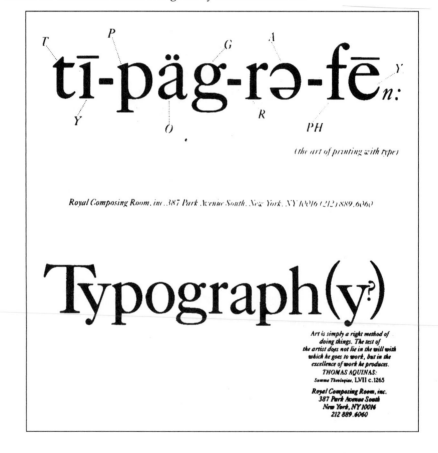

FIGURE 9.

FIGURE 10.

(212) 254-1177

(212) 254-1177

212/254-1177

212 254-1177

212 254·1177

212 254.1177

Punctuation marks need not be considered only in relation to texts in which they are an obvious part of the design. The sensitive application of punctuation in even the most commonplace unit changes the entire feeling of a design. One frequent application in which punctuation is taken for granted is the telephone number (Figure 10). *Telephone numbers traditionally have been indicated by parentheses enclosing the area code and a hyphen separating the next three numbers from the last four: (212) 987–6543.* Punctuation marks such as parentheses and hyphens are designed to center on the x-height letters and, as a result, sit low in relation to lining numbers, which are designed to correspond to the height of uppercase letters. Adjusting the position of such punctuation marks can be done in the type specifications. This grouping of numbers can be simplified by omitting the parentheses and inserting a slash or a word space after the area code: *212 987-6543.* The grouping can further be changed by substituting a bullet for the hyphen: *212 987•6543.* Base aligning a period is a better option, because the powerful circular shape of a bullet is noncommittal to the area it occupies and is unrelated to type style and spacing. If preferred, a wide variety of devices such as ballot boxes, triangles, arrows, and dingbats can work better in concert with respective letter form shapes (Figure 11). An additional option is to omit all punctuation or punctuation marks: *212 987 6543.*

Designers must understand the subtleties involved in working with punctuation. These subtleties include refinements in spacing and position. Spacing refinements maintain the optical alignment and tonal value continuity of a typographical composition. Hanging minor weight punctuation partially outside a flush left and right pica measure, for example, will maintain optical column alignment (Figure 12). Hanging punctuation on centered lines maintains vertical optical consistency between lines (Figure 13). Ellipses set with too much space between the dots appear too light in tonal value in relation to the

FIGURE 11.

FIGURE 12.

"Formative art" is what matters most in our time, where the new means of production—the machine—has changed the whole social background of our life, depriving the old forms of their former vital expression. Only formative art can create new genuine expression. A new conception towards formative art is beginning to make itself felt. Today we insist upon the form of a thing following the function of that thing; upon its creator's desire for expression following the same direction as the organic building-up processes in nature and not running counter to that direction. We insist upon harmony again being achieved between intellect and desire.

Statement by Walter Gropius.

FIGURE 13.

Typography:
the art of
printing.

rest of the copy and therefore should be specified with no additional letter space between the dots. All of these refinements contribute to the totality of a composition by creating an harmonious interrelation between punctuation and words.

Punctuation is to typography what perspective is to painting. It introduces the illusion of visual and audible dimension, giving words vitality. Whether prominent or subtle, punctuation marks are the heartbeat of typography, moving words along in proper timing and with proper emphasis.

18 Repetition and the Rhetoric of Visual Design

JAMES E. PORTER AND PATRICIA A. SULLIVAN

This chapter examines the role repetition plays in professional writing. It reports on a longitudinal study of a developing professional writer who wrote, tested, and revised a tutorial for using the page layout program Aldus PageMaker. We observed how this writer ("Max") conceived, collected information from, and then reconceived the audience for his tutorial. In doing this, we noticed (a) how the writer relied on the repetition of design elements in the manual to provide a familiar look that he thought would comfort and assist his users; and (b) how the users' orientations toward the manual were influenced, both positively and negatively, by the design pattern he employed. We use these observations to argue that repetition is a vital element in the design of professional documents — but that its use has to be guided by rhetorical considerations. Repetition can help readers, but certain uses of it can also hinder understanding and learning. Writers need to learn the important difference between helpful and nonhelpful repetition.

Our chapter begins by providing some background into the theoretical perspective of rhetoric and professional writing, moves to considering design theory as rhetoric, and then focuses on the study of Max. We conclude with some observations about the desirability of "design repetition" (or "design consistency") in professional writing.

THE THEORETICAL PERSPECTIVE OF RHETORIC AND PROFESSIONAL WRITING

Traditionally, composition has had little to say about repetition, other than the typical advice one can find in the ubiquitous and infamous handbooks, which treat repetition simply as reappearance of words and phrases within a given discourse. The stock advice concerning repetition in written discourse is to avoid it, because it wastes space and the reader's time, except when it

From *Repetition in Discourse: Interdisciplinary Perspectives*. Vol. 2. Ed. Barbara Johnstone. Vol. XLVIII in the Series Advances in Discourse Processes. Ed. Roy O. Freedle. Norwood, NJ: Ablex, 1994. 114–129.

might be desirable for emphasis. In the 1970s and 1980s, as the field of composition developed a sense of its own theoretical and historical roots in rhetoric (and as "composition" became "rhetoric and composition"), its focus changed to considering more the *effects* of various textual strategies, including repetition.

As a practical art (*techne*), rhetoric is concerned with how a discourse can be constructed to achieve a certain effect. Other forms of textual analysis describe discourse with the aim of building general theories or models of language use. To some extent, rhetoric does the same thing, but with an additional aim: Rhetoric applies such descriptions to the end of practice, and so complicates discourse studies. This means that rhetoric is a situational discipline: We can do a post hoc empirical analysis to determine what effect the letter we wrote yesterday had on its readers — but how will that analysis help us write another letter today? Obviously writers call upon prior experience, upon rhetorical principles and compositional practices to guide their efforts, but since writers are always in new situations, they must select and interpret prior experience to build new writing plans. Rhetoric and composition are interested in how writers build plans, or "representations of situated actions" (Suchman, 1987, p. 50).

Because rhetoric is a situated and applied art, it generates *principles*, not *rules*. The difference is significant: principles are always interpreted and adjusted for situations (and rarely survive in pure form); rules circumscribe absolute boundaries. "Rather than actions being determined by rules, actors effectively use the normative rules of conduct that are available to produce significant actions" (Suchman, 1987, p. 66). This situational premise is stated in different ways by different theorists — e.g., knowledge is local (Geertz, 1983); the significant level of inquiry is practice (Bourdieu, 1977; Phelps, 1988) — but the position is generally that

> The significance of a linguistic expression on some actual occasion . . . lies in its relationship to circumstances that are presupposed or indicated by, but not actually captured in, the expression itself. . . . The communicative significance of a linguistic expression is always dependent upon the circumstances of its use. (Suchman, 1987, pp. 58, 60)

Suchman articulates here the premise of intertextuality, the principle that recognizes the interconnected, networked characteristic of discourse. Intertextuality notes that any given discourse is influenced by its relationship to other discourses and is composed of *traces*, pieces of other texts that help constitute its meaning in a given situation (see Culler, 1981). Intertextually speaking, then, all discourse is in some sense repetitious. For example, in the Declaration of Independence the phrase "Life, Liberty, and the pursuit of Happiness" appears only once. Yet the phrase appeared in numerous political documents of its era and was, in fact, a cliche of the times. Though the phrase was not explicitly repetitious within the document, it is intertextually repetitious — and may have achieved its persuasive force precisely for that reason (Porter, 1986).

The object of analysis for those in rhetoric and composition is not only the written text, but the writer-in-the-act-of-writing, and also the audience. We examine the text, not as an autonomous structure, so much as a stage in an overall process of action involving the writer and the audience, as well as numerous other discourses. Rhetoric complicates discourse study by involving matters related to situation and process — the setting for discourse as well as the means by which it is produced and received. From this disciplinary perspective, then, the significant questions involving repetition have to do with its inter- and con-textual, rather than simply its textual, features.

Professional writing is a newly developing field that encompasses what used to be labeled *business writing* or *technical writing*, but that extends beyond to include other concerns. Like rhetoric, professional writing is a practical discipline focusing on how general strategies are interpolated locally. Some characteristics of professional writing, as a disciplinary orientation, are that

- it draws upon rhetorical theory of language and persuasion;
- it concerns itself with the everyday practice of writing, especially writing within the parameters of the organization (or *workplace writing*);
- it calls upon resources from a variety of disciplines not typically associated with rhetoric and composition (e.g., human–computer interaction studies, graphic design);
- it focuses especially on the roles various technologies (especially computer-aided publishing) play in composing processes; and
- its focus of interest is mainly the *career writer*, the professional whose job responsibility is mainly the design, testing, and development of documents. (This orientation is different from that of traditional technical and business writing, whose orientation is not as much the *professional writer* as the *professional who writes*.)

Thus, inquiries in professional writing often examine connections between rhetorical situation, document design, computer use, and audience — as does our study.

RHETORIC AND VISUAL DESIGN THEORY

The basic premise of the rhetoric of visual design is this: Any page of text is composed of visual as well as verbal elements, and those visual patterns themselves exert a rhetorical effect. The words on a page are always laid out in certain spatial patterns (if only block paragraph form, with simple one-inch margins), and those patterns not only cue the reader as to how the material is to be comprehended, but also attempt to persuade, or argue that the reader should adopt a certain posture toward the material (see Buchanan, 1989; Bernhardt, 1986). Layout directs seeing, which influences learning and thinking — and behavior generally (see Arnheim, 1969).

FIGURE 1. Warning Box

> ### • WARNING! •
>
> **Reading this passage before reading the previous discussion**
>
> **will only prove the authors' point.**

We can look at an obvious example of how design influences reading. It is fairly easy to get a reader's attention with a warning label (see Figure 1).

The box will garner your attention, but can we predict when or how you will read the warning box? Can we accurately predict that you will read it before you read anything else on its page? It would not require much insight to predict that anything boxed and centered on a page of otherwise dense, gray, academic prose would get noticed. Before we jump to conclusions about reading processes, though, it would be best to consider contextual factors: Our article is thus far laid out so as to invite a conventional linear reading, and if you arrived at that page committed to that pattern (both because the text promotes this reading and because you are accustomed to reading academic prose) you may *not* have read the warning box first.

We include this example to point to the problem of predicting the effects of design. Contextual complexities create problems which can frustrate information designers (see Easterby & Zwaga, 1984). Readability research notes that machine operators who receive too many warnings begin disregarding them. Laws mandate warnings, and companies post warnings, to promote the safety of their employees (and to protect themselves from law suits). But the more warnings there are, the less effective they may be. Despite the importance or "newness" of the message, repetition of a familiar message or design can lead a machine operator to ignore it. The standardized medicine label is another instance where design repetition can both help and hurt (see Hartley, 1985). Standardized labels assure that information will be positioned in a uniform way from bottle to bottle — and that, ideally, is supposed to promote safe use of medicines. But as consumers become inured to the design, will they read labels as carefully?

The issue of repetition emerges for the field of professional writing under the rubric *design consistency* — and the conventional thinking supports design consistency as a positive feature of documents. *Design* in this context refers to format in the physical sense (i.e., page layout) and to typographical elements. *Design consistency* refers to repetition of basic patterns throughout a document, to the repeatability of basic page formats, styles and positioning of headings, and so on. In the field of information design, it is thought that design consistency assists comprehension and memory. The simple cognitive principle invoked here is that readers will understand new material best in relationship to old material. A familiar design, then, can help writers process complicated and/or new information.[1] At times, even redundancy is recommended.[2]

In desktop publishing, writers are encouraged to create page templates and style sheets that will assist them in maintaining design consistency throughout an entire publication.[3] The very idea of a template is that it establishes a master page format which is repeatable through a publication: "Templates speed up the production cycle and help maintain consistency. In addition, they add a 'family resemblance' to your . . . publications, thereby increasing their effectiveness" (Parker, 1988, p. 126). Design consistency and conformity are strong and established values in the field of professional writing (see Polson, 1988). Lay says that:

> Frames [on a page] should be consistently designed; the same element should appear in the same place for continuity and if possible be identified by borders or symbols unique to that element. . . . To have "findability," a layout should be consistent and predictable, with information blocked and labeled and with easy-to-scan internal heads (1989, p. 76)

Consistency and conformity are positive qualities, but page designers are also urged to develop variation within established patterns. Lay recognizes that consistency alone does not make for effective writing: "a general design rule is that meaning lies in contrast; the unusual, the irregular, or the large attracts our attention" (1989, p. 80). "Creativity," as well as conformity, is recommended. But despite such recommendations to establish diversity, the dominant value — especially in the writing of instructional (as opposed to promotional) text — urges consistency of page template, heading format, user interface, and so on. Though each page may have separate unique elements, the overriding advice to the instructional designer is to situate those elements within an established template.

DISCUSSION OF STUDY

In part, our study aims to determine whether overall page design consistency — from page to page through a manual, for instance — is desirable in computer documentation. Does a repeated page design promote or conflict with the aims of computer documentation? In 1989 we began a longitudinal study of a developing professional writer's involvement with a page-layout tutorial he was producing for use in a desktop publishing class at Purdue University. Much audience theory in rhetoric argues that sensitivity to audience is slow to develop in writers, and we were particularly interested in the question of how user testing of documents might promote sensitivity to audience (see Sullivan & Porter, 1990a,b). Max, our longitudinal subject, developed an allegiance to the document he produced in that class and kept working on it for another year. Our study tracks various aspects of Max's involvement with his tutorial.

Here we report on one of the later segments of the longitudinal case study, Max's April 1990 user testing of his Aldus PageMaker tutorial. In this segment of the study Max is anticipating what users will do with his tutorial and is observing five users trying to complete his tutorial.

METHODOLOGY

The Subject

Max, the central subject of this study, graduated from Purdue's Professional Writing program in December 1989, with the technical writing option. At the time of the user testing he had taken a documentation job at a major computer company, but had not yet begun working. Max is a bit older (almost 25) than other graduates of the program; he started as an engineering student, dropped out of school a couple times, and did not seem to focus until he "found" technical writing. His grade point average is lower than that of most of our students, though he has good grades in writing classes taken during his last year. We think he is typical of technical writers, as he has come to it from something else; he is eclectic; he is an independent learner; he values system accuracy. Max has the traditional value of "system first" that is instilled in computer scientists and engineers, and often technical writers.

The Document

The document is a sixteen-page tutorial that introduces Aldus PageMaker by having the user recreate the cover page of the tutorial. The page that users produce has a graphic, some headlines, and two-column text; it is designed to have the basic elements of a simple newsletter. The tutorial itself is produced in 8½″ × 11″ format (single-sided pages). It is comprised of three pages of introductory material, twelve pages of instructions, and a one-page conclusion (listing suggestions for future learning). Max's goal in the tutorial is to have people move through the basic tasks fairly quickly, get some experience, and have some success. He wants to give users enthusiasm for the task of learning Aldus PageMaker. We have some measure of the quality of the tutorial: it received an A in an upper-level professional writing class; it won third place in its division in a publications contest (the Chicago chapter of the Society for Technical Communication); it was successfully completed (and praised) by all five users.

The Users

Max tested his tutorial with five users, all of whom were women in an advanced professional writing class (taught by J. Porter) that was using PageMaker to format a class project. Max selected these users based on a screening survey the teacher distributed to the class. He wanted people with no experience with PageMaker, with some knowledge of computers, but with a sincere interest in (or a good reason to learn) PageMaker. All five users were familiar with basic word-processing functions on the Macintosh computer. We concur with Max's judgment that these are appropriate subjects for his tutorial.

The Researchers

We are participants as well as observers. Max is our student; if he runs into profound difficulties in one area or another, we are honor bound to try to help him. And, even though he has now graduated, he takes our opinions as having more authority (in some areas) than his do. This does not mean he is not a maturing adult; nor does it mean that we "tell" him what to do all the time. In fact, we try to allow student discovery in our classes rather than dispensing knowledge, so Max does not really expect us to give him answers—we never have. The users were at the time students in J. Porter's class. So we are bound up with everyone in this study, as the professional writing community at Purdue.

The Data Collected

Our data for this portion of the study include audiotaped interviews, audiotaped user test sessions, and printed material. We interviewed Max twice regarding planning for the user test sessions, and we interviewed him immediately before and after each session. Written data include the tutorial itself; our and Max's notes during the user test sessions; surveys about the backgrounds of the users; and the printed pages the users produced.

The User Test Sessions

Each of the five users was tested on separate days in April 1990. The test was held at an isolated table in a corner of a computer lab, with observers at the user's side. The test procedure was modeled after Atlas's (1981) recommended "user edit," Max briefly introduced each test and asked the user to work alone and to talk aloud as she worked. Each user then worked through the tutorial, finishing by printing out a facsimile of the cover page of the tutorial. After each user finished, Max asked for her comments, suggestions, and responses.

RESULTS/DISCUSSION

The Document

The tutorial follows the standard conventions for computer documentation, maintaining a consistent tone, style, and design throughout. The rhetorical posture Max adopts in the tutorial is also conventional: it assumes that absolute authority lies in the program, and that the role of the manual (and its author) is to explain that authority and its proper procedures to the user (who begins in ignorance). Max does assume that the user has a certain amount of computer background (e.g., basic word-processing background; familiarity with the Macintosh), but that the user has near-total ignorance about PageMaker. This turns out to be an accurate assessment of the audience, but is it ever rhetorically sound to remind an audience of their ignorance for any length of time? The tutorial's adherence to convention that is reflected in the visual consistency of the pages may have conflicted with the changes in the users, who are not static entities but people who change through the course of the tutorial.

The physical design of the tutorial supports the conventional rhetorical posture. Max uses fairly conventional instructional design elements for his tutorial (see Figure 2 for mock-up): two-column page, with headings in larger and bold type, numbered directions, explanations in smaller plain type, numerous illustrations (mostly computer screens), and one task per page. The reading pattern this design encourages is well established: You (a) read each direction in order, (b) perform the function, (c) check results (either against a description or an illustration and (d) proceed to next step. Max repeats this basic pattern on twelve of the sixteen pages of the tutorial. Earlier in his composing process, he wondered whether there was a better "track" for the manual—but he stayed with the step-by-step procedure, in part because he could always group related steps into a page.

The single most repetitious element in the tutorial is the numbered, single-sentence, imperative instruction: e.g., "When the Page Setup window appears, click the OK box." Max gives sixty-five separate imperative commands in the twelve pages of directions. This is not unusual for documentation—in fact, it is quite the norm. The commands are often followed by a computer screen illustrating the action the user is to perform. At other points, the commands are followed by verification statements—such as "The Placing Tool for paint files will appear as your mouse pointer"—intended to provide a way for the user to determine whether she has successfully implemented the command.

The physical design helps maintain the consistency of the rhetorical posture: command, illustration, verification, next command. The user is treated as an operating system—and in fact in one interview Max referred to his intended users as "compilers." The users experienced some impatience with the tutorial toward the end—and especially when they were instructed to type out what they perceived as an unnecessarily long sample text. They followed the directions, but expressed various forms of frustration at doing so (e.g., sighing in two cases, snickering in another).

The Users

All five of the users tested successfully completed the tutorial by printing out a reasonable facsimile of the cover page of Max's tutorial—though two of the five encountered obstacles that required Max's intervention. Four of the five users reported feeling good about what they had learned about PageMaker; these four indicated that they felt confident enough to try PageMaker on their

FIGURE 2. Mock-up of Representative Tutorial Page

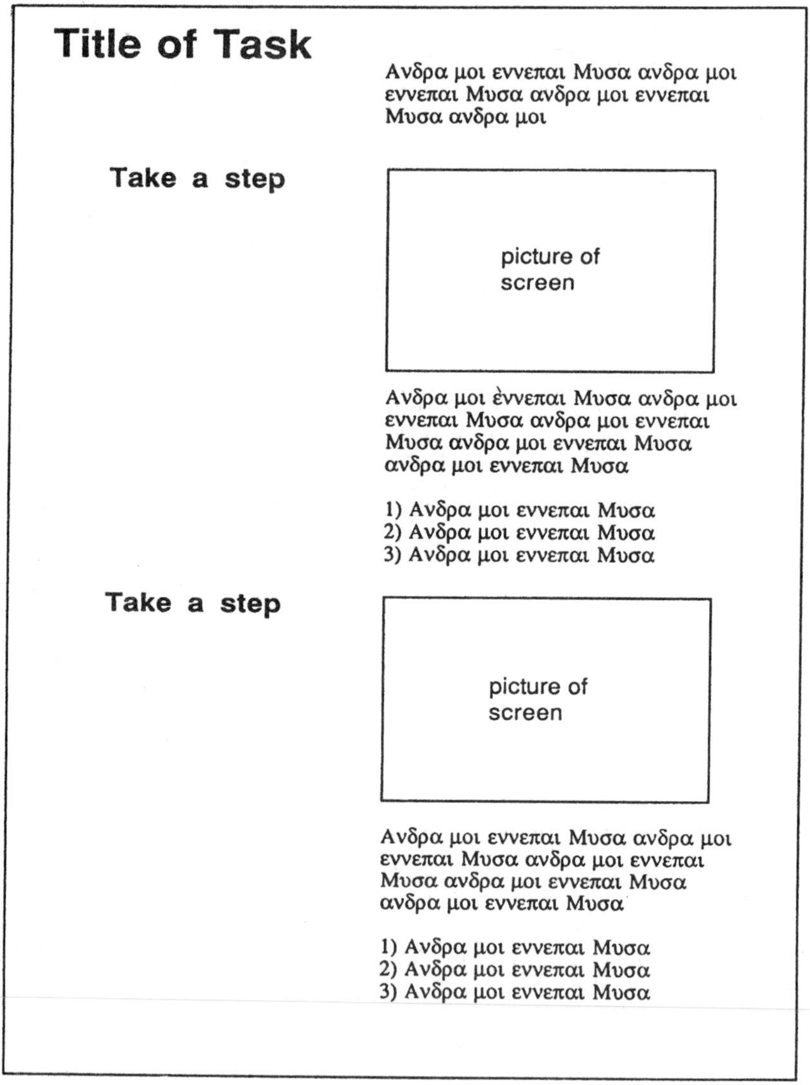

Title of Task

Ανδρα μοι εννεπαι Μυσα ανδρα μοι εννεπαι Μυσα ανδρα μοι εννεπαι Μυσα ανδρα μοι

Take a step

picture of screen

Ανδρα μοι εννεπαι Μυσα ανδρα μοι εννεπαι Μυσα ανδρα μοι εννεπαι Μυσα ανδρα μοι εννεπαι Μυσα ανδρα μοι εννεπαι Μυσα

1) Ανδρα μοι εννεπαι Μυσα
2) Ανδρα μοι εννεπαι Μυσα
3) Ανδρα μοι εννεπαι Μυσα

Take a step

picture of screen

Ανδρα μοι εννεπαι Μυσα ανδρα μοι εννεπαι Μυσα ανδρα μοι εννεπαι Μυσα ανδρα μοι εννεπαι Μυσα ανδρα μοι εννεπαι Μυσα

1) Ανδρα μοι εννεπαι Μυσα
2) Ανδρα μοι εννεπαι Μυσα
3) Ανδρα μοι εννεπαι Μυσα

own in the future. None of the five users took longer than forty minutes to complete the tutorial (the quickest took thirty-two minutes).

It is difficult to isolate page design as the significant variable influencing users' behaviors, since any particular reading behavior can probably be attributed to multiple influences. Our five users' reactions to the PageMaker tutorial could well be reactions to the overall rhetorical posture of the text, as well as to its page design. But there is a point where rhetorical posture and page design overlap.

In part, our discussion demonstrates what we mean when we say that design is rhetorical. Even though instructional text is typically thought to be neutral, it is not (see Kinross, 1989). Max's page design and rhetorical posture are interconnected, and the two work in unison to establish and maintain authority over the users. The users seemed willing, even glad, for the lock-step, directional guidance early in the tutorial, when they were least confident. One user commented positively to Max about how he had arranged the tutorial: "step by step . . . you didn't make a lot of presumptions about how to do it. I like that." But especially later in the tutorial the users became impatient with the user test. As they felt that they had the "idea" of using PageMaker, they became more impatient to be through with this and start their own projects.

We noticed that as Max's users worked through his documentation, they began to miss messages that were visually deemphasized on the page. As they became more familiar with the page design, they became less careful readers. (Since none of the user sessions lasted more than forty minutes, we doubt that physical fatigue was a significant factor in their responses.) Repetition provides a familiar orientation for the reader; but an overly familiar design can also lead readers to conclude (mistakenly) that they are familiar with the material. People ignore instructions when "they believe that they already know how to proceed" (Suchman, 1987, p. 166). Ramey's research on computer users tells us what our own experience affirms: "about one-half to three-quarters of computer users want to spend very little time reading, and especially do not want to read continuous discourse. . . . They skip sections that look like overviews, introductions, and so on, and scan down the page" (1988, p. 148). At some stage in the user's development, a more open-ended design allowing for user independence might be more suitable.

The Developing Writer

Max's project, which he views as his attempt to learn how to design pages and how to write for users, is one he is committed to. That is clear from his conduct: he wrote and rewrote the document for an advanced writing class he took in Spring 1989, and he revised it for his portfolio in Fall 1989. He revised it again for submission in the publications contest of the Society for Technical Communication (STC). Based on feedback he got from the STC, he continued to revise the document into Spring 1990, and agreed to let us observe him testing the document with five users.

Max's expressed goals in writing the documentation were complex and potentially contradictory. Max wanted to motivate novices to learn and to use PageMaker. He wanted to help novice users understand the basics of PageMaker and to learn enough that they would be encouraged to learn more. His step-by-step tutorial design choice seemed to work against the "understanding" goal by placing the user not in the role of learner so much as the role of doer simply performing actions without understanding them. He thought that by doing, the novices would come to understand. Interestingly, we observed several points at which the users would continue to follow directions even when they recognized it as arbitrary or stupid to do so. For instance, three of the users typed their PageMaker headlines in miniature, even though they knew this was probably wrong, simply because the tutorial did not prompt them to select the "Actual Size" view. The design of the directions promoted a dependent doing, rather than the independent learning Max expressed as his aim. Such a design asks the user to surrender independent thinking and to simply follow directions. It is a design that suits "reading-to-do" rather than "reading-to-learn" (see Porter, 1989).

Max's page design represents his version of an ideal path of human-computer interaction. We suspect that he chose his design based on his familiarity with other similar designs for instructional text. He repeats the design because he expects that the familiar pattern will direct users in predictable ways. There are other design options Max could have chosen to encourage different types of human-computer interactions (for example, a more open-ended type of tutorial that would not demand specific responses). But Max seemed committed to the directional design. Despite evidence from the user test that indicated that different designs, or multiple designs, might have been appropriate, Max remained committed to his established template, choosing design consistency over user needs.

Max's approach to documentation reflects his systems orientation. In an interview early in our study, Max told us that, until Spring 1989, he never bothered with page design, because he was too busy getting the content into the manual. In this remark, Max reflects a conventional attitude that content is what counts most in writing. He thinks good documentation is comprehensive, covering all the necessary material and providing a complete and accurate description of a procedure. Users must be told everything to do; the tutorial provides lock-step directions for performing the tasks—and either the users get it "right" or they get it "wrong." When they encounter problems, Max's answer is to provide more clarifying information, or to "fix" sentences. His orientation toward users seems to block him from making global changes that might have helped his documentation.

CONCLUSION

The key question we ask, then, is this: Should page design (which always conveys a rhetorical posture) change through an instructional tutorial or publication to suit the changing reader? Our tentative answer is, yes, this might be desirable—though anticipating whether and how fast a user is likely to develop will pose yet another challenge to professional writers. Repetition of page design through an entire publication and consistency of rhetorical stance may suit some situations and may satisfy some abstract aesthetic principle. But strict adherence to such consistency may not be suitable for readers whose needs change as they learn. McDonald and Schvaneveldt (1988, p. 291) warn us that "it would be a mistake to conclude that standardization is a good solution to the most important interface design problems."

Now, we do not want to suggest that page designers begin eschewing consistency on a large scale. We agree that certain forms of consistency are helpful to users—for instance, certain typographic consistencies (such as using bold type for computer commands) serve a metadiscourse function, indicating how readers are supposed to react to the language. Extended repetition of overall page layout, however, may bespeak an infelicitous commitment to a single rhetorical posture. And a single rhetorical posture—especially if that posture is one of authority over the supposed ignorant user—may not be tolerated for very long by the user who is learning and developing.

Writing usable computer documentation is more challenging than most people imagine. It involves more than simply explaining all the steps of a procedure or listing out directions in neat sequential order. Writers need to be aware, not only of the system they are describing, but of the situation of the user—and use this knowledge to build suitable designs (see Rubens & Rubens, 1988; Winograd & Flores, 1986). Partly this art requires an appreciation of the role and effect of repetition within the rhetorical situation. Repetition can help establish a common and/or familiar framework for the audience, but in some situations familiarity can also undermine the aims of the discourse.

NOTES

1. The basic component of the page, in terms of design, is the *grid*, a "skeletal understructure [that] brings cohesiveness to a visual piece" (Berryman, 1984, p. 38). The grid a designer sets up for a page establishes a basic pattern providing cohesiveness and continuity. The psychological presumption here is that "humans tend to prefer organized visual and verbal information. Grid systems allow the designer to satisfy viewer groups with respect to equilibrium, similarity, and continuation. They help the designer to avoid visual ambiguity" (Berryman, 1984, p. 38).

2. For example, Weiss (1985, p. 133) advises that "Redundancy [in computer documentation], although it complicates maintenance and seems inefficient and wasteful, reduces the number of skips, jumps, branches, and loops in a publication."

3. The very history of the book supports the importance of repetition to design consistency. As W. J. Ong (1982, p. 127) asserts, a printing press can print an "exactly repeatable visual statement." He points out that, in the printing press culture, a book is less of an utterance and more of a thing, bringing with it labels, title pages, complex lists, maps, charts, and alphabetical indexing. Ong goes on to say that

> Because visual surface had become charged with imposed meaning and because print controlled not only what words were put down to form a text but also the exact situation of the words on the page and their spatial relationship to one another, the space itself on a printed sheet—"white space" as it is called—took on high significance that leads directly into the modern and post-modern world (p. 128).

REFERENCES

Arnheim, R. (1969). *Visual thinking.* Berkeley: University of California Press.
Atlas, M. (1981). The user edit: Making manuals easier to use. *IEEE Transactions on Professional Communication*, PC 24, 28–29.
Bernhardt, S. A. (1986). Seeing the text. *College Composition and Communication, 37*(1), 66–78.
Berryman, G. (1984). *Notes on graphic design and visual communication.* (Rev. ed.) Los Altos. CA: William Kaufmann.
Bourdieu, P. (1977). *Outline of a theory of practice.* Cambridge: Cambridge University Press.
Buchanan, R. (1989). Declaration by design: Rhetoric, argument, and demonstration in design practice. In V. Margolin (Ed.), *Design discourse: History, theory, criticism* (pp. 91–109). Chicago: The University of Chicago Press.

Culler, J. (1981). *The pursuit of signs: Semiotics, literature, deconstruction.* Ithaca: Cornell University Press.

Easterby, R., & Zwaga, H. (Eds.). (1984). *Information design: The design and evaluation of signs and printed material.* New York: Wiley and Sons.

Geertz, C. (1983). *Local knowledge: Further essays in interpretive anthropology.* New York: Basic Books.

Hartley, J. (1985). *Designing instructional text* (2nd ed.). London: Kogan Page.

Kinross, R. (1989). The rhetoric of neutrality. In V. Margolin (Ed.), *Design discourse: History, theory, criticism* (pp. 131–143). Chicago: University of Chicago Press.

Lay, M. M. (1989). Nonrhetorical elements of layout and design. In B. E. Fearing & W. K. Sparrow (Eds.), *Technical writing: Theory and practice* (pp. 72–85). New York: MLA.

McDonald, J. E., & Schvaneveldt, R. W. (1988). The application of user knowledge to interface design. In R. Guindon (Ed.), *Cognitive science and its applications for human-computer interaction* (pp. 289–338). Hillsdale, NJ: Erlbaum.

Ong, W. J. (1982). *Orality and literacy: The technologizing of the word.* London: Methuen.

Parker, R. C. (1988). *Looking good in print: A guide to basic design for desktop publishing.* Chapel Hill, NC: Ventana Press.

Phelps, L. W. (1988). *Composition as a human science: Contributions to the self-understanding of a discipline.* New York: Oxford University Press.

Polson, P. G. (1988). The consequences of consistent and inconsistent user interfaces. In R. Guindon (Ed.), *Cognitive science and its applications for human-computer interaction* (pp. 59–108). Hillsdale, NJ: Erlbaum.

Porter, J. E. (1986). Intertextuality and the discourse community. *Rhetoric Review, 5*(1), 34–47.

Porter, J. E, (1989). Assessing readers' use of computer documentation: A pilot study. *Technical Communication, 36*(4), 422–423.

Ramey, J. (1988). How people use computer documentation: Implications for book design. In S. Doheny-Farina (Ed.), *Effective documentation: What we have learned from research* (pp. 143–158). Cambridge, MA: MIT Press.

Rubens, P., & Rubens, B. K. (1988). Usability and format design. In S. Doheny-Farina (Ed.), *Effective documentation: What we have learned from research* (pp. 213–233). Cambridge, MA: MIT Press.

Suchman, L. A. (1987). *Plans and situated actions: The problem of human-machine communication.* Cambridge: Cambridge University Press.

Sullivan, P. A., & Porter, J. E. (1990a). How do writers view usability information? A case study of a developing documentation writer. *SIGDOC '90 Conference Proceedings, 14*(4), 29–35.

Sullivan, P. A., & Porter, J. E. (1990b). User testing: The heuristic advantages at the draft stage. *Technical Communication, 37*(1), 78–80.

Weiss, E. H. (1985). *How to write a usable user manual.* Philadelphia: ISI Press.

Winograd, T., & Flores, F. (1986). *Understanding computers and cognition: A new foundation for design.* Norwood, NJ: Ablex Publishing Corp.

PART FOUR

Visual Rhetoric and Argument

Introduction to Part Four

An established convention of composition pedagogy holds persuasive discourse or argument as a foundation of both classical and revisionist rhetoric and even of composition studies itself. Meanwhile, composition and classical rhetoric as disciplines tend to approach rhetoric and, by extension, argument in strictly verbal terms. Within composition, then, to say nothing of philosophy or semiotics, scholars by no means agree universally on the question of whether or not images can make arguments, especially as arguments are classically defined: linear sequences of claims, counter-claims, and evidence. Whether images can argue on their own or only in conjunction with words is an even more contentious subject. The readings in this section examine the objections to visuals being capable of persuading and sustaining traditional linear arguments consisting of claims, counter-claims, and supporting evidence, and they describe what visual arguments might look like. All of them offer ways to expand our notions about whether visual argumentation and persuasion are possible.

Those of us with language arts backgrounds — rhetoric, expository writing, and literature — may be more inclined to focus on the *text* in hybrid documents at the expense of the *images*, but rhetoric as a lens or means of analysis might just as well extend to hybrid texts. The selections included here argue that we must resist overlooking the rhetorical function of graphics, small or large, which we might often find so easy to ignore or to dismiss subconsciously as decoration. When analyzing hybrid texts and constructing them with our students, we need to constantly remind ourselves that images, as much as text, can be analyzed rhetorically, can be connotative, for instance, in addition to being denotative.

Traditionally, the formal area of study we call "Argumentation Theory" has not included visual elements. But instead of holding to the tradition and refusing to consider visuals at all, David Birdsell and Leo Groarke believe traditional Argumentation Theory to be too strict and intellectually binding in a world filled with visual elements. In "Toward a Theory of Visual Argument," they advocate extending the theory to account for visual portrayals that are persuasive and argumentative. Without such a move, they claim,

Argumentation Theory cannot help us understand the increasingly visual modes of communication emerging in our digital world. The authors refute claims of theorists who deny that visuals can conduct arguments simply because these theorists believe visuals to be inherently indeterminant. Words, according to Birdsell and Groarke, can be just as indeterminate as pictures, and this indeterminacy is, in fact, what allows theoretic arguments to take place in all academic fields. In order to have a workable theory of visual argument, Birdsell and Groarke argue that we need to be able to "(a) identify the internal elements of a visual image, (b) understand the contexts in which images are interpreted, (c) establish the consistency of an interpretation of the visual, and (d) chart changes in visual perspectives over time." They urge the study of fields as diverse as art history and cognitive psychology in order to fully address the complexity of visual argument.

If, for compositionists, the major stumbling block to accepting visual argument is still that arguments seem impossible to construct based on images alone, Keith Kenney's "Building Visual Communication Theory by Borrowing from Rhetoric" works from a different angle to help dismantle this objection. Explaining that visual communication is rhetorical, Kenney at first shows that we can find elements of classical rhetoric in different types of visual texts. Cartoons and magazine ads are rhetorical; cartoonists and magazine ad creators are true rhetoricians. Cartoonists use inventional *topoi*, formal organizing principles, and a particular rhetorical style. In addition, these graphic artists apply the canons of memory and delivery — just not in ways that verbal rhetoricians do.

Kenney also tackles head-on the troublesome accusation that visual elements cannot form rational arguments. Words, the accusers insist, have explicit meanings, but visuals cannot. Kenney cites Birdsell and Groarke's argument that words are just as imprecise as images since explicitness for both rests on the contexts in which we use them. So if context lends explicitness to words, it does so, too, for images. To refute the underlying claim for the objections that visual images cannot state clear *premises*, Kenney identifies the assumption it rests on: that pictures do not have the "two-part relationship of premises leading to conclusions." Kenney includes an extensive account of a communications professor's campaign against billboards to illustrate how framing devices, such as substitution and transformation, can form both premises and conclusions by focusing our attention on a single part of an image or on a series of objects. Kenney's use of a range of rhetorical terms, such as *topoi, scheme, metaphor*, and *disposition*, models ways in which traditional rhetoric might be used by composition teachers and students to understand and produce hybrid documents.

Philosopher J. Anthony Blair also wonders — but skeptically — whether strictly visual arguments are theoretically possible. More to the point, he asks whether, given their philosophic possibility, such arguments can exist. Searching for answers in "The Possibility and Actuality of Visual Arguments," he delineates two types of arguments: One consists of a claim supported by reasons, while the other is constituted by disagreements between interacting parties. Blair shows that visual arguments tend to be the first type of argument. He then distinguishes between persuasion and formal argument, between communicating a point of view and constituting an argument, and finally between visual assertions and visual arguments. After reasoning that such a creature is theoretically possible, Blair presents a test case: a series of Benetton ads. In them we see how a visual argument could operate. Blair's analysis of the ads lead him to an important conclusion: Hybrid ads combining text with images often leave readers exposed to the affective power of visuals while these same readers concentrate solely on the ads' text. Blair distinguishes, most importantly, between rational and nonrational means of persuasion. In the real world, an image may persuade, but through affect rather than a reasoned choice. Therefore, it can be rhetorical, strictly speaking, but not argumentative. Blair does allow that visual arguments may tend to be one-dimensional and therefore urges that readers examine them especially critically.

Blair is the last of the scholars in this section who present theoretical and philosophical interrogations of the existence and/or legitimacy of visual arguments. In "The Problem of Electronic Argument: A Humanist's Perspective," Michele Shauf never questions the possibility or existences of visual arguments. As a rhetorician, she worries whether combining images with text in electronic creations causes students to use images as mere decoration instead of as rhetorically considered elements. Especially for technologically advanced students, the kind who attend technological universities and easily manipulate the most difficult visual packages and scripting for the World Wide Web, technology's superficial glamor easily overshadows any study of rhetorical foundations. Shauf contends that in order to focus students' attention on the importance of rhetoric, Composition Studies must pay attention to the design of arguments in any media, not just textual, and, as a discipline, take up the study of both "the logic of the image" and "the logic of space," or "the logic of subordination or the logic of proportion." For Shauf, traditional rhetorical concepts, such as metaphor, metonymy, analogy, and description, can form the basis of a visual digital rhetoric. Her work furthers the argument that using familiar rhetorical terms in the context of our students' more unfamiliar electronic practices offers us new ways to teach and critique our students' electronic work.

Shauf's major concern is that our students not adopt the rhetoric of commerce and entertainment, that is, the never-ending desire to "go-beyond" and to upgrade. She wants students to recognize as shallow such models for their electronic creations and to understand the degree to which technological discourse implicitly contradicts the values of humanistic discourse, which revisits eternal conceptual, aesthetic, and ethical questions. The humanist's rhetoric will provide the richest, most thoughtful, layered creations, ones befitting the caliber of critical thinking we expect of our students.

The final two selections, the first by Richard Lanham, and the second by Robert Horn, discuss stylistic features, or figures of rhetoric. They fit nicely together as a discussion and a literal illustration of that discussion: Horn's selection shows visual equivalents of figures that Lanham discusses. Richard Lanham's volume, *A Handlist of Rhetorical Terms*, is particularly useful for identifying rhetorical figures and understanding their effects not just on style but also on critical thinking. In the entry included here, "Figures of Rhetoric," Lanham emphasizes that rhetorical figures are more than decorative ornamentation: They are essential to seeing and thinking. They afford us a way of looking *at* the surface of language rather than *through* it for ideas: Recognizing the visual patterns of words as reflecting patterns of thoughts can help us to grasp an author's ideas.

Lanham argues that the many classifications of rhetorical figures distract from the point that we, as humans, have needed to invent verbal figures in order to focus on the verbal surfaces of written documents. They help us express arguments but also provide a way to play or entertain with language and mold language in a way that we can recognize as elegant. Figures of rhetoric also provide structures that enlarge or widen the capacity of the human brain to remember language. If figures of rhetoric serve such a function for written communication, they can also function similarly for hybrid texts combining the verbal and visual, or even for completely visual texts. Whether communicating verbally or visually, our intellects still want to engage in playful, entertaining, elegant modes of delivery that help us retain the ideas being conveyed.

If we do accept that rhetorical figures are inescapable, perhaps even necessary, for communication, we may still find ourselves wondering how to identify in images those figures we have grown accustomed to identifying only in words. Robert Horn's "Rhetorical Devices and Tight Integration" provides visual explanations for synecdoche, metonymy, and metaphor in order to make clear what shapes these three figures might take. Such concrete visual explanations might suggest ways for writing teachers to explain rhetorical concepts to their students and ultimately empower them to use rhetorical figures in their own work.

Although the forms and stories—the syntax, vocabularies, and literacies—of hybrid texts look to be new and different, the rhetoric and rhetorical strategies that digital texts embody, their visual figures and tropes, arise from ones with which we are already familiar. And more, those familiar techniques from classical rhetoric—invention, arrangement, style, delivery, and ethos—can all be communicated visually. The hybrid, multilayered texts in our posttypographic, visual world clearly involve persuasion and argumentation. By turning to the vocabulary of argument, and understanding that it also applies to the visual, we provide for ourselves a new way to think about the role of the visual in hybrid texts.

19   *Toward a Theory of Visual Argument**

DAVID S. BIRDSELL AND LEO GROARKE

These special, two issues are motivated by the conviction that argumentation theorists do not pay enough attention to the visual components of argument and persuasion. A better understanding of these components is especially important if we want to understand the role of advertising, film, television, video, multi-media, and the World Wide Web in our lives. A decision to take the visual seriously has important implications for every strand of argumentation theory, for they all emphasize a verbal paradigm which sees arguments as collections of words. Most scholars who study argumentation theory are, therefore, preoccupied with methods of analyzing arguments which emphasize verbal elements and show little or no recognition of other possibilities, or even the relationship between words and other symbolic forms. Students of argumentation emerge without the tools needed for proficiency in assessing visual modes of reasoning and persuasion. We hope that these essays will help spur the development of a more adequate theory of argument which makes room for the visual.

Though we are committed to the development of a theory of visual argument, we have chosen to begin with an article in which David Fleming details his skepticism. Visual images ("pictures") cannot, he claims, be arguments. We have begun with his paper because we want to recognize that many theorists explicitly or implicitly reject this possibility (Fleming has provided a useful bibliography), and because an answer to their objections must be the basis of a convincing account of visual argument. The rest of our issue therefore

---

From *Argumentation and Advocacy* 33 (Summer 1996): 1–10.
*Articles referred to in this chapter include the following: Barbatsis, G. S. (Fall 1996) "Look, and I will show you something you will want to see": Pictorial engagement in negative political campaign commercials. *Argumentation and Advocacy*, 33:2, 69–80. Blair, J. A. — reprinted as Chapter 21 in this volume or see (Summer 1996) The possibility and actuality of visual arguments. *Argumentation and Advocacy*, 33:1, 23–39. Fleming, D. (Summer 1996) Can pictures be arguments? *Argumentation and Advocacy*, 33:1, 11–22. Shelley, C. (Fall 1996) Rhetorical and demonstrative modes of visual argument: Looking at images of human evolution. *Argumentation and Advocacy*, 33:2, 53–68.

answers these objections. J. Anthony Blair attempts to meet them in a defense of the possibility and the nature of visual arguments. Cameron Shelley and Gretchen Barbatsis (appearing in the fall issue) examine cases which illuminate different kinds of visual argument, and propose conceptual distinctions necessary for dealing with different kinds of visual materials. The review essay by Lenore Langsdorf discusses an important book on images and persuasion and reflects more generally on the questions raised by contemporary attempts to understand visual persuasion.

In the present introduction we would like to add some comments on those concerns that strike us as most important when one considers the development of a theory of visual argument. The first issue which must be addressed is a prevalent prejudice that visual images are in some intrinsic way arbitrary, vague and ambiguous. This presumption encourages the view that visual images are less precise than words, and especially the written word. We think that this prejudice is a dogma that has outlived its usefulness, and that the first step toward a theory of visual argument must be a better appreciation of both the possibility of visual meaning and the limits of verbal meaning.

Visual images can, of course, be vague and ambiguous. But this alone does not distinguish them from words and sentences, which can also be vague and ambiguous. The inherent indeterminacy of language is one of the principal problems that confront us when we try to understand natural language argument. This is why historians endlessly debate the interpretation of historical documents, law courts struggle continuously with the implications of written and spoken claims, and personal animosities revolve around who said what and what was meant. The point that visual images are frequently vague and indeterminate cannot, in view of the demonstrable indeterminacy of verbal expressions, show that images are intrinsically less precise than spoken or written words (especially as we often clarify the latter with visual cures–as we may make the tone and meaning of a statement clear with a smile or a wink).

We can best illustrate the possibility of verbal meaning with some simple examples. We will begin with the following anti-smoking poster, which was produced by the U.S. Department of Health, Education and Welfare (now the U.S. Department of Health and Human Services). We must begin by noting that this poster is an amalgam of the verbal and the visual (see Figure 1). The important point is that this does not make its visual components redundant or superfluous. Without the visual elements, we could not understand the poster, for the verbal message it contains—"don't you get hooked!"—is vague and ambiguous. It does not explicitly refer to smoking or cigarettes and could as easily refer to drugs, alcohol, or anything else which is potentially addictive. We know it is a message about smoking only because it depicts a fish which is "hooked" to a cigarette. The message of the poster is straightforward. It can plausibly be rendered as "You should be wary of cigarettes because you could get hooked and—like a fish on a lure—endanger your health." This is a quaint argument by analogy. It does not

FIGURE 1. Anti-Smoking Poster
Source: U.S. Department of Health, Education and Welfare (1976)

match the sophistication of the visuals which crowd our television sets — and increasingly, our computer screens — but it is an argument in the standard sense: it provides a reason for a conclusion.

This and countless similar examples make it difficult to sustain the kind of skepticism of those who maintain that the visual is radically indeterminate and cannot, therefore, sustain an argument. Consider Fleming's claim that a picture itself "makes no claim which can be contested, doubted, or otherwise improved upon by others. If I oppose the 'position' you articulate in a picture, you can simply deny that your picture ever articulated that, or any other, position." As common as such views are in academic discussions of the visual, they make little sense in the context of examples like the present one. Here the argument that you should be wary of cigarettes because they can hook you and endanger your health is forwarded by means of visual images, even though it is just the sort of claim that can be contested, doubted and improved upon. We too easily forget that there was a time when debates raged about the addictive qualities and the health effects of cigarettes. If someone viewing our sample poster did not "read" it as an attack on smoking (or arbitrarily denied that it "ever articulated that, or any other position"), then we are forced to the conclusion that they have radically misunderstood the visual image — to a point where we might reasonably wonder about their ability to comprehend the visual (much as we would wonder about someone's ability to understand English if they did not understand the corresponding verbal argument to be an attack on smoking).

Consider a second case which also illustrates the point that visual meaning can be in some cases neither arbitrary nor indeterminate. The following drawing is based on a 1926 editorial cartoon by S.K. Suvanto. The original cartoon was published in *The Daily Worker*, a socialist newspaper published in Chicago from 1924–1958 (see Figure 2). Though we are far removed from the context which produced this cartoon, we still readily understand it, even if we ignore its title (the words in the title add nothing which is not obvious in the image itself). In the background we see the flag of the former Soviet

FIGURE 2. "The Model and the Painting" (After K. A. Suvanto)

Union—a hammer and sickle—and the silhouette of a Russian worker. The sky suggests dawn. The lattice of new buildings suggests the new industrial communist society. In the foreground we see a painter with an easel. His exaggerated obesity, his suit and his bald head are standard symbols of the capitalist. He is painting the scene in the background but what he paints bears scant resemblance to the "actual" image we see. In his canvas, the hammer and sickle in the flag—symbols of work—become a skull and cross bones. The hammer in the worker's hand becomes a bloody dagger which the worker—who has become a ruthless soldier—is plunging into a victim he grasps with his other hand.

Once again, meaning in our example is straightforward. We can discern a whole set of visual claims: Soviet communism is hard at work building a new industrial society; commentators who portray the Soviets as bent on violence and repression distort the facts; they themselves are greedy and self-interested capitalists. Taken together, these claims lead to the obvious conclusion that we should not listen to those who attack the new Soviet experiment.

Such examples leave little room for the presumption that visual meaning is necessarily arbitrary or indeterminate. The claims Suvanto makes in his cartoon are, moreover, just the sorts of claims which are open to debate, confirmation, and argument. Someone who does not see his cartoon as an answer to criticisms of Soviet communism has radically misunderstood the point. Of course, one might debate specific points of interpretation (whether there is, for example, some significance in the fact that the *left* hand of the soldier in the painter's painting clutches his victim's throat) and one might fail to understand the visual vocabulary (a teenager might, for example, not understand the references to the Soviet Union or to capitalism). But these issues of interpretation are comparable to the issues that arise in the attempt to interpret verbal claims—the remarks of a political speaker, for example—and cannot be used to show that visual claims are radically indeterminate.

What we have said about these two examples applies equally well to more sophisticated visual images. In the articles in this double issue, Blair shows how a Benetton ad can reasonably be deciphered, Barbatsis illustrates how a television camera can convey an argument and Shelley shows how drawings taken from articles on paleontology forward two different kinds of visual arguments. Fleming is right to point out that argumentation theory lacks a well developed account of the distinction between visual premises and conclusions, but this is because we have not taken seriously the possibility of visual meaning, not because visual images are—as so many commentators presume—necessarily indeterminate.

It does not follow that verbal and visual meanings are equivalent or identical. There are good reasons for questioning whether they have a similar capacity to convey relatively precise meanings. We merely observe that both can be ambiguous or cogent and that both can convey claims and arguments. The meaning of a visual claim or argument obviously depends on a complex set of relationships between a particular image/text and a given set of interpreters. The recognition that visual meaning is not necessarily arbitrary is the crucial first step that we must take in our development of a theory of visual argument.

The importance of context is the second issue that we feel must be addressed in developing such a theory. We do not expect words (at least not all words) to have solid, unassailable meanings of their own. Instead, we look to companion sentences and paragraphs to ascertain contextual meanings which may or may not be corroborated by dictionary definitions. The word "well," standing alone, could refer to my health, my skepticism, or the municipal water supply. If you read the sentence "I am well, thank you," then the context makes it clear that the first meaning is intended. Context plays a similar role when you hear someone ask me how I feel, in which case the single word "well" would be a terse but perfectly intelligible reply.

There is of course more to the process of assessing meaning and its context than examining words on a page or puzzling through sounds we hear. "Context" can involve a wide range of cultural assumptions, situational cues, time-sensitive information, and/or knowledge of a specific interlocutor. The immediate verbal context of a sentence is only one source of information interpreters use in determining the meaning of a string of words. Imagine that you overhear the following exchange:

JONATHAN: Do you think the faculty will get a raise this year?

MARYANN: Oh, sure. Now that we have a growing deficit, enormous new demands on our operating budget, flat revenues, and a government hostile to public education, I expect 15%!

In such circumstances, it is hard to imagine Jonathan concluding that Maryann actually means that a 15% raise is in the offing, or, more naively still, that Maryann has made a poor argument. Assuming minimal communicative competency on Maryann's part, tone of voice alone will indicate her sarcasm. Assuming that there has never been a raise as significant as 15%, the contextually initiated will recognize that Maryann's response should not be taken at face value. The words alone do not convey these meanings, which are instead conveyed by the contextual cues.

Considered against the background of this familiar feature of verbal communication, there is no reason to assume that a visual image must conduct its contributions to argument in perfect isolation. Yet this assumption undergirds David Fleming's examination of visual argument and drives a good deal of the thinking that presupposes significant, inherent, and universal differences separating the verbal and the visual. We would never banish the consideration of contextual evidence when we consider verbal arguments, especially if we wish to understand their real-world efficacy. It would make no sense to take single words as units of argumentation unless they were clearly understandable as truncated references to more complete propositions. Why then would we assume that photographs should be examined in isolation from one another, or from verbal statements with which they are juxtaposed?

At least three kinds of context are important in the evaluation of visual arguments: immediate visual context, immediate verbal context, and visual culture. The significance of immediate visual context is most obvious in film, for it incorporates a progression of images which allows us to recognize a single frame as part of an overarching argument. Depending on the sequence of frames of which it is a part, an image of a man holding a knife may represent someone preparing to cook, a knife salesman, or, more insidiously, evidence that someone is prepared to commit a murder. Sequences of images also play a role in other contexts. Instructional diagrams often use a progression of images to show viewers how to perform simple tasks. Cameron Shelley (in part two of this issue) shows that such diagrams can forward arguments.

Immediate visual contexts, however, encompass more than sequences of images. In judging such contexts we must often pay attention to visual cues beyond a single message source. Elements of the ambient visual environment can be equally influential in providing contextual cues to the interpretation of visual materials.

Immediate verbal context also provides a basis for the interpretation of visual images. A number of commentators (see Fleming in this issue) treat captions and other direct verbal references acting in concert with images as special cases, as indeed they are. It does not follow that the role of the image in a verbal-visual equation is unimportant, or secondary. Words can establish a context of meaning into which images can enter with a high degree of specificity while achieving a meaning different from the words alone. We see this in our first example, in which the words tell us that we are dealing with something which is addictive and harmful, while the visual image establishes that the topic is smoking.

Fleming explains another verbal-visual relationship in his remarks about visual evidence. But Fleming's formulation is limited by his emphasis on immediate verbal contexts which incorporate explicit claim/image interactions. The drawing based on the Suvanto cartoon invokes a much richer relationship between a larger and more general verbal context (communist narratives of the hostility of capital to the achievements of labor) and a specific visual rendition of the assertion that capitalists lie about communism. The implicit verbal backdrop that allows us to derive arguments from images is clearly different from the immediate context created by the placement of a caption beside an image.

When we incorporate conventionalized, situation-specific meanings within the process of interpreting visual arguments, we effectively extend the traditional verbal enthymeme. Suvanto's capitalist, for example, is a conventionalized image, easily recognizable as a type that could be invoked in a narrative description as readily as a visual depiction, particularly in the pages of *The Daily Worker*. But the imagistic recall is likely to be different from the verbal; we still need to be attentive to the way that a given image calls attention to the type. In this case, the drawing emphasizes physical characteristics, implicitly arguing against romantic images of capitalism—the beauty, glamor, and power of Hollywood, for example—by emphasizing "undesirable" physical traits like corpulence, baldness, and age. In other images, the dyslogies of depiction extend to demonizing qualities, such as the appearance of fangs and claws. In part two of this double issue, Shelley shows how subtle physical characteristics portrayed in a visual image can convey arguments about human evolution.

A third kind of context is supplied by visual culture, which differs from the first two categories principally in its indirect influence on the production of visual meaning. Many scholars have argued that visual culture changes significantly over time, and that developments in art, technology, philosophy, and science promote different ways of seeing over time. These scholars are for the most part careful to distinguish between the notions of "change" and "progress." They argue not that painting, or sculpture, or any other form of art has necessarily improved over time, but quite precisely that it differs, reflecting different values, production, and habits of interpretation. Cultural conventions of vision in this sense include what it means to see, or to represent seeing, as well as changes in the meaning of particular elements of visual vocabulary.

This is not the place for a comprehensive discussion of such complex ideas, but the basic concept can be illustrated readily by changes in television styles over the past thirty years. In the 1960s, television shots were considerably longer than those we find in the jumpy, quick edits typified by music videos in the 1990s. This change reflects something more than the difference between the evening news and MTV. Shot length has been reduced in almost all commercial television, and the number of shots per minute has surged. Much as cubism tried to present multiple perspectives unfolding over time and/or space on a single, two-dimensional frame, the quick-cut video editing style of the 1990s prefers several quiet perspectives on a subject over the single, probing, shot that holds an image for minutes at a time. The result is a combination of visuals that decenters a unitary perspectivalism. No one camera is all-knowing and the subject is deliberately distorted with the use of negative effects or other filters that "reveal" different elements of the subject-as-source for videographic play.

Visual culture provides the broad master narratives of design which are the background for more specific visual (or for that matter, verbal) texts which perpetuate or challenge those narratives. Martin Jay's work identifies "scopic regimes" peculiar to historical periods. Students of argumentation have accepted since Aristotle the influence of acculturation in the production of verbal enthymemes. We are now arguing that the same allowances must be made for visual commonplaces as well, allowing potential visual arguments to draw on the same range of resources that we afford potential verbal arguments.

The changes in visual meaning made plain in studies of visual culture suggest a third issue which must be the basis of a satisfactory theory of visual argument. It concerns the meaning of "resemblance." In his article, David Fleming restricts his analysis to images that are created in an effort to resemble what they represent. We do not dispute the existence of a category of imagery that purports to represent reality, but we want both to problematize the notion and note that argumentation plays a key role in determining resemblance and representation (which constitute another way in which visuals are linked to argument). At issue here is a complex set of relationships having to do with representation and resemblance per se. The topic is too large to address thoroughly in this introduction, but three of its elements bear mention: the disjunction between resemblance and representation, the consequent conventionalization of representation, and the susceptibility of resemblance to visual and verbal challenge.

While most observers would say that a well-executed "realistic" portrait *resembles* the sitter, it may or may not adequately *represent* the sitter. If I sit for a portrait wearing a gorilla suit, a realistic painting, even a photograph, will resemble me (sitting in front of the artist, in a gorilla suit). But does it represent me? A caricaturist's line drawing (consider the famous profile of Alfred Hitchcock that became the lead-in to his television series) that cannot be said to resemble anyone in any detailed way may serve as a good representation of a sitter. Such examples show that while representation is a more ambiguous concept than resemblance, resemblance is itself fraught with judgment. What, exactly, should a successful visual image of a sitter "resemble"? Should it be the sitter's present attitude, the sitter's most common expression, a characteristic gesture?

These difficult questions posed by resemblance and representation have encouraged a wide reliance on conventionalized representations that are easily used in arguments. Heraldry is a conventionalized representation of a family. King Francis I of France was represented by the salamander, though he could hardly be said to have resembled one. In the sixteenth century, the Visconti family was visually represented by a serpent eating a child. While there is no "photographic" resemblance one might say that this demonstration of raw power represents (or metaphorically "resembles") the family's own. Likewise, the President of the United States is represented by his seal, which does not "resemble" him. In fact, because the seal's eagle motif is highly abstracted, appearing in a posture that no "real" eagle could attain in life, it is debatable whether the symbol even resembles a real eagle.

The shifting standards applied to resemblances make them subject to challenge on two argumentative levels. First, they may not in fact resemble (anyone who has argued with a photographer over the quality of a graduation or a wedding picture will have no trouble coming up with cases), and second, they may not represent. The kinds of arguments this implies can be conducted either visually or verbally. In this double issue they are reflected in Barbatsis' analysis of visual images in advertisements aired during the 1988 presidential campaign. One of the principal visual techniques she identifies is the deconstruction of an apparent resemblance in favor of an allegedly more accurate representation in political advertising. The point is not that the preferred alternative is or is not "genuinely" more accurate, but that through the application of visual techniques rather than verbal narrative, the question of resemblance has entered directly into the argument.

So far, we have suggested three prerequisites for a satisfactory account of visual argument: we must accept the possibility of visual meaning, we must make more of an effort to consider images in context, and we must recognize the argumentative aspects of representation and resemblance. We want to finish by more tentatively noting another issue raised by the attempt to formulate a theory of visual argument. Blair raises the issue in his article when he offers an account of visual argument which places significant limits on the visuals we can classify as arguments. In part, these limits are imposed by his distinction between argument and persuasion, suggesting that many of the visuals one might consider arguments are instances of persuasion *rather* than argument. Intuitively, there is something to his suggestion that such visual presentations are attempts to convince in a way that purposely circumvents argumentation and the reflection it implies. Considered from this point of view, the attempt to convince a dieter to eat a piece of cake by holding it under his or her nose is not, it seems, an argument.

Or is it? Why not take the holding of the cake in front of the dieter's nose to be a particularly forceful way of expressing the argument that "Eating this cake would be wonderful, therefore you should forget your diet and eat it"? So construed this is an argument. One might compare the ancient story that Diogenes the Cynic is said to have responded to Zeno's famous arguments against motion by walking a few steps and declaring "I refute Zeno thus." Surely this *is* an argument. But it is also an attempt to circumvent the reasoning and the reflection that accompanies Zeno's paradoxes.

Forbes I. Hill (1983) locates, in Aristotle's *Rhetoric*, support for the notion that visual appeals to desire influence our actions. As Hill puts it, "Aristotle's view of the pathe [feelings] is extremely intellectualized. To come into a state of feeling an auditor must make a complex judgment about himself in relation to external events. If he is incapable of making this judgment, he will not come into the state of feeling" (p. 47). Such a view collapses the distinction between "psychological and logical proof" by making appeals to feelings appeals to certain kinds of judgments. From this point of view, we "argue a person into a state of feeling."

At the very least it must be said that this way of extending the theory of visual argument has some intriguing consequences that are worth exploring. Most importantly, it allows for a significant expansion of the theory of argument. Without this expansion, argumentation theory has no way of dealing with a great many visual ploys that play a significant role in our argumentative lives — even though they can frequently be assessed from the point of view of argumentative criteria. Aristotle's notions of logos, ethos, and pathos can, for example, frequently be used to shed light on such circumstances, even when we have something that falls short of what we would normally count as a fully fledged argument. It is in view of this that the standard distinction between argument and persuasion needs to be reconsidered in the realm of visual argument.

Any account of visual argumentation must identify how we can (a) identify the internal elements of a visual image, (b) understand the contexts in which images are interpreted, (c) establish the consistency of an interpretation of the visual, and (d) chart changes in visual perspectives over time. These issues have been explored at length — albeit without a full appreciation of their relevance to argumentation studies — in the fields of art history, cognitive psychology, media studies, semiotics, and visual culture. The rich diversity of perspectives discussed in Langsdorf's review in this issue provides a good starting point for fruitful explorations of the literature this implies, but students of argument interested in the visual should obviously go beyond the single collection she discusses if they wish to engage the burgeoning scholarship in visual theory.

In the highly selective annotated bibliography that follows, we have chosen a few titles that speak very clearly to concerns that parallel the sort of broad understanding any argumentation scholar would want to bring to the examination of a verbal enthymeme. It is a literature to which we may reasonably expect to contribute ourselves. Missing from much of the analysis of visual imagery is the careful consideration of argumentation evidenced in the close readings of cases provided by Blair, Shelley, and Barbatsis. Though arriving at different conclusions about the project of visual argumentation, David Fleming exhibits much the same kind of concern by insisting that we actually find elements of something recognizable as argument before proceeding to an "argumentative" analysis of a picture, a condition that we feel the other three authors have amply demonstrated in their essays.

Our contributions to understandings of the visual will come from our ability to flesh out theories of visual argumentation as rich and as rigorous as those we have developed for verbal argumentation. In the process of developing a theory of visual argument, we will have to emphasize the frequent lucidity of visual meaning, the importance of visual context, the argumentative complexities raised by the notions of representation and resemblance, and the questions visual persuasion poses for the standard distinction between argument and persuasion. Coupled with respect for existing interdisciplinary literature on the visual, such an emphasis promises a much better account of verbal and visual argument which can better understand the complexities of both visual images and ordinary argument as they are so often intertwined in our increasingly visual media.

SELECTED ANNOTATED BIBLIOGRAPHY

Brennan, T. and Jay, M. (Eds.). (1996). *Vision in context: Historical and contemporary perspectives on sight*. New York: Routledge. A highly eclectic collection of essays on vision from scholars in a wide range of disciplines. Argumentation scholars will find particularly useful the first five essays on the changed and changing roles of vision at different points in history. Later essays address issues relating to vision and gender, vision and subjectivity, and visual studies and interpretation.

Bryson, N., Holly, M. and Moxey, K. (1991). *Visual theory: Painting and interpretation*. New York: HarperCollins. The articles in this collection range from elements of semiology to situated seeing. Every article is followed by at least one commentary, making this volume a particularly rich exploration of the issues raised. Argumentation scholars will want to pay close attention to the authors' treatment of arguments about visual materials and visual theory.

Foster, H. (1988). *Vision and visuality*. Seattle: Bay Press. This collection sponsored by the Dia Art Foundation, is a brief (135 pp.) introduction to several important themes in the study of visual culture. Particularly valuable are Martin Jay's essay "Scopic Regimes of Modernity," and Norman Bryson's discussion of interpretive subjectivity in "The Gaze in the Expanded Field."

Gombrich, E. H. (1989). *Art and illusion: A study in the psychology of pictorial representation*. Princeton: Princeton UP. This classic work, originally published in 1960, sets out to explore the relationships among culture, perception, and forms of artistic production. Written before the development of most visual theories based on postmodernism or electronic media, *Art and Illusion* is a useful starting point for those who find the latter perspectives uncongenial.

Horace, B., Blakemore, C., and Weston-Smith, M. (Eds.). (1990). *Images and understanding*. Cambridge: Cambridge UP. This collection of essays, based on the Rank Prize Funds' International Symposium in October 1986, emphasizes cognitive approaches to visual understanding in the context of commentary from art historians and theorists.

Jay, M. (1993). *Downcast eyes: The denigration of vision in 20th century French thought*. Berkeley: U or California P. Here Jay explores vision as a cultural product, and particularly as the product of intellectual/artistic culture. The analyses of Bataille's and Lacan's contributions to perspectives on vision are invaluable.

Jenks, C. (Ed). (1995). *Visual culture*. London: Routledge. This volume contains essays on visual culture from a British cultural studies perspective. Readers interested in visual issues in electronic media will find this study particularly useful.

Melville, S. and Readings, B. (Eds.). (1995). *Vision and textuality*. Durham: Duke UP. This volume collects essays oriented around questions of disciplinarity in visual studies. Argumentation scholars hoping to understand academic institutionalization of vision will find several essays useful. Helpful as well is a repeated emphasis on verbal/visual issues.

Mitchell, W. J. T. (1986). *Iconology: Image, text, ideology*. Chicago: U of Chicago P. This is an enormously influential study of the shifting fortunes of visually and verbally based systems of meaning in western culture. Mitchell provides a lucid explanation of the stakes in preferring the visual to the verbal and vice versa. His is also the best single-volume exploration of the broad sweep of intellectual history on these issues.

Panofsky, E. (1995). *Meaning in the visual arts*. Garden City, NY: Doubleday Anchor. This is in part Panofsky's most accessible text on the nature of pre-iconographic, iconographic, and iconological analysis. These distinctions are very helpful for anyone attempting to "read" an image.

Sherman, C. R (1995). *Imaging Aristotle: Verbal and visual representation in fourteenth century France*. Berkeley: U of California P. This richly illustrated volume examines the use of manuscript illumination in the first French translations of Aristotle. Sherman shows how the illuminations themselves conveyed important arguments about state power generally and Charles V in particular. The fact that the analysis focuses on the works of Aristotle makes this book uniquely accessible to argumentation scholars.

SOURCE CITED

Hill, F. I. (1983). The rhetoric of Aristotle. In J.J. Murphy (Ed.), *A Synoptic History of Classical Rhetoric* (pp. 19–76). Davis CA: Hermagoras Press.

20   Building Visual Communication Theory by Borrowing from Rhetoric

KEITH KENNEY

Robert T. Craig (1999) argues that a field of communication theory does not yet exist. Instead, scholars work within narrow disciplines or "traditions." He distinguishes seven traditions of communication theory: rhetorical, semiotic, phenomenological, cybernetic, socio-psychological, socio-cultural, and critical. Craig believes that each tradition derives from certain commonplace beliefs, and each tradition challenges other beliefs. To become a coherent field of communication, these traditions cannot develop in total isolation from each other, but must engage each other in argument as their beliefs are compared and contrasted. If all goes well, "dialogical-dialectical coherence" results. The goal of this special issue of *Journal of Visual Literacy* is to begin to look at the key issues, concepts, and research questions of the various traditions of VISUAL communication theory so that the "argument" may begin for scholars investigating photographs, video, film, paintings, cartoons, and other visual media.

This article begins by examining rhetoric's traditional and symbolic perspectives. A selective review of the visual rhetoric literature then shows how key rhetorical concepts have been applied to visual means of communication. The value of using a traditional rhetorical perspective is demonstrated with a case study of how photographs and video were used to persuade a county council to limit the number of additional billboards. The value of a symbolic rhetorical perspective is demonstrated by re-analyzing the work of David Perlmutter (1998) concerning the effects of four famous photographs upon American foreign policy.

TRADITIONAL (CLASSICAL) PERSPECTIVE

The *traditional perspective*, based upon Aristotle's teachings, assumes that people are, by nature, subject to and capable of persuasion because, unlike other species, we have the capacity to be rational. Of course emotional,

From *Journal of Visual Literacy* 22:1 (Spring 2002): 53–80.

321

psychological, and physiological factors also affect persuasion, but classical rhetoric insists that such appeals are subsidiary to, or contingent upon, judgments resulting from rational means of persuasion. Rhetoric is viewed as a battle of words, in which speakers attempt to overcome resistance to a course of action, an idea, or a particular judgment by effectively expressing their thoughts in particular situations.

Rhetoric traditionally was considered to be public, contextual, and contingent. It was *public* because it affected the entire community and was typically performed before law courts, legislative assemblies, and celebratory gatherings of citizens. Rhetoric was *contextual* because the meaning of a particular figure of speech or example derived from the particular experiences of a particular audience addressed by a particular speaker at a particular moment. Situations were *contingent* because the speaker couldn't know ahead of time what was most important or most necessary to say in order to persuade an audience. Unlike scientists who use systematic, empirical, and objective investigation, or artists who wish to create works with timeless quality, rhetors rely on probability and they seek timely and fitting action (Lucaites, Condit, & Caudill, 1999).

All choices, from the arguments to the style of delivery, were assumed to be conscious decisions made to produce an intended effect on listeners. Critics sought an understanding of both a speaker's intentions and the potential effects upon an audience by asking why a speaker chose to talk about certain topics, why the artistic elements of his speech were structured as they were, why certain styles of speech were followed, and so forth. The critic's job was to assess how closely the speaker came to accomplishing what could have been achieved given the circumstances.

The typical approach to neo-Aristotelian criticism was to use classical rhetorical categories to describe and explain oral persuasive messages. Wichelns explains:

> Rhetorical criticism is necessarily analytical. The scheme of a rhetorical study includes the element of the speaker's personality as a conditioning factor; it includes also the public character of the man—not what he was but what he was thought to be. It requires a description of the speaker's audience, and of the leading ideas with which he plied his hearers—his topics, the motives to which he appealed, the nature of proofs he offered. These will reveal his own judgment of human nature in his audiences, and also his judgment on the questions which he discussed. Nor can rhetorical criticism omit the speaker's mode of arrangement and his mode of expression, nor his habit of preparation and his manner of delivery from the platform; though the last two are perhaps less significant. "Style"—in the sense which corresponds to diction and sentence movement—must receive attention, but only as one among various means that secure for the speaker ready access to the minds of his auditors. Finally, the effect of the discourse on its immediate hearers is not to be ignored, neither in the testing of witnesses, nor in the record of events. And throughout such a study one must conceive of the public man as influencing the men of his own times by the power of his discourse (1980, pp. 69, 70).

Neo-classical critics, following what they believed to be Aristotle's lead, disregarded many manifestations of symbolic meaning that were nonverbal and non-oral as being irrelevant to their concerns, and they further disregarded those oral modes of discourse that did not appear to exhibit patterns of (rational) reasoning. Beginning in 1970, however, the scope of rhetorical criticism was expanded to include nondiscursive subjects, and the next sections describe a few of the more important examples of traditional perspective applied to visual forms of communication.

APPLICATION OF NEO-CLASSICAL PERSPECTIVE TO CARTOONS

Medhurst and DeSousa (1981) used slightly modified versions of Aristotle's five *canons*—invention, disposition, style, memory and delivery—as a means to understand graphic persuasion in political cartoons. The first three canons were easy to "translate" into a new medium. Like speakers, cartoonists draw upon a storehouse of inventional *topoi*—political commonplaces, cultural allusions, character traits—and use those *topoi* to construct arguments. Like speakers, cartoonists use contrast, commentary, and contradiction as formal organizing principles, or *disposition*. For style, rather than finding equivalences for verbal figures and tropes, the authors explained how use of line and form, exaggeration of physiognomical features, placement within the frame, relative size of objects, relation of text to visual imagery, and rhythmic montage have persuasive potential.

Medhurst and DeSousa were ingenious when applying the canons of memory and delivery. In the classical tradition, a speaker had a good *memory* if he (normally a man) could construct a mental image filled with specific icons, which the rhetor then associated with particular ideas, and the placement of the icons correlated with the order in which the ideas were to be presented. Movement was from visual mental construction, to specific idea, to oral discourse. With political cartoons, Medhurst and DeSousa write, the movement is reversed. The cartoonist starts with the universe of discourse—oral, written and pictorial—from which he (again, cartoonists are usually male) selects a specific idea and then draws a visual sign to represent that idea. In graphic expression, therefore, memory is primarily an art of evocation. The cartoonist attempts to compress into a single image the various streams of cultural consciousness from which he has drawn his idea. Readers then are expected to unpack one or more layers of available cultural consciousness that the cartoon has evoked from them. The cartoons "work" to the extent that readers and cartoonists share cultural symbols.

In the classical tradition, speakers could use volume, tone, rate, pitch, and so forth to get and keep listeners' interest when *delivering* their message. When applied to the medium of newspapers, the canon of delivery is reconceptualized as image placement, size, and typeface to get and keep readers' attention. Although others have used rhetoric to analyze editorial cartoons, no one (including Medhurst and DeSousa) has applied this typology to critique a particular set of cartoons.

APPLICATION OF RHETORICAL STYLE TO MAGAZINE ADVERTISEMENTS

Rhetorical *figures,* defined as artful deviations, are considered a stylistic device, and rhetorical critics of oral, written, or visual messages frequently note their presence and categorization. McQuarrie and Mick (1996) provide a sophisticated analysis of why advertisements with visual figures are more memorable and give consumers greater pleasure than ads without figures. They distinguish two types of rhetorical figures: schemes and tropes. *Schemes* occur when a text contains excessive order or regularity, so schemes add internal redundancy to advertising messages, and readers will have multiple possibilities to retrieve the message. Examples of schemes are rhyme, alliteration, and antithesis. *Tropes* contain a deficiency of order or irregularities, so tropes lack closure, and readers will be invited to *elaborate,* or engage or interpret a text. Examples of tropes are hyperbole, metonym, metaphor, pun, irony, and paradox. The additional cognitive activity of schemes and tropes, therefore, increases the number of associative pathways stored in memory and makes retrieval of messages easier.

Later, McQuarrie and Mick (1999) used four test magazine advertisements with different visual figures, as well as four manipulated copies of the ads without visual figures, in order to test their theory. For example, a mascara ad originally used *visual rhyme* in that the eyelashes of the model echoed the contours of her fur coat. Visual rhyme is an example of a *scheme* because it has "excessive order or regularity," so it was expected to add internal redundancy to the advertising message and provide multiple opportunities for retrieval. In the manipulated ad, the fur ends were airbrushed to remove their texture, eliminating the repetition of contours. A motion sickness remedy ad, on the other hand, originally used *visual metaphor* by depicting a package of Dramamine as a seat belt buckle. Visual metaphor is an example of a *trope* because it has a "deficiency of order," so it was expected to increase the number of associations and to make retrieval easier. In the manipulated ad, a buckle was added to the seat belt and the package was moved further away to break the metaphor. An experiment with seventy-two undergraduates then demonstrated that the manipulated ads indeed led to greater elaboration. The authors then conducted a second experiment, which supported their theory that visual rhetoric leads to a positive attitude to the advertisements. Between the two experiments, they showed that the persuasive effect of visual figures held across samples and product categories.

CAN VISUALS FORM RATIONAL ARGUMENTS?

When rhetorical critics use the word *argument* they mean the presentation of premises followed by a conclusion, and they mean a debate in which disagreement is expressed. By such standards, it is not obvious whether or not pictures can argue.

Some scholars deny the possibility of visual arguments because visual images do not have explicit meanings, so they lack clear premises. Birdsell and Groarke (1996), however, write that if visuals lack explicit meanings, then so do words—the meanings of both are dependent upon their context. For visual images, three kinds of context are important—immediate visual context, immediate verbal context, and visual culture. Most people have no trouble understanding *immediate* visual and verbal contexts, but they may have problems with visual culture because visual culture changes significantly over time, and some people may lack visual cultural literacy. In order for visuals to have more explicit meanings, therefore, the authors recommend charting changes of visual culture over time.

Scholars also deny the possibility of visual arguments because pictures are perceived as a whole, rather than processed sequentially; therefore, pictures lack the two-part relationship of premises leading to conclusions. The solution to the problem of finding both premises and conclusions within a visual, Blair (1996) writes, is the interplay between the visual itself and the visual's context. The eight-page block advertising for Benetton clothing, he explains, is an example of a visual argument against racism (but not an argument for buying from Benetton). The first two-page spread shows three hearts, suggesting we're all human. The next spread shows a white girl and black girl hugging, suggesting innocent children have no racial prejudices. The third spread shows a black hand manacled to a white one, suggesting we are locked together, and there is no escaping our condition and we are prisoners of our own prejudices. From these suggestive photos, we get the following premises:

1. We are all the same under our skin;

2. Racism is a construct, not an inborn attitude;

3. We are joined together, black and white, inescapably; we are prisoners of our attitudes. The conclusion is that racism is unjustified and should be ended.

Finally, some scholars deny the possibility of visual arguments because they believe pictures cannot point out the weaknesses in opposing arguments. Lake and Pickering (1998), however, contend that visual arguments can refute one another even though they do not, strictly speaking, negate one another. Such refutation can be accomplished:

1. through *substitution*, in which one image is replaced within a larger visual frame by a different image with an opposing polarity; and

2. through *transformation*, in which an image is "recontextualized in a new visual frame, such that its polarity is modified or reversed through association with different images" (p. 82).

Lake and Pickering (1998) illustrate the concept of substitution with an account of Planned Parenthood's rebuttal film, which was created after the anti-abortion film *Silent Scream* received much media attention. In *Silent Scream*, women seemed limited to their ability to bear children. No woman speaks in the entire film. Visually, they are depicted as passive, pregnant objects victimized by "abortionists." In the response film, however, audiences see images of women as active professionals. They speak extensively and authoritatively on a number of issues. Planned Parenthood's film also shifts viewer attention from the *act* of abortion to the *reasons* for abortion, so women's motivations become visible for the first time. The active, outspoken achieving women in Planned Parenthood's film, therefore, serve as a counterargument to the original lack of presence of women in *Silent Scream*.

The concept of transformation is vividly illustrated by "reframing" and "mobile framing," two techniques used by filmmakers when photographing still images for their movies or videos. Ken Burns, for example uses reframing when he only shows part of an original photograph. He uses mobile framing when pans, tilts, or tracking shots prolong, beyond normal expectations, the time it takes viewers to decipher exactly what they are seeing. Lancioni (1996) explains that both techniques are used to foreground ideological implications. With "reframing," the same photo can have several meanings, depending on which aspects of it are foregrounded. With "mobile framing," delayed recognition obliges us to reflect on the meaning of the images. The techniques of mobile framing and reframing demonstrate that the social relationships previously regarded as "real" and constant are, in fact, susceptible to change.

Visuals, therefore, can be said to persuade by argument when we have the ability to choose. Visuals also must:

1. provide reasons for choosing one way or another;
2. counter other arguments, perhaps via substitution or transformation; and
3. cause us to change our beliefs or to act.

A BILLBOARD CAMPAIGN

A journalism and mass communications professor, Dan (name changed), has been leading a group of local citizens in an effort to stop the proliferation of billboards (see Figure 1). This section will apply a traditional rhetorical perspective to critique his efforts to visually persuade the local county council that there are too many billboards and they are visual clutter.

Traditional criticism evaluates the various choices that were made throughout the persuasion process and, of course, the final effects. Was Dan the best possible visual communicator (speaker)? In this case, yes. He knows how to do research, so he is well informed about the billboard problem around the country. He teaches graphics and public relations, so he knows how to create visually effective messages that the media will want to use. He has been a community activist for years, so he has credibility within the community, and he can link the community's efforts to similar efforts around the state and country. He can take pictures and shoot video that are easily understood by general audiences, but he is NOT a professional photographer, so the images do not appear to have been (and were NOT) taken by someone hired to make a certain point. Dan's images seem more "realistic," "documentary," and, therefore, "truthful" because they lack the slick, high production quality that would occur if an advertising or public relations photographer was given the job.

FIGURE 1. Protesting Billboard Clutter

Van Kornegay

Evidence of his effectiveness as a visual communicator came from his opponents, the billboard industry. At one point in the hearing, a billboard spokesperson told the audience that Dan had introduced himself but had not told them who he was; that he was a journalism professor who knows "how to manipulate the media." True, Dan knows how to get his views into the newspaper better than many people. For example, during one presentation, he showed a photograph of a river with the city's skyline in the background and a billboard sign in the middle of the river. Then he showed the same image after he had digitally removed the billboard, visually depicting how much nicer the view would be without "visual clutter." (See Figures 2 and 3.) This is an example of "antithesis," a *scheme* that is a type of visual figure that helps people remember messages. After the presentation, he handed the reporter a computer disk that contained the before-and-after images of the billboard in the river. Rather than bringing editors a bland meeting picture, the reporter (easily) delivered two emotionally powerful images for the next day's newspaper.

Dan understood his audience, a group of conservative politicians, as demonstrated by the first visual image in his PowerPoint presentation of an interstate billboard promoting a strip club. He knew the council would find the image of a stripper offensive and would be embarrassed, which was the entire point; billboards make (some) people uncomfortable, yet people cannot get away from billboards. The NIMBY (not-in-my-backyard) attitude towards the sex industry might carry over to billboards in general.

FIGURE 2. City River and Skyline with Billboard

Van Kornegay

FIGURE 3. City River and Skyline with Billboard Removed

Van Kornegay

Another major idea (*topoi*), and a good choice, was that billboards are a form of litter. Local football coach Lou Holtz is known not only for football and motivational speaking, but also for his dislike of litter. Holtz informally leads a publicity campaign to clean up trash (on the ground) of the state's roads, so litter is a high-profile issue. This idea was visually communicated two ways. First, Dan went around town photographing billboards with peeling signs, and to each picture he added the bold headline "Litter on a Stick." This effective element of *style* used the *metaphor*, "litter on a stick," to compare billboards to oversized pieces of trash raised up high. Another effective element of style was *repetition*. The audience saw many photographs of peeling billboards and these repetitions made the billboard problem seem to grow and grow. Certainly the billboard people found the message effective because the next day every peeling billboard shown in Dan's presentation was replaced with a new sign, generally a public service advertisement to prevent forest fires (see Figures 4 and 5). At their next encounter, Dan teased that the number of forest fires had recently declined (the area is an urban environment where forest fires do not pose a risk).

Dan also shot video of billboard-related litter. The sequence begins with a light shot of litter on the ground. The camera then tilts up and zooms out to reveal a medium shot of a billboard with a peeling sign. This device evokes *memories* of a searchlight as the audience sees the "problem" (trash on the ground) and then the camcorder jerkily moves up and around until it has the "villain" (billboard) in its "beam." The ground litter obviously came from the peeling billboard above.

Dan's visuals appealed to people's need to exercise some control over their environment and to their desire to have an attractive home. The billboard industry claimed that only two areas had a high density of billboards—Decker and Two-Notch roads. To refute this claim, Dan used pictures from locations around the city to show the intrusiveness of billboards. He also went to an area with a high concentration of billboards and used a telephoto lens to compress distance, making the density of billboards seem even higher. The pictures make it seem as if the billboards are multiplying beyond anyone's control. They *say*: "Look at what's happening in our own backyard—and we aren't doing anything about it!" Then Dan showed pictures of beautiful streets without billboards. These pictures *say*: "If we work together to limit billboards, we can have an attractive city." The *disposition*, therefore, was "contrast" between the tree-lined and billboard-cluttered streets.

Dan copied a technique commonly used by *60 Minutes* investigative reporters. He first showed the home page of the Outdoor Advertising Association's Web site. Dan then enlarged and added dramatic drop shadows to selected portions of the site's text. One passage said, "Billboards grab you; they make you look." Another said, "Billboards operate in the people's space, creating a veritable theater of the streets." So Dan used the billboard industry's words to make his point that the billboard industry is using something of value (people's space) and that they are intrusive (they make you look),

FIGURE 4. Billboard with Peeling Sign, Depicting "Litter on a Stick"

Van Kornegay

FIGURE 5. Site with Peeling Billboard Removed

Van Kornegay

but, of course, Dan's conclusion differs; rather than invest in more billboards, he argues for additional regulation.

Normally when citizens and industry representatives "voice" their concerns on an issue, people will stand at the microphone and make a passionate plea. Dan used a portable computer and a projection unit to display pictures and video for the audience. Industry representatives were caught unaware; in other words, they lacked visual images and could only stomp their feet in frustration. At the next meeting, however, the billboard representative displayed visuals on an oversize plasma screen, so its visuals would be even larger than Dan's. An important element of *delivery*, therefore, was "image size" as the size of the pictures became a competitive struggle between the opposing persuading forces.

One *style* Dan used was low camera angles, which forced viewers to look up at dominating billboards. In one case, however, the billboards were not high enough (to their owners). To make the drive into the city more attractive, the city planted palmetto trees along the road from the airport to downtown. As the trees grew, the company that owned the billboard behind the trees asked for the trees to be cut down. Citizens heard about the request and protested. So the owner of the billboard changed the sign to show apes looking over the trees accompanied by type that reads "Here's Looking At You . . . the Billboard People." The intended message seems to be that the city had planted trees and blocked drivers' view of the billboard, but the billboard company could still look back at the drivers. Dan, however, put the sign into a new context. A video sequence opened with a tight shot on "The Billboard People" text part of the sign and then the camera panned over to the apes. The recast message is that the billboard people are like apes, or at least the billboard people used a clumsy image to make their point.

One way to measure the effectiveness of Dan's visual presentation would be to wait for the city council's decision about the pending billboard law, and if it decides to stop companies from adding billboards or increasing the size of billboards, then "victory" was obtained. But even if the council was logically persuaded by Dan's presentation, it may not stop the addition of billboards. Politicians seem to cast their votes on the basis of getting re-elected, and Dan's visual presentation did not show that many voters care about the billboard issue. The presentation, however, could be effective without ultimate victory. The council must have noticed the agitated reactions of the billboard representatives, who obviously found Dan's presentation distressingly compelling. The billboard industry hired a political consultant to counter Dan's presentations and to develop a new strategy to persuade the city council and the public. They thought that the visuals were particularly convincing; actually, they would say the visuals were "misleading." Dan was accused of running a smear campaign.

To analyze the presentation in terms of visual *arguments*, three *premises* are considered:

(a)   Billboards clutter our landscape;

(b) Billboards are like trash; and

(c) Clean, natural environments are more attractive places to live.

The *conclusion*, therefore, is to eliminate billboards (or at least not add more billboards). A possible counter-argument to industry's claims that people need billboards to become aware of services and products they desire could be (but wasn't) shown by *substituting* "nothingness" for billboards. Dan could go to other states that ban all billboards and show their businesses are prospering without the "benefits" of advertising on billboards.

Symbolic Perspective

The symbolic perspective, based upon Burke's writings, explains that we are rhetorical because we use symbols. More than other species, he writes, we assign meaning to stimuli, and that meaning determines our subsequent behavior. Rhetoric considers how people use symbols to alter perception, to reinforce and channel belief, to initiate and maintain action, as well as to foster or undermine a competing ideology (Rosteck, 1994). With the symbolic perspective, the scope of rhetoric expanded to include all forms of communication, including gestural, visual, musical, and dance.

Working within symbol perspective, McGee (1980) redefined the concept of audience. He believes we live together in a community because we can agree to the visions and images of ourselves created by those we select as our public leaders. Rather than think of an audience as the people attending a discourse, or as an abstract phenomenon such as public opinion, McGee argues that speakers call an audience into being, urging potential members of a collectivity to see themselves in the specific visions sketched by the rhetor. From this perspective, rhetoric can speak to issues such as ideology, power, leadership, and social change.

Within the symbol perspective, understanding the intentions of the communicator is less important because meaning is now the result of an audience's efforts as much as, if not more than, whoever created the message. The effects of the message, therefore, are not always judged from the perspective of the message maker. Moreover, symbolic messages may work at the unconscious level. An active audience may unconsciously identify with, or associate feelings with, a message.

Why do people sometimes evaluate arguments and evidence (traditional perspective), and other times are persuaded based on associations (symbolic perspective)? The Elaboration Likelihood Model (Petty & Cacioppo, 1986) explains that a message can change attitudes in one of two ways: by getting the person to do a great deal of thinking about the message (central route), or by getting the person to focus on simple, but compelling, cues that are more superficial to the message content (peripheral route). A person's motivation and ability to process the message will influence his or her choice of processing strategy.

Some scholars believe that visuals are always processed peripherally. With visuals, they argue, information is NOT "transported" from the source to the receiver's conscious memory, where it is stored and later retrieved for weighing against existing attitudes and input from others until a logical decision can be made. Instead, visual messages are brought out of people by striking responsive chords. Visual communication follows a "mosaic model" with massive parallel processing that creates chains of reaction with other stored memories so that entire experiences, including feelings, are recalled (Larson, 1982). Metaphoric, narrative, mythic, and fantasy theme analyses fit well with the mosaic, or "evoked recall," models.

IDENTIFICATION, APPOSITION, CLICHES, STEREOTYPES, CULTURETYPES, ARCHETYPES, MYTHS

Identification is defined as: "The act of crossing individual boundaries to gain another person's or group's perspective through shared characteristics, experiences, objects, assumptions, beliefs, goals, or languages" (Youngdahl and Warnock, 1996, 337). Rhetoric, therefore, becomes the act of discovering or creating the common interests that make persuasion possible. The degree of identification may vary from pure identification—*consubstantiality*, meaning sharing the same nature or essence—to a mere sense of recognition because of a shared bumper slicker.

Identification occurs via a common (visual) language, shared assumptions, stereotypes, and universal appeals. Olson (1983) found that to create posters with broad appeal, Norman Rockwell used symbols from diverse American populations, situations, and actions, and he also omitted details that could have limited the potential number of identifications.

Visual identification often is used to separate "us" from "them." It occurs in politics when one candidate appears in front of the flag and the opponent appears to be scowling and shaking hands with the enemy. Countering such simple presentations of virtue and villainy is difficult, writes Jamieson (1992), whereas capitalizing on them is too easy.

Apposition is similar to identification, but rather than visually depict the candidate as virtue or villain, campaigns try to associate their candidate's name with everything the electorate cherishes and to transform the opponent into an antonym of those treasured values. After associating one's candidate with "good" and the opponent with "evil," all a campaign has left to do is remind voters of the resulting contrasts (Jamieson, 1992). Of course, visuals in print advertisements perform the same affective, psychological identification, and thus do the real selling job.

Identification also occurs via the telling of stories and myths. Myths are a special kind of story that captures the imagination of people and provides resources for both interpreting and explaining "reality." The myth must seem to be the answer to some compelling question, the dramatis personae must seem larger-than-life, and the myth must convey the sense of the sacred (Osborn, 1990). For example, the Adamic Myth was used to explain Oliver Stone's movie, *JFK* (Medhurst, 1993). Successful myths must include both culturetypes and archetypes in harmonious combination. Archetypes are ideal examples of a universal type, and culturetypes are culture-specific symbols that resonate important values. They complement each other, with culturetypes expressing the special values and meanings of a society, and archetypes anchoring the cultural system in enduring meaningfulness. Culturetypes, for example, remind us of what it means to be American, while archetypes remind us of what it means to be human.

EPIDEICTIC GENRE

Although the concept epideictic genre goes back to Aristotle and classical rhetoric, it is included in the symbolic perspective because evocative words and images are used to display values rather than to force audiences to submit to the power of cold logic. The epideictic genre was devoted to celebration. Its goals were to glorify and promote in order to achieve benevolence, goodwill, jubilation, and generosity of spirit. The epideictic genre also was devoted to memorializing the nobility so they would live forever in the sensibilities of the community. Unfortunately, over time, the messages for celebration and memorialization were over-used and they became empty rituals and hollow clichés. Instead of inspiring a community, too often epideictic rhetoric now gives honor in a detached, even platitudinous spirit (Rosenfield, 1989).

Whereas arguments have a definite structure of premises—conclusion within a context shared by the rhetor and audience, images in the epideictic genre are juxtaposed in novel ways and decontextualized. Images, for example, may follow each other consecutively but without a clearly marked temporal relationship. Epideictic discourses work by unifying audiences around a common set of values. These clichés, stereotypes, and myths create a favorable, reassuring impression through associations. The resulting images are pleasurable because they are so effortlessly recognizable. They reinforce conventional images of social reality and one's place in it and are perceived to represent truths.

Morreale (1991) uses epideictic rhetoric to explain how the political campaign film functions so effectively. In 1984, for example, the Reagan campaign aired the lushly produced film, *A New Beginning*, in place of the nominating speech at the Republican National Convention. The half-million dollar, fifteen-minute film borrows truth-like devices from the documentary genre as well as persuasive elements from the advertising business. Filmmakers used actors, props, staged settings, lighting, color, and camera work to give the film a soothing feel. The film was ordered thematically rather than chronologically, and its message was entirely upbeat. It used mythic images such as the American flag and the Statue of Liberty to depict American values such as work, family, and patriotism.

DEPICTION

Depiction is a complex concept that includes the ideas of identification, culturetypes, archetypes, myths, epideictic genre, etc. discussed above. Osborn

(1986) defines depiction as "strategic pictures, verbal or nonverbal visualizations that linger in the collective memory of audiences as representative of their subjects" (p. 79). Their meanings can be influential even if neither the rhetor nor the audience are fully aware of them.

According to Osborn, the five functions of depiction are:

- presentation,
- intensification of feeling,
- facilitation of identification,
- application of identification, and
- reaffirmation of identity.

Presentation is the way we experience the world via messages (rather than direct experience). Presentations range from highly reflective (resembling "reality") to highly symbolic (colored by the communicator). Presentations can be *repetitive* or *innovative*. Repetitive presentations show us what we already know, and they attempt to reinforce our acceptance. Examples include icons, culturetypes, archetypes, narratives, myths, stereotypes, and the like. Metaphors, on the other hand, are *innovative* symbolic presentations that link the familiar with the novel, and they disturb expectations that had been established by repetitive representation.

The second function of depiction is *intensification of feeling*. When a vast number of subjects are reduced to a few synecdochal instances, intensification of feeling occurs. Likewise, when vague subjects are given form through metaphors, intensification occurs because now we can transfer feelings from something we know and care about to something new and difficult to define.

Facilitation of identification is defined as creating a feeling of closeness in a community. To Osborn, identification occurs via culturetypes and archetypes transmitted quickly by mass media and understood easily by a mass audience.

The fourth function is *implementation*, defined as applied identification. Examples are a form of implementation because they either offer illustrations of a principle, or they embody the consequences of following or not following some potential course of action. "For example," rhetors can use graphic lessons from the past to influence and lend urgency to present decisions.

The fifth function is to *re*affirm identity, "often in ceremonies during which heroes, martyrs, villains, and the role of the people are recalled and renewed in common appreciation" (Osborn, p. 95). In other words, reaffirming identity is the same as epideictic rhetoric.

REPRESENTATIVE FORM

Building upon depiction, Edwards and Winkler (1997) introduce the concept of "representative form." They contend that the 1945 photograph of the flag-raising at Iwo Jima has been used and parodied in editorial cartoons and has become a special type of symbolic form; it is an instance of depictive rhetoric that functions as a visual ideograph (p. 303). Edwards and Winkler define representative form as an image that "transcends the specifics of its immediate visual references and, through a cumulative process of visual and symbolic meaning, rhetorically identifies and delineates the ideals of the body politic" (p. 295). A representative form originates in actuality and specificity, but is abstracted into a symbol or concentrated image, and provides an explanatory model for human motive.

Edwards and Winkler explain how the Iwo Jima image meets the same (slightly adapted) criteria established by McGee for (verbal) ideographs: (1) it must be an ordinary image found in political discourse, and both the elite and the non-elite must be influenced by the image; (2) it must be a high-order abstraction representing collective commitment to a particular, yet ill-defined normative goal; (3) it must warrant the use of power and guide behavior into acceptable and laudable channels; and (4) it must be culture-bound.

An excellent example of criticism using visual ideographs is the work of DeLuca (1999), who studied how environmental activists controlled the way they were verbally and visually presented to the general public and how they shifted the parameters of discussion about the environment. He writes that social movements are changes in the meanings of the world, and such redefinitions of reality are always constructed through rhetoric. DeLuca believes environmental groups also are attempting "to disarticulate and rearticulate" the links between ideographs in order to create a new discourse. In other words, they are challenging the links between progress and nature, as well as the links between humanity, technology, and reason.

Environmental groups change the meaning and linkages of ideographs by creating image events that call attention to mass extinctions, deforestation, toxic wastes, nuclear radiation, etc. They use shock (dis-identification) to shatter familiar landmarks of thought. For example, when Greenpeace confronts a Soviet whaling ship, we see a hulking, black ship dwarfing the Greenpeace rafts. With modern industrial technology, the nature/culture dichotomy has been reversed and now the huge ship towers over the whales (and Greenpeace). The whaling ships are the new leviathans of the deep. By arguing against reducing animals to economic resources and instead proposing that animals have intrinsic value and inalienable rights, Greenpeace contests the linking of economic progress with nature as a storehouse of resources, thus challenging the discourse of industrialism that warrants the use of technology to exploit nature in the name of progress.

INVITED AUDIENCE

Rhetorical critics generally focus on the context of production and they generally pay little attention to how people receive the message. Rhetorical critics know that other people may interpret the same message in a different way, and they even acknowledge that other readings may be more productive and responsible, but they do not investigate how audiences experience messages. Critics simply evaluate how well the rhetor chose between various options when creating a message, and then pronounce that the effects will be great/(minimal) because the right/(wrong) choices were made. Rhetorical critics do not generally consider differences in how messages are consumed because they assume texts are straightforward containers of meaning.

Like other critics, Thomas Benson does not ask moviegoers about their interpretations of films, but he goes to greater lengths than many others to identify structures that "invite" audiences to particular interpretations. He wants to know how people can, did, or should use a film. He is interested not only in *what* meaning emerges from a film, but also *how* it emerges. To do this, he pays attention to the details of films, to the internal and external contexts that give the film meaning, and to ways symbolic forms connect to create meanings.

Benson begins his review of *High School* (1980) with two arguments about interpretation. He argues that because *High School* is an audio-visual experience, and because it is an example of cinema verité that borrows from actuality, it resists linear, prepositional argument, and so Benson himself refuses to reduce the film to "an oversimplified pseudolinearity." If filmmaker Wisemen had wanted to be explicit, he would have written an essay, writes Benson. By making a film, with inexplicit messages, Wisemen could appeal to a larger shared experience.

Benson also argues that to avoid over-interpretation, which could happen by selecting a detail here or there and calling it a symbol, critics should only interpret elements as symbols if one of three conditions exist: (a) the element's context requires such an interpretation; (b) the same or contrasting elements appear repeatedly; or (c) failure to account for the symbol makes the element incoherent, implausible, or distracting. Benson explains how Wisemen invites readers to experience a particular group of meanings by analyzing two levels of symbolic activity: the film as a structure, and the social behavior recorded in the film as another structure.

All the themes Benson discussed had been mentioned by other writers. Benson's role was to develop the themes in more detail, to show how those details related to one another to form a structure, and to offer an account of how the structure might invite a rhetorical response. He proceeds sequence by sequence through the film, presenting a detailed explication that suggests the ways in which Wisemen invites viewers to experience the meanings of *High School* as structures. One useful idea is that a *meaning*, once established, begins to absorb neutral or ambiguous signs. For example, one of the themes of the movie is that schoolteachers and administrators are aware of students' heightened sexual awareness and they use students' hormones for their own power plays. Once viewers become aware of this sexual theme, gestures that are, in themselves, neutral, seem to take on special (sexual) relevance.

EVALUATION OF VISUAL MESSAGES

According to Foss (1994), semiotics is similar to rhetoric in that both deal with how meaning is constructed from signs and symbols. Semiotics is concerned with the codes needed to understand a text. Rhetoric, on the other hand, attempts to persuade a specific audience, so both the intended and perceived messages are contingent upon the situation, and a fixed code cannot be used. Berger (1991) provides a good metaphor to explain the difference. Semiotics judges a meal by the kinds of ingredients (i.e., pork instead of chicken, lamb, beef; with rice instead of potatoes, cous-cous, bread, etc.) and what it would mean if you chose those particular ingredients. Rhetoric not only considers the ingredients, but also how they were cooked that particular evening and how they tasted for those particular diners.

For rhetorical criticism, Foss believes that a visual image should be judged in terms of the functions of the image. She also believes that the audience rather than the creator determines the function of an image. A message, once completed, stands independent of its production, she writes.

To evaluate an image from a rhetorical perspective, therefore, involves three kinds of judgments: (a) identification of a function communicated in the image; (b) assessment of how well that function is communicated; and (c) evaluation of the legitimacy of that function. Identification of a function occurs via a critic's interpretation of the physical data of the image. The function the critic names is but one possible function. The critic must support his/her choice by showing the steps taken from the physical data to the claim. The next step explores the connections made between the identified function and the means available in the image to support it. The critic looks at subject matter, medium, forms, colors, organization, craftsmanship, and context, for example. A visual image is compared to other images with the same or a similar function in an effort to highlight available options in communicating such a function. Finally, the third step involves scrutiny of the function itself — Is the function legitimate? If the function is judged to be problematic in terms of its likely consequences, other functions may be suggested as more legitimate than the one communicated by the image.

Foss also has used a rhetorical background to explain why a visual image arouses interest in viewers, which leads to a positive evaluation of the image (1993). She believes that construction of appeal in a visual image is triggered by an element of technical novelty that results in a displacement of the image from its usual interpretive context. The violation of expectations and lack of context in which to place an image could generate confusion and frustration for viewers, causing viewers to abandon their efforts to understand the image. But the element of technical novelty makes abandonment of the image unlikely. Viewers want to resolve the tension created by the technical novelty, which they do by associating the appealing image's form or context (or both) with familiar contexts of events, objects, and qualities. These associations, such as delight, affection, nostalgia, or other positive qualities, are likely to result in viewers' assignment of a positive meaning to the appealing image.

EFFECTIVENESS OF PHOTOGRAPHIC ICONS OF OUTRAGE

Can iconic visual images emotionally sway world opinion, which then forces American policy makers to respond? David Perlmutter has written a thought-provoking book, *Photojournalism and Foreign Policy*, that challenges this idea.

He is skeptical about the power of images and encourages greater prudence "before automatically attributing to a news photograph, icon or not, the power to change the world, scar the nation, outrage the people or make or break policy" (p. xiii). The purpose of this section of the essay is to examine what Perlmutter describes as the theory of "visual determinism," as well as his challenge to the theory, and then apply some of the concepts of the symbolic rhetorical perspective to a critique of photographic "icons of outrage."

The theory of visual determinism seems to include the following statements:

(a) Policy makers and the public get their understanding of world events from the news media, especially TV.

(b) TV (and print media) use a lot of news pictures.

(c) These news pictures have universal, denotative meanings that reflect "reality."

(d) These fixed meanings evoke viewers' emotions rather than rational thoughts.

(e) These emotion-laden pictorial messages are transmitted to the public quickly.

(f) Quick transmission bypasses channels of public decision making; therefore, news pictures deliver messages like hypodermic needles.

(g) Some of these pictures demand our attention and become the center of public discourse.

(h) These "icons of outrage" have a subject content that is stored in our collective memories.

(i) Our memories do not include the original contexts of the images.

(j) Without context, meaning is framed via the media, following public political arguments.

(k) Picture content, (lack of) context, and media framing (irrationally) affect public opinion.

(l) Public opinion causes the nation's leaders to alter public policy.

(m) New public policy changes the world.

Perlmutter's first challenge to this "lay" theory arises from a questionnaire he gave to 146 students in a college introductory mass communication course. He found that they could neither name nor describe "famous" photographs from the Tet offensive in 1968 (ten years before their birth). In a reverse experiment, Perlmutter showed a different class of students a set of famous photographs and found they could correctly associate an image with an event, but few could provide any detail about the exact context and circumstance of the picture's creation and provenance. These results dejected Perlmutter, who concluded that the icons of one generation are the enigmas, or shadows, of another generation. If a picture is not well known, can it be an icon, he asks? (Of course, college students do not affect current government policy and they will have their own icons when they are elected officials.) Perlmutter concludes there is a major difference between scholars/media workers who comment on images and the general public, and that those who study images for a living are the least qualified to talk about them.

Perlmutter also challenges the idea that iconic pictures have clear meanings. He believes that people *project* meanings onto the pictures rather than simply *inspecting* the pictures for meanings. In other words, Perlmutter seems to say that these icons have connotative as well as denotative meanings, and that much (visual) meaning is in the eye of the beholder. He adds that "photographers, editors, commentators, and historians try to direct us to an approved meaning." From "approved meaning" Perlmutter quickly moves to the idea that images are prone to ideological manipulation "to almost any degree and in almost any direction" (p. 28). He implies that a dictator controls unanimous agreement about the meaning of a photographic icon. Regarding the image of a man blocking a line of tanks at Tiananmen in 1989, Perlmutter wrote:

> A consensus exists in the West that the picture was important, well known, and influential, and that the event was a metonym of Beijing Spring; but is no other interpretation possible? If everyone agrees an image means something, then must they be correct? . . . In dictatorships when only one approved meaning is attached to an event, but people, in their own minds, may refute the official story, how may we judge the consensus of truth? (p. 74)

Perlmutter sets tough standards for measuring the effects of photographs. Pictures do not affect policy, he implies, unless politicians use ALL of their influence to react upon the outrage AND their actions have long-term success. Perlmutter cites the "man against tanks at Tiananmen" picture as an example of how pictures can affect policy, "but only marginally." "The losers of the media battle won on the ground, and eight years later have triumphed in all areas of their foreign policy interests save the capturing of the Olympic Games for Beijing in the year 2000" (p. 83). The reaction to images in the press may be strong, but are shallow, he writes, because "few political elites are willing to expend their total political capital and influence on reacting to the outrage, especially from a foreign land," and certainly not when the lives of Americans are involved (p. 83).

With the picture of the naked body of an American soldier dragged through the streets of Mogadishu by jeering Somalis, there seems clear evidence that the photograph affected public opinion. Perlmutter cites a survey, which found that fifty percent of respondents who had seen the images favored withdrawal from Somalia as opposed to only thirty-three percent who had not. Perlmutter, however, does not find the image "powerful." He writes that pictures do not affect policy because people are not reacting to pictures; instead they are reacting to the people-objects-events portrayed in the pictures.

> People reacted to the events; the icons focused their reaction. This is a crucial distinction in assessing the power of an image. Pictures are not just forms and shapes; they show things and people. How much we care about those things and people affects the power of the image over us (p. 115).

With this line of reasoning, no representational photograph, video, or film could have much effect.

If Perlmutter had applied rhetorical concepts to understand the impact of photojournalism on foreign policy, would his conclusions have changed? To attempt to answer this question, the effectiveness of the same four images — Eddie Adams' picture of a South Vietnamese policeman firing a pistol at the head of a prisoner on the streets of Saigon in 1968; Kevin Carter's picture of a Sudanese child bending over the parched savanna with a vulture lurking in the background in 1993; Charles Cole's picture of a man blocking a line of tanks at Tiananmen in 1989; and the picture from Somalia — are analyzed from a symbolic perspective.

Rhetoricians might argue that the photographs were persuasive because they helped American audiences identify with foreign events. The Somalia image, for example, quickly separated "us" (Americans) against "those people" who had been so ungrateful and were now killing "our" soldiers. The Beijing image resonated with American stereotypes of rebellion and defiance against authority. It took on mythic qualities of "David versus Goliath." The Sudan image was an archetype that appealed to anyone with a nurturing spirit who wants to protect vulnerable children. The Saigon picture helped transform an ally (South Vietnamese military policeman) into a villain and an enemy (North Vietnamese prisoner) into an object of sympathy. This process of identification, of who is "good" and who is "evil," lays the foundation for subsequent actions by political leaders for decades.

The concept of depiction is helpful because it recognizes that images may be highly reflective or symbolic and they can be REPETITIVE or innovative. Photographs such as the one of the starving child and vulture reinforce what we already know about the problems of starvation in war-torn regions, but they also INTENSIFY our feelings. As every journalist knows, it is easier to make the public care about one suffering person than to write about the thousand or million or more who suffer from the same problems. Because the vast number of people are reduced to one synecdochal instance, we care more. We begin to IDENTIFY with the child and a feeling of closeness in a (world) community develops. Perhaps a MYTH will be generated. In this case the photojournalist, Kevin Carter, became a Christ-like figure after committing suicide. He had suffered great pain ("I am haunted by the vivid memories of killings & corpses & anger & pain . . . of starving or wounded children") in order to enlighten others with his images, and the pain proved to be overwhelming, so he took his own life. The picture, therefore, became an EXAMPLE of the consequences of war. Perlmutter is correct that the picture "does not tell us who is really to blame for the girl's plight" (p. 28), but I would argue that people have some CONTEXT for the image, and that the image serves as an example for that context. So, finally, the picture MAGNIFIES and reveals the shame of fighting between the Arab and Muslim-dominated government of the north and the black and Christian rebels of the south.

Like the Iwo Jima image, the picture of the public execution in Saigon is probably an example of a representative form. Perlmutter seemed disturbed that photographic icons became separated from their original context (and therefore, he implies, the icons do not affect policy). Rhetoricians, in contrast,

would applaud a visual ideograph that "transcends the specifics of its immediate visual references and, through a cumulative process of visual and symbolic meaning, rhetorically identifies and delineates the ideals of the body
politic." Because a visual ideograph becomes a concentrated symbol of a normative goal for a particular culture, it warrants the use of power. After all,
doesn't the ideology of a culture affect public policies more than policies
affect ideology?

According to Foss, these four photographic icons should be evaluated
in terms of their functions as determined by their audiences. For most
Americans, I would argue, the function of the Somalia image was to settle
an ongoing debate about the U.S. military's humanitarian role in Somalia
and other countries without many social-economic-political-defense ties to
America. I would argue that the functions of the Saigon execution image
were to show the barbarity of war and to question whether the U.S. was in
the "right war." Although these are not the only potential functions of the
two images, they are reasonable choices given the extensive list of comments on the two images provided by Perlmutter in his book's appendixes
(pp 137–41; 145–48). These functions were more clearly communicated in
the execution and dragging photos than in other photographs of war, or stories of war, or speeches, movies, books, etc. Finally, the third step in Foss'
evaluation process involves scrutiny of the functions themselves. In the case
of the Somalia photograph, certainly the debate about using American military personnel for humanitarian missions in countries involved in civil
wars is legitimate. But would any one image be adequate for a debate? This
picture effectively shows the costs of the worst-case scenario. Where is the
photo showing the benefits? With the Saigon photo, no photographer in the
history of photography would argue against the legitimacy of using images
to show the brutality of war. Moreover, the photo's function of questioning
America's involvement in Vietnam was sound since neither the U.S. military nor government seemed to avoid self-interest when examining the
question.

In summary, Perlmutter seemed to evaluate the effectiveness of "famous"
photographic icons according to the same "hypodermic needle" theory of
communication he derided in his text. Since scholars cannot clearly establish
a cause-effect relationship between a particular image and long-term foreign
policy, the commonly held belief in the effects of those images is unjustified,
he writes. On the other hand, from a rhetorical perspective, which emphasizes
a ritual model of communication and a social construction of reality, these
images seemed to have both immediate and long-lasting effects upon citizens
and leaders. Foreign policy debates still take account of the "Vietnam syn-
drome" partly defined by Adams' photograph, and U.S. relations with China
remain influenced by the Tiananmen incident best remembered by Cole's
image. The genocide of Rwanda without intervention by the U.S. has been
attributed to the ideological climate established in Somalia characterized by
the dragging photo. These symbolic effects are more difficult to measure over
short time periods, but they still exist.

REFERENCES

Benson, T. W. (1980). The rhetorical structure of Frederick Wiseman's *High School. Communication Monographs, 47,* 233–261.

Berger, A. A. (1991). *Media analysis techniques,* rev. ed. Newbury Park, CA: Sage.

Birdsell, D. S. & Groarke, L (1996). Toward a theory of visual argument. *Argumentation and Advocacy, 33,* 1–10.

Blair, J. A (1996). The possibility and actuality of visual argument. *Argumentation and Advocacy, 33,* 23–39.

Burke, K. (1950). *A rhetoric of motives.* Englewood Cliffs, NJ: Prentice-Hall.

Craig, R. T. (1999). Communication theory as a field. *Communication Theory, 9,* 199–261.

DeLuca, K. M. (1999). *Image politics: The new rhetoric of environmental activism.* New York: Guilford Press.

Edwards, J. L. & Winkler, C. K. (1997). Representative form and the visual ideograph: The Iwo Jima image in editorial cartoons. *Quarterly Journal of Speech, 83,* 289–310.

Foss, S. K. (1993). The construction of appeal in visual images: A hypothesis. In D. Zarefsky (Ed.), *Rhetorical movement: Essays in honor of Leland M. Griffin* (210-224). Evanston, IL: Northwestern University Press.

Foss, S. K. (1994). A rhetorical schema for the evaluation of visual imagery. *Communication Studies, 45,* 213–224.

Jamieson, K. H. (1992). *Dirty politics: Deception, distraction, and democracy.* New York: Oxford University Press.

Lake, R. A. and Pickering, B. A. (1998). Argumentation, the visual, and the possibility of refutation: An exploration. *Argumentation, 12,* 79–93.

Lancioni, J. (1996). The rhetoric of the frame revisioning archival photographs in *The Civil War. Western Journal of Communication, 60,* 397–414.

Larson, C. U. (1982). Media metaphors: Two models for rhetorically criticizing the political television spot advertisement. *Central States Speech Journal, 33,* 533–546.

Lucaites, J. L., Condit, C. M. and Caudill, S, (1999). *Contemporary rhetorical theory: A reader.* New York: Guilford Press.

McGee, M. C. (1980). The ideograph: A link between rhetoric and ideology. *Quarterly Journal of Speech, 66,* 1–16.

McQuarrie, E. F. and Mick, D. G. (1996). Figures of rhetoric in advertising language. *Journal of Consumer Research, 22,* 424–437.

McQuarrie, E. F. and Mick, D. G. (1999). Visual rhetoric in advertising: Text-interpretive, experimental, and reader-response analyses. *Journal of Consumer Research. 26,* 37–54.

Medhurst, Martin J. (1993), The rhetorical structure of Oliver Stone's *JFK. Critical Studies in Mass Communication, 10,* 128–143.

Medhurst, M. J. & DeSousa, M. A. (1981). Political cartoons as rhetorical form: A taxonomy of graphic discourse. *Communication Monographs, 48,* 197–237.

Morreale, J. (1991). The political campaign film: Epideictic rhetoric in a documentary frame. In F. Biocca (Ed.), *Television and Political Advertising, Vol.2* (187–210). Hillsdale, NJ: Lawrence Erlbaum.

Olson, L. C. (1983). Portraits in praise of a people: A rhetorical analysis of Norman Rockwell's icons in Franklin D. Roosevelt's "Four Freedoms" Campaign. *Quarterly Journal of Speech, 69,* 15–24.

Osborn, M. (1986). Rhetorical depiction. In H. W. Simons & A. A. Aghazarian (Eds.), *Form, genre, and the study of political discourse* (79–107). Columbia: University of South Carolina Press.

Osborn, M. (1990). In defense of broad mythic criticism — A reply to Rowland. *Communication Studies, 41,* 121–127.

Perlmutter, D. D. (1998). *Photojournalism and foreign policy: Icons of outrage in international crises.* Westport, CT: Praeger.

Petty, R. E, & Cacioppo, J. T. (1986). The Elaboration Likelihood Model of persuasion. In L. Berkowitz (Ed.), *Advances in experimental social psychology, Vol. 19* (123–205) New York: Academic Press.

Rosenfield, L. W. (1989). Central Park and the celebration of civic virtue. In T. W. Benson (Ed.) *American rhetoric: Context and criticism* (221-265). Carbondale: Southern Illinois University Press.

Rosteck, T. (1994). *"See It Now" confronts McCarthyism.* Tuscaloosa: University of Alabama Press.

Wichelns, H. A. (1980). The literary criticism of oratory. In R. T. Oliver & M. G. Bauer (Eds.), *The speech profession: The first fifty years.* New York: SAES.

Youngdahl, P. & Warnock, T. (1996). Identification. In T. Enos (Ed.), *Encyclopedia of rhetoric and composition* (337–339). New York: Garland Publications.

21 *The Possibility and Actuality of Visual Arguments*

J. ANTHONY BLAIR

For the last thirty years the very concept of argument has come under fairly intense examination by the speech communication community (see Gronbeck, 1980, for the early years). Sometimes the focus has been inward, upon its central features (Brockriede, 1975; O'Keefe, 1977, 1982; Trapp, 1983; Hample, 1985). More recently, its more global features have been scrutinized (Willard, 1983, 1989; van Eemeren & Grootendorst, 1984). The present paper is intended as a contribution to the investigation of the extension of argument into a realm hitherto given scant attention. The study of argument since Aristotle has assumed it to be paradigmatically verbal, if not essentially and exclusively so. At a time when technological and cultural developments are increasingly enhancing visual communication, it behooves us to consider whether argument can partake visual expression.

There is no doubt that images can be influential in affecting attitudes and beliefs. A single visual image can probably be more powerful than a single verbal assertion, other things being equal, although broader claims should be made with caution: probably nothing in history has been more influential than the great verbal religious works, such as the Bible and the Koran. However, it is obvious that paintings and sculptures, and the visual component of movies, television programs, and commercial and political advertising, are enormously powerful influences on attitudes and beliefs. Still, from the fact that images influence beliefs and attitudes it does not follow that such images are arguments, for there is any number of other ways of influencing attitudes and beliefs besides arguing.

Indeed, it would be a mistake to assimilate all means of cognitive and affective influence to argument, or even to assimilate all persuasion to argument. In that case, shock therapy becomes indistinguishable from a syllogism; crowd mania merges with a carefully crafted case for a conclusion; and fear-mongering or appeals to blind loyalty cannot be separated from clear-eyed appeals to interests or to evidence. There is no pedantry, no hairsplitting, in

From *Argumentation and Advocacy 33* (Summer 1996): 23–39.

recognizing that a loss of clarity and understanding attends such blurring of conceptual boundaries. So we should at the outset investigate whether there can be visual arguments, not just take it for granted that they exist.

To determine whether they exist, we need to know what a visual argument would look like if we encountered one. How, if at all, are visual and verbal arguments related? An account of a concept of visual argument serves to establish the possibility that they exist. By analogy, knowing what a symphony is tells us that symphonies are auditory, not visual; so a "visual symphony" must be a metaphor. Are visual arguments like visual symphonies? If they are possible in a non-metaphorical way, are there any visual arguments? By analogy, an adult person who is totally free of self-deception is surely possible; but has any such person lived yet? Are all the things that look as though they might be visual arguments the genuine article? These are the questions addressed in this paper.

1. Properties of Visual Arguments

Let us turn first, then, to what would count as a visual argument. We are exploring new territory: little has been written about visual arguments (see Groarke, in press). Like the Norse adventurers, who are said to have kept a landfall in sight behind them when they sailed into the North Atlantic,[1] it would be best to keep in mind a clear conception of argument and a clear conception of what "visual" means here, when we investigate the *terra* relatively *incognita* of visual argument. That approach sounds a prioristic, which can be a Bad Thing. But the preferred method, starting the analysis from clear and indisputable cases of visual arguments and observing their salient properties, is unavailable here because it would beg the question: the issue before us is precisely whether the paradigm of verbal arguments has room for, or can be extended to include, visual arguments. The latter constitute a new candidate for inclusion in the concept of argument. And the only other alternative seems to be to list all sorts of "examples," or candidates for membership in this class, without any way of deciding which ones really belong and which ones don't. So let us begin by setting, first, what counts as an argument and, second, what counts as visual.

A. Argument

For the purpose of the present investigation, O'Keefe's concept of argument$_1$ serves admirably. O'Keefe describes the paradigm case of argument$_1$ as involving "a linguistically explicable claim and one or more linguistically explicable reasons" (O'Keefe, 1982, p. 17). Let it be clear that O'Keefe's argument$_1$ is not the logician's abstraction. Such arguments are made and used. O'Keefe suggests that, "a paradigm case of making an argument$_1$ involves the communication of both (1) a linguistically explicable claim and (2) one or more overtly expressed reasons which are linguistically explicit" (p. 14).

I use O'Keefe's argument$_1$ because if anything is an argument, then arguments$_1$ are. And I use his concept of argument$_1$ rather than his concept of argument$_2$ (argument as "overt disagreement . . . between interactants" [1982, p. 11]), because visual arguments are more plausibly akin to reasons for claims (arguments$_1$) than to open disagreements between interacting parties (arguments$_2$).

The explicit properties of arguments$_1$ are the following:

(1) There is a claim; that is, the assertion has been made that something has to be believed, or chosen, or done;

(2) There is a reason or there are reasons for the claim; that is, the assertion has been made of something supporting what is to be believed, chosen or done;

(3) The reason(s) is(are) linguistically explicable and overtly expressed;

(4) The claim is linguistically explicable;

(5) There is an attempt to communicate the claim and reason(s).

These explicit properties entail the following implicit properties of arguments$_1$:

(6) There is some person who uses the claim and its reason(s) (this person may, but need not be, its author);

(7) There is some intended recipient audience or interlocutor(s) to whom the claim and reason(s) are addressed.

Although not entailed by O'Keefe's descriptions of the paradigms of argument$_1$ and of making arguments$_1$, I think it is in the spirit of his account that one further property be included:

(8) It is the intention of the "user" to bring the recipient to accept the claim on the basis of the reason(s) offered.

The concept of argument$_1$ has two implications of importance to the present discussion.

One is that such arguments are "propositional." Arguments$_1$ are propositional because claims and reasons have to be propositions. That is, the reasons and claims making them up have propositional content, using "propositional content" in a broad way, so as to include as propositions value judgments and action prescriptions as well as descriptions, predictions, and so on. An expression has propositional content in the sense used here if it has a truth value, or (and this is a weaker but broader requirement) if it can be affirmed or rejected. Thus, "The economy is in a recession," "It is unfortunate that the economy is in a recession," and "Steps should be taken to get the economy out of the recession" all count here as expressing propositions.

The second implication of the concept of argument$_1$ that is important for present purposes is that arguments$_1$ are not necessarily linguistic or verbal arguments. All that is required by O'Keefe's account for something to qualify as an argument$_1$ is that reasons be *overtly expressed*, and that reasons and claim be linguistically *explicable*. That means we have to be able to state or restate them in language, not that they have to be expressed in language in the first place. Thus O'Keefe's concept of argument is not inimical to the possibility of visual arguments.

What these two further implications add up to is that for something to count as an argument$_1$, we have to be able to say what the claim is and what the reasons are, and we have to be able to say so clearly enough that the claims or reasons can be accepted or rejected. (You cannot accept or reject "Yuck!"; you can accept or reject the claim, "This steak tastes like shoe leather!")

B. Visual

When we are interested in visual argument as a distinct and distinctive species, I take it that we mean to emphasize the contrast between the visual and the verbal. To be sure, verbal communication can be transmitted visually, by print or writing, but what is essential to it is the use of words and a language. Visual communication, when understood in contradistinction to verbal communication, occurs without the mediation of words or language in the literal sense. It is true that what is communicated visually can be described verbally, or translated into verbal communication. (Whether such descriptions or translations can be complete or fully adequate is a separate question.) However, such description or translation is not a *reduction* of the visual to the verbal. The visual communication stands on its own feet.

Visual communication may entail the use of conventions, as exemplified by the rich visual symbolism to be found in medieval church sculpture and stained glass images, and medieval and renaissance paintings (Ferguson, 1954); however, these conventions are not a language in the literal sense. There is no grammar, just signs and symbols: conventionalized images. Communication through visual imagery is not verbal.

It is also true that we now know that certain causal properties are supervenient on certain visual properties, which thus affect their viewers in predictable ways. For example, colors invoke feelings of warmth (reds, oranges) or coolness (blues, greens); photographs of young animals (puppies, kittens, children) evoke tender-heartedness; photographs of adults in different garb or uniform (physician, police officer, teenager) evoke standard responses according to stereotypes; and certain scenery (the open desert, the mountains, the seashore, hills and forests) evoke feelings of freedom and escape in their viewers. However, once again, while such properties can be and are exploited effectively to cause feelings and attitudes and to evoke responses (for example, in advertising), that does not imply that the visual images to which they attach are languages in any literal sense, for they are not verbal, and so such communication is not verbal communication.

I have been arguing that the fact and the effectiveness of visual communication do not reduce it to verbal communication. What would visual communication have to be like in order to count as arguments$_1$, or else to have some claim to the title of argument by virtue of a degree of family resemblance to arguments$_1$? The answer is, first, that it would have to have all, or some, of the salient properties of arguments$_1$, and second, that it would have to be non-verbal visual communication. We have thus at least conditionally answered our question, "What would be the properties of visual arguments?"

2. THE POSSIBILITY OF VISUAL ARGUMENT

The next question is, "Are there any?" But first we must determine that they are possible in our world. There seems to be no reason in principle for thinking there cannot be visual arguments.

Visual arguments are to be understood as propositional arguments in which the propositions and their argumentative function and roles are expressed visually, for example by paintings and drawings, photographs, sculpture, film or video images, cartoons, animations, or computer-designed visuals. Is it possible to express argumentation visually?

Propositions can be expressed in any number of ways, including by silence (the standard response to, "Anybody want to take out the trash?"), but also by signs or signals (a one-way street arrow sign, a nod at an auction), or by facial and other body-language expressions (wrinkled brow: "I'm skeptical"; squirming: "I want this lecture to be over."). So already we have examples of their being expressed visually. "Is June at home?" can be answered negatively (in some cultures) by shaking one's head from side to side just as well as by saying, "No." The fact that the communicative function of some of these signs and symbols is conventional–and symbols, at least, are by definition conventions–does not make them *ipso facto* verbal. Even granting a continuum from written languages using words, through written languages using pictograms, to conventional signs (such as traffic signs: one-way, no parking, no passing, curve ahead), and on to communication by facial expressions (such as smiles, grins, wide-open eyes and mouth), does not imply that all items on the continuum are reducible to one type, verbal language. The visual expression of propositions, then, is familiar and relatively unproblematic.

All we need in addition, in order to get visual arguments from propositions expressed visually ("visual propositions"), is for it to be possible to communicate visually the functions of the propositions, so that it can be communicated that some visual propositions are intended as claims and others as reasons for those claims–or that some visual propositions are intended as reasons for unexpressed but expressible claims. Since, "X is a reason for Y," and "You should accept Y, given X" are themselves propositions, and given that propositions can be expressed visually, there is nothing in principle preventing the "reason for" or illative function from being expressible visually. As for the assertion function, which is what turns the statement of a proposition into a claim–a claim being a proposition asserted or put forward as to be accepted–we can readily do that by adopting certain visual conventions, for certainly in verbal communication we have conventions for identifying claims, when there is any doubt about it. So there seems to be no problem in principle in having visual assertions, including the assertion of illation.

In practice, however, there is in this connection the following difference between verbal and visual expression. Asserting or claiming is the default function in spoken or written language. That is, to utter or write a declarative sentence is, in the absence of any counter-indication, to assert its propositional content. The same is not true for all visual expression. When we go to an art gallery or to the movies, we do not at the outset take it that what we are encountering is likely to be visual assertion. In fact, although this is an empirical question, I suspect that there is no default function for visual expression, but instead a range of possibilities which we usually must sort through on each occasion. Sometimes the context is labelled for us: an exhibition of paintings is billed as " abstract expressionist," for example. But more often we must infer what we can from the external and internal contextual cues. Thus the movie *Batman* is taken to be sheer entertainment, not argumentative; whereas the movies *Dances With Wolves* or *J.F.K.* are not only given advanced billing as "making a statement," but are dramatically structured so as to leave no doubt that they express a point of view, and thereby become candidates for, or locales for possible, visual arguments. Thus there is a systematic tendency to indeterminacy about visual expression, at least in our culture at the present time, that is absent from verbal expression.[2] To put this point more precisely, in most instances in our culture the conditions of interpretation of visual expression are indeterminate to a much greater degree than is the case with verbal expression.[3]

What distinguishes visual argument from verbal argument, then, are the differences in argument expression facing the arguer, and the hermeneutical differences of identification and interpretation facing the interlocutor, audience, or critic. These are likely to create formidable practical problems for arguer and audience, but they do not make visual arguments impossible in principle.

3. THE OCCURRENCE OF VISUAL ARGUMENTS

Visual arguments are possible, if we are right so far, but are there any in fact? It would be nice to find some examples. That turns out to be more easily said than done. We might expect to find visual arguments in such things as dramatic paintings and sculptures, magazine and other static advertisements, television commercials, and political cartoons. Consider each of these in turn.

A. Arguments in Dramatic Painting and Sculpture

It is important to keep in mind the difference between an argument and a statement, even a complex set of related statements. Many works of art that convey a message, that communicate points of view, emotions, or attitudes, do not provide or constitute arguments. Expressing a proposition, even forcefully and dramatically, is not arguing for it.

Consider as examples four famous dramatic paintings. Goya's portrayal of the execution of Spanish patriots by Napoleon's troops, "The Third of May, 1808, At Madrid: The Shootings on Principle Pio Mountain" (1808), portrays human cruelty, fear, terror, hopelessness, and courage; but it gives no reasons for favoring the loyalists or opposing Napoleon. Géricault's "The Raft of the Medusa" (1818–19) expresses the despair and misery of being adrift at sea after a shipwreck, and shows us the fifteen survivors of the 150 who had clung to the raft twelve days before when the Medusa foundered; but it gives no reasons for drawing any conclusions, for example about a need for life-boats, safer vessels, or less risk-taking in trans-oceanic trade, nor is it a justi-fication of the cannibalism that allegedly took place on the raft. Picasso's "Guernica" (1937) depicts and expresses the horrors of the German bombing of women and children in the town of Guernica in the Spanish civil war; but what conclusion are we to draw? That this was a terrible, cruel, destructive act? But that is what Picasso's painting expresses; there is no argument. Munch's "The Cry" (1893) expresses anxiety and dread, but tenders no con-clusion. It may render the alienation of modern life, but it isn't an argument against it.

In order to reconstruct any of these paintings as an argument, it is neces-sary not only to give propositional expression to it–to treat the picture as delivering a message–but also to identify and distinguish premises (reasons, evidence: grounds) from conclusions, whether asserted visually or unex-pressed (and discoverable from the context). This is the main difficulty in interpreting any of these four dramatic paintings as an argument. There is no way to have confidence in any one conclusion that the painter wanted his viewers to draw. Clearly the painters sought to communicate. At least the first three of these paintings have narrative intent: they are records of events, they tell stories. The artist in each case intended to send a message and to evoke a reaction. I think these artists are inviting us to ponder, or to agree with, their statements. They wish us to feel or identify with the terror or fear or horror their paintings convey. It does not follow that they are presenting us with arguments.

Any assertion whatever can be placed in a context which renders it the premise of an argument. Indeed, Anscombre and Ducrot (1983) see all dis-course as argumentative. Take our earlier example, "June is not at home." Imagine it uttered in circumstances when we knew that normally June would be sure to be at home. We may then be expected to infer that something out of the ordinary has happened. The utterance of "June is not at home" is then, in that situation, the assertion of an argument (or a part of one), with a con-clusion expressible as, "Something (unusual? untoward?) has happened." But in the absence of such contextual information, all we have is the possibility of argument, or possible arguments. It's easy to think of an indefinite number of possible conclusions to draw from the assertion of "June is not at home" in the absence of any context: "June is at her office," "June has run off with Chris," "June has already left for the airport," and so on. The possibility of a conclu-sion following from it in some imaginable context does not turn an assertion into an argument.

In the case of the dramatic paintings in question, nothing in principle rules out an argument-creating context. My point is that, in none of these four cases is there a context that permits anything more than speculation about a range of possibilities. Perhaps Picasso meant to argue that the Nazis were vicious, but he equally might have meant to argue that war is hell; or he might not have meant to argue at all, but just to express his own horror and evoke ours. That any of these paintings might have been an argument in other circumstances does not make it an argument as things stand.

Will no work of art be an argument? I haven't made that claim. Indeed, as I have argued, nothing in principle prevents a painting or other art from expressing an argument. But I think that to do so the work of art has to satisfy the condition that we are able to identify its premise(s) and its intended conclusion (whether expressed of not).

A nice example of exactly how such conditions can be met is Groarke's (in press) case that Jacques-Louis David's famous painting, "Death of Marat" (1793), was an argument for the conclusion that "Marat was, like Christ, a great moral martyr." Groarke points out that David painted in an historical context which "saw art as a vehicle for 'the edification and uplifting of mankind'" (quoting Kelder, 1976), and that "he was committed to works that encouraged high moral standards and a sense of patriotic self-sacrifice." But Groarke goes beyond showing that David might have been painting an argument, by identifying three particular statements that may be inferred from the painting,[4] and showing how–in the context of the time–these are best explained as premises in an argument. Premise 1: "Marat gave his last penny to the poor" (supported by the alm on the box beside Marat's bath and the adjacent note, portrayed as written with Marat's dying hand, which reads: "You will give this assignat to this mother of five children whose husband died in defense of the fatherland" plus the widely held belief that this was Marat's total wealth when he died). Premise 2: "Marat was a benefactor of the unfortunate" (supported by the note from Marat's assassin, Charlotte de Corday, that David painted gripped in Marat's hand, which appeals to him as a benefactor of the unfortunate). Premise 3: "Marat was a poor man of great dignity and composure," supported by numerous details in the painting which portray Marat in this way. Although Groarke takes these premises and the conclusion (that "Marat was, like Christ, a great moral martyr") to be expressed, not implicit, whereas it seems to me that all are unstated inferences which David, by his painting, invites the viewer to draw, nevertheless, I think Groarke makes a compelling case that this is one conclusion of the argument which David uses the painting to make. Notice that in establishing his interpretation of "The Death of Marat" as an argument, Groarke has identified the propositions expressed or implied visually and their logical roles in the argument.

Another example of argument in art are the stone sculptures of the Last Judgment which adorn the tympanums above doorways in many Gothic cathedrals (see Mâle, 1898/1958, chap. VI). To the right of Christ the judge, and the Archangel Michael holding the scales to weigh the good actions against the sins of the resurrected souls, are dynamic, dramatic portrayals of the elect, clothed in royal garments and crowned as they enter heaven; and to the left are the condemned, being led off in chains to the burning mouth of hell. Although these sculptures are portrayals of biblical themes and contemporary theological writings, dramatized by the individual sculptors, it seems plausible to regard them at the same time as conveying the message to the illiterate populace: "Here is what will happen to you at the time of the Last Judgment if you are virtuous, and here is what will happen to you if you are a sinner." The unexpressed assumptions, "No one wants to experience everlasting tortures; everyone wants to experience everlasting joy," and the implied conclusions, "You would be well advised not to sin, but to be virtuous" are unproblematic in the context of the times.

So I certainly agree that visual arguments in art exist; I just think they are not to be conflated with visual assertions which are expressed without argument, and thus not to be found automatically in every dramatic work of art.

B. Arguments in Magazine and Other Static Visual Ads

Many magazine advertisements combine words with pictures. The case for visual arguments in advertising will be more convincing if it can be made with purely visual ads. There are plenty of them. One striking recent example was an eight-page block advertising the Benetton clothing company that appeared in the April 29 and May 6, 1996 issue of *The New Yorker* magazine (pp. 51–58). This was a special, double-issue of the magazine devoted to the theme, Black in America. I want to discuss the Benetton ad in some detail because it seems to be a strong candidate for purely visual argument in an ad.

The Benetton block began with a blank all-black right-hand page. The following six pages consisted of three full two-page spreads, in color, reproduced here as Figures 1 through 3 in the order in which they appeared in *The New Yorker*.[5] On each set, the tag "United Colors of Benetton" was in white print on a bright green background; the other colors appeared natural, undoctored. The page after the Figure 3 picture, a left-hand page, was blank, all-white.

The overt messages are richly evocative. (1) The three hearts (see Figure 1) suggest: we're all humans, with hearts (and all that they symbolize) under our skin; skin color of donor and recipient is irrelevant to a heart transplant;

FIGURE 1.

the distinctions of color are just labels put onto us (by others); and much more. (2) The little girls (see Figure 2) suggest: innocent children have no racial prejudices; those come from adults; and adult racist attitudes destroy possibilities children represent for interracial harmony (a kind of Rousseauian thesis); and much more. (3) The manacled hands (see Figure 3) suggest: we are locked together, whites and blacks; there is no escaping our condition of whites-and-blacks together in the country and the world; we are the prisoners of our own prejudices. The identical clothing suggests equality. It is possible to find in the photo a reminder of Hegel's master-slave commentary: the uninformativeness of the picture as to which man is the controller and which is the controlled (if either) reminds us of Hegel's point that the master is controlled by the relationship by which he supposedly exerts control, and the slave has a measure of control in the relationship whereby he supposedly is denied any control, and that thus freedom for either one entails freedom for the other.

The three two-page spreads are brilliant in their suggestiveness, but are they an argument (or a set of arguments)? It is easy to supply further claims that are supported by the propositions suggested by the photographs, especially in the context of the ad's appearing in the special issue of *The New Yorker* on Black in America in 1996: racism is unjustified, harmful; we should be rid of it.[6] It is plausible, therefore, to interpret these photographs as a set of visual arguments against racism. Premise I (see Figure 1): we are all the same under our skin; we are biologically the same species, and we are all human. Premise 2 (see Figure 2): racism is a construct, not an inborn attitude; adults

FIGURE 2.

FIGURE 3.

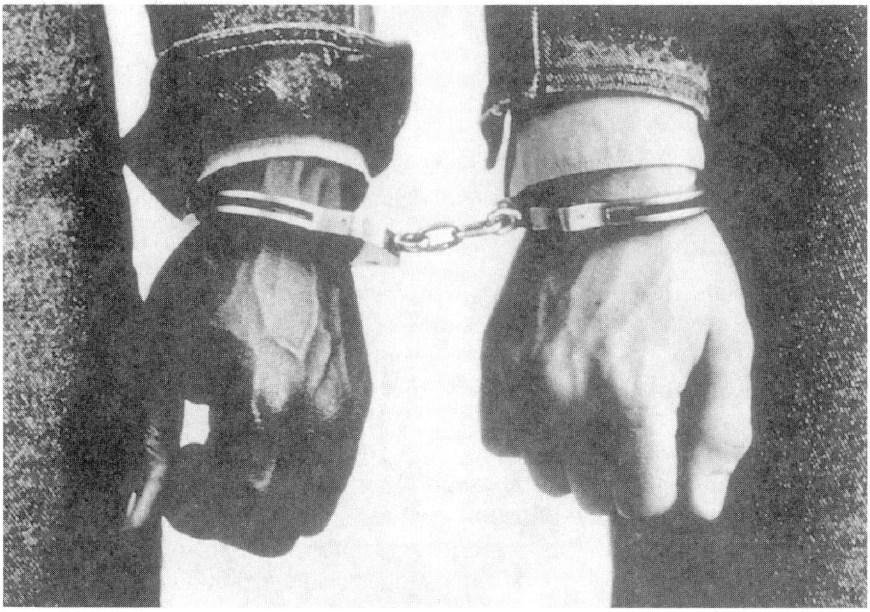

impose its ugliness on the innocence of children. Premise 3 (see Figure 3): we are joined together, black and white, inescapably; we are prisoners of our attitudes. Conclusion: racism is unjustified and should be ended.

Let us not forget, however, that this is a very expensive advertisement by the Benetton clothing company. How does it sell Benetton clothes? Virtually no clothing, and nothing distinctive, is shown. Factor in the Black in America theme and the fact that the readership of *The New Yorker* is predominantly upper middle class and wealthy, mostly white, liberals, judging by the advertisements typically found in its pages and its standard editorial content. What the ad does is identify Benetton with the self-image of their racial attitudes held by *The New Yorker* readers. One thing that is going on is that through the ad, Benetton is conveying the message, "We share your color-blind ideals, your opposition to racism, and your recognition of the problems facing the ideal of blacks and whites living in harmony and your desire to see them overcome." And it does so with powerful images and symbols. The Benetton ad is a paradigm case of the classical advertising ploy: create an ad that the viewer feels good about or identifies with and the viewer will transfer those feelings and that identification to your company or products(s). One particular concrete way the identification in this case might transfer to the act of purchasing is that the consumer who makes it will want to act on his or her solidarity with Benetton's powerful anti-racism message by buying Benetton: "I support your stand, and I want to put my money where my mouth is—I'll take a couple of those shirts."[7]

But is the ad an argument for buying Benetton clothes? My contention is that the way this and similar visual ads work is precisely by NOT being arguments designed to persuade or convince us to buy the product or patronize the company. They do not engage our intellects in critical thinking about purchasing or product choices; they supply no reasons for buying the product or patronizing the company. They sell precisely by creating and trading on unconscious, unexamined identifications. In the case of the Benetton ad, just as soon as the viewer realizes what these ads are doing, she or he will see that they constitute a clever, perhaps even a cynical, attempt to trade on her or his attitudes. The now more fully aware viewer might very well reason as follows: "Benetton is a company that sells clothing. Its purpose in paying a lot of money for the creation of this ad and its placement here is to sell Benetton in order to sell Benetton clothes. Hence its evocation of my feelings and attitudes is self-serving manipulation. I don't want to give my business to a company that tries to do that to me." In other words, the moment the viewer's focus escapes from the overt message and his or her reasoning becomes engaged, the selling power of the ad begins to weaken. (To be sure, the unconscious identifications may be more powerful than the conscious rejection of the manipulation, so exposing the manipulation may not defuse the effectiveness of the identifications.) The ad works best by being an argument at the superficial level, but above all by *not* being an argument at the deeper, affective level. In fact, the stark, spare simplicity of the Benetton ad is extremely clever as a means of avoiding reminding the viewer that this is an ad to sell clothing, while the green tag keeps the company name identification prominent.[8]

Let me sum up my theses about the Benetton ad. First, the ad presents a powerful, multi-premise, visual argument against racism. Second, the ad presents no argument, visual or otherwise, for buying from Benetton. Third, the way (or at least one principal way) that the ad is likely to contribute to an increase in Benetton sales is through the unconscious effect on viewers of the statement about Benetton that the visual argument of the ad presents. Fourth, while this effect can take various forms (simultaneously), essential to them all is the identification of the viewer with the values expressed by the argument, and the transfer of that identification to Benetton as a company and to Benetton products.

Many print ads that combine texts with photographs or other pictures use the text to convey an overt argument, thereby disguising the fact that the visuals serve up the affective, psychological identification, and thus do the real selling job. It's a clever shell game: suspicious of a non-rational sell, we get an (apparently) rational sell, which disarms us, thus leaving us vulnerable to the covert non-rational sell. Of course, if the argument (verbal or visual) sells by itself, or reinforces the non-argumentative identifications of the pictures, so much the better.

The interaction between text and visuals in advertising and elsewhere (in television news, and in documentary reporting like *60 Minutes*, for instance) is extremely important, and deserves careful study that is beyond the scope of this paper. I speculate, however, that such study will not reveal arguments to play more than a disguising role in effective visual advertising. Recall, for example, the old STP ad that *showed* someone with STP-slicked fingers unable to hold onto a screwdriver by the tip. The voice-over *said*, "STP reduces friction in your engine." Was the ad an argument from analogy: "The friction between fingers and a screwdriver tip is like that between a piston and a cylinder; as you can see, STP reduces the former friction; therefore it will reduce the latter?" I don't think so. Seeing the ad in terms of an argument from analogy made explicit provides the viewer with hooks on which to hang critical questions, such as, "*Are* the two kinds of friction at all comparable?" Much more likely, I suspect, is the hope that the viewer will think, "Wow! Look how slippery that stuff is: the voice-over claim is true." In any case, there is a fruitful field for case studies here.

C. Television Commercials

What has just been said about print ads goes in spades for TV commercials. The latter have enormously powerful means of evoking identifications that are independent of the text. They have music, which in a few seconds can create a mood. A familiar tune can flash us back to earlier experiences, evoking floods of feelings. The dynamics that TV images provide mean that, instead of giving us just a snapshot to identity with, we can get an entire drama, with plot and character development, structure of crisis, climax, and dénoument, all in thirty seconds. It is easier with TV than print to use humor, which is disarming and misdirecting. Many more evocative symbols (such as children, animals, nature, family, mother, doctor, or scientist) can be packed into a thirty-second clip than into a static one-page magazine ad. It is also easy to use the overt, surface, verbal argumentation of the spoken script to mask the manipulation of feelings by the music, the drama, and the visuals.

Again, I am not at all saying that TV ads never use visual arguments directly to sell a product or a brand. But I would hypothesize that the effective ones either don't use arguments at all, or else they get their efficacy not directly from any arguments they proffer, but from the underlying and hidden identifications and feelings they evoke. Should we call such manipulation "persuasion," if not argument? That is a question taken up in Section 5., below.

D. Arguments in (Political) Cartoons

A good case can be made that political cartoons can and do present us with arguments. (Notice how cartoon-like are the medieval cathedral sculptures of the Last Judgment.) Groarke has found an excellent example in a 1938 David Low cartoon. In it, a man is shown sitting on a steep hillside reading a newspaper, with his back to a pile of big boulders poised above him, all prevented from tumbling down on him by one key boulder, labelled "Czechoslovakia." The boulders above it are labelled, "Poland," "Romania," "French Alliances," and "Anglo-French Security." The man is saying, "What's Czechoslovakia to me anyway?" Low's visual argument was clearly that anyone who thought the Nazi psychological war against Czechoslovakia did not matter to England was wrong, because if it fell (to Hitler's bullying), then Poland and Romania would be next, followed by the French alliances, and finally the Anglo-French security pact would come crashing down. As Groarke points out, this is an obvious example of a slippery-slope argument.

Not all political cartoons present arguments; many simply make statements. What is the difference? Again, as with paintings and advertisements, enough information has to be provided visually to permit an unambiguous verbal reconstruction of the propositions expressed, so that, combining that with contextual information, it is possible to reconstruct a plausible premise-and-conclusion combination intended by the cartoonist.

Let me sum up this part of the discussion. While visual arguments are possible, they seem not to be widespread. More significantly, they seem not to constitute a radically different kind of argument from verbal ones. What makes visual messages influential, taking television advertisements as the most striking examples, is not any argumentative function they may perform, but the unconscious identifications they invoke. There is no reason to ignore or overlook visual arguments. However, their existence presents no theoretical challenge to the standard sorts of verbal argument analysis. They are easily assimilated to the paradigm model of verbal argument characterized by O'Keefe's concept of argument$_1$. The difficulties they do present are practical ones of exegesis or interpretation. Moreover, we have to translate them into verbal arguments in order to analyze and criticize them. So verbal arguments retain their position of primacy.

In the process of answering the question, "Are there any instances of visual arguments?" (Answer: Yes), we have answered the further question, "Are visual arguments significantly different from verbal arguments?" (Answer: No).

4. Non-Propositional Argument

For visual argument to represent a radically different kind of argument, it would have to be non-propositional. But what kind of argument could that conceivably be? Let us consider some candidates.

There is a use of "argument" which counts states of affairs and complex entities as arguments. "The way those two dress is an argument that opposites attract," "*All Quiet on the Western Front* is an argument against war," "Some critics think that Mailer's oeuvre (*malgré lui*) is an argument for authorial absence," or "The horrible final six months of Zoë's cancer-racked life is an argument for legalizing euthanasia." But the use of "argument" exemplified by such cases is a handy shorthand for, or summation of, an extended case consisting of verbally expressible propositions. In each case, someone can ask, "What do you mean?" and would, and should, expect in answer a fuller account showing how a propositional argument making the case would run.

We also naturally speak of narratives as arguments, or at least as having an argumentative or else at least a persuasive function. Striking examples are the great religious narratives, or the historical stories in terms of which we justify national policies, both domestic and foreign (for example, "The Opening Up of the West," or "The Cold War"). Certainly narratives can be powerfully persuasive; they may be the most persuasive kinds of discourse that exist. Yet, on the one hand, they too are propositional, however complex their propositional structure may be; and on the other hand, they accomplish their influence not by argument in any traditional sense, but by connecting our beliefs and experience into meaningful stories which we adopt as elements of our personal or collective worldviews.

Metaphors are another powerfully persuasive force. Lakoff and Johnson (1980) have shown how pervasively they shape our conceptual schemes, and hence the perceptions, interpretations, and choices in terms of which we construct our lives. However, (a) metaphors can function independently of argument, but in any case, (b) metaphors too are propositional.

As we review the various extended concepts or kinds of argument or persuasion, we discover that what distinguishes them from the paradigm is not that the paradigm is propositional whereas they are not. They turn out either to be propositional, or else not arguments.

5. Reprogramming, Persuasion, Argument, and Rhetoric

Various ways of influencing beliefs, attitudes, and behavior can be placed along a continuum. A course of treatments consisting of electrical impulses delivered to key locations in the brain that causes a pedophile to lose his sexual interest in children is not an example of argument or persuasion. A physical seduction (kissing, stroking, licking, nibbling) which causes someone to act very much against his or her better judgment is persuasion of one sort, but it cannot be classified as argument in any sense. The offer of a cigarette to a smoker trying to quit, or the dessert tray shown to a struggling dieter, may persuade the person (even if not persuasive in intent and made in ignorance of the interlocutors' conditions); but again, there is no argument involved. We come to a case bordering on argument with the example of the robber who points a gun at you and demands your wallet or purse.

The significant variable in all these cases is the nature and degree of mediation by the agent. Imagine a mediation mechanism that has a beep function that sounds to alert us when we have a choice to make (think of the loud warning klaxon activated when commercial vehicles are in reverse gear), and a "Yes" and "No" pair of buttons we can press to make the choice. With the brain implant treatment, the choice mechanism is by-passed: the beep does not even go off. With the seduction, the static from the stimulation of our erogenous zones interferes with our hearing the beep. (The real possibility that we make a prior choice to allow the interference to mask the choice beep is what leads us to suspect self-deception in the case of "seduction.") The habits, perhaps the addiction, in the smoking or overeating examples, seem not to camouflage the choice beep (it sounds loud and clear), but to draw us inexorably to push the "Yes" button. Most of us know first-hand the phenomenology of temptation: the sense of being pulled by a force-field to say "Yes," while the faint voice that urges us to say "No" is overwhelmed by another more powerful and seemingly reasonable one, citing ever-so-good reasons for making an exception this time. What makes the robbery case different is that, at least on some occasions, for a moment we clearly experience the opportunity to choose and the choice seems open: we do a quick cost-benefit analysis (which normally makes it clear that refusal to comply is not worth the risk).

The paradigm for persuasion is verbal persuasion, as it is for its subspecies, argument. As a result, we are more comfortable identifying as persuasion those cases of belief/attitude/behavior influence in which speech is involved, even if we admit that it can be other factors than the speaker's arguments, such as her ethos or the figures she used, which are persuasive. Still, we do permit locutions like, "The mouth-watering aroma of its sauce persuaded me to try the fish," which implies that verbal factors are not necessary to persuasion. According to the Oxford English Dictionary, almost all definitions of the word "persuade" focus on the result produced. The only reference to the means used identifies persuasion with "inducing" to (believe, act, and so on). Now, to *induce* someone to believe or act is to act upon their will, which brings us back to the factor of the agent's mediation which distinguishes the brain surgery from the other cases in our examples above.

We refuse the label "persuasion" to behavior modification through brain surgery, because the agent has no mediating role to play: nothing acts on his will. We classify the cases of seduction and the temptations of smoking and dessert as persuasion precisely because the agent knew there was a choice, and could and did in some sense make a choice. The distraught cuckold or the disappointed dietitian would be entirely right to counter our protestations with: "Nonsense! You had a choice and you made it!" The salient difference between these two cases and the robbery case is phenomenological — namely the experience of having a choice that accompanies the latter more than the former. That is what, to my mind, associates the robber's threat with argument, for in the case of argument the agent's mediation is essential: the audience or interlocutor must identify the premise and conclusion propositions and make a determination about the degree of the support the former lends to the latter.

Some might want to assimilate the offer of dessert or a cigarette to argument, too. In most restaurants that show a dessert tray, the point is either to inform the diner (visually) of what is available, or to tempt the diner, or both. The person offering a cigarette is normally just being polite, or (sometimes) mean. It strikes me as forced to view these as attempts to get someone to accept a proposition on the basis of reasons offered. However, admittedly I have not offered a formal analysis of the difference between argumentative and non-argumentative persuasion.

To the extent that visual communication causes us to change our beliefs or attitudes, or to act, without engaging our choice buttons, it is assimilable neither to persuasion nor argument. Once the choice light flashes, persuasion is occurring. And once we have identified expressible reasons that are provided for pressing one button rather than the other, we are being persuaded by argument. In sum, the act of argument is a species of persuasion, and both entail the attempt to engage the agent as mediator in a decision to act or to change an attitude or belief. (We can be persuaded against our better judgment, but not against our will.) Persuasion by argument entails the making explicit of propositions and their alleged illative relations.

If all this is right, then the psychological sell of the advertiser who manipulates our unconscious identifications can be classified neither as argument nor as non-argumentative persuasion, visual or otherwise: we don't get to choose or decide. If we reach or ask for a Coke or a Coors instead of a Pepsi or a Bud, most of us don't really know why. Many ads provide no reasons whatever for preferring one brand to the other, or one type of product to alternatives; the "reasons" others supply often cannot withstand even cursory critical analysis. Yet we claim to have preferences, and since the principal differences are between the ads, not the products, presumably somehow the ads get to us. How exactly they do so is a question eminently worthy of study. The hypothesis that I have ventured, namely manipulation of unconscious ego-identification, is undeveloped and may turn out to be untestable or false, but the idea that these ads work by persuading us with visual arguments is barking up the wrong tree, and even the hypothesis that they persuade us (perhaps non-rationally), is not plausible either, unless the concept of persuasion is stretched to include causally efficacious influence in general. Such an extension of the concept then runs into the difficulty of distinguishing that kind of persuasion from behavior modification by brain surgery.

At this point one may well ask, Where is rhetoric on this map? Even mentioning rhetoric opens a Pandora's box, yet failing to do so in the present discussion would be culpable, so I will timorously and briefly venture a proposal. Reboul (1991, p. 4) notes a range of definitions of rhetoric, and states his own preference to be "the art of persuading by speech [*l'art de persuader par le discours,*]" thereby agreeing, in general, with Foss, Foss, and Trapp (1985, p. 12), who say, "the paradigm case of rhetoric is the use of the spoken word to persuade an audience." If these authorities are right, and if the above points about persuasion are correct, then (a) the study of rhetoric includes the study of argument, (b) the concept of visual argument is an extension of rhetoric's paradigm into a new domain. Whether the realm of rhetoric is identical to that of persuasion, or instead just partially overlaps it, depends on how tightly the concept of rhetoric is tied to that of persuasion. If rhetoric in a broader sense is the use of symbols to communicate (see Foss, Foss, and Trapp, 1985, p. 11), so that symbolic communication rather than persuasion is its fundamental property, then some but not all rhetoric will be persuasive in intent and some but not all persuasion will be rhetorical in nature; there will be non-persuasion-oriented rhetoric and non-rhetorical persuasion. On the other hand, if the persuasive function lies at the heart of rhetoric, then any form of persuasion, including visual persuasion, belongs within rhetoric's province.

6. THE IMPORTANCE OF VISUAL ARGUMENT

What is lost by foregoing or overlooking visual argument? The question asks what can be accomplished only or best by using visual arguments. And what are the disadvantages of visual arguments? Like much else, visual arguments have correlative virtues and vices.

The incredibly evocative power of a movie (even more than a novel) can bring us as close to actual experiential knowledge as it is possible to get, short of living the experience. Thus movies can make the truth of premises more "real" than can any assemblage of evidence in, say, a legal brief. For example, by getting us to feel what it is like to be exploited or discriminated against, they can provide enormously powerful arguments against these treatments and the attitudes and systems that foster them. Of course, the same power can be used to distort or misrepresent, and thus to argue falsely. Movies can bring us to experience the panoply of emotions–impatience, fear, disappointment, joy, rage, frustration, contentment–but the reality of those feelings does not vouch for their legitimacy. People can be furious when they should be understanding, complacent when they should be angry; and so on. By creating false experiences, movies can convince us of conclusions that should not be drawn.

To be sure, with argument-containing films, and plays too, we have a hybrid of the visual and the verbal, not purely visual argument. It is therefore hard to extract the argumentative force of just the visual dimension of the communication. However, the dramatic difference in effect between reading a film script or a play and watching the movie or the play in the theater is familiar to us all. The nature of the visual contribution may be difficult to describe, but its force is undeniable. (The relation between the textual, the visual, and the auditory dimension of film deserves study.)

The power of the visual granted, visual arguments tend to be one-dimensional: they present the case for one side only, without including the arguments against it, or without doing so sympathetically, and without representing alternative standpoints and their merits and defects. The demands of the movie or TV dramatic form include pressures for simplicity and for closure. Painting or sculpture are even more limited in this regard. Visual arguments, then, must always be suspect in this respect, and their power countered by a degree of skepticism and a range of critical questions: "Is that the whole story?" "Are there other points of view?" "Is the real picture so black and white?" Visual argument will tend to be one-sided, uni-dimensional argument.

While visual communication can be concrete and particular, it can also, even simultaneously, be vague or ambiguous. If suggestiveness is the aim, this is a virtue; where clarity or precision are desiderata, it is a disadvantage. The sender of the message lacks the power to have his or her intentions well understood, since the receiver is free to interpret in various ways. To be sure, this is a problem with written and spoken argument too, but less so than with visual argument. So visual argument has both the strength and the weakness of its form.

In sum, while there can be no doubt that visual argument is important by virtue of its ability to be powerfully influential, its responsible deployment calls for great skill and integrity, and its responsible consumption requires alert critical interaction.

7. Conclusion

The main point that I draw from these reflections is that visual arguments are not distinct in essence from verbal arguments. The argument is always a propositional entity, merely expressed differently in the two cases. Therefore visual arguments are not a particularly exciting conceptual novelty; they do not constitute a radically different realm of argumentation. The need to give visual arguments premise-conclusion propositional embodiment has the consequence that plenty of dramatic visual statements fall short of being arguments. And the non-propositional character of the truly effective psychological manipulation in much advertising has the implication that such powerful visual persuasion comes no closer to argument than the decoys or facades of argument that, by disguising the manipulation, enhance it. The attempt to conceive of the possibility of non-propositional argument (as distinct from non-propositional persuasion) comes up empty. Finally, the great advantages of visual argument, namely its power and its suggestiveness, are gained at the cost of a loss of clarity and precision, which may not always be a price worth paying.

While the preceding contentions downplay the theoretical distinctness of visual arguments, they are not meant to understate the differences inherent in its medium of communication. Just how visual images and visual forms in general can and do communicate propositions, just how the important ancillary concept of context is to be understood and how in practice context is to be interpreted and combined with the visual, and just how text and visuals (and sound) interact to produce meaning are all questions which strike me as important, difficult and unanswered by the present paper.[9]

NOTES

1. According to Mowat (1965, see pp. 356–57), that was one of the navigational methods they used in sailing first from the Outer Islands to Iceland, and later thence to Greenland, and thence to Labrador and Newfoundland.

2. This fact makes visual irony more difficult to achieve, or detect, than verbal irony, since irony requires the reversal of surface assertion.

3. Thanks to David Birdsell for this formulation.

4. Groarke says these statements are made by the painting, but what the painting actually depicts is the evidence for them.

5. Figure 1., "Hearts," United Colors of Benetton, Concept: O. Toscani, Spring 1996; Figure 2., "Angel/Devil," United Colors of Benetton, Concept: O. Toscani, Fall/Winter 1991/92; Figure 3., "Handcuffs," United Colors of Benetton, Concept: O. Toscani, Fall/Winter 1989/90.

6. Even though the three photos were not initially conceived as a unit, but on different occasions over the past seven years, their grouping here in this special issue of *The New Yorker* supplies

a new context.

7. This last point is due to David Birdsell. He recalled a discussion of the effectiveness of Nike's ads with kids. The point made was that kids didn't think buying Nikes would transform them into Michael Jordans, but they wanted to declare their allegiance. I believe one such discussion occurred in an article devoted to the agency responsible for those Nike ads, that appeared in *The New Yorker* a few years ago.

8. This general position on advertising is developed more fully in Johnson and Blair, 1994, Ch. 11.

9. I wish to thank an anonymous referee, Leo Groarke, and David Birdsell for numerous corrections, constructive criticisms, and suggestions, all of which I have tried to respond to in revising the paper and which have much improved it.

REFERENCES

Anscombre, J. & Ducrot, O. (1983). *Lárgumentation dans la langue. Liège*: Pierre Mardaga.
Brockriede, W. (1975). Where is argument? *Journal of the American Forensic Association, 11*, 179–182.
Eemeren, F.H., van, & Grootendorst, R. (1984). *Speech acts in argumentative discussions: A theoretical model for the analysis of discussions directed towards solving conflicts of opinion*. Dordrecht: Foris.
Ferguson, G. (1954). *Signs & symbols in Christian art*. Oxford: Oxford UP.
Foss, S. K., Foss, K. A., & Trapp, R. (1985). *Contemporary perspectives on rhetoric*. Prospect Heights, IL: Waveland Press.
Groarke, L. (in press). Logic, art and argument. *Informal Logic*.
Gronbeck, B. (1980). From argument to argumentation: Fifteen years of identity crisis. In J. Rhodes & S. Newell (Eds.), *Proceedings of the Summer Conference on Argumentation* (pp. 8–19). Annandale, VA: Speech Communication Association.
Hample, D. (1985). A third perspective on argument. *Philosophy and Rhetoric, 18*, 1–22.
Johnson, R. H. & Blair, J.A. (1994) *Logical self-defense* (U.S. ed.). New York: McGraw-Hill.
Kelder, D. (1976). *Aspects of "official" painting and philosophic art, 1789–1799*. New York: Garland.
Lakaoff, G. & Johnson, M. (1980). *Metaphors we live by*. Chicago: U of Chicago P.
Mâle, E. (1958). *The Gothic image: Religious art in France of the thirteenth century*. (D. Nussey, Trans.). New York: Harper & Row. (Original work published in 1898)
Mowat, F. (1965). *Vestviking: The ancient Norse in Greenland and North America*. Toronto: McClelland & Stewart.
O'Keefe, D.J. (1977). Two concepts of argument: *Journal of the American Forensic Association, 13*, 121–128.
O'Keefe, D. J. (1982). Two concepts of argument and arguing. In J. R. Cox and C. A. Willard (Eds.), *Advances in argumentation theory and research* (pp. 3–23). Carbondale, IL: Southern Illinois UP.
Reboul, O. (1991). *Introduction à la rhétorique*. Paris: Presses Universitaires de France.
Trapp, R. (1983). Generic characteristics of argumentation in everyday discourse. In D. Zarefsky, M. O. Sillars & J. Rhodes (Eds.), *Argument in transition: Proceedings of the third summer conference on argumentation* (pp. 516–530). Annandale, VA: Speech Communication Association.
Willard, C. A. (1983) *Argumentation and the social grounds of knowledge*. Tuscaloosa, AL: U of Alabama P.
Willard, C.A. (1989). *A theory of argumentation*. Tuscaloosa, AL: U of Alabama P.

22   *The Problem of Electronic Argument: A Humanist's Perspective*

MICHELE S. SHAUF

1. INTRODUCTION

In a way, but only in a way, I want to examine the challenge of creating visualized arguments in electronic domains. I teach multimedia design at both the graduate and undergraduate levels at a large, public, technological university, and am constantly frustrated by what I once thought was the unwillingness of students to undertake argument in their work. When I give students a chance to invent their own multimedia projects—and I refer here to both Web sites and stand-alone CD-ROMs—they come up with a curiously limited array of topics, namely three: multimedia narratives about their families (usually their grandparents); educational multimedia for very young children (lessons in multiplication, for instance); or purely expository works laying out the facts of some topic in an old-school "who, what, where, when, and how" journalistic style. I have even specifically assigned multimedia arguments, but in each case what I got from students was a neutral setting-out of data with little rhetorical impetus. What I have come to believe, though, is that students in my classes cannot conceive of such a thing as an electronic argument because they engage the computer in a language unlike mine.

In my language, "composition" returns to its classical roots in the rhetorical notion of discursive arrangement. Restricted in the age of literacy to writing, composition should now more broadly refer to the design of arguments —in whatever media. And, because contemporary media are decidedly visual, Composition Studies now ought to mean something like visual rhetoric or visual literacy. Again, in my language, or my vocabulary, this latest repurposing of the ancient art of rhetoric involves two visual grammars: one, the logic of the image; and two, the logic of space. In my classes, therefore, I begin with the rhetoric of the image, with particular emphasis on the photograph's way of meaning.

Unfortunately for instructors of electronic rhetoric, clip art, animated GIFs, and the painting software that comes free with flatbed scanners have

---

From *Computers and Composition* 18:1 (March 2001): 33–37.

made it so easy to include images in electronic artifacts that they are used compulsively. Many of these images are generic in the most literal sense of the word, which is to say they are nothing more than denotative information: two people (one sitting, one standing) at a computer terminal. That is the kind of imagery I mean. We have all seen it. Today, students are most likely adept enough at the rudiments of layout that they will place the image effectively on the screen and achieve a nicely-balanced visual composition. But the image will often be mere decoration, a graphical weight to offset the pull of a text field or row of buttons. In itself, this ability is very much an accomplishment, and certainly a welcomed improvement by students who only three or four years ago had not yet built a home page or worked with graphics software and were completely new to making these kinds of design choices. Once a student can see visual weight, then the more complex matter of the rhetoric of the image can be introduced and with it the most robust tools of composition: metaphor and metonymy, analogy and description. This is the first visual grammar of electronic rhetoric.

The second visual grammar is the logic of space, which is perhaps another way of saying the logic of subordination or the logic of proportion. This visual grammar is one we have practiced and taught for a long time, though where we once called it "outlining" we now call it *information architecture* or *discursive architectonics*. Certainly I don't tell students they are outlining—we talk about flow charts with varying degrees of data granularity—but when they are planning a site for electronic discourse, outlining is precisely what they are doing. Outlines as blueprints are the cognitive basis of every flow chart, which in turn is simply a geometric visualization of an outline. Once students become proficient in spatializing abstractions such as arguments, they ought to be able to draw again upon metaphor and analogy to build an electronic essay traversed by the user as a space—rooms in a house, for instance; galleries in a museum; or drawers in a desk.

But all of this, as I have said, comes out of my language, a vocabulary not common to everyone. A specific example might prove helpful: Last semester I taught a course in the grammar of the photograph. It was a critical survey, exploring photography both as a medium and as a cognitive frame, meaning that just as it is possible to take a photograph, it is also possible to see and to think photographically. And, if it is possible to think photographically, then it ought to be possible to develop a photographic style that may be expressed in a variety of media—in writing, for instance. Early on, the class was able to dispense with photography's public relations problem, its habit of prevarication and tenuous (at best) relation to reality. The reason we were able to dispense with this problem early on in the semester is that no one believes it anyway. We have all taken (and been captured in) too many reality-twisting snapshots to believe that the image is true. This is just one of photography's many fine paradoxes. We know it isn't a transcript, yet we wish ever so much that it was.

What was more difficult, though, was setting each student on an idiosyncratic track toward discovering (that is, inventing) a photographic style. To encourage a writing style that performed a photographic esthetic, I engaged the class in some distinctions between the essay and the article as literary genres and tried to get at the idea that the essay, like the photograph, has a pronounced point of view—a shading, a cropping, an apparent process of selection. The talented, technically proficient students of my institution are impressively skillful with the article mode, written in the voice-of-no-voice, so it seemed to me that with some practice they could also skillfully cultivate other, more audible writing voices. The idea finally took, but it was initially quite difficult for me to explain the idea of style as rhetoric.

One class discussion stands out in particular. The students had already read two collections of "photographic" writing—Susan Sontag's (1977) *On Photography* and George Trow's (1997) awe-inspiring *Within the Context of No Context*—and I was attempting to jump-start the inductive process: "If these are examples of the essay, then what are some characteristics of the essay as a genre?" I was plainly making little headway, so a student with a facilitator temperament, asked: "Can you just tell us the functionality of the essay?"

Now *functionality* is a programmer's word, and it is a good one in the context of computer programming because the slightest oversight—failing to assign a value to a variable, let's say—might result in zero functionality. Your program won't work. What is interesting about functionality is that the difference between none and 100% could be a mere keystroke or two, an omitted "if" in a crucial if-then statement.

Obviously, functionality makes no sense in the context of the essay; nor does it make much sense in the humanist's vocabulary. An additional example might further illustrate: Shopping around for suitable texts for my photography class, I noticed a narrative common to many media histories that might be titled "The March of Time." The story begins with the ideologically suspect linear perspective, which is mechanized in photography and then finds its moving groove in film which, in turn, is democratized in video. These events are condensed into a single "before" as the narrative reaches its climax in New Media. It is a story in which photography supersedes drawing, film supersedes photography, video supersedes film, and new media supersedes video.

As a humanist, I cannot understand this narrative. Or rather, I understand the plot line, just not with these particular agents. By way of contrast, I quite understand that techniques of bridge building in the 1990s supersede the way bridges were built in the 1920s, but that seems to me an entirely different story. What I do not see is that photography "wants to be" film or that video is finally "fulfilled" in 360 degree × 360 degree × 360 degree virtual space.

One final example: I used David Siegel's (1997) *Creating Killer Web Sites* in a graduate class. Many people consider Siegel the premier Web design guru and his book a classic. Certainly it is single-handedly responsible for the generational distinction so often invoked in the critique of Web sites. According to Siegel, first generation sites (the typical site in the early days of the Web) are characterized by a relentless textuality broken only by strategically placed horizontal rules. Second generation sites add images, but third generation sites, today's cutting-edge, open with introductory "splash" screens. And they never, ever use horizontal rules, horizontal rules being, so, "over."

Anyone interested in composition (again, synonymous with "design") knows, of course, that nothing is ever "over." Composers, in whatever medium, are always looking to the past for ideas, to Montaigne or Depression-era painting or aleotoric music or Christian Dior fashions of the 1950s. I can only conclude that in saying third generation sites "go beyond" text and graphics as logical cues, Siegel cannot be speaking as a humanist. He conceptualizes digital space in the vocabulary of the technologist and this, I think, is why electronic argument presents such a problem.

What I am talking about through these examples are ways of talking, of vocabularies. I recognize that talking about ways of talking is tricky, possibly suspect, maybe even futile, because the twentieth century was largely about exposing the absence of foundational vocabularies, but I am no French minister of culture bemoaning the adulteration of languages. In principle, interlinguisitic borrowings are a good idea as long as no inquiry is confined to a single frame of reference; in any event, they are unavoidable. I do want to suggest, however, that because technology gives rise to new media applications, multimedia comes predisposed to the vocabulary most germane to the technologist's work. And the problem with this bundled vocabulary is that it reads chronologies as advancements, which is rather anathema to the humanist point of view. Indeed, one way to describe the humanities might be to say that it is the record of human attempts to address questions in which no advance whatever has been made. What is good, why is death the truest and the falsest thing, where is beauty, what is just, how has history made us? Surely these are problems quite unlike the problems of scripting rollovers and preloading video into cache if only because we cannot be sure that our current solutions will, in the long run, turn out to be any better than those offered by Raphael or Kierkegaard or Woolf or Satie or Arbus or Muddy Waters.

In fact, I would argue that the most vital role of humanists in our technological age is to maintain a skeptical eye and a cautious attitude toward the early adoption of technologies simply because they "go beyond." Our goal is to foster not technical invention but rhetorical invention, and yet the composition (or design) classroom is increasingly given over to technical troubleshooting—why does the spin work in Netscape COMMUNICATOR but not Microsoft's INTERNET EXPLORER?—or, even worse, software instruction. What I fear is that the art of rhetoric is not helping shape the content and form of multimedia artifacts but rather that new media technologies, and the considerable cognitive demands they place on composers, are instead subsuming entirely the practice of rhetoric. What we naturally see, then, is a distinctive pattern in multimedia composition with plenty of technical ambition (3-D modeling, sound, animation) but very little rhetorical ambition (hence the virtual nonexistence of electronic essays or arguments). This is because students approach electronic composition through the language of technology, not rhetoric.

To assert its pertinence to electronic composition, a rhetorical approach to new media must begin by rebuffing the seductions of cutting-edge technologies because the seduction amounts to the humanities finally admitting the irrelevance of their vocabularies and capitulating to the go-beyond vocabulary of technology. Most unfortunately for us, this go-beyond language is also the language of administrators, who too often measure programs and even individual instructors in terms of a gizmo quotient, the wow-factor of the wired classroom. Nevertheless, it is our job to foster carefully considered rhetorical (which is to say conceptual and esthetic and ethical) ambitions in students so they are continually asking, as we do, what lies beyond "beyond."

This is a question that needs to be posed relentlessly, as evidenced by the strange narrowness of purpose to which new media has so far been put. As we all know, the most successful examples of professional multimedia, in terms of exposure and impact, are the Amazon.com Web site and the MYST adventure game. These are natural enough artifacts to come out of a culture of perpetual adolescence suffering from NASDAQ ADD, and they have been fast answers—six years out of the box since NCSA's MOSAIC first made multimedia widely available through the World Wide Web. But if retail and kids' entertainment are the obvious answers to the question of how multimedia might be used and to what end, then the humanist vocabulary has enormous contributions to make in new media. First, however, we must restrict students to a limited technical palette to focus their attention on the idea that rhetoric, not JavaScript, is the core challenge in electronic composition.

To speak metaphorically (a habit of the humanist), I am reminded of the several times I've sat down with friends to watch a wedding video. Video technology is widely available, easy to use, and inexpensive. Why not videotape your wedding? Well, in each instance it was clear to the viewing lot of us that a videotaped wedding is on all accounts insufferable. It is easy enough to engage the technology, but one must ask to what end, for what rhetorical purpose. Going beyond the photo album is, of course, no reason at all.

REFERENCES

Siegel, David. (1997). *Creating killer web sites*. Indianapolis, IN: Hayden.
Sontag, Susan. (1977). *On photography*. New York: Noonday.
Trow, George W. S. (1997). *Within the context of no context*. New York: Atlantic Monthly.

23 *Figures of Rhetoric*

RICHARD LANHAM

"Every definition," Erasmus tells us, "is a misfortune." Certainly the lists of rhetorical terms which have appeared since the beginnings of formal rhetoric—which have from time to time seemed to *be* formal rhetoric—have been viewed as one long series of misfortunes. As every historian of rhetoric points out, even the historians of figures seem to hate the figures. Almost no one has a good thing to say about them, but almost no one could resist arguing about them and, if possible (and often if not), adding a new term to the list. In a self-conscious age like our own, the very existence of the terminology, and of lists of it like this one, deserves a comment. Why has the nomenclature loomed so large and confused so many?

Perhaps the confusion began because Rome was bilingual. The Greek rhetorical terminology put on a Latin doubleture, and then in the Renaissance both sets of terms absorbed the numinosity of classical culture itself. No wonder Puttenham's wonderful terms hadn't a chance. They must have seemed—they still seem to us—somehow *impious*. It is those confusing, conflicting, overlapping Greek and Latin terms that we cling to. Everyone from Quintilian onward, of course, has complained about the imprecision and proliferation, regretting the absence of a clear, brief, and definitive set of terms, a nomenclature fixed once and for all. Curtius remarks, for example: "The study of figures has never been satisfactorily systematized. . . . This lack of a settled terminology, and, in short, the endless variations in enumerating and defining the figures, are to be explained historically by contacts between various schools" (*European Literature and the Latin Middle Ages*, p. 45).

To counteract this historical drift, some critics have suggested informal basic classifications. W. K. Wimsatt, Jr., for example, practiced the reduction this way:

> To put the matter simply yet, I believe, essentially: the figures of speech found in classical prose and poetry and described by Aristotle and the Roman rhetoricians, though multiplied during the centuries and often

From *A Handlist of Rhetorical Terms*. 2nd ed. Berkeley: U of California P, 1991. 78–80.

confused, fell into a few classes of main importance: 1. logical patterns of parallel and contrast in syllable, word, and phrase; 2. metaphoric meanings (often and correctly taken as figures of thought); and 3. a series of non-logical phonetic auxiliaries of metaphor, variously graded as pun, "turn" (or *traductio*), and alliteration.
(*Alexander Pope: Selected Poetry and Prose*, p. xxix)

And Alexander Bain had suggested a not wholly dissimilar three-part categorization in the previous century:

A classification of the more important Figures may be based on the three leading divisions of the Human Understanding . . . :

(1) Discrimination, or Feeling of Difference, Contrast, Relativity. . . .

(2) Similarity, or the Feeling of Agreement. . . .

(3) Retentiveness, or Acquisition.
(*English Composition and Rhetoric*, pp. 135–136)

But needful as such historical and classificatory thinking is, it may overlook the central point about the nomenclature of rhetorical figuration: that the confusion has been a *creative* one. We have *needed* to create it. The vast pool of terms for verbal ornamentation has acted like a gene pool for the rhetorical imagination, stimulating us to look at language in another way. When Gombrich wants to find out how Constable's painting of *Wivenhoe Park* creates the illusion of life, he superimposes a grid upon it, to break up the three-dimensional illusion into a series of surface squares which can then be studied in a new way. Doesn't rhetorical terminology work in much this way, testifying to a kind of verbal attention which looks *at* the verbal surface rather than *through* it? The figures have worked historically to teach a way of seeing—have supplied, if you will, a theory of reader response. If, as the postmodern Derridean theorists argue, rhetorical analysis is required for all kinds of reading, philosophical and ordinary as well as poetical, might we not argue that the terms have formed the central theory for such a general theory of verbal attention?

The act of inventing ever more finely tuned discriminatory figures has formed an excuse for a different activity altogether, the establishment of a domain of expressivity opposite to argumentation. We continually underestimate the degree of self-consciousness with which the world before Newton spoke and listened, read and wrote. Speeches were also entertainments, and it was the doctrine of the figures, the ability to create them and to spot them on the wing, that set up the oscillation between argumentation and ornamentation which has always provided the *diastole* and *systole* of the Western verbal imagination. As a dozen different fields of inquiry are telling us in one way or another today, ornament matters. It is not "merely ornamental." It feeds a genuine human hunger, the hunger for style. The great Greek scholar Eric Havelock once wrote that "Our species seems to have an inner biologic motivation which seeks to vary its own forms of expression" (*The Liberal Temper in Greek Politics*, p. 30). The rhetorical figures have been the central testimony, for language, to this inner motivation. Perhaps we should not repine that they have been so many and so various. Much has been done with such variety.

We might also project rhetorical figures onto a yet larger scale. They may represent a basic evolutionary strategy for our species. The biologist Edward O. Wilson writes: "The brain depends upon elegance to compensate for its own small size and short lifetime. As the cerebral cortex grew from apish dimensions through hundreds of thousands of years of evolution, it was forced to rely on tricks to enlarge memory and speed computation. The mind therefore specializes on analogy and metaphor, on a sweeping together of chaotic sensory experience into workable categories labeled by words and stacked into hierarchies for quick recovery" (*Biophilia*, p. 60). Such a raison d'être for figured language would make it finally into a kind of data-compression, an immensely rapid substitute for iterative searching. As such, it would be a part of our original evolutionary equipment, not an add-on; essential rather than ornamental.

WORKS CITED

Bain, Alexander. *English Composition and Rhetoric*. 2nd ed. New York: American Book Co., 1887.
Curtius, Ernst Robert. European Literature and the Latin Middle Ages. Translated by Willard R. Trask. Bollingen Series, 36. New York: Pantheon, 1953.
Erasmus, Desiderius. *Collected Works of Erasmus*, vols. 23–24: *Literary and Educational Writings*, 1–2. Edited by Craig R. Thompson. Vol. 23, *Antibarbari*, trans. Margaret Mann Phillips, and *Parabole*, trans. R. A. B. Mynors. Vol. 24, *Decopia*, trans. Betty I. Knott, and *De ratione studii*, trans. Brian McGregor. Toronto: University of Toronto Press, 1978.
Gombrich, E. H. *Art and Illusion: A Study in the Psychology of Pictorial Representation*. Vol. 5. A. W. Mellon Lectures in the Fine Arts. Princeton, NJ: Princeton UP, 1969. 305.
Havelock, Eric A. *The Liberal Temper in Greek Politics*. New Haven: Yale University Press, 1957.
Pope, Alexander, *Selected Poetry and Prose*. Edited by William K. Wimsatt, Jr. New York: Rinehart, 1952.
Puttenham, George. *The Arte of English Poesie* [1589]. Edited by Gladys Doidge Willcock and Alice Walker. Cambridge: Cambridge University Press, 1936.
Quintilian. *Institutio oratoria*. Translated by H. E. Butler, 4 vols. LCL, 1920–22.
Wilson, Edward O. *Biophilia*. Cambridge, Mass., and London: Harvard University Press, 1984.

24   *Rhetorical Devices and Tight Integration*

ROBERT HORN

Semantic relationships between visual and verbal elements are also created via classical rhetorical devices such as metaphor, metonymy, and synecdoche. Close examination of communication units that utilize these rhetorical devices reveals that they exhibit one or more of the types of integration cataloged on the preceding pages in addition to exhibiting a particular rhetorical device. In one sense, then, a kind of multiple integration occurs.

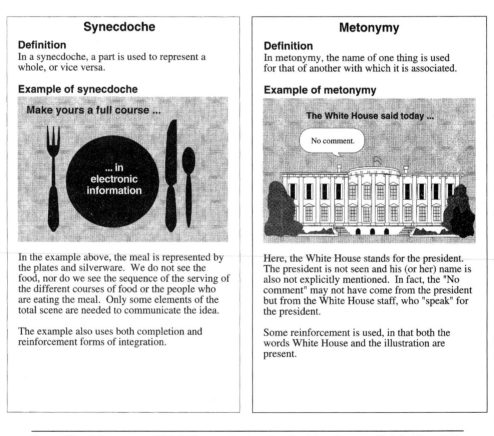

Synecdoche

Definition
In a synecdoche, a part is used to represent a whole, or vice versa.

Example of synecdoche

Make yours a full course ...

... in electronic information

In the example above, the meal is represented by the plates and silverware. We do not see the food, nor do we see the sequence of the serving of the different courses of food or the people who are eating the meal. Only some elements of the total scene are needed to communicate the idea.

The example also uses both completion and reinforcement forms of integration.

Metonymy

Definition
In metonymy, the name of one thing is used for that of another with which it is associated.

Example of metonymy

The White House said today ...

No comment.

Here, the White House stands for the president. The president is not seen and his (or her) name is also not explicitly mentioned. In fact, the "No comment" may not have come from the president but from the White House staff, who "speak" for the president.

Some reinforcement is used, in that both the words White House and the illustration are present.

From *Visual Language: Global Communication for the 21st Century*. Bainbridge, WA: MacroVU, Inc., 1998. 105–106.

Metaphor

Definition

In metaphor, one meaning or idea is used to represent a 2nd meaning or idea in order to suggest an analogy or likeness between the 2. Metaphors enable us to think about complex or abstract ideas in terms of more familiar or concrete ideas or experiences.

Visual language metaphor has the capacity to incorporate multiple meanings. The visual elements often provide the impact, emphasis, mood, or tonality that reinforces the main idea but that also triggers supporting or relevant ideas.

In visual language, different mixtures of verbal and visual components make the metaphor a very rich and expressive tool.

At this juncture, we are interested in simply seeing that metaphor functions as a rhetorical device in the tight integration of visual and verbal elements. The next section (➔113–122) contains a deeper analysis of metaphorical integration.

Example of metaphor

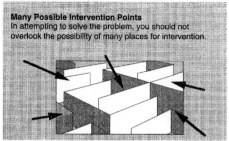

Many Possible Intervention Points
In attempting to solve the problem, you should not overlook the possibility of many places for intervention.

The visual conveys the problem via the spacial metaphor of a labyrinth. The arrows indicate the possible intervention points.

In this example the ideas are probably expressed clearly enough with the text so that the visual cannot be classified as disambiguation. The visual does reinforce the ideas presented by the words.

Example of metaphor

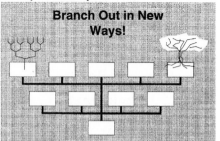

Branch Out in New Ways!

In this example, pictures of a conceptual tree and a natural tree are integrated metaphorically with the idea of "branching out" applied in an advertising firm. It suggests corporate growth or creativity coming out of a traditional organizational chart portrayed upside down.

This metaphor also shows integration with reinforcement.

PART FIVE

Visual Rhetoric and Culture

Introduction to Part Five

The power of the visual pervades our culture, dramatically shaping our perceptions of the world. The more we study the visual, the more we realize that what we see and how we interweave images with texts depend on the cultures, times, and places we live in. Our vision, our texts, our rhetoric are never neutral; our minds do not function in a vacuum devoid of subjectivity, political agendas, and points of view. As both visual and verbal rhetoricians, we should think deeply about cultural contingency and situated knowledge, about the ways in which we are embedded in our cultures and our historical time periods. We should recognize, furthermore, that rhetoric is not merely a neutral tool for analyzing and influencing culture, but is itself a cultural product. This final section samples contemporary academic work that studies the visual in culture, if not explicitly addressing visual rhetoric itself. The readings offer theoretical, architectural, artistic, and scientific enterprises (among others) that may influence or be influenced themselves by visual rhetoric.

Visual culture as a subfield of cultural studies focuses on vision as a starting point for tracing the ways cultural meanings form. Visual-culture studies also analyzes how the visual affects an audience, or a particular culture, and the degree to which that culture influences the meaning of the visual. Visual rhetoric, on the other hand, might be defined as a discipline that focuses on the visual elements that persuade, taking culture as just one element among many: culture, along with images, sounds, and space, work together rhetorically to convince an audience.

Visual-culture studies asks questions about cultural shifts initiated by the increase of the visual in our lives. In "Studying Visual Culture," theorist Irit Rogoff articulates some of these questions as "[w]ho we see and who we do not see; who is privileged within the regime of specularity; which aspects of the historical past actually have circulating visual representations and which do not; whose fantasies of what are fed by which visual images?" Such questions may also help rhetoricians identify and analyze visual rhetoric as it functions in culture. Rogoff believes that visual culture fosters a branch of study where we can read different kinds of texts, ones with "images, sounds, and spatial delineations" onto and through each other. According to Rogoff, approaching visual culture intertextually, incorporating the totality of images, sounds, and space that comprise the visual, rather than privileging a single strain to the exclusion of others, will allow the field to ask new questions, approach problems from unconventional intellectual angles, and, most important, unframe discussions from conventional values, histories, and methodologies.

If space, as Rogoff argues, is part of the intertextual mix that needs to be studied, we can learn much from those who critique, imagine, dictate, and analyze how spaces are inhabited, especially those working in fields such as architecture, ethnography, and anthropology. In "Black Vernacular: Architecture as Cultural Practice," cultural critic bell hooks lays out the extent to which architecture and geographic location reflect and influence cultural, political values. In high school, hooks was asked to invent a dream house as an art assignment. Reflecting on the assignment now, hooks realizes that for working-class, poor, and black people in the South, architecture "exist[ed] only in the location of dream and fantasy." In architecture, space often constitutes a physical expression of cultural and political power, equally capable of enabling or restricting a people's hopes and dreams, in effect a form of rhetoric "creating a sense of entitlement for some and deprivation for others." In order to better theorize black experience, hooks argues that critics need to acknowledge and analyze "vernacular" architecture, the very real spaces that families occupy. Understanding these spaces, according to hooks, may offer new ways to move beyond "the limits and confines of fixed locations" to construct places that embody real political gains. hooks' observations about architecture could just as well extend to our classroom spaces. If we are working in wired classrooms, we might also ask how cyberspace reflects cultural preferences, its ideals as well as its shortcomings.[1] If we accept the structures and designs we are most accustomed to, ones created by those who first occupy that space, we may be accepting designs that privilege a certain culture, race, sex, or age group to the detriment of the most vulnerable.

Instead of focusing on the ways in which culture influences artists or architects, Marita Sturken, a professor of communication studies, analyzes the influence of culture on the reception of the Vietnam Veterans Memorial, which triggered more disagreement than any other monument or architecture on the Washington Mall. In "The Wall, the Screen, and the Image: The Vietnam Veterans Memorial," Sturken argues that Maya Lin's "silent" modernist design of the Vietnam Memorial became a screen for viewers to project any and all of the conflicting political views circulating in the United States after the Vietnam War. For many who supported the war, Lin's untraditional, un-triumphalist memorial has seemed an icon critiquing the United States' engagement in Vietnam. Sturken's methodology of examining the various groups' responses in their different cultural contexts suggests one way to introduce composition students to the idea that visuals exist within both rhetorical and cultural contexts.

Anthropologists and ethnographers bring their own cultures to bear on their visual studies, filmed records, and scholarly interpretations of others. The recent field of visual anthropology reflects changes within the wider discipline of anthropology toward understanding the intercultural politics of viewing and being viewed. Instead of traveling to distant places to film "exotic" cultures, anthropologists are focusing on their own cultures. They do so in order to avoid the form of domination and hegemonic relations that accompany filming "the other" and interpreting these others' observed actions according to the anthropologists' own preferences. Nancy Lutkehaus and Jenny Cool's analysis of visual ethnography and anthropology in "Paradigms Lost and Found: The 'Crisis of Representation' and Visual Anthropology" is important to composition and rhetoric in two ways: It bears on the studies of compositionists who conduct ethnographic research, whether or not they record their subjects visually, and it can serve as an analytic tool for those who allow students to include short video or film clips as part of a composition class's requirements. If students can learn to recognize and reflect on the authorial, cultural bias evident in their own visual portfolios or papers, they will be well on their way toward developing a more sophisticated idea of both verbal and visual rhetoric.

While we need to consider whether or not we are reading ourselves into what we see and what we study visually, professor of communication Mark J. P. Wolf suggests that we also need to consider how a temporal element might affect visual representations in "Subjunctive Documentary: Computer Imaging and Simulation." In a medium such as film, we can easily recognize a filmmaker's ideas as imaginary, as what could or what might be. In the case, however, of a medium such as computer simulation, we may have more trouble distinguishing what we can actually see from what someone has imagined, and sometimes such an inability could cost lives. Wolf explains the world of computer simulations, a world of possibility, using the conditional verb tense, as in what *might* have been or what *might* be, rather than the present tense, or what *is*. By presenting us with what we cannot possibly see with the human eye, the visual equivalent of the subjunctive tense projecting the possible, computer simulations are seductive and tricky. As Wolf explains, these simulations are the end result of perhaps dozens of human interventions by software designers, computer programmers, mathematicians, scientists, and many other disciplinary representatives. What we see is conditional, or subjunctive, because the simulations embody conceptual or theoretical points of view, assumptions, human prejudices, and human error. In science, medicine, and law — institutions heavily impacting people's very real lives — not recognizing how culture and the abstract have influenced images that we both perceive and allow to affect our lives could be fatal.

Finally, our study of visual rhetoric, our move toward a pedagogy of the visual, and our granting to images the same respect we give to words, still need to go further. An impressively prescient work from 1994, Richard Lanham's "The Implications of Electronic Information for the Sociology of Knowledge," helps us ask how the heightened visuality of the digital medium, as opposed to print culture, alters our inherited notions of the "transparent" verbal text, and, in fact, the entire landscape of our interactions with texts. We also need to anticipate, like Lanham does, the ways in which acceptance of the visual will affect how we teach and how we think. Will digital media enable enhanced visuality and greater levels of participation in textual production and consumption? Or is it possible that those raised within this visual medium will have newly and differently structured brains than those of us reared on the printed text? Digital media will also emphasize how much educators need to remain open to change. The wake of such a change could fundamentally alter entire disciplines and curricula, as well as the relations among them.

NOTE

1. While not focusing on the visual specifically, Cynthia Selfe and William Wresch have pointed to the social and political discrepancies that have begun to mark cyberspace. See Selfe's *Technology and Literacy in the Twenty-First Century: The Importance of Paying Attention* (Carbondale: Southern Illinois University Press, 1999) and Wresch's *Disconnected: Haves and Have-nots in the Information Age* (New Brunswick, NJ: Rutgers UP, 1996).

25   *Studying Visual Culture*

IRIT ROGOFF

I raise my eyes and I see America.

> (Newt Gingrich, *New York Times*, 19 April 1995)

"And please remember, just a hint of starch in Mr. Everett's shirts." For one brief moment their eyes actually met, Blanche was the first to look away. "Yes ma'am." After Grace left the kitchen, Blanche sat down at the table. Was it just the old race thing that had thrown her off when her eyes met Grace's? Her neighbor Wilma's father said he'd never in his adult life looked a white person in the eye.

> (Barbara Neely, *Blanche on the Lam*, 1992)

His smoldering eyes saw right through my tremulous heart.

> (Barbara Cartland, *The Pirate's Return*, 1987)

How can we characterize the emergent field "visual culture"? To begin with, we must insist that this encompasses a great deal more than the study of images, of even the most open-ended and cross-disciplinary study of images. At one level we certainly focus on the centrality of vision and the visual world in producing meanings, establishing and maintaining aesthetic values, gender stereotypes, and power relations within culture. At another level we recognize that opening up the field of vision as an arena in which cultural meanings get constituted, also simultaneously anchors to it an entire range of analyses and interpretations of the audio, the spatial, and of the psychic dynamics of spectatorship. Thus visual culture opens up an entire world of intertextuality in which images, sounds, and spatial delineations are read on to and through one another, lending ever-accruing layers of meanings and of subjective responses, to each encounter we might have with film, TV, advertising, art works, buildings, or urban environments. In a sense we have produced a field of vision version of Derrida's concept of *différance* and its achievement has had a twofold effect both on the structures of meaning and

---

From *The Visual Culture Reader*. Ed. Nicholas Mirzoeff. London: Routledge, 1998. 14–26.

interpretation and on the epistemic and institutional frameworks that attempt to organize them. Derrida's conceptualization of *différance* takes the form of a critique of the binary logic in which every element of meaning constitution is locked into signification in relation to the other (a legacy of Saussurian linguistics' insistence on language as a system of negative differentiation). Instead what we have begun to uncover is the free play of the signifier, a freedom to understand meaning in relation to images, sounds, or spaces not necessarily perceived to operate in a direct, causal, or epistemic relation to either their context or to one another. If feminist deconstructive writing has long held the place of writing as the endless displacement of meaning, then visual culture provides the visual articulation of the continuous displacement of meaning in the field of vision and the visible.

This insistence on the contingent, the subjective, and the constantly reproduced state of meanings in the visual field is equally significant for the institutional or disciplinary location of this work. If we do not revert exclusively to ascribing meaning exclusively to an author, nor to the conditions and historical specificities of its making, nor to the politics of an authorizing community, then we simultaneously evacuate the object of study from the disciplinary and other forms of knowledge territorialization. Perhaps then we are at long last approaching Roland Barthes's description of interdisciplinarity not as surrounding a chosen object with numerous modes of scientific inquiry, but rather as the constitution of a new object of knowledge. The following brief attempt to engage with the arena of visual culture will touch on some of these themes as well as on the thorny politics of historical specificity: its advantages, its limitations, and the dangers and freedoms inherent in attempting to move out of a traditional and internally coherent and unexamined model of what it means to be historically specific.

VISION AS CRITIQUE

In today's world meanings circulate visually, in addition to orally and textually. Images convey information, afford pleasure and displeasure, influence style, determine consumption and mediate power relations. Who we see and who we do not see; who is privileged within the regime of specularity; which aspects of the historical past actually have circulating visual representations and which do not; whose fantasies of what are fed by which visual images? Those are some of the questions which we pose regarding images and their circulation. Much of the practice of intellectual work within the framework of cultural problematics has to do with being able to ask new and alternative questions, rather than reproducing old knowledge by asking the old questions. (*Often in class the students complain that the language of theoretical inquiry is difficult, that "it is not English." They need considerable persuasion that one cannot ask the new questions in the old language, that language is meaning. In the end almost always their inherent excitement at any notion of "the new" wins the day and by the end of the trimester someone invariably produces a perfectly formulated remark about discourse, representation, and meaning usually followed by a wonder-filled pause at the recognition that they have just uttered something entirely "different."*)

By focusing on a field of vision and of visual culture operating within it, we create the space for the articulation of (but not necessarily the response to) such questions as: What are the visual codes by which some are allowed to look, others to hazard a peek, and still others are forbidden to look altogether? In what political discourses can we understand looking and returning the gaze as an act of political resistance? Can we actually participate in the pleasure and identify with the images produced by culturally specific groups to which we do not belong? These are the questions which we must address to the vast body of images that surrounds us daily. Furthermore we need to understand how we actively interact with images from all arenas to remake the world in the shape of our fantasies and desires or to narrate the stories which we carry within us. In the arena of visual culture the scrap of an image connects with a sequence of a film and with the corner of a billboard or the window display of a shop we have passed by, to produce a new narrative formed out of both our experienced journey and our unconscious. Images do not stay within discrete disciplinary fields such as "documentary film" or "Renaissance painting," since neither the eye nor the psyche operates along or recognizes such divisions. Instead they provide the opportunity for a mode of new cultural writing existing at the intersections of both objectivities and subjectivities. In a critical culture in which we have been trying to wrest representation away from the dominance of patriarchal, Eurocentric, and heterosexist normativization, visual culture provides immense opportunities for rewriting culture through our concerns and our journeys.

The emergence of visual culture as a transdisciplinary and cross-methodological field of inquiry means nothing less and nothing more than an opportunity to reconsider some of the present culture's thorniest problems from yet another angle. In its formulation of both the objects of its inquiry and of its methodological processes, it reflects the present moment in the arena of cultural studies in all of its complexities. How would I categorize this present moment? From the perspective I inhabit it seems to reflect a shift from a phase of intensely analytical activity we went through during the late 1970s and the 1980s, when we gathered a wide assortment of tools of analysis to a moment in which new cultural objects are actually being produced. While deeply rooted in an understanding of the epistemological denaturalization of inherited categories and subjects revealed through the analytical models of structuralist and poststructuralist thought and the specific introduction of theories of sexual and cultural difference, these new objects of inquiry go beyond analysis towards figuring out new and alternative languages which reflect the contemporary awareness by which we live out our lives. All around us fictions such as Toni Morrison's *Beloved*, autobiographies such as Sara Suleri's *Meatless Days*, films such as Terry Zwygoff's *Crumb* and complex multimedia art installations such as Vera Frenkel's *Transit Bar*, live out precarious and immensely creative relations between analysis, fiction, and the uneasy conditions of our critically informed lives.

One of the most important issues cultural studies has taken on is to provide a "hands-on" application of the epistemological shift which Gayatri Spivak has characterized thus: "It is the questions that we ask that produce the field of inquiry and not some body of materials which determines what questions need to be posed to it." In doing so we have affected a shift from the old logical-positivist world of cognition to a more contemporary arena of representation and of situated knowledges. The emergence of a relatively new arena such as visual culture provides the possibility of unframing some of the discussions we have been engaged in regarding presences and absences, invisibility and stereotypes, desires, reifications and objectifications from the disciplinary fields — art history, film studies, mass media and communications, theoretical articulations of vision, spectatorship, and the power relations that animate the arena we call the field of vision — which first articulated their status as texts and objects. Thereby unframing them from a set of conventional values as *either* highly valued *or* highly marginalized *or* outside of the scope of sanctioned vision altogether. Equally they are unframed from the specific histories of their making and the methodological models of analyses which have more recently served for their unmaking. The field that I work in, which labors heavy-handedly under the title of the critical theorization of visual culture (or visual culture for short) does not function as a form of art history or film studies or mass media, but is clearly informed by all of them and intersects with all of them. It does not historicize the art object or any other visual image, nor does it provide for it either a narrow history within art nor a broader genealogy within the world of social and cultural developments. It does not assume that if we overpopulate the field of vision with ever more complementary information, we shall actually gain any greater insight into it.

(*When I was training as an art historian, we were instructed in staring at pictures. The assumption was that the harder we looked, the more would be revealed to us; that a rigorous, precise, and historically informed looking would reveal a wealth of hidden meanings. This belief produced a new anatomical formation called "the good eye." Later, in teaching in art history departments, whenever I would complain about some student's lack of intellectual curiosity, about their overly literal perception of the field of study, or of their narrow understanding of culture as a series of radiant objects, someone else on the faculty would always respond by saying "Oh, but they have a good eye.")*

Nor does this field function as a form of art (or any other visual artifact) criticism. It does not serve the purpose of evaluating a project, of complementing or condemning it, of assuming some notion of universal quality that can be applied to all and sundry. Furthermore it does not aim at cataloguing the offenses and redressing the balances, nor of enumerating who is in and who is out, of what was chosen and what was discarded. These were an important part of an earlier project in which the glaring exclusions, erasures, and distortions of every form of otherness — women, homosexuals, and non-European peoples to mention a few categories — had to be located and named and a judgment had to be passed on the conditions of their initial exclusion.

All of this, however, would constitute a "speaking about": an objectification of a moment in culture such as an exhibition or a film or a literary text, into a solid and immutable entity which does not afford us as the viewing audience, the possibilities of play, the possibilities of rewriting the exhibition (or the site of any other artifact) as an arena for our many and different concerns. It would assume that the moment in culture known as the exhibition should ideally dictate a set of fixed meanings rather than serve as the site for the continuous (re)production of meanings.

In fact the perspectives that I would like to try and represent, the critical analysis of visual culture, would want to do everything to avoid a discourse which perceives of itself as "speaking about" and shift towards one of "speaking to." In the words of Trinh T. Min-ha, "Tale, told, to be told/Are you truthful?", acknowledging the complexities inherent in any speech act does not necessarily mean taking away or compromising the qualities of a fine story.

> Who speaks? What speaks? The question is implied and the function named, but the individual never reigns, and the subject slips away without naturalizing its voice. S/he who speaks, speaks to the tale as S/he begins telling and retelling it. S/he does not speak about it. For without a certain work of displacement, "speaking about" only partakes in the conservation of systems of binary opposition (subject/object I/it, we/they) on which territorialized knowledge depends.

Trinh suggests here not merely that in reading/looking we rewrite ("speak about") the text. More importantly, she recognizes that in claiming and retelling the narratives ("speaking to"), we alter the very structures by which we organize and inhabit culture.

It is this questioning of the ways in which we inhabit and thereby constantly make and remake our own culture that informs the arena of visual culture. It is an understanding that the field is made up of at least three different components. First, there are the images that come into being and are claimed by various, and often contested histories. Second, there are the viewing apparatuses that we have at our disposal that are guided by cultural models such as narrative or technology. Third, there are the subjectivities of identification or desire or abjection from which we view and by which we inform what we view. While I am obviously focusing here on the reception rather than the production of images and objects or environments, it is clearly one of the most interesting aspects of visual culture that the boundary lines between making, theorizing, and historicizing have been greatly eroded and no longer exist in exclusive distinction from one another.

For some years I have been wondering about the formation of a counter viewing position to that old art historical chestnut "*the good eye.*" Are we developing "the mean eye, the jaundiced, skeptical eye"? Is the critical eye one that guards jealously against pleasure? Hardly so, if we are to engage with the fantasy formations that inform viewing subjectivities. For the moment, and following some of Laura Mulvey's later work within feminist film theory, I have settled on the notion of "*the curious eye*" to counter the "good eye" of connoisseurship. Curiosity implies a certain unsettling; a notion of things outside the realm of the known, of things not yet quite understood or articulated; the pleasures of the forbidden or the hidden or the unthought; the optimism of finding out something one had not known or been able to conceive of before. It is in the spirit of such a "curious eye" that I want to open up some dimension of this field of activity.

Perhaps one of the best indications of just how destabilizing this form of "curiosity" for the not-yet-known can be, is the alarm which seems to be caused by the clearly emerging institutional formations of this new field of "visual culture." A recent issue of the journal *October* contained a questionnaire on the subject of this emergent arena of inquiry. All of the statements to which correspondents were asked to reply indicated some profound sense of loss — the loss of historical specificities and of material groundings and of fixed notions of quality and excellence, etc., which the editors who had set them seem to view as the loss of the grounding navigational principles for their activities. Apparently the most alarming of all has been the infiltration of the field of art history by something termed the "anthropological model." I puzzled long and hard over both this analysis and the dread it seemed to provoke. I spoke to all my sophisticated cultural anthropologist acquaintances to try and understand what they may have foisted on us unawares. I read all the predictable responses to the questionnaire set by the *October* editors, and still not the slightest glimmer of comprehension emerged. Finally, reading through Tom Conley's very refreshing and extremely well-judged response "Laughter and Alarm," it seemed that all this fuss was being provoked by the growing presence or preference for a "relativist" model of cultural analysis. As far as I could make out, the so-called "relativism" of this assumed anthropological model involves a nontransferable specificity for the context of any cultural production. Thus the ability to establish a set of inherent values or criteria of excellence for images or cultural objects which would transcend the conditions of their making and constitute a metacultural relationality (as for example in the traditional modernist model for the historical avant-garde of Europe and the United States as a set of international, interlinked, innovative art movements sharing a particular confrontational spirit and a commitment to formal experimentation) is seemingly negated or sacrificed through this more current relational model.

Now, the editors of *October* who have articulated all of these anxieties about the erosion of good old art history through the encroaching dangers of so-called anthropological relativism are hardly an intellectually naïve lot; indeed they were in part responsible for acquainting my generation of art historians and critics with important analytical models and with important cultural criticism from both France and Germany as well as debates carried on in the U.S. Nor are they in any way provincial intellectuals, locked up within the confining frameworks of one single, national, cultural discussion. They are clearly more than aware that the notion of "relativist" carries within it all kinds of intimations of cultural conservatism. One of the most publicized cases of polemics for and against historical relativism was the case of the

1980s German *Historikerstreit,* in which a group of conservative German historians such as Nolte and Broszat began making claims for a study of German fascism in the 1930s and 1940s as relational to all the other fascisms and totalitarian regimes around at that same historical moment. The German neoconservative historians' project was underpinned by a politics that aimed at lessening guilt through undermining historical specificity both at the level of cause and of effect. The accusations of "relativism" with which this writing project was greeted by more left-liberal historians in the West were due largely to the fact that much of this writing was aimed at a *re-evaluation,* in moralizing terms, of the events and policies of the period. Thus nationalist-socialist fascism was graded in relation to other Western fascisms and to Soviet totalitarian regimes and was found either to have been a response to them or to have similarities with them, or to compare not quite so horrifically with these other models. What it did not attempt was to reframe understandings of a very notion of fascism or to think it away from a national history, or to understand it in relation to certain values and aesthetics within the modern period, or any of the other possibilities available for unframing a discussion of fascism and gaining an alternative set of understandings into it, of actually questioning the certainty that we *know* what fascism, the object of inquiry, is. Cultural specificity in this particular historical discussion takes the form of two fixities: (a) a discrete, stable, and clearly known object of study and (b) discrete, stable, and fixed contexts (in this case of national cultures with clear lines of division between them) which contain and separate their histories. It presumes to know, in no uncertain terms, what a political movement is, where a national culture begins and ends, and it assumes that endlessly complex social, cultural, racial, and sexual differences might actually coalesce around such a dramatic articulation of a subject known as "fascism." In contrast the cultural studies project which *October* characterizes as having been infiltrated by a so-called "anthropological model" aims at establishing internal cultural specificities which can in turn attempt intercultural conversations while maintaining the necessary regard for the value and serious significance of *anyone*'s cultural production. There is a world of acute political difference between the politics of these two cultural/analytical projects which seems to be conflated here. So how to explain what is clearly a most confusing political slippage?

I could adopt a mean-spirited and pragmatic attitude and say that all this is simply about the loss of territories of knowledge and reputations established in given disciplinary fields which are being called into question (the fields, not the reputations) by the emergence of other, newer fields. But that would be disrespectful to a publication that contributed much to my own intellectual development and it would only serve the purpose of personalizing a serious political issue and thereby devaluing its importance. To address the argument as presented in *October* both in its stated terms and with attention to the alarm underlying it is to take issue with the cautioning against undifferentiated relativism and unsituated knowledges being put forward by its editors. Clearly, notions of "relativism" cannot be dragged around from one discussion to another with complete disregard to the politics that inform each of these. To unframe hierarchies of excellence and of universal value that privilege one strand of cultural production while committing every other mode to cultural oblivion, as claims the not fully articulated accusation in *October*, does not mean that one is launching an undifferentiated universalism in which everything is equal to everything else. Rather it opens up the possibilities for analyzing the politics that stand behind each particular relativist model and of differentiating between those rather than between the supposed value of objects and images. The history whose loss the editors of *October* seem to be lamenting has not disappeared, it has simply shifted ground. In visual culture the history becomes that of the viewer or that of the authorizing discourse rather than that of the object. By necessity this shift in turn determines a change in the very subject of the discussion or analysis, a shift in which the necessity for having the discussion in the first place and for having it in a particular methodological mode and at a particular time become part of this very discussion. This conjunction of situated knowledge and self-reflexive discourse analysis accompanied by a conscious history for the viewing subject hardly seems grounds for such a pessimistic lament, simply an opportunity for a bit of self-consciousness and a serious examination of the politics inherent in each project of cultural assessment. (*The whole discussion reminds me of a dreadful sociology conference I attended a few years ago at Berkeley in which a very authoritative and very senior woman sociologist complained that without standards of excellence how would she be able to hire and fire people or accept or dismiss students? A fellow attendee at the conference who happened to be sitting next to me kept muttering under his breath in a very heavy Swedish accent "Why don't you already stop hiring and firing?"* (Enough said.)

SPECTATORSHIP IN THE FIELD OF VISION

The space this investigation inhabits is the field of vision, which is a much wider arena than a sphere for the circulation of images or questions regarding the nature of representation. This space, the field of vision, is to begin with a vastly overdetermined one. In the West, it bears the heavy burden of post-Enlightenment scientific and philosophical discourses regarding the centrality of vision for an empirical determination of the world as perceivable. In these analyses we find the gaze described as an apparatus of investigation, verification, surveillance, and cognition, which has served to sustain the traditions of Western post-Enlightenment scientificity and early modern technologies. The limitations of such historical accounts of the field of vision as central to the continuing Western Enlightenment project (such as Martin Jay's exceptionally scholarly and informative recent book *Downcast Eyes*) is that it is vacated of any political dynamics or models of subjectivity. It becomes a neutral field in which some innocent objective "eye" is deployed by an unsituated viewer. Therefore the kind of looking that was sanctioned and legitimated by scientific imperatives or the kind of surveillance which claimed its necessity through the establishment of civility through a rooting out of criminality, can now be understood through questions about who is allowed to look, to what purposes, and by what academic and state discourses it is legitimated. The recent spate of literature regarding "vision" as it appears in numerous learned discourses does precisely the opposite of what "visual culture" sets out to do. It reproduces a tedious and traditional corpus of knowledge and tells us how each great philosopher and thinker saw the concept of vision within an undisputed philosophical or other paradigm. Most ignominiously, feminist theorists such as Luce Irigaray (who in their writing undid territorialities of hierarchized, linear knowledge), get written into this trajectory in some misguided form of tribute to feminism via its inclusion within the annals of Western thought. By contrast, a parallel discussion in visual culture might venture to ask how bodies of thought produced a notion of vision in the service of a particular politics or ideology and populated it with a select set of images, viewed through specific apparatuses and serving the needs of distinct subjectivities.

The discussion of spectatorship *in* (rather than *and*) sexual and cultural difference, begun within feminist film theory and continued by the critical discourses of minority and emergent cultures, concerns itself with the gaze as desire, which splits spectatorship into the arena of desiring subjects and desired objects. Currently such binary separations have been increasingly tempered by the slippages between the ever-eroding boundaries of exclusive objecthood or coherent subjecthood. At present we have arrived at an understanding that much of initial sexual and racial identity in the field of vision is formed through processes of negative differentiation: that whiteness needs blackness to constitute itself as whiteness; that masculinity needs femininity or feminized masculinity to constitute its masculinity in agreed upon normative modes: that civility and bourgeois respectability need the stereotypical unruly "others" — be they drunks or cultural minorities or anyone else positioned outside phantasmatic norms — to define the nonexistent codes of what constitutes "acceptable" behavior. However, at the same time we have understood that all of these are socially constructed, "performative" rather than essentially attributed, and therefore highly unstable entities. Thus the field of vision becomes a ground for contestation in which unstable normativity constantly and vehemently attempts to shore itself up. Films such as *The Crying Game* or *The Last Seduction* played precisely with the erosion of assumptions that something — gender identity in both cases — "looks like" that which names it and the cataclysmic results which such processes of destabilization produce. Spectatorship as an investigative field understands that what the eye purportedly "sees" is dictated to it by an entire set of beliefs and desires and by a set of coded languages and generic apparatuses.

Finally the field of vision is sustained through an illusion of transparent space. This is the illusion of transparency which is claimed in the quote from Newt Gingrich with which I began this essay: "I raise my eyes and I see America." In this scenario, he has the ability to see. America — in all its supposed unity and homogeneity — is there available to his vision; it can be seen by him and the space between them is a transparent entity in which no obstacles obscure the directness and clarity of (his) vision. Politically and philosophically this condition has been best theorized by Henri Lefebvre in *The Production of Space* (1991) when he says:

> Here space appears as luminous, as intelligible, as giving action free rein. What happens in space lends a miraculous quality to thought, which becomes incarnate by means of a *design* (in both senses of the word). The design serves as a mediator—itself of great fidelity—between mental activity (invention) and social activity (realization); and it is deployed in space. The illusion of transparency goes hand in hand with a view of space as innocent, as free of traps or secret places. Anything hidden or dissimulated—and hence dangerous—is antagonistic to transparency, under whose reign everything can be taken in by a single glance from the mental eye which illuminates whatever it contemplates.

To some extent the project of visual culture has been to try and repopulate space with all the obstacles and all the unknown images, which the illusion of transparency evacuated from it. Space, as we have understood, is always differentiated: it is always sexual or racial; it is always constituted out of circulating capital; and it is always subject to the invisible boundary lines that determine inclusions and exclusions. Most importantly it is always populated with the unrecognized obstacles which never allow us to actually "see" what is out there beyond what we expect to find. To repopulate space with all of its constitutive obstacles as we learn to recognize them and name them, is to understand how hard we have to strain to see, and how complex is the work of visual culture.

The Visual Conditions of Historicizing

I have attempted to map out some constitutive components of the arena of visual culture. Most importantly I need to try to articulate the importance of its operations as a field of knowledge. In the first instance I would argue that the unframing operations I have described above might lead towards a new object of study which would be determined around issues. Those issues in turn are determined by the various urgent cultural conditions and cultural problematics with which we are faced every day. To be able to assemble a group of materials and a variety of methodological analyses around an issue that is determined out of cultural and political realities rather than out of traditions of learned arguments, seems an important step forward in the project of reformulating knowledge to deal responsibly with the lived conditions of highly contested realities, such as we face at the turn of this century in the West.

This is however also a cautionary moment: as we divest ourselves of historical periods, schools of stylistic or aesthetic affiliation, national cultural locations, or the limitations of reading objects through modes and conditions of production, we run the danger of divesting ourselves of self location. It is at this point that we enter perhaps the thorniest and most contentious aspect of this entire project, for it has become clear to each and every one of us — though we may belong to radically different collectives and cultural mobilizations within the arena of contemporary feminist, multicultural, and critically/theoretically informed culture — that historic specificity is a critically important part of coming into cultural recognition and articulation. Every movement that has attempted to liberate marginalized groups from the oppressions of elision and invisibility has, to all intents and purposes, insisted on having something to say, on having a language to say it in, and on having a position from which to speak.

My own coming into critical consciousness took place within the feminist theory of the 1980s in Europe and the United States. Without doubt, the historical uncovering and location of earlier female subjects and their numerous histories and the insistence on speaking as women were a very important part of feminist critique, just as emergent cultural minority discourses are presently important in the rewriting of culture by previously colonized peoples. Having established these as both intellectually important and institutionally legitimate, the next phase moved to using gender as a category for the analysis of such categories as style or periodicity or such overall categories as "modernism," which enfold both. (*And this was not at all simple — I will never forget the comments of a Vassar art history professor after a lecture I gave there on the visual construction of masculinity and masculine artistic privilege through self-portraiture. He announced uncategorically that my few comments on the subsidiary female figures within these paintings were far more interesting than my efforts at theorizing the visual constructions of masculinity and that as a feminist art historian I should stick with those.*)

At stake therefore are political questions concerning who is allowed to speak about what. These can set up limitations to our intellectual capacity to engage with all the texts, images, and other stimuli and frameworks we encounter; to break down the barriers of permissible and territorialized knowledge rather than simply redraw them along another formalized set of lines. The answer lies, to my mind at least, in substituting the historical specificity of that being studied with the historical specificity of he/she/they doing the studying. In order to effect such a shift without falling prey to endless anecdotal and autobiographical ruminating which stipulates experience as a basis for knowledge, we attempt to read each culture through other, often hostile and competitive, cultural narratives. This process of continuous translation and negotiation is often exhausting in its denial of a fixed and firm position, but it does allow us to shift the burden of specificity from the material to the reader and prevents us from the dangers of complete dislocation. Perhaps it might even help us to understand that at the very moment in which historical specificity can provide liberation and political strength to some of the dispossessed, it also imprisons others within an old binary structure that no longer reflects the conditions and realities of their current existence.

I should like to demonstrate this process by presenting a condensed version of a long project in which I have been involved over the past three years. The project is in several parts and involves different types of activity, both historical and critical, often involving a certain amount of fiction writing. The starting point for me has been my need to think through some issues regarding projects of public commemoration and the political uses they serve in different cultures at different times. My need to think through these problems, in relation to one another and against their official articulation by the commemorating culture, has to do with my location as a native of Israel, as someone who has for many years spent long periods of time in Germany and has been very involved with political culture on the German left, and most recently as a teacher and cultural organizer in the U.S. where I have become acquainted with, and shaped by, discussions of multiculturalism and cultural difference. As a native of Israel I grew up in the shadow of a trauma, the genocide of European Jews during the Second World War and of its consequences in the establishment of the modern state of Israel. Simultaneously this history served in covert and unacknowledged ways to legitimate numerous acts of violence; against the indigenous population of Palestine and for the marginalization of Arab Jews, who were not perceived as part of this European horror, which perversely came to define rights of inclusion and participation within the Jewish state of Israel. Perhaps even more importantly, the plethora of commemoration practices of this horror within Israel became extremely important in maintaining a culture of constant and high anxiety within the population of the country, a kind of manifest haunting which could not be shaken despite all evidence of military and technological supremacy in the eastern Mediterranean. No matter how many battles were won and how many enemies vanquished, no matter how often the U.S. assured the population of its undying support and loyalty, not to mention huge and constant influxes of cash and privileged markets, people in Israel have continued to live out their days driven by a fear of annihilation which the ever-present Holocaust monuments have sustained and maintained. So that has been one part of the political urgency of my project, to question the contemporary political uses of commemoration practices.

At the same time I have had to face the recent spate of commemoration activities in Germany and to contend with German discourses of guilt and of compulsory public memory. Operating in this other context, I understood that discourses of guilt and monumental public commemoration affect a form of historical closure. To begin with they assume that one can replace an absence (many millions of murdered subjects) with a presence (a column or a statue or a complex conceptual set of public space interrogations). Second, the protagonists are frozen into binary, occupying positions of victim and perpetrator, both of whom have seemingly come to a miserable end. The newly hybridized and continuing cultural development of not only Jewish and German but also many other lives affected by the cataclysmic events of fascism and war, elsewhere around the globe and in relation to other geographies and cultures, is denied in its entirety. Finally the historic trauma of the Holocaust linked to the specter of European fascism becomes the index of all political horror and its consequence, imposing once again a Eurocentric index of measure and political identity on the very concept of political horror.

Viewed from the perspective of the U.S. I have watched with dismay the emergence of more and more Holocaust museums across the country over the past four years. Situated within the contexts of the current culture wars exemplified by the multicultural contestation of the traditional and ongoing supremacy of European American cultural legacies, these museums have begun to take on an extremely disturbing dimension: a form of rewriting of the recent past in which a European account of horror would vie with the locally generated horror of slavery and the annihilation of native peoples. It also assumes the form of a "re-whitening" of the migrant heritage of the United States at a moment in which immigration is constantly discussed through non-European and racially marked bodies. This is disturbing in more ways that I can recount in this quick summary of a problematic, but primarily I have been thinking of the ways in which this account writes all of the Jewish world as European, which of course it never has been, and the ways in which it sets up contestations of horror within U.S. histories, between Jewish, African-American, and Native American populations.

As a culturally displaced person I move between all of these cultures and languages and inhabit positions within all of their political discourses. My displacement being neither tragic nor disadvantaged but rather the product of restless curiosity, I have an obligation to write all these problematics across one another and to see whether they yield insights beyond their specific cultural and political location. As anyone who inhabits an intercultural or cross-cultural position (which increasingly, with ever-growing self-consciousness, is most of us) knows, this constant translation and mediation process is a deeply exhausting business and one would like to put it to some productive use so that the permanent unease might unravel some other possible perspective on problems viewed almost exclusively from within each of the cultures involved. While I have had the opportunity to write each one within its own context, that was merely the reproduction of an analysis situated within a culture. What then are the possibilities of unframing these problematics and seeing how they interlink and inform one another? Perhaps even more importantly I would like to see if I can find a model of opening up a uniquely European horror to a relationality with all the political horror experienced by migrating populations elsewhere around the globe around the same time. I think that the loss of historical specificity in this instance will be compensated for by the undoing of an indexical hierarchy of horrors, in which one is culturally privileged over others. I hope that in the process some understanding of the degree to which "Trauma" informs all of our originary myths, means that some patterns and symptoms are shared by the culture at large, even if its populations have radically different specific histories. It might even help me to think through the constant state of cultural haunting, the underlying conditions of unease emanating from shared but denied histories between the West and non-West, that silently ruffle the surfaces of our daily lives.

That, in a nutshell, constitutes the political urgency of the specific project I am describing, and in writing projects published elsewhere, I hope to demonstrate a possible model for its exploration within the arena of visual culture. These have taken the form of long-term collaborations with conceptual artist Jochen Gerz, with video and multimedia artist Vera Frenkel, and with computer and electronic artist George Legrady. These are collaborations in which I approach the work with my specific issues at hand and invariably find in it a set of thoughts and images that allow me to formulate the next stage of my investigation. In turn my theoretical articulations locate the artists' work within a set of cultural debates in which the visual arts rarely find representation. It assumes the form of a practice, of a "writing with" an artist's work rather than about it, a dehierarchization of the question of whether the artist, the critic or the historian, the advertising copywriter or the commercial sponsor, the studio or the director, has the final word in determining the meaning of a work in visual culture. (*Oddly this lesson was learned far from the field of dealing with contemporary objects, through Derek Jarman's extraordinary film* Caravaggio *which, more than anything I had encountered in the early 1980s, produced a model for "contemporizing history" and reading historical artifacts through current preoccupations such as the instability of the sexual nature of gender categories. After seeing this film I experienced the very necessary delights of uncertainty, of never being quite sure of what I was looking at.*)

One of the many advantages of encountering and analyzing issues of commemoration across a broad range of visual representations that function in public and in private spaces, that tease the viewer with their reluctant visible presence or with their entire physical absence, that broadcast on monitors or lie within the bowels of the computer waiting to be unfolded in real time, is that they straddle the spatial trajectory between memory and commemoration: a trajectory that seems parallel to our dilemma within the intellectual work of the academy. In the unframed field of vision there exist possibilities for simultaneously remembering as we structure solid commemorative arguments, amass fact, and juggle analytical models.

26 Black Vernacular: Architecture as Cultural Practice

bell hooks

Designing the house of my dreams in a high school art class, I did not think that any decisions I made were political. Indeed, every thought I had about the aesthetics of this project was rooted in imaginative fantasy. Beginning with the idea of a world of unlimited freedom where space, and in particular living space, could be designed solely in relation to "desire," I greatly wanted most to move away from concrete "political" realities, such as class, and just dream. When we were given the assignment—to build a dream house—our art teacher encouraged us to forget about dwellings as we knew them and to think imaginatively about space, about the link between what we desire, dream about, and what is practical.

We were to design, as I understood it, a dwelling place of dreams. I began this assignment by making a list of all the aspects of a house I found most compelling: stairways, window seats, hidden nooks and crannies. On paper, my house exposed and revealed my obsessions. I was a constant reader, living with a huge family, in small space. To me, reading was a deliciously private experience, one that allowed me to be secluded, walled in by silence and thought. In my dream house there were many places designed to enhance the pleasure of reading, places for sitting and lying down, places for reading and reverie. Every bit of space was shaped to be subordinate to these desires. Thus, there were endless stairways, window seats, and small rooms everywhere. On paper, in structure and design the house I imagined was a place for the fulfillment of desire, a place with no sense of necessity.

Although I have no clear memory of where this design ended up, I know this assignment affected me deeply. More than twenty years later, I can close my eyes and see the image of this house as I drew it. Loving flowers, I had designed the different floors to be like petals. It fascinates me now to think about why a white male Italian immigrant high school art teacher in the segregated South would encourage students to think of artistic practice solely in relation to fantasy and desire. In retrospect it is clear that this was precisely

From *Art on My Mind: Visual Politics*. New York: The New Press, 1995. 145–151.

the kind of assignment that was meant to deflect attention from political realities, from the class, race, and gender differences that separated and divided us from one another. Through this sort of a project, we could work harmoniously, focusing on dreams; we could see ourselves as connected — as the same.

This would have been a radically different assignment had we been encouraged to think critically about the actual spaces we inhabited, the neighborhoods and houses that were our world. Had we been given such an assignment, we would have learned to think about space politically, about who controls and shapes environments. This assignment might have compelled recognition of class differences, the way racial apartheid and white supremacy altered individuals' space, overdetermined locations and the nature of structures, created a sense of entitlement for some and deprivation for others. Doing this assignment, we might have come face to face with the politics of property, not only who owns and controls space but the relationship between power and cultural production.

We were not given such an assignment because it would not only have disrupted and subverted the idea of artistic endeavor and creative expression as politically neutral acts, it would have at the same time fundamentally challenged the idea of art as a site for transcendence, of art as emerging from an unfettered free zone of the imagination. Even though I did not see myself as thinking politically then, the very fact that I designed my dream house to counter the experience of growing up in a small overcrowded space, a circumstance that reflected my families' economic standing, meant that undergirding my dreams, my fantasies and desires, were class-based longings. This dream house, then, was not solely the outcome of abstract musings about dwellings; it was equally rooted in a concrete acknowledgment of my reality. Despite its limitations, this assignment did teach us that, irrespective of our location, irrespective of class, race, and gender, we were all capable of inventing, transforming, making space. It would have been exciting to have designed this dream house, then to have done another assignment in which we worked on designing space to meet concrete needs within the limitations of our lived experiences.

Had we done an assignment that required us to think critically and imaginatively about our homes and neighborhoods, those of us from nonprivileged backgrounds would have had an opportunity to think about architecture and design in relation to our lives both in the present and in the future. Growing up working-class and black in the South, I do not remember any direct discussion of our architectural realities. If our earliest understanding of architecture was that it exists only in the location of dream and fantasy, of "impossibility," it is no wonder then that many children of the working class and poor tend not to grow to maturity understanding architecture as a professional and cultural practice central to our imaginative and concrete relationship to space.

Although the dream house I designed had no direct connection to the dwellings in my community — which were separate, distinct, segregated spaces inhabited by the black working and non-working poor—the link between that fantasy place and the actual world I lived in was grounded in generations of concern with space, with the shaping and construction of environments. Poor Southern black folks were often land rich. Owning land, they were concerned with the use of space, the building of dwellings. Many narratives of resistance struggle from slavery to the present share an obsession with the politics of space, particularly the need to construct and build houses. Indeed, black folks equated freedom with the passage into a life where they would have the right to exercise control over space on their own behalf, where they would imagine, design, and create spaces that would respond to the needs of their lives, their communities, their families.

Growing up in a world where black working-class and "po' folk," as well as the black well-to-do, were deeply concerned with the aesthetics of space, I learned to see freedom as always and intimately linked to the issue of transforming space. I have chosen to write about this concern with space in order both to acknowledge the oppositional modes of psychic decolonization that marginalized, exploited, and oppressed black folks envisioned and to document a cultural genealogy of resistance. This project is distinct from those forms of nostalgic remembering of the past that simply appropriate colorful touristic images of "the darkies way back then." Framing this cultural genealogy of resistance in relation to space is necessary for the "cognitive mapping" Fredric Jameson speaks about when he insists that "it is at least empirically arguable that our daily life, our psychic experience, our cultural languages, are today dominated by categories of space rather than categories of time." It is my conviction that African-Americans can respond to contemporary crises we face by learning from and building on strategies of opposition and resistance that were effective in the past and are empowering in the present.

It is empowering for me to construct, in writing, the continuum that exists between the exploration of space and architecture that was a fundamental aspect of poor black rural Southern life even though it was not articulated in those terms. When my father's father, Daddy Jerry, a sharecropper and farmer, talked in concrete terms about his relationship to land, his longing to own and build, he spoke poetically about working with space so that it would reveal and mirror the texture of his longings. I never understood how Daddy Jerry "came by" a piece of land; that was the way folks talked about it then. The phrase could define a number of transactions. It could mean that he bought, traded, inherited, or exchanged work for land. On this land Daddy Jerry built a house. I can still remember the way he and my father would sit on the porch and have deep discussions about that house; their talk evoked a poetics of space, the joy of thinking imaginatively about one's dwelling. And I can recall my disappointment when I finally saw the small square brick house that he built. In my childhood imagination this space seemed so utterly closed and tight. Had I understood the interconnected politics of race, gender, and class in the white-supremacist South, I would have looked upon this house with the same awe as I did my favorite house.

My awe was reserved for the house of my mother's father, Daddy Gus, and her mother, Baba. An artist/quiltmaker, Baba shaped this house to meet her needs, those of her husband of more than seventy years, and the extended family that stayed or visited there. Like Toni Morrison's fictional character Eva Peace in *Song of Solomon*, Baba's wood-frame dwelling was a place where rooms were continuously added in odd places, tacked on, usually to accommodate the desires of the individual who was destined to inhabit that space. At Baba's house there was always an excitement about space — a sense of possibility. There dwellings were seen as in a constant state of change. Significantly, the absence of material privilege did not mean that poor and working-class black folks (such as my grandparents) did not think creatively about space. While lack of material privilege limited what could be done with one's surroundings, it was nevertheless always possible to make changes.

My grandmother's house was not unlike the small shacks that were the homes of many Southern black folks. Her place was just a bigger, more elegant shack. Wood-frame dwellings that were fragile or sturdy shaped my sense of meaningful vernacular architecture. Many of these structures, though fragile and therefore altered by time and the elements, remain and offer a wealth of information about the relationship of poor and working-class rural black folks to space. African-American professor of architecture LaVerne Wells-Bowie highlights in her writings the significance of architecture created by folks who were not schooled in the profession or even in the arts of building. She offers the insight that "vernacular architecture is a language of cultural expression" that "exemplifies how the physical environment reflects the uniqueness of a culture." Little railroad shacks in the South were often peopled by large families. When I was a child, I entered the home of an elderly black woman who lived in a lovely shack and was most impressed and delighted by the small cot-size beds placed here and there. I carry in my memory the serenity this woman's utterly neat and sparse place evoked. This experience helped shape my relationship to interior design and dwellings.

Often the rural black folks who lived in shacks on the edges and margins of town conceptualized the yard as a continuation of living space. Careful attention might be given to the planting of flowers, the positioning of a porch or a rope-hung swing. In the recent autobiography of the more-than-a-hundred-year-old Delaney sisters, they describe their migration north, their purchase of a small house, and the amazement of white folks that they wanted to add on a porch. Reading this, I recalled overhearing the conversations between my father and his dad as they sat on the porch and shared thoughts, ideas, dreams. Often, exploited or oppressed groups of people who are compelled by economic circumstance to share small living quarters with many others view the world right outside their housing structure as liminal space where they can stretch the limits of desire and the imagination.

Recording these memories seems absolutely essential, because in today's world we are led to believe that lack of material privilege means that one can have no meaningful constructive engagement with one's living space and certainly no relationship to aesthetics. I am often disturbed when folks equate a concern with beauty, the design and arrangement of space, with class privilege. Unfortunately, so many poor people have been socialized by the mass media and the politics of consumerism to see themselves as lacking "taste and style" when it comes to issues of architecture and aesthetics that they have surrendered their capacity to imagine and create. They explain this surrender as the unavoidable consequence of poverty. Yet lack of material privilege need not be synonymous with poverty of spirit or imagination. Significantly, in the past, even during the most dire circumstances of oppression and exploitation, African-Americans could find ways to express their creativity—to display artistry. They dared to use their imagination in ways that were liberatory.

Few critics have attempted to look at poor and working-class black folks' relationship to space. We need studies of housing that talk about the way in which the construction of "projects"—state-owned and -designed dwellings for the economically disadvantaged—brought an end to the dwelling in shacks that allowed for individual creativity and an assertion of aesthetic engagement with space and one's environment. The state-built dwellings erase all chances for unique perspectives to shape living space and replace these with a blueprint of sameness—everyone's place structured similarly. Clearly, these structures inform the ways poor folk are allowed to see themselves in relationship to space. No matter how poor you were in the shack, no matter if you owned the shack or not, there you could allow your needs and desires to articulate interior design and exterior surroundings. Poverty could not be viewed as a circumstance that suppresses creativity and possibility, for all around you were expressions of unique sensibility. Standardized housing brought with it a sense that to be poor meant that one was powerless, unable to intervene in or transform, in any way, one's relationship to space. In many areas of the rural South the shack still remains as a dwelling that counters and subverts the messages of this dehumanization of the spatial imagination of folks who are not materially privileged.

Mapping a cultural genealogy of resistance, we can see ways poor African-Americans used their imaginations to transcend limits. This history increasingly becomes subjugated knowledge as black folks embrace notions of victimhood that suggest our reality can be defined only by the circumstances of our oppression. In the essay "Race and Architecture," the philosopher and cultural critic Cornel West suggests that "the major challenge of a new architectural historiography is that its conception of the 'past' and 'present' be attuned to the complex role of difference—nature, primitive, ruled, Dionysian, female, black and so on." To rise to this challenge, spaces must exist for us to think and talk about, and theorize architecture as it reflects and informs culture.

In this expansive and more inclusive understanding of architecture, the vernacular is as relevant as any other form of architectural practice. This perspective allows critics to theorize black experience in ways that promote documentation of our historical and contemporary relationship to space and aesthetics. Few scholars theorize black experience from a standpoint that centralizes the perspectives of poor and working-class folks. Yet to ignore this standpoint is to reproduce a body of work that is neocolonial insofor as it violently erases and destroys those subjugated knowledges that can only erupt, disrupt, and serve as acts of resistance if they are visible, remembered. Documentation of a cultural genealogy of resistance invites the making of theory that highlights the cultural practices which transform ways of looking and being in a manner that resists reinscription by prevailing structures of domination. Subversive historiography connects oppositional practices from the past with forms of resistance in the present, thus creating spaces of possibility where the future can be imagined differently — imagined in such a way that we can witness ourselves dreaming, moving forward and beyond the limits and confines of fixed locations.

27 The Wall, the Screen, and the Image: The Vietnam Veterans Memorial

MARITA STURKEN

The forms remembrance takes indicate the status of memory within a given culture. In these forms, we can see acts of public commemoration as moments in which the shifting discourse of history, personal memory, and cultural memory converge. Public commemoration is a form of history-making, yet, it can also be a contested form of remembrance in which cultural memories slide through and into each other, merging and then disengaging in a narrative tangle.

With the Vietnam War, discourses of public commemoration are inextricably tied to the question of how war is brought to closure in American society. How, for instance, does a society commemorate a war for which the central narrative is one of division and dissent, a war whose history is still formative and highly contested? The Vietnam War, with its lack of a singular, historical narrative defining clear-cut purpose and outcome, has led to a unique form of commemoration.

Questions of public remembrance of the Vietnam War can be examined through the concept of the screen: a screen is a surface that is projected upon; it is also an object that hides something from view, that shelters or protects. The kinds of screens that converge in the case of the Vietnam Veterans Memorial in Washington, DC both shield and are projected upon: the black walls of the memorial act as screens for innumerable projections of memory and history — of the United States' participation in the Vietnam War and the experience of the Vietnam veterans since the war.

A singular, sanctioned history of the Vietnam War has not coalesced, in part because of the disruption of the standard narratives of American imperialism, technology, and masculinity that the war's loss represented. The history of the Vietnam War is still being composed from many conflicting histories, yet particular elements within the often opposing narratives are uncontested — the divisive effect the war had on American society and the

From *The Visual Culture Reader*. Ed. Nicholas Mirzoeff. London: Routledge, 1998. 163–178.

marginalization of the Vietnam veteran. This essay is concerned with how narratives of the war have been constructed out of and within the cultural memory of the Vietnam Veterans Memorial. I shall examine how the screens of the memorial act to eclipse — to screen out — personal and collective memories of the Vietnam War in the design of history, and how the textures of cultural memory are nevertheless woven throughout, perhaps over and under, these screens.

The Status of a Memorial

Although now administered under the aegis of the National Park Service of the federal government, the impetus for the creation of the Vietnam Veterans Memorial came from a group of Vietnam veterans who raised the funds and negotiated a site on the Washington Mall. Situated on the grassy slope of the Constitutional Gardens near the Lincoln Memorial, the Vietnam Veterans Memorial, which was designed by Maya Lin, consists of a V shape of two walls of black granite set into the earth at an angle of 125 degrees. Together, the walls extend almost five hundred feet in length, with a maximum height of approximately ten feet at the central hinge. These walls are inscribed with 58,196 names of men and women who died in the war, listed chronologically by date of death, with opening and closing inscriptions. The listing of names begins on the right-hand side of the hinge and continues to the end of the right wall; it then begins again at the far end of the left wall and ends at the center again. Thus, the name of the first American soldier killed in Vietnam, in 1959, is on a panel adjacent to that containing the name of the last American killed in 1975. The framing dates of 1959 and 1975 are the only dates listed on the wall; the names are listed alphabetically within each "casualty day," although those dates are not noted. Eight of the names on the wall represent women who died in the war. Since 1984 the memorial has been accompanied by a flag and a figurative sculpture of three soldiers, both facing the memorial from a group of trees south of the wall. In 1993 a statue commemorating the women who served in Vietnam was added 300 feet from the wall.

The memorial functions in opposition to the codes of remembrance evidenced on the Washington Mall. Virtually all the national memorials and monuments in Washington are made of white stone and constructed to be seen from a distance. In contrast, the Vietnam Veterans Memorial cuts into the sloping earth: it is not visible until one is almost upon it; if approached from behind, it seems to disappear into the landscape. Although the polished black granite walls of the memorial reflect the Washington Monument and face the Lincoln Memorial, they are not visible from the base of either structure. The black stone creates a reflective surface, one that echoes the reflecting pool of the Lincoln Memorial, and allows the viewers to participate in the memorial; seeing their own image reflected in the names, they are implicated in the listing of the dead. The etched surface of the memorial has a tactile quality, and viewers are compelled to touch the names and make rubbings of them.

Its status as a memorial, rather than a monument, situates the Vietnam Veterans Memorial within a particular code of remembrance. Monuments and memorials can often be used as interchangeable forms, but there are distinctions in intent between them. Arthur Danto writes: 'We erect monuments so that we shall always remember, and build memorials so that we shall never forget.'[1] Monuments are not generally built to commemorate defeats; the defeated dead are remembered in memorials. Whereas a monument most often signifies victory, a memorial refers to the life or lives sacrificed for a particular set of values. Memorials embody grief, loss, and tribute. Whatever triumph a memorial may refer to, its depiction of victory is always tempered by a foregrounding of the lives lost.

Memorials are, according to Charles Griswold, "a species of pedagogy" that "seeks to instruct posterity about the past and, in so doing, necessarily reaches a decision about what is worth recovering."[2] The Lincoln Memorial is a funereal structure that gains its force from its implicit reference to Lincoln's untimely death. It embodies the man and his philosophy, with his words on its walls. The Washington Monument, by contrast, operates purely as a symbol, making no reference beyond its name to the mythic political figure. The distinction between the two outlines one of the fundamental differences between memorials and monuments: memorials tend to emphasize specific texts or lists of the dead, whereas monuments are usually anonymous.

The Vietnam Veterans Memorial is unmistakably representative of a particular period in Western art. In the uproar that accompanied its construction, it became the focus of a debate about the role of modernism in public sculpture. Just one month prior to the dedication of the memorial in November 1982, Tom Wolfe wrote a vitriolic attack on its design in the *Washington Post*, calling it a work of modern orthodoxy that was a "tribute to Jane Fonda."[3] Wolfe and other critics of modernism compared the memorial to two infamously unpopular, government-funded public sculptures: Carl Andre's *Stone Field Piece* (1980) in Hartford, Connecticut, and Richard Serra's *Tilted Arc* (1981) in downtown Manhattan. Andre's work, which consists of thirty-six large boulders positioned on a lawn near Hartford's city hall, is widely regarded with derision by residents as a symbol of the misguided judgements of their city government.[4] Serra's now notorious *Tilted Arc*, an oppressive, leaning slab of Cor-Ten steel that bisected the equally inhospitable Federal Plaza, inspired several years of intense debate and was dismantled in March 1989 after workers in the Federal Building petitioned to have it removed.[5] In the media, these two works came to symbolize the alienating effect of modern sculpture on the viewing public and people's questioning of the mechanisms by which tax-funded sculpture is imposed upon them.

In situating the Vietnam Veterans Memorial purely within the context of modernism, however, Wolfe and his fellow critics ignore fundamental aspects of this work, an omission which, it might be added, the sketches of the design may have aided. The memorial is not simply a flat, black, abstract wall; it is a wall inscribed with names. When members of the "public" visit this memorial, they do not go to contemplate long walls cut into the earth but to see and touch the names of those whose lives were lost in this war. Hence, to call this a modernist work is to overemphasize its physical design and to negate its commemorative purpose.

Modernist sculpture has been defined by a kind of sitelessness. Yet, the Vietnam Veterans Memorial is a site-specific work that establishes its position within the symbolic history embodied in the national monuments on and around the Washington Mall. Pointing from its axis to both the Washington Monument and Lincoln Memorial, the Vietnam Veterans Memorial references, absorbs, and reflects these classical forms. Its black walls mirror not only the faces of its viewers and passing clouds but the obelisk of the Washington Monument, thus forming a kind of pastiche of monuments. The memorial's relationship to the earth shifts between context and decontextualization, between an effacement and an embracement of the earth; approached from above, it appears to cut into the earth; from below, it seems to rise from it. The site specificity of the Vietnam Veterans Memorial is crucial to its position as both subversive of and continuous with the nationalist discourse of the mall.

It is as a war memorial that the Vietnam Veterans Memorial most distinguishes itself from modernist sculpture. As the first national memorial to an American war built since the Second World War memorials, it makes a statement on war that diverges sharply from the traditional declarations of prior war memorials. The Vietnam Veterans Memorial Fund (VVMF), which organized the construction of the memorial, stipulated only two things in its design—that it contain the names of all of those who died or are missing in action, and that be apolitical and harmonious with the site. Implicit within these guidelines was the desire that the memorial offer some kind of closure to the debates on the war. Yet, with these stipulations, the veterans set the stage for the dramatic disparity between the message of this memorial and that of its antecedents. The stipulation that the work not espouse a political stand in regard to the war—a stipulation that, in the ensuing controversy, would ultimately appear naive—ensured that in the end the memorial would not glorify war.

The traditional war memorial achieves its status by enacting closure on a specific conflict. This closure contains the war within particular master narratives either of victory or the bitter price of victory, a theme dominant in the "never again" texts of First World War memorials. In declaring the end of a conflict, this closure can by its very nature serve to sanctify future wars by offering a complete narrative with cause and effect intact. In rejecting the architectural lineage of monuments and contesting the aesthetic codes of previous war memorials, the Vietnam Veterans Memorial refuses to sanction the closure and implied tradition of those structures. Yet, it can be said to both condemn and justify future memorials.

THE BLACK GASH OF SHAME

Before the memorial was completed, its design came under attack not only because of its modernist aesthetics but, more significant, because it violated unspoken taboos about the remembrance of wars. When it was first unveiled, the design was condemned by certain veterans and others as a highly political statement about the shame of an unvictorious war. The memorial was termed the "black gash of shame and sorrow," a "degrading ditch," a "tombstone," a "slap in the face," and a "wailing wall for draft dodgers and New Lefters of the future." These dissenters included a certain faction of veterans and members of the "New Right," ranging from conservative activist Phyllis Schafly to future presidential candidate Ross Perot, who had contributed the money for the design contest. Many of these critics saw the memorial as a monument to defeat, one that spoke more directly to a nation's guilt than to the honor of the war dead and the veterans.

The criticism leveled at the memorial's design showed precisely how it was being 'read' by its opponents, and their readings compellingly reveal codes of remembrance of war memorials. Many saw its black walls as evoking shame, sorrow, and dishonor and others perceived its refusal to rise above the earth as indicative of defeat. Thus, a racially coded reading of the color black as shameful was combined with a reading of a feminized earth connoting a lack of power. Precisely because of its deviation from traditional commemorative codes — white stone rising above the earth — the design was read as a political statement. In a defensive attempt to counter aesthetic arguments, an editorial in the *National Review* stated:

> Our objection . . . is based upon the clear political message of this design. The design says that the Vietnam War should be memorialized in black, not the white marble of Washington. The mode of listing the names makes them individual deaths, not deaths in a cause: they might as well have been traffic accidents. The invisibility of the monument at ground level symbolizes the "unmentionability" of the war. . . . Finally, the V-shaped plan of the black retaining wall immortalizes the antiwar signal, the V protest made with the fingers.[6]

This analysis of the memorial's symbolism, indeed a perceptive reading, points to several crucial aspects of the memorial: its listing of names does emphasize individual deaths rather than the singular death of a body of men and women; the relationship of the memorial to the earth does refuse to evoke heroism and victory. Yet these conservative readings of the memorial, though they may have been accurate in interpreting the design, did not anticipate the effects of the inscription of names.

The angry reactions to the memorial design go beyond the accusation of the elite pretensions of abstraction — the uncontroversial Washington Monument itself is the epitome of abstraction. Rather, I believe that the memorial's primary (and unspoken) subversion of the codes of war remembrance is its antiphallic presence. By "antiphallic" I do not mean to imply that the memorial is somehow a passive or "feminine" form, but rather that it opposes the codes of vertical monuments symbolizing power and honor. The memorial does not stand erect above the landscape; it is continuous with the earth. It is contemplative rather than declarative. The V shape of the memorial has been interpreted by various commentators as V for Vietnam, victim, victory, veteran, violate, and valor. Yet one also finds here a disconcerting subtext in this debate in which the memorial is seen as implicitly evoking castration. The V of the two black granite walls, it seems, is also read as a female V. The "gash" is not only a wound, it is slang for the female genitals. The memorial contains all the elements that have been associated psychoanalytically with the specter of woman—it embraces the earth; it is the abyss; it is death.

Indeed, some of the criticism of the memorial was direct in calling for a phallic memorial. James Webb, who was a member of the Fund's sponsoring committee, wrote:

> Watching then the white phallus that is the Washington Monument piercing the air like a bayonet, you feel uplifted. . . . That is the political message. And then when you peer off into the woods at this black slash of earth to your left, this sad, dreary mass tomb, nihilistically commemorating death, you are hit with that message also. . . . That is the tragedy of this memorial for those who served.[7]

To its critics, this antiphallus symbolized this country's castration in an unsuccessful war, a war that "emasculated" the United States. The "healing" of this wound would therefore require a memorial that revived the narrative of the United States as a technologically superior military power and rehabilitated the masculinity of the American soldier.

The person who designed this controversial, antiphallic memorial was unlikely to reiterate traditional codes of war remembrance. At the time her anonymously submitted design was chosen by a group of eight art experts, Maya Ying Lin was a twenty-one-year-old undergraduate at Yale University. She had produced the design as a project for a funerary architecture course. She was not only young and uncredentialed but also Chinese-American and female. Initially, the veterans of the VVMF were pleased by this turn of events; they assumed that the selection of Lin's design would only show how open and impartial their design contest had been. However, the selection of someone with "marginal" cultural status as the primary interpreter of a controversial war inevitably complicated matters. Eventually, Maya Lin was defined, in particular by the media, not as American but as "other." This otherness became an issue not only in the way she was perceived by the media and some of the veterans, it became a critical issue of whether or not that otherness had informed the design itself. Architecture critic Michael Sorkin wrote:

> Perhaps it was Maya Lin's "otherness" that enabled her to create such a moving work. Perhaps only an outsider could have designed an environment so successful in answering the need for recognition by a group of people—the Vietnam vets—who are plagued by a sense of "otherness" forced on them by a country that has spent ten years pretending not to see them.[8]

Lin's marginal status as a Chinese-American woman was thus seen as giving her insight into the marginal status experienced by Vietnam veterans, an analogy that noticeably erased other differences in race and age that existed between them.

When Lin's identity became known, there was a tendency in the press to characterize her design as passive, as having both a female and an Asian aesthetic. There is little doubt that in its refusal to glorify war, it is an implicitly pacifist work, and, by extension, a political work. In its form, the memorial is emphatically antiheroic. Yet as much as it is contemplative and continuous with the earth, it can also be seen as a violent work that cuts into the earth. Lin has said, "I wanted to work with the land and not dominate it. I had an impulse to cut open the earth . . . an initial violence that in time would heal. The grass would grow back, but the cut would remain, a pure, flat surface, like a geode when you cut into it and polish the edge.[9] The black walls cannot connote a healing wound without also signifying the violence that created that wound, cutting into the earth and splitting it open.

Trouble began almost immediately between Maya Lin and the veterans. 'The fund has always seen me as a female—as a child', she has said. 'I went in there when I first won and their attitude was—O.K. you did a good job, but now we're going to hire some big boys—boys—to take care of it.'[10] Lin was situated outside the veterans' discourse, because she was a woman and an Asian-American and because of her approach to the project. She had made a decision deliberately not to inform herself about the war's political history to avoid being influenced by debates about the war. According to veteran Jan Scruggs, who was the primary figure in getting the memorial built,

> She never asked, "What was combat like?" or "Who were your friends whose names we're putting on the wall?" And the vets, in turn, never once explained to her what words like "courage," "sacrifice," and "devotion to duty" really meant.[11]

In the larger political arena, discourses of aesthetics and commemoration were also at play. Several well-placed funders of the memorial, including Ross Perot, were unhappy with the design, and Secretary of the Interior James Watt withheld its permit. It became clear to the veterans of the VVMF that they had either to compromise or to postpone the construction of the memorial (which was to be ready by November 1982, in time for Veterans Day). Consequently, a plan was devised to erect a statue and flag close to the walls of the memorial; realist sculptor Frederick Hart was chosen to design it. (Hart was paid $330,000, compared to the $20,000 fee that Maya Lin received for her design from the same fund.)[12]

Hart's bronze sculpture, placed in a grove of trees near the memorial in 1984, consists of three soldiers—one black, one Hispanic, and one white—standing and looking in the general direction of the memorial. The soldiers' military garb is realistically rendered, with guns slung over their shoulders and ammunition around their waists, and their expressions are somewhat bewildered and puzzled. Hart, one of the most vociferous critics of modernism in the debate over the memorial, said at the time:

My position is humanist, not militarist. I'm not trying to say there was anything good or bad about the war. I researched for three years—read everything. I became close friends with many vets, drank with them in bars. Lin's piece is a serene exercise in contemporary art done in a vacuum with no knowledge of its subject. It's nihilistic—that's its appeal.[13]

Hart bases his credentials on a kind of "knowledge" strictly within the male domain—drinking with the veterans in a bar—and unavailable to Maya Lin, whom he had on another occasion referred to as "a mere student." She describes the addition of his statue as "drawing mustaches on other people's portraits."[14] Hart characterizes Lin as having designed her work with no "knowledge" and no "research," as a woman who works with feeling and intuition rather than expertise. He ultimately defines realism as not only a male privilege but also an aesthetic necessity in remembering war. Ironically, the conflict over Lin's design forestalled any potential debate over the atypical expression of Hart's soldiers.

The battle over what kind of aesthetic style best represents the Vietnam War was, quite obviously, a battle of the discourse of the war itself. In striving for an "apolitical" memorial, the veterans of the VVMF had attempted to separate the memorial, itself a contested narrative, from the contested narratives of the war, ultimately an impossible task. The memorial could not be a neutral site precisely because of the divisive effects of the Vietnam War. Later, Maya Lin noted the strange appropriateness of the two memorials: "In a funny sense the compromise brings the memorial closer to the truth. What is also memorialized is that people still cannot resolve that war, nor can they separate issues, the politics, from it.[15] However, after Lin's memorial had actually been constructed, the debate about aesthetics and remembrance surrounding its design simply disappeared. The controversy was eclipsed by a national discourse on remembrance and healing. The experience of viewing Lin's work was so powerful for the general public that criticism of its design vanished.

THE VIETNAM VETERAN: THE PERENNIAL SOLDIER

The incommunicability of the experience of the Vietnam veterans has been a primary narrative in Vietnam War representation. This silence has been depicted as a consequence of an inconceivable kind of war, one that fit no prior images of war, one that the American public would refuse to believe. The importance of the Vietnam Veterans Memorial lies in its communicability, which in effect has mollified the incommunicability of the veterans' experience.

Though the Vietnam Veterans Memorial most obviously pays tribute to the memory of those who died during the war, it is a central icon for the veterans. It has been noted that the memorial has given them a place—one that recognizes their identities, a place at which to congregate and from which to speak. Vietnam veterans haunt the memorial, often coming at night after the crowds have dispersed. Many veterans regard the wall as a site where they visit their memories. Hence, the memorial is as much about survival as it is about mourning the dead. The construction of an identity for the veterans has become the most conspicuous and persistent narrative of the memorial. The central theme of this narrative is the veterans' initial marginalization, before the memorial's construction generated discussion about them.

Unlike the Second World War veterans, Vietnam veterans did not arrive home en masse for a celebration. Some of the most difficult stories of the veterans' experience are about their mistreatment upon their return, and these incidents serve as icons for the extended alienation and mistreatment felt by the veterans. Many veterans ended up in underfunded and poorly staffed Veterans' Administration Hospitals. They were expected to put their war experiences behind them and to assimilate quickly back into society. That many were unable to do so further exacerbated their marginalization—they were labeled social misfits and stereotyped as potentially dangerous men liable to erupt violently at any moment.

The scapegoating of the veteran as a psychopath absolved the American public of complicity and allowed the narrative of American military power to stand. Implied within these conflicting narratives is the question of whether or not the veterans are to be perceived as victims or complicit with the war. Peter Marin writes, "Vets are in an ambiguous situation—they were the agents and victims of a particular kind of violence. That is the source of a pain that almost no one else can understand."[16] Ironically, their stigma has resulted in many Vietnam veterans' assumption of hybrid roles; they are both, yet neither, soldiers and civilians.

Although the marginalization of the Vietnam veterans has been acknowledged in the current discourse of healing and forgiveness about the war, within the veterans' community another group has struggled against an imposed silence: the women veterans. Eight women military nurses were killed in Vietnam and memorialized on the wall. It is estimated that 11,500 women, half of whom were civilians and many of whom were nurses, served in Vietnam and that 265,000 women served in the military during the time period of the Vietnam War. The experience of the women who served in Vietnam was equally affected by the difference of the war: an unusually large proportion of them, three-quarters, were exposed to hostile fire. Upon their return, they were not only subject to post-traumatic stress like the male veterans but they were also excluded from the veteran community. Many have since revealed how they kept their war experience a secret, not telling even their husbands about their time in Vietnam.

These women veterans were thus doubly displaced, unable to speak as veterans or as women. In response, several women veterans began raising funds for their own memorial, and in November 1993, the Vietnam Women's Memorial was dedicated near the Vietnam Veterans Memorial. The statue, which was designed by Glenna Goodacre, depicts three uniformed women with a wounded soldier. The two women who direct the VWMP, Diane Carlson Evans and Donna Marie Boulay, say that it is Hart's depiction of three men who make the absence of women so visible, and that they would not have initiated the project had Lin's memorial stood alone. Says Evans, "The wall in itself was enough, but when they added the men it became necessary to add women to complete the memorial."[17] Hence, the singular narrative of Hart's realist depiction is one of both inclusion and exclusion.

One could argue that the widespread discourse of healing around the original memorial led women veterans to speak of their memorial as the beginning rather than the culmination of a healing process. Yet the radical message of commemorating women in war is undercut by the conventionality of the statue itself. A contemporary version of the *Pietà*, the statue presents one woman nurse heroically holding the body of a wounded soldier, one searching the sky for help, and one looking forlornly at the ground. Benjamin Forgery, who called this memorial in the *Washington Post* "one monument too many," has criticized the women's memorial for cluttering up the landscape with "blatheringly sentimental sculpture." He wrote that the sculptor's "ambition is sabotaged by the subject and the artist's limited talent—compared with Michelangelo's Christ figure, this GI is as stiff as a board. The result is more like an awkward still from a *M*A*S*H* episode."[18]

The decision to build the women's memorial was not about aesthetics (except in so far as it reaffirms the representational aesthetic of Hart's statue) but about recognition and inclusion. However, by reinscribing the archetypal image of woman as caretaker, one that foregrounds the male veteran's body, the memorial reiterates the main obstacle to healing that women veterans face in recognizing their needs as veterans. Writes Laura Palmer, "After all, these women had *degrees* in putting the needs of others before their own."[19]

The difficulty of adequately and appropriately memorializing the women veterans falls within the larger issue of masculine identity in the Vietnam War. The Vietnam War is depicted as an event in which American masculinity was irretrievably damaged, and the rehabilitation of the Vietnam veteran is thus also a reinscription of American masculinity. This has also taken the form of re-enacting the war at the memorial itself through the Veterans' Vigil of Honor, which keeps watch there, and the "battles" over its construction and maintenance. As a form of re-enactment, this conflation of the memorial and the war is a ritual of healing, although one that appears to be stuck in its ongoing replay, with a resistance to moving beyond narratives of the war. For the men of the Veterans' Vigil, only the war can provide meaning. In refighting that war every day, they are also reinscribing narratives of heroism and sacrifice. But, for others, there is a powerful kind of closure at the memorial. The one story for which the memorial appears to offer resolution is that of the shame felt by veterans for having fought in an unpopular war, a story that is their primary battle with history.

THE MEMORIAL AS A SHRINE

The Vietnam Veterans Memorial has been the subject of an extraordinary outpouring of emotion since it was built. Over 150,000 people attended its dedication ceremony and some days as many as 20,000 people walk by its walls. It is presently the most visited site on the Washington Mall with an estimated twenty-two to thirty million visitors. People bring personal artifacts to leave at the wall as offerings, and coffee-table photography books document the experiences of visitors as a collective recovery from the war. It has also spawned the design or construction of at least 150 other memorials, including the Korean War Veterans Memorial, which was dedicated in July 1995.

The rush to embrace the memorial as a cultural symbol reveals not only the relief of voicing a history that has been taboo but also a desire to reinscribe that history. The black granite walls of the memorial act as a screen for myriad cultural projections; it is easily appropriated for a variety of interpretations of the war and of the experience of those who died in it. To the veterans, the wall makes amends for their treatment since the war; to the families and friends of those who died, it officially recognizes their sorrow and validates a grief that was not previously sanctioned; to others, it is either a profound anti-war statement or an opportunity to recast the narrative of the war in terms of honor and sacrifice.

The memorial's popularity must thus be seen in the context of a very active scripting and rescripting of the war and as an integral component in the recently emerged Vietnam War nostalgia industry. This sentiment is not confined to those who wish to return to the intensity of wartime; it is also felt by the news media, who long to recapture their moment of moral power—the Vietnam War was very good television. Michael Clark writes that the media nostalgia campaign,

> . . . healed over the wounds that had refused to close for ten years with a balm of nostalgia, and transformed guilt and doubt into duty and pride. And with a triumphant flourish it offered us the spectacle of its most successful creation, the veterans who will fight the next war.[20]

Though the design of Maya Lin's memorial does not lend itself to marketable reproductions, the work has functioned as a catalyst for much of this nostalgia. The Vietnam Veterans Memorial is the subject of no fewer than twelve books, many of them photography collections that focus on the interaction of visitors with the names. The memorial has tapped into a reservoir of need to express in public the pain of this war, a desire to transfer the private memories of this war into a collective experience. Many personal artifacts have been left at the memorial: photographs, letters, poems, teddy bears, dog tags, combat boots and helmets, MIA/POW bracelets, clothes, medals of honor, headbands, beer cans, plaques, crosses, playing cards. At this site, the objects are transposed from personal to cultural artifacts, as items bearing witness to pain suffered.

Thus, a very rich and vibrant dialogue of deliberate, if sometimes very private, remembrance takes place at the memorial. Of the approximately 40,000 objects that have been left at the wall, the vast majority have been left anonymously. Relinquished before the wall, the letters tell many stories:

> Dear Michael: Your name is here but you are not. I made a rubbing of it, thinking that if I rubbed hard enough I would rub your name off the wall and you would come back to me. I miss you so.

FIGURES 1 and 2. Vietnam Veterans Memorial, Washington, DC

Photos courtesy Marita Sturken.

Dear Sir: For twenty-two years I have carried your picture in my wallet. I was only eighteen years old that day that we faced one another on that trail in Chu Lai, Vietnam. Why you didn't take my life I'll never know. You stared at me for so long, armed with your AK-47, and yet you did not fire. Forgive me for taking your life, I was reacting just the way I was trained, to kill VC.

Hence, the memorial is perceived by visitors as a site where they can speak to the dead (where, by implication, the dead are present). Many of these letters are addressed not to visitors but to the dead, though intended to be shared as cultural memory. Many of the artifacts at the memorial also represent a catharsis in releasing long-held objects to memory: a can of C-rations, a "short stick," worn Vietnamese sandals, a grenade pin. For those who left

FIGURES 3 and 4. Vietnam Veterans Memorial, Washington, DC

Photos courtesy Marita Sturken.

these objects, the memorial represents their final destination and a relinquishing of memory.

The National Park Service, which is now in charge of maintaining the
memorial, operates an archive of the materials that have been left at the
memorial. Originally, the Park Service classified these objects as lost and
found." Later, Park Service officials realized the artifacts had been left inten-
tionally, and they began to save them. The objects thus moved from the cultural status of being "lost" (without category) to historical artifacts. They have
now even turned into artistic artifacts; the manager of the archive writes:

> These are no longer objects at the Wall, they are communications, icons
> possessing a subculture of underpinning emotion. They are the products
> of culture, in all its complexities. They are the products of individual

selection. With each object we are in the presence of a work of art of individual contemplation. The thing itself does not overwhelm our attention since these are objects that are common and expendable. At the Wall they have become unique and irreplaceable, and, yes, mysterious.[21]

Labeled "mysterious," and thus coded as original works of art, these objects are given value and authorship. Some of the people who left them have since been traced. This attempt to tie these objects and letters to their creators reveals again the shifting realms of personal and cultural memory. Assigned authorship and placed in an historical archive, the objects are pulled from cultural memory, a realm in which they are presented to be shared and to participate in the memories of others.

The memorial has become not only the primary site of remembrance for the Vietnam War, but also a site where people pay homage to many current conflicts and charged public events. Artifacts concerning the abortion debate, the AIDS epidemic, gay rights, and the Persian Gulf War have all been left at the memorial. Hence, the memorial's collection inscribes a history not only of the American participation in the Vietnam War but also of national issues and events since the war. It is testimony to the memorial's malleability as an icon that both prowar and antiwar artifacts were left there during the Persian Gulf War.

One of the most compelling features of the Vietnam Veterans Memorial collection is its anonymity, mystery, and ambiguity. It appears that many of the stories behind a substantial number of artifacts may never be known, and that the telling of these stories to history was never the purpose of their being placed at the memorial. Though couched within an official history and held by a government institution, these letters and offerings to the dead will continue to assert individual narratives, strands of cultural memory that disrupt historical narratives. They resist history precisely through their obscurity, their refusal to yield specific meanings.

THE CONSTRUCTION OF A HISTORY

The politics of memory and history of the Vietnam Veterans Memorial shift continuously in a tension of ownership and narrative complexity. Who, in actuality, is being allowed to speak for the experience of the war? Has the Vietnam Veterans Memorial facilitated the emergence of the voices of veterans and the families and friends of veterans in opposition to the voice of the media and the government? The process of healing can be an individual process or a national or cultural process; the politics of each is quite different.

Much of the current embrace of the memorial amounts to historical revisionism. The period between the end of the war and the positioning of the memorial as a national wailing wall has been long enough for memories and culpability to fade. Ironically, the memorial allows for an erasure of many of the specifics of history. It is rarely noted that the discussion surrounding the memorial never mentions the Vietnamese people. This is not a memorial to their loss; they cannot even be mentioned in the context of the Mall. Nor does the memorial itself allow for their mention; though it allows for an outpouring of grief, it does not speak to the intricate reasons why the lives represented by the inscribed names were lost in vain.

Thus, remembering is in itself a form of forgetting. Does the remembrance of the battles fought by the veterans in Vietnam and at home necessarily screen out any acknowledgment of the war's effect on the Vietnamese? In its listing of the U.S. war dead, and in the context of the Mall, the memorial establishes Americans, rather than Vietnamese, as the primary victims of the war. For instance, questions about the 1,300 American MIAs are raised at the memorial, yet in that space no mention can be made of the 300,000 Vietnamese MIAs. Does the process of commemoration necessitate choosing sides?

Artist Chris Burden created a sculpture in 1991, *The Other Vietnam Memorial*, in reaction to the memorial's nonacknowledgment of the Vietnamese. Burden's piece consists of large copper leaves, twelve by eight feet, arranged as a kind of circular standing book, on which are engraved three million Vietnamese names to commemorate the three million Vietnamese who died in the war. He says: "Even though I feel sorry for the individuals named on [the Vietnam Veterans Memorial], I was repulsed by the idea. I couldn't help but think that we were celebrating our dead, who were aggressors, basically, and wonder where were the Vietnamese names?"[22] Burden's listing of names is not unproblematic; he was unable to get the actual listing of names, so he took 4,000 names and repeated them over and over again. However, Burden's sculpture exposes a fundamental limit of commemoration within nationalism. Why must a national memorial re-enact conflict by showing only one side of the conflict? What is the memory produced by a national memorial?

The memorial's placement on the Washington Mall inscribes it within nationalism, restricting in many ways the kinds of memory it can provide. Its presence indicates both the limitations and the complexity of that nationalist discourse. Lauren Berlant writes:

> When Americans make the pilgrimage to Washington they are trying to grasp the nation in its totality. Yet the totality of the nation in its capital city is a jumble of historical modalities, a transitional space between local and national cultures, private and public property, archaic and living artifacts . . . it is a place of national *mediation*, where a variety of nationally inflected media come into visible and sometimes incommensurate contact.[23]

The memorial asserts itself into this "jumble of historical modalities," both a resistant and compliant artifact. It serves not as a singular statement but a site of mediation, a site of conflicting voices and opposing agendas.

However, the act of commemoration is ultimately a process of legitimation and the memorial lies at the center of a struggle between narratives. It has spawned two very different kinds of remembrance: one a retrenched historical narrative that attempts to rewrite the Vietnam War in a way that reinscribes U.S. imperialism and the masculinity of the American soldier; the other a textured and complex discourse of remembrance that has allowed the Americans affected by this war — the veterans, their families, and the families and friends of the war dead — to speak of loss, pain, and futility. The screens of the memorial allow for projections of a multitude of memories and individual interpretations. The memorial stands in a precarious space between these opposing interpretations of the war.

NOTES

1. Arthur Danto, "The Vietnam Veterans Memorial," *The Nation*, August 31, 1985, p. 152.

2. Charles Griswold, "The Vietnam Veterans Memorial and the Washington Mall," *Critical Inquiry*, Summer 1986, p. 689.

3. Tom Wolfe, "Art Disputes War," *Washington Post*, October 13, 1982, p. B4.

4. Kenneth Baker, "Andre in Retrospect," *Art in America*, April 1980, pp. 88–94.

5. See Robert Storr, "'Tilted Arc': Enemy of the People," in Arlene Raven (ed.), *Art in the Public Interest* (Ann Arbor: University of Michigan Press, 1989).

6. "Stop That Monument," *National Review*, September 18, 1981, p. 1064.

7. Quoted in Mary McLeod, "The Battle for the Monument," in Helene Lipstadt (ed.), *The Experimental Tradition* (New York: Princeton Architectural Press, 1989), p. 125.

8. Michael Sorkin, "What Happens When a Woman Designs a War Monument?" *Vogue*, May 1983, p. 122.

9. Quoted in "America Remembers: Vietnam Veterans Memorial," *National Geographic*, May 1985, p. 557.

10. "An Interview With Maya Lin," in Reese Williams (ed.), *Unwinding the Vietnam War* (Seattle: Real Comet Press, 1987), p. 271.

11. Jan Scruggs and Joel Swerdlow, *To Heal a Nation* (New York: Harper & Row, 1985), p. 79.

12. Mary McLeod, op. cit., p. 127.

13. "An Interview With Frederick Hart," in Reese Williams (ed.), *Unwinding the Vietnam War* (Seattle: Real Comet Press, 1987), p. 274.

14. Quoted in Rick Horowitz, "Maya Lin's Angry Objections," *Washington Post*, July 7, 1982, p. B1.

15. Quoted in Scruggs and Swerdlow, op. cit., p. 133.

16. Peter Marin, "Conclusion," in Harrison Salisbury (ed.), *Vietnam Reconsidered* (New York: Harper & Row, 1984), p. 213.

17. Quoted in Benjamin Forgery, "Battle Won for War Memorials," *Washington Post*, September 20, 1991.

18. Benjamin Forgery, "One Monument Too Many," *Washington Post*, November 6, 1993, p. D7.

19. Quoted in Laura Palmer, "How to Bandage a War," *New York Times Magazine*, November 7, 1993, p. 40.

20. Michael Clark, "Remembering Vietnam," *Cultural Critique* 3, Spring 1986, p. 49.

21. David Guynes, quoted in Lydia Fish, *The Last Firebase* (Shippensburg, PA: White Mane, 1987), p. 54.

22. Quoted in Robert Storr, "Chris Burden," *MoMA Members Quarterly*, Fall 1991, p. 5.

23. Lauren Berlant, "The Theory of Infantile Citizenship," *Public Culture* 5, 1993, p. 395.

28

Subjunctive Documentary: Computer Imaging and Simulation

MARK J. P. WOLF

Whereas most documentaries are concerned with documenting events that have happened in the past, and attempt to make photographic records of them, computer imaging and simulation are concerned with what *could be, would be,* or *might have been*; they form a subgenre of documentary we might call *subjunctive* documentary, following the use of the term *subjunctive* as a grammatical tense. At first glance such a term might appear to be an oxymoron, but there is no more contradiction here than in any other form of documentary. The last of the above conditionals, *what might have been*, applies to all documentary film and video, because all are subjective and incomplete, reconstructing events to varying degrees through existing objects, documents, and personal recollections. However, by translating invisible entities (beyond the range of human vision) or mathematical ideas into visible analogues, computer simulation has allowed the conceptual world to enter the perceptual one. It has created new ways in which an image can be linked to an actual object or event, with mathematically reconstructed simulacra used as representations, standing in for photographic images. By narrowing and elongating the indexical link and combining it with extrapolation or speculation, computer imaging and simulation may suggest that there is a difference between what is called "documentary film" and "nonfiction film," especially when one is documenting the subjunctive.

In this era of computer simulation, there is a greater willingness to trade close indexical linkage for new knowledge that would otherwise be unattainable within the stricter requirements of indexical linkage that were once needed to validate knowledge empirically. Many of these requirements have to do with observation, the visual verification of one's data. In *Techniques of the Observer*, Jonathan Crary describes transformations in the notion of visuality that occurred in the first half of the nineteenth century. Writing about the relationship between the eye and the optical apparatus, he states:

From *Collecting Visible Evidence*. Ed. Jane M Gaines and Michael Renov. Minneapolis: U of Minnesota P, 1999. 274–291.

During the seventeenth and eighteenth centuries that relationship had been essentially metaphoric; the eye and the camera obscura or the eye and the telescope or microscope were allied by a conceptual similarity, in which the authority of an ideal eye remained unchallenged. Beginning in the nineteenth century, the relation between eye and apparatus becomes one of metonomy: both were now contiguous instruments on the same plane of operation, with varying capabilities and features. The limits and deficiencies of one will be complemented by the other, and vice versa.[1]

The notion that observation could be performed through the mediation of instruments did not find immediate acceptance; Auguste Comte, the founder of positivism, deprecated the microscope, the use of which he did not consider to be direct observation.[2] In *Instrumental Realism*, Don Ihde writes that seventeenth-century Aristotelians objected to Galileo's telescope, and Xavier Bichat, the founder of histology (the study of living tissues), distrusted microscopes and would not allow them into his lab.[3] Ihde points out, however, that some of the objection was due to imperfect technology, which produced blurred images. In one sense, a blurred image is an indication that the technology has reached its limits; sharp images with dubious indexical linkages may be more harmful in that their shortcomings are less noticeable. The instrument does not indicate what it does not see, and so one must take this into account when studying objects viewed with it.

The use of imaging technologies is essential to much of modern science, but the issues regarding the status of the entities studied through them are still a matter of debate. In his discussion of instrumental realism, Ihde describes the work of philosopher Patrick Heelan:

> Heelan's position regarding instrumentation is clearly an enthusiastic endorsement of a "seeing" with instruments, albeit cast in the hermeneutic terms of "reading" a "text" provided by instruments. Nevertheless, this "reading" is held to have all the qualities of a perceptual "seeing." Thus, one can say that Heelan's is a specialized but liberal interpretation of "seeing with" an instrument.[4]

Ihde gives Heelan's example of a measured perception that is both hermeneutical and perceptual: that of reading a thermometer to learn the temperature, an act that requires no knowledge of thermodynamics, but rather an understanding of how the instrument is read. Ihde points out that Robert Ackerman's position is more cautious:

> [Ackerman] argues both for the largest degree of ambiguity relating to what he calls "data domains" which are text-like, and for considerable skepticism relating to the (hermeneutic) interpretative process. "Instrumental means only produce a data text whose relationship to nature is problematic." And, "the features of the world revealed to experiment cannot be philosophically proven to be revealing of the world's properties." (I am not sure whether Ackerman holds any counterpart thesis that other means of analyzing world properties can be

philosophically proven.) Yet, examination of the interpretive result relating to such data domains turns out to be the same as for other knowledge claims.[5]

Thus, along with optical instruments like the microscope and telescope, we could include the camera and the record it produces. Photographic technology and processes, since their invention, have come to be valued as records and evidence in the areas of science, law, and medicine.[6] Most people's reliance on media for knowledge of the world is another instance of belief in the recorded image.

Photography, as a source of instrumental realism, differed from prior instruments because of its ability to store an image. The viewing of entities using telescopes, microscopes, and other optical apparatuses was done in real time, an unbroken link between subject and observer, both physically present on either end of the link. The camera, as a system of lenses, was similar to the telescope and microscope, but it had the ability to record the images seen, saving them for later examination, even after the subject was gone. The photograph's image was not "live" like the images viewed in other optical instruments, but its fixity provided a means of making a record that could be analyzed later, like a scientific journal. The photograph bridged the gap between *observation* and *documentation*.

The documentary value accorded the photograph was due in part to the acceptance of other optical apparatuses as epistemologically sound instruments, and could be seen as an extension of them. Other imaging technologies, such as video, were also accorded similar status. As the computer came to be trusted as a scientific tool, it was only a matter of time before it, too, would be combined with the imaging apparatus, especially in its revolutionization of the idea of the retrievable document. The concept of the stored image is analogous to the concept of the stored program, and the digital image can be seen as the marriage of the two.

Computer imaging, however, is often indexically less direct than film-based photography, due to the active mediation of hardware and software, as well as the storage of the image as a signal instead of a fixed record. Like the magnification produced by the microscope or telescope, computer imaging is often an extension of the camera into realms indirectly available to human experience. One of the functions of the *Voyager* spacecraft, for example, was to send back images of the outer planets of the solar system. Images of the planets taken by its onboard camera were transmitted electronically back to Earth, composited, and arranged in sequence to produce moving imagery, which contained far more detail than what an Earth-bound observer could produce. Physical distance is not the only boundary overcome; many forms of computer imaging record light waves or energies that fall outside the spectrum of visible light—infrared, ultraviolet, radio waves, and so on—and transduce them into the visible portion of the spectrum, creating visual imagery from recorded data. Likewise, forms of medical imaging such as computerized axial tomography (CAT) scans, positron emission tomography (PET) scans, and magnetic resonance imaging (MRI) use radio waves (and ultrasound, which uses sound waves) to construct images or three-dimensional models, with different tones or colors representing different intensities.

The rendering of these transduced waves into the visible spectrum means tones or colors must be assigned to various frequencies to make them visible. The false coloring making up the image, however, is a step into the subjunctive, because the image is not a record of how the subject appears to the observer, but rather how it *might* appear, if such frequencies were substituted for frequencies (light waves) within the visible spectrum. Thus it is the differences between frequencies that are being documented, not the frequencies themselves. Also, false colors in computer imaging are usually assigned to make the data displayed clearer, representing another level of mediation between subject and observer.[7]

In some ways, the false coloring found in computer imaging is only one step removed from black-and-white photography, which shows us things not as they appear to us (in color) but rather as a map of tonal intensities. In this sense, black-and-white photography could also be considered subjunctive, showing us what things would look like if our retinas contained only rods and no cones, making us sensitive to tonality but not to hue and saturation. Ironically, the emphasis on computer imaging processes can lead to neglect of the real, visible colors that exist in the universe. David F. Malin has described how the visible spectrum is often overlooked by astronomers, who often prefer to use charged-coupled devices (CCDs), electronic detectors that collect light far more efficiently than do photographs:

> One of the key advantages [film-based] photography has over electronic imaging is that photographic plates can capture high-resolution, sensitive images over an area of virtually unlimited size, for example, across the entire wide field view of the U. K. Schmidt telescope in Australia. In comparison, the largest CCDs measure only a few centimeters across. Photography therefore offers a superior means for recording images of extended astronomical objects such as nebulae and nearby galaxies.

> Furthermore, the photographic layer serves as a compact medium for storing vast amounts of visual information. A single 35.6-by-35.6-centimeter plate from the U. K. Schmidt telescope, which records a patch of sky 6.4 degrees on a side, contains the equivalent of several hundred megabytes of data.

> Color images present the information packed into an astronomical photograph in an attractive and intuitively obvious way. Indeed, measuring the colors of nebulae, stars and galaxies is central to understanding their composition and physical state.[8]

In the computer age, film-based photography now seems like a direct process of observation, compared with computer imaging, quite a far cry from the days when the microscope was considered a step beyond direct observation. At the same time, computer imaging technologies have changed the nature of "observation" and what is considered observable.

Many of the entities or energies imaged by the computer are ones that are too small, too large, or too fast to be visible to traditional optical instruments or the unaided eye. In the photographic world, microphotography, time-lapse, and high-speed photography serve similar purposes, although to a much lesser degree; but in several cases they can be seen as precursors of computer imaging techniques. The electron microscope, for example, is an extension of the optical microscope and the camera, using a focused beam of electrons rather than light to create an image; the scanning electron micro-scope produces an image from scan lines in a manner similar to television images. The scanning tunneling microscope, which uses computer imaging, produces an image by scanning a very small area with a fine, microscopic probe that measures surface charge. The closer the probe is to an atom, the stronger the charge. The charge on the probe changes during the scan, and a reconstructed image of the surface emerges when different colors are assigned to different charge intensities and displayed. Although the process presents a visual image of the atoms, it is not an image in the traditional pho-tographic sense, because traditional photography is impossible on a sub-atomic scale.[9]

The recording of high-speed events in particle physics also evolved from photographic techniques to computer imaging techniques in which twenty-five billion bits of data are produced in one second. The earliest detectors used for monitoring particle collisions were cloud chambers, bubble cham-bers, and streamer chambers, all of which were similar in principle. In these chambers, charged particles were detected when they moved through a medi-um leaving a trail of ionized atoms behind them. These trails (composed of water droplets, bubbles, or sparks, depending on the chamber) could then be recorded on film. Photographic records were highly detailed and could be interpreted easily, and during the late 1960s computers were used in the analyses of the photographs, although more complicated images required human assistance. However, according to a 1991 article in *Scientific American*:

> Capturing events on film became impossible when accelerators were developed that produced thousands of particles in a second. To record particles at this rate, physicists designed complicated electronic detectors. Because information was gathered in electronic form, computers became an essential tool for making quick decisions during data collection.

> Yet physicists still cannot rely exclusively on computers to analyze the data. Computers that automatically inspect events are limited by the expectations of programmers. Such systems can selectively suppress information or obscure unusual phenomena. Until scientists invent a pattern recognition program that works better than the human brain, it will be necessary to produce images of the most complicated and inter-esting events so that physicists can scrutinize the data.[10]

Toward the end of the article, the authors state that "the detectors, like all complex mechanisms, have certain quirks." And they add that during the test runs of the detectors, "the programs occasionally produce images showing inconsistencies between the data and the laws of physics. These inconsistencies can arise because of a malfunction in part of the detector, in the data acquisition system or in the data analysis software."[11] In this instance, the desire for more data and finer detail necessitated a move away from conventional media, which proved to be too limited for scientific purposes. Although the data may not be as reliable, there are several thousand times more data to examine.

Sensor technology is also used on larger scales as well, for tracking and imaging planes with radar, submarines with sonar, or weather patterns imaged by satellite. Electronic signals and sensors have been used to track whole flocks of birds, and even human beings, some of whom owe their lives to these sensors.[12] NASA's Mission to Planet Earth (MPTE) involves sending up nineteen Earth-orbiting satellites over a fifteen-year period (1998–2013) that will collect data on environmental conditions such as the greenhouse effect, desertification, ozone depletion, weather cycles, and other ecological information. Garrett Culhane, writing about these satellites in *Wired*, states:

> One of the largest will generate a terabyte (1,012 bytes) of data about the earth every ten days—that's enough to fill 2,000 CDs or 500,000,000 pages of text. "The EOS will produce data on the scale of that contained in the Library of Congress about every ten days," says [MPTE director Robert] Price.[13]

The data imaged are collected from all over the globe, and the sheer numbers of them are far too extensive to be represented in any single image or sequence of images; and if the satellites are collecting continuously, the data may be coming in faster than anyone can analyze it.

In this string of examples, computer imaging gradually moves further and further away from conventional photographic methods of documenting events as the phenomena being studied slip out of visibility, because they are too far away, too small, or too quick, or because they lie outside of the visible spectrum. And unlike infrared, ultraviolet, or even X-ray photography, computer imaging involves more interpretation and often must reconstruct objects or events in order to visualize them. Although often displayed in two-dimensional images, the data collected in medical scanning, astronomy, particle physics, and meteorology represent complex events and structures in three dimensions. These reconstructed events can be rendered and viewed from any angle, and replayed repeatedly for further analysis, as computer simulations.

Computer-generated three-dimensional representations that change over time are more than just reconstructions of images, they are reconstructions of a system's behavior. In these reconstructions, still imagery becomes moving imagery, and computer imaging becomes computer simulation; like the photograph as a stored image that can be analyzed in the absence of its subject, a computer simulation made from recorded data allows an event to be reconstructed and analyzed after it has occurred. The data in a computer simulation are a series of measurements combining disparate forms of other data, many of which are nonphotographic. These data are linked to their referents in a variety of ways, recording the values of whatever variables they are programmed to represent.

If computer simulations are documentary, they are subjunctive documentary. Their subjunctive nature lies not only in their flexibility in the imaging of events, but in their staging as well; computer simulations are often made from data taken from the outside world, but not always. Just as the digital image does not always have a real-world referent, computer simulation can be used to image real or imaginary constructs, or some combination of the two. Computer simulations go beyond the mere recording of data; they are frequently used to study the behavior of dynamic systems and become the basis of decisions, predictions, and conclusions made about them. As a simulation is constructed, and the data set becomes larger and more comprehensive, its indexical link to the physical world grows stronger, until the simulation is thought to be sufficiently representative of some portion or aspect of the physical world. The computer allows not only physical indices like visual resemblance but conceptual indices (like gravity or the laws of physics) to govern simulated events. Like the photograph, computer simulation can combine observation and documentation, and as the embodiment of a theory, it can document what *could be, would be,* or *might have been.* In many cases, actual experiments and events are represented as measurements and relationships; these are abstracted into a set of laws governing the phenomena, and these laws become the basis for creating the *potential events* of the simulation. Thus the simulation documents possibilities or probabilities instead of actualities.

Computer simulation has been used in a wide range of applications: for the visualization of purely mathematical constructs, architectural walk-throughs, job training, product design and testing, and experimental scientific research. The basis for all of these simulations is mathematical reconstruction, in which a mechanical, simplified version of the events being studied is created in the computer's memory. Mathematical visualization can give visual form to purely mathematical constructs, such as fractal objects, rotating hypercubes, and other higher-dimensional forms.[14] It can also be used to illustrate the hypothetical; for example, to show how relativistic distortions would appear to an extremely high-speed traveler (buildings would shift in color and appear to lean in toward the observer). A simulation can give the hypothetical an appearance of feasibility, by virtue of its visualization; such concrete imagery can be useful in swaying belief, especially in a society that tends to rely on the image as evidence. Although mathematical visualizations seek to give concrete visual form to abstract ideas, most visualizations seek to re-create objects and situations that are thought to have existed or that could exist in the material world.

Architectural walk-throughs—or fly-throughs, as they are called—are computer simulations of hypothetical buildings that the user can "move through" and view from any angle, under various lighting conditions, and with different styles of decor and furniture. They allow a user to get a sense of what a building and its interior will be like before it is built, to make changes, and to decide on a final design. Architects designing on the computer may work closely with these tools while creating the plans for buildings. The limitations inherent in a simulation program, then, may subtly influence the design of a building, and the way the building is depicted as a three-dimensional space will also influence the choices shaping its design. While computer simulation allows the visualization of possibilities, it limits those possibilities by providing the language of speculation used to create their visual analogues.

Architectural simulations can be used to speculate about the past as well as the future. Structures that are partially destroyed, no longer exist, or were designed but never built can be visually (and aurally) re-created.[15] The Taisei Corporation, Japan's third-largest construction firm, uses computer modeling in the design of large-scale structures, including skyscrapers and power plants. The company has also made a series of architectural fly-throughs of ancient cities, which it reconstructed for the British Museum.[16] Reconstructed from archaeological data, a fly-through of the Sumerian city of Ur begins with a rotating bird's-eye view of the city. The point of view revolves around a ziggurat and over rooftops, and then eventually drops down to street level, moving through an alley, under canopied doors, and finally through the interior of one of the buildings, where pottery and furniture can be seen. The sequence combines a map of the city, architecture of individual buildings, and artifacts such as pottery into one unified illustration. Similarly, computer animation is used to bring a reconstructed city of Tenochtitlan back to life in *500 Nations* (1995), a television series documenting Native American history. Although the virtue of such reconstructions is a more holistic presentation of disparate data, it is difficult to tell from the imagery alone where historical evidence ends and speculation begins; the problem is similar to that faced by paleontologists who reconstruct dinosaur skeletons from incomplete collections of bone fragments. It would seem that computer simulations are not so different, after all, from the constructed interpretations found in documentary film and video, where editing constructs a world and a point of view; they are all representations of partial reconstructions of the past, and can be considered subjunctive to some degree. No simulation or film can ever provide enough information for a reconstruction of past events free of speculation. There are always gaps filled in by the person who constructs the re-creation, as well as by those who study it; and these may range from educated guesses to unacknowledged assumptions.

History, however, is not the only thing at stake; the belief that computer simulations can represent reality is often relied upon to the point that people's lives may depend on the accuracy of those simulations. For example, the flight simulators used in training pilots are deemed close enough to the real experience that pilots can obtain their licenses without ever having left the ground. During an actual flight, weather conditions may produce zero visibility, forcing pilots to fly entirely by their instruments and radar; when this happens, the cockpit completely mediates the experience of the pilots, much as a training simulator would. In such cases, ironically, actual conditions simulate the simulator.

Pilots and their passengers are not the only ones whose lives might depend on the accuracy of simulations. On the ground, surgeons can now perform lifesaving operations without having practiced on animals or cadavers. One medical simulator developed by High Techsplanations of Rockville, Maryland, allows users to open up a digital torso that contains three-dimensional organs such as kidneys, urethra, and prostate, all in vivid color. The organs can even be programmed to simulate various illnesses.[17] The attempt at realism even extends to the purely visual side of the simulation. According to a newsletter from Viewpoint Datalabs:

> For the opening of a new digestive center, Traveling Pictures produced an animation featuring Revo Man, showing the intricacies of the digestive system. Viewpoint's anatomy datasets were implemented to produce a result that was almost too real. "We reached our goal of making the sequence look realistic," says Dave Burton, animation director. "When we showed our clients the initial animation, it made some people ill because of the realism. We had to tone it down a little by using transparent and glassy materials."[18]

Even if the simulations look as real as Burton claims, will these abstractions prepare medical students psychologically for the real thing? Can virtual blood replace real blood, and the cutting of an incision in a human being with a sharp metal tool? No matter how accurately human organs can be simulated, there will always be an *experiential* gap between real and virtual.

Medical simulations are most useful for analysis and visualization when the data used to construct them are taken directly from life. As with an x ray, the data are taken from the patient's body and analyzed on-screen. One simulation, of the treatment of an ocular tumor, was shown at a SIGGraph convention, and some of the methods were described. The clip had the following voice-over:

> The physical form of the eye for this simulation comes from diagnostic ultrasound scans. The shapes of the eye and tumor are captured as digitized slices by using digitized pulse echo ultrasound. The digital slices are stretched into a rectangular format and used as the basis for reconstructing solid models. A typical section is shown indicating the tumor and retina. Sweeping through the volume gives the doctors a feel for the data integrity. The model eye is constructed from the image slices by hand tracing. As data slices are peeled away, outlines of the tumor and retina are shown being converted into polygonal objects. The shape of the other structures in the eye are obtained from standard database structures and B scan ultrasoundly.[19]

The simulation described above combines data gathered from a real source (the patient) with data from outside the patient ("from standard database structures"). The patient's body has become a series of interchangeable parts, for which standardized structures can be substituted — an instance of filling in the gaps with default assumptions.

The substitution of a generalized, "standard" computer model for a specific existing object is common throughout computer simulation. The general model acts as a stand-in for all specific physical versions of the model. Many industries use computer simulation in designing their products, and an increasing number are doing product testing with computer simulation as well. Originally, the purpose of product testing was to see how well a product stood up to forces in the physical world, so there is perhaps a certain irony in simulating such tests on the computer—today product testing could be done physically in order to test not the product itself, but rather how well the simulation simulates the product.

Computer-simulated product testing is used for everything from simple containers to complex large-scale products like automobiles, where people's lives may be at stake if the product fails. In 1991, "the world's first digital smashup involving two complete automobiles" occurred inside a computer in Germany.[20] Describing it, Gene Bylinsky writes:

> Such simulations are so accurate and economical that engineers at many automakers now conduct most of their crash tests using computers instead of real cars. In one that models a broadside collision of two Opels, the cars appear on the screen as ghostly X-ray images produced by a Cray supercomputer and software from Mecalog of Paris. The crash unfolds in slow motion. The engineers can freeze the action at any point and study the effect of the impact on the bodywork, the key internal parts, and the dummies inside. Such tests yield detailed results at a cost of about $5,000 per crash—vs. roughly $1 million using real cars.[21]

The cars, crashes, and human beings are all simulated by the computer, and now even the test-driving of cars under various conditions is being simulated on the computer.

> Since Renault can't test a new model under real conditions without the risk of leaking its designs to its competitors, it has created a digital test-bed for prototyping the aesthetics, road-holding, and drivability of new vehicles.
>
> The first step is to build a database of virtual driving routes. Then designers mock up a complete virtual car with digitized features: weight, size, shock absorption, steering-lock coefficient, and tire profiles. Using a simulator program, the design team then drives the prototype through the database to find out how it behaves.[22]

Rather than bring the virtual product into a real environment for testing, manufacturers simulate the environment along with the product.

Computer simulations and reconstructions are depended on not only in industry, but in experimental science and law as well, where they are routinely given a status that is almost that of real events. In the courtroom, computer simulations have been admitted as substantive evidence with independent probative value—that is, they may be used as evidence or proof. In 1985, computer simulations were pivotal in the case concerning the crash of Delta Flight 191. This fourteen-month trial was the longest in aviation history, and more than $150 million in claims were at stake.[23] Lawyers from both sides made extensive use of computer simulation to support their case, and they were able to establish a precise chronology of events and replay them from multiple perspectives. Most crucial were the films made from the digital onboard flight recorder that survived the crash. These "black boxes" record flight path and instruments, audio of pilots' voices, and airborne radar imagery; newer versions can log as many as seven hundred different variables, including the positions of five hundred switches. When these data are combined with a map of the terrain, simulations can be made from whatever point of view is desired.[24]

Simulations used to reconstruct events are sometimes used even to reconstruct the crime itself, resulting in a bizarre form of visible evidence. Since 1992, Alexander Jason, an expert witness in ballistic events, has been producing computer-generated reconstructions that are used as evidence during criminal proceedings. Ralph Rugoff describes Jason's productions:

> The Mitchell video, which reconstructs the movements of a homicide victim during a sequence of eight gunshots, looks like a primitive video game: the protagonist resembles a faceless robot with orange hair, while bullets appear as bright-red spikes identifying entry and exit wounds. Terse data flash on the screen following each gunshot, but the aura of scientific investigation is occasionally punctured by oddly realistic details—like the way a beer bottle bounces and rolls when it's dropped by the victim. The result is an unnerving viewing experience where a relatively innocent cultural form—the cartoon—is made to serve within a grisly documentary context.
>
> . . . In other videos, some figures are depicted with clothing, and in a few cases race is also indicated, yet this realism is tempered by the use of uncanny effects: a torso may abruptly dissolve to reveal the underlying skeletal structure, tracing a bullet's path through the body. In one stunning cinematic flourish, Jason creates a shot from the bullet's point of view, taking us from a policeman's gun, through the victim's chest, and into the wall beyond.[25]

Despite the strange iconic and geometrical appearances of the simulations, people's unquestioning faith in both the documentary quality of the presentations and the scientific and mathematical means of producing them make it necessary for judges to remind jurors of the unreal and speculatory nature of such simulations. In this sense, some of the abstractions of computer graphics are desirable, because they can act as a reminder of the simulation's construction. They can also be used to distance the jury from the events, in the same way that judges will often allow black-and-white photographs of a victim's injuries to be used but will not allow color photos because they are felt to unduly influence a jury.

Simulations like Jason's may look nothing like the actual crime, but they are believed to represent the events of the crime. Similarly, in experimental science, abstract representations are made to represent events—in many cases, events that never even happened. In chemistry, computer simulation is used to model such things as molecular bond energies and enzyme catalysis; the objects being modeled are molecules, atoms, and particles, whose individual properties can be satisfactorily defined with a small number of variables, and are visually represented in a variety of ways, one of the more familiar being a three-dimensional array of balls and sticks, similar to the wooden or plastic physical models used before the development of computer modeling. Here, the generalized models used in the simulations come closest to what they represent, because individual atoms have no specificity apart from position (like pixels and phonemes, they too are subject to "double articulation").

Experiments simulated on a computer come a long way from traditional means of documentation, such as the photograph or eyewitness reports, and one may ask what indexical connection to the real-world referent remains. It certainly isn't one of visual resemblance, because molecules don't really look like wiggling balls and sticks, as they are so often depicted. Nor are the simulated reactions reconstructions of specific reactions that actually took place; they are only possible scenarios based on chemical properties and the laws of physics. Molecular simulations are based on such things as bond angles, binding energies, and other elementary data, and are used to test and develop theories in a manner similar to physical experiments. In effect, the re-creation of dynamics and behavior is their only link to the outside world and the only thing being documented; the referents are not objects, but laws of physics and descriptions.

In this indexical shift, as mentioned above, actual experiments and observations have been reduced to measurements and relationships, which are in turn abstracted into a set of laws. These laws then become the basis for the *potential events* seen in the simulation. Theories based on these laws, which fill in incomplete data and understanding of the laws of physics, stretch the indexical link even further. There is a shift from the *perceptual* to the *conceptual*; the image has become an illustration constructed from data, often representing an idea or speculation as much as or more than existing objects or actual events.

All simulations are subjunctive to some degree, subjective, and prone to ideological manipulation. Yet in science and in many public sectors, as well as in the public's imagination, the mathematical basis behind computer simulation has given it a status similar to (or greater than) photography, despite the often much more tenuous indexical linkage. One of the reasons is computer simulation's obscuring of point of view. Documentary theory has shown, in a wide array of writings, how the camera is not objective but subjective, because every image contains an inherent point of view. Simulations, however, do not come with an inherent visual point of view; they can be rendered and replayed from any angle, and reconstructed events can be seen from any point of view desired, including from the insides of objects. Although this omniscience lends an air of objectivity to the displays, it effaces the fact that *point of view* more importantly refers to the programs, theories, and assumptions controlling the simulations, in much the same way that a particular theoretical stance may steer an authorial voice in a photographic documentary.

The "point of view" is not visual or perceptual, but conceptual and theoretical, the speculation behind the simulation structuring how everything is seen. As Albert Einstein is said to have remarked, "So far as the laws of mathematics refer to reality, they are not certain. And so far as they are certain, they do not refer to reality."

No simulated "virtual world" can be free of a worldview, and the assumptions behind such a world are often difficult to discern, given only the visuals. Even barring digital legerdemain and computer simulations deliberately slanted in one direction or another, assumptions and speculations will be shaping the results they produce. Indeed, due to the complexity of the science, mathematics, and program code involved, it may be the case that no single person is aware of all the assumptions involved in a particular simulation. The simulation's subjectivity is a multiple one, layered with the assumptions of multiple people and disciplines: the designers, the programmers, the company that sells it, and the field expert who uses it. And, of course, the potential for deliberate manipulations will always remain. It is usually assumed that computer simulations are at least unfolding on a sound mathematical basis, but how can anyone but the programmers be sure?

Computer simulation's speculative nature blurs the line between fiction and nonfiction and complicates the question of how far an indexical link can be stretched and displaced and still be considered valid in society, as facts get skewed, left out, misinterpreted, or filled in by theory and speculation. As Jack Weber cautions:

> Precisely because it allows you to see the invisible, the capabilities of visualization, with its pizzazz and drama, can also blind you to what it reveals. To watch the dynamic ebb and flow of market forces or to reach out and touch an enzyme molecule is a seductive experience—so seductive that you can easily forget the approximations and interpolations that went into it.

> "One of the problems with data exploration and visualization," says Paul Velleman, president of Data Description (Ithaca, NY), a maker of visualization software, "is that these technologies make it easy to find patterns that may or may not be real." Color, shading, sound, and other dimensions that add realism to visualization are equally capable of making the unreal seem more plausible.[26]

Even the most honest and accurate computer simulations can succumb to software glitches, hardware flaws, and human or computer error, making them unreliable and sometimes potentially dangerous. As in the examples of car testing, medical simulations, court cases, and pilot training, people's lives can depend on computer simulations.[27] And, as Theodore Roszak points out, political leaders often make decisions based on computerized representations and simulations of situations, complete with predicted outcomes, so world affairs may actually depend on software intricacy and accuracy, and the way the software develops the user's worldview of the events the simulation supposedly represents.[28]

Computer simulations and systems are enormously long chains, and they are only as strong as their weakest links. The interconnectedness of computer systems means that errors can propagate to enormous size before they are corrected. Peter Neumann, the moderator of RISKS-forum on the Internet (which is a compendium of reports of disasters due to computer error), describes the collapse of the ARPANET in 1980:

> There was a combination of problems: You had a couple of design flaws, and you had a couple of dropped bits in the hardware. You wound up with a node contaminating all of its neighbors. After a few minutes, every node in the entire network ran out of memory, and it brought the entire network down to its knees. This is a marvelous example because it shows how one simple problem can propagate. That case was very similar to the AT 10:52 AMT collapse of 1990, which had exactly the same mechanism: A bug caused a control signal to propagate that eventually brought down every node in the network repeatedly.[29]

Software glitches can occur due to small errors in source code; in one case, a string of failures at a telephone company resulted from three faulty instructions in several million lines of code.[30] Complexity is one of the main reasons for software bugs; there may be thousands or even several million lines of code and thousands of decisions and alternate paths of execution, making it nearly impossible to test everything before the program is put into operation. And with multiple programmers working over long periods of time, human error is also a likelihood.[31] According to the authors of an article published in 1992 in *Scientific American*, the very nature of digital technology itself is partly responsible for the computer's vulnerability:

> The intrinsic behavior of digital systems also hinders the creation of completely reliable software. Many physical systems are fundamentally continuous in that they are described by "well-behaved" functions—that is, very small changes in stimuli produce very small differences in responses. In contrast, the smallest possible perturbation to the state of a digital computer (changing a bit from 0 to 1, for instance), may produce a radical response. A single incorrect character in the specification of a control program for an Atlas rocket, carrying the first U.S. interplanetary spacecraft, Mariner I, ultimately caused the vehicle to veer off course. Both rocket and spacecraft had to be destroyed shortly after launch.[32]

Not only is computer source code ultrasensitive to error, but the creation of software is, according to some, not yet even a science. Even after fifty years of refinement, the NATO Science Committee's goal of a field of "software engineering," defined as "the application of a systematic, disciplined, quantifiable approach to the development, operation and maintenance of software," has yet to emerge fully. "It's like musket making was before Eli Whitney," says Brad J. Cox, a professor at George Mason University.[33]

In the computer industry, the design of integrated circuits and microchips has grown so complex that much of it is done on—or by—computers. As in so many other industries, testing of the designs is also done on the computer.[34] Computers are being used to simulate computers; thus, if errors occur and go undetected during the design phase, software glitches in today's computers could become hardware flaws in tomorrow's computers. Of course, this doesn't mean the process would be more error-free without computers; the chips are simply too complex to be manufactured perfectly in any event. For example, Intel Corporation's Pentium microprocessor received sudden media attention when Thomas Nicely, a mathematics professor in Lynchburg, Virginia, discovered that the chip had a flaw in its floating point divider.[35] The story got a lot of press and inspired some jokes in the computer community (Q: What's another name for the "Intel Inside" sticker they put on Pentiums? A: Warning label), but Intel's promise to replace the chip seemed to quell any fears that might have arisen; the "new" replacement chip, by virtue of its being the "replacement," was seen as being better. But can anyone prove that it is really more error-free than the chip it replaces?

At any rate, computer imaging and simulation represent a shift from the *perceptual* to the *conceptual*, a shift that underscores a willingness to exchange direct experience for abstractions that open up the wide vistas not directly available to the senses. As subjunctive documentary, computer simulation reconstructs and preserves, but not without speculation; several layers of assumptions (concerning the computer hardware, the software, the expert witness, and the applied theories) will always be present. The data used in simulations are often much more selective and abstract than the images and sound of conventional film documentary, which take in background scenery and sound, recording the subject's milieu along with the subject. Thus a lack of context may occur in some simulations, limiting the means of cross-checking data and limiting the data to only what was thought to be important at the time—or, worse, what could be afforded. The epistemological problems of computer simulation can shed new light on the speculative nature of documentary film and video, when they are viewed as "simulations" of events. However, unlike film and video, computer simulations are relied upon in medicine, science, industry, law, and other institutions in which human lives may depend on decisions based on computer simulations.

Through its translation of the invisible into a visible analogue, computer simulation has allowed the conceptual world to enter the perceptual one, by concretizing the imaginary or speculatory through visualizations. It has created new ways in which an image can be linked to an actual object or event and ways to make that link as flexible and selective as the user wishes to program it. Mathematically reconstructed simulacra are used as representations, standing in for photographic images, and the faith in logic accorded to mathematics may well spill over into the simulations, making them seem more credible in the process. In any event, computer simulations are routinely given the same status as real events, and are relied upon as such. Thus it makes sense to consider computer simulation as a special form of documentary, albeit a subjunctive one. By limiting and elongating the indexical link and combining it with extrapolation or speculation, computer imaging and simulation may suggest that there is a difference between "documentary film" and "nonfiction film," especially when one is documenting the sub-junctive.

NOTES

1. Jonathan Crary, *Techniques of the Observer* (Cambridge: MIT Press, 1990), 129.

2. From the "Positivism" entry by George Boas in *Collier's Encyclopedia*, vol. 19, *Phyfe to Reni* (New York: P. F Collier, 1993), 292.

3. Don Ihde, *Instrumental Realism: The Interface between Philosophy of Science and Philosophy of Technology* (Bloomington: Indiana University Press, 1991), 87–88.

4. Ibid., 85.

5. Ibid., 107–8. The Ackerman quotes come from Robert Ackerman, *Data, Instruments, and Theory* (Princeton, N.J.: Princeton University Press, 1985), 31, 9

6. The video camera has likewise been given the status of reliable witness, in the courtroom as well as in psychotherapy sessions, where it has been shown to help mental patients whose responses and behavior are recorded and analyzed. As early as 1977, video's potential was recognized, as in Dr. Arthur Parkinson's "Videocassettes Used as Diagnostic Tools for the Mentally Ill," *Millimeter* (June 1977): 28. Not only were patients recorded, but a computer was then used to analyze their behavior: "It permits us to compare facial expression and physical attitude with specific responses."

7. According to Ihde, an early use of false coloring was for the study of transparent tissue, in order to make cells more visible. *Instrumental Realism*, 88.

8. David F. Malin, "A Universe of Color," *Scientific American*, August 1993, 73, 75.

9. The useful magnification power of the light-based microscope is limited by the wavelength of light in the visible spectrum, which cannot be used to image objects smaller than the light waves themselves, any more than a person could determine much about the shape of a small porcelain figurine while wearing boxing gloves. Because traditional photography also is light based, it suffers the same limitations.

10. Horst Breuker, Hans Dreverman, Christoph Grab, Alphonse A. Rademakers, and Howard Stone, "Tracking and Imaging Elementary Particles," *Scientific American*, August 1991, 58–63. The illustration on p. 61 is especially interesting, as it shows images from three different types of image technologies side by side.

11. Ibid., 63.

12. Brad Warren, "The Winged Wired," *Wired*, August 1994, 36; Kevin M. Baerson, "NOAA Aids in Global Search and Rescue," *Federal Computer Week* 6, no. 3 (February 3, 1992): 8(2). According to Baerson, some 2,262 individuals owe their lives to the Cospas/Sarsat, a satellite tracking system used for locating downed aircraft and sinking boats and ships.

13. Garrett Culhane, "Mission to Planet Earth," *Wired*, December 1993, 94.

14. Of course, there is no way to represent objects of more than three dimensions adequately in visual form; only the "shadow" of a hypercube can be represented in three dimensions. In order to represent more than three dimensions, one must apply some set of visual conventions, placing such images further into the symbolic realm than the iconic. For a discussion of some of these conventions, see Lloyd A. Treinish. "Inside Multidimensional Data," *Byte*, April 1993, 132–35.

15. B. J. Novitski, "Visiting Lost Cities: Using 3D CAD and Rendering Tools, Archaeologists and Architects Are Making Famous Buildings and Cities Accessible to a Wide Audience of "Travelers,'" *Computer Graphics World* 16, no. 1 (January 1993): 48. On the aural recreation of architectural spaces, see Mark Frauenfelder, "Listening to a Blueprint," *Wired*, February 1995, 47.

16. The fly-throughs of ancient cities are shown on a demo tape produced by the Taisei Corporation. For a description of the Taisei Corporation, see Paul Gillin, "Mixing High Tech and High Rises," *Computerworld* 24, no. 33 (August 13, 1990): S25(2).

17. Gene Bylinsky, "The Payoff from 3-D Computing," *Fortune*, autumn 1993, 40.

18. From "Take the Guesswork Out of Modeling," *Exchange*, spring 1994, 12. *Exchange* is a newsletter produced by Viewpoint Datalabs, and is available from the company.

19. From "Simulated Treatment of an Ocular Tumor," *SIGGraph Video Review* no. 9849 *Visualization in Scientific Computing*, (contact: Wayne Lytle, Cornell National Supercomputer Facility, B49, Caldwell Hall, Garden Avenue, Ithaca, NY 14853).

20. Bylinsky, "The Payoff from 3-D Computing," 34.

21. Ibid., 40.

22. Andrew Joscelyne, "A Totally Unreal Car," *Wired*, August 1994, 35.

23. Paul Marcotte, "Animated Evidence: Delta 191 Crash Recreated through Computer Simulations at Trial," *ABA Journal* (December 1989): 52–56. This article was the journal's cover story. Marcotte describes a number of other cases in which computer simulations of events became the deciding factors in the case outcomes and also tells of a company, Graphic Evidence of L.A., that specializes in producing computer-simulated evidence for the courtroom.

24. Daniel Clery, "Black Box Flight Recorder 'Film' of Crashes," *New Scientist*, October 7, 1992, 19.

25. Ralph Rugoff, "Crime Storyboard: Welcome to the Post-rational World," *L.A. Weekly*, December 2–8, 1994, 39. For other examples of the use of computer simulations in the courtroom, see David Sims, "Virtual Evidence on Trial," *IEEE Computer Graphics and Applications* (March 1993): 11–13. On Legal Video Services, a company producing products for video and computer use in the courtroom, see Jordan Gruber, "Persuasion on the Fly," *Wired*, April 1995, 48.

26. Jack Weber, "Visualization: Seeing is Believing; Grasp and Analyze the Meaning of Your Data by Displaying it Graphically," *Byte*, April 1993, 128.

27. For more examples of dangers to public safety caused by software glitches, see Bev Littlewood and Lorenzo Strigini, "The Risks of Software," *Scientific American*, November 1992, 62; W. Wayt Gibbs, "Software's Chronic Crisis," *Scientific American*, September 1994, 86.

28. Theodore Roszak, *The Cult of Information: A Neo-Luddite Treatise on High Tech, Artificial Intelligence, and the True Art of Thinking*, 2d ed. (Berkeley: University of California Press, 1994). Computer simulation-based decision making has being going on for some time; for a look at what it was like more than twenty-five years ago, see U.S. General Accounting Office, *Advantages and Limitations of Computer Simulation in Decisionmaking* (report to the Congress by the Comptroller General of the United States) (Washington, DC: U.S. Department of Defense, 1973).

29. Quoted in Simson L. Garfinkel's interview with Peter G. Neumann, "The Dean of Disaster," *Wired*, December 1993, 46.

30. See "Faulting the Numbers," *Science News*, August 24, 1991, 127.

31. Littlewood and Strigini, "The Risks of Software," 62.

32. Ibid., 63.

33. Quoted in Gibbs, "Software's Chronic Crisis," 86–87.

34. Jozef Kalisz, "General-Purpose Languages Simulate Simple Circuits," *EDN* 35 (September 17, 1990): 205–14.

35. Peter Baker, "Flawed Chip Brings Fame," *Milwaukee Journal*, December 17, 1994, 1.

29 Paradigms Lost and Found: The "Crisis of Representation" and Visual Anthropology

NANCY LUTKEHAUS AND JENNY COOL

The "paradigms lost" of our title refers to the "crisis of representation" that beset anthropology and other fields in the humanities during the 1980s. This postmodern, postcolonial, postfeminist erosion of paradigmatic authority posed significant challenges to anthropology—a discipline grounded in the Enlightenment project of rationality and objectivity and intimately bound up in the history of Western imperialism. Beginning with the critiques of Dell Hymes, Edward Said, Johannes Fabian, Clifford Geertz, James Clifford, and George Marcus and Michael Fischer, anthropologists have been called to task for their unself-conscious production of cultural representations.[1] Descriptions and analyses written from observations and field notes—the very heart of ethnography—have come into serious question, epistemologically as well as politically. Criticism has been made of anthropologists' naive assertions of objectivity in the construction of their ethnographic representations. Even more pointedly, Said and others have suggested that through their inability, or refusal, to appreciate sufficiently the discipline's imperial legacy, anthropologists continue to "act to shut and block out the clamor of voices on the outside asking for their claims about empire and domination to be considered."[2] The implications of this statement are several: that, on the one hand, anthropologists have systematically misrepresented social reality by presenting images of homogeneous cultural "wholes"; that hegemonic relations of authority and representation have silenced alternative visions and voices in favor of those toward which anthropologists, for whatever personal, professional, or political reasons, are most disposed; and that the very act of representing others not only bears with it moral responsibility, but, more sinisterly, is a form of domination.

Anthropologists, however, have not remained silent in the face of these attacks on the discipline. The most extreme response to the crisis of representation has been the stance that anthropology as a social practice in general and

From *Collecting Visible Evidence*. Ed. Jane M. Gaines and Michael Renov. Minneapolis: U of Minnesota P, 1999. 116–139.

ethnographic film as a particular extension of it are colonialist enterprises that have no place in a postcolonial world. Those who take this view would put an end to anthropology's cross-cultural tradition, arguing that the most valid cultural representations are those made by indigenous ethnographers (or image makers) working *in* and *on* their own cultures.[3] Although we are sympathetic to the reasons underlying this view, we argue that it represents an unnecessary abandonment of anthropology's cross-cultural aims.[4] Far from heralding the end of anthropology, in this essay we show that the crisis of representation has given rise to both written and filmic ethnographies that incorporate critiques of Enlightenment thinking while still maintaining the moral, social, and epistemological validity of cultural representations made by "outsiders."

We begin with the premise that written and visual representations of culture have long shared a dialectical relationship of interaction and impact, each affecting the other, but seldom overtly referencing this interrelationship. Moreover, we assert that this cross-fertilization has played, and can continue to play, an important role in the revitalization and transformation of the creation of cross-cultural representations. In presenting a brief overview of the "new ethnography" (the experiments in anthropological writing catalyzed by the critique of the so-called realist representations characteristic of traditional ethnography), we also describe examples of their counterparts in ethnographic film — what might be called, in homage to ethnographic filmmaker Jean Rouch and his influence on French fictional film, "a new wave" of ethnographic film. The new ethnographies we refer to have not only influenced recent ethnographic films, but they in turn bear evidence of the impact of cinema in general, and ethnographic film to a lesser extent, on the writing of ethnography.[5]

The majority of the films and videos we discuss in this chapter are the products of filmmakers and anthropologists associated with the Center for Visual Anthropology (CVA) at the University of Southern California. This is no mere coincidence, as both of us are or have been associated with the center.[6] Nor is it simply a matter of self-promotion; rather, we feel that it is important to be able to write about the relationship between ethnography and ethnographic film from the perspective not only of film critics, but as practitioners of both anthropology and filmmaking. Both of us are trained as professional ethnographers, and we have both made ethnographic films. Lutkehaus, in her capacity as professor of visual anthropology at the CVA, has been involved in aspects of the production (i.e., research, filming, editing) of most of the films described in this essay. However, by limiting the films discussed here to those produced at the Center for Visual Anthropology, we do not mean to imply that these are the only ethnographic films and videos produced recently that reflect the changes in ethnographic film that we describe. More specifically, our decision to limit the range of films discussed reflects our desire to document a historical movement in the development of ethnographic film and visual anthropology that began at the University of Southern California during the late 1970s as the result of the intellectual and aesthetic influence of anthropologist Barbara Myerhoff and ethnographic filmmaker Timothy Asch, two of the founding forces behind the creation of the Center for Visual Anthropology.[7] Through the examples of their own films, several of which we mention below, as well as their interest in developing an institutional space for the production and analysis of visual anthropology, Myerhoff and Asch helped to create the Center for Visual Anthropology as a site of experimentation and the rethinking of the genre of ethnographic film.

After a brief discussion of the dialectical relationship between written ethnography and ethnographic film, we describe two recent trends in ethnographic film that we interpret as a response to the crisis of representation in anthropology: first, the trend toward indigenous and autobiographical films, and second, the trend toward global/transnational films. Although at first glance these two trends appear almost to be diametrically opposed, we suggest that they are united by the common denominator that each involves a new relationship to the subject of ethnographic film. Finally, we present a detailed discussion of Jenny Cool's video *Home Economics* (1993) as one example of an ethnographic film that preserves the cross-cultural tradition, yet also successfully negotiates the epistemological and political minefield of contemporary anthropology.

THE DIALECTICAL RELATIONSHIP BETWEEN ETHNOGRAPHY AND ETHNOGRAPHIC FILM

New ethnographies are characterized by a rejection of the anthropological paradigm that posited the omnipotent authority of the ethnographic observer vis-à-vis his or her distanced object of observation. Although these ethnographies take a number of different forms, they share in a self-conscious effort to portray the socially constructed nature of ethnographic knowledge. They also attempt to portray new subjects of ethnographic investigation, such as contemporary Western society itself. And they share the assumption that ethnography can serve to enable intelligent dialogue across ethnic, class, and cultural lines, among individuals different from one another, but who nonetheless can benefit from attempts to convey their differences.

Some of the earliest examples of experimental ethnography focused precisely on the dialogical nature of ethnographic inquiry. Books such as Vincent Crapanzano's *Tuhami* and Kevin Dwyer's *Moroccan Dialogues* attempted to reproduce the dialogical relationship between ethnographer and informant(s) as part of their literary exposition.[8] These representations aimed not only to present the socially constructed nature of ethnographic knowledge, but also to present consciously the ethnographer and his or her "subjects" as specific individuals encountering one another within specific social contexts. Thus, in contrast to the disguised and distant voice of the narrator/anthropologist in traditional realist ethnographies, dialogical ethnographies sought to represent distinct voices engaged in conversation. (One might include yet a third work based on research in Morocco, Paul Rabinow's *Reflections on Fieldwork in Morocco*, as transitional, bridging the gap between the genre of fictionalized or

disguised fieldwork narratives exemplified by Laura Bohannan's pseudony-
mous classic *Return to Laughter* and the "new ethnographies" that integrate
the anthropologist as actor within the ethnography itself.)[9]

This practice of representing the ethnographer as a particular individual — rather than an omnipotent, authorial voice whose identity is disguised — has been referred to as "reflexivity."[10] Other reflexive texts include
Jean-Paul Dumont's *The Headman and I*, Paul Friedrich's *The Princes of Naranja*,
Tanya Luhrmann's *Persuasions of the Witch's Craft*, and Kamala Visweswaran's
Fictions of Feminist Ethnography.[11] Visweswaran's book also represents another trend within anthropology — the overt development of new agents of investigation, such as anthropologists of mixed cultural heritage using their own
cultural bifurcation as a means of empathy in their exploration of other cultural worlds.[12]

Through their very praxis, prompted in part by the development in the
late 1960s of portable synchronous sound, ethnographic filmmakers experimented even earlier than ethnographic authors with this issue of voice. Thus,
for example, in their African trilogy *Turkana Conversations*, shot in Kenya in
1973–74, David and Judith MacDougall allowed the recorded conversation to
give dramatic shape and tension to their ethnographic films. In contrast to
these films that sometimes have the quality of eavesdropping on other people's conversations, Jean Rouch, the French ethnographic filmmaker, working
almost twenty years before, collaborated with his West African informants in
producing innovative films such as *Les Maîtres Fous* (1955), *Moi, Un Noir*
(1957), and *Jaguar* (1967). In these films Rouch lets his subjects speak for themselves, while his own voice is not an omniscient, anonymous narrator, but
that of a distinct individual, the ethnographer/filmmaker. Even more experimental was Rouch's decision, as in *Jaguar*, to film semifictional sequences created by his collaborators. These films were also innovative in that they dealt
with then nontraditional ethnographic subjects such as migration, urbaniza-
tion, and indigenous responses to colonialism in West Africa. Both Rouch,
with his cinema verité, and the MacDougalls practiced a form of "participatory cinema" in which the camera was acknowledged, indeed encouraged, to
provoke action and responses in a manner we can now identify as a precursor to the notion of reflexivity in written ethnography; in both instances the
presence of the ethnographer and/or camera is acknowledged as a significant
participant in the event or interaction represented.[13]

Also focusing on the issue of voice, in the late 1960s Tim Asch began to
shift his thinking about narration in his films. Like the MacDougalls, he
thought that the filmmaker could present a "truer" representation of filmic
subjects if they were allowed to speak for themselves on-screen without the
presence of a narrator or voice-over. This shift also allowed for a shift in the
content of his films, from a focus on observable behavior to a foregrounding
of voice as a means of conveying cultural interpretation and indigenous
meaning.[14] Asch and Myerhoff also produced early examples of ethnographic films that employed reflexivity to portray the process and personal
dynamics through which ethnographic knowledge is obtained. These include

Asch and Chagnon's *The Ax Fight* (1975), Barbara Myerhoff and Lynne Littman's Academy-Award-winning documentary *Number Our Days* (1977) as well as their *In Her Own Time* (1985), and *Jero on Jero: "A Balinese Trance Séance" Observed* (1984) by Patsy and Timothy Asch, produced in conjunction with anthropologist Linda Connor.

The Ax Fight is a precursor to these other films. Unlike their explicit portrayal of the anthropologist in dialogue with ethnographic subjects, in *The Ax Fight* we are made privy only to Asch's voice, as cameraman, in conversation with the anthropologist Napoleon Chagnon. We do, however, hear Chagnon's speculation about the behavior we have witnessed on-screen. His explanation, which later proves to have been incorrect, provides the overall framework for the film: the discovery of how anthropological explanation is constructed through the process of fieldwork and analysis.

In subsequent films such as *Number Our Days*, the anthropologist plays an on-camera role. We see Barbara Myerhoff interacting with the subjects of her film—the elderly men and women who congregate at a Jewish community center in Venice, California—and hear her reflect upon her initial interest in these individuals. The product of ongoing ethnographic research, *Number Our Days* was not shot strictly as cinema verité, but was filmed after Myerhoff had been working for some time with the people at the Aliyah Community Center and thus knew which individuals she wanted to focus on in the film. Nevertheless, through Myerhoff's interaction with people such as Shmuel, a former tailor, and Rebekah, who had once been a seamstress and still loved to dress up in fanciful hats, we hear the dialogue the anthropologist engaged in with her informants and see their sometimes emotional responses to her questions.

In the film *In Her Own Time*, the concept of reflexivity and the nature of ethnographic inquiry is carried a dramatic step further. Here, in Myerhoff's last film, the anthropologist's increasingly deteriorating health—her ultimately unsuccessful fight against cancer—becomes the focus of her investigation into the beliefs and practices of a community of Hasidic Jews who live in the Fairfax district of Los Angeles. Through their efforts to help her in her struggle with her illness, we gain insight into the world of the Hasidim and their religious practices, as well as the meaning of spirituality in their lives and their belief in its power to help others. Part of the dramatic tension in this film lies in the ambiguity between Myerhoff's roles as distanced ethnographic observer and earnestly engaged participant. The anthropologist becomes as much the subject of this film as the Hasidim she is studying.[15]

In contrast, *Jero on Jero: "A Balinese Trance Séance" Observed* offers the viewer an opportunity to observe the anthropological subject—a Balinese woman named Jero who is a skilled masseuse and healer—view and comment on her own previously filmed performance documented in *A Balinese Trance Séance*. In *Jero on Jero* we see Jero watching herself on film and observe her responses to seeing herself possessed as she conducts a séance in which she converses with the dead relatives of her clients. We also hear the dialogue she carries on with the anthropologist, Linda Connor, who poses questions to her as Jero watches the film on a small monitor.[16] The presentation of these multiple levels of reflexivity — of Jero witnessing her own performance, of the anthropologist questioning her informant — allows skeptical Western viewers the opportunity to evaluate this post-performance discussion of Jero's previous behavior.

Besides dialogism and reflexivity, the new ethnography has been characterized by a conscious focus on the narrative structure of ethnography as a genre. Sometimes referred to as "the literary turn" in anthropology and other social sciences, this focus on ethnographic representation qua literary production has led scholars such as Marcus and Cushman, Marcus and Fischer, Clifford, Fabian, Geertz, and Strathern to look at the ethnographies of earlier anthropologists — Malinowski, Benedict, Frazer, Lévi-Strauss — and to analyze their narrative and rhetorical strategies.[17]

Anthropologists' self-conscious reflection on narrative structure has parallels in recent ethnographic films. Works such as Sylvia Sensiper's *Films Are Dreams That Wander in the Light of Day* (1989) and Wilton Martinez's *Viewing Cultures* (1991) series challenge our naive assumptions about the objectivity of ethnographic representations through their visual investigation of the sources and impact of cross-cultural images. Sensiper's video, for example, explores Hollywood's portrayal of Tibet as Shangri-La in classic films such as *Lost Horizons* in order to demonstrate the impacts such stereotypical representations have had on ethnographic films. Bringing herself into the picture — literally and figuratively — she also discusses the effects of these romanticized images on her own interest in Tibetan culture and their contrast with the political and social reality of contemporary Tibet. Creating an even more complexly dialogic film, Sensiper includes the representation of her friendship with a Tibetan refugee whom she accompanies on his return to his homeland for the first time since his departure as a child in the late 1950s. Through his words, we also learn the "native's" point of view, hear his thoughts in anticipation of his return to his homeland, view his reunion with his family, and are privy to his post hoc ruminations about the visit. The juxtaposition of the two perspectives, Sensiper's and the refugee's, as well as the video's "before-and-after" narrative structure provide an additional layer of irony and hindsight to the simplistic images and hopes presented at the beginning of the video.

Striking even closer to home, Martinez's series *Viewing Cultures* probes the academic world of teaching anthropology with film and attempts to represent aspects of the processes of film production, circulation (the use of ethnographic film by professors), and reception (students' responses to a variety of ethnographic films).[18] One of the only studies to document the reception of ethnographic film, and the only one to present such evidence visually, *Viewing Cultures* presents a complex message about the social process of film spectatorship as well as an analysis of genres of ethnographic film. Both Sensiper's and Martinez's films force us to reflect upon the social factors that contribute to visual stereotypes of the idyllic and exotic Other in ethnographic and documentary film, as well as the effects of these stereotypes on viewers.

MONTAGE IN ETHNOGRAPHIC WRITING AND ETHNOGRAPHIC FILM

Returning to the topic of written ethnography, although anthropological theory may have been influenced by postmodern discourse, Marcus reminds us that as textual strategies, these self-conscious experimental moves away from realist representation in the writing of ethnography are merely modernist in the classic literary sense.[19] Referring to the historical development of the modernist style, and following the literary critic Keith Cohen, who has written about the historical relation of film to modern fiction,[20] Marcus argues that there is a strong cinematic basis to the contemporary experiments in ethnographic writing. Both Marcus and Cohen consider the cinematic technique of montage — the physical juxtaposition of images in the editing of film — to have had primary influence in creating the transformations identified with classic literary modernism and, by extension, according to Marcus, with the new ethnography.

Montage provides a technique that allows a break with existing rhetorical conventions and narrative modes that in turn allows for the problematizing of the construction of space, temporality, and perspective or voice in ethnography. For example, Marcus points out that not only does Taussig's ethnography *Colonialism, Shamanism, and the Wild Man* explicitly draw upon the concept of montage to analyze shamanic performances, but aspects of Taussig's verbal representation of these performances also assume the effects of montage. By calling attention through the use of verbal montage to the essentially oral conventions and techniques of other cultures, ethnographers such as Taussig are better able to give voice to the qualities of oral genres of communication in performance.[21]

Whereas mundane montage provides the building blocks of narrative structure in film, intellectual montage — as distinguished by Eisenstein and exemplified in his films — has been used less creatively by ethnographic filmmakers. Its primary function — for example, in films such as John Marshall's *N!ai: The Story of a !Kung Woman* (1979) — has been to provide flashbacks to earlier events, either prior to the ethnographic present of the film or within the film itself.[22] More recently, however, ethnographic filmmakers have begun to break with the time-space convention of realist film practice to experiment consciously with montage as a means of conveying specific ideas; for example, to represent visually concepts such as memory, identity, and class differences. In their short film *Pepino Mango Nance* (1995), Bann Roy and Gillian Goslinga effectively use intellectual montage to portray the unequal relationship between a young urban male Chicano composer living in a loft in downtown Los Angeles and the illegal Latin American immigrant women fruit vendors whose street chants have provided inspiration for his avant-garde music. The juxtaposition of images eliminates the need for any narration to spell out the contrast in lifestyles, the gap of class differences that separate them, and allows the viewer to muse upon the irony of their uneasy — and unequal — relationship.

In another, lengthier example, in the film *Bui Doi* (Life of Dust) (1993), about a group of teenage Vietnamese gang members in Orange County, California, filmmakers Ahrin Mishan and Nicholas Rothenberg use montage as a means of exploring aspects of identity and memory. Undoubtedly influenced by Trinh T, Minh-ha's striking use of found footage in her documentary film *Surname Viet Given Name Nam* (1989), and unable to film in Vietnam themselves or gain access to any earlier footage of the youths' childhoods there, Mishan and Rothenberg used stock footage of the Vietnamese countryside and newsreel images of the war in combination with voice-over reminiscences by the gang members in order to provide dreamlike flashbacks to their former lives in Vietnam. These sequences are interspersed with actual footage of the gang members' everyday lives together. The mundane activities of eating, sleeping, and horsing around are eerily juxtaposed with images of the gang members casually fondling guns and striking macho poses with them. These images — as well as the youths' comments about the violent acts they perform to support their independent lifestyle — reverberate ironically with their statements that their life is "just like a movie." To what extent has the camera provoked their posturing? To what extent is it merely capturing on film an accurate projection of their own self-images? While far removed from the realist conventions of traditional ethnographic/documentary film — yet evocative of Rouch's earlier work — the stylized black-and-white format of *Bui Doi* evokes a sense of lost innocence, the poignancy and quiet desperation of alienation, and the thrill of crime and violence that infuses the communal life of the surrogate "family" the gang members have created for themselves.

NEW ETHNOGRAPHIC SUBJECTS

In addition to experimentation with narrative structure, new ethnography also has been characterized by a shift in subject matter. Rather than the so-called exotic or primitive Other, contemporary ethnographers have increasingly turned to the study of their own society, or aspects of it, thereby "bringing anthropology home." Thus Tanya Luhrmann's *Persuasions of the Witch's Craft* looks at the phenomenon of contemporary witchcraft among the middle class in England; Faye Ginsburg, Emily Martin, Rayna Rapp, and Marilyn Strathern have explored the gender and class dynamics of the pro-choice/anti-abortion movements, the female body, and new reproductive technologies in Euro-American societies; Sharon Traweek, Bruno Latour, and Paul Rabinow have studied the culture of theoretical physicists, research scientists, and biotechnology, respectively; and George Marcus has turned an ethnographic eye on the lives and fortunes of American dynastic families and the institutions they beget.[23]

In a similar manner, ethnographic film has also been shifting its traditional focus away from the foreign and exotic toward the familiar and near. Both of Myerhoff's films, *Number Our Days* and *In Her Own Time*, are early examples of an anthropologist's attempt to study her own culture. Although her previous work had fit the traditional cross-cultural model—she had studied the religious pilgrimages of the Huichol Indians in northern Mexico[24]—Myerhoff later turned her ethnographic gaze toward the elderly Jews of Venice Beach, California, partly out of a desire to know something more about the lives of these old people because, as she remarks in *Number Our Days*, she would someday be "a little old Jewish lady" herself.[25]

Although not all new ethnographic films that focus on American culture have turned so personally toward exploration of the ethnographer's own ethnic identity, ethnographic filmmakers have focused with increasing frequency on segments of their own society and on social classes other than those of the ethnic subcultures, deviants, or underprivileged that have characterized more traditional sociological and ethnographic films.

In *Gang Cops* (1989), for example, Toby Fleming and Daniel Marks follow a special unit of the Los Angeles Sheriff's Department as they patrol the turf of gang members in South-Central L.A. In traditional ethnographic fashion, for more than a year Fleming and Marks were participant observers, accompanying the officers on their patrols, hanging out with them during off-hours and in their barracks, attending their public appearances as spokesmen for law and order, to present a compelling and insightful portrait of the symbiotic relationships among cops, gang members, and neighborhood residents.

In yet another portrait of middle-class Americans—ironically titled *Natives* (1993)—Jessie Lerner and Scott Sterling focus their camera on the activities of participants in the Light Up the Border movement in San Diego, allowing audiences not only to see the protesters' picket lines, but also to hear the point of view of these staunchly conservative, predominantly white Americans who see it as their patriotic duty to keep illegal aliens from entering the United States from Mexico. Although there is no voice-over narration that comments on the opinions and activities of the individuals shown, the odd camera angles sometimes used to shoot the interviews, the expressionistic use of sound in repeated sequences showing close-ups of a border fence in the process of being locked, and the use of intellectual montage serve to create the film's distinct point of view.

More recently, Gillian Goslinga, curious about the human dimensions of the new reproductive technologies, used a video camera to record and analyze the social dynamics of the relationship between a gestational surrogate and the biological parents of the infant she was carrying in *The Baby the Stork Brought Home* (1997). We watch as the pregnancy unfolds, witness the birth of the baby girl, and see the bitter disappointment of the surrogate as she is left alone, feeling like "a breed cow," after the parents—no longer wanting to acknowledge the surrogate's role in the birth process—have achieved their goal: a healthy baby girl. Aside from the documentary value of the film, which allows us to get to know both sets of partners in the relationship—the surrogate and her husband and the biological parents—over a nine-month period, *The Baby the Stork Brought Home* is enriched by a companion thesis that analyzes surrogacy as a new form of social and kinship relationship, questions traditional feminist critiques of surrogacy and motherhood, and probes the class dynamics of the new reproductive technologies.[26]

SUBJECTS: TWO NEW TRENDS IN ETHNOGRAPHIC FILM

In addition to these examples of changes in the traditional subject matter of ethnographic films—epitomized in the past by either the portrayal of exotic and/or visually resplendent rituals or the exact opposite, the lengthy recording of prosaic, everyday activities—the homeward turn in ethnographic writing is paralleled in visual anthropology by two other seemingly unrelated, but paradoxically kindred, trends. The first is found in the production and analysis of indigenous media and "autobiographical" films, the second in explorations of the signifying practices and transnational nature of postmodern consumer society. We will first briefly characterize these trends, then identify the source of their kinship in their radically altered conception of the relationship between ethnographer and subject. Finally, we explore the impact of this changed relationship on the practice of ethnographic filmmaking with a detailed discussion of the video *Home Economics*.

The First Trend

The fact that indigenous filmmakers from the Amazon to the Arctic and Aboriginal Australia have begun to produce their own filmic representations of their cultures has not only created a new corpus of visual representations, it has generated new subject matter for anthropologists and documentarians to explore. Thus, on the one hand, an increasing number of films and videos are made by indigenous filmmakers, working either independently or in collaboration with outside anthropologists.[27] On the other hand, just as an increasing number of studies by anthropologists, and other media scholars, aim to document and analyze the cultural products and social organization of indigenous media production,[28] there is also a new genre of ethnographic film and video that documents indigenous film- and videomakers' use of filmic images as a political and cultural tool. Thus we have films such as *Kayapo: Out of the Forest* (1987), by the American anthropologist Terence Turner, made in conjunction with British TV, and *Taking Aim* (1992), by Brazilian ethnographic filmmaker Monica Frota, that document the use the Kayapo Indians have made of video images in their struggle against outside encroachment in the Amazon.[29]

   The inverse of this trend to put the camera into the hands of the proverbial non-Western Other—whose focus is often social in character, looking at group experience rather than that of the subjective individual—is the production of autobiographical films and videos that make the Self the focus of the camera. Michael Renov has recently explored this burgeoning genre of new ethnographic "life history" films. Both developments, as different forms of self-representation, alter the social distance between the observer and observed by conflating it. Work produced under the rubric of ethnographic film that fits this category includes So Yun Roe's *My Husband's Families* (1994) and Ju-hua Wu's *Worlds Incomplete: From Nation to Person* (1997). A step removed from a purely autobiographical voice, yet clearly still speaking from the filmmaker's own experiences, in the video My *Husband's Families* recently married Korean American visual anthropologist So Yun Roe uses her camera to allow the multiple members of her new husband's two families of origin — one the Swiss-German/Italian family in which he was raised through adoption, the other his Korean birth family — to speak about the meaning of kinship and family. In order to do so, the video moves from Europe to the United States and then to Korea. Ultimately, this exploration of cross-cultural adoption is not only a comment on the nature of the post-modern family, but also a means for the filmmaker to explore the complexity of her husband's personal background and her relationships to the individuals who make up her new, extensive set of in-laws.[30]

In *Worlds Incomplete: From Nation to Person*, Ju-hua Wu uses video footage of her Chinese father in Taiwan and China in combination with personal narrative in the form of a voice-over commentary that reflects upon her transnational identity, her feelings of filial betrayal evoked by her marriage to an American, and her father's return to China to visit his home village forty-six years later — only to find it submerged beneath a lake that was created by a dam. Her commentary questions the nature of identity and the roles that the cultural construction of the nation and national identity play in the determination of personal identity. Wu creates a personal narrative that transcends the simplistic formula of "one can only know oneself" as an ethnographic subject to probe personal memories and kinship relation in order to understand more fully the complexity of the relationship between personal and political identities.[31]

The Second Trend

Less well-known is the second trend in ethnographic film that has responded to Marcus and Fischer's clarion call for a postmodern ethnography, one that in the manner of such theorists as Jameson, Harvey, and Baudrillard explores contemporary societies through the crossing of national boundaries and covers the vast global culture of consumerism and transnational identities.[32] Recent examples of this type of film that break out of the insular time-space frame of traditional ethnographies and ethnographic films that remain bound to a single community, locale, or event include *Transnational Fiesta: 1992* (1993) by anthropologist Paul Gelles and Peruvian filmmaker/anthropologist Wilton Martinez, *A Chief in Two Worlds* (1993) by Micah van der Ryn, *For Here or To-Go?* (1997) by Bann Roy, and *In and Out of Africa* (1992) by anthropologist Christopher Steiner and ethnographic filmmakers Ilisa Barbash and Lucien Taylor.

Transnational Fiesta: 1992 follows a group of Peruvian immigrants currently living in Washington, DC, as they return to their former home, the Andean village of Cabanaconde, to sponsor an annual fiesta in honor of the village's patron saint. Afterward, we return with the Peruvian sponsors — and, in some cases, their American spouses — to their homes in Washington, DC. We see them at their daily jobs, learn of why they left Peru, and listen as they discuss their reasons for continuing to return to Peru and to sponsor the village ritual. In seeing the same individuals first in their home village in Peru and then in their suburban houses in Washington, DC, not only do we hear them talk about their multiple identities as Peruvian villagers and American immigrants, we are also privy to the social and cultural contexts, experiences, and relationships that produce these identities. In a second example of this genre, *A Chief in Two Worlds*, working-class Samoans in Los Angeles parlay their wages into chiefly titles that assure them access to land back in Samoa. In this case prestige — in the form of chiefly status — can be acquired only in Samoa, in exchange for goods and money more easily acquired by wage earners in Hawaii, the mainland United States, and New Zealand. Finally, in *For Here or To-Go?* filmmaker Roy, himself from India, focuses on the story of Amitabh, an Indian graduate student studying architecture in Los Angeles. The film cuts back and forth between interviews with Amitabh in L.A. and with his father, girlfriend, colleagues, and mentor in India. Through the juxtaposition of these various dialogues, we gain insight into the complex set of issues concerning home and identity that many foreign students face when they are given the opportunity to study abroad. As Amitabh says, "The FI [student visa] becomes the beginning of a new way of life for many," but not without conflicts over where one's loyalties and heart lie and how one creates a bicultural identity.

Whereas it is people who cross national boundaries in *Transnational Fiesta: 1992, A Chief in Two Worlds,* and *For Here or To-Go?* it is objects (and people) that travel between different worlds in *In and Out of Africa.* The video moves between Côte d'Ivoire and the United States, visually exploring the creation and transformation of value in cultural artifacts as so-called indigenous art moves from its source of production and distribution in Côte d'Ivoire to its circulation in the art markets of New York and Los Angeles.[33] Here objects are transformed by their location in different social contexts, their fluctuating value dependent upon the particular set of social relations in which they are embedded. The video documents the activities and attitudes of the traders who facilitate the transport of the objects from one cultural milieu to another, for they are the middlemen who, through their knowledge of the different social contexts, profit from the fluctuating values of the different spheres of exchange. All four of the videos discussed here as examples of the second trend focus on an inherently anthropological topic — exchange and the creation of value — with a decidedly postmodern twist: the visual representation of transnational forms of consumption and the circulation of goods and people.

Although the first trend discussed above, a turn toward self-representation, stands in contrast to the second, which looks at global social processes and phenomena, the two share certain views on the relationship between filmmaker and filmed, certain views about the *connectedness* of groups on either side of the screen.[34] Both recognize the political, situated nature of representation, and both posit a more intimate relationship between knower and known than is assumed in the Enlightenment scheme. Both genres recognize, and here we crib from Geertz, that "one of the major assumptions upon which anthropological . . . [work] rested until only yesterday, that its subjects and its audience were not only separable but morally disconnected, that the first were to be described but not addressed, the second informed but not implicated has fairly well dissolved."[35]

The indigenous, autobiographical, and reflexive works of the first trend tend to handle this dissolution by asserting an identity of subject and author, whereas those of the second handle it in a more typically anthropological way. They engage in research and representation across lines of cultural difference, not in an effort to produce totalizing depictions of "how the [fill in the blank] live," but in an attempt to *enable conversation* across those lines. Such attempts, moreover, rest on the conviction that because difference proliferates—even as the world's peoples are drawn ever more tightly into each other's affairs and into the vast transnational processes of postmodernity—working toward mutual understanding and the construction of some common ground is a valid anthropological endeavor. Here the connection between author and subject takes the form not of a given identity, but of an affinity that must be constructed during the fieldwork and filmmaking process.

Home Economics

Researched and produced between 1990 and 1994 at the Center for Visual Anthropology, Jenny Cool's video *Home Economics* draws on both the critical insights of "new ethnography" and the legacy of the "new wave" in ethnographic film that was passed to a generation of visual anthropologists trained at the center that Myerhoff and Asch helped to found in the late 1970s. Though its choice of subject and approach to representing that subject in film are clearly informed by the "crisis of representation," *Home Economics* looks at the ideal of home ownership in suburban Los Angeles County and makes a quintessentially anthropological argument—it seeks to show the logic and validity of a particular way of life, that of petit bourgeois, suburban home owners, and it turns this showing into a critique of contemporary American society. As Marcus and Fischer have argued, this two-step process of critiquing the Self via a detour through the Other has been a mainstay of anthropological writing from the outset.[36]

Subtitled *A Documentary of Suburbia, Home Economics*, like a number of recent ethnographic works discussed in this essay, deliberately eschews the exotic, spectacular otherness of classical anthropology in favor of the domestic and the everyday.[37] Anthropologist/filmmaker Cool and the video's three subjects are all white American women deeply concerned with the social costs of the American Dream of home ownership. Yet the film is neither autobiographical nor the work of an indigenous suburbanite—the identities shared by author and subject are divided and crosscut by class difference and

A homeward turn in anthropology, Home Economics *(1994) bursts the bubble of the suburban American Dream.*

by the division between expert and lay inherent in any attempt at anthropological representation. Like the films discussed above that explore the transnational circulation of goods and people, *Home Economics* recognizes the multiple, fluid, and overlapping identities of the postmodern subject. Cool's video negotiates the multifarious relationships of otherness and connectedness between anthropologist/filmmaker and informants/subjects in two important ways, which we discuss in detail below because they represent Cool's strategy for responding to postmodernist critiques of anthropology without abandoning that discipline's cross-cultural mission.

Subjects Addressed, Not Described

Home Economics contains no voice-over narration, but consists of "real-time takes" (i.e., single runs of the camera uninterrupted by cutaways) in which the video's three subjects give lengthy responses to Cool's short prompts and questions. Shot in the subjects' kitchens, living rooms, and backyards and recorded with a camera carefully set up on a tripod and left to run unattended for long periods of time, the interview portions of *Home Economics* take on the tone of "kitchen conversations" rather than interviews proper. These dialogue sections run from two and a half to five minutes in length and are connected by much shorter montage sequences of the surrounding landscape that alternately illustrate and comment upon each woman's words. Although

Cool's preoccupation with the meaning and value of home ownership conveys an implicit critique of consumerism in late-twentieth-century America (as the video's title ironically signals), her filmmaking technique serves to foreground her subjects' experiences as home owners, to reveal the meanings that home ownership holds for them, and to present their perceptions of the logic and contradictions of their lives and social relations.[38]

This avoidance of voice-over narration and the impulse to present subjects who speak for themselves in real time have a long history in documentary and ethnographic filmmaking that begins in 1960 with the development of portable synchronous sound.[39] As Erik Barnouw has written in his history of the nonfiction film:

> The documentarist's conquest of synchronized sound decisively influenced the makers of ethnographic films. . . . Such works as *Tidikawa and Friends* (1971), made among the Bedamini of New Guinea by Jef and Su Doring; *Last of the Cuiva* (1971), made by Brian Moser in eastern Colombia; *Kula* (1971), made by Yasuko Ichioka among the Trobriand islanders of the Western Pacific; and *To Live With Herds* (1973), made in northern Uganda by David MacDougall, gave audiences—whether the language was understood or not—a sense of immersion in the societies they portrayed. . . .
>
> Synchronized sound affected editing style. The silent film editing tradition, under which footage was fragmented and then reassembled, creating "film time," began to lose its feasibility and value. With speech, "real time" reasserted itself. . . . This resulted in long films depicting long

Subjects addressed: intimate portraits from suburbia. Home Economics *(1994).*

rituals, as in [Roger] Sandall's *Gunabibi* (1971), made in Australia; some-times in short episodic films such as *Dedeheiwa Weeds His Garden* (1971) and *Dedeheiwa Washes His Children* (1971), and numerous others of the same sort made by Napoleon Chagnon and Timothy Asch among the Yanomamo Indians of southern Venezuela.[40]

Cool's technique in *Home Economics* of presenting long, uninterrupted shots of speaking subjects owes as much to the films the MacDougalls and the Asches made during the 1970s and 1980s as it does to the dialogical mode of textual production characteristic of "new ethnography." *Home Economics's* rhetorical power as ethnography and as social documentary draws heavily on the persuasive power of its subjects, its characters, and on the immersive sense of "being there" that the video constructs. Yet it moves beyond obser-vational cinema to situate the anthropologist/filmmaker within the video and to acknowledge the authored nature of the representations it presents.

Authorship Acknowledged

Influenced by the cinema verité of Rouch, by the MacDougalls' "participato-ry cinema," and by the reflexivity practiced by Myerhoff, Asch, and their stu-dents at the CVA, *Home Economics* openly acknowledges its own constructed nature. Cool appears on camera several times, and when she is not in the shot, either her voice is heard asking questions from just outside the frame or her presence there is indicated by her subjects' gestures. In *Home Economics* Cool acknowledges her authorship but does not present herself as a subject in the text, in the manner of more intensely reflexive films and writings. Instead, the video's quiet reflexivity and straightforward narrative structure serve to remind the audience that *Home Economics* is presenting an ethnographic argu-ment. As Cool explains:

> Making *Home Economics*, I tried to close the strange distance between expert and lay person, representor and represented, by talking to — rather than watching — my informants; and by taking their words — not as raw data — but as the interpretations and insights of reasoning social actors who might well have something to teach me about the world I sought to represent. In keeping with ethnographic tradition, I looked upon my informants' discourse as expressing a specific cultural logic and worked to demonstrate its rationality. . . . In *Home Economics* I do not claim to be telling my informants' stories, rather I give them room and time to emerge as expert witnesses whose thoughts and experiences cor-roborate, but also enlarge, my own story about the nature of the society in which we live together.[41]

In addition to reflexivity, *Home Economics* uses montage sequences to break free of the real-time dialogue and create an overarching "film time." Cool edits her subject's interviews so that they present a clear narrative arc. The ideals and expectations driving the American Dream of suburban home ownership, built up in the first half of *Home Economics*, are eroded in the

Kitchen conversations and relaxed reflexivity: the "key witness," center, talks to the anthropologist/filmmaker, at right. Home Economics *(1994).*

second half by stories of "latchkey kids," stressful commutes, racism, and social atomization that reveal the deep human costs of suburbanization. Cool's rhetorical aim in acknowledging her authorship and craft was to avoid creating a documentary that might be read in observational or realist terms as "a slice of life." By representing the anthropologist/filmmaker as a voice in dialogue with—but distinct from and *external to*—the film's subjects, *Home Economics* creates a place from which to advance its anthropological critique, namely, that home ownership in contemporary, suburban America is often achieved at the expense of the very values a home is said to represent.

Reviewed in *Variety* as "a pure use of the documentary format and a model of how to evoke the general from the particular," *Home Economics* consciously works to negotiate between the particularities of its subjects' testimony and the generalities of its author's argument, and thus to incorporate each informant's voice—as the voice of an active, rational social agent—into the anthropologist's interpretive narrative.[42] In this way, Cool responds to critiques of Enlightenment modes of representation while still maintaining the moral, social, and epistemological validity of cultural representations made by "outsiders."

Conclusion

Recently, visual anthropologist Jay Ruby sounded an alarm. "To survive," he asserts, "ethnographic film must find a new relationship to its subject, perhaps find a new subject, and abandon its slavish attachment to the realist conventions of the documentary and broadcast journalism."[43] We have argued here that in some arenas this is exactly what has been going on within ethnographic film: new subjects have been found (from middle-class white Americans in suburbia to art dealers in Manhattan and surrogate mothers at high-tech fertility clinics), and new relationships of mutuality and interconnection have been developed between filmmaker and subject.

While acknowledging that these new conceptions of the relationship between ethnographer and subject owe much to critiques of the traditional anthropological paradigm, we have also suggested that the sort of recognition about ordinary human actors that Cool and others have emphasized in their films has actually been central to the ethnographic paradigm since it emerged in anthropology.[44] From Evans-Pritchard's classic explanation of Zande witchcraft as natural philosophy to Lévi-Strauss's resplendent account of the science of the concrete, anthropologists have long sought to demonstrate the existence and validity of "other" cultural logics.[45] It is this sense of human agency, this apperception of a certain empirical quality among all humans, be they expert or lay, tribesmen or citizens, that the filmmakers of the second trend we have described work to evoke. What makes it empirical rather than ethical is that its apperception does not rest on assumed identity but on evidence and insight gathered in the fieldwork and filmmaking process.

We have also suggested that the relationship between ethnographic film and written ethnography has not simply been one-way, nor have the changes in ethnographic film simply been derivative, mere applications of insights from written to filmic representations. Although many of the recent ethnographic films we have described have indeed been influenced by the self-conscious critique of written representations of culture, creating new subject matter and new relationships between ethnographers and their subjects, ethnographic filmmakers foreshadowed and experimented with some of the same issues of representation—in particular those concerned with dialogism, reflexivity, and narrative structure—that later came under scrutiny by critics of the realist conventions of written ethnography.

Rather than abandoning anthropology—whether textual or visual—in the wake of the crisis of representation, we argue that critiques Enlightenment ways of knowing and representing can provide a new understanding of the relationship between ethnographers and their subjects. This new understanding should, in turn, serve to deepen and extend the most valuable aspects of the ethnographic enterprise: our knowledge of ourselves and of others.

NOTES

1. Dell Hymes, *Reinventing Anthropology* (New York: Vintage, 1974); Edward Said, *Orientalism* (New York: Pantheon, 1978); Edward Said, "Representing the Colonized: Anthropology's Interlocutors," *Critical Inquiry* 15 (1989): 205–25; Johannes Fabian, *Time and the Other: How Anthropology Makes Its Object* (New York: Columbia University Press, 1983); Clifford Geertz, *Works and Lives: The Anthropologist as Author* (Stanford, Calif.: Stanford University Press, 1988); James Clifford, *The Predicament of Culture: Twentieth-Century Ethnography, Literature, and Art* (Cambridge: Harvard University Press, 1988); James Clifford and George E. Marcus, eds., *Writing Culture: The*

Poetics and Politics of Ethnography (Berkeley: University of California Press, 1986); George E. Marcus and Michael M. J. Fischer, *Anthropology as Cultural Critique: An Experimental Moment in the Human Sciences* (Chicago: University of Chicago Press, 1986).

2. Said, *Orientalism*, 219.

3. For example, visual anthropologist Jay Ruby's comments from the first Visible Evidence conference in 1993 are representative of a less extreme version of this position. Although Ruby sees three possible roles the visual ethnographer can play now that "the natives speak for themselves," he is skeptical of the first two — ethnographers as facilitators and cultural brokers for indigenous media makers or collaborators with them — and thus finds the third alternative — the filmic exploration of the ethnographer's own culture — ultimately to be the most viable. Jay Ruby, "The Moral Burden of Authorship in Ethnographic Film," *Visual Anthropology Review* 11, no. 2 (1995): 77–82. For a provocative critique of indigenous media as a panacea for ethnographic film, see Rachel Moore, "Marketing Alterity," In *Visualizing Theory*, ed. Lucien Taylor (New York: Routledge, 1994), 126–39.

4. For a similar point of view specifically with regard to ethnographic film, see Terence Turner, "Representation, Collaboration and Mediation in Contemporary Ethnographic and Indigenous Media," *Visual Anthropology Review* 11, no. 2 (1995): 102–6.

5. See George E. Marcus, "The Modernist Sensibility in Recent Ethnographic Writing and the Cinematic Metaphor of Montage," in *Fields of Vision: Essays in Film Studies, Visual Anthropology, and Photography*, ed. Leslie Devereaux and Roger Hillman (Berkeley: University of California Press, 1995), 35–55.

6. Nancy Lutkehaus is currently codirector of the Center for Visual Anthropology as well as associate professor in the Department of Anthropology at the University of Southern California. Cool is a graduate of the center's master's degree program in visual anthropology.

7. Myerhoff died in 1984 and Asch in 1994.

8. Vincent Cropanzano, *Tuhami: Portrait of a Moroccan* (Chicago: University of Chicago Press, 1980); Kevin Dwyer, *Moroccan Dialogues* (Baltimore: Johns Hopkins University Press, 1982).

9. Paul Rabinow, *Reflections on Fieldwork in Morocco* (Chicago: University of Chicago Press, 1977); Elenore Smith Bowen [Laura Bohannan], *Return to Laughter* (New York; Harper & Row, 1954).

10. Jay Ruby, ed., *A Crack in the Mirror: Reflexive Perspectives in Anthropology* (Philadelphia: University of Pennsylvania Press, 1982).

11. Jean-Paul Dumont, *The Headman and I* (Austin: University of Texas Press, 1978); Paul Friedrich, *The Princes of Naranja: An Essay in Anthropological Historical Method* (Austin: University of Texas Press, 1986); Tanya Luhrmann, *Persuasions of the Witch's Craft: Ritual Magic in Contemporary England* (Cambridge: Harvard University Press, 1989); Kamala Visweswaran, *Fictions of Feminist Ethnography* (Minneapolis: University of Minnesota Press, 1994).

12. See also Lila Abu-Lughod, "Writing against Culture," in *Recapturing Anthropology*, ed. Richard Fox (Santa Fe, NM: School of American Research Press, 1991), 140; Lila Abu-Lughod, *Writing Women's Worlds: Bedouin Stories* (Berkeley: University of California Press, 1993); Ruth Behar, *Translated Woman: Crossing the Border with Esperanza's Story* (Boston: Beacon, 1993).

13. See David MacDougall, "Beyond Observational Cinema," and Jean Rouch, "The Camera and Man," both in *Principles of Visual Anthropology*, ed. Paul Hockings (Chicago: Aldine, 1975). Rouch's best-known work outside of anthropology is probably *Chronicle of a Summer* (1960), filmed in Paris during the period of the Algerian War. Not only did Rouch's work influence documentary filmmakers, his cinematic style — which came to be known as cinema verité — was of crucial influence on the Parisian "New Wave" feature filmmakers of the 1960s, who had in turn been influenced by aspects of modernist fiction.

14. Patsy Asch, personal communication, May 1995.

15. For further discussion of Myerhoff and her films, see Gelya Frank, "The Ethnographic Films of Barbara G. Myerhoff: Anthropology, Feminism, and the Politics of Jewish Identity," in *Women Writing Culture*, ed. Ruth Behar and Deborah A. Gordon (Berkeley: University of California Press, 1995), 207–32; Riv-Ellen Prell, "The Double Frame of Life History in the Work of Barbara Myerhoff," in *Interpreting Women's Lives: Feminist Theory and Personal Narratives*, ed. Personal Narratives Group (Bloomington: Indiana University Press, 1989), 241–58.

16. See Patsy Asch and Linda Connor, "An Exploration of Double-Voicing in Film," *Visual Anthropology Review* 10, no. 2 (1994): 14–28.

17. George E. Marcus and Dick Cushman, "Ethnographies as Texts," *Annual Review of Anthropology* 11 (1982): 25–69; Marcus and Fischer, *Anthropology as Cultural Critique*; Clifford, *The Predicament of Culture*; Fabian, *Time and the Other*; Geertz, *Works and Lives*; Marilyn Strathern, "Out of Context: The Persuasive Fictions of Anthropology," *Current Anthropology* 28, no. 3 (1987): 251–81.

18. See Nancy Lutkehaus and Wilton Martinez, "The Visual Translation of Culture" (unpublished report to the Spencer Foundation, 1990); Wilton Martinez, "Who Constructs Anthropological Knowledge: Toward a Theory of Ethnographic Film Spectatorship," in *Film as Ethnography*, ed. Peter Ian Crawford and David Turton (Manchester: Manchester University Press, 1992), 131–61.

19. Marcus, "The Modernist Sensibility," 40.

20. Keith Cohen, *Film and Fiction: The Dynamics of Exchange* (New Haven, Conn.: Yale University Press, 1979).

21. Marcus, "The Modernist Sensibility." 47; Michael Taussig, *Colonialism, Shamanism, and the Wild Man: A Study in Terror and Healing* (Chicago: University of Chicago Press, 1987).

22. Jean Rouch's use of montage is more complex. For example, in *Lea Maîtres Fous* he also uses montage didactically to illustrate a relationship between the ritual participants' practice of cracking an egg on the symbolic head of the colonial governor and the plume on the hat of the actual governor.

23. Luhrmann, *Persuasions of the Witch's Craft*; Faye Ginsburg, *Contested Lives: The Abortion Debate in an American Community* (Berkeley: University of California Press, 1989); Emily Martin, *The Woman in the Body* (Boston: Beacon, 1987); Rayna Rapp, "Constructing Amniocentesis: Maternal and Medical Discourses," in *Uncertain Terms: Negotiating Gender in American Culture*, ed. Faye Ginsburg and Anna Tsing (Boston: Beacon, 1990), 28–42; Marilyn Strathern, *Reproducing the Future: Essays on Anthropology, Kinship and the New Reproductive Technologies* (New York: Routledge, 1992); Sharon Traweek, *Beamtimes and Lifetimes* (Cambridge: Harvard University Press, 1989); Bruno LaTour, *The Pasteurization of France* (Cambridge: Harvard University Press, 1989); Paul Rabinow, *Making PCR: A Story of Biotechnology* (Chicago: University of Chicago Press, 1996); George E. Marcus, ed., *Elites: Ethnographic Issues* (Albuquerque: University of New Mexico Press, 1983); George E. Marcus, with Peter Dobkin Hall, *Lives in Trust: The Fortunes of Dynastic Families in Late Twentieth-Century America* (Boulder, CO: Westview, 1992).

24. Barbara Myerhoff, *Peyote Hunt: The Sacred Journey of the Huichol Indians* (Ithaca, NY: Cornell University Press, 1974).

25. See also Barbara Myerhoff and Jay Ruby, "A Crack in the Mirror: Reflexive Perspectives in Anthropology," in *Remembered Lives: The Work of Ritual, Storytelling, and Growing Older*, ed. Barbara Myerhoff (Ann Arbor: University of Michigan Press, 1992). (This paper appeared originally as the introduction to Ruby, *A Crack in the Mirror*.)

26. Like the other CVA-produced films mentioned thus far, Goslinga's film—while able to stand on its own as a visual text—is enhanced by the existence of a written text that describes the filmmaker's research, her involvement with her research subjects, and her anthropological interpretation of her research results. It is this dual product—a film/video and a written text to accompany it—that Tim Asch, in particular, has asserted is essential to ethnographic film. Timothy Asch, "Using Film in Teaching Anthropology: One Pedagogical Approach," in *Principles of Visual Anthropology*, ed. Paul Hockings (The Hague: Mouton, 1975), 385–420.

27. See Pat Aufderheide, "The Video in the Villages Project: Videomaking with and by Brazilian Indians," *Visual Anthropology Review* 11, no. 2 (1995): 83–93; Sarah Elder, "Collaborative Filmmaking: An Open Space for Making Meaning, a Moral Ground for Ethnographic Film," *Visual Anthropology Review* 11, no. 2 (1995): 94–101; Jacqueline Urla, "Breaking All the Rules: An Interview with Frances Peters," *Visual Anthropology Review* 9, no. 2 (1993): 98–106.

28. See Aufderheide, "The Video in the Villages Project"; Faye Ginsburg, "Indigenous Media: Faustian Contract or Global Village?" in *Rereading Cultural Anthropology*, ed. George E. Marcus (Durham, NC: Duke University Press, 1992), 356–76; Debra Spitulnik, "Anthropology and Mass Media," *Annual Review of Anthropology* 22 (1993): 293–815.

29. Some of Vincent Carelli's material on the Kayapo also falls into this category as well. See Aufderheide, "The Video in the Villages Project"; Vincent Carelli, "Video in the Villages: Utilization of Video-tapes as an Instrument of Ethnic Affirmation among Brazilian Indian Groups," *Commission on Visual Anthropology Newsletter*, May 1988, 10–15.

30. For a detailed discussion of adoption and the postmodern family, see SoYun Roe, "My Husband's Families: Kinship in an International Korean Adoptive Superextended Family" (master's thesis, University of Southern California, 1994).

31. For a theoretical discussion of the relationship between the anthropology of the self and the nation-state, see Ju-hua Wu, "Worlds Incomplete: From Nation to Person" (master's thesis, University of Southern California, 1997).

32. Fredric Jameson, "Postmodernism, or the Cultural Logic of Late Capitalism," *New Left Review* 146 (July-August 1984): 53–92; David Harvey, *The Condition of Post-modernity: An Enquiry into the Origins of Cultural Change* (Oxford: Basil Blackwell, 1989); Jean Baudrillard, *For a Critique of*

the Political Economy of the Sign, trans. Charles Levin (St. Louis, MO: Telos, 1981); Jean Baudrillard, *Jean Baudrillard: Selected Wirings,* ed. Mark Poster (Cambridge: Polity, 1988).

33. Christopher B. Steiner, *African Art in Transit* (Cambridge: Cambridge University Press, 1994).

34. Given that the filmmaker Roy is himself a graduate student from India, his film *For Here or To-Go?* contains a submerged autobiographical theme — Amitabh is to a great extent his alter ego. Thus Roy's film bridges the two trends we discuss here.

35. Geertz, *Works and Lives,* 132.

36. Marcus and Fischer, Anthropology as *Cultural Critique.*

37. Cool's focus on everyday life reflects the impact of cultural studies and the work of contemporary theorists such as Bourdieu, de Certeau, and Jameson rather than the continuation of anthropology's traditional description of the quotidian practices of a particular culture transferred to a postmodern venue. See Pierre Bourdieu, *The Logic of Practice,* trans. Richard Nice (Stanford, Calif.: Stanford University Press, 1980); Pierre Bourdieu, *Distinction: A Critique of the Judgement of Taste,* trans. Richard Nice (Cambridge: Harvard University Press, 1984); Michel de Certeau, *The Practice of Everyday Life* (Berkeley: University of California Press, 1984); Jameson, "Postmodernism." For an analysis of the different dimensions of "the everyday" as a prominent ideological construct of academic writing about the social, see George E. Marcus, *Everything. Everywhere: The Effacement of the Scene of the Everyday* (Brasília: University of Brasília, 1993). Marcus suggests that there are three distinct discursive functions of the construct: as a site of moral order, as a site of resistance, and as a site of the experientially real and mundane (4). It is this last function that attracts Cool's attention, for she attributes everyday life with providing her informants with the experiential basis for moral insights.

38. As she describes in detail in her master's thesis, "The Experts of Everyday Life: Cultural Reproduction and Cultural Critique in the Antelope Valley" (University of Southern California, 1993), Cool ascribes to her subjects the status of "experts of everyday life" and finds them paradoxically to be simultaneously critical and perpetuating of dominant middle-class American ideologies. Cool's ethnographic data show that the requirements of home ownership, which her informants have wholeheartedly embraced, conflict with the very ideals of family and community that home is said to represent.

39. For further discussion of the crucial role played by portable synchronous sound in observational cinema, direct cinema, and cinema verité, see Erik Barnouw, *Documentary: A History of the of the Non-fiction Film* (Oxford: Oxford University Press, 1974), 234–41.

40. Ibid., 251.

41. Jenny Cool, "Automatic Borders," unpublished research notes, 1994, n.p.

42. John P. McCarthy, "P.O.V. Home Economics," *Variety* (Los Angeles ed.), July 17–23, 1995, 28. *Home Economics* was broadcast nationally in the United States in July 1997, on the Public Broadcasting Service's independent documentary series *POV*.

43. Ruby, "The Moral Burden of Authorship," 77–78.

44. For a similar statement regarding ethnography, see Marcus and Fischer, *Anthropology as Cultural Critique,* 129.

45. E. E. Evans-Pritchard, *Witchcraft, Oracles and Magic among the Azande* (Oxford: Clarendon, 1976); Claude Lévi-Strauss, *The Savage Mind,* 2d ed. (Chicago: University of Chicago Press, 1966).

30 The Implications of Electronic Information for the Sociology of Knowledge

RICHARD A. LANHAM

The basic operating system for humanistic knowledge from the Renaissance until the present has been the codex book. Two forces converged at that time to establish it as the central system, one technological and one ideological. The technology of print created in the codex book a vehicle of miraculous versatility from which have descended alembicated variants like broadsides, magazines, even scholarly conference proceedings. Onto this technological marvel the humanist ideology grafted the concept of the authoritative text. Humanistic scholarship existed to rescue, edit, and annotate the great texts of antiquity and to publish them in definitive editions. Cultural authority flowed from these texts and thus their dissemination mattered; the great humanistic efforts to found grammar schools, write textbooks, and establish libraries, institutional and private, sought to insure such dissemination. This dual explosion of a technology of expression and an operating system of cultural authority gained additional force at every point, as we all know, by the translation of the Bible into the vernacular languages and its "publication," its democratization, in the new form. This heroic democratization, with all its triumphs and mortal perils, can be followed in the career of William Tyndale, the principal, if unacknowledged, translator of the King James Version.

We still operate under this system and take for granted its rules. Books are stored in libraries, taught in schools, carry on learned debate, enshrine the truth, as we have been given to know it. After books have been printed and bound, they are unchangeable. Thus the idea of a single author can be protected. Because books can be *physical property*, they can be *intellectual property*, protected by some version of copyright law. Thus the career of authorship becomes possible. And books create a natural authority: you can quarrel with them but only marginally or by writing another book. If you are dealing with the *ipsissima verba* of God, as in the Bible, you cannot quarrel with the Author at all. (The quarrel about interpretation will continue, presumably, until

From *Leonardo* 27:2 (1994). 155–163.

Doomsday.) Books have always been centered in the word; illustrations can be reproduced but they require a different radical of expression, one which has almost always been much more expensive than setting text; color has always been an expensive ornament, not an essence. Sounds cannot be reproduced at all.

"We are coming to the end of the culture of the book," O. B. Hardison has written. "Books are still produced and read in prodigious numbers, and they will continue to be as far into the future as one can image. However, they do not command the center of the cultural stage. Modern culture is taking shapes that are more various and more complicated than the book-centered culture it is succeeding" (*Disappearing Through the Skylight: Culture and Technology in the Twentieth Century* [Penguin Books, 1989], p. 264). What happens when this occurs, when humanistic knowledge moves from book to screen? The operating system changes fundamentally. Texts are not fixed in print but projected on a phosphor screen in volatile form. They can be amended, emended, rewritten, reformatted, set in another typeface, all with a few keystrokes. The whole system of cultural authority we inherited from Renaissance Humanism thus evaporates, literally, at a stroke. The "Great Book," the authoritative text, was built on the fixity of print technology. That fixity no longer operates. The reader defined by print—the engrossed admiration of the humanist scholar reading Cicero—now becomes quite another person. He can quarrel with the text, and not marginally, or next year in another book, but right now, integrally. The reader thus becomes an author. Author and authority are both transformed.

The possibility of such instantaneous disagreement changes the time-scale of humanistic debate. We can compare the old diastole and systole with the new by juxtaposing the stately pace of humanistic publication—years to write a book, a year at least to publish it, years to review it, more years for it to affect the debate—with online special interest groups, where the interchange happens daily. To change the time-scale of humanistic knowledge affects its essence, not only its pace. It changes, to take the simplest example, the paradigmatic expressive form from the essay (another Renaissance creation) to online conversation (a return, on a faster time scale, of the paradigmatic medieval form, the letter).

And, as we have now all discovered, the protective carapace of copyright law simply cannot apply. Copyright law was created to regulate a market in printed books. Because digital information has physical expression but no physical embodiment, it cannot be owned in the same way as a printed book. You can eat your cake, give it away, and still have it too. A new marketplace must be devised. The new digital bounty, by denying the laws of substance, changes fundamentally both the career and the cultural authority of authorship. For properties in the arts and letters, existing copyright law seeks to focus on a central question—substantial similarity. To make such a distinction, you need a substance. Electronic text, unlike books, has none. Copyright law must have a fixed text, with a fixed order. Such an order is an integral part of a literary text and essential for making the comparisons copyright litigation always involves. Yet a digital electronic text, because of its intrinsic volatility, can leave the order up to the reader.

As a brilliant recent book, *Writing Space* (Erlbaum Associates, 1991), by the classical scholar Jay Bolter, has made clear, the natural form of electronic expression is not linear but hypertextual. Hypertext leaves the organization up to the user. Beginnings, middles, and ends are what he or she makes them out to be. The final "reading" order represents a do-it-yourself collage, a set of user-selected variations, around a central theme. The idea of beginning-middle-end—the fundamental Aristotelian laws of artistic creation and indeed of rational thought itself—is called into question. Narrative and logical order, in such a world, are not fixed in the text, but a boundary-condition which the reader can apply when and how she wants to. This change in the fundamental nature of literary structure, and of the human "reason" a common reader is assumed to possess, subverts utterly the kinds of textual comparisons any copyright jury can be expected to understand.

Consider for a moment a mock trial in which I participated at the 1991 "Digital World" meeting. The case at bar: An academic "author" decides to develop a multimedia program on gangs in the inner city. As one segment of this program, he uses, without permission (it was requested but denied), the famous gang knife-fight scene from the film *West Side Story*. (In the *Romeo and Juliet* original, this is the duel between Tybalt and Romeo.) The scene is short, and forms part of a program segment on gang fights which is much longer. A "reader" of the program need not look at this scene at all, or need not look at all of it. It may not even be noticed. Each "reader" makes his way through the program in an idiosyncratic way—no central guidance. How much of the "substance" of the program does the borrowed segment represent? Is it prominent, because it comes from a famous movie, or *de minimis*, because it lurks in a corner easy to overlook? In a program basically scholarly in nature, can it be reckoned "fair use"? If the "substance" is not fixed in book form, nor the "reader's" trajectory of attention implied, the true nature of the taking simply cannot be measured.

Electronic information, then, affects the organization of humanistic knowledge and the social basis of its production in some fundamental ways.

- It changes the central humanistic artifact (the CPU, we might call it) from printed book to digital display.
- It changes what we mean by author.
- It undermines the basic idea of originality we inherited from the Romantic Movement.
- It changes what we mean by text.
- It radically compromises the cultural authority of the text.
- It metamorphoses the marketplace of humanistic inquiry in ways so radical we can scarcely yet find our way.
- It *desubstantializes* the arts and letters in much the same way that the information society has desubstantialized the industrial revolution.

The operating system we inherited from the Renaissance, then, undergoes digital metamorphosis: book, author, authoritative text, book market, library, all become something else. But this metamorphosis only begins the digital transformation. Consider the center of the humanistic enterprise, the arts and letters themselves. We can do this in three parts. First, we'll consider the current state of their new expressive medium — what people now call "multimedia." Second, we'll sample the state of play in music, the visual arts, and letters. Third, we'll ponder the implications for the arts of their new fundamental boundary condition: in a digital universe, words, images, and sounds share an isomorphic representative code.

(1) THE CURRENT STATE OF MULTIMEDIA

If the basic mode of cultural expression is moving from the book to some electronic form, what does this form look like? Do not confuse it with broadcast television. Broadcast TV is an analogue form, a fundamentally different affair. I have no doubt that Nicholas Negroponte is right in prophesying its imminent, and let's hope, eminent, demise. This new expressive form that is replacing the book is emerging from a cluster of technologies which people now call, for better or worse, "multimedia." In trying to explain it, I am severely constrained because I am trying to explain in print, to people who have internalized print into an unalterable condition of human life, a fundamentally different medium. There ought to be, in every such presentation, a demonstration. But circumstances do not permit it, so we must try to explain a dynamic medium in a static one, an imagistic medium in words only, a hypertextual one in linear text, a color one in black and white, a speaking one in the echoing voice of prose style.

How, thus constrained as we are by putting new wines into an old bottle, can I describe the current expressive vehicle for the arts and letters? It is a composite of techniques. Start with an electronic screen. This screen can do everything that a computer can do. It can display and manipulate type. Unlike print, it permits the reader to change the display from one typeface to another, for ornamental effect, for expressive effect, or simply to enlarge it for easier reading. (The ability to magnify print has to date been thought simply an aid for the near-blind, but it goes much further than that. How many books have vanished down the oubliette because of minute type? I first read the poetry of Edmund Spenser in type 1/32 of an inch high, and it took me half a dozen years to get back to the poetry.) Thus type becomes, instead of the famous crystal goblet of Victorian typesetting theory, an expressive parameter in itself, an iconic surface that interacts continually with the words which it bodies forth.

This new self-conscious expressive dimension isn't just a visual joke, like a ransom note assembled from a dozen different typefaces. It introduces a fundamentally different meaning for literacy itself. The late Eric Havelock, the great Hellenist, argued that the Greek alphabet enfranchised modern literacy because it was simple enough to be internalized in early childhood. The reader thus looked through the words on the page to the thoughts expressed. Thought was, thus, unintermediated or at least made to seem so. (Greek and ancient Latin manuscript notation, written without word spaces, was of course much less transparent than modern type, or even than a fine Renaissance italic hand, but the principle remains.) This transparent medium was for humanism what Newtonian physics was for science—a fundamental paradigm. Pure conceptual thought, unintermediated by expression, was possible and indeed ideal. The printed page was a transparent window onto the world of thought.

The computer screen constitutes a more opaque surface altogether. We have to decide how we are going to constitute our "reality." Much more self-consciousness enters into the occasion. This self-consciousness affects "the organization of humanistic knowledge" at the most intimate level. Both author and audience, citizen and society in the world of letters, become fundamentally more self-conscious about themselves, about writing, about how social decorum is constituted. We have to do here not with an ornamental elegance but a fundamental state-change in how the social imagination works.

A multimedia "page" can manipulate printed text not only in visual scale but in conceptual scale. We can construct a text, using an outlining program, in layers, and the reader can choose which level of generality within which to read. Typographical formatting of books tries this but within very severe limits. Its basic cognitive scale is fixed, and with it the reader's time scale; the reader follows the argument on the level of generality the author has chosen to employ. With the new medium, the *scale* at which conceptual thought is pursued now becomes a user-selectable parameter. Such a scaled reading is "hypertextual," but in a particularly ordered, top-down way. It would seem to be a natural for such written discourse as the law, for example, though to my knowledge no one has yet used it for this purpose. It offers some obvious pedagogical applications, but here, too, we seem to have missed the boat.

In the new expressive medium, text can also be in color. We see in magazine formats and advertisements how such a text might look, but we dismiss it for conceptual thought. I don't think we should. It seems far different in the context of, for example, a digital magazine published on a CD-ROM disk. We have proverbialized black-and-white expression as a guarantee of the truth ("I've got it down here in black-and-white!"), but the proverbs can't hide the technological base of this metaphysical verity. "Black and white," like print technology as a whole, works by sensory exclusion; there is nothing intrinsically truthful about such a technique.

Freedom of the press, the cynical proverb hath it, means owning a printing press. Now, through desktop publishing programs, such ownership has been radically democratized. This democratization indeed constitutes a revolution in "the social basis of production and dissemination" for humanistic knowledge. But desktop publishing brings other changes as well. In a print world, we think of print as fixed, "cold type" even when it has been produced by photography. You *set* it. In a desktop publishing world, you *flow* type. The fundamental metaphor shifts from static to dynamic. This "liquidity" of our basic alphabet will affect in profound ways how we think about reading, about literacy itself. What becomes, for example, of the stability of spelling, punctuation, and syntax? Will we return to the chaotic days of Elizabethan orthography?

But all these changes, enzymatic though they are, only hint at the fundamental change that screen brings to page: a radical alteration in the alphabet/icon ratio of ordinary discursive prose. In a desktop publishing program, you not only "flow" your text, you usually flow it around pictures. To find the critical machinery needed to analyze such an alphabetic/iconic convention, we have to go to previously marginal expressive conventions like shape poetry. (We might also, if our humanistic respectability didn't forbid it, consider the new genre of "serious" comic book.) Such a mixture of word and image is not utterly new, to be sure, but digital expression poses it with a resurgent force. The new humanistic "page" can reproduce images as easily as text, and it can manipulate them to an equal depth. And the white space is free. The playing field for word and image thus finds a miraculous enlargement. We can now process images as easily as we do words, and this ability has called forth horrified perturbations of dismay. Because we have thought photographs, like "black-and-white" words, to be unalterable talismans of truth, like long-time prisoners we shudder when our chains are removed. But all these fixities are technological conventions, not eternal truths.

Our allegiance to the truths of alphabetic expression, in the humanistic world especially, has become so strong that we denigrate iconic communication as "comic book culture." But the power of the visual cortex to organize experience, not to mention the power of visual art to render it joyful, surely indicates that this prejudice must dissipate. We are in for a complete renegotiation of the relationship between verbal and visual thinking. This renegotiation, like the others we have considered, goes deep. The two sides of the brain are being brought into a new—and, perhaps, we may find, more balanced—relationship. This rebalancing finds its scientific counterpart in the emergent discipline of "visualization," the use of computer graphics to think through, to conceptualize problems rather than simply to illustrate solutions arrived at through other means. I am not sure what an imagistic, or iconic, or iconographic "organization of humanistic knowledge" will look like, but it will certainly be different from our present one. Perhaps we should look to the patterns of thought built up by logographic languages like Chinese or Japanese for guidance. At all events, "visual thinking" will become much more than an oxymoron, or even a paradox. The growth stock, in such a new humanistic world, will have to be the visual arts and art history, will it not?

Classical rhetoric spoke often of the "colors of rhetoric," and we are now equipped to literalize this metaphor. But with even greater urgency it urged the power of the "speaking picture." We can now literalize that ideal too, for we can on the multimedia "page" add sound to word and image. Even entry-level computers can now add the spoken word to the written text. Soon it will be a common mix. Voice, written word, image. And music too. It is hard to wrap your mind around such a complex sensory mix, but I don't see why it should dismay us, although it does remind one a little of the Greek rhapsodic performance which so disconcerted Plato!

So. We have an expressive surface which can mix word, written and spoken, with image and music. A Wagnerian *gesamtkunstwerk* for the common reader. To this rich expressive surface, now add a dynamic digital video signal—that is, mix in movies as well as still photos. The "capture boards" which enable us to do this, although some impoverished English professors still cannot afford them, have been steadily declining in price. Thus the history of film and television dynamic imagery becomes available, part of our new system of humanistic "production and dissemination." The film and television world's treatment of its rich archive has always been a scandal, but a digital universe makes it worse than that—a financial blunder. The VCR democratized the history of film and television, stormed the archival Bastille, as it were. Now a further democratization offers itself: the digitization of filmic record into an archival form where it can be stored more safely and dispensed more widely and at less expense. More than all this, though, the digitization of our visual archive, both still and moving, democratizes it still further, for it offers the power to reconfigure, to reconstitute. We have always had this with words. Why not with pictures?

At this point, the great cookie monster of humanistic angst, broadcast TV, has entered our new expressive surface. Once we get it on screen, we can manipulate it as easily as we manipulate every other digital signal. We can invert beginnings, middles, and endings to make up new stories. We can use the basic art form of our time, collage, to our heart's content. Talk about zapping the commercials—we can zap the programs! Thus we disarm the monster that threatens to devour us. Surely even Neal Postman could not object to this.

The multimedia developers have chosen as their "God-term" the word interactivity, and rightly so. At the deepest level, humanistic expression, and the means which disseminate it, have moved from a static to a dynamic medium. Is this not, as well, a fundamental movement of Western art in our time? A building for us now is not a timeless monument but, like the Centre Pompidou, for example, a structure built to change and interact with its environment and its inhabitants. From the sculpture garden we move to Christo's *Running Fence*, and to Happenings. From the gallery Madonna we move to Jean Tinguely's interactive junk-machines. From the tranquil landscapes of Poussin and Lorrain, we move to the minimalist paintings and room environments of Robert Irwin, where not only surfaces and walls and colors but the very nature and palpability of light itself change as we watch, and gaze, and ponder, and enter into the surface. And from there, to continually changing, algorithmically composed computer "paintings."

The multimedia developers keep claiming that they have created a form so new that neither they nor anyone else knows what to make of it. But the aesthetic we need to interpret the new expressive surface that humanism now wields can be found just here, in the history of the visual arts from Futurism and Dada to the present. Scale-change, repetition, collage, chance-based creation, volatility, interchange of reader and writer, creator and perceiver, the radical democratization of signage, etc.—all these and more reveal the extraordinary fact that the visual arts have, once again, miraculously imagined an expressive explosion before it took place, before digital electronic means made it possible. People who develop the kinds of arguments I am sketching out are always reproached with being "futuristic," prophets of a sci-fi future that stable feet-on-the-ground people should beware of. Two answers present themselves to this ever-green reproach. First, the new multimedia humanistic expressive surface *already exists.* None of these expressive possibilities is rare or unknown or undeveloped, some of them are quite cheap, and all of them are getting cheaper. But the stronger argument for this new expressive surface, and distribution system, for the arts and letters is never brought forward—the very history of the twentieth-century arts. If the digital revolution has not really happened to the humanities, if the changes I have been charting have not occurred, then the history of twentieth-century art is a meaningless aberration. It may be so, but it takes some temerity to make such a claim.

(2) THE STATE OF PLAY IN MUSIC, THE VISUAL ARTS, AND LETTERS

The arts are "humanistic information" in its most characteristic form. How, in creation, performance, and teaching, have they been digitally transformed? We might find our footing in the performing arts by considering music. Over half of the music performed in America these days has a digital base. Recording and playback are entirely digitized, with the consequences for listener-directed reconfiguration that the CD has made familiar to us all. Musical publication has been vastly democratized by electronic means. The nature of musical instruments has been fundamentally changed. There seem to be only three basic ones: the electronic keyboard, horn, and drum pad. From these, all the effects that carefully tuned brass and magically varnished wood create can now issue. The sound is not yet the same but the transformation has occurred. Musical composition now proceeds as a collage, specific sounds or bits of performed music are "sampled" into a single piece of music. Often the sampling proceeds, as John Cage predicted it would, from the world of ordinary, non-musical sounds. It needs no extraordinary mother-wit to extrapolate from these slate-changes to the alterations required in music education.

In such a digital electronic world, "the social basis of production and dissemination" has indeed changed. "Musical talent" in such a world means something quite different from that in the world created by the Renaissance. The physical talents and training necessary for performance have been radically democratized in range and altered in kind. And the "performance" of a piece of music resembles far more the act of writing than the high-wire act of professional concertizing. The digital performer depends, as does the writer, on a rush of power created by time-scale. As a writer, I work for twenty hours to create what you read in one; the power comes from the compression of effort and design that writing allows. That compression now can occur in musical *performance*. And the performance, the act of dissemination, now occurs in private as well as in public; since the signal is digitized from the beginning, to replay it at home is as "authentic" as to replay it in a concert hall. All of this sampling, collaging, and replaying creates horrendous copyright confusion, of course.

In the visual arts, let me single out two exemplary transformations. I take the first one directly off the screen upon which I now project these words. Like many other people, I use a screen-darkener program called *After Dark*. It takes over when the muse deserts me. After the keystrokes have stopped for a specified time, to protect the screen from burn-in it creates, through various algorithms, wonderful moving visual patterns on my screen. Some are narrative and cute, one or two even cutesy — prowling cats, flying toasters, and the like. The most beautiful ones, however, draw abstract patterns of ever-changing catenary curves, boxes, ever-vanishing and reappearing perspectives, Mondrians, and so on. They rival the best conventional geometrical abstractions done with oils on canvas. I happened the other day to look at a reproduction of a real Mondrian: it wasn't the color differences that I noticed, but the *absence of motion*. Will this not happen to anyone who is used to a dynamic visual medium? What of how we look at still pictures? How we teach about them? Research them? Will not all of these change radically? (You can see the changes in research techniques peeping through in conventional art history here and there. Consider, for example, the resurvey of the Rembrandt *oeuvre* now underway. Does such a survey not, as a programmatic assumption, transfer the final reality of "Rembrandt" to a dynamic creative energy we choose to call by the artist's name, while the individual pictures become simply printouts, temporary static expressions of a dynamic center?)

After Dark has always included means for the user to vary the patterns, combine them according to taste, repaint them as it were. These opportunities have not gone unremarked, and customizing the *After Dark* patterns is now a cottage industry. In such a world of viewer customization, conventional still "paintings" will never be the same. The time dimension they lack will be keenly felt, just as the noises Tinguely's machines make in a gallery make us *feel* the disturbed ritual silence of a conventional gallery. And much of the artistic "originality" we have been brought up to admire in this breathless silence now comes from a new, algorithmic creator. If a painting is a kind of humanistic knowledge, as I hope we can agree it is, then we have a new way of organizing and disseminating it.

As a second heuristic example, let me discuss for a moment what I will call "virtual architecture." This genre has always existed — plans, sketches, and renderings of an architect's unbuilt work. In very rare cases, like that of Frank Lloyd Wright, designs unbuilt during the architect's lifetime are built later, as a cultural *homage*. Now the "social basis of production" has changed here too. Instead of huge rooms full of drafting-table drudges working out half-inch details with pen and ink, we have a computer-graphics program within which the building can be designed, and then reconfigured at will, to be printed out, with whatever scaling manipulation needed. And then, through the simulation technique called "virtual reality," we can "walk" through a simulation of the building's three-dimensional space. This is no blue-sky affair; in Japan, kitchen planners sell their designs to housewives this way. These techniques are being extended to larger civic spaces. Thus architectural design is radically democratized. Architects without clients can yet "build," and clients without architects can yet "design." All of us, not only those with acute powers of spatial reconstruction, can walk through these unbuilt architectural, and civic, spaces and see how we like them. Again, the critic can become a creator. These computer-assisted design techniques represent an extraordinary metamorphosis in the sociology of architectural design; they fulfill and genuinely empower the "behavioral design" movement, which has beaten so often in vain upon the cold glass edges of the International Style.

In the literary world, the patterns of postmodern fiction have anticipated electronic display, too. Postmodern narrative patterns are hypertextual rather than linear. The typographical manipulations in Kenneth Burke's *Flowerishes* on Derrida's *Glas* remind us of Marinetti and the Italian Futurists at the beginning of the century. But the real revolution in the production and dissemination of fiction has come in participatory forms, in video games, theme parks, and museum simulations. We discount these in the literary academy because, like the novel when it first began, they are an emergent popular art rather than *belles lettres*. When we talk about "democratizing" literary experience, we usually mean taking our regular seminars and teaching them to audiences which normally don't or can't attend them. This is a fine thing to do, but the real, the radical democratization of literary experience is taking place elsewhere, in the recreational areas I've just noted and, indeed, in the almost universal use of dramatic simulation for all the processes in the world of work.

And not only in the world of work. We might reflect parenthetically for a moment on the implications of computer simulation for writing history. New powers of data searching and sifting only begin the story. Historical events can be reenacted, with the "reader" acting either as participant "making" history or as interpreter "writing" history by choosing among various possible weightings of character and event. We can, dyslogistically, call this the "fictionalizing" of history, or view it eulogistically as an alternative to Ranke's positivistic history "as it really happened." Interactive videodiscs like the CBS program on the San Francisco earthquake, or more complex programs like the IBM *Columbus*, supply the raw materials from which a student can construct her own historical essays in video form. The use of illustrative live video clips now often accessed in medical texts through light pen barcodes surely will be used for historical illustration and citation. (A reader who wants an illustration of a particular heart operation uses the light pen to call up a real-time video of that operation on a video monitor.) But this is an interim technology. The mature one will interpolate live video clips into the historical text; we can do this now on a moderately sophisticated home computer. But looming larger than these specific technologies is the whole idea of historical simulation as a basic learning technique. Again, broad-scale democratization.

(3) AN ISOMORPHIC REPRESENTATIVE CODE FOR WORDS, IMAGES, AND SOUNDS

In a digital universe, word, sound, and image share a common notation. They are, at a fundamental level, *convertible into one another*. I have a program which traces drawings and makes them into music. You can make music from any imagistic source this way—it has been done with hospital charts, to pluck a pleasingly *outré* example from the current scene. And you can move the other way, to derive images from music. Plato dreamed of a common mathematical basis for the Forms. Digital notation creates it, or something very like. And Mandelbrot seems to have found another digital path to this goal, finding the key to visual form in the arts in the self-similar fractal patterns described by chaos theory. Thus the arts draw together, and together with mathematics, in a truly wondrous way. What does this convergence mean? We don't altogether know yet, but certainly the traditional areas of creativity now overlap, with consequences for the democratization of the arts, and for the academic organization within which they are taught. How can we keep apart the practice of arts with common methods of input and a common digital base? Here are grounds for a genuine revolution in the social basis of production. How can we keep apart the study of these arts? How long can we keep the teaching of these arts in separate departments? Here are grounds for a genuine revolution in the "social basis of dissemination."

It is time for another internal summary. We have seen that digital expression has changed in fundamental ways what art is, how it is *created*, and how it is *disseminated*. We have seen that the common digital base brings the arts into a fundamentally new relationship, one that transforms how they are studied and taught. We have seen that, if you wish to study how electronic information affects the sociology of humanistic inquiry, you must start by pondering the enormous changes that have occurred in the arts and letters. It makes no sense to talk about how digitization has transformed our scholarship and teaching about the arts and letters without confronting the massive changes that have come to the arts and letters themselves.

Having done that, at least in a preliminary way, let's switch our gaze from the organization, production, and dissemination of the arts and letters themselves to the academic humanism which studies and teaches them. What the "humanities" *are* nowadays is largely what the Renaissance humanists defined them to be: to study "humankind" is to study the great texts, literary, historical, and philosophical, and to a lesser degree the art and music which accompany them. We have grown so accustomed to this definition of "humanism" that we have failed to see how narrow it has become. The narrow focus is a product of rhetorical education. The rhetorical *paideia* which governed Western education until the explosion of the modern subjects a century and a half ago taught through a centripetal system. Every type of inquiry was included in the corpus of great texts, and the formal system of study and performance built on them. History was studied through formal speeches recreating famous historical occasions. Psychology was studied through acts of personification. Political science was studied through the dynamics of verbal persuasion. Thus to study these texts in this way was to study all that pertained to humankind. All the great subjects were drawn inward into the verbal center. Needless to say, we proceed nowadays on the opposite system, a centrifugal one in which new subjects are continually being thrown out into discrete orbits.

As a result of this rhetorical centripetality, the name "humanism" perhaps claims more than it should. It claims a theoretical centrality it no longer possesses. Either this centrality must be renounced or we must include in the humanities some fundamental areas of inquiry which we now omit. These omissions, as I see it, constitute the great suppressed agenda of the humanities, not the current race-gender-class obsessions. Let me discuss three segments of this suppressed agenda: behavioral biology, behavioral neuroscience, and the study of nonlinear systems—what is now called "chaos theory." I choose these because, instead of being drawn into "humanism" by conceptual affinity, as ought to have happened, they are now being *driven into collision with it* by the logic of digital technology. I must address this up-to-now unremarked technological pressure because it constitutes the most profound way in which to return once again to the agenda of this session—digital technology is affecting "the organization of humanistic knowledge."

Electronic technology has prompted so hostile a response from the humanities establishment because it creates a different literacy from our customary print-based one. As we have seen, electronic "text" mixes word, sound, and image in new ways. It thus draws on different areas of the brain, and lays down different neural pathways within it. In so doing, it affects "the organization of humanistic knowledge" at the most fundamental organic level. Jane Healy has argued, in a thoughtful recent book (*Endangered Minds: Why Children Don't Think and What We Can Do About It* [Simon & Schuster, 1990]), that we are educating a generation of children whose brains lack the neural networks needed for higher-level cognitive processing. Their brains have not received the social and verbal stimulation needed during the brain's critical periods of development. The villains rounded up for this—impoverishment, broadcast TV, high-decibel rock music, the decline of family nurturance, drugs—also include the new alphabet/image ratio I have been discussing. No one I know thinks the electronic universe will *go away*. If we are to understand the "literacy" it creates, we will have to school ourselves in the work now being done by behavioral neuroscience, which teaches us how the brain processes the various components of that new literacy. Humanist inquiry of all sorts depends on such an understanding. Nothing less than human reason itself stands at risk. Electronic technology is driving the humanities toward learning how our knowledge is organized at the neural level—the "sociology" of neuroanatomy.

Digital information drives the humanities toward behavioral biology as well as toward behavioral neuroscience. I must now make an argument essential if we are to understand how digital information affects the sociology of humanist inquiry — that is, the social matrix within which that inquiry proceeds. But to do so, I will have to use a very high compression ratio — about 100/1. Bear with me.

It is apparent, I think, to anyone who has worked in the computer world that the spirit of play and game works there more strongly than it does in the world of print. We have to do here with a fundamental change in motivational balance. The three basic areas of human motivation — game, play, and purpose — are mixed in different ways by different technologies. The history of that mixture — genetic, evolutionary, behavioral — is what behavioral biology studies. As more and more of our communications become digitally based, we will more and more need to master a new mix of human motive. The humanities come into vital play because they exist to balance and remix human motive, to infuse the world of purpose with the world of play and game. Behavioral biology gives humanistic inquiry its evolutionary history — a history we desperately need to understand the new motivational mix that humanistic expression will now embody. Thus, in the effort to devise a new sociology of knowledge for digital communication, electronic technology drives humanistic inquiry toward behavioral biology as well as behavioral neuroscience.

As if this weren't difficult enough, we must confront a third area of inquiry which the digital computer has made essential to humanistic inquiry: chaos theory. Whatever else it may be, the new mixture of word, image, and sound that digital communication brings with it will be radically non-linear, associative, discontinuous, interactive. As postmodern art has predicted, such communications procedures will depend heavily on scale-changes. As it happens, we now have a new way of thinking about such non-linear systems of organization, and especially about scale-changes. It is called "chaos theory." It may be, according to this way of thinking, that the arts are non-linear systems. Mandelbrot argues that the forms of visual art constitute one such system. Certainly, if you are trying to write the intellectual history of a computer network, you will have to use chaos theory to do it. When we think about the "organization" of anything in the world of digital communication, we will go greatly astray if we apply to it Newtonian patterns of thought. It is fatally easy to do this. We thus touch here a potential reorchestration of intellectual history itself.

We've pondered, in considering Jane Healy's work, whether electronic text actually forms the brain in different ways than does printed text. Might we not scale such a question up to network level? This reordering of how the brain is affected by verbal, imagistic, and auditory input during its formative stages must model in little, must it not, how we will communicate about the humanities at the digital-library network level? May it not be the case that the nature of scholarly communication, of how we write and read about the arts, as well as create and socialize them, will be similarly altered? That our scholarly communication will mix words, images, and sounds in the same way that digital "artistic" texts do? Gregory Ulmer has written a provocative book on this subject (*Teletheory: Grammatology in the Age of Video* [Routledge, 1989]). He argues that we must invent a new mode of scholarly conversation based on the new mix of word and moving image. Will not such a new mix inevitably become part of how digital library networks process information? Might scholarly communication become iconic in ways never seen before? It is fun to think about.

Learned societies, like academic departments and at about the same time, were formed as part of an academic specialization based on print communication. They started journals. Now we have special interest groups communicating online. Do these SIGs not constitute the "learned societies" of the digital future? Their communication is already radically hypertextual — discontinuous, associative, based on oral conversation rather than print. SIGs are fissiparous. They form and re-form continually, work on the formative edge of interdisciplinary inquiry. They model, too, the way multicultural perspectives invade and invigorate traditional professional specializations. Print publication encourages disciplinary differences by its very fixity and by the time-scale of its scholarly interchange. Computer-based "publication" works the other way, encourages the mixture of fields, of perspectives, of "publication" channels, which lies at the heart of both interdisciplinary and multicultural scholarship. Both the "national society" and the "national meeting" are more print-based than we customarily think. It seems unlikely that they will remain unchanged in a digital universe.

Let me turn now to humanistic teaching. What will change under the new operating system? Let's start with the idea of a "class." I'll use an example close to home, my Shakespeare class. I give it once a year. I always recommend additional reading which the students never do. Partly they are lazy, but partly they can't get to the library for they work at outside jobs for twenty to thirty hours a week and commute from pillar to post. Each year's class exists in a temporal, conceptual, and social vacuum. They do not know what previous classes have done before them. They don't know how other instructors teach their sections of the same class. They seldom know each other before they take the class. They never read each other's work though sometimes they appropriate it in felonious ways. I read all their work myself, and mark it up extensively, often to their dismay. A few of them take me up on my rewrite options but most don't, and hence don't learn anything much from my revisions, since they are not made to take them into account. They thus have an audience they know, but it is a desperately narrow one.

Imagine what would happen were I to add an electronic library to this class. Students access it by modem or through a CD-ROM or whatever. On it, they read papers good, bad, and indifferent submitted in earlier sections on the topics I suggest. They read scholarly articles good, bad, and indifferent on these same topics. They read before-and-after examples of prose style revision. A revision program is available for them to use — licensed by me to UCLA, since it depends on my own textbooks! They can do searches of the

Shakespearean texts, also available online, when they study patterns of imagery, rhetorical figuration, etc. They can make QuickTime™ movie excerpts from the videos of the plays and use them to illustrate their papers. (The papers will not be "papers," of course, but "texts" of a different sort.) They needn't go to the campus library to do any of this. They can access this library wherever and whenever they find time to do their academic work. All their work—papers, exams, stylistic analyses—is "published" in the electronic library. You got a "C" and feel robbed? Read some "A" papers to see what went wrong. Read some other papers, just to see what kind of work your competitors are producing. Lots of other neat things happen in such a universe. But you can fill in the blanks yourself.

Such a course—here is the vital point—now has a *history*. Students join a tradition. It is easy to imagine how quickly the internets *between* such courses would develop. We can see a pattern in the hypertextual literary curriculum developed by George Landow and his colleagues at Brown University. The isolation of the course, not only in time, but in discipline, is broken. The course *constitutes a society*, and it is a continuing one. The students become citizens of a commonwealth and act like citizens—they publish their work for their fellow scholars. The mesmeric fixation on the instructor as the only reader and grader is broken.

Now imagine another course—the independent study or "honors" course. A student in my Shakespeare course is interested in music and wonders what I mean when I keep using analogies between musical ornament and verbal ornament. When I talk about sonata form vs. theme-and-variations in a lecture on the *Sonnets*, she comes in and asks for a fuller explanation. Could she do a special study with me on this topic? Well, I'm not a musicologist. What do I do now? "Next time Prof. Winter teaches his Haydn, Mozart, and Beethoven course, you ought to take it." I'm certainly not competent to teach such a course. In a multimedia environment, I'd pursue a different route. "Sure, I'll do this course with you. We'll construct it around Winter's wonderful new multimedia programs on Beethoven's *Ninth Symphony*, Stravinsky's *Rite of Spring*, Mozart's *Dissonant String Quartet*, and Bach's *Brandenburg Concertos*. You can play them all on the equipment in the music school or the library. Using them, you can teach yourself the fundamentals of music harmony, find out all you need to know about classical sonata form, learn about what happened to music when sonata form no longer predominated, and so on. You can play these pieces theme and motif at a time, dissect them, learn how the orchestra is constructed, what the instruments are, etc." I am, with Winter's help, perfectly competent to teach such a course. Such a procedure not only generates new kinds of disciplinary relationships; if used widely it would save money for both student and school.

Now, the classroom itself. The "electronic classrooms" in use now, at least the ones which give each student a computer, have generated some reliable generalizations. Just as "author" and "authority" change meaning in electronic text, they change meaning in the classroom. The professor ceases to be the cynosure of every eye: some authority passes to the group constituted by the electronic network. You can of course use such a configuration for self-paced learning, but I would use it for verbal analysis. Multimedia environments allow you to anatomize what "reading" a literary text really means. This pedagogy would revolutionize how I teach Shakespeare. (Again, in suggesting how, I run up against the difficulties of discussing a broadband medium with the narrowband one of print.)

Now the textbook. Let me take another example from my backyard. Let us consider the dreariest textbook of all, the Freshman Composition Handbook. You all know them. Heavy, Shiny coated paper, Pyroxylin, peanut-butter-sandwich-proof cover. Imagine instead an online program available to everyone who teaches, and everyone who takes, the course. The apoplexy that comp handbooks always generate now finds more than marginal expression. Stupid examples are critiqued as such; better ones are found. Teachers contribute their experience on how the book works, or doesn't work, in action. The textbook, rather than fixed in an edition, is a continually changing, evolutionary document. It is fed by all the people who use it, and continually made and remade by them.

And what about the literary texts themselves? It is easy to imagine (copyright problems aside) the classic literary texts all put on a single CD-ROM, and a device to display them which the student carries with her. What we don't often remark is the manipulative power such a student now possesses. Textual searching power, obviously. But also power to reconfigure. Imagine for a moment students *brought up* on the multimedia electronic "texts" I have been discussing. They are accustomed to interacting with texts, playing game/s with them. Won't they want to do this with *Paradise Lost?* And what will happen if they do? Will poems written in a print-based world be compromised? Will poems which emerged from an oral world, as with so much Greek and Latin literature, be rejuvenated and re-presented in a more historically correct way? And what about the student's license to re-create as well as read? If Marcel Duchamp can mustache the *Mona Lisa*, why can't they? Once again, questions of cultural authority.

Now the "major." If electronic text threatens the present disciplinary boundaries in the arts and letters, it threatens the major in the same way. The "major" is constructed, at least when it retains any disciplinary integrity, on a hierarchical and historical basis. Such means of organization and dissemination, as we have seen, do not last long in a digital domain.

Now the curriculum, or at least two words about it. First, the debate about the university curriculum has centered, in the last century, on what to do about a "core" curriculum in a fragmented and disciplinary world. Various "core curricula" have been devised and, in some times and places, taken over the first two or even, at St. John's, all four undergraduate years. We have, in all these programs, hearkened back to a linear course of study. For all kinds of reasons, practical and theoretical, such a pre-planned program has rarely worked. What digital networks suggest is a new core constituted hypertextually, on a non-linear basis. None of the obstacles to the traditional core curriculum apply.

Second, the current streetfight about the undergraduate curriculum—Great Books or Politically Correct Books—ignores the probability that our "texts" won't be books at all. Both sides base their arguments on the fixity of print, and the assumptions that fixity induces in us. Thus they both, and the curricular debate they generate, depart from obsolete, indeed otiose, operating principles.

What about graduate training? Will digital information systems change how graduate students do their work? This is the wrong question. It presumes, as do many of the questions asked about the new operating system, that digital communications changes our tools but not our products. In framing the proper question, and an answer to it, I'll stick again to my own backyard. The crucial question for graduate training in literature is not whether students will become skillful in online searches and database manipulations, important though that is. We should be asking rather whether the subject they study will continue to exist. I taught a graduate seminar last year called "The Death of Literature." The class took its name from Alvin Kernan's recent book, wherein he argues that electronic communication, with some help from theory, is killing literature, at least print-based literature. The class considered three other new books that, in very different ways, debated the same proposition. I myself don't think literature will die, but clearly it will change as it moves from page to screen. Graduate programs in English ought to be considering that movement. I know of none that does. Even as we are conducting "literacy" campaigns based on a print-based literacy which is, as Hardison argues, disappearing up the skylight, so we are educating graduate students to read and teach literature in the same print-based way in which literature will no longer be written or read. We are indeed, to borrow Charles Horton Cooley's wonderful phrase for ossified instruction, educating "clerks of a forgotten mood."

I cannot help thinking that the same thing is happening in other fields of humanistic inquiry. It certainly seems to be so in music and the fine arts. Surely someone ought at least to be talking about this vital metamorphosis.

The matrix of cultural grasp represented by the arts and letters, is now dominated by three convergent forces: technology, theory, and democracy. Technology—digital communications technology—we have now considered "Theory"—by which I mean the postmodern critique, whether pursued in literary studies, art history, linguistics, or the law—lies outside our present discussion, though it informs it at every point. (I have, after all, argued that the aesthetics of electronic expression were laid out by twentieth-century visual art before the computer was invented.) What of democracy? Clearly higher education has been democratized in the United States since World War II. We need not debate that. Does electronic technology constitute an exclusionary force, as many people now argue? Certainly in some ways it does. Inner-city schools have fewer computers than Andover and Exeter. But in the long run, indeed in the short run too, I would argue, digital technology democratizes the arts and letters, rather than the reverse. Simply by opening discourse out from a strictly verbal base, it enfranchises not only the left-handed but the right-brained of all sorts. It will have, in my field, an extraordinary impact on what we still call "remedial" training. It opens out both artistic composition and performance to people formerly excluded from it, and it has enormously expanded the audience for artistic expression of all sorts. Our discussion of the "access" question has been far too narrowly based, and far too unimaginative.

But how, you may well ask, does such theorizing as I have been doing affect our daily decision-making life in this time of deep financial crisis for the higher learning in America? Here is a quick list of some decisions which, according to the arguments posed in this paper, are affected by the digitization of the arts and letters.

The fundamental change in operating system which the humanities are now undergoing

- affects libraries because it affects books, and in the most intimate way
- affects, therefore, library buildings and the budgets thereof
- affects all the issues of intellectual property
- affects professional specializations and departmental structures, and therefore university administrative structures at all levels
- affects "access" in all its aspects, especially in the most profound ones, access to creation and performance of the arts and letters, as well as learning about them
- affects "literacy," literacy programs, and every social impact they exert
- affects the neural pathways of the brain, and how they are being irreversibly laid down; thus it affects whether students will be able to pursue any intellectual work which requires the higher processes of symbolic thought
- affects a "class" and how it works
- affects what a "classroom" is and how it works
- affects what a "textbook" is and how it works
- affects the undergraduate "major"
- affects what the undergraduate curriculum will become
- affects what traditional graduate disciplines will study as well as how they will study it.

In *The Aims of Education*, Whitehead argues that higher education should always be concerned with "the insistent present." This list constitutes a pretty insistent present, it seems to me. I've tried to sketch out a theoretical context to explain or at least contain the items on it, but there is nothing theoretical about the list itself. It should affect at every point how the university handles reinventing itself, as this process of reengineering is now called, in a new financial universe.

When you talk about digital technology, someone will always dismiss it as "futuristic." None of the technology I have talked about is futuristic. It all exists now. It is the budget cutting that involves planning for the future. Why not use the occasion for some long-term planning in terms of this new oper-ating system for the humanities we have been discussing? The planning I read about at my own institution and others like it amounts to keeping on the same way, with as few changes as possible. Review departments, drop the weak ones—but don't rethink what a department is. Ditto "programs." Review majors, drop the weak or obscure ones, but don't rethink what a "major" is. Review courses, cut out frivolous and ornamental ones, but don't rethink what a "course" is. Ditto graduate programs. Nothing new or prom-ising can emerge from any of this fire-fighting.

The short-term approach—how do I keep on doing what I have been doing in the ways I have been doing it, but with much less money?—hasn't worked for the rest of American enterprise. Why should it work for us? It has all been done over and over in America in the last two decades, in the auto-mobile industry, the steel industry, the railroads, the farm machinery busi-ness—the list goes on and on. Department stores are worrying about which departments to phase out while the traditional idea of a department store is drifting down the stream of mercantile history. In the academy we are pris-oners of the same inert patterns of thinking that have dominated the rest of American corporate enterprise. There is nothing "futuristic" about trying to break out of these patterns; it is the most insistent present one can possibly imagine. It will be our own fault, not the fault of our funders, if we continue to imitate the Post Office and worry about moving letters around in an elec-tronic way, when it is not only the delivery system but the "letters" them-selves which have fundamentally changed.

SELECTED READINGS FOR FURTHER STUDY

GENERAL BACKGROUND

Aristotle. *On Rhetoric: A Theory of Civic Discourse*. Trans. and Intro. George A. Kennedy. New York: Oxford UP, 1991.

Arnheim, Rudolph. *Visual Thinking*. Berkeley: U of California P, 1969.

Berger, John. *Ways of Seeing*. London: BBC and Penguin Books Ltd. 1972.

Dondis, Donis. *A Primer of Visual Literacy*. Cambridge, MA: MIT Press, 1973.

Gaines, Jane M., and Michael Renov, eds. *Collecting Visible Evidence*. Minneapolis: U of Minnesota P, 1999.

Gombrich, E. H. *Art and Illusion: A Study in the Psychology of Pictorial Representation*. Vol. 5. A. W. Mellon Lectures in the Fine Arts. Princeton: Princeton UP, 1969.

Horn, Robert. *Visual Language: Global Communication for the 21st Century*. Bainbridge, WA: MacroVU, Inc., 1998.

Journal of Visual Literacy. Ed. Nancy Nelson Knupfer. East Lansing, MI: MATRIX; Michigan State University. <http://www.cameron.edu/jvl>

Kress, Gunther. *Literacy in the New Media Age*. London: Routledge, 2003.

Kress, Gunther, and Theo van Leeuwen. *Reading Images: The Grammar of Visual Design*. London: Routledge, 1996.

Lanham, Richard A. *The Electronic Word: Democracy, Technology and the Arts*. Chicago: U of Chicago P, 1994.

———. *A Handlist of Rhetorical Terms*. 2nd ed. Berkeley: U of California P, 1991.

MacPhee, Graham. *The Architecture of the Visible: Technology and Urban Visual Culture*. London: Continuum, 2002.

Margolin, Victor. *Design Discourse: History | Theory | Criticism*. Chicago: U of Chicago P, 1989.

Margolin, Victor and Richard Buchanan, eds. *The Idea of Design: A Design Issues Reader*. Cambridge, MA: MIT Press, 1995.

McCloud, Scott. *Understanding Comics: The Invisible Art*. New York: Harper Collins, 1994.

Mirzoeff, Nicholas, ed. *The Visual Culture Reader*. London: Routledge, 1998.

Mitchell, W. J. T. *Iconology: Image, Text, Ideology*. Chicago: U of Chicago P, 1986.

Monmonier, Mark. *How to Lie with Maps*. 2nd ed. Chicago: U of Chicago P, 1996.

Reinking, David, Michael C. McKenna, Linda D. Labbo, and Ronald D. Kieffer, eds. *Handbook of Literacy and Technology: Transformations in a Post-Typographic World*. Mahwah, NJ: Lawrence Erlbaum, 1998.

Stafford, Barbara Maria. *Good Looking: Essays on the Virtue of Images*. Cambridge, MA: MIT Press, 1996.

Tufte, Edward R. *Envisioning Information*. Cheshire, CT: Graphics Press, 1990.

———. *The Visual Display of Quantitative Information*. 2nd ed. Cheshire, CT: Graphics Press, 2001.

———. *Visual Explanations: Images and Quantities, Evidence and Narrative*. Cheshire, CT: Graphics Press, 1997.

Venturi, Robert, Denise Brown, and Steven Izenour. *Learning from Las Vegas*. Rev. ed. Cambridge, MA: MIT Press, 1977.

PART ONE: TOWARD A PEDAGOGY OF THE VISUAL

Braden, Roberts A, "Twenty-Five Years of Visual Literacy Research." *Visual Literacy in the Digital Age*. Ed. Darrell G. Beauchamp, Roberts A. Braden, and Judy Clark Baca. Blacksburg, VA: International Visual Literacy Association, 1994. 1–14.

Burnett, Ron. "Technology, Learning, and Visual Culture." *Silicon Literacies: Communication, Innovation and Education in the Electronic Age*. Ed. Ilana Snyder. London: Routledge, 2002. 141–153.

George, Diana. "From Analysis to Design: Visual Communication in the Teaching of Writing." *College Composition and Communication* 54:1 (September 2002), 11–39.

Goldfarb, Brian. *Visual Pedagogy: Media Cultures in and beyond the Classroom*. Durham, NC: Duke UP, 2002.

Hocks, Mary E. "Understanding Visual Rhetoric in Digital Writing Environments." *College Composition and Communication* 54:4 (Jun 2003), 629–656.

Lanham, Richard A. "Digital Literacy." *Scientific American* 273:3 (September 1995), 98, 200.

New London Group, The. "A Pedagogy of Multiliteracies: Designing Social Futures." *Harvard Educational Review* 66:1 (Spring 1996), 60–92.

Titen, Jennifer. "Application of Rudolf Arnheim's Visual Thinking to the Teaching of Technical Writing." *The Technical Writing Teacher* 7:3 (1980), 113–118.

Tyner, Kathleen. "Splintering Literacies." *Literacy in a Digital World: Teaching and Learning in the Age of Information.* Mahwah, NJ: Lawrence Erlbaum, 1998. 60–68.

Williams, Sean. "Thinking Out of the Pro-Verbal Box." *Computers and Composition* 18:1 (March 2001), 21–32.

PART TWO: THE RHETORIC OF THE IMAGE

Abbott, Chris. "Writing the Visual: The Use of Graphic Symbols in Onscreen Texts." *Silicon Literacies: Communication, Innovation and Education in the Electronic Age.* Ed. Ilana Snyder. London: Routledge, 2002. 31–46.

deMan, Paul. "Semiology and Rhetoric." *Allegories of Reading: Figural Language in Rousseau, Nietzsche, Rilke, and Proust.* New Haven: Yale UP, 1979. 3–19.

Gombrich, E. H. "Standards of Truth: The Arrested Image and the Moving Eye." *The Language of Images.* Ed. W. J. T. Mitchell. Chicago: U of Chicago P, 1980. 181–217.

Mitchell, W. J. T. "Beyond Comparison: Picture, Text, and Method." *Picture Theory: Essays on Verbal and Visual Representation.* Chicago: U of Chicago P, 1994. 83–107.

Sontag, Susan. *On Photography.* 1977. New York: Anchor Books, 1990.

———. *Regarding the Pain of Others.* New York : FSG, 2003.

Stafford, Barbara Maria. "Think Again: The Intellectual Side of Images." *The Chronicle of Higher Education,* XLIII:41 (20 June 1997), B6–7.

Woods, Denis. "Each Sign Has a History." *The Power of Maps.* New York: Guilford Press, 1992. 143–181.

PART THREE: THE RHETORIC OF DESIGN

Fenlon, Kevin. "The New Typographer Muttering in Your Ear." *Looking Closer 2: Critical Writings on Graphic Design.* Ed. Michael Beirut, William Drentell, Steven Heller, and D. K. Holland. New York: Allworth Press, 1997. 31–33.

Horn, Robert E, "Visual Language" and "Semantic Investigations." *Visual Language: Global Communication for the 21st Century.* Bainbridge, WA: MacroVU, Inc., 1998. 20, 99–100.

Ilyin, Natalia. "Fabulous Us: Speaking the Language of Exclusion." *Looking Closer 2: Critical Writings on Graphic Design.* Ed. Michael Beirut, William Drentell, Steven Heller, and D. K. Holland. New York: Allworth Press, 1997. 37–39.

Kinross, Robin. "The Rhetoric of Neutrality." *Design Discourse: History | Theory | Criticism.* Ed. Victor Margolin. Chicago: U of Chicago P, 1989. 131–143.

Monmonier, Mark. "Introduction." *How to Lie with Maps.* 2nd ed. Chicago: U of Chicago P, 1996. 1–4.

Tufte, Edward R. "Parallelism: Repetition and Change, Comparison and Surprise." *Visual Explanations: Images and Quantities, Evidence and Narrative.* Cheshire, CT: Graphics Press, 1997. 79–103.

Part Four: Visual Rhetoric and Argument

Barton, Ben F. and Marthalee S. Barton. "Towards a Rhetoric of Visuals for the Computer Era." *The Technical Writing Teacher* 12:2 (1985), 126–145.

Brent, Doug. "Rhetorics of the Web: Implications for Teachers of Literacy." *Kairos: A Journal for Teachers of Writing in Webbed Environments* 2:1 (Spring 1997). Available at http://english.ttu.edu/kairos/2.1/features/brent/bridge.html. Verified 28 October 2003.

Burbules, Nicholas C. "Rhetorics of the Web: Hyperreading and Critical Literacy." *Page to Screen: Taking Literacy into the Electronic Era.* Ed. Ilana Snyder. London: Routledge, 1998. 102–122.

———. "The Web as a Rhetorical Place." *Silicon Literacies: Communication, Innovation and Education in the Electronic Age.* Ed. Ilana Snyder. London: Routledge, 2002, 75–84.

Carter, Locke. "Argument in Hypertext: Writing Strategies and the Problem of Order in a Nonsequential World." *Computers and Composition* 20.1 (2003): 3–22.

Shirk, Henrietta Nickels. "Hypertext and Composition Studies." *Evolving Perspectives on Computers and Composition Studies: Questions for the 1990s.* Ed. Gail E. Hawisher and Cynthia L. Selfe. Urbana, IL: NCTE, 1991. 177–202.

Tufte, Edward R. "Parallelism: Repetition and Change, Comparison and Surprise." *Visual Explanations: Images and Quantities, Evidence and Narrative.* Cheshire, CT: Graphics Press, 1997. 79–103.

Part Five: Visual Rhetoric and Culture

Doane, Mary Ann. "Ideology and the Practice of Sound Editing and Mixing." *The Cinematic Apparatus.* Ed. Teresa de Laurentis and Stephen Heath. New York: St. Martin's Press, 1980. 47–56.

Hutchins, Edwin. "Cultural Cognition." *Cognition in the Wild.* Cambridge, MA: MIT Press, 1996. 353–374.

Law, John and John Whittaker. "On the Art of Representation: Notes on the Politics of Visualization," *Picturing Power: Visual Depiction and Social Relations.* Sociological Review Monograph 35. Ed. John Law and John Whittaker. London: Routledge, 1988. 160–183.

Selfe, Cynthia L. *Technology and Literacy in the Twenty-First Century: The Importance of Paying Attention.* Carbondale, IL: Southern Illinois UP, 1999.

Sibley, David. "Images of Difference." *Geographies of Exclusion: Society and Difference in the West.* London: Routledge, 1995. 14–31.

Trend, David. "Nationalities, Pedagogies, and Media." In *Between Borders: Pedagogy and the Politics of Cultural Studies.* Ed. Henry A. Giroux and Peter McLaren. London: Routledge, 1994. 225–241.

Wresch, William. *Disconnected: Haves and Have-nots in the Information Age.* New Brunswick, NJ: Rutgers UP, 1996.

NOTES ON THE AUTHORS

Rudolf Arnheim is most well known for his influential works including *Art and Visual Perception* (1954/1974) and *The Power of Center* (1982/1988). As one of the great psychologists of our time, Arnheim has made significant contributions in the fields of psychology of art, aesthetics, art education, and media studies. From 1946–1968 he taught at Sarah Lawrence College and in 1968 was invited to serve as Chair in Psychology of Art at Harvard University. Currently, Arnheim lives in Ann Arbor, Michigan and continues, after retirement, to contribute to the field.

Roland Barthes was a French intellectual whose life's work made a lasting impact in critical and literary theory, Barthes is most well known for his theory of occidentalism and for his landmark strides in the field of semiotics. As a professor, Barthes spent time at Lycees in Biarritz, Bayonne, Paris, Bucharest, and Alexandria, Egypt. His most famous works include *Le Degre Zero De L'Ecriture* (1953, *Writing Degree Zero*), *Michelet Par Lui-Meme* (1954), *Sur Racine* (1963), *Le Plasir De Texte* (1973), and *Elements De Semiologie* (1964).

Stephen A. Bernhardt is Professor of English and the Kirkpatrick Chair in Writing at the University of Delaware. As Senior Consultant with McCulley/Cuppan LLC, he works with pharmaceutical companies on document development. He has interests in computers and writing, document design, and training in technical writing. Bernhardt has published in many of the leading journals of scientific and technical communication. Much of his focus is devoted to workplace communication and how technology has and does influence language use.

David Birdsell's work centers on the nexus of communication, media, and information technology in politics, government, and nonprofit administration. He studies public access to information technology; presidential debates; political discourse and its relationship to civic engagement; and nonprofit leadership. He is Professor and Executive Director of Academic Programs in the Baruch College School of Public Affairs. He received BA and MA degrees from the University of Virginia and his Ph.D. in Public Communication from the University of Maryland.

J. Anthony Blair, a University Professor at the University of Windsor, Ontario, Canada, studied Philosophy at McGill University and the University of Michigan. He co-authored the textbooks, *Logical Self-Defense and Reasoning, a Practical Guide,* and is co-founder and a co-editor of the journal, *Informal Logic.* He has published extensively in informal logic and theory of argument, and helped organize many international argumentation conferences in the Netherlands and Canada.

Richard Buchanan is Professor of Design and former Head of the School of Design at Carnegie Mellon University. He teaches interaction design, communication planning, and the philosophy and theory of design. His research interests address issues of interaction design, verbal and visual communication, communication planning and design, and product development. Dr. Buchanan is editor of *Design Issues,* a journal of design history, theory, and criticism. He is also President of the Design Research Society.

Jenny Cool is an educational media producer and social anthropologist who has been working in multimedia since 1990. Her documentary work aired on P.B.S. and she has developed online media for Netscape, Silver Burdett Ginn, Computer Curriculum Corporation, and Disney/ABC. Her film, *Home Economics,* examines the social costs of suburbia.

Hanno H. J. Ehses is Professor at Nova Scotia College of Art and Design. His specialty is in graphic and communication design as well as in visual semiotics and rhetoric. Since 1996 Ehes has been teaching in the Master of Information Design program at the Universidad de las Americas in Puebla. His publications include "Semiotic Foundation of Typography," "Design and Rhetoric: An Analysis of Theatre Posters," and "Rhetorical Handbook: An Illustrated Manual for Graphic Designers."

Leo Groarke is the Dean of the Brantford Campus of Wilfrid Laurier University. He is the author of a number of works on applied logic. His recent publications include *Good Reasoning Matters!* (with Chris Tindale, Oxford University Press, 2003); "Toward a Pragma-Dialectics of Visual Argument" (in Van Eemeren, ed. *Advances in Pragma-Dialectics, Sic Sat,* 2002); "Logic, Informal" (in the *Stanford Encyclopedia of Philosophy,* http://plato.stanford.edu, 2002); and "Logic, Art, and Argument" (*Informal Logic,* 1996).

Jessica Helfand is a partner of William Drenttel/Jessica Helfand, a multimedia and print media company. Her publications include *Six Essays (to 12) on Design and New Media* (William Drenttel, 1997) and *Paul Rand: American Modernist* (William Drenttel, 1998).

Charles A. Hill received his Ph.D. in Rhetoric from Carnegie Mellon University and currently teaches courses in writing, rhetoric, linguistics, and literature at the University of Wisconsin, Oshkosh, where he is also the Director of the Writing Center, Computer Lab, and the Writing Across the Curriculum program. Hill's work has been published in numerous anthologies and journals including *Computers and Composition* and *Reading Research Quarterly*.

Catherine L. Hobbs is professor and director of first-year composition at University of Oklahoma. She is the editor of a collection of essays *Nineteenth-Century Women Learn to Write* (University of Virginia Press, 1995). She is also the author of the book *Rhetoric on the Margins of Modernity* (Southern Illinois University Press, 2002).

bell hooks is Distinguished Professor of English at City College in New York. Her writings cover a broad range of issues surrounding gender, race, teaching, and the significance of media in culture. Her works include *Ain't I a Woman: Black Women and Feminism* (South End Press, 1981), *Talking Back: Thinking Feminist, Thinking Black* (Between the Lines, 1989), *Art on My Mind: Visual Politics* (New Press, 1995), *Remembered Rapture: The Writer at Work* (Henry Holt, 1999).

Robert Horn is Visiting Scholar at the Center for the Study of Language and Information at Stanford University and Distinguished Consulting Faculty at the Saybrook Graduate School and Research Center. He is also president and founder of Macro VU Inc. Currently, Horn is working on two projects: *New Maps for Public Policy* and *Visual Language and Information Design*.

Jeffery Keedy teaches at the Program in Graphic Design at California Institute of the Arts. He is a designer, writer, type designer, and educator. His designs and essays have been published in *Eye*, *I.D.*, *Emigre*®, *Critque*, *Idea*, *HOW*, *Design Quarterly*, and *Looking Closer One and Two*.

Keith Kenney has been teaching photojournalism, communication theory, and graphic design at the University of South Carolina since 1988. An active member of the National Press Photographers Association since 1980, Keith was founding editor of *Visual Communication Quarterly* and was editor of the journal for three years. His articles were published in *Journalism and Mass Communications Quarterly*, *Visual Anthropology*, *Gazette*, *Journalism Educator*, *Newspaper Research Journal*, *Journal of Visual Literacy*, and *American Journalism*.

Gunther Kress is professor of Education/English at the Institute of Education, University of London. He has a specific interest in the interrelations in contemporary texts of different modes of communication—writing, image, speech, music—and their effects on shapes of knowledge and forms of learning, and in the changes—and their effects and consequences—brought by the shift in the media of communication from the page to the screen.

Some of his recent books are *Reading Images: The Grammar of Graphic Design* (Routledge, 1996), *Multimodal Discourse* (Edward Arnold, 2001) (both with Theo van Leeuwen), *Literacy in the New Media Age* (Routledge, 2003),

Multimodal Teaching and Learning: The Rhetorics of the Science Classroom (Continuum, 2002), and *Multimodal Literacy* (Peter Lang, forthcoming).

Richard Lanham taught in the English department at UCLA, where he is currently Professor Emeritus. Lanham explores the changes in the use of textual information in the electronic environment, looking specifically at the role of graphics and animation. His most well-known work, *The Electronic Word: Democracy, Technology and the Arts* (University of Chicago Press), published in 1993. Lanham has also published numerous texts and articles on literary criticism and prose stylistics.

J. L. Lemke is Professor in the School of Education at the University of Michigan. Discourse linguistics, social semiotics, language in education, and science education are his specialties. Co-editor of both *Linguistics and Education: An International Journal* (Elsevier Science) and *Critical Discourse Studies* (Routledge/Taylor & Francis), Lemke's publications include *Textual Politics: Discourse and Social Dynamics* (Taylor & Francis), *Talking Science: Language, Learning, and Values* (Ablex Publishing), and *Using Language in the Classroom* (Oxford University Press).

Nancy Lutkehaus is Associate Professor of Anthropology and Chair of the Gender Studies Program at the University of Southern California. She authored *Zaria's Fire: Engendered Moments in Manam Ethnography* (Carolina Academic), co-edited *Gender Rituals: Female Initiation in Melanesia* (Routledge), *Gendered Missions: Women and Men in Missionary Discourse* (Michigan), and is a former editor of *Visual Anthropology Review*. Her current project is titled *Margaret Mead and the Media: Anthropology and the Making of an American Icon*.

Scott McCloud is a comic book artist, theorist, and author of *Understanding Comics and Reinventing Comics*. McCloud examines the inner workings of comics, concepts of visual communication, and comics and computers. He has also authored numerous online comics, *Zot!* (36-issue series), and is an active public speaker around the country.

Dr. Punyashloke Mishra is Assistant Professor of Learning, Technology, and Culture at the College of Education, Michigan State University. His research has focused on the cognitive, aesthetic, and social aspects related to the design and use of digital technologies. His other interests include online learning, teacher education around technology, visual literacy, creativity, and the cognitive psychology of science. You can find out more about his work by going to http://punya.educ.msu.edu or by emailing punya@msu.edu.

James E. Porter is a Professor in the Department of Writing, Rhetoric, and American Cultures at Michigan State University, where he also serves as Director of the Rhetoric and Writing graduate program in the College of Arts and Letters. His research interests include rhetoric theory, technical and professional communication, and digital writing theory. Porter has authored or co-authored four books: *Rhetorical Ethics and Internetworked Writing* (Ablex and Computers and Composition); *Open Spaces: Writing Technologies and*

Critical Research Practices (with Patricia Sullivan, Ablex and Computers and Composition); *Audience and Rhetoric: An Archaeological Composition of the Discourse Community* (Prentice Hall); and the textbook *Professional Writing Online* (with Patricia Sullivan and Johndan Johnson-Eilola, Longman).

Irit Rogoff holds a university chair in Visual Culture at Goldsmiths College, London University and is director of an AHRB-funded international research project "Cross Cultural Contemporary Arts." She writes extensively on conjunctions of critical theory and contemporary arts with particular interest in issues of performativity and cultural difference. Rogoff has written on German Modernism ("The Divided Heritage" 1992), museums, and the politics of display ("Museum Culture—Histories/Theories/Spectacles" 1994) She is the author of "Terra Infirma—Geography's Visual Culture" (2001) and is currently working on a study of the participatory entitled "Looking Away—Participations in Visual Culture."

Michele S. Shauf works at the intersection of word and image in the context of new media as well as traditional book arts. She has presented her work on humanism, rhetoric and media, visual argument, and information design in both academic and industry forums. Shauf is the senior editor of *Computers, Ethics, and Society*, published by Oxford University Press, now in its third edition, and she is the principal of a communication arts consultancy in Atlanta.

Martin Solomon studied Communication design at New York University and Pratt Institute and is now a graphic designer, artist, and educator. Author of *The Art of Typography* and published by *Graphics*, *Design Issues*, *The Idea of Design*, and *Step by Step Graphics*, Solomon has contributed much to the field of contemporary graphic design. Currently, he is the director and founder of the Martin Solomon Company, specializing in teaching, exhibiting art, and participating in conferences.

Barbara Stafford is William B. Ogden Distinguished Service Professor at The University of Chicago. She has authored *Symbol and Myth* (Associated University Presses, 1979), *Voyage into Substance* (MIT Press, 1984), *Body Criticism* (MIT Press, 1991), *Artful Science* (MIT Press, 1994), *Good Looking* (MIT Press, 1996), *Visual Analogy* (MIT Press, 1999), and *Devices of Wonder: From the World in a Box to Images on a Screen* (with Frances Terpak, Getty Research Institute, 2001). Stafford's new work focuses on tying together cognitive science, neurobiology, and the new philosophy of mind with the history of imaging. Visit her Web site at http://home.uchicago.edu

Craig Stroupe teaches information design at the University of Minnesota-Duluth. He formerly served as Associate Director of San Jose State University's Online Campus. His work has appeared in *College English*, *Pedagogy*, *Computers and Composition* and the book collection *Defining Visual Rhetorics*. His e-mail address is cstroupe@d.umn.edu

Marita Sturken is Associate Professor for the Annenberg School for Communication at the University of Southern California, where she teaches cultural studies, popular culture, visual culture, and the culture of technology. She is the author of *Tangled Memories: The Vietnam War*, the *AIDS Epidemic*, and the *Politics of Remembering* (California, 1997), co-author of *Practices of Looking: An Introduction to Visual Culture* (Oxford, 2001), and co-editor of *Technological Visions* (Temple, 2004).

Patricia Sullivan has directed Technical Writing and currently directs the Graduate Program in Rhetoric and Composition at Purdue. Curriculum-wise, she has been instrumental in starting the B.A. in Professional Writing and secondary areas for the Ph.D. in Technical and Professional Writing and in Rhetoric, Technology, and Digital Writing. Her publications include *Electronic Literacies in the Workplace* (co-edited with Jennie Dautermann), *Opening Spaces* (co-authored with James Porter), *Professional Writing Online* (co-authored with James Porter and Johndan Johnson-Eilola), and *Technology, Labor, and Writing* (co-edited with Pamela Takayoshi, forthcoming). Syllabi from her recent graduate classes and several recent conference papers are available at her Web page.

John Trimbur is Professor of Writing and Rhetoric and Co-Director of the Technical, Scientific, and Professional Communication program at Worcester Polytechnic Institute. He has published extensively in writing theory and cultural studies of literacy. The article "English Only and US College Composition," coauthored with Bruce Horner, won the Richard Braddock Award in 2003.

Mark J. P. Wolf received his Ph.D in the Critical Studies Division of the School of Cinema/Television at the University of Southern California and is currently Associate Professor in the Communication Department at Concordia University Wisconsin. His most recent publication is *The Video Game Theory Reader* (Routledge), an anthology co-edited with Bernard Perron. Wolf's interests are in film and multimedia, graphic design, technology studies, animation, science fiction, world building, and fiction writing.

NOTE ON THE EDITOR

Carolyn Handa is Professor of English Language and Literature and Director of Expository Writing at Southern Illinois University Edwardsville. She has been interested in the influence of culture and visual rhetoric on the world wide web for nearly a decade.

In 2001 she was the guest editor for two special issues of *Computers and Composition* devoted to the subject of digital literacy, digital rhetoric, computers and composition. She has co-authored a chapter on the cultural and literacy implications of the World Wide Web for Greece and has also published several pieces on computer pedagogy and classroom design. She edited the volume *Computers and Community Teaching Composition in the Twenty-first Century* (Boynton/Cook, 1990) and has also published articles on the contemporary poet Elizabeth Bishop in *American Poetry,* the *South Atlantic Quarterly*, and *Contemporary Authors*.

Her other research interests include the social and political implications of computers in the writing classroom, collaborative learning, basic writing, and contemporary Irish poetry.

ACKNOWLEDGMENTS *(continued from page ii)*

Rudolph Arnheim. "Pictures, Symbols and Signs." From *Visual Thinking* by Rudolph Arnheim. Copyright © 1969 The Regents of the University of California. Reprinted by permission of the University of California Press.

Roland Barthes. "Rhetoric of the Image." From *Image–Music–Text* by Roland Barthes, translated by Stephen Heath. English translation copyright © 1977 by Stephen Heath. Reprinted by permission of Hill and Wang, a division of Farrar, Straus and Giroux, LLC.

Stephen Bernhardt. "Seeing the Text." From *College Composition and Communication*, Volume 37, Number 1, (Feb. 1986), pp. 66–78. Copyright © 1986 by the National Council of Teachers of English. Reprinted by permission of the publisher.

David Birdsell and Leo Groarke. "Toward a Theory of Visual Argument." From *Argumentation and Advocacy* 33 (Summer 1996) pp. 1–10. Copyright © 1996. Reprinted by permission of the American Forensics Association.

J. Anthony Blair. "The Possibility and Actuality of Visual Arguments." From *Argumentation and Advocacy* 33 (Summer 1996), pp. 23–39. Copyright © 1996. Reprinted by permission of the American Forensics Association.

Richard Buchanan. "Rhetoric Humanism, and Design." From *Discovering Design: Explorations in Design Studies*, edited by R. Buchanan and V. Margolin. Copyright © 1995 by The University of Chicago Press. Reprinted by permission of the publisher and the author.

Hanno H.J. Ehses. "Representing Macbeth: A Case Study in Visual Rhetoric." From *Design Issues* 1:1 (Spring, 1984), pages 53–63. Copyright © 1984 by Massachusetts Institute of Technology. Reprinted by permission of the MIT Press Journals.

Jessica Helfand. "Electronic Typography: The New Visual Language." From *Looking Closer 2*, Edited by Michael Bierut, William Drenttel, Steven Heller, D.K. Holland. Copyright © 1997 by Jessica Helfand. Reprinted by permission of the author.

Charles Hill. "Reading the Visual in College Writing Classes." From *Intertexts*, Edited by Marguerite Helmers. Copyright © 2003. Reprinted by permission of Lawrence Erlbaum Associates, Inc.

Catherine Hobbs. "Learning From the Past: Verbal and Visual Literacy in Early Modern Rhetoric and Writing Pedagogy." From *Language and Image in the Reading-Writing Classroom: Teaching Vision*, edited by Kristie S. Fleckenstein, Linda T. Calendrillo, and Demetrice A. Wovley. Copyright © 2002. Reprinted by permission of Lawrence Erlbaum Associates, Inc.

bell hooks. "Black Vernacular: Architecture as Cultural Practice." From *Art on My Mind: Visual Politics*. Copyright © 1995. Reprinted by permission of The New Press.

Robert Horn. "Rhetorical Devices and Tight Integration." From *Visual Language: Global Communication for the 21st Century*. Copyright © 1998 by Robert Horn. Reprinted by permission of the author and Macro VU, Inc.

Jeffery Keedy. "The Rules of Typogrpography according to Crackpots Experts." From *Looking Closer 2: Critical Writings on Graphic Design*, edited by Michael Beirut, William Drentell, Steven Heller, and D.K. Holland. Copyright © 1997. Reprinted by permission of the author.

Keith Kenny. "Building Visual Communication Theory by Borrowing from Rhetoric." From *Journal of Visual Literacy* 22:1 (Spring 2002) pp. 53–80. Copyright © 2002 by the Journal of Visual Literacy. Reprinted by permission.

Gunther Kress. "Multimodality, Multimedia, and Genre." From *Literacy in the New Media Age*. Copyright © 2003 by Gunther Kress. Reprinted by permission of the author.

Richard Lanham. "Figures of Rhetoric." From *A Handlist of Rhetorical Terms*, 2/e by Richard Lanham. Copyright © 1968, 1991 by Regents of the University of California. Reprinted by permission of the University of California Press.

Richard A. Lanham. "The Implications of Electronic Information for the Sociology of Knowledge." From *Leonardo* 27:2 (April, 1994), pp. 155–163. Copyright © 1994 by the International Society for the Arts, Sciences and Technology (ISAST). Reprinted by permission of the publisher.

J. L. Lemke. "Metamedia Literacy: Transforming Meaning and Media." From *Handbook of Literacy and Technology: Transformations in a Post-Typographic World*, edited by David Reinking, Michael C. McKenna, Linda D. Labbo, and Ronald D. Kieffer. Copyright © 1998. Reprinted by permission of Lawrence Erlbaum Associates, Inc.

Nancy Lutkehaus and Jenny Cool. "Paradigms Lost and Found: The 'Crisis of Representation' and Visual Anthropology." From *Collecting Visible Evidence* edited by Jane M. Gaines and Michael Renov. Copyright © 1999 by the University of Minnesota Press. Reprinted by permission of the publisher.

INDEX